D1334282

Introduction

Welcome to *Edexcel GCSE Mathematics Modular Foundation Student Book and ActiveBook*. Written by Edexcel as an exact match to the new Edexcel GCSE Mathematics Foundation Tier specification these materials give you more chances to succeed in your examinations

The Student Book

Each chapter has a number of units to work through, with full explanations of each topic, numerous worked examples and plenty of exercises, followed by a chapter summary and chapter review questions.

There are some Module 3 topics that may also be assessed in Modules 2 or 4. These are identified in the contents list with the symbol: +M4

These topics are also highlighted within the chapters themselves,

also assessed in Module 4

using this flag by the relevant unit headings:

The text and worked examples in each unit have been written to explain clearly the ideas and techniques you need to work through the subsequent exercises. The questions in these exercises have all been written to progress from easy to more difficult.

At the end of each chapter, there is a Chapter Summary which will help you remember all the key points and concepts you need to know from the chapter and tell you what you should be able to do for the exam.

Following the Chapter Summary is a Chapter Review which comprises further questions. These are either past exam questions, or newly written exam-style questions – written by examiners for the new specifications. Like the questions in the exercise sections, these progress from easy to hard.

In the exercise sections and Chapter Reviews

 by a question shows that you may use a calculator for this question or those that follow.

 by a question shows that you may NOT use a calculator for this question or those that follow.

The ActiveBook

The ActiveBook CD-ROM is found in the back of this book. It is a digital version of this Student Book, with links to additional resources and extra support. Using the ActiveBook you can:

● Find out what you need to know before you can tackle the unit

● See what vocabulary you will learn in the unit

● See what the learning objectives are for the unit

● Easily access and display answers to the questions in the exercise sections (these do not appear in the printed Student Book)

● Click on glossary words to see and hear their definitions

● Access a complete glossary for the whole book

● Practice exam questions and improve your exam technique with *Exam Tutor* model questions and answers. Each question that has an *Exam Tutor* icon beside it links to a worked solution with audio and visual annotation to guide you through it

Recommendation specification

Pentium 3 500 Mhz processor
128MB RAM
8× speed CD-ROM
1GB free hard disc space
800 × 600 (or 1024 × 768) resolution screen at 16 bit colour
sound card, speakers or headphones

Windows 2000 or XP. This product has been designed for Windows 98, but will be unsupported in line with Microsoft's Product Life-Cycle policy.

Installation

Insert the CD. If you have autorun enabled the program should start within a few seconds. Follow on-screen instructions. Should you experience difficulty, please locate and review the readme file on the CD.

Technical support

If after reviewing the readme you are unable to resolve your problem, contact customer support:

● telephone 0870 6073777 (between 8.00 and 4.00)

● email schools.cd-romhelpdesk@pearson.com

● web http://centraal.uk.knowledgebox.com/kbase/

Collecting and recording data

Statistics is the area of mathematics in which information is

collected and recorded   displayed and then used

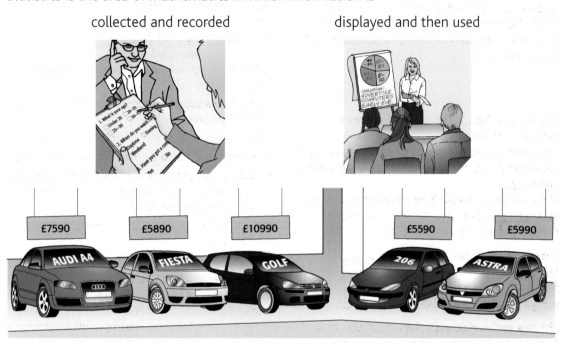

The table shows some information about second-hand cars.

Make	Model	Year	Engine	Doors	Miles	Colour	Price
Ford	Fiesta	2004	1.2 litres	3	7050	Silver	£5890
Vauxhall	Astra	2002	1.6 litres	5	10 000	Silver	£5990
VW	Golf	2005	1.4 litres	5	6040	Black	£10 990
Peugeot	206	2002	1.4 litres	3	27 500	Blue	£5590
Audi	A4	2000	2.0 litres	4	41 000	Red	£7590

In statistics, information like this is called **data**.
In the table, some of the data is given in words – for example the colour of each car. Some of the data is also given as numerical values – for example the number of doors and the number of miles travelled.

1.1 Collecting data by observation and by experiment

Which type of fruit do most people buy?
To answer this question data needs to be collected. Observing the type of fruit people buy and recording this information is called **collecting data by observation**.

A **data collection sheet** is a way of recording information. This one can be used to show the total number of people buying different types of fruit.

Type of fruit	Tally	Frequency

Twenty people buy the following types of fruit.

Apples	Bananas	Plums	Apples	Bananas
Oranges	Oranges	Apples	Pears	Pears
Bananas	Bananas	Oranges	Bananas	Apples
Bananas	Bananas	Pears	Apples	Oranges

The completed data collection sheet shows these results.

Type of fruit	Tally	Frequency
Apples	卌	5
Bananas	卌 ‖	7
Oranges	‖‖	4
Pears	‖‖	3
Plums	‖	1

Frequency shows the total number of people buying each type of fruit. Four people buy oranges.

These are **tally marks**.
There is one tally for each type of fruit chosen.

卌 is another way of writing 5 tally marks.

The total of the frequency column = 20. This is equal to the total number of people who buy fruit.

Since tally marks are used, this is also called a **tally chart**.

It is sometimes called a **frequency table** because it shows the frequency of each type of fruit.

Another way of collecting data is **by experiment**.

An experiment can be carried out to find out if this spinner is **biased** or **fair**.

The spinner is fair if it lands on each of the four numbers about the same number of times. Otherwise, the spinner is said to be biased.

The spinner is spun 80 times.
For each spin, the number that the spinner lands on is recorded in a tally chart.

Since the four frequencies are about the same, the spinner is likely to be fair.

Number	Tally	Frequency
1	卌 卌 卌 IIII	19
2	卌 卌 卌 卌 II	22
3	卌 卌 卌 卌	20
4	卌 卌 卌 IIII	19

Example 1

Rachel wants to find out the number of letters in each word of an article in a local newspaper.

She chooses one paragraph and counts the number of letters in each word. Some of her results are shown in the tally chart.

The information from this final sentence of the paragraph has not been included in the table.

'Most of his fortune is held
in his wife's name'

a Count the number of letters in each word of the final sentence and complete the tally chart.

b Work out the total number of words in the paragraph.

Number of letters	Tally	Frequency
1	III	
2	卌 卌	
3	卌 IIII	
4	卌 卌 III	
5	卌 IIII	
6	卌 II	
7	IIII	
8	II	
9	I	

Solution 1

a   'Most of his fortune is held in his wife's name'
           4   2   3   7   2   4 2 3   5   4

b The total number of words is equal to the total of the frequency column.

$3 + 13 + 11 + 16 + 10 + 7$
$+ 5 + 2 + 1 = 68$

Number of letters	Tally	Frequency
1	III	3
2	卌 卌 III	13
3	卌 卌 I	11
4	卌 卌 卌 I	16
5	卌 卌	10
6	卌 II	7
7	卌	5
8	II	2
9	I	1

Exercise 1A

1 Tyler asked 25 people where they spent their last holiday in England. Here are their answers.

Blackpool	Newquay	Brighton	Blackpool	Newquay
Whitby	Skegness	Blackpool	Brighton	Skegness
Whitby	Brighton	Newquay	Newquay	Blackpool
Skegness	Blackpool	Skegness	Blackpool	Skegness
Blackpool	Brighton	Newquay	Newquay	Skegness

a Copy and complete the data collection sheet to show this information.

b Write down the name of the most popular resort.

Holiday resort	Tally	Frequency

2 Here is a data collection sheet. It shows information about the colours of cars in a school car park. The frequency column has not been completed.

Colour of car	Tally	Frequency
Blue	JHT III	8
Green	JHT JHT JHT	15
Red	JHT JHT JHT JHT II	
White	JHT IIII	
Yellow	IIII	

a Write down the number of red cars in the school car park.

b Write down the number of yellow cars in the school car park.

c Write down the number of white cars in the school car park.

d Which colour of car is the most popular?

e Work out the total number of cars in the school car park.

3 Amy spins a coin 30 times. She records in a table which side the coin lands on. The entries in the tails row have been rubbed out.

Coin lands on	Tally	Frequency
Heads	JHT JHT II	12
Tails		

Copy and complete the table for the 30 spins.

4 Matthew asks each of his friends which football team they support. Draw a suitable data collection sheet that Matthew could use to record this information.

5 Nadia throws a dice 40 times.
Here are the scores on the dice for each of the 40 throws.

a Draw a tally chart to show this information.

b Is the dice fair or biased? Explain your answer.

3	4	1	3	5	6	3	1	2	1
5	5	1	3	4	4	2	4	1	3
3	2	6	4	3	1	2	3	5	4
1	2	1	4	3	6	3	2	3	1

6 Mr. Singh asks some students to name their favourite type of food. He records their answers in this data collection sheet.

He then asks another five students. Here are their answers.

Chinese   English   Indian
Indian   Chinese

Type of food	Tally	Frequency
Chinese	IIII	
Italian	IHT III	
Indian	IHT IIII	
English	IIII	

a Copy and complete the frequency table.

b Write down the most popular favourite type of food.

c Work out the total number of students Mr. Singh asks.

1.2 Questionnaires

A **questionnaire** is a list of questions which help to collect data in a survey. Here is an example of part of a questionnaire.

What Year are you in?   Year 10 ☐   Year 11 ☐

Are you male or female?   Male ☐   Female ☐

4 to 6 means shoe sizes 4, $4\frac{1}{2}$, 5, $5\frac{1}{2}$, 6

What is your shoe size?

Under 4 ☐   4 to 6 ☐ $6\frac{1}{2}$ to 8 ☐ $8\frac{1}{2}$ to 10 ☐   over 10 ☐

What is your height?

Under 1.5 m ☐   1.5 m up to 1.6 m ☐   1.6 m up to 1.7 m ☐

1.7 m up to 1.8 m ☐   1.8 m and over ☐

1.5 m up to 1.6 m means heights of 1.5 m and over but less than 1.6 m

What is your weight?

Under 40 kg ☐   40 kg up to 50 kg ☐   50 kg up to 60 kg ☐

60 kg up to 70 kg ☐   70 kg and over ☐

Numerical data can either be **discrete data** or **continuous data**.

● Discrete data has definite values – for example shoe size, number of doors, scores on a dice.

● Continuous data can be measured; it can take *any* value – height, weight and time are all examples of continuous data.

What types of fruit do people buy most in a large town?
This can be answered by carrying out a survey using a questionnaire.
These are examples of good and bad questions that could appear on the questionnaire.

1 'Which types of fruit do you eat?'
(You may choose more than one.)

| This question is short and clear. This will help show which types of fruit are eaten. |

Apples   Bananas   Pears   Oranges   Plums   Others (please state)   Do not eat fruit

☐ ☐ ☐ ☐ ☐ ☐ ☐

Every question on a questionnaire must have response boxes.
A **response box** is where a person can answer the question, usually by writing a tick (✓) in the box. This question has seven response boxes.

These two response boxes make sure that everyone can complete at least one box.

2 'How often do you eat fruit?'

Often   Sometimes   Now and then

☐ ☐ ☐

In this question the response boxes could mean different things to different people. Using, for example, 'Less than once a week'. 'Once or twice a week' and 'More than twice a week' would be better.

3 'Have you ever stolen fruit?'

Yes   No

☐ ☐

It is unlikely that anyone would admit to a question like this. The question will not help find out which types of fruit people buy.

4 'How much do you usually spend on fruit each week?'

£1 up to £3   £3 up to £5   £5 up to £10

☐ ☐ ☐

There is no response box to tick for anyone spending less than £1 or more than £10 each week. This could be improved by adding two more response boxes 'Less than £1' and '£10 and over'.
It is important that the intervals cover *all* amounts, and that each person can tick just *one* box.

5 'Do you agree that to be healthy you should eat more fruit?'

Yes   No

☐ ☐

By asking 'Do you agree ...', this question suggests that the correct answer is 'Yes'. This is called a biased question.

Example 2

The manager of a restaurant has made some changes. She uses these questions as part of a questionnaire to find out what the public think of these changes.

Write down what is wrong with each of these questions.

a 'What do you think of the improvements to the restaurant?'

    Excellent   Very good   Good

    ☐   ☐   ☐

b 'How much money do you normally pay for a main course?'

    A lot   Average

    ☐   ☐

c 'How often do you come to the restaurant?'

    Not very often   Often

    ☐   ☐

Solution 2

a
- The question is biased because it only allows positive responses to be recorded.
- The question is too vague because, 'excellent', 'very good' and 'good' may mean different things to different people.
- There is no response box for the customers who do not like the changes.

b
- A 'lot' and 'average' may mean different things to different people. She should specify different amounts of money.

c
- This question does not make it clear if she is asking how often a customer comes to the restaurant each month or each year. She needs to specify the time period.
- The response boxes are not very helpful because they are too vague.

Example 3

Angela carries out a survey of the amount of television watched by some people. She uses this question on a questionnaire.

    'How much time do you spend watching television?'

    A lot   Average   A bit

    ☐   ☐   ☐

a Design a better question that Angela could use.

b State if the data used here is discrete data or continuous data.

Solution 3

a How much time do you spend watching television each week?

    Under 5 hours   5 up to   10 up to   20 hours and over

                   10 hours   20 hours

    ☐   ☐   ☐   ☐

b Since time can be measured and can take any value, the data is continuous data.

1.3 Sampling

It is difficult to ask every person in a large town what fruit they eat. It is easier to ask a small number of people. This is called a **sample**.

It is important that this sample is not biased towards any group of people – for example, adults only, or men only. Recording information about the person answering the questions will tell you whether your sample is biased or unbiased.

A **random sample** is one in which every person has an equal chance of being chosen.

To make sure that a sample is random and unbiased, choose the best place and time to ask questions. A good place to stand to ask about buying fruit is in a busy part of the town centre during the daytime. This is because most people shop in the town centre during the day.

Example 4

The manager of a leisure centre wants to find out what sporting activities people prefer. He asks the first 100 people who enter the leisure centre one Saturday morning. Explain what is wrong about this way of sampling.

Solution 4

This way of sampling is biased because

- Choosing the first 100 people is no guarantee that all ages and both sexes are represented; they may all be children.
- Just sampling on a Saturday morning may not include people who use the leisure centre at other times.
- Choosing only people who use this leisure centre may exclude people who prefer sporting activities that are not available at this leisure centre.

Exercise 1B

1   Mary carries out a survey of swimmers. The data collected includes colour of eyes, length of arm, shoe size and fastest time to swim 100 metres.
   Which of these data are **a** discrete, **b** continuous?

2   Write down one thing that is wrong with each of the following questions.
   a 'How much time do you spend doing homework?'
   b 'How much pocket money do you get each week?'   A lot ☐   Not much ☐

   c 'Do you agree that exercise is good for you?'
      Yes   No
      ☐   ☐

   d 'How much do you usually spend on your lunch each day?'
      under £1   £1–£2   £3–£4   over £4
      ☐   ☐   ☐   ☐

e 'Have you ever been in trouble with the police?'   Yes ☐   No ☐

f 'What is your favourite colour?'   Red ☐   Blue ☐   Yellow ☐   Green ☐

3 The manager of a cinema asks these two questions in a questionnaire.

'Do you go to the cinema?'   Often   Sometimes   Never

☐   ☐   ☐

'How old are you?'   0 to 10 years   10 to 20 years   20 to 40 years   over 40 years

☐   ☐   ☐   ☐

There is something wrong with each question.
For each one design a better question for the manager to use.

4 A company is going to open a new adventure playground. They want to know what type of activity would be most popular.

a **i** Design a suitable question to find out which activity most people would use in an adventure playground.

ii Draw a suitable data collection sheet to record the answers.

b A worker for the company stands in the town centre one Monday morning and asks the first 100 people she meets to complete the questionnaire. Explain fully what is wrong with this method of sampling.

5 Melissa wants to find out how students in her Year travel to school.

a Design a suitable question to find out how students in her Year travel to school.

There are 240 students in her Year. Melissa decides to use a sample of 40 students only from her Year. She gives a questionnaire to each of the 30 members of her class and also a questionnaire to each of 10 friends from different classes.

b **i** What is wrong with this sample?

ii How could Melissa get a better sample?

6 Write down five questions that might appear in a questionnaire on the types of holiday people prefer. Describe how this information might be collected and recorded.

1.4 Databases

A **database** is a collection of information. It is organised so that any piece of data can be found quickly. This information is usually stored on a computer but it can also be stored on paper.

So far all the data that has been considered has been collected and recorded by the person carrying out a particular survey or experiment. This is called **primary data**.
The data in a database that has usually been collected and recorded by someone else is called **secondary data**.

Example 5

This database contains information about some students.

Name	Gender	Age	Key stage 3 English level	Key stage 3 Maths level	Key stage 3 Science level
David	Male	16	4	3	4
Samantha	Female	14	5	5	5
Daniel	Male	16	4	4	4
Yousef	Male	15	6	6	5
Amir	Male	15	7	6	6
Kirsty	Female	15	3	4	4
Nadia	Female	16	4	6	4
Clive	Male	14	5	6	6
Natasha	Female	16	6	8	7
Joshua	Male	16	3	3	4

Using the database

a write down Kirsty's age.

b write down Clive's key stage 3 Maths level.

c write down Nadia's key stage 3 English level.

d write down who got the only level 8.

e which students got the same level in all three subjects?

f how many students are under 16 years of age?

g how many boys got level 5 in key stage 3 English?

h list the girls in order of key stage 3 Maths level, highest level first.

i write down the age of the boy whose Maths level was higher than his English level.

Solution 5

a 15

Name	Gender	Age
Kirsty		15

b 6

Name	Gender	Age	Key stage 3 English level	Key stage 3 Maths level
Clive				6

c 4

Name	Gender	Age	Key stage 3 English level
Nadia		'	4

d Natasha

Name	Gender	Age	Key stage 3 English level	Key stage 3 Maths level
Natasha				8

e Samantha (5, 5, 5) and Daniel (4, 4, 4)

Name	Gender	Age	Key stage 3 English level	Key stage 3 Maths level	Key stage 3 Science level
Samantha			5	5	5
Daniel			4	4	4

f 5 (Samantha, Yousef, Amir, Kirsty and Clive)
g 1 (Clive)
h Natasha (8), Nadia (6), Samantha (5), Kirsty (4)
i 14

Name	Gender	Age	Key stage 3 English level	Key stage 3 Maths level
Clive	Male	14	5	6

Example 6

'Teenage girls watch more TV soaps than any other group.'
Bill wants to test if this statement is true.
Here is part of a database that Bill finds on the internet.

Name	Age	Month of birth	Gender	Colour of hair	Favourite colour	Favourite music	Favourite sport	Favourite TV programme	TV hours watched per week	Number of pets
Asif	20	April	Male	Black	Red	R & B	Rugby	The Simpsons	42	0
Ben	15	June	Male	Black	Orange	Pop	Rounders	Coronation Street	14	2
Cath	16	March	Female	Red	Black	Rock	Tennis	The News	27	10
Deb	12	May	Female	Blonde	Blue	Rock	Baseball	Coronation Street	22	3
Eric	35	June	Male	Brown	Pink	Rock	Judo	Crimewatch	22	5

Bill does not need to use all of this database.
Which parts of the database should Bill use?

Solution 6

Age	Gender	Favourite TV programme	TV hours watched per week
20	Male	The Simpsons	42
15	Male	Coronation Street	14
16	Female	The News	27
12	Female	Coronation Street	22
35	Male	Crimewatch	22

Exercise 1C

1   The table gives some information about the matches played by five football teams.

Team	Played	Won	Drawn	Lost	Points
Chad Rovers	16	11	3	2	36
Turton Lane	16	9	5	2	32
Pine United	16	9	2	5	29
Grafton Town	16	5	5	6	20
Workston	16	1	3	12	6

   a   Write down the number of matches that Pine United won.
   b   Write down the number of matches that Grafton Town drew.
   c   Write down the number of points that Turton Lane have.
   d   Which team lost six matches?
   e   Which two teams drew more matches than they lost?

2   The database contains some information about second-hand cars.

Make	Model	Year	Engine	Doors	Miles	Colour	Price
Ford	Fiesta	2004	1.2 litres	3	7050	Silver	£5890
Vauxhall	Astra	2002	1.6 litres	5	10 000	Silver	£5990
VW	Golf	2005	1.4 litres	5	6040	Black	£10 990
Peugeot	206	2002	1.4 litres	3	27 500	Blue	£5590
Audi	A4	2000	2.0 litres	4	41 000	Red	£7590

   a   Write down the colour of the Peugeot 206.
   b   Write down the price of the Audi A4.
   c   Write down the make of car which is silver and has 5 doors.
   d   Write down the makes of the cars which have travelled more than 10 000 miles.
   e   Write down the make of the car which has 5 doors and costs less than £6000.

3   The database contains some information about houses for sale.

	Type of house	Bedrooms	Bathrooms	Garage	Garden size in square metres	Price
A	Detached	5	2	Yes	120	£244 000
B	Semi-detached	3	1	No	40	£109 000
C	Town house	2	1	No	20	£98 000
D	Semi-detached	3	1	Yes	50	£128 000
E	Detached	4	2	Yes	200	£285 000
F	Detached	3	1	No	90	£165 000
G	Terraced	2	1	No	none	£95 000
H	Semi-detached	4	1	Yes	60	£205 000
I	Semi-detached	5	3	No	240	£324 000
J	Flat	1	1	No	none	£130 000

a Write down the letter of the house
   i with a price of £95 000
   ii which has a garden size greater than 200 square metres.
b Write down the letters of the houses that have
   i no garden and no garage
   ii more than one bathroom.
c Write down the number of semi-detached houses that have no garage.
d List the houses in order of price, starting with the lowest price.
e List the houses which have a garden, in order of garden size, starting with the largest.

4   The table shows information about 20 students.

Name	Gender	Age	Colour of hair	Colour of eyes
Angus	Male	16	Blonde	Brown
Caroline	Female	14	Blonde	Blue
Stuart	Male	16	Ginger	Green
Mark	Male	15	Blonde	Blue
Tahir	Male	15	Black	Brown
Fatima	Female	15	Black	Brown
Brenda	Female	16	Brown	Hazel
Damian	Male	14	Brown	Blue
Shirley	Female	16	Ginger	Blue
Kyle	Male	16	Brown	Hazel
Mumtaz	Male	15	Black	Brown
Nosheen	Female	16	Brown	Hazel
Helen	Female	14	Blonde	Blue
Parvinder	Male	16	Black	Brown
Viv	Female	15	Brown	Hazel
Arshad	Male	14	Black	Brown
Alex	Male	14	Black	Green
Asia	Female	16	Blonde	Green
Summer	Female	15	Black	Blue
Dale	Male	16	Brown	Brown

a Write down the name of the 14 year old male who has brown eyes.
b Write down the name of the 16 year old female who has blonde hair.
c How many students are male?
d How many female students are 15 years of age?
e Write down the names of all the males with blue eyes.
f Write down the names of all the females who are over 15 years of age and have brown hair.
g Draw and complete a tally chart to show the different colours of eyes.

5 'Teenage boys who like rugby prefer rock music.'
Viv wants to test if this statement is true. Here is part of a database she finds on the internet

Name	Age	Month of birth	Gender	Colour of hair	Favourite colour	Favourite music	Favourite sport	Favourite TV programme	TV hours watched per week	Number of pets
Asif	20	April	Male	Black	Red	R&B	Rugby	The Simpsons	42	0
Ben	15	June	Male	Black	Orange	Pop	Rounders	Coronation Street	14	2
Cath	16	March	Female	Red	Black	Rock	Tennis	The News	27	10
Deb	12	May	Female	Blonde	Blue	Rock	Baseball	Coronation Street	22	3
Eric	35	June	Male	Brown	Pink	Rock	Judo	Crimewatch	22	5

Viv does not need to use all of this database.
Which parts of the database should she use?

Chapter summary

You should know

★ **Data** is information which can be recorded in words or in numbers.

★ Data can be collected by **observation**, by **experiment** and by using **questionnaires**.

★ How to record data using **data collection sheets** and **tally charts**.
  • **Tally marks** are used to record each piece of information.
  • **Frequency** means the same as total.

★ Numerical data is either **discrete data** (for example key stage Maths level, number of goals scored and shoe size) or **continuous data** (for example height, weight and time).

★ How to write questions for a questionnaire avoiding **bias** and including **response boxes** which cover all possible answers.

★ The **sample** of people to take part in a survey must be carefully chosen to avoid bias.

★ A **random sample** is one where every person has an equal chance of being chosen.

★ **Primary data** is data collected by yourself and **secondary data** is data collected by someone else.

★ A **database** is an organised collection of information which can be stored in a computer or on paper.

★ How to recognise the parts of a database that are needed to solve a problem and be able to answer questions using a database.

Chapter 1 review questions

1 The table shows information about five television programmes.

Programme	Channel	Running time	Star rating
Wildlife on One	BBC1	30 minutes	***
World Sport	ITV1	35 minutes	**
Casualty	BBC1	50 minutes	****
Top of the Pops	BBC2	35 minutes	***
Self Portraits	Channel 4	60 minutes	*

  a Write down the running time of *Top of the Pops*.

  b Write down the programme that is on ITV1.

  c Write down the programme that is on BBC1 and has a 3-star rating

2 Nazia is going to carry out a survey of the types of videos her friends have watched. Draw a suitable data collection sheet that Nazia could use.   (1385 June 2000)

3 Wayne is going to carry out a survey to record information about the type of vehicles passing the school gate. Draw a suitable data collection sheet that Wayne could use.   (1385 May 2002)

4 Miles rolls a dice 60 times and each time records the number that the dice lands on. The tally chart shows the first 50 results.

The remaining ten results are

4 5 3 4 2 1 3 4 4 6

  a Copy and complete the tally chart.

  b Which number does the dice land on the most times?

Number	Tally	Frequency
1				
2	IIII IIII	
3	IIII IIII	
4	IIII IIII III	
5	IIII IIII	
6	IIII ||	

5 Daniel carried out a survey of his friends' favourite flavour of crisps. Here are his results.

Plain	Chicken	Bovril	Salt & Vinegar	Plain
Salt & Vinegar	Plain	Chicken	Plain	Bovril
Plain	Chicken	Bovril	Salt & Vinegar	Bovril
Bovril	Plain	Plain	Salt & Vinegar	Plain

  a Copy and complete the table to show Daniel's results.

  b Write down the number of Daniel's friends whose favourite flavour was Salt & Vinegar.

  c What was the favourite flavour of most of Daniel's friends?

Flavour of crisps	Tally	Frequency
Plain		
Chicken		
Bovril		
Salt & Vinegar		

(1387 June 2005)

6 Angela asked 20 people in which country they spent their last holiday. Here are their answers.

France	Spain	Italy	England
Spain	England	France	Spain
Italy	France	England	Spain
Spain	Italy	Spain	France
England	Spain	France	Italy

Design **and** complete a suitable data collection sheet that Angela could have used to show this information.

(1388 March 2004)

7

Subject	Number of students 1997	Number of students 1998
Religious studies	2860	3358
Law	4389	4617
German	2007	2481
Statistics	1999	2491

The table shows the numbers of students who took examinations in four different subjects in 1997 and 1998.

a Which of these subjects had the least number of students taking the exam in 1998?

b How many more students took the Statistics exam in 1998 than in 1997?

c Which of these subjects had the greatest increase in the number of students taking the exam from 1997 to 1998?

(1385 June 1999)

8 The manager of a school canteen has made some changes.
She wants to find out what students think of these changes.
She uses this question on a questionnaire.
'What do you think of the changes in the canteen?'

Excellent	Very good	Good

a Write down what is wrong about this question.

This is another question on the questionnaire.

'How much money do you normally spend in the canteen?'

A lot	Not much

b **i** Write down one thing that is wrong about this question.

ii Design a better question for the canteen manager to use. You should include some response boxes.

(1387 June2004)

9 A student wanted to find out how people used the cinema in his town. He used this question on a questionnaire.

'How many times have you visited the cinema in town?'

A lot	A bit

a Explain two things that are wrong with this question.

b Write an improved question. You should include some response boxes.

10 Mr Beeton is going to open a restaurant. He wants to know what type of restaurant people like. He designs a questionnaire.

a Design a suitable question he could use to find out what type of restaurant people like.

He asks his family 'Do you agree that pizza is better than pasta?'
This is **not** a good way to find out what people who might use his restaurant like to eat.

b Write down **two** reasons why this is **not** a good way to find out what people who might use his restaurant like to eat.

(1387 June 2003)

11 Write down five questions that might be included in a questionnaire on the types of films people prefer. Describe how this information might be collected and recorded.

12 Hamid wants to find out what people in Melworth think about the sports facilities in the town. Hamid plans to stand outside the Melworth sports centre one Monday morning. He plans to ask people going into the sports centre to complete a questionnaire. Carol tells Hamid that his survey will be biased.

i Give **one** reason why the survey will be biased.

ii Describe **one** change Hamid could make to the way in which he is going to carry out his survey so that it will be less biased.

(1388 Jan 2004)

Processing, representing and interpreting data

Data is often easier to understand if it is presented in the form of a graph or a diagram.

The information for a graph or diagram is often given in a **frequency table**.

A frequency table gives the name of each category of data as well as its **frequency**. The frequency is the number of times that each category of data occurs.

This frequency table shows the colour of cars in a car park.

It shows that there were 12 blue cars, 4 yellow cars, 8 black cars and 10 red cars in the car park.

Colour	Blue	Yellow	Black	Red
Number of cars	12	4	8	10

2.1 Pictograms

A **pictogram** uses symbols to represent discrete data. A pictogram must have a **key** to show how many items of data each symbol represents.

The pictogram shows the information from the frequency table about the cars in the car park.

Colours of cars in car park

Blue is the car colour that occurs most often and so is called the **mode** (or **modal colour**).

When drawing pictograms, it is sometimes necessary to use part of a symbol.

Example 1

Joni asked some of her friends which sport they liked best.

The table shows the results.

Draw a pictogram to show this information.

Use ⊕ to represent four friends.

Sport	Number of friends
Tennis	16
Swimming	6
Hockey	11
Netball	8

Solution 1

Sport	Number of friends	Number of symbols
Tennis	16	$16 \div 4 = 4$
Swimming	6	$6 \div 4 = \frac{6}{4} = \frac{3}{2} = 1\frac{1}{2}$
Hockey	11	$11 \div 4 = \frac{11}{4} = 2\frac{3}{4}$
Netball	8	$8 \div 4 = 2$

> Work out the number of symbols needed for each sport by dividing the number of friends by 4 If the answer is not a whole number, write it as a fraction.

Favourite sports

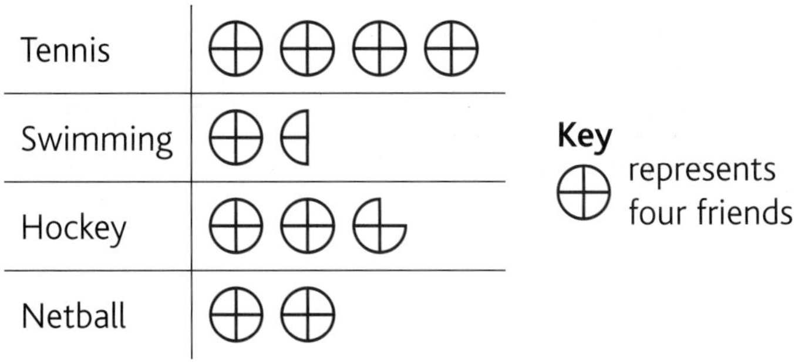

Tennis	⊕ ⊕ ⊕ ⊕
Swimming	⊕ ◖
Hockey	⊕ ⊕ ◔
Netball	⊕ ⊕

Key
⊕ represents four friends

Exercise 2A

1 The pictogram shows the number of letters received by a school in one week.

Number of letters

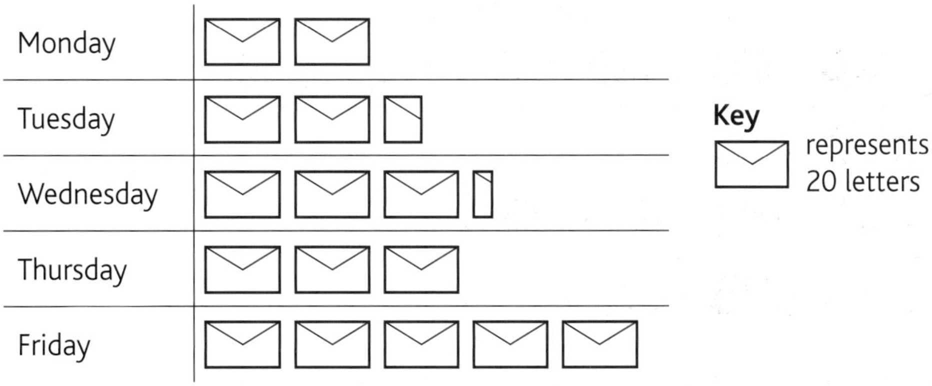

Monday	✉ ✉
Tuesday	✉ ✉ ◹
Wednesday	✉ ✉ ✉ ▯
Thursday	✉ ✉ ✉
Friday	✉ ✉ ✉ ✉ ✉

Key
✉ represents 20 letters

   a On which day did the school receive the greatest number of letters?
   b How many letters did the school receive on Monday?
   c How many letters did the school receive on Tuesday?
   d How many letters did the school receive on Wednesday?

2 The pictogram shows the number of drinks sold in one day at a café.

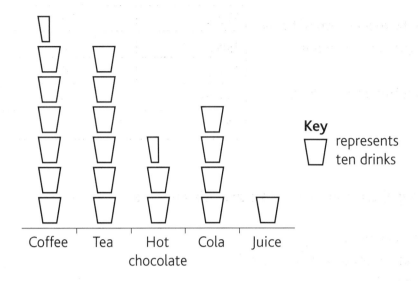

Key
◻ represents ten drinks

Coffee   Tea   Hot chocolate   Cola   Juice

a Which drink was the least popular?
b Which drink was the mode?
c How many drinks of tea were sold?
d How many drinks of hot chocolate were sold?
e Work out the total number of drinks sold.

3 The pictogram shows the number of three different types of pizza sold in one day.

20 salami pizzas were also sold.

a Complete the pictogram on the resource sheet.
b How many of each type of pizza were sold?
c Which type of pizza is the mode?

Pizzas sold

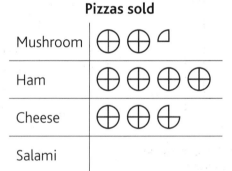

Mushroom

Ham

Cheese

Salami

Key
⊕ represents eight pizzas

4 40 students were asked which of five subjects was their favourite.
The table shows the results.

Draw a pictogram to show this information.

Use 🧍 to represent two students.

Subject	Number of students
English	14
Maths	7
French	5
Games	10
Art	4

5 The table shows how 60 students travel to school.

a Write down the modal form of travel.

b Draw a pictogram to show this information.

Use to represent 4 students.

Form of travel	Number of students
Walk	24
Bus	13
Train	6
Cycle	10
Car	7

2.2 Bar charts

A **bar chart** (or bar graph) can also be used to display discrete data.

In a bar chart:

- all the bars are the same width
- both the vertical and horizontal axes have labels
- there is a gap between the bars
- the bars can be drawn horizontally or vertically.

This frequency table shows the eye colours of 40 adults.

The two bar charts also show this information.

Eye colour	Blue	Hazel	Brown	Green
Frequency	12	8	15	5

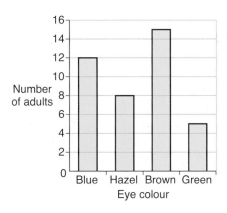

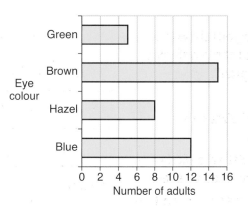

A vertical line graph can be drawn instead of a bar chart. In this type of graph the bars are replaced by vertical lines.

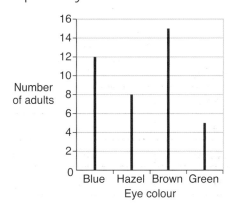

Dual bar charts can be drawn to compare data.
In a dual bar chart two (or more) bars are drawn side by side.
The bars can be horizontal or vertical.

Example 2

The dual bar chart shows Rachel's and Emily's marks in each of four subjects.

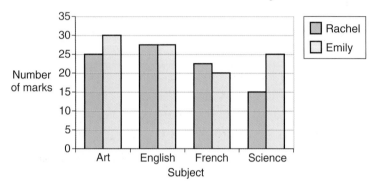

a   In which subject did Emily and Rachel score the same number of marks?
b   Which girl scored the higher mark in French?
c   How many marks did Emily score in art?
d   How many marks did Rachel score in art?
e   How many more marks than Rachel did Emily score in science?

Solution 2

a   Emily and Rachel scored the same mark in English.

> The bars are the same height for English.

b   Rachel scored more marks in French.

> Rachel's bar is higher than Emily's bar.

c   Emily scored 30 marks in art.

> Look carefully at the key to see which colour represents Emily's score.

d   Rachel scored 25 marks in art.

e $25 - 15 = 10$
    Emily scored 10 more marks than Rachel in science.

> Emily scored 25 marks in science.
> Rachel scored 15 marks in science.

Exercise 2B

1 The bar chart shows information about the hair colour of all the students in a class.

  a   Which hair colour is the mode?
  b   How many students have black hair?
  c   How many students are in the class?

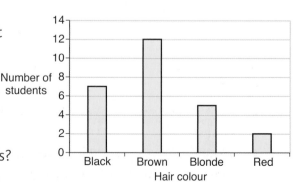

2 The bar chart shows the number of hours that Sarah spent watching television on each day one week.

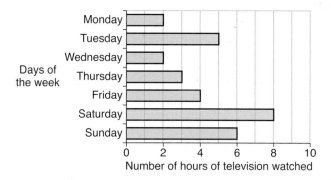

a On which day did Sarah watch the most hours of television?

b Write down the number of hours of television she watched on Thursday.

c Write down the two days on which she watched the same number of hours of television.

d On which day did she watch four hours of television?

3 Sanjeev collected data on the meals that students bought in the school canteen. Here are his results. Draw a bar chart to show this information.

Meal	Fish and chips	Lasagne	Pie and chips	Cheese salad	Sausage and mash
Frequency	55	27	34	12	43

4 The bar chart shows the maximum temperatures, in °C, in Mallorca and Turkey each month from April to October.

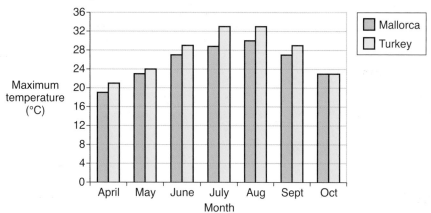

a Write down the maximum temperature in Turkey in May.

b Write down the maximum temperature in Mallorca in July.

c Write down the month in which Mallorca and Turkey have the same maximum temperature.

d Write down the months in which the maximum temperature in Turkey was 29°C.

e Write down the month in which the maximum temperature in Mallorca was 19°C.

5 The table shows the maximum monthly temperatures, in °C, in Spain and Florida each month from July to December.

Month	July	Aug	Sept	Oct	Nov	Dec
Maximum monthly temperature in Spain (°C)	30	29	24	18	15	12
Maximum monthly temperature in Florida (°C)	28	28	27	25	22	20

Draw a dual bar chart to illustrate this information.

6 The vertical line graph shows how often each number on a dice was thrown.

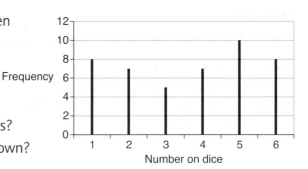

   a How many times was the number 2 thrown?

   b Which number is the mode?

   c Which number was thrown 5 times?

   d How many times was the dice thrown?

2.3 Pie charts

A **pie chart** shows the proportions of the different categories of data.

A pie chart is a circle that is divided into **sectors**.
The whole circle represents all the data.
Each sector represents the number of items in that category of data.

This pie chart shows that a dog is the favourite pet of $\frac{1}{2}$ the people asked and that a cat is the favourite pet of $\frac{1}{4}$ of them.

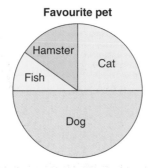

Favourite pet

To draw a pie chart you must work out the size of the angle for each sector.

Example 3

The table shows the favourite colour of each of 30 students.
Draw a pie chart to represent this information.

Colour	Red	Blue	Yellow	Green
Frequency	9	14	4	3

Solution 3
Method 1
360 ÷ 30 = 12

> There are 360° in a full circle. There are 30 students. To work out the size of the angle that will represent 1 student, divide 360° by 30

12° represents 1 student

Red	9 × 12 = 108°
Blue	14 × 12 = 168°
Yellow	4 × 12 = 48°
Green	3 × 12 = 36°

> Multiply the frequency of each colour by 12

Method 2

Red $\frac{9}{30}$ × 360° = 108°

Blue $\frac{14}{30}$ × 360° = 168°

Yellow $\frac{4}{30}$ × 360° = 48°

Green $\frac{3}{30}$ × 360° = 36°

> 9 out of 30 students chose red as their favourite colour. Write this as the fraction $\frac{9}{30}$ and then find $\frac{9}{30}$ of 360°.
>
> The same method can be used to find the angle for each of the other colours.

To draw the pie chart, draw a circle and mark the centre.

Draw a radius and from this line, use a protractor to measure the angle of the sector for the colour red.

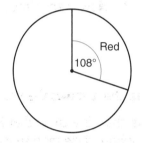

Use a protractor to measure the angles for all the other sectors. Remember to label each sector of the pie chart.

Favourite colour

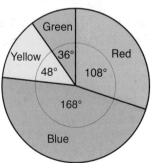

Exercise 2C

1 40 passengers at a train station were asked which city they were travelling to. The table shows this information.

City	York	Durham	Newcastle	Edinburgh
Frequency	10	6	7	17

a Work out the sector angle for each city.

b Draw an accurate pie chart to show this information.

2   Jasmin asked 30 friends to name their favourite flavour of ice-cream.
The table shows her results.

Flavour	Vanilla	Chocolate	Strawberry	Coffee	Mint
Frequency	6	10	7	2	5

   a   Work out the sector angle for each flavour.
   b   Draw an accurate pie chart to show this information.

3   The table shows the time it takes each of 60 pupils to travel to school.

Time in minutes	Frequency
Less than 10	11
Between 10 and 15	24
Between 15 and 30	18
More than 30	7

Draw an accurate pie chart to show this information.

4   The table shows information about the 540 fiction books in a school library.

Category	Romance	Thriller	Classics
Frequency	120	90	330

Draw an accurate pie chart to show this information.

5   The table shows the numbers of the different types of houses in one street.

Type of house	Detached	Semi-detached	Terraced	Bungalow
Frequency	24	30	27	9

Draw an accurate pie chart to show this information.

6   The table shows the number of hours that Saul worked on each of 5 days.

Day	Monday	Tuesday	Wednesday	Thursday	Friday
Number of hours worked	7	8	10	6	5

Draw an accurate pie chart to show this information.

2.4 Using pie charts

If the total number of items is known, the number of items in each category can be worked out.

Example 4

There are 20 trees in a park.
Alex counted the number of each type of tree in the park.
The pie chart shows this information.

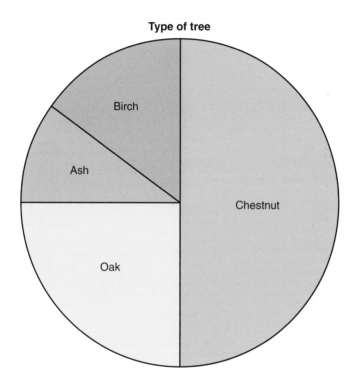

Type of tree

a   Which type of tree is the most common in the park?

b   Work out the number of each type of tree.

Solution 4

a   Chestnut is the most common type.

> It has the biggest sector.

b   Chestnut 180°
       Oak   90°
       Ash   36°
       Birch   54°

> Measure the angle of each sector with a protractor.

There are two methods that can be used to work out the number of each type of tree.

Method 1

$360 \div 20 = 18$

| There are 360° in a full circle. There are 20 trees in the park. |
| Divide 360 by 20 to work out how many degrees represent one tree. |

18° represents one tree.

$180 \div 18 = 10$
$90 \div 18 = 5$
$36 \div 18 = 2$
$54 \div 18 = 3$

| Divide each of the four angles by 18 |
| This gives the number of each type of tree. |

There are 10 chestnut, 5 oak, 2 ash and 3 birch trees in the park.

Method 2

$\frac{180}{360} = \frac{1}{2}$ $\frac{1}{2} \times 20 = 10$
$\frac{90}{360} = \frac{1}{4}$ $\frac{1}{4} \times 20 = 5$
$\frac{36}{360} = \frac{1}{10}$ $\frac{1}{10} \times 20 = 2$
$\frac{54}{360} = \frac{3}{20}$ $\frac{3}{20} \times 20 = 3$

| The sector for the chestnut trees is $\frac{180}{360}$ of the full circle. |
| Write this fraction in its simplest form and then multiply by 20 to work out the number of chestnut trees. |
| Do the same for all the other types of tree. |

There are 10 chestnut, 5 oak, 2 ash and 3 birch trees in the park.

If the number of items in one category is known, the number of items in other categories and the total number of items can be worked out.

Example 5

The pie chart shows information about the number of girls in each year of Lampton School.
There are 30 girls in Year 8

a   Which year is the mode?

b   How many girls are there in Year 7?

c   How many girls are there altogether in Lampton School?

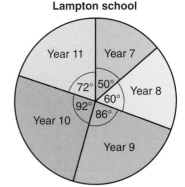

Lampton school

Solution 5

a   The mode is Year 10

b $60 \div 30 = 2$
    2° represent 1 girl

| The sector for Year 10 is the largest sector. |
| There are 30 girls in Year 8 |
| The angle for Year 8 is 60°. |
| Divide 60 by 30 to work out how many degrees represent 1 girl. |

$50 \div 2 = 25$
There are 25 girls in Year 7

| The angle for Year 7 is 50°. |
| 2° represent 1 girl. |
| Divide 50 by 2 to work out the number of girls in Year 7 |

c $360 \div 2 = 180$
    There are 180 girls in Lampton School.

| There are 360° in a full circle. |
| 2° represents each girl so divide 360 by 2 |

Exercise 2D

1 120 adults were asked where they went on holiday last summer. The pie chart shows the results of this survey.

   a Which was the most popular holiday destination?

   b Which holiday destination was the least popular?

   c What fraction of the adults went to France? Give your fraction in its simplest form.

   d How many of the adults went to France?

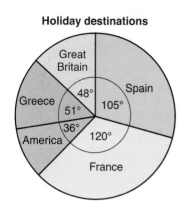

Holiday destinations

2 The pie chart shows the favourite sports of 90 girls.

   a Which sport is the mode?

   b How many degrees represent one person on the pie chart?

   c How many girls said netball was their favourite sport?

   d What angle represents hockey on the pie chart?

   e How many girls said hockey was their favourite sport?

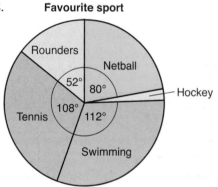

Favourite sport

3 The pie chart shows information about how Oliver spends his time in one 24-hour day.

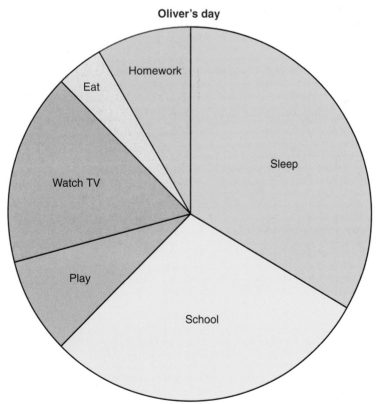

Oliver's day

Copy and complete the table. You will need to measure the angles in the pie chart.

Activity	Angle (degrees)	Number of hours
Sleep		
School		
Play		
Watch TV		
Eat		
Homework		

4 The pie chart shows information about the makes of car driven by 900 people.

a What fraction of the 900 people drive a Vauxhall? Give your fraction in its simplest form.

b How many people drive a Vauxhall?

c How many people are represented by 1 degree in the pie chart?

d How many people drive a Toyota?

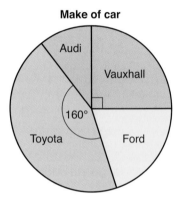

Make of car

5 In a survey, some adults were asked to name their favourite chocolate centre. The results are shown in the pie chart.

30 adults said that fudge was their favourite chocolate centre.

a How many degrees represent one person in the pie chart?

b How many adults took part in the survey?

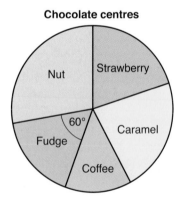

Chocolate centres

6 In a survey, some students were asked to name their favourite fruit. The pie chart shows information about their answers.

a Write down the fraction of the students who answered 'apple'. Write your fraction in its simplest form.

12 students answered 'apple'.

b Work out the number of students that took part in the survey.

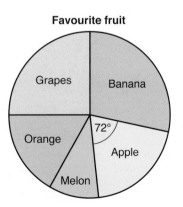

Favourite fruit

2.5 Time series

A **time series** is a set of readings taken over a period of time.
Some examples of time series are:

● the amount of money spent on food each week

● the number of days of sunshine each month

● electricity readings taken every quarter (three months).

A time series can be used to draw a **line graph**. This is sometimes called a time series graph.
The line graph shows the change in a quantity over a period of time.
The scale on the horizontal axis represents time.
The line graph below shows the number of holiday brochures sent out by a holiday company each month over one year.

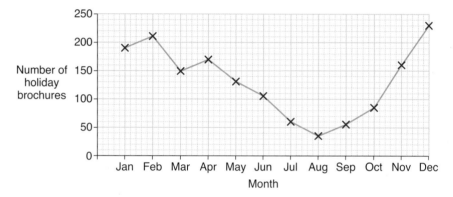

When a line graph is drawn from a time series, only the points that are plotted represent actual values.
The points are joined with straight lines to show the **trend** of the data.

Example 6

Lesley joins a diet club.
She records her weight at the end of every week for eight weeks.
This is shown in the line graph.

a What was Lesley's weight at the end of week 1?

b What was Lesley's weight at the end of week 6?

c What happened to Lesley's weight between the end of week 6 and the end of week 7?

d Is it possible to tell how much Lesley weighed in the middle of week 2?
Give a reason for your answer.

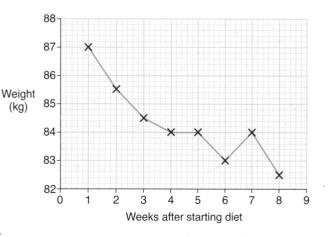

Solution 6

a   87 kg   b   83 kg   c   Her weight went up.

d   No. Lesley's weight goes down during week 2 but it is not possible to work out what she weighs on any single day, except on the days when she records her weight.

Exercise 2E

1   The Retail Price Index shows how prices change over a period of years. The graph shows the Retail Price Index for the years 1987 to 2005

   a   What was the Retail Price Index for 1995?

   b   What was the Retail Price Index for 1998?

   c   What does the graph tell you about the Retail Price Index?

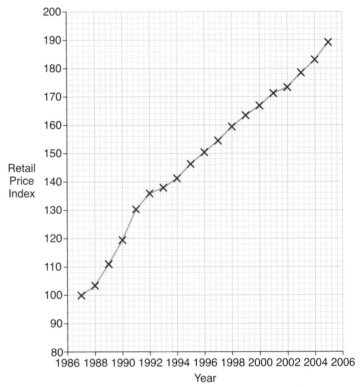

data from www.statistics.gov.uk

2   The graph shows the average monthly rainfall in Edinburgh.

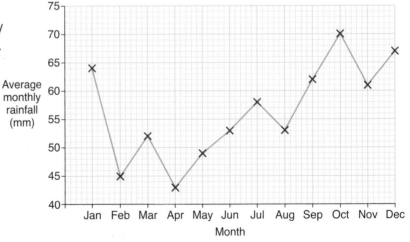

   a   In which month is the average monthly rainfall highest?
   b   In which month is the average monthly rainfall lowest?
   c   What was the average monthly rainfall in July?
   d   In which month is the average monthly rainfall 53 mm?

3   The table shows the maximum monthly temperature, in °C, in Blackpool.

Jan	Feb	Mar	Apr	May	Jun	Jul	Aug	Sep	Oct	Nov	Dec
7	7	9	12	15	17	19	19	17	14	10	8

Draw a line graph to show this information.

4   The graph shows the number of books sold by two shops each month for six months.

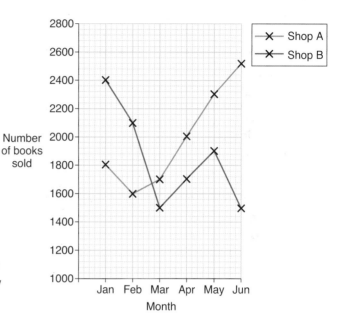

a   How many books were sold by shop A in May?

b   How many books were sold by shop B in January?

c   Which shop sold more books in April?

d   How many more books than shop A were sold by shop B in February?

e   Sales for shop A appear to be improving. How do you know this from the graph?

5   The table shows the average monthly temperature, in °C, in Croatia and Sicily each month for six months.

	Apr	May	Jun	Jul	Aug	Sep
Croatia	20	22	27	29	24	14
Sicily	15	20	24	29	34	32

Draw two line graphs on the same set of axes to show these temperatures.

2.6 Grouping data

When there is a large amount of data, the data is often grouped.
A **grouped frequency table** contains data that has been put into different groups.

The table shows information about the heights of 30 people. The heights have been grouped.

$160 \leqslant h < 165$ means 160 cm or more but less than 165 cm.

Height (h cm)	Frequency
$160 \leqslant h < 165$	9
$165 \leqslant h < 170$	15
$170 \leqslant h < 175$	6

Each group is called a **class interval** and, in this table, each class interval is of equal width (5 cm).
There are 9 people with heights in the class interval $160 \leqslant h < 165$

The **modal class interval** is the class interval with the highest frequency.
So the modal class interval for the heights is $165 \leqslant h < 170$

A **frequency diagram** can be drawn from grouped discrete data. A frequency diagram looks the same as a bar chart except that the label underneath each bar represents a group.

Example 7

20 students took a maths test. Their test marks are shown below.

17	9	6	12	19
4	13	12	15	16
20	14	5	10	11
17	8	14	12	18

a Complete the grouped frequency table.

b Draw a frequency diagram to show this information.

Mark	Tally	Frequency
1–5		
6–10		
11–15		
16–20		

Solution 7

a

Mark	Tally	Frequency
1–5	||	2
6–10	||||	4
11–15	ЖГ |||	8
16–20	ЖГ		6

b

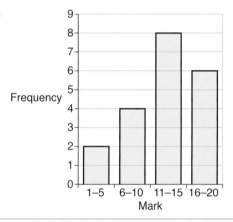

A **histogram** can be drawn from grouped continuous data. A histogram is similar to a bar chart but represents continuous data so there is no gap between the bars. There is a scale on the horizontal axis rather than a label under each bar.

Example 8

The grouped frequency table shows information about the heights of 42 students.

a Write down the modal class interval.

b Jenny's height is 177.2 cm. In which class interval is her height recorded?

c Charlie's height is exactly 180 cm. In which class interval is his height recorded?

d Draw a histogram to represent this information.

Height (h cm)	Frequency
$160 \leqslant h < 165$	10
$165 \leqslant h < 170$	14
$170 \leqslant h < 175$	8
$175 \leqslant h < 180$	5
$180 \leqslant h < 185$	3
$185 \leqslant h < 190$	2

Solution 8

a The modal class interval is
$165 \leqslant h < 170$

> This class interval has the highest frequency, 14

b Jenny's height is in the class interval
$175 \leqslant h < 180$

> 177.2 is greater than 175 but less than 180.

c Charlie's height is in the class interval
$180 \leqslant h < 185$

> 180 is shown at the end of one class interval and at the beginning of another. The sign for 'less than or equal to' ($\leqslant$) shows that 180 should go in the class interval $180 \leqslant h < 185$

d The histogram has a scale on the horizontal axis and no gaps between the bars.

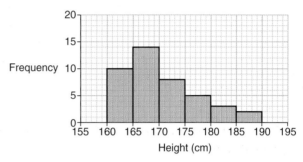

2.7 Frequency polygons

A **frequency polygon** is another graph which shows data.

To draw a frequency polygon for the data in Example 8, mark the midpoint of the top of each bar and join these points with straight lines.

This is the frequency polygon.

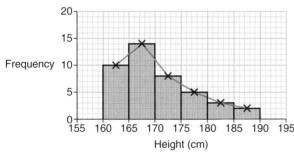

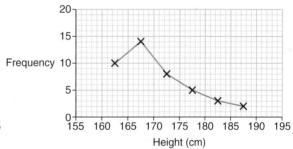

Example 9

The weight, in grams, of each of 30 apples is shown below.

98	110	103	94	104
91	92	114	96	100
102	99	95	103	116
118	113	108	114	99
105	103	112	91	93
90	105	103	109	97

a Complete the grouped frequency table.

b Write down the modal class interval.

c Use the information to draw a histogram.

d Draw a frequency polygon to represent the information.

Weight (w grams)	Tally	Frequency
$90 \leqslant w < 95$		
$95 \leqslant w < 100$		
$100 \leqslant w < 105$		
$105 \leqslant w < 110$		
$110 \leqslant w < 115$		
$115 \leqslant w < 120$		

Solution 9

a

Weight (w grams)	Tally	Frequency
$90 \leqslant w < 95$	̶I̶I̶I̶I̶ I	6
$95 \leqslant w < 100$	̶I̶I̶I̶I̶ I	6
$100 \leqslant w < 105$	̶I̶I̶I̶I̶ II	7
$105 \leqslant w < 110$	IIII	4
$110 \leqslant w < 115$	̶I̶I̶I̶I̶	5
$115 \leqslant w < 120$	II	2

Note that a weight such as 95 grams is included in the $95 \leqslant w < 100$ group and not the $90 \leqslant w < 95$ group.

b The modal class interval is $100 \leqslant w < 105$

c and **d** As the question has asked for both a histogram and a frequency polygon to be drawn, draw the frequency polygon on the histogram.

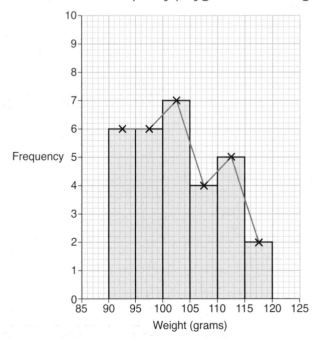

More than one frequency polygon can be drawn on the same grid to compare data.

Example 10

The two frequency polygons show the heights of a group of girls and the heights of a group of boys.

Compare the heights of the two groups. Give a reason for your answers.

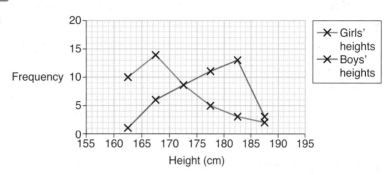

Solution 10

The boys are generally taller than the girls.

The line showing the boys' heights is above the line for the girls' heights towards the right of the graph.

There are more tall boys than tall girls.

There are two girls and three boys in the 185–190 cm class interval.

There are more short girls than short boys.

There are ten girls and one boy in the 160–165 cm class interval.

Example 11

This graph shows the percentage of Mathstown buses that arrived on time each year from 2000 to 2003

Explain why this graph is misleading.

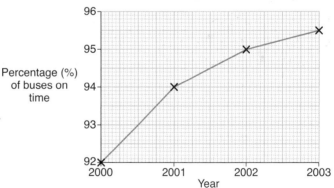

Solution 11

The steep line between 2000 and 2001 suggests that a *much higher* percentage of buses were on time in 2001 than in 2002 but it is only 2% more.

If the vertical scale starts from 0, the lines are all less steep, showing that the increases are small. The disadvantage of this is that a large area of the graph is empty.

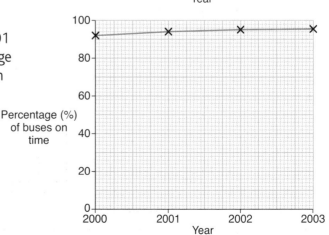

A zig-zag in the vertical axis can be used to show that the scale does not start at 0

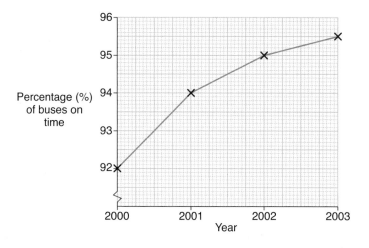

Exercise 2F

1 Jason records how many copies of a daily newspaper his shop sells each day in September.

56	43	51	54	49	42
57	60	67	52	52	47
42	61	65	58	50	54
65	54	63	62	61	53
55	59	61	45	68	61

a Copy and complete the grouped frequency table.

b Write down the modal class interval.

Number of newspapers	Tally	Frequency
41–45		
46–50		
51–55		
56–60		
61–65		
66–70		

2 The grouped frequency table shows the test marks of a class of 32 students.

a Write down the modal class interval.

b Draw a frequency diagram for this information.

Test marks	Frequency
1–4	2
5–8	5
9–12	6
13–16	11
17–20	8

3 The histogram shows information about the times taken by some girls to run 100 m.

a Write down the modal class interval.

b Work out the total number of girls.

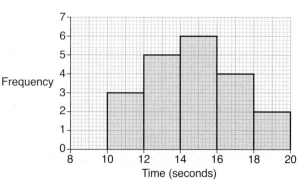

Some boys also ran 100 m. The grouped frequency table shows information about their times.

Time (t seconds)	Frequency
$10 \leqslant t < 12$	6
$12 \leqslant t < 14$	5
$14 \leqslant t < 16$	5
$16 \leqslant t < 18$	3
$18 \leqslant t < 20$	1

c   Draw a histogram to show this information.

d   Draw a frequency polygon to show this information.

4   In one month Julie went to the Post Office 20 times and to the bank 20 times. The frequency polygons show information about the amount of time Julie spent waiting in a queue at the post office and at the bank.

a   At the bank, how many times did Julie wait for between 15 and 20 minutes?

b   At the post office, how many times did Julie wait for between 5 and 10 minutes?

c   For what fraction of the times Julie went to the post office did she wait for less than 10 minutes? Give your fraction in its simplest form.

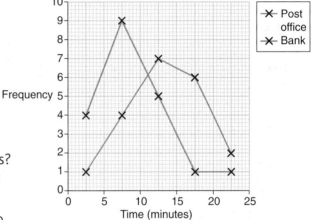

d   Where did Julie generally have to wait the longest time, the bank or the post office? You must give a reason for your answer.

5   The graph shows the number of cars sold in 3 years.

Give two reasons why the graph is misleading.

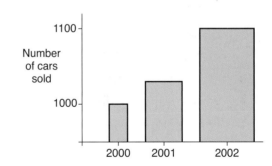

Chapter summary

You should know

★   That **pictograms** and **bar charts** are used to show discrete data

★   How to interpret and draw pictograms and bar charts

★   That the **mode** is the value that occurs most frequently

★   That **pie charts** show the proportions of the different categories of data.

★   How to draw and interpret pie charts

★ That **time series graphs** can be used for discrete data to show change over a period of time

★ How to draw and interpret time series graphs

★ That a **grouped frequency table** contains data in class intervals

★ That the **modal class interval** is the class interval with the highest frequency

★ That **line graphs** can be used to represent continuous data

★ How to draw and interpret line graphs

★ That **frequency diagrams** can be used to represent grouped discrete data

★ How to draw and interpret frequency diagrams

★ That **histograms** can be used to represent continuous data

★ How to draw and interpret histograms

★ That **frequency polygons** can be used to compare two or more sets of data

★ How to draw frequency polygons.

Chapter 2 review questions

1   Here is a pictogram.
    It shows the number of letters delivered to High School on each of four days.

Monday	⊞ ⊞ ⊞ ⊞
Tuesday	⊞ ⊞
Wednesday	⊞ ⊞ ⊞ ⊟
Thursday	⊞ ⊞ ⊞ ⊞ ▫
Friday	

    Key
    ⊞ represents 20 letters

    a   Write down the number of letters delivered to the school on
        i Tuesday   ii Wednesday
    On Friday 55 letters were delivered to the school.
    b   Show this on a copy of the pictogram.
    c   Work out the total number of letters delivered to the school on the five days.

2   The table shows the number of DVDs borrowed from a shop each day from Monday to Friday one week.

Monday	Tuesday	Wednesday	Thursday	Friday
60	90	100	85	115

    Draw a pictogram to represent this information.
    Use ⊞ to represent 20 DVDs.

3   A shop has a sale. The bar chart shows some information about the sale.

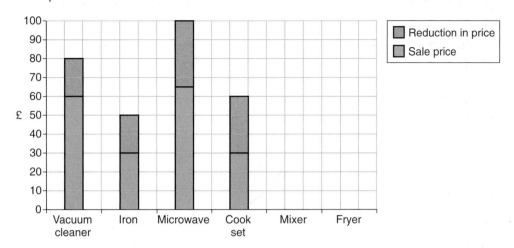

The normal price of a vacuum cleaner is £80
The sale price of a vacuum cleaner is £60
The price of a vacuum cleaner is reduced from £80 to £60

a   Write the sale price of a vacuum cleaner as a fraction of its normal price.
Give your answer in its simplest form.

b   Find the reduction in the price of the iron.

c   Which **two** items have the same sale price?

d   Which items has the greatest reduction in price?

Mixer	
Normal price	£90
Sale price	£70

Fryer	
Normal price	£85
Sale price	£70

e   On the resource sheet, complete the bar chart for the mixer and the fryer.
(1387 June 2004)

4   The bar chart shows information about the favourite drink of each student in a class.

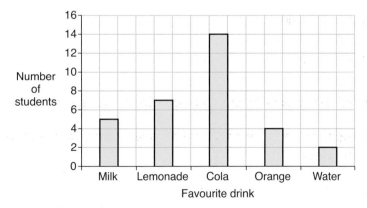

a   Which was the favourite drink of the greatest number of students?

b   Write down the number of students whose favourite drink was lemonade.

c   Work out the **total** number of students in the class.   (1388 June 2003)

5 Ray and Clare are pupils at different schools.
They each did an investigation into their teachers' favourite colours.

Here is Ray's bar chart of his teachers' favourite colours.

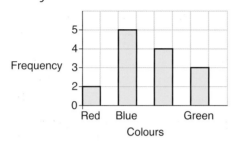

a Write down two things that are wrong with Ray's bar chart.

Clare drew a bar chart of her teacher's favourite colours.

Part of her bar chart is shown below.

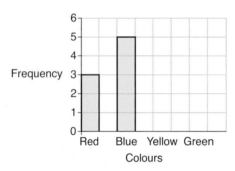

4 teachers said that yellow was their favourite colour.

2 teachers said that green was their favourite colour.

b Complete Clare's bar chart on the resource sheet.

(1387 Jan 2003)

6 Six students each sat a history test and a geography test.

The marks of five of the students, in each of the tests, were used to draw the bar chart.

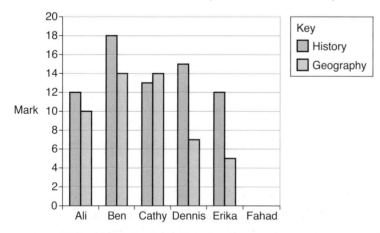

a How many marks did Ali get in his history test?

b How many marks did Dennis get in his geography test?

  c One student got a lower mark in the history test than in the geography test. Write down the name of this student.

Fahad got 16 marks in the history test. She got 11 marks in the geography test.

  d Use this information to complete the bar chart on the resource sheet.

(1388 March 2004)

7 In a survey, some students were asked what their favourite leisure activity was.
Their answers were used to draw this pie chart.

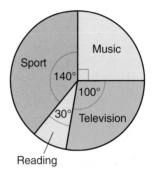

  a Write down the fraction of the students who answered 'Television'.
Write your answer in its simplest form.

18 students answered 'Music'.

  b Work out the number of students who took part in the survey.

(1388 March 2003)

8 Sam sells second hand cars.
Sam has 36 cars in his showroom.

The table gives information about the makes of cars in his showroom.

Draw a pie chart to show this information.

Make of car	Frequency
Ford	7
Toyota	6
Rover	8
Renault	15

9 Barry's pulse rate is taken every 6 hours over 3 days.
The graph shows his pulse rate in beats per minute.

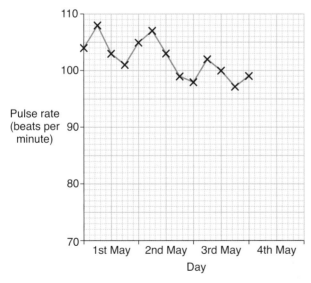

  a Write down the first pulse rate shown on the graph.

  b Write down Barry's highest pulse rate shown during the three days.

  c Work out the difference between his highest and lowest pulse rates shown on 3rd May.

(1385 June 2001)

10 A railway company wanted to show the improvements in its train service over 3 years. This graph was drawn.

Explain why this graph may be misleading.

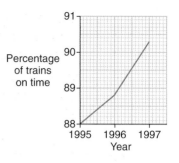

(1385 Nov 2001)

11 The table shows the frequency distribution of student absences for a year.

Absences (d days)	Frequency
$0 \leqslant d < 5$	4
$5 \leqslant d < 10$	6
$10 \leqslant d < 15$	8
$15 \leqslant d < 20$	5
$20 \leqslant d < 25$	4
$25 \leqslant d < 30$	3

Draw a frequency polygon for this frequency distribution on the resource sheet.

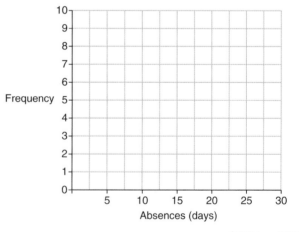

(1385 June 2001)

12 Alan recorded the pulse rate of 25 of his friends. The information he recorded is shown below.

54	59	64	72	58
70	83	67	98	92
88	85	73	87	82
93	99	72	63	68
82	80	77	79	90

Pulse rate	Tally	Frequency
50–59		
60–69		
70–79		
80–89		
90–99		

a Copy and complete the grouped frequency table.

b Write down the modal class interval.

c Draw a frequency polygon to represent this information.

13 Jackie recorded the heights of 30 of her friends. The grouped frequency table shows information about these heights.

Height (cm)	Frequency
$150 \leqslant h < 155$	4
$155 \leqslant h < 160$	7
$160 \leqslant h < 165$	10
$165 \leqslant h < 170$	4
$170 \leqslant h < 175$	5

   a Mary's height is 154.4 cm. In which class interval is Mary's height recorded?

   b Declan's height is 170 cm. In which class interval is Declan's height recorded?

   c Write down the modal class interval.

   d Draw a histogram to represent the information.

Averages and range

"I've got to improve my batting **average**"

"Yes madam you have an **average** shoe size"

sale

Giorgio Shoes

"The lowest test mark was 3 and the highest was 19. That's a **range** of 16 marks."

"That's not the **average** wage for my workers!"

3.1 Mean, mode, median and range

What is the average of the five numbers   1   7   1   5   6?

In statistics there are three different measures of average – the **mean**, the **mode** and the **median**.

To find the mean, add the five numbers together and divide by 5

The mean is $\dfrac{1+7+1+5+6}{5} = \dfrac{20}{5} = 20 \div 5 = 4$

In general, mean = (sum of all the numbers) ÷ (how many numbers there are).

The mode is the number in the list which occurs the most times. The mode in the list above is 1

To find the median, list the numbers in order and the median is the middle number.

In order, the numbers are 1   1   5   6   7 . The **median** is 5

If there are two middle numbers the median is halfway between them.

In statistics, **range** is a measure of how spread out the numerical data is.
To find the range work out the difference between the highest number and the lowest number.

For the five numbers, 1, 7, 1, 5 and 6 the range is $7 - 1 = 6$

Example 1

Tony and Andrew play cricket. The numbers of runs Tony scores in each of ten innings are

| 20 | 35 | 17 | 1 | 14 | 15 | 5 | 13 | 2 | 6 |

a Work out Tony's mean score.

b Andrew's mean score for his last ten innings is 9
Work out the total number of runs Andrew scored in his last ten innings.

Solution 1

a Mean score $= \dfrac{20 + 35 + 17 + 1 + 14 + 15 + 5 + 13 + 2 + 6}{10}$

$= \dfrac{128}{10} = 12.8$

b Mean = (total number of runs scored) ÷ (number of innings)
$9 = \text{total} \div 10$
$\text{Total} = 9 \times 10 = 90$
Andrew has scored a total of 90 runs.

In cricket, a batsman's 'average' score is his mean score.
The mean does not have to be a whole number.

A calculator can be used to find a mean. Check that you know how to calculate means using your own calculator.

Example 2

Here is a pictogram about ladies' shoes.
It shows how many pairs of each shoe size were sold in a shop last week.

a **i** Which shoe size is the mode?
ii How many pairs of size 6 shoes were sold last week?

b Work out the range of these shoe sizes.

Shoe size		Key
3	θ θ θ θ	θ represents four pairs
$3\frac{1}{2}$	θ θ	
4	θ θ θ θ	
$4\frac{1}{2}$	θ θ θ	
5	θ θ θ θ θ θ θ	
$5\frac{1}{2}$	θ θ θ θ θ	
6	θ θ θ θ θ θ	
$6\frac{1}{2}$	θ θ θ	
7	θ θ	

Solution 2

a **i** 5   Shoe size 5 has the most symbols in the pictogram.
    ii 6 × 4   Size 6 has 6 symbols. Each symbol represents 4 pairs of shoes
                 = 24 pairs of size 6 shoes.

b 7 is the largest shoe size.
    3 is the smallest shoe size.
    The range is 7 − 3 = 4

It is more useful for the shopkeeper to know which shoe sizes are most popular.
So finding the mode is the most appropriate average in this case.

Example 3

Seven people work in an office. The table shows
their income last year.

a Work out the mean income last year.
b Find the median income last year.
c Leaving out Julian's income, work out for
    the remaining six office workers
      i their mean income
     ii their median income.

Name	Income last year
Arthur	£12 000
Bob	£8500
Bradley	£30 000
Jim	£11 000
Julian	£73 000
Pamela	£29 500
Tracey	£11 000

Solution 3

a Mean income $= \dfrac{12\,000 + 8500 + 30\,000 + 11\,000 + 73\,000 + 29\,500 + 11\,000}{7}$

$= \dfrac{175\,000}{7} = £25\,000$

b List the seven incomes in order

$\boxed{£8500 \quad £11\,000 \quad £11\,000}$ £12 000 $\boxed{£29\,500 \quad £30\,000 \quad £73\,000}$

Median income = £12 000

c **i** Mean income $= \dfrac{12\,000 + 8500 + 30\,000 + 11\,000 + 29\,500 + 11\,000}{6}$

$= \dfrac{102\,000}{6} = £17\,000$

ii List the six incomes in order.

$\boxed{£8500 \quad £11\,000}$ £11 000 • £12 000 $\boxed{£29\,500 \quad £30\,000}$

Find the number which is halfway between
11 000 and 12 000

Median income $= \dfrac{11\,000 + 12\,000}{2} = \dfrac{23\,000}{2} = £11\,500$

11 500 is the mean of the middle two numbers.

One extreme value (£73 000) has a big effect on the mean but little effect on the median.
The median can be used for average income to avoid this effect.

Exercise 3A

1 Here is a list of five numbers: 2   6   3   7   2
  a Write down the mode.   **b** Find the median.
  c Find the range.   **d** Work out the mean.

2 Here is a list of six numbers: 2   5   3   7   2   11
  a Find the median.   **b** Work out the mean.

3 The list shows the number of cars sold at a garage in the last ten days.

| 3 | 2 | 7 | 8 | 4 | 9 | 7 | 5 | 7 | 3 |

  a Write down the mode.
  b Find the range.
  c Find the median.
  d Work out the mean number of cars sold per day.
  e In the previous ten days, the lowest number of cars sold on any day was 3
      The range of the numbers of cars sold was 9. Find the greatest number of cars
      sold on any of these ten days.

4 A rugby team plays 12 games. Here are the number of points they score.

| 24 | 10 | 23 | 16 | 12 | 8 | 19 | 23 | 16 | 37 | 16 | 27 |

  a Write down the mode.
  b Work out the range.
  c Work out the mean number of points per game.

5 Here are the lengths, in centimetres, of five used matchsticks.

| 2.7 | 2.8 | 3.0 | 3.2 | 2.8 |

  a Work out the range of these lengths.
  b Work out the mean length of these matchsticks.
  c The mean length of ten other matchsticks is 3.0 cm. Find the total of the lengths
      of these ten matchsticks.

6 Five people work in a canteen.
  The table shows their incomes last year.
  a Work out the mean income last year.
  b Find the median income last year.
  c Pamela is the canteen manager.
      How much more was Pamela's income
      than the mean income of the remaining
      four workers?

Name	Income last year
Leanne	£2500
Mike	£3200
Nazia	£5800
Owen	£4100
Pamela	£22 400

3.2 Using frequency tables to find averages

Example 4

A dice is rolled ten times. Here are the scores, in order of size.

| 1 | 2 | 2 | 2 | 3 | 3 | 4 | 4 | 5 | 6 |

a Show this information in a frequency table.
b Find the median for the ten scores.

Solution 4

a

Score	Frequency
1	1
2	3
3	2 (fifth and sixth)
4	2
5	1
6	1

b *Method 1*

                    5th 6th

| 1 | 2 | 2 | 2 | 3 • 3 | 4 | 4 | 5 | 6 |

The median score is 3

Method 2
The frequency table shows the scores in order. Since there are ten scores the median will be halfway between the fifth and sixth scores. The median score is 3.

For a large amount of data method 2 is quicker.

Example 5

The frequency table shows information about the number of certificates awarded to each student in a class last month.

Number of certificates	Frequency
0	3
1	7
2	3
3	9
4	8

a Write down the modal number of certificates awarded.
b Work out the range of the number of certificates awarded.
c How many students were in the class?
d Work out the total number of certificates awarded.
e Work out the mean number of certificates awarded to students.
f Work out the median number of certificates awarded to students.

Solution 5

a The highest frequency is 9
The number of certificates with this frequency is 3
The modal number of certificates = 3

b Students were each awarded 0 or 1 or 2 or 3 or 4 certificates.
The highest number of certificates is 4 and the lowest number of certificates is 0
The range = 4 − 0 = 4

c Total number of students = 3 + 7 + 3 + 9 + 8 = 30

d 3 students were each awarded 0 certificates; number of certificates = 3 × 0 = 0
7 students were each awarded 1 certificate; number of certificates = 7 × 1 = 7
3 students were each awarded 2 certificates; number of certificates = 3 × 2 = 6
9 students were each awarded 3 certificates; number of certificates = 9 × 3 = 27
8 students were each awarded 4 certificates; number of certificates = 8 × 4 = 32
Total number of certificates awarded = 0 + 7 + 6 + 27 + 32 = 72

e Mean number of certificates = $\dfrac{\text{total number of certificates}}{\text{total number of students}} = \dfrac{72}{30} = 2.4$

f

Number of certificates	Frequency
0	3
1	7
2	3
3	9
4	8

1st to 3rd students received **0** certificates

4th to 10th (3 + 7) students received **1** certificate

11th to 13th (3 + 7 + 3) students received **2** certificates

14th to 22nd (3 + 7 + 3 + 9) students received **3** certificates

23rd to 30th students received **4** certificates

Splitting the group of 30 students in half (30 ÷ 2 = 15) gives

| The number of certificates received by the lower 15 students | | The number of certificates received by the higher 15 students |

or | Number of certificates received by the **1st to 14th** students | **15th** 3 certficates | **16th** 3 certficates | Number of certificates received by the **17th to 30th** students |

The median number of certificates is 3

Exercise 3B

1 The table shows the results of rolling a dice 10 times.

  a Find the median score.

  b Work out the mean score.

Score	Frequency
1	3
2	3
3	1
4	2
5	1
6	0

2 The table shows the numbers of cakes sold in a shop to 30 customers.

   a Write down the modal number of cakes sold.

   b Work out the total number of cakes sold to these 30 customers.

   c Work out the mean number of cakes sold.

   d Find the median number of cakes sold.

Number of cakes	Number of customers
0	2
1	9
2	6
3	6
4	5
5	2

3 The table shows the numbers of goals scored by a hockey team in each of 25 matches.

   a Write down the mode of the number of goals scored.

   b Work out the mean number of goals scored per match.

Number of goals	Frequency
0	9
1	5
2	5
3	4
4	2

4 Mrs Fox does a survey of the number of books each pupil in her class borrowed from the library last month. The frequency table shows her results.

   a Work out the number of pupils that Mrs Fox asked.

   b Ben thinks that the average number of books borrowed in this survey is 6. Explain why Ben cannot be correct.

   c Find the median number of books borrowed.

   d Work out the mean number of books borrowed.

Number of books borrowed	Frequency
0	4
1	6
2	6
3	8

5 A wedding photographer records the number of weddings he attended each week last year. The table shows his results.

   a Find the median number of weddings he attended per week.

   b Find the mean number of weddings he attended per week.

   c The photographer is paid £250 for each wedding he attends. Work out the total amount the photographer was paid last year.

Number of weddings	Frequency
0	10
1	14
2	4
3	2
4	13
5	5
6	3
7	1

3.3 Stem and leaf diagrams

Data can be shown in a **stem and leaf diagram**. From this, the mode, median and range can be found easily.

The ages, in years, of eleven people are

| 12 | 9 | 20 | 24 | 15 | 17 | 31 | 4 | 15 | 17 | 28 |

Here is a stem and leaf diagram showing these ages. The key is part of the stem and leaf diagram.

Stem   Leaves

Stem	Leaves
0	4 9
1	2 5 5 7 7
2	0 4 8
3	1

The data is ordered from $0 \mid 4$ (= age 4) to $3 \mid 1$ (= age 31).

In this case, the **stem** shows the **tens** and the **leaves** show the **units**.

Key

$1 \mid 2$ means age 12

Example 6

Here is a stem and leaf diagram showing the ages, in years, of 15 office workers. Find

a the range of the 15 ages

b the median age.

1	6 7 9
2	1 2 5 5 9 9
3	0 4 5 8
4	1 7

Key

$1 \mid 6$ means age 16

Solution 6

a The data is ordered from
$1 \mid 6$ (= age 16) to $4 \mid 7$ (= age 47)
Range = 47 − 16 = 31 years

b The median is the 8th age which is $2 \mid 9$.
(The middle of 15 numbers is the eighth number.)
The median age is 29 years.

1	6 7 9
2	1 2 5 5 **9** 9
3	0 4 5 8
4	1 7

Example 7

Twenty boys are timed over a 10 metre sprint.
Here are their times to the nearest tenth of a second.

| 2.6 | 3.8 | 3.0 | 4.7 | 2.9 | 4.1 | 2.9 | 2.1 | 3.1 | 3.9 |
| 4.0 | 2.4 | 4.4 | 3.7 | 2.7 | 3.8 | 5.1 | 2.8 | 4.7 | 2.9 |

a Draw a stem and leaf diagram to show these results.

b Use your stem and leaf diagram to find
  i the range of the times   **ii** the median time.

Solution 7

a

2	1 4 6 7 8 9 9 9
3	0 1 7 8 8 9
4	0 1 4 7 7
5	1

Key

3 | 9 means 3.9 seconds

b **i** Range = 5.1 − 2.1 = 3.0 seconds.

ii The median is halfway between the **10th** and **11th** times, **3.1** and **3.7** seconds.

4 is halfway between 1 and 7, since $\dfrac{1+7}{2} = 4$, so 3 | 4 gives the median time, which is 3.4 seconds.

Exercise 3C

1 The stem and leaf diagram shows number of minutes taken by each student in a class to complete a puzzle.

0	8 9 9
1	0 1 3 3 8 8 9
2	1 4 4 4 6 6 9
3	0 2 3 4 7 7 8 8
4	1 1 2 2 4

Key

4 | 1 stands for 41 minutes

a Find the number of students in the class.

b Write down how many students took 24 minutes to complete the puzzle.

c Write down how many students took 10 minutes longer than the quickest student to solve the puzzle.

d Find the range of the times.

e Find the median time.

2 Here are the numbers of minutes a sample of 15 patients had to wait before seeing a hospital doctor.

49	23	34	10	28
39	28	25	45	20
35	15	14	48	10

a Draw a stem and leaf diagram to show this information.

b Use your stem and leaf diagram to find

i the range of the times

ii the median time.

3 Tony records the number of e-mails he receives each day. Here are his results for the last 20 days.

178	189	147	147	166
167	153	171	164	158
189	166	165	155	152
147	158	148	151	172

a Draw a stem and leaf diagram to show this information.

b Use your stem and leaf diagram to find the median number of e-mails.

4   The table gives the number of days each of
25 people had been on holiday in Spain.

    a   Draw a stem and leaf diagram to show
this information.

    b   Use your stem and leaf diagram to find
the median number of days.

    c   Use your stem and leaf diagram to find the range of the number of days.

0	7	14	38	26
16	13	21	35	30
9	10	21	25	22
7	15	7	21	14
25	31	30	7	7

5   Nicki weighs 20 parcels.
Here are her results, in kilograms.

    a   Draw a stem and leaf diagram to show
this information.

    b   Use your stem and leaf diagram to find the
range of the weights.

    c   Use your stem and leaf diagram to find the median weight.

0.7	1.6	2.3	3.4	2.8
1.7	1.5	1.1	1.4	0.8
3.3	2.6	1.6	1.1	2.7
2.7	1.8	2.0	0.9	3.0

3.4 Data logging and comparing distributions

Data logging is the collection and
storage of data for later use.

Data is usually collected electronically
at equal time intervals. For example,
in hospital, a patient's temperature,
pulse rate and blood pressure can be
monitored continuously throughout
the day. Graphs of these results are
produced electronically.

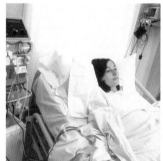

Example 8

Weather stations in Florida and Spain record the midday temperatures. The diagram shows
the average monthly temperatures in Florida and in Spain for the six month period from
July to December.

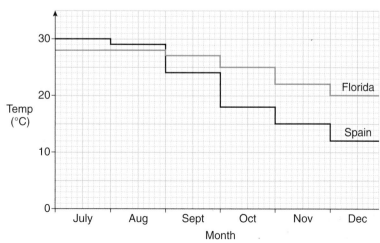

a Write down the average temperature in Spain during September.

b Work out the mean of the average monthly temperatures for this six month period in
  i Florida   **ii** Spain.

c Work out the range of the average monthly temperatures for this six month period in
  i Florida   **ii** Spain.

d Comment on your answers to **b** and **c**.

Solution 8

a 24°C

b **i** Florida: mean $= \dfrac{28 + 28 + 27 + 25 + 22 + 20}{6} = \dfrac{150}{6} = 25°C$

  ii Spain: mean $= \dfrac{30 + 29 + 24 + 18 + 15 + 12}{6} = \dfrac{128}{6} = 21.3°C$ (to 1 d.p.)

c **i** Florida: range $= 28 - 20 = 8°C$
  ii Spain: range $= 30 - 12 = 18°C$

d Even though the average temperatures in July and August are higher in Spain than Florida, Florida has the higher mean during the six month period. The spread of monthly temperatures is less in Florida than in Spain, as shown by the range in Florida being less than in Spain.

Example 9

Jenny buys a rock CD and a pop CD. There are 10 tracks on each.
The length, in minutes, of each track on the rock CD are

| 3 | 5 | 6 | 4 | 12 | 9 | 7 | 6 | 4 | 5 |

The length, in minutes, of each track on the pop CD are

| 6 | 5 | 6 | 7 | 6 | 6 | 7 | 6 | 7 | 5 |

a For each CD work out the mean length of track.

b For each CD work out the range of the lengths of tracks.

c Comment on your answers to parts **a** and **b**.

Solution 9

a Rock CD: mean $= \dfrac{3 + 5 + 6 + 4 + 12 + 9 + 7 + 6 + 4 + 5}{10} = \dfrac{61}{10} = 6.1$ minutes.

  Pop CD: mean $= \dfrac{6 + 5 + 6 + 7 + 6 + 6 + 7 + 6 + 7 + 5}{10} = \dfrac{61}{10} = 6.1$ minutes.

b   Rock CD: range $= 12 - 3 = 9$ minutes.   Pop CD: range $= 7 - 5 = 2$ minutes.

c   Both CDs have the same mean length of track but the range of the lengths of the tracks on the pop CD is much smaller. This means that there is much less variation in the lengths of the tracks on the pop CD.

Comparing distributions

Back-to-back stem and leaf diagrams can be used to compare two distributions.

Example 10

David chooses a sample of 30 girls and 30 boys in Year 10 to compare their weights.

This back-to-back stem and leaf diagram shows his results.

Girls		Boys
9 9 8 7 7 0	**4**	
9 9 9 8 8 7 7 6 4 4 3 2 1	**5**	6 7 7 8 9
8 7 6 6 6 5 4 4 3 2	**6**	0 1 1 2 4 5 6 6 6 6 8 9
2 1	**7**	0 0 1 2 2 3 4 4 5 6 7
	8	0 1

Key **5** $\mid$ 1 means 51 kg

Compare the weights of the girls and boys by finding

a   the range   **b**   the median of each distribution.

Solution 10

a   For the girls, the data is ordered from 0 $\mid$ **4** ($= 40$ kg) to 2 $\mid$ **7** ($= 72$ kg).
The range $= 72 - 40 = 32$ kg.

For the boys, the data is ordered from **5** $\mid$ 6 ($= 56$ kg) to **8** $\mid$ 1 ($= 81$ kg).
The range $= 81 - 56 = 25$ kg.

This shows that the weights of the girls are more spread out.

b   The median is in the middle of the 30 weights for each distribution.
This is halfway between the 15th weight and 16th weight.

For the girls, the 15th weight is **8** $\mid$ **5** which is 58 kg
                 the 16th weight is **9** $\mid$ **5** which is 59 kg.

The median for the girls $= 58.5$ kg.

For the boys, the 15th weight is **6** $\mid$ 6 which is 66 kg
              the 16th weight is **6** $\mid$ 8 which is 68 kg.

The median for the boys $= 67$ kg.

This shows that in general the boys are heavier than the girls.

Look back at the stem and leaf diagram. The distribution of the weights of the boys is towards the higher values.

Exercise 3D

1   The graph shows some readings of Wendy's temperature when she was in hospital.

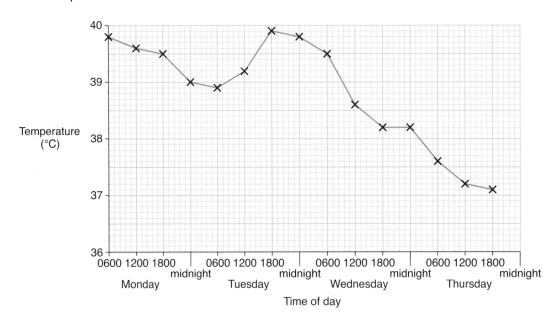

a   How many hours were there between each reading?

b   i   Write down each of the four readings of Wendy's temperature on Monday.
   ii   Write down the range of these temperatures.
  iii   Work out the mean of these temperatures.

c   i   Write down each of the four readings of Wendy's temperature on Wednesday.
   ii   Write down the range of these temperatures.
  iii   Work out the mean of these temperatures.

d   Comment on your results to parts **b** and **c**.

2   Kevin and Joe play golf. The table shows the number of shots taken by each of them at the 18th hole over their last 20 rounds of golf.

Number of shots	Kevin	Joe
2	0	3
3	2	5
4	9	4
5	6	4
6	3	1
7	0	3

a   Write down the range of the number of shots for each player.

b   Write down the modal number of shots for each player.

c   Work out the mean number of shots for each player.

d   Which golfer plays the 18th hole better? Give reasons for your answer.

3 The back to back stem and leaf diagram shows the percentage marks of a group of boys and girls in a science test.

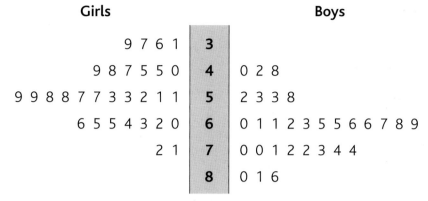

	Girls		Boys
	9 7 6 1	**3**	
	9 8 7 5 5 0	**4**	0 2 8
9 9 8 8 7 7 3 3 2 1 1		**5**	2 3 3 8
	6 5 5 4 3 2 0	**6**	0 1 1 2 3 5 5 6 6 7 8 9
	2 1	**7**	0 0 1 2 2 3 4 4
		8	0 1 6

Key **5** | 2 means 52%

a Find the range of percentage marks for **i** the boys **ii** the girls.

b Find the median of percentage marks for **i** the boys **ii** the girls.

c Compare and comment on the marks for the boys and girls.

3.5 Estimating the mean of grouped data

This table appeared in the *Burwich Guardian*.

It shows some information about the number of road accidents in Burwich each day last September.

There were 7 days on which there were fewer than 5 accidents.

It is impossible to tell from the table the exact number of accidents on each day so an exact value for the average number of accidents per day cannot be found.

Number of accidents	Number of days
0 to 4	7
5 to 9	14
10 to 14	8
15 to 19	1

It is possible to find an estimate for the mean number of accidents per day. We use the middle of each class interval. For example, we assume that there were $\dfrac{0 + 4}{2} = 2$ accidents on each of the 7 days. This gives a total of $7 \times 2 = 14$ accidents.

Example 11

This table shows some information about the number of road accidents in Burmage last April.

Work out an estimate for the mean number of accidents per day in Burmage last April.

Number of accidents	Number of days		
0 to 4	7		
5 to 9	9		
10 to 14	12		
15 to 19	2		

Solution 11

Number of accidents	Number of days	Middle of class interval	Number of accidents
0 to 4	7	$\dfrac{0+4}{2} = 2$	$7 \times 2 = 14$
5 to 9	9	$\dfrac{5+9}{2} = 7$	$9 \times 7 = 63$
10 to 14	12	$\dfrac{10+14}{2} = 12$	$12 \times 12 = 144$
15 to 19	2	$\dfrac{15+19}{2} = 17$	$2 \times 17 = 34$

The total number of accidents in April is $14 + 63 + 144 + 34 = 255$
The total number of days in April is $7 + 9 + 12 + 2 = 30$
Estimated mean $= \frac{255}{30} = 8.5$ accidents per day.

Example 12

The table shows some information about the annual earnings of 140 employees of a company.

The figures in the first column are called **class intervals**.

$10\,000 < x \leqslant 20\,000$ means earnings above £10 000 up to and including £20 000
See Section 2.6

a Work out an estimate for the mean earnings.

b Find the class interval that contains the median earnings.

Annual earnings (£)	Frequency
$0 < x \leqslant 10\,000$	30
$10\,000 < x \leqslant 20\,000$	42
$20\,000 < x \leqslant 30\,000$	28
$30\,000 < x \leqslant 40\,000$	20
$40\,000 < x \leqslant 50\,000$	18
$50\,000 < x \leqslant 60\,000$	2

Solution 12

a

Annual earnings (£)	Frequency	Middle of class interval	Totals of earnings
$0 < x \leqslant 10\,000$	30	5000	$5000 \times 30 = 150\,000$
$10\,000 < x \leqslant 20\,000$	42	15 000	$15\,000 \times 42 = 630\,000$
$20\,000 < x \leqslant 30\,000$	28	25 000	$25\,000 \times 28 = 700\,000$
$30\,000 < x \leqslant 40\,000$	20	35 000	$35\,000 \times 20 = 700\,000$
$40\,000 < x \leqslant 50\,000$	18	45 000	$45\,000 \times 18 = 810\,000$
$50\,000 < x \leqslant 60\,000$	2	55 000	$55\,000 \times 2 = 110\,000$
	Total = 140		Total = 3 100 000

Estimated mean $= \dfrac{\text{total earnings}}{\text{total number of employees}} = \dfrac{3\,100\,000}{140} = £22\,143$ (to the nearest £).

b 140 ÷ 2 = 70. The median is in the middle of the 70th and the 71st earnings.

Annual earnings (£)	Frequency
$0 < x \leqslant 10\,000$	30
$10\,000 < x \leqslant 20\,000$	42

1st to the 30th earnings.

31st to 72nd earnings.

Both the 70th and the 71st earnings lie in the class interval $10\,000 < x \leqslant 20\,000$, so the median lies in the class interval $10\,000 < x \leqslant 20\,000$

Exercise 3E

1 Twenty people take part in a competition. The points scored are grouped in the frequency table.

a Find the class interval which contains the median.

b Work out an estimate for the mean number of points scored.

Points scored	Number of people
1 to 5	1
6 to 10	2
11 to 15	2
16 to 20	6
21 to 25	7
26 to 30	2

2 The table shows information about the number of minutes that 125 students spent doing homework.

a Find the class interval which contains the median.

b Work out an estimate for the mean number of minutes that the students spent doing homework.

Number of minutes (t)	Frequency
$0 < t \leqslant 20$	10
$20 < t \leqslant 40$	20
$40 < t \leqslant 60$	30
$60 < t \leqslant 80$	35
$80 < t \leqslant 100$	25
$100 < t \leqslant 120$	5

3 The table shows some information about the lifetimes, in hours, of 50 light bulbs.

a Find the class interval which contains the median.

b Work out an estimate for the mean number of hours.

Number of hours (t)	Number of light bulbs
$0 < t \leqslant 50$	2
$50 < t \leqslant 100$	3
$100 < t \leqslant 150$	6
$150 < t \leqslant 200$	9
$200 < t \leqslant 250$	19
$250 < t \leqslant 300$	11

4   The table shows some information about
    the number of text messages Simon
    received each day in December.
    a   Find the class interval which
        contains the median.
    b   Work out an estimate for the
        mean number of points scored.
        Give your answer correct to
        one decimal place.

Number of text messages	Frequency
0 to 4	3
5 to 9	11
10 to 14	12
15 to 19	3
20 to 24	0
25 to 29	2

5   Jack grows onions. The table shows some
    information about the weights (w) of
    some onions.
    a   Work out an estimate for the mean
        weight of these onions. Give your
        answer correct to the nearest gram.
    b   Find the class interval that contains
        the median.

Weight (w grams)	Frequency
$0 \leqslant w < 40$	10
$40 \leqslant w < 60$	16
$60 \leqslant w < 80$	25
$80 \leqslant w < 100$	28
$100 \leqslant w < 120$	17
$120 \leqslant w < 150$	8

Chapter summary

You should know

★   For a list of numbers
    the **mean** = (sum of all the numbers) ÷ (how many numbers there are)
    the **mode** is the number which occurs most times
    the **median** is the middle number when the numbers are written in order
    the **range** is the difference between the highest and lowest numbers

★   That **data logging** is the collection of data at regular intervals, usually by electronic
    means.

You should also be able to

★   Find the mean, mode and median of a list of numbers

★   Find the mean, mode, median and range of data given in a frequency table

★   Draw single and back-to-back **stem and leaf diagrams** and use them to find the
    median and range

★   Use average and range to compare distributions

★   Estimate the **mean of grouped data** by using the middle value of each **class interval**.

Chapter 3 review questions

1 Here are ten numbers

    3   2   5   4   2   4   6   2   1   2

Find the mode of these numbers.   (1388 March 2004)

2 Here are the shoe sizes of 15 men.

    5 6 8 6 5 4 7 9 7 11 8 8 10 8 7

  a Find the mode of these shoe sizes.

  b Find the median of these shoe sizes.

3 **a** Kuldip records the numbers of people getting off his tram at ten stops.
Here are his results for Monday.

      3 5 4 7 4 7 4 9 8 12

Work out
   i the range   **ii** the median   **iii** the mean.

  b On Tuesday, the mean number people getting off his tram at the same ten stops
is 8.6 How many more people got off the tram on Tuesday at these ten stops?

4 Annie and Billy take part in a
competition. Annie fires at the
target ten times. Her scores are

  8 8 9 5 6 6 5 8 8 6

  a Work out
    i the range of her scores
    ii the mean of her scores.

Billy fires at the target ten times. The frequency
table gives information about his scores.

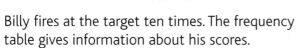

Score	Frequency
5	2
6	1
7	3
8	1
9	2
10	1

  b **i** Write down the modal score.
     ii Work out his total score.

                                             (1385 June 2000)

5 The table shows Mae's five test marks.

  a Find her median mark.

  b Work out the range of her marks.

  c Work out her mean mark.

English	44
French	60
History	72
Mathematics	67
Science	32

                                             (1386 Jan 2000)

6 Fred does a survey on the number of televisions people had in their houses. Information about the results is given in the table.

   a Work out the total number of televisions that were in the survey.

   b Work out the median number of televisions in the survey.

Number of televisions in the house	Frequency
0	5
1	8
2	12
3	21
4	7

7 20 students scored goals for the school hockey team last month. The table shows the number of goals they scored.

   a Work out the modal number of goals scored.

   b Work out the range of the number of goals scored.

   c Work out the mean number of goals scored.

Goals scored	Number of students
1	9
2	3
3	5
4	3

(1387 June 2004)

8 Andy did a survey of the number of cups of coffee some pupils in his school had drunk yesterday. The frequency table shows his results.

   a Work out the number of pupils that Andy asked.

   Andy thinks that the average number of drinks pupils in his survey had drunk is 7

   b Explain why Andy cannot be correct.

Number of cups of coffee	Frequency
2	1
3	3
4	5
5	8
6	5

(1387 June 2003)

9 Mrs Chowdery gives her class a maths test. Here are the test marks for the girls.

   7   5   8   5   2   8   7   4   7   10   3   7   4   3   6

   a Work out the mode.

   b Work out the median.

   The median mark for the boys was 7, and the range of the marks for the boys was 4
   The range of the girls' marks was 8

   c By comparing the results, explain whether the boys or the girls did better in the test.

(1385 June 1988)

10 Anil counted the number of letters in each of 30 sentences in a newspaper.
Anil showed his results in a stem and leaf diagram.

```
0 │ 8  9  9                        Key
1 │ 1  2  3  4  4  8  9            4│1 stands for 41 letters
2 │ 0  3  5  5  7  7  8
3 │ 2  2  3  3  6  6  8  8
4 │ 1  2  3  3  5
```

a Write down the number of sentences with 36 letters.

b Work out the range.

c Work out the median.

(1387 Nov 2004)

11 Jan measures the heights, in millimetres, of 20 plants in her greenhouse.
Here are her results.

178   189   147   147   166   167   153   171   164   158
189   166   165   155   152   147   158   148   151   172

Draw a stem and leaf diagram to show this information.

(1387 Nov 2003)

12 Here are the weights, in kilograms, of 15 parcels.

1.1   1.7   2.0   1.0   1.1   0.5   3.3   2.0   1.5   2.6   3.5   2.1   0.7   1.2   0.6

Draw a stem and leaf diagram to show this information.

(1388 March 2004)

13 A teacher asked 50 children how much pocket money they got each week.
The table shows some information about their replies.

Work out an estimate for the mean amount of pocket money the children got.

Pocket money (£x)	Frequency
$0 < x \leqslant 2$	1
$2 < x \leqslant 4$	10
$4 < x \leqslant 6$	23
$6 < x \leqslant 8$	14
$8 < x \leqslant 10$	2

(1388 March 2004)

14 The table shows information about the number of hours that 120 children used a computer last week.

Work out an estimate for the mean number of hours that the children used a computer. Give your answer correct to two decimal places.

Number of hours (h)	Frequency
$0 < h \leqslant 2$	10
$2 < h \leqslant 4$	15
$4 < h \leqslant 6$	30
$6 < h \leqslant 8$	35
$8 < h \leqslant 10$	25
$10 < h \leqslant 12$	5

(1388 June 2005)

Probability

Favourites to seize the Olympic flame

As the day for decision approaches it seems **unlikely** that London will win the battle to host the 2012 Olympic Games. The **probability** that Paris will win this race has always been high. It is felt that Madrid, Moscow and New York have little **chance** of success as the final presentations are made.

London team defies all the odds

London won with their bid to host the 2012 Summer Olympic Games. Yesterday's vote saw **likely** winners Paris stumble at the final hurdle. A spokesperson said 'Everyone thought that Paris was **certain** to win the vote, but I always felt that we had a greater than **even chance** of success.'

Probability is a measure of how likely it is that an event will happen.

An event could be **certain** to happen. For example, if it is Friday today, it is certain to be Saturday tomorrow.

An event could be **impossible** or have **no chance** of happening. For example, it is impossible for a baby to weigh 1000 kg.

An event which is as likely to happen as it is not to happen is said to have an **even** chance of happening. For example, there is an even chance of a spun coin coming down heads.

4.1 The probability scale

For an event, the probability of an outcome which is *certain* to happen is said to be **1**
The probability of an outcome which is *impossible* is said to be **0**
The probability of an outcome which has an *even chance* of happening is said to be **0.5** or $\frac{1}{2}$

This **probability scale** shows these.

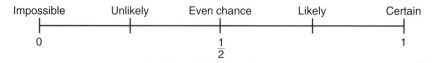

An outcome which has less than an even chance of happening is said to be **unlikely**.
An outcome which has more than an even chance of happening is said to be **likely**.

Example 1

On the probability scale, mark with an arrow the probability that it will rain in Manchester during April.

Solution 1

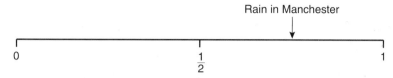

As it is likely that it will rain in Manchester during April, the probability is between $\frac{1}{2}$ and 1. So the arrow can be anywhere between $\frac{1}{2}$ and 1.

Exercise 4A

1 In each of the following choose the word from the list below that best describes the probability of each outcome happening.

| Impossible | Unlikely | Even chance | Likely | Certain |

a   The sun will never shine again.

b   It will snow in Scotland next year.

c   The roll of a dice will show an odd number.

d   The next baby to be born will weigh less than two tons.

e   It will snow in London in July.

f   The colour of a card picked from a pack of playing cards will be red.

g   December will be the next month after November.

h   Your maths teacher will be on television tonight.

2 Draw a probability scale like the one in Example 1. Mark with a ↓ the probability of each of the following outcomes. Label your arrows with the letters **a–d**.

a   A spun coin will come down tails.

b   This evening, in Wales, the sun will set in the West.

c   Great Britain will win more gold medals than the USA in the next Summer Olympic Games.

d   You will score more than 10% in your GCSE maths exam.

3 Write down one example of an event the outcome of which is:

a   impossible   b   unlikely   c   even chance

d   likely   e   certain to happen.

4.2 Writing probabilities as numbers

The diagram shows a three-sided spinner.

The spinner can land on red or blue or yellow.
It is equally likely to land on each of the three
colours, so the spinner is said to be **fair**.

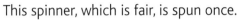

This spinner, which is fair, is spun once.
This is called a single **event**.
The colour that it lands on is called the **outcome**.
The outcome can be red or blue or yellow. There are three possible outcomes.

The probability that the spinner will land on blue $= \dfrac{1 \text{ successful outcome}}{3 \text{ possible outcomes}} = \dfrac{1}{3}$

Similarly, the probability that the spinner will land on red $= \dfrac{1}{3}$

and the probability that the spinner will land on yellow $= \dfrac{1}{3}$

When all the possible outcomes are equally likely to happen,

$$\text{probability} = \frac{\text{number of successful outcomes}}{\text{total number of possible outcomes}}$$

Probability can be written as a fraction or a decimal.

Example 2

A fair five-sided spinner is numbered 1 to 5
Jane spins the spinner once.

a Find the probability that the spinner will land on the
number 4

b Find the probability that the spinner will land on an even
number.

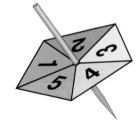

Solution 2

a The possible outcomes are 1, 2, 3, 4 and 5 There are **5 outcomes**.
The successful outcome is the number 4, just **1** outcome.

The probability that the spinner will land on 4 $= \dfrac{\text{number of successful outcomes}}{\text{total number of possible outcomes}} = \frac{1}{5}$
or 0.2

b 2 and 4 are even numbers.
The number of successful outcomes is **2**
The total number of possible outcomes is **5**
So the probability that the spinner will land on an even number $= \frac{2}{5}$ or 0.4

Example 3

Six coloured counters are in a bag.

3 counters are red, 2 counters are green and 1 counter is blue.

One counter is chosen at random from the bag.

a Write down the colour of the counter which is

    i most likely to be chosen   **ii** least likely to be chosen.

b Find the probability that the counter chosen will be

    i red   **ii** green   **iii** blue.

Solution 3

In this question, at **random** means that each counter is equally likely to be chosen.

a   **i** Red is the most likely colour to be chosen since there are more red counters than green or blue.

    ii Blue is least likely to be chosen since there are fewer blue counters than red or green.

b There are 6 possible outcomes.

Outcome   1   2   3   4   5   6

  i Number of successful outcomes = 3 (3 red counters).
The probability that the counter will be red $= \frac{3}{6} = \frac{1}{2}$

  ii Number of successful outcomes = 2 (2 green counters).
The probability that the counter will be green $= \frac{2}{6} = \frac{1}{3}$

  iii Number of successful outcomes = 1 (1 blue counter).
The probability that the counter will be blue $= \frac{1}{6}$

Exercise 4B

1 Nicky spins the spinner. The spinner is fair.
Write down the probability that the spinner will land on a side coloured

    a blue   **b** red   **c** green.

2 John spins the fair spinner.
Write down the probability that the spinner will land on

    a 2   **b** a number more than 5

    c an even number   **d** a number bigger than 10.

3

Jim has a bag of 6 counters. 3 of the counters are green, 1 is red, and the others are blue. Jim chooses a counter at random from the bag. Find the probability that Jim will choose

    a a red counter   **b** a blue counter   **c** a green counter.

4 Samantha Smith has eight cards which spell 'Samantha'.

She puts the cards in a bag and chooses one of the cards at random. Find the probability that she will choose a card showing

a a letter S

b a letter A

c a letter which is also in her surname 'SMITH'.

5 Ben has 15 ties in a drawer.
7 of the ties are plain, 3 of the ties are striped, and the rest are patterned.
Ben chooses a tie at random from the drawer. What is the probability that he chooses a tie which is

a plain   **b** striped   **c** patterned?

6 Lisa has 5 cards numbered 1 to 5
Lisa shuffles the cards and chooses one of them at random.
What is the probability that the card will show

a a 4   **b** an even number

c an odd number   **d** a number bigger than 3

e a number less than 10   **f** a 6?

7 Peter has a bag of 8 coins. In the bag he has one 10 p coin, five 20 p coins and the rest are 50 p coins. Peter chooses one coin at random. What is the probability that Peter will choose

a a 10 p coin   **b** a 20 p coin

c a 50 p coin   **d** a £1 coin

e a coin worth more than 5 p?

8 Rob has a drawer of 20 socks.
4 of the socks are blue, 6 of the socks are brown, and the rest of the socks are black.
Rob chooses a sock at random from the drawer.
Find the probability that he chooses

a a blue sock   **b** a brown sock

c a black sock   **d** a white sock.

9 Verity has a box of pens.
Half of the pens are blue, 11 of the pens are green, 10 of the pens are red, and the remaining 4 pens are black.
Verity chooses a pen at random from the box.
Find the probability that she chooses

a a blue pen   **b** a green pen

c a red pen   **d** a black pen.

4.3 Two-way tables

This **two-way table** shows some information about the numbers of girls and boys in Year 10 and in Year 11 in a school.

	Year 10	Year 11	Total
Girls	80	90	170
Boys	75	105	180
Total	155	195	350

One of the ways shows information about the numbers of girls and boys.
The other way shows information about the number of students in Year 10 and the number of students in Year 11

Example 4

From the table, find the probability that a student chosen at random from all the students in Years 10 and 11 will be a Year 10 girl.

Give your answer in its simplest form.

Solution 4
The number of successful outcomes is 80 (because there are 80 Year 10 girls).
The number of possible outcomes is 350 (the total number of students in Years 10 and 11).
The probability that the student chosen will be a Year 10 girl $= \frac{80}{350} = \frac{8}{35}$

Sometimes a given two-way table is incomplete and the table has to be completed before probability questions can be answered.

Example 5

This two-way table gives information about the ages of students in a school.

	Under 12	12 to 15	Over 15	Total
Boys	96		35	
Girls		275		444
Total		500	100	

a Complete the two-way table.

b One of the students is to be picked at random.
  i Find the probability that the student picked will be 12 to 15
  ii Find the probability that the student picked will be a boy who is under 12

Give your answers in their simplest forms.

Solution 5

	Under 12	12 to 15	Over 15	Total
Boys	96	225	35	356
Girls	104	275	65	444
Total	200	500	100	800

a The total number of girls over 15 is $100 - 35 = 65$
The total number of girls under 12 is $444 - (275 + 65) = 104$
The total number of students under 12 is $104 + 96 = 200$
The total number of boys 12 to 15 is $500 - 275 = 225$
The total number of students $= 200 + 500 + 100 = 800$
The total number of boys $= 800 - 444 = 356$

Check: The total number of boys is $96 + 225 + 35 = 356$

b   **i** The probability that a student aged 12 to 15 will be picked $= \frac{500}{800} = \frac{5}{8}$
  ii The probability that a boy under 12 will be picked $= \frac{96}{800} = \frac{3}{25}$

Example 6

Here is some information about the way that the boys and girls in class 10C travel to school.

Boys
Walk	Bus	Car	Bus
Car	Bus	Bus	Bus
Walk	Walk	Bus	Walk

Girls
Bus	Bus	Car	Walk	Bus	Bus
Bus	Car	Walk	Bus	Car	Car
Bus	Bus	Car	Walk	Bus	Car

a Show this information in a suitable two-way table.

b One of the students in 10C is to be chosen at random.
Find the probability that this student will travel to school by bus.
Give your answer in its simplest form.

c One of the students in 10C who travels to school by car is to be chosen at random.
Find the probability that this student will be a girl.
Give your answer in its simplest form.

Solution 6

a

	Walk	Bus	Car	Total
Boys	4	6	2	12
Girls	3	9	6	18
Total	7	15	8	30

b The probability that the student chosen will travel to school by bus $= \frac{15}{30} = \frac{1}{2}$

c 8 students travel to school by car. 6 of these 8 students are girls.
The probability that the student chosen will be a girl $= \frac{6}{8} = \frac{3}{4}$

Exercise 4C

1   The two-way table gives some information about the weather on a number of days in the months of April, May and June.

   a   Write down the total number of rainy days.

   b   Write down the number of sunny days in June.

   c   Write down the number of days in May which were neither sunny nor rainy.

	Sunny	Rainy	Total
April	4	20	24
May	9	12	21
June	18	7	25
Total	31	39	70

2   The two-way table gives some information about the favourite fruit of a group of children.

   a   Copy and complete the two-way table.

   b   A child is chosen at random from the group. Find the probability that the child's favourite fruit will be oranges. Give your answer in its simplest form.

   c   Find the probability that a child chosen at random from the group will be a girl whose favourite fruit is bananas. Give your answer in its simplest form.

	Bananas	Oranges	Apples	Total
Boys	2	5		14
Girls		4	2	
Total	6			

3   The two-way table gives some information about the colours of some vehicles in a car park.

   a   Copy and complete the two-way table.

   b   Find the probability that a vehicle chosen at random will be a car. Give your answer in its simplest form.

   c   Find the probability that a vehicle chosen at random will be a white van. Give your answer in its simplest form.

	Silver	Black	White	Total
Cars		7		
Vans	3		8	
Total	15	12		40

4   80 students were asked which football team they support. The two-way table shows some of their answers.

   a   Copy and complete the two-way table.

   b   Find the probability that a girl chosen at random will support Rovers. Give your answer in its simplest form.

   c   Find the probability that a boy chosen at random will support United. Give your answer in its simplest form.

	United	City	Rovers	Total
Boys			9	
Girls	10			32
Total		31	15	

5 A group of 17 boys and 15 girls were asked at what time they went to lunch yesterday.

> 12 boys went to lunch before 12 30
> 13 students, of which 8 were girls, went to lunch from 12 30 to 13 00
> 3 girls went to lunch after 13 00

	Before 12 30	From 12 30 to 13 00	After 13 00	Total
Boys				
Girls				
Total				32

a Copy and complete the two-way table.

b A girl is chosen at random. Find the probability that the girl went to lunch before 12 30 Give your answer in its simplest form.

c A boy is chosen at random. Find the probability that he went to lunch after 13 00

4.4 Sample space diagrams

A **sample space diagram** shows all the possible outcomes of a single event or all the possible outcomes of more than one event.

For this three-sided spinner, the sample space when the spinner is spun once is

1	2	3

Example 7

The 3-sided spinner is spun and a coin is tossed at the same time.
Draw the sample space of all possible outcomes.

Solution 7
There are six possible outcomes.
The possible outcomes are 1 and a head, 1 and a tail, and so on.
The sample space is:

> (1, head)   (1, tail)   (2, head)   (2, tail)   (3, head)   (3, tail).

Example 8

Two fair dice are thrown.

a Draw the sample space showing all the possible outcomes.

b Find the probability that the numbers on the two dice will be
  i both the same   **ii** both even numbers   **iii** both less than 3

Solution 8

a   (1, 1)   (2, 1)   (3, 1)   (4, 1)   (5, 1)   (6, 1)
       (1, 2)   (2, 2)   (3, 2)   (4, 2)   (5, 2)   (6, 2)
       (1, 3)   (2, 3)   (3, 3)   (4, 3)   (5, 3)   (6, 3)
       (1, 4)   (2, 4)   (3, 4)   (4, 4)   (5, 4)   (6, 4)
       (1, 5)   (2, 5)   (3, 5)   (4, 5)   (5, 5)   (6, 5)
       (1, 6)   (2, 6)   (3, 6)   (4, 6)   (5, 6)   (6, 6)

A total of 36 possible outcomes.

b   **i**   (1, 1) (2, 2) (3, 3) (4, 4) (5, 5) and (6, 6) are the successful outcomes with both numbers the same.

The probability that the numbers on both dice will be the same $= \frac{6}{36} = \frac{1}{6}$

ii   (2, 2) (2, 4) (2, 6) (4, 2) (4, 4) (4, 6) (6, 2) (6, 4) (6, 6) are the successful outcomes with both numbers even.

The probability that the numbers on both dice will be even $= \frac{9}{36} = \frac{1}{4}$

iii   (1, 1) (2, 1) (1, 2) (2, 2) are the successful outcomes with both numbers less than 3.

The probability that the numbers on both dice will be less than 3 is $\frac{4}{36} = \frac{1}{9}$

Exercise 4D

In each of these questions give all probabilities in their simplest forms.

1   Two coins are spun at the same time.

   a   Draw the sample space showing all possible outcomes.

   b   Find the probability that both coins will come down heads.

   c   Find the probability that one coin will come down heads and the other coin will come down tails.

2   A bag contains 1 blue brick, 1 yellow brick, 1 green brick, and 1 red brick.
   A brick is chosen at random from the bag and its colour noted.
   The brick is then replaced in the bag.
   A brick is again chosen at random from the bag and its colour noted.

   a   Draw a sample space to show all the possible outcomes of the colours of these two bricks.

   b   Find the probability that
     i   the two bricks will be the same colour
    ii   one brick will be red and the other brick will be green.

3   Two fair dice are thrown.
   The sample space containing all the possible outcomes is shown in Example 8
   The numbers on the two dice are added together.

   a   Find the probability that the sum of the numbers on the two dice will be
     i   greater than 10   **ii**   less than 6   **iii**   a square number.

   b   **i**   What sum of the numbers on the two dice is most likely to occur?
     ii   Find the probability of this sum occurring.

4 Daniel has four cards – the ace of hearts, the ace of diamonds, the ace of spades and the ace of clubs.
Daniel also has a fair dice.
He rolls the dice and chooses a card at random.

  a Draw the sample space showing all possible outcomes. One possible outcome, ace of diamonds and 4 has been done for you.

     (D, 4)

  b Find the probability that a red ace will be chosen.

  c Find the probability that he will choose the ace of spades and roll an even number on the dice.

5 Three normal coins are spun.

  a Draw a sample space showing all eight possible outcomes.

  b Find the probability that the three coins will land on the same side.

  c Find the probability that the coins will show two heads and a tail.

  d Write down the number of possible outcomes when
    i four coins are spun   **ii** five coins are spun.

4.5 Mutually exclusive outcomes and the probability that the outcome of an event will not happen

Five coloured counters are in a bag.
3 counters are red and 2 counters are green.
One counter is chosen at random from the bag.

The probability of choosing a red counter $= \frac{3}{5}$

The probability of choosing a green counter $= \frac{2}{5}$

Mutually exclusive outcomes are outcomes which cannot happen at the same time.

When one counter is chosen at random from the bag, the outcome 'red' cannot happen at the same time as the outcome 'green'. The two outcomes are mutually exclusive.

Probability of red + probability of green $= \frac{3}{5} + \frac{2}{5} = \frac{5}{5} = 1$

The sum of the probabilities of all the possible mutually exclusive outcomes of an event is 1

There are 5 possible outcomes, 2 of which are green.

The probability that the counter will be green is $\frac{2}{5}$

Out of the 5 possible outcomes, $5 - 2 = 3$ outcomes are NOT green.

The probability that the counter will NOT be green is $1 - \frac{2}{5} = \frac{3}{5}$

If the probability of something happening is p, then the probability of it NOT happening is $1 - p$.

Example 9

David buys one newspaper each day. He buys the Times or the Telegraph or the Independent. The probability that he buys the Times is 0.6 The probability that he buys the Telegraph is 0.25 Work out the probability that David will buy the Independent.

Solution 9

P(Times) = 0.6   P(Telegraph) = 0.25   P(Independent) = ?

> P(Times) means the probability that David buys the Times.

As David only buys one newspaper each day, the three outcomes are mutually exclusive.
P(Independent) + 0.6 + 0.25 = 1
P(Independent) + 0.85 = 1
P(Independent) = 1 − 0.85
The probability that David will buy the Independent = 0.15

Example 10

The probability that Julie will pass her driving test next week is 0.6
Work out the probability that Julie will NOT pass her driving test next week.

Solution 10
The probability that Julie will NOT pass = 1 − 0.6 = 0.4

Exercise 4E

1 Nosheen travels from home to school. She travels by bus or by car or by tram. The probability that she travels by bus is 0.4 The probability that she travels by car is 0.5 Work out the probability that she travels by tram.

2 Roger's train can be on time or late or early. The probability that his train will be on time is 0.15 The probability that his train will be early is 0.6 Work out the probability that Roger's train will be late.

3 The probability that Lisa will pass her maths exam is 0.8
Work out the probability that Lisa will not pass her maths exam.

4 A company makes batteries. A battery is chosen at random. The probability that the battery will **not** be faulty is 0.97 Work out the probability that the battery will be faulty.

5 Kevin has a bag of sweets. He takes a sweet at random from the bag. The probability that the sweet will be orange is 0.64 Work out the probability that the sweet will not be orange.

6 Four athletes, Aaron, Ben, Carl and Des, take part in a race. The table shows the probabilities that Aaron or Ben or Carl will win the race.

Aaron	Ben	Carl	Des
0.2	0.14	0.3	x

   a Work out the probability that Aaron will not win the race.
   b Work out the probability that Ben will not win the race.
   c Work out the probability, x, that Des will win the race.

7   A roundabout has four roads leading from it. Michael is driving round the roundabout. The roads lead to Liverpool or Trafford Park or Eccles or Bolton. The table shows the probabilities that Michael will take the road to Liverpool or Trafford Park or Bolton.

Liverpool	Trafford Park	Eccles	Bolton
0.49	0.18	x	0.23

   a   Work out the probability that Michael will not take the road to Liverpool.
   b   Work out the value of x.

8   Sam has red, white, yellow and green coloured T-shirts only. She chooses a T-shirt at random. The probabilities that Sam will choose a red T-shirt or a white T-shirt are given in the table. Sam is twice as likely to choose a green T-shirt as she is to choose a yellow T-shirt.

   Work out the value of x.

Red	White	Yellow	Green
0.5	0.14	x	$2x$

4.6 Estimating probability from relative frequency

The diagram shows two three-sided spinners.

One spinner is fair and one is biased.

A spinner is **biased** if it is not equally likely to land on each of the numbers.

This can be tested by experiment.

If a spinner is spun 300 times, it is fair if it lands on each of the three numbers approximately 100 times.

John spins one spinner 300 times and Mary spins the other spinner 300 times.

John's spinner			Mary's spinner		
300 spins			300 spins		
1	2	3	1	2	3
97	104	99	147	96	57

John's spinner is fair because it lands on each of the three numbers approximately the same number of times.

Mary's spinner is biased because it is more likely to land on the number **1** (147 times out of 300). It is least likely to land on the number **3** (only 57 times out of 300).

To estimate the probability that Mary's spinner will land on a particular number, the **relative frequency** of each number is found using

$$\text{relative frequency} = \frac{\text{number of times the spinner lands on the number}}{\text{total number of spins}}$$

The relative frequency that Mary's spinner will land on the number **1** $= \frac{147}{300} = 0.49$

The relative frequency that Mary's spinner will land on the number **2** $= \frac{96}{300} = 0.32$

The relative frequency that Mary's spinner will land on the number **3** $= \frac{57}{300} = 0.19$

An **estimate** of the probability that the spinner will land on the number **1** is 0.49
An estimate of the probability that the spinner will land on the number **2** is 0.32
An estimate of the probability that the spinner will land on the number **3** is 0.19

Example 11

In a statistical experiment, Brendan throws a dice 600 times. The table shows the results.

Number on dice	1	2	3	4	5	6
Frequency	48	120	180	96	54	102

Brendan throws the dice again.

a Estimate the probability that he will throw a 2

b Estimate the probability that he will throw an even number.

Zoe now throws the same dice 200 times.

c Estimate the number of times Zoe will throw a 6

Solution 11

a Relative frequency of a 2 is $\frac{120}{600}$

Estimated probability of a 2 is $\frac{120}{600} = 0.2$

b The number of times he throws an even number $= 120 + 96 + 102 = 318$

Relative frequency of an even number $= \frac{318}{600}$

Estimated probability of an even number $\frac{318}{600} = 0.53$

c Relative frequency of a 6 is $\frac{102}{600} = 0.17$

$$\text{Relative frequency} = \frac{\text{number of times Zoe throws a 6}}{\text{total number of throws}}$$

So an estimate for the number of times Zoe throws a 6 is $0.17 \times 200 = 34$

Exercise 4F

1 A coin is biased. The coin is tossed 200 times.
   It lands on heads 140 times and it lands on tails 60 times.

   a Write down the relative frequency of the coin landing on tails.

   b The coin is to be tossed again. Estimate the probability that the coin will land on
      i tails   **ii** heads.

2 A bag contains a red counter, a blue counter, a white counter and a green counter. Asif chooses a counter at random. He does this 400 times. The table shows the number of times each of the coloured counters are chosen.

Red	Blue	White	Green
81	110	136	73

   a Write down the relative frequency of Asif choosing the red counter.

   b Write down the relative frequency of Asif choosing the white counter.

   Asif chooses a counter one more time. Estimate the probability that this counter will be

   c   **i** blue   **ii** green.

3 Ian throws a dice 400 times. He scores three 100 times. Is the dice fair? Explain your answer.

4 Tyler carries out a survey about the words in a newspaper. He chooses an article at random. He counts the number of letters in each of the first 150 words of the article. The table shows Tyler's results.

Number of letters in a word	1	2	3	4	5	6	7	8	9	10
Frequency	7	14	42	31	21	13	10	6	4	2

   A word is chosen at random from the 150 words.

   a Write down the most likely number of letters in the word.

   b Estimate the probability that the word will have
         i 1 letter   **ii** 7 letters   **iii** more than 5 letters.

   c The whole article has 1000 words. Estimate the total number of 3-letter words in this article.

5 A bag contains ten coloured bricks. Each brick is white or red or blue. Alan chooses a brick at random from the ten bricks in the bag. He does this 500 times. The table shows the numbers of each coloured brick chosen.

White	Red	Blue
290	50	160

   a Estimate the number of red bricks in the bag.

   b Estimate the number of white bricks in the bag.

6 The probability that someone will pass their driving test at the first attempt is 0.45 On a particular day, 1000 people take the test for the first time. Work out an estimate for the number of these 1000 people who pass.

7 Gwen has a biased coin. When she spins the coin, the probability that it will come down tails is $\frac{3}{5}$. Work out an estimate for the number of tails she gets when she spins her coin 400 times.

8 The probability that a biased dice will land on a one is 0.09. Andy is going to roll the dice 300 times. Work out an estimate for the number of times the dice will land on a one.

Chapter summary

> **You should know that:**
>
> ★ **probability** is a measure of how likely it is that the outcome of an event will happen.
>
> ★ probabilities are written as fractions or decimals between 0 and 1
>
> ★ an outcome which is **impossible** has a probability of 0; an outcome which is **certain** to happen has a probability of 1
>
> ★ probabilities can be shown on a **probability scale**
>
> ★ in an event, outcomes which are equally likely have equal probabilities
>
> ★ when all outcomes of an event are equally likely to happen
>
> $$\text{probability} = \frac{\text{number of successful outcomes}}{\text{total number of possible outcomes}}$$
>
> ★ two-way tables can be used to find probabilities; you should know how to complete a two-way table
>
> ★ outcomes can be listed in an ordered way using **sample space diagrams**
>
> ★ **mutually exclusive outcomes** are outcomes which cannot happen at the same time
>
> ★ **the sum of the probabilities of all the possible mutually exclusive outcomes is 1**
>
> ★ if the probability of something happening is p, then the probability of it NOT happening is $1 - p$
>
> ★ from a statistical experiment, for each outcome
>
> $$\text{relative frequency} = \frac{\text{number of times the outcome happens}}{\text{total number of trials of the event}}$$
>
> ★ relative frequencies give good estimates of probabilities when the number of trials is large
>
> ★ if the probability that an experiment will be successful is p and the experiment is carried out a number of times, then an estimate for the number of successful experiments is $p \times$ number of experiments.

Chapter 4 review questions

1   On a probability line, mark the following probabilities.

    a   It will rain sometime next year in England. Use the letter R.

    b   The Sun will collide with the Earth tomorrow. Use the letter S.

    c   A fair coin when tossed will come down tails. Use the letter T.

2   Here is a spinner.
The spinner is spun.

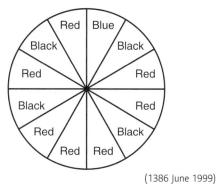

  a   **i** Which colour is least likely?
       ii Give a reason for your answer.

  b   On a probability line, mark with an X the
       probability that the colour will be Red.

  c   Write down the probability that the colour will
       be Blue.

(1386 June 1999)

3   Some bulbs were planted in October.
The ticks in the table show the months in which each type of bulb grows into
flowers.

		Month					
		Jan	Feb	March	April	May	June
Type of bulb	Allium					✓	✓
	Crocus	✓	✓				
	Daffodil		✓	✓	✓		
	Iris	✓	✓				
	Tulip				✓	✓	

  a   In which months do tulips flower?
  b   Which type of bulb flowers in March?
  c   In which month do most types of bulb flower?
  d   Which type of bulb flowers in the same months as the iris?

Ben puts one of each type of these bulbs in a bag.
He takes a bulb from the bag without looking.

  e   **i** Write down the probability that he will take a crocus bulb.
       ii On a probability scale, mark with a cross (✗) the probability that he
          will take a bulb which flowers in February.

(1387 June 2005)

4   Richard has a box of toy cars. Each car is red or blue or white.
3 of the cars are red. 4 of the cars are blue. 2 of the cars are white.
Richard chooses one car at random from the box.
Write down the probability that Richard will choose a blue car.   (1388 Jan 2004)

5   Shreena has a bag of 20 sweets. 10 of the sweets are red. 3 of the sweets are black.
The rest of the sweets are white.
Shreena chooses one sweet at random.
What is the probability that Shreena will choose a

  a   red sweet   **b**   white sweet?   (1385 June 1999)

6   30 students were asked if they liked coffee.
20 of the students were girls.
6 boys liked coffee.
12 girls did **not** like coffee.

Use this information to copy and complete the two-way table.

	Boys	Girls	Total
Liked coffee			
Did not like coffee			
Total			

(1388 Jan 2004)

7   80 students each study one of three languages.
The two-way table shows some information about these students.

	French	German	Spanish	Total
Female	15			39
Male		17		41
Total	31	28		80

a   Copy and complete the two-way table.

One of these students is to be picked at random.

b   Write down the probability that the student picked studies
French.

(1387 June 2005)

8   80 students were each asked to name their favourite swimming stroke.
The two-way table shows some information about these students' answers.

	Breaststroke	Front crawl	Backstroke	Total
Boy		28	7	
Girl	23			36
Total			12	80

a   Copy and complete the two-way table.

One of these 80 students is picked at random.

b   Write down the probability that this student's favourite stroke is backstroke.

9 Zen has two fair spinners.

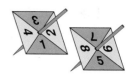

One of the spinners is numbered 1, 2, 3, 4
The other spinner is numbered 5, 6, 7, 8

Zen is going to spin the two spinners.
He multiplies the numbers on the two spinners to get the score.

a Copy and complete the table to show all the possible scores.

×	1	2	3	4
5	5	10	15	20
6	6			24
7	7			28
8	8	16	24	32

b What is the probability of getting a score of 28?

c What is the probability of getting a score of more than 25?   (1386 Nov 2001)

10 Here are two sets of cards. Each card has a number on it as shown.
A card is selected at random from Set A and a card is selected at random from Set B.

The difference between the number on the card selected from Set A and the number on the card selected from Set B is worked out.

Set A

Set B

a Copy and complete the table to show all the possible differences.

Set A

		1	2	3	4
	1	0		2	
Set B	**2**		0		
	3		1		
	4				

b Find the probability that the difference will be zero.

c Find the probability that the difference will **not** be 2

11 A company makes hearing aids. A hearing aid is chosen at random.
The probability that it has a fault is 0.09
Work out the probability that a hearing aid, chosen at random,
will **not** have a fault.

                                                                                (1388 March 2004)

12 There are 20 coins in a bag.
7 of the coins are pound coins.
Gordon is going to take a coin at random from the bag.

   a Write down the probability that he will take a pound coin.

   b Find the probability that he will take a coin which is **not** a pound coin.

13 Asif's bus could be on time or late or early.
The probability that his bus will be on time is 0.9
The probability that his bus will be late is 0.03
Work out the probability that Asif's bus will be early.

(1385 Nov 1998)

14 Mr Brown chooses one book from the library each week.
He chooses a crime novel or a horror story or a non-fiction book.
The probability that he chooses a horror story is 0.4
The probability that he chooses a non-fiction book is 0.15
Work out the probability that Mr Brown chooses a crime novel.

(1387 June 2005)

15 Martin bought a packet of mixed flower seeds.
The seeds produce flowers that are red or blue or white or yellow.
The probability of a flower seed producing a flower of a particular colour is:

Colour	Red	Blue	White	Yellow
Probability	0.6	0.15		0.15

   a Write down the most common colour of a flower.

   Martin chooses a flower seed at random from the packet.

   b   **i** Work out the probability that the flower produced will be white.
   ii Write down the probability that the flower produced will be orange.

(1385 June 1998)

16 Here is a 4-sided spinner.
The sides are labelled red, blue, yellow and green.
The spinner is biased.
The probability that the spinner will land on each of the
colours red, blue, and green is shown in the table.

Colour	Red	Blue	Yellow	Green
Probability	0.45	0.3	x	0.1

Jo spins the spinner once.

   a Work out the probability, x, that the spinner will land on yellow.

Daniel spins the spinner 100 times.

   b Work out an estimate for the number of times the spinner will land on blue.

17 Here is a 4-sided spinner.
The sides of the spinner are labelled 1, 2, 3 and 4
The spinner is biased.
The probability that the spinner will land on each of the
numbers 2 and 3 is given in the table.
The probability that the spinner will land on 1 is equal to the probability
that it will land on 4

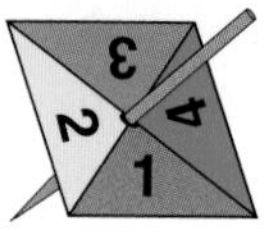

Number	1	2	3	4
Probability	x	0.3	0.2	x

a Work out the value of x.

Sarah is going to spin the spinner 200 times.

b Work out an estimate for the number of times the dice will land on 2

(1387 June 2005)

18 The probability that a biased dice will land on a four is 0.2
Pam is going to roll the dice 200 times.
Work out an estimate for the number of times the dice will land on 4

(1387 June 2004)

19 Meg has a biased coin.
When she spins the coin, the probability that it will come down heads is 0.4
Meg is going to spin the coin 350 times.
Work out an estimate for the number of times it will come down heads.

20 Julie does a statistical experiment. She throws a dice 600 times.
She scores six 200 times.
Is the dice fair? Explain your answer.

(1387 June 2003)

Scatter graphs

5.1 Scatter graphs and relationships

Scatter graphs can be used to investigate whether there is a relationship between two quantities. For example, a scatter graph could show the marks of twelve students who took a test in science and in maths. One of the students, Cath, scored 27 in science and 16 in maths. On the grid, the cross shows her pair of marks.

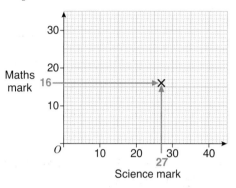

The table shows the test marks of the other eleven students.

Science mark	5	19	35	7	33	29	23	9	36	17	32
Maths mark	6	15	21	10	22	21	18	7	25	13	19

Here is the completed scatter graph for all twelve students.

The pattern of the crosses on the scatter graph suggests that there is a relationship between the science marks and the maths marks.

One way of describing the relationship is

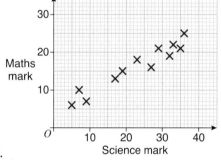

As the science mark increases, the maths mark increases.

Scatter graphs can suggest other sorts of relationship between two quantities or even that there is no relationship at all.

Example 1

The table shows, for each of ten men, his age and the number of his own teeth he has.

Age (years)	22	28	33	37	41	49	52	56	64	68
Number of own teeth	29	29	26	28	26	21	23	21	17	15

a Draw a scatter graph to show this information.

b Describe the relationship between the men's ages and the number of their own teeth they have.

Solution 1

a

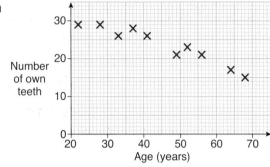

b The older a man is, the fewer of his own teeth he has.

(This relationship is true for these ten men but, in the whole country, there are many men who do not fit this pattern.)

Example 2

The table shows the ages, in years, and the heights, in cm, of twelve women.

Age (years)	21	25	30	34	39	42	46	54	57	63	66	68
Height (cm)	175	162	173	154	177	148	157	152	168	164	143	171

a Draw a scatter graph to show this information.
b Describe the relationship, if any, between the women's ages and their heights.

Solution 2

a

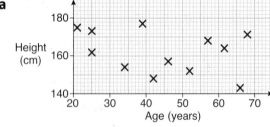

b There is no pattern to the points and so there is no obvious relationship between the women's ages and their heights.

Exercise 5A

1 The table shows the height, in cm, and the weight, in kg, of each of ten men.

Height (cm)	173	153	187	183	179	166	176	165	181	158
Weight (kg)	68	57	92	97	78	76	81	67	85	59

a On the resource sheet, complete the scatter graph to show the information in the table.
The first two points in the table have been plotted for you.

b Describe the relationship between the men's heights and their weights.

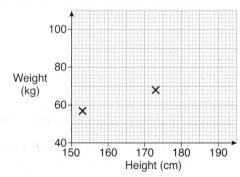

2 The table shows the birth weights, in kg, of ten babies and the average number of cigarettes per day their mothers smoked during pregnancy.

Number of cigarettes	2	19	11	29	0	6	14	23	5	8
Birth weight (kg)	3.53	3.37	3.48	3.24	3.62	3.51	3.38	3.31	3.56	3.46

a On the resource sheet, complete the scatter graph to show the information in the table. The first two points in the table have been plotted for you.

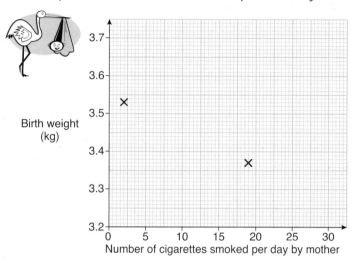

b Describe the relationship between the number of cigarettes smoked per day by the mothers during pregnancy and their babies' birth weights.

3 The table shows the number of goals scored and the number of goals conceded by each of twelve Premier League football teams in a recent season.

Number of goals scored	45	52	49	53	47	47	45	42	40	52	47	32
Number of goals conceded	46	41	44	46	39	41	52	58	46	60	57	43

a On the resource sheet, complete the scatter graph to show the information in the table. The first point in the table has been plotted for you.

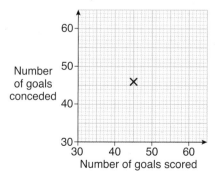

b Describe the relationship, if any, between the number of goals scored by the teams and the number of goals they conceded.

4   Nick sells ice creams. The table shows the noon temperature and the number of ice creams he sells each day for a fortnight.

Noon temperature (°C)	20	28	18	24	30	22	21	16	29	19	27	26	23	27
Number of ice creams	70	86	58	76	97	78	65	58	91	63	93	91	79	82

   a   On the resource sheet, complete the scatter graph to show the information in the table. The first two points in the table have been plotted for you.

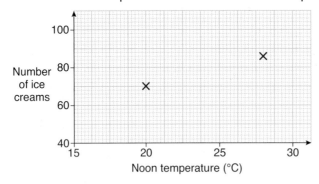

   b   Describe the relationship between the noon temperatures and the number of ice creams Nick sells.

5   The table shows the number of hours of sunshine and the rainfall, in mm, each month in England in 2004.

Month	Jan	Feb	Mar	Apr	May	Jun	Jul	Aug	Sep	Oct	Nov	Dec
No of hours of sunshine	51	87	107	136	204	200	169	176	160	97	50	53
Rainfall (mm)	152	49	48	78	43	56	67	148	53	131	47	59

   a   On the resource sheet, complete the scatter graph to show the information in the table. The first two points in the table have been plotted for you.

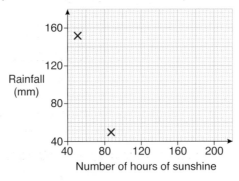

   b   Describe the relationship, if any, between the number of hours of sunshine and the rainfall.

6 The table shows some annual mileages of a car and the running costs per mile, in pence, of the car for those mileages.

Annual mileage	4000	6500	8000	10 000	12 000	14 500	18 500	22 000	27 500	29 500
Running costs per mile (pence)	53	48	42	34	32	31	25	24	21	23

a On the resource sheet, complete the scatter graph to show the information in the table. The first two points in the table have been plotted for you.

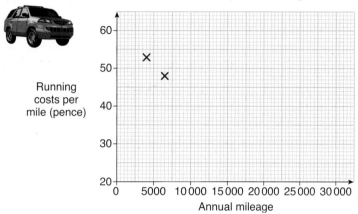

b Describe the relationship between the car's annual mileage and its running costs per mile.

5.2 Lines of best fit and correlation

On the scatter graph at the beginning of this chapter, it is possible to draw a straight line which passes near all the points. This line is called a **line of best fit**.

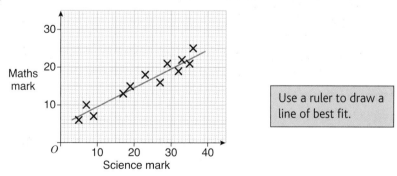

Use a ruler to draw a line of best fit.

A line of best fit does not have to pass through any of the points, although it can, and there should be roughly equal numbers of points on each side of the line.

If a line of best fit can be drawn, then there may be a relationship, called a **correlation**, between the quantities.

Maths marks increase as science marks increase. When one quantity increases as the other increases, the correlation is called **positive correlation**.

When one quantity decreases as the other increases, the line of best fit slopes in the opposite direction to the one above and the correlation is called **negative correlation**. The scatter graph in Example 1 shows negative correlation.

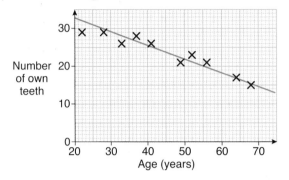

It is not possible to draw a line of best fit on the scatter graph in Example 2, as there is no pattern to the points. So there is **no correlation** or **zero correlation** between a woman's age and her height.

If the points are all close to the line of best fit, the correlation is called **high** or strong.

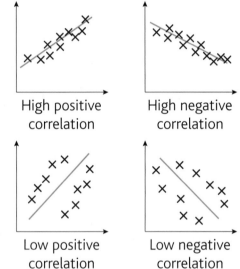

High positive correlation

High negative correlation

If the points are not all close to the line of best fit, the correlation is called **low** or weak.

Low positive correlation

Low negative correlation

5.3 Using lines of best fit

If the value of only one of the two quantities is known, lines of best fit can be used to estimate the value of the other quantity. For example, to estimate the maths mark of a student whose science mark is 13, draw a vertical line up from 13 to the line of best fit. Then draw a horizontal line across and read off the maths mark, 11.

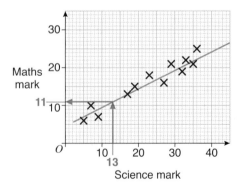

Using lines of best fit outside the range of the plotted points can give estimates which are unreliable or even ridiculous. Extending the line of best fit on the scatter graph in Example 1 and using it to estimate the number of teeth for a 20-year-old man gives an answer of 33 but people with *all* their own teeth normally have only 32!

Exercise 5B

1 The table shows the marks scored by ten students in an English exam and a History exam.

English	20	87	56	42	96	92	41	32	86	52
History	8	49	32	22	55	52	14	10	52	23

    a On the resource sheet, draw a scatter graph to show the information in the table.

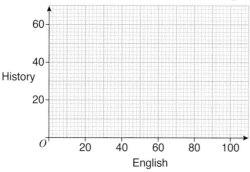

    b Describe the correlation between the marks scored in the two exams.

> 'Describe the correlation' means state whether it is positive or negative. It is not necessary to say whether it is high or low. A description of the *relationship* is not acceptable.

    c Draw a line of best fit on your scatter graph.

    d Use your line of best fit to estimate

      i the History mark of a student whose English mark is 70,

      ii the English mark of a student whose History mark is 44

2 The table shows the outdoors temperature, in °C, at noon on ten days and the number of units of electricity used in heating a house on each of those days.

Noon temperature (°C)	9	2	0	4	11	10	12	5	3	1
Units of electricity used	25	39	44	34	23	24	21	32	36	42

    a On the resource sheet, draw a scatter graph to show the information in the table.

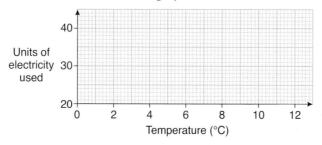

    b Which of these three terms best describes the relationship between the temperature and the number of units of electricity used?

      positive correlation   **negative correlation**   **no correlation**

    c Draw a line of best fit on your scatter graph.

    d Use your line of best fit to estimate

      i the number of units of electricity used when the outdoors temperature was 8 °C,

      ii the outdoors temperature when 30 units of electricity were used.

3 The table shows the inflation rate and the unemployment rate in the UK every two years from 1982 to 2000

Year	1982	1984	1986	1988	1990	1992	1994	1996	1998	2000
Inflation rate (%)	8.6	5.0	3.4	4.9	9.5	3.7	2.5	2.5	3.4	3.0
Unemployment rate (%)	9.0	10.1	10.5	7.6	5.5	9.2	8.8	7.0	4.5	3.6

a On the resource sheet, draw a scatter graph to show the information in the table.

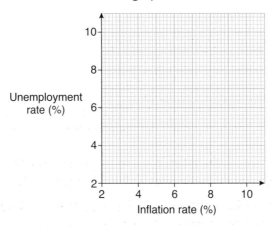

b Which of these three terms best describes the relationship between the inflation rate and the unemployment rate?

positive correlation   negative correlation   zero correlation

4 Complete the table on the resource sheet to show whether there is a positive correlation, a negative correlation or no correlation between the quantities. The first one has been done for you.

	Positive correlation	Negative correlation	No correlation
ages of cars and their value		✓	
heights of women and their weekly pay			
the number of students and the number of teachers in a school			
the distance a motorist drives and the amount of petrol used			
the hat sizes of students and their GCSE maths marks			
the amount of rain one day at a seaside town and the number of people on the beach			

5   The table shows, for ten cities, the highest temperature, in °C, and the number of hours of sunshine one day in September.

Highest temperature (°C)	20	33	14	21	29	25	16	26	19	24
Number of hours of sunshine	6	10	5	7	9	8	5	8	6	7

a   On the resource sheet, draw a scatter graph to show the information in the table.

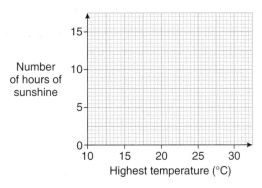

b   On the same day, in St. Petersburg, the highest temperature was 16 °C and there were 13 hours of sunshine. Plot this information on the scatter graph.

c   For the eleven cities, comment on the relationship between the highest temperature and the number of hours of sunshine.

6   The scatter graph shows the age and the price of 15 *Vector* cars.
A line of best fit has been drawn.

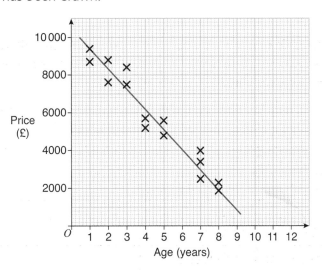

a   Describe the correlation between the age of the *Vector* and its price.

b   Use the line of best fit to find
   i   the price of a 6-year-old *Vector*,
   ii the age of a *Vector* that costs £6200

c   Why would it not be sensible to use the line of best fit to estimate the price of an 11-year-old *Vector*?

Chapter summary

> **You should now know**
>
> ★ how to draw a **scatter graph**
>
> ★ how to describe the relationship, if any, suggested by a scatter graph
>
> ★ how to draw a **line of best fit**
>
> ★ how to use a line of best fit
>
> ★ the meaning of **correlation** and how a line of best fit can be used to show it
>
> ★ how to recognise **positive** correlation, **negative** correlation and **no** correlation or **zero correlation**

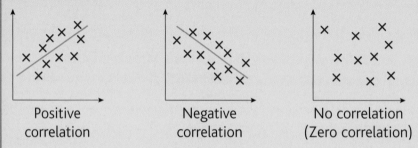

Positive correlation   Negative correlation   No correlation (Zero correlation)

Chapter 5 review questions

1 The scatter graph shows information about eight countries.

For each country, it shows the birth rate and the life expectancy, in years.

The table shows the birth rate and the life expectancy for six more countries.

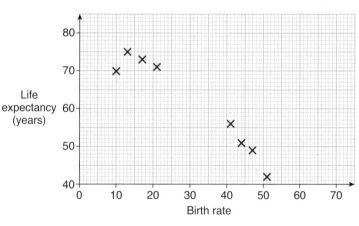

Birth rate	25	28	30	31	34	38
Life expectancy (years)	68	65	62	61	65	61

a On the scatter graph on the resource sheet, plot the information from the table.

b Describe the relationship between the birth rate and the life expectancy.

c Draw a line of best fit on the scatter graph.

The birth rate in a country is 42.

d Use your line of best fit to estimate the life expectancy in that country.

The life expectancy in a different country is 66 years.

e Use your line of best fit to estimate the birth rate in that country. (1385 June 2000)

2 Ten men took part in a long jump competition.
The table shows the heights of the ten men and the best jumps they made.

Best jump (m)	5.33	6.00	5.00	5.95	4.80	5.72	4.60	5.80	4.40	5.04
Height of men (m)	1.70	1.80	1.65	1.75	1.65	1.74	1.60	1.75	1.60	1.67

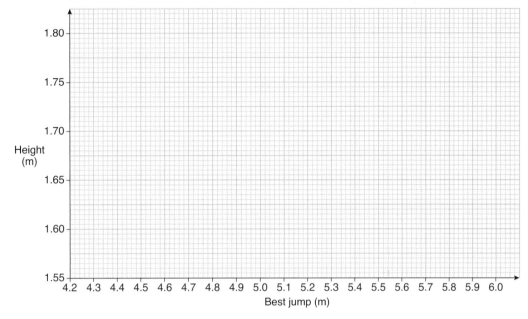

a On the grid on the resource sheet, plot the points as a scatter diagram.
b Describe the relationship between the height and the best jump.
c Draw in a line of best fit.
d Use your line of best fit to estimate
    i the height of a man who could make a best jump of 5.2 m,
    ii the best jump of a man of height 1.73 m.
    (1385 Nov 1998)

3 The scatter graph shows some information about six new-born baby apes.

For each baby ape, it shows the mother's leg length and the baby ape's birth weight.

The table shows the mother's leg length and the birth weight for two more baby apes.

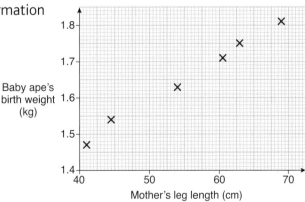

a On the scatter graph on the resource sheet, plot the information from the table.
b Describe the correlation between a mother's leg length and the baby ape's birth weight.

Mother's leg length (cm)	50	65
Baby ape's birth weight (kg)	1.6	1.75

c Draw a line of best fit on the diagram.

A mother's leg length is 55 cm.

d Use your line of best fit to estimate the birth weight of the baby ape.   (1387 June 2005)

4   A park has an outdoor swimming pool. The scatter graph shows the maximum temperature and the number of people who used the pool on ten Saturdays in summer.

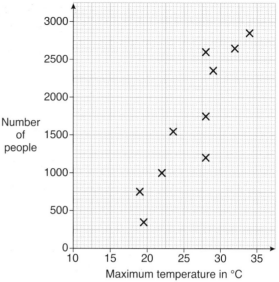

a   Describe the correlation between the maximum temperature and the number of people who used the pool.

b   Draw a line of best fit on the scatter graph on the resource sheet.

The weather forecast for next Saturday gives a maximum temperature of 27 °C.

c   Use your line of best fit to estimate the number of people who will use the pool.

(1385 Nov 1999)

5   The scatter graph shows some information about seven children.
It shows the age of each child and the number of hours sleep each child had last night.

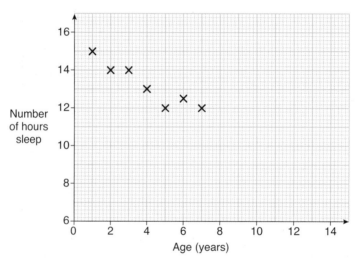

The table shows the ages of four more children and the number of hours sleep each of them had last night.

Age (years)	10	11	12	13
Number of hours sleep	11	10	10.5	9.6

a   On the scatter graph on the resource sheet, plot the information from the table.

b   Describe the correlation between the age, in years, of the children and the number of hours sleep they had last night.

c   Draw a line of best fit on the diagram.

d   Use your line of best fit to estimate the number of hours sleep for an 8 year old child.

(1385 June 2002)

6 a Here is a scatter graph. One axis is labelled 'weight'.

    i For this graph state the type of correlation.

    ii From this list choose an appropriate axis for the other axis.

    shoe size, length of hair, height, hat size, length of arm.

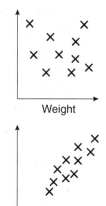

b Here is another scatter graph with one axis labelled 'weight'.

    i For this graph state the type of correlation.

    ii From this list, choose an appropriate label for the other axis.

    shoe size, distance around neck, waist measurement, GCSE Maths mark

(1385 June 2000)

7 The table shows information about the percentage share of daily viewing hours of ITV1 and cable/satellite channels from 1992 until 2002.

Year	ITV1	Cable/satellite channels
1992	41	5
1993	40	6
1994	39	7
1995	37	9
1996	35	10
1997	33	12
1998	32	13
1999	31	14
2000	29	17
2001	27	20
2002	24	22

Here is a scatter graph for the information from 1992 to 1998

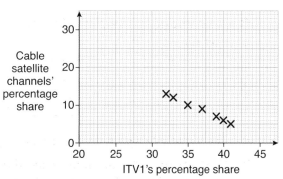

a On the scatter graph on the resource sheet, plot the information for 1999, 2000, 2001 and 2002

b Describe the relationship between ITV1's percentage share of the daily viewing hours and the percentage share of cable/satellite channels.

c Draw a line of best fit on the scatter graph.

In 2003, cable/satellite channels had a 24% share of daily viewing hours.

d Use your line of best fit to estimate ITV1's percentage share in 2003

Introducing number

6.1 Numbers and place value

The number 2825 in words is 'Two thousand, eight hundred and twenty five'.

Thousands	Hundreds	Tens	Units
2	8	2	5

Each figure has a different **value** as shown in the table.

Example 1

Write the number eight thousand and fifty three in figures.

Solution 1

Put the figures in the number under the column headings shown above.

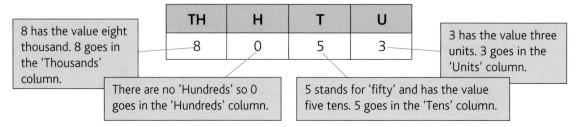

8 has the value eight thousand. 8 goes in the 'Thousands' column.

TH	H	T	U
8	0	5	3

3 has the value three units. 3 goes in the 'Units' column.

There are no 'Hundreds' so 0 goes in the 'Hundreds' column.

5 stands for 'fifty' and has the value five tens. 5 goes in the 'Tens' column.

The answer is 8053

Numbers are put in order of size by looking at the value of the figures in each number.

Example 2

Put these numbers in order: 347   50   678   9030   400   Start with the smallest.

Solution 2

50 contains only tens and units so this is the smallest number.

347, 678 and 400 all contain hundreds, tens and units.

347 only has three hundreds so this is the smallest of the three numbers.

400 has four hundreds so this is the next largest number.

678 has six hundreds so this is the largest number of the three.

9030 has nine thousands so this is the largest number.

The correct order is 50, 347, 400, 678, 9030

TH	H	T	U
	3	4	7
		5	0
	6	7	8
9	0	3	0
	4	0	0

Exercise 6A

1 Write in words the numbers shown in the table.

	TH	H	T	U
a	4	2	1	3
b	2	3	1	0
c	3	2	0	6
d	4	0	5	4
e	5	0	0	2

2 The number 214 written in hundreds, tens and units is 200 + 10 + 4
Write the following numbers in hundreds, tens and units.

a 315 **b** 256 **c** 432 **d** 329 **e** 156

3 The number 3126 written in thousands, hundreds, tens and units is
3000 + 100 + 20 + 6
Write the following numbers in thousands, hundreds, tens and units.

a 2315 **b** 6483 **c** 1267 **d** 7452 **e** 2383

4 Written as a single number   100 + 50 + 6 = 156
Write the following as single numbers.

a 200 + 30 + 7 **b** 400 + 50 + 8 **c** 600 + 40 + 3
d 500 + 90 **e** 400 + 6 **f** 1000 + 200 + 30 + 4
g 2000 + 500 + 40 + 7 **h** 5000 + 600 + 70 + 8 **i** 3000 + 40 + 7
j 2000 + 300 + 8 **k** 5000 + 9

5 Copy the table of column headings. Use it to write these numbers in figures.

Thousands	Hundreds	Tens	Units

a four hundred and eighty five
b five thousand, two hundred and sixty seven
c eight hundred and four
d four thousand and twenty one
e six thousand and eight.

6 Copy the table of column headings above and use it to write these numbers in words.

a 25 **b** 369 **c** 409 **d** 6429 **e** 4079 **f** 6004

7 Copy the table of column headings.
Use it to put these whole numbers in order. Start with the smallest.

a 356 48 7 3466 **b** 566 345 67 8 **c** 65 56 404 232
d 345 3800 2333 999 **e** 367 361 1001 34

8 Write the following numbers in order. Start with the smallest.

a 486 32 533 21 4 **b** 333 234 108 32 47
c 438 444 423 430 407 **d** 207 270 720 277 727

9 Write the following numbers in order. Start with the smallest.

   a thirty eight, 407, sixty four, 397, four hundred and twenty

   b 507, four hundred and thirteen, 366, two hundred and three

10 Write down the value of the 3 in the number 356

11 Write down the value of the 8 in the number 3589

12 Write down the value of the 3 in the number 3070

13 Here are 4 cards. Each card has a figure on it.
The cards show the number 2643.

   a Arrange the four cards to make the
biggest number possible.

   b Arrange the four cards to make the
smallest number possible.

   c Put a number in the last card to make
the answer 10 times bigger.

14 Write the following numbers in figures

   a ten thousand

   b fourteen thousand, eight hundred and twenty four

   c eighteen thousand, four hundred and seven

   d twenty three thousand and forty eight

   e forty two thousand and six

   f one hundred thousand

   g two million

15 Here are some numbers on a display.
Write down the numbers in words

6.2 Number lines

Whole numbers can be shown as positions on a number line.

Here is a number line which stretches from 0 to 100

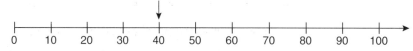

The arrow points to the number 40

This number line starts at 120 and ends at 140

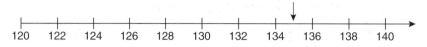

The arrow points to the number 135

Number lines can be used to add one number to another.

Example 3

Calculate 34 + 15, using a number line.

Solution 3

On a number line which begins at 30 and ends at 50, mark 34 with an arrow.
Count 15 divisions from 34

The diagram shows 34 + 15 = 49

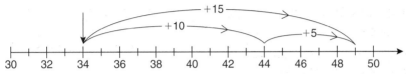

Another way of doing this is to add 10 onto 34 to get 44 and then add 5 onto 44 to get 49

Number lines can also be used to subtract one number from another.

Example 4

Calculate 45 − 17 using a number line.

Solution 4

On a number line which begins at 20 and ends at 50 mark 45 with an arrow.
Count 17 divisions back from 45

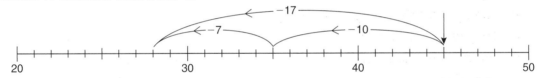

Another way of doing this is to go back 10 to 35 then go back 7 to end at 28

Exercise 6B

1 Copy the number line and mark the following numbers with an arrow.

    a 11   **b** 19   **c** 15   **d** 13   **e** 17

    10   11   12   13   14   15   16   17   18   19   20

2 Copy the number line and mark the following numbers with an arrow.

    a 3   **b** 6   **c** 11   **d** 14   **e** 19

    0   2   4   6   8   10   12   14   16   18   20

3 Copy the number line and mark the following numbers with an arrow.

    a 50   **b** 75   **c** 62   **d** 88   **e** 91

    50   55   60   65   70   75   80   85   90   95   100

4 Write down the numbers marked on the number line.

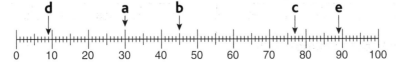

5 Copy the number line and mark the following numbers with an arrow.

    a 2200   **b** 2400   **c** 2050   **d** 2480   **e** 2150

6 Write down the numbers marked on the number line.

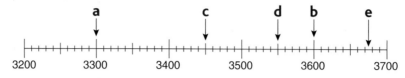

7 Use the number line to work out 24 + 17

8 Use the number line to work out 16 + 32

9 Use the number line to work out 46 − 28

10 Use the number line to work out 42 − 18

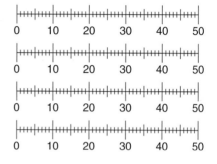

6.3 Rounding numbers

There are 783 students in a school. There are *about 800* students in the school.
The number of students has been **rounded** to the nearest 100

There are 22 sweets in a bag. There are *about 20* sweets in the bag.
The number of sweets has been rounded to the nearest 10

There are 3500 people at a concert. There are *about 4000* people at the concert.
If the number is exactly halfway between the two end points then **round up**.
The number of people at the concert has been rounded up to the nearest 1000

Example 5

The number of people in a football ground at the start of the game is 6536

a Write 6536 correct to the nearest 1000   **b** Write 6536 to the nearest 100

Solution 5

a 6536 is between 6000 and 7000 6500 is halfway between these two numbers.
    6536 is more than 6500 so it is nearer to 7000 than 6000 and the answer is 7000

b 6536 is between 6500 and 6600 6550 is halfway between these two numbers.
    6536 is less than 6550 so it is nearer to 6500 than 6600 and the answer is 6500

Exercise 6C

1 Write each of the following numbers to the nearest 10
   a 48   **b** 56   **c** 73   **d** 85   **e** 8   **f** 98

2 Write each of the following numbers to the nearest 100
   a 459   **b** 766   **c** 333   **d** 450   **e** 88   **f** 969

3 Write each of the following numbers to the nearest 1000
   a 3400   **b** 2410   **c** 6600   **d** 4870   **e** 3333   **f** 9896

4 Write each of the following numbers to the nearest 1000
   a 4399   **b** 7378   **c** 6904   **d** 5050   **e** 9500   **f** 6499

5 **a** Write 2340 to the nearest 100   **b** Write 28 680 to the nearest 1000
   c Write 5876 to the nearest 10   **d** Write 677 to the nearest 1000
   e Write 4579 to the nearest 10   **f** Write 24 589 to the nearest 100

6 **a** There are 1483 students in a school. Write down the number of students correct to the nearest 100 students.
   b Rob drove a distance of 942 miles on holiday. Write down the distance Rob drove correct to the nearest 100 miles.
   c There are 366 days in a leap year. Write down the number of days in a leap year correct to the nearest 10 days.
   d Liz lives 18 kilometres from her work. Write down the distance Liz lives from work to the nearest 10 kilometres.
   e Anis earns £454 in a month. Write down how much Anis earns correct to the nearest £100.

7 **a** Write 24 000 correct to the nearest 10 000
   b Write 28 500 correct to the nearest 10 000
   c Write 23 600 correct to the nearest 1000
   d A car is advertised for sale for £13 999. What is the sale price correct to the nearest £1000?
   e The distance from London to Sydney is 13 642 miles. Write this distance correct to the nearest 100 miles.

8 **a** During Comic Relief day twenty eight million, three hundred and twenty four thousand, four hundred and eighty pounds had been promised. Write this amount to the nearest million pounds.
   b The attendance at a football ground is 41 879. Write this to the nearest 10 000
   c The number of people living in a town is 18 345. Write this number to the nearest 1000
   d The number of passengers carried on one day by a railway company is 13 479. Write this number to the nearest 100
   e Fred wins a prize of £13 487. Write this amount to the nearest £100
   f A catering company delivers 56 845 meals each day. Write this number to the nearest 100

9   There are 800 people, correct to the nearest 100, living in a village.

    a   What is the largest number of people that could be living in the village?

    b   What is the smallest number of people that could be living in the village?

10   There are 14 000 people, correct to the nearest 1000, at a football match.

    a   What is the largest number of people that could be at the football match?

    b   What is the smallest number of people that could be at the football match?

6.4 Mental methods

Often you can work out the answer to a calculation by doing it in your head.
To do this you must know your **number bonds** to 100
This is useful when you are working out change from £1, for example.

In the table are some ways of
doing calculations mentally.

Example 6

Fred buys a drink for 54p.
Work out his change from £1

Solution 6
Count up to the next ten.
$54 + \mathbf{6} = 60$
Count on to the next 100
$60 + \mathbf{40} = 100$
So the change is $\mathbf{6 + 40} = 46$p.

Example 7

Work out $136 + 58$

Solution 7
$130 + 50 = \mathbf{180}$ Add up the tens.
$6 + 8 = \mathbf{14}$ Add up the units.
$\mathbf{180 + 14} = 194$ Add the two results
                          together.

Example 8

Work out $84 - 38$

Solution 8
$84 - 30 = \mathbf{54}$ Subtract 30 first.
$\mathbf{54} - 8 = 46$ Then subtract the 8

Add 9	Add 10 then subtract 1
Add 99	Add 100 then subtract 1
Add 90	Add 100 then subtract 10
Add 48	Add 50 then subtract 2
Add 42	Add 40 then add 2
99×8	$100 \times 8 - 1 \times 8$ $= 800 - 8$ $= 792$
$£1.99 \times 5$	$£2 \times 5 - 1p \times 5$ $= £10 - 5p$ $= £9.95$
$£1.48 \times 3$	$£1.50 \times 3 - 2p \times 3$ $= £4.50 - 6p$ $= £4.44$
Change from £10	Add on when giving change e.g. $£10 - £5.86$ Add on 4p to make £5.90 Add on 10p to make £6 Add on £4 to make £10 This gives £4.14
$100 - 34$	Add on 6 to 34 to make 40 Add on 60 to 40 to make 100 This gives $100 - 34 = 66$
$142 - 76$	Add on 4 to 76 to make 80 Add on 60 to 80 to make 140 Add on 2 to 140 to make 142 This gives $142 - 76 = 66$

Exercise 6D

1   Work out the following mentally and write down your answer. Jot down anything you need.

   a 23 + 58   **b** 38 + 24   **c** 45 + 43

   d 38 + 46   **e** 57 + 68   **f** 49 + 68

   g 36 + 76   **h** 45 + 78   **i** 76 + 89

   j 55 + 36 + 20   **k** 40 + 37 + 39

2   Work out the following mentally and write down your answer.

   a 26 − 13   **b** 38 − 21   **c** 47 − 24

   d 68 − 34   **e** 98 − 16   **f** 43 − 29

   g 23 − 14   **h** 54 − 29   **i** 55 − 29

   j 64 − 29   **k** 74 − 28   **l** 93 − 27

3   Work out the following and write down your answer. Jot down anything you need.

   a Add the answer to 10 × 6 to the answer to 4 × 6

   b Add the answer to 5 × 7 to the answer to 3 × 8

   c Add the answer to 4 × 8 to the answer to 9 × 4

   d Add the answer to 3 × 7 to the answer to 5 × 9

   e Add the answer to 6 × 7 to the answer to 4 × 9

4   Work out the following and write down your answer. Jot down anything you need.

   a Subtract the answer to 4 × 5 from the answer to 9 × 6

   b Subtract the answer to 2 × 8 from the answer to 8 × 5

   c Subtract the answer to 6 × 5 from the answer to 7 × 6

   d Subtract the answer to 4 × 9 from the answer to 7 × 7

   e Subtract the answer to 5 × 9 from the answer to 7 × 8

5   Copy and complete this multiplication table.

×	2		7
		15	35
8			
	20		

6   **a** Find the cost of two tins of paint at £1.99 each.

   b Find the cost of three cans of drink at 49p each.

   c Find the cost of six packets of sweets at 99p each.

   d Find the cost of four boxes of cereal at 98p each.

   e Find the cost of six litres of petrol at 95p each litre.

6.5 Written calculations

also assessed in Module 4

Some calculation are too hard to be done mentally. It helps to write them down.
The four **operations** are **addition, subtraction, multiplication and division.**

Addition

Example 9

Work out 345 + 48

Solution 9

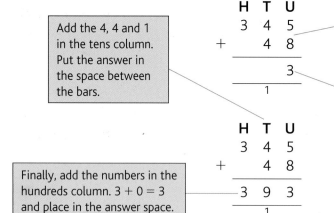

Add the 4, 4 and 1 in the tens column. Put the answer in the space between the bars.

Put the numbers in columns. Figures with equal place value go in the same column. For example, 5 and 8 are units so they go in the same column.

$$
\begin{array}{ccc}
\text{H} & \text{T} & \text{U} \\
3 & 4 & 5 \\
+ & & 4 & 8 \\
\hline
 & & 3 \\
 & 1 &
\end{array}
$$

5 + 8 = 13
Put 3 in the answer space in the units column and 1 'ten' in the tens column.

Finally, add the numbers in the hundreds column. 3 + 0 = 3 and place in the answer space.

$$
\begin{array}{ccc}
\text{H} & \text{T} & \text{U} \\
3 & 4 & 5 \\
+ & & 4 & 8 \\
\hline
3 & 9 & 3 \\
 & 1 &
\end{array}
$$

The result of adding two or more numbers is called the **sum** of those numbers.

Subtraction

Example 10

Work out 365 − 258

Solution 10

$$
\begin{array}{ccc}
\text{H} & \text{T} & \text{U} \\
3 & 6 & 5 \\
- & 2 & 5 & 8 \\
\hline
\end{array}
$$

Put the numbers in columns.

$$
\begin{array}{ccc}
\text{H} & \text{T} & \text{U} \\
3 & 5 & {}^{1}5 \\
- & 2 & 5 & 8 \\
\hline
 & & 7
\end{array}
$$

5 − 8 you cannot do so borrow one ten from the tens column to make 15
15 − 8 = 7. Put 7 in the answer space.

$$
\begin{array}{ccc}
\text{H} & \text{T} & \text{U} \\
3 & 5 & {}^{1}5 \\
- & 2 & 5 & 8 \\
\hline
1 & 0 & 7
\end{array}
$$

Subtract the numbers in the tens and hundreds columns.

When a smaller number is subtracted from a larger number, the result is called the **difference** between the two numbers.

Exercise 6E

1   Work out the following additions
    a   367 + 128   **b**   249 + 178   **c**   255 + 24
    d   387 + 68   **e**   567 + 128

2   Work out the following additions
    a   2367 + 2444   **b**   1286 + 4306   **c**   3457 + 345   **d**   2039 + 768
    e   4506 + 967   **f**   679 + 3888   **g**   49 + 7608

3   Work out the following subtractions
    a   648 − 123   **b**   459 − 320   **c**   877 − 434   **d**   561 − 186
    e   674 − 128   **f**   345 − 137   **g**   767 − 293   **h**   856 − 173
    i   637 − 261   **j**   543 − 181

4   Work out the following subtractions
    a   351 − 179   **b**   427 − 289   **c**   535 − 168   **d**   422 − 175
    e   734 − 178   **f**   852 − 653   **g**   402 − 229   **h**   646 − 188

5   Work out the following subtractions
    a   400 − 168   **b**   305 − 213   **c**   704 − 178
    d   505 − 256   **e**   903 − 387

6   Find the sum of
    a   387 and 269   **b**   1256 and 965   **c**   267 and 8799

7   Find the difference between
    a   344 and 167   **b**   704 and 367   **c**   436 and 59

8   Find the missing numbers.
    a   234 + ? = 476   **b**   312 + ? = 508   **c**   278 + ? = 566
    d   ? + 255 = 400   **e**   ? + 363 = 532   **f**   ? + 419 = 722

9   Find the missing numbers.
    a   213 − ? = 80   **b**   235 − ? = 122   **c**   428 − ? = 244
    d   ? − 235 = 300   **e**   ? − 534 = 121   **f**   ? − 129 = 236

10   The sum of two numbers is 564. One of the numbers is 128
     Work out the other number.

11   The sum of three numbers is 425. Two of the numbers are 124 and 138
     Work out the other number.

12   The sum of three numbers is 238. Two of the numbers are 89 and 90
     Work out the other number.

13   The difference between two numbers is 120. The larger of the two numbers is 200
     Work out the smaller number.

14 The difference between two numbers is 100. The smaller of the two numbers is 150
Work out the larger number.

15 The difference between two numbers is 140. One of the numbers is 200
Work out the other number.

Multiplication

The result of multiplying two numbers is called the **product.**

Example 11 shows how to multiply a two or three figure number by a single figure number.

Example 11

Work out 243 × 6

Solution 11

```
  H  T  U
  2  4  3
×       6
_____
        8
     1
```

Put the numbers in columns.
Start with the units column, 3 × 6 = 18
Put the 8 in the units column and the 1 in the tens column.

```
  2  4  3
×       6
_____
     5  8
  2  1
```

Work out '4 tens' × 6 = 24 tens. Add in the 1 ten to get 25 tens.
Put the 5 in the tens column and the 2 in the hundreds column.

```
  2  4  3
×       6
_____
1  4  5  8
  2  1
```

Work out '2 hundreds' × 6 = 12 hundreds.
Add the other 2 in the hundreds column to get 14 hundreds.

The calculation can also be done by splitting the
243 into 2 hundreds, 4 tens and 3 units
and multiplying each by 6.

$$3 \times 6 = 18$$
$$40 \times 6 = 240$$
$$200 \times 6 = 1200$$
$$\overline{1458}$$

Exercise 6F

1 16 × 4   **2** 32 × 3   **3** 25 × 5   **4** 38 × 5   **5** 64 × 4

6 23 × 6   **7** 34 × 7   **8** 43 × 8   **9** 27 × 8   **10** 43 × 9

11 234 × 5   **12** 213 × 4   **13** 354 × 6   **14** 352 × 7   **15** 158 × 7

16 215 × 6   **17** 473 × 6   **18** 648 × 7   **19** 438 × 8   **20** 365 × 9

Examples 12 and 13 show the two main methods for multiplying a two or three figure number by a single figure number.

Each method multiplies by a number in the 10 times table. This is easy as multiplying a number by 10 means adding a nought on to the number for the answer.

For example $10 \times 24 = 240$

Example 12

Work out 20×40

Solution 12

$20 \times 40 = 2 \times 10 \times 40 = 2 \times 400$ because $10 \times 40 = 400$

$\qquad = 800$

Example 13

Work out 23×45

Solution 13

Method 1 – The box method

$23 = 20 + 3$

$45 = 40 + 5$

Write this in a box and complete the box as shown.

$40 \times 20 = 800$

×	20	3
40	800	120
5	100	15

$5 \times 20 = 100$ $\qquad$ $40 \times 3 = 120$ $\qquad$ $5 \times 3 = 15$

The answer is $800 + 100 + 120 + 15 = 1035$

Method 2 – The column method

$$
\begin{array}{ccc}
 & 2 & 3 \\
\times & 4 & 5 \\
\hline
1 & 1 & 5 \\
9 & 2 & 0 \\
\hline
1 \quad 0 & 3 & 5 \\
\hline
\end{array}
$$

$5 \times 23 = 115$
$40 \times 23 = 920$

The answer is $115 + 920 = 1035$

To multiply any whole number by 100 add two noughts to the number.

$31 \times 100 = 3100$

To multiply any whole number by 1000 add three noughts to the number.

$76 \times 1000 = 76\,000$

Exercise 6G

1	10 × 9	**2**	10 × 16	**3**	10 × 27	**4**	10 × 60	**5**	20 × 60
6	20 × 70	**7**	32 × 21	**8**	42 × 21	**9**	35 × 23	**10**	31 × 35
11	43 × 32	**12**	44 × 33	**13**	53 × 45	**14**	42 × 44	**15**	76 × 87
16	64 × 86	**17**	45 × 77	**18**	99 × 99				

Division

There are many different methods of carrying out division.
Example 14 shows two methods for dividing by a single figure number.

Example 14

Work out 748 ÷ 5

Solution 14

Method 1

```
      7  4  8
   -  5  0  0          Take off 100 5s
   ─────────
      2  4  8
   -  2  0  0          Take off another 40 5s
   ─────────
         4  8
   -     4  5          Take off 9 5s and you are left
   ─────────           with a remainder of 3
            3
   ─────────
```

748 ÷ 5 = 149 remainder 3   100 + 40 + 9 = 149

Method 2

$$\begin{array}{r} 1 \\ 5\overline{)7\,{}^2 4\,8} \end{array}$$

7 in the hundreds column divided by 5 is 1 in the hundreds column with a remainder of 2

$$\begin{array}{r} 1\ 4 \\ 5\overline{)7\,{}^2 4\,{}^4 8} \end{array}$$

24 in the tens column divided by 5 is 4 in the tens column with a remainder of 4

$$\begin{array}{r} 1\ 4\ 9 \\ 5\overline{)7\,{}^2 4\,{}^4 8} \end{array}$$

48 in the units column divided by 5 is 9 in the units column with a remainder of 3

748 ÷ 5 = 149 remainder 3

Exercise 6H

1	48 ÷ 4	**2**	49 ÷ 7	**3**	47 ÷ 3	**4**	58 ÷ 3
5	64 ÷ 4	**6**	124 ÷ 4	**7**	276 ÷ 5	**8**	568 ÷ 6
9	387 ÷ 6	**10**	354 ÷ 6	**11**	427 ÷ 7	**12**	538 ÷ 8

Example 15 shows how you can use the same method to divide by a two figure number.

Example 15

Work out $776 \div 24$

Solution 15

Method 1

```
    7  7  6
 -  2  4  0        from 10 times 24
 _____
    5  3  6
 -  2  4  0        from 10 times 24 again
 _____
    2  9  6
 -  2  4  0        from 10 times 24 one more time
 _____
       5  6
 -     4  8        from 2 times 24
 _____
          8
 _____
```

$776 \div 24 = 32$ remainder 8 $10 + 10 + 10 + 2 = 32$

Method 2

$$\overset{\displaystyle 3}{24 \overline{)\, 7\ 7\ ^5 6}}$$

Write out the first few multiples of 24: 24 48 72 96
24 goes into 77 three times with a remainder of 5

$$\overset{\displaystyle 3\ 2}{24 \overline{)\, 7\ 7\ ^5 6}}$$

56 in the units column divided by 24 is 2 in the units column with a remainder of 8

$776 \div 24 = 32$ remainder 8

Exercise 6I

1	$345 \div 15$	**2**	$480 \div 25$	**3**	$369 \div 23$	**4**	$487 \div 24$	**5**	$567 \div 32$
6	$388 \div 18$	**7**	$364 \div 26$	**8**	$669 \div 53$	**9**	$807 \div 47$	**10**	$1354 \div 36$

6.6 Solving problems with and without a calculator

also assessed in Module 4

Problems can be solved using a calculator. You need to decide which operations are needed and make sense of the calculator display.

Example 16

A box holds 25 exercise books. Use a calculator to work out how many boxes are needed to hold 1450 exercise books.

Solution 16

To solve this, you need to use division.

$1450 \div 25$ Using a calculator, divide 1450 by 25 to find the number of boxes and press the equals button.

$= 58$ The calculator displays 58, so this is the answer.

58 boxes are needed.

Exercise 6J

1 A tin of paint costs £2.39. Find the cost of 16 cans of paint.

2 A box of chocolates contains 25 chocolates. How many boxes are needed for 10 000 chocolates?

3 Doris gets paid £6.35 for each hour she works. Find how much she gets paid for 23 hours work.

4 A machine fills 287 paint cans in an hour. How many cans does it fill in 14 hours?

5 There are 24 hours in a day and 365 days in a year. How many hours are there in a year?

6 23 367 people each paid £23 to watch a football match. How much was paid altogether?

7 182 adults and 374 children visited a museum. Each adult paid £4.10 and each child paid £2.40. Work out the total amount paid.

8 A shop sells 45 CDs at £7.99 each and 28 CDs at £12.49 each. How much money is taken?

9 The price of a concert ticket is £18. The total takings from ticket sales for one concert is £7614. How many people attend one concert?

10 Billy works for 38 hours and is paid £241.30. How much does he earn in an hour?

Sometimes you will have to do number problems without a calculator.

Example 17

The number of students in a school is 1250
All of the students are going on a school trip by bus.
Each bus holds 47 students.
Work out the number of buses that are needed to take students on the trip.

Solution 17

1250 ÷ 47

> This is a division by 47 because each bus can carry 47 students.

$$\begin{array}{r} 2\ 6 \\ 47\overline{)\ 1\ 2\ 5\ ^31 0} \end{array} \text{ remainder 28}$$

The number of buses = 26 + 1 (to carry the 28 remaining students)

The number of buses = 27

Example 18

A can of cola costs 46p. A sandwich costs 98p. Work out the total cost of five cans of cola and two sandwiches.

Solution 18

Sandwiches $2 \times 98p = 196p$

Cola $5 \times 46p = 230p$

                                    $\overline{426p}$

> Use multiplication to work out the total cost of the sandwiches and then the total cost of the cola.
> Write the problem in columns and add the two totals.

The total cost is £4.26

Exercise 6K

1 There are 19 girls and 15 boys in a room. How many children are there in the room?

2 James has £103 in his bank account. He takes out £38. How much is left?

3 Work out how many 25p stamps can be bought for £2

4 A can of cola costs 39p. Work out the cost of three cans.

5 A sandwich costs 99p and a coffee costs 45p. Work out the total cost of two sandwiches and two coffees.

6 A bus can carry 54 students. How many students can four buses carry?

7 Fred earns £28 for 7 hours work. How much does he earn in an hour?

8 A crate holds 36 cans of drink. How many cans will 16 crates hold?

9 £252 is to be shared equally amongst seven people. How much money will each person get?

10 13 buses are used on a school trip. Each bus holds 36 students. How many students can go on the school trip?

11 A packet contains 26 biscuits. How many biscuits are there in 32 packets?

12 A book has 287 pages. Work out the number of pages in eight copies of the book.

13 John is packing cakes into boxes. Each box holds six cakes. How many full boxes can he pack if he has 154 cakes?

14 A new car costs £7450. Work out the cost of seven new cars.

15 The number of students in a school is 1300. All the students go on a school trip. How many buses are needed if one bus holds 48 students?

16   There are 32 pencils in a box. How many pencils are in 12 of these boxes?

17   Work out the number of seconds in 24 minutes.

18   A box of 16 calculators costs £448. Find the cost of one calculator.

19   A full toy pack contains 12 toys. Zoe has 850 toys to pack and makes as many full toy packs as she can. How many toys will be left over?

Checking calculations

To check whether an answer is correct, use the opposite or **inverse** operation of the operation that gave that answer.

The inverse (or opposite) of multiplying is dividing.
The inverse (or opposite) of dividing is multiplying.
The inverse (or opposite) of adding is subtracting.
The inverse (or opposite) of subtracting is adding.

Example 19

A student thinks that 46 $\times$ 54 = 2484
Check his answer.

Solution 19
The inverse operation to $\times$ is $\div$
Calculate 2484 $\div$ 54.

The answer is 46 so the student was correct.

Another way of checking is to round the numbers to find a rough answer.
Round tens to the nearest 10 (for example round 11 to 10).
Round hundreds to the nearest 100 (for example round 189 to 200).
Round thousands to the nearest 1000 (for example round 3004 to 3000).

Example 20

A bottle of lemonade costs 98p. Shane thinks that the cost of 12 bottles is £117.60
Check his answer.

Solution 20
Round the 12 to 10 and the 98p to £1
10 $\times$ £1 = £10
The cost should be about £10

Shane has got the answer wrong.

Exercise 6L

1 Check these calculations by rounding and write down a rough answer.

    a $38 \times 51 = 1938$ **b** $23 \times 19 = 2093$ **c** $424 \times 32 = 13\,568$

    d $167 \times 28 = 13\,694$ **e** $456 \times 125 = 581$

2 Check these calculations by using the inverse operation.

    a $487 - 238 = 251$ **b** $366 - 228 = 124$ **c** $956 - 237 = 721$

    d $601 - 124 = 527$ **e** $3004 - 1025 = 1979$

3 A litre of fuel costs 96p. Grant thinks the cost of 48 litres of fuel is £393.60
Use rounding to check whether he is correct.

4 Check these calculations using the inverse operation.

    a $46 \times 54 = 2484$ **b** $38 \times 28 = 3116$ **c** $124 \times 32 = 3968$

    d $245 \times 36 = 88\,200$ **e** $456 \times 105 = 478\,080$

5 Check these calculations using the inverse operation.

    a $3024 \div 36 = 84$ **b** $4096 \div 64 = 64$ **c** $2187 \div 27 = 81$

    d $5184 \div 144 = 63$ **e** $1932 \div 42 = 46$

6.7 Factors, multiples, squares and cubes

Factors are numbers which divide exactly into a bigger number.

5 is a factor of 15 because 5 divides exactly 3 times into 15.

6 is not a factor of 15 because 6 does not divide exactly into 15.

Since $12 = 3 \times 4$, both 3 and 4 are factors of 12

    $20 = 1 \times 20$

    $20 = 2 \times 10$

    $20 = 4 \times 5$

There are no other pairs of numbers which have a product of 20

So the factors of 20 are 1, 2, 4, 5, 10 and 20

Common factors

The factors of 10 are 1, 2, 5 and 10. The factors of 15 are 1, 3, 5 and 15

1 and 5 are factors of both 10 and 15. We say that 1 and 5 are **common factors** of 10 and 15

Multiples

A **multiple** of a number is found by multiplying it by any whole number.

To find the multiples of 3, multiply 3 by any whole number. Here are some of the multiples of 3

    $3 \times 1 = 3$

    $3 \times 2 = 6$

    $3 \times 3 = 9$

    $3 \times 4 = 12$

These are all in the 'three times' multiplication table.

Multiples of 2 are called **even** numbers.
Any number that ends in 2, 4, 6, 8 or 0 is even.
Whole numbers which are not even are called **odd** numbers.
Any number that ends in 1, 3, 5, 7 or 9 is odd.

Square numbers

Nine is a **square number** because it can be arranged
into a *square* pattern of dots of 3 rows of 3

Square numbers are numbers that can be arranged into *square* patterns of dots.

9 is the third square number because it can be found from 3×3
16 is the fourth square number because it can be found from 4×4

The first ten square numbers are 1, 4, 9, 16, 25, 36, 49, 64, 81 and 100

Multiplication can be used to work out higher square numbers. For example, to find the
14th square number, work out 14×14, which is 196

Cube numbers

Multiplying a number by itself three times gives a **cube number**.
$2 \times 2 \times 2 = 8$ 8 is a cube number.

The first five cube numbers are 1, 8, 27, 64 and 125
These are calculated from $1 \times 1 \times 1, 2 \times 2 \times 2, 3 \times 3 \times 3, 4 \times 4 \times 4$ and $5 \times 5 \times 5$

The tenth cube number is 1000 ($10 \times 10 \times 10$)

Exercise 6M

1 Which of the following numbers are factors of 12 ?
   a 12   **b** 6   **c** 9   **d** 3   **e** 24

2 Which of the following numbers are factors of 30?
   a 1   **b** 20   **c** 15   **d** 3   **e** 6

3 List all of the factors of the following numbers
   a 8   **b** 10   **c** 16   **d** 24   **e** 28   **f** 32
   g 36   **h** 40   **i** 50   **j** 60   **k** 100

4 For the following numbers find the factor which goes with the given factor.
   a 24, factor 12   **b** 22, Factor 2   **c** 18, factor 3   **d** 14, factor 2
   e 25, factor 5   **f** 34, factor 2   **g** 39, factor 3   **h** 42, factor 6
   i 42, factor 3   **j** 64, factor 4

5 List all the common factors of the following pairs of numbers.
   a 6 and 8   **b** 6 and 9   **c** 6 and 10   **d** 8 and 12
   e 12 and 15   **f** 10 and 20   **g** 15 and 20   **h** 18 and 24

6 Write down the first three multiples of the following numbers.
   a 5   **b** 10   **c** 8   **d** 7   **e** 24

7 Write 'true or false' for the following statements.

   a 12 is a multiple of 2   **b** 14 is a factor of 7

   c 24 is a multiple of 3   **d** 72 is a multiple of 9

   e 12 is a multiple of 6 and a factor of 36   **f** 9 is a factor of 27

   g 6 is a multiple of 1   **h** 4 is a multiple of 12

8 Write down

   a the fourth square number

   b the cube of 3

   c twice the sixth square number

   d a multiple of the tenth square number

   e the tenth cube number divided by the tenth square number

9 Work out

   a 2 times the fourth square number

   b 3 times the seventh square number

   c the sum of the third square number and the fifth square number

   d the difference between the fifth cube number and the fifth square number

   e the eighth square number multiplied by the third square number

   f the fourth cube number multiplied by the fourth square number.

10 **a** Ricky thinks of an odd number that is a factor of 12. The number is not 1. What number is Ricky thinking of?

     b Doris thinks of an even number that is a factor of 28. The number is not 2. What number is Doris thinking of?

     c Joe thinks of an odd number that is a multiple of 5. The number is between 8 and 22. What number is Joe thinking of?

     d Samir thinks of a square number between 30 and 40. What number is Samir thinking of?

     e Sanjit thinks of a cube number between 20 and 40. What number is Sanjit thinking of?

11 Here are the first nine square numbers

      1   4   9   16   25   36   49   64   81

Write each of the numbers below as the sum of two square numbers taken from the list above.

   a 5   **b** 8   **c** 13   **d** 34   **e** 20

   f 29   **g** 61   **h** 80   **i** 90   **j** 97

6.8 Order of operations

A calculation can contain more than one operation.

The operations that could be in a calculation are addition ($+$), subtraction ($-$), multiplication ($\times$) and division ($\div$).

An expression like $2 + 3 \times 4$ can be worked out in two different ways.

$2 + 3 = 5$

$5 \times 4 = 20$

OR

$3 \times 4 = 12$

$2 + 12 = 14$

We use a set of rules to tell us which operations to do first so that so that everyone gets the same answer.

- If **brackets** appear, work out the value of the expression in the brackets first.
- If there are no brackets, do **multiplication and division before addition and subtraction** no matter where they come in an expression.

The rules can be remembered using the word **BIDMAS** which gives the order in which the operations are carried out.

Brackets

(Indices)   (Indices are explained in Chapter 20)

Division

Multiplication

Addition

Subtraction

- If an expression has only addition and subtraction then work from left to right to work it out.

Example 21

a   Work out $4 + 24 \div 2 + 4$ **b**   Work out $20 - 8 + 5$

Solution 21

a $24 \div 2 = 12$ | Do the division first. |

$4 + 12 + 4 = 20$ | Then work from left to right. |

b $20 - 8 = 12$ | Start at the left with the subtraction, as the expression has only addition and subtraction. |

$12 + 5 = 17$ | Then do the addition. |

Example 22

Work out $(6 + 4) \times 5$

Solution 22

$6 + 4 = 10$ | Work out the brackets first. |

$10 \times 5 = 50$ | Then do the multiplication. |

If the numbers are large then the expression can be worked out using a calculator. Calculators are either 'scientific' or 'non-scientific'. If the calculator is scientific the expression can be entered in the order it is written. If the calculator is non-scientific, each part of the expression must be worked out and written down before the calculation can be completed.

You can test whether your calculator is a scientific one or not by working out $2 + 3 \times 4$
If it is a scientific calculator you should get the answer 14

Example 23

Work out $\dfrac{63 \times 36}{23 + 31}$

Solution 23

$63 \times 36 = 2268$ — Work out the top of the expression and write the answer down.

$23 + 31 = 54$ — Work out the bottom of the expression and write the answer down.

Work out $2268 \div 54 = 42$ — Writing one number over another means dividing the top by the bottom.

Exercise 6N

1 Work out

  a $3 \times 5 + 4$ **b** $4 \times 4 - 4$ **c** $3 + 5 \times 4$ **d** $5 + 3 \times 6$

  e $20 - 2 \times 7$ **f** $16 - 3 \times 5$ **g** $37 - 4 \times 5$ **h** $38 - 5 \times 6$

  i $63 - 7 \times 8$ **j** $54 + 32 \times 2$

2 Work out

  a $17 - 5 - 3$ **b** $20 - 13 - 5$ **c** $23 - 5 + 8$ **d** $25 - 13 + 5$

  e $32 + 8 - 15$ **f** $29 + 18 - 20$ **g** $24 - 24 + 12$

3 Work out

  a $8 \div 2 + 2$ **b** $16 \div 4 + 8$ **c** $20 + 8 \div 4$

  d $32 + 8 \div 4$ **e** $36 + 8 \div 2$

4 Work out

  a $4 \times (6 + 2)$ **b** $5 \times (12 - 4)$ **c** $(3 + 7) \times 12$ **d** $(7 - 5) \times 9$

  e $(6 - 3) - 3$ **f** $6 - (3 - 3)$ **g** $(8 + 4) - 2$ **h** $8 + (4 - 2)$

5 Work out

  a $(6 + 4) \div 2$ **b** $(15 - 6) \div 3$ **c** $20 \div (10 - 5)$ **d** $36 \div (12 - 10)$

  e $24 \div (6 - 4)$ **f** $30 \div (15 - 10)$ **g** $640 \div (20 - 10)$

6   Add brackets so that each answer is correct.

    a $8 + 2 \times 3 = 30$ **b** $4 \times 5 + 6 = 44$ **c** $20 - 2 \times 2 = 36$

    d $18 + 2 \times 4 = 80$ **e** $14 - 3 \times 3 = 33$ **f** $20 \div 2 + 3 = 4$

    g $30 + 4 \div 2 = 17$ **h** $20 - 2 \div 2 = 9$ **i** $40 - 10 \div 2 = 15$

    j $48 \div 4 - 2 = 24$ **k** $16 - 8 - 6 = 14$ **l** $24 - 4 + 6 = 14$

    m $36 \div 6 \div 3 = 18$ **n** $24 \div 12 \div 2 = 4$ **o** $45 \div 5 \div 5 = 45$

7   Use a calculator to work out the following

    a $(65 + 81) \times 47$ **b** $(57 + 234) \times 46$ **c** $45 + 56 \times 13$

    d $1234 - 24 \times 36$ **e** $1728 \div 18 + 54$ **f** $432 \div 18 + 6$

    g $225 + 5280 \div 15$ **h** $(645 - 258) \div 3$

8   Use a calculator to work out the following

    a $(234 + 123) \times (39 + 56)$ **b** $(39 - 18) \times (638 - 239)$

    c $(248 + 169) \times (102 - 67)$ **d** $(24 \times 33) \div (346 - 322)$

    e $(672 + 368) \div (201 - 196)$

    f $\dfrac{36 \times 24}{16}$ **g** $\dfrac{48 \times 66}{36}$ **h** $\dfrac{726}{11 \times 2}$ **i** $\dfrac{1792}{56 \times 16}$

    j $\dfrac{1452}{182 - 116}$ **k** $\dfrac{48 \times 54}{321 - 249}$ **l** $\dfrac{169 + 273}{721 - 695}$ **m** $\dfrac{14\,820 - 7530}{135}$

6.9 Writing a number as a product of its prime factors

A **prime number** is a whole number which has only two factors.

2 is a prime number because 1 and 2 are its only factors.
3 is also a prime number because 1 and 3 are its only factors.

1 is **not** a prime number, because its only factor is 1
9 is **not** a prime number because it has more than two factors 1, 3 and 9

Here are the first eight prime numbers. The list continues for ever.

               2   3   5   7   11   13   17   19

Example 24

Which of the following numbers are prime numbers?

    21   23   25   27   29

Solution 24

$21 = 7 \times 3$ and 1×21 $25 = 5 \times 5$ and 25×1 $27 = 9 \times 3$ and 1×27

so they have more than two factors.

23 and 29 are the prime numbers in the list.

Prime numbers are the building blocks of all of the whole numbers because all whole numbers are either prime or can be written as a product of prime numbers.

For example, 15 is not prime, but can be written as the product 3×5
3 and 5 are prime numbers which are factors of 15 and so are called the **prime factors** of 15

12 is not prime, but can be written as the product of its prime factors.
$12 = 2 \times 2 \times 3$

Example 25

Write 18 as the product of its prime factors.

Solution 25

$18 = 2 \times 9$ (2 $\times$ 9 is not the answer, as 9 is not a prime number.)
$18 = 2 \times 3 \times 3$

Writing large numbers as the product of prime factors

Divide a large number by one of its prime factors to produce a smaller number.
Repeat this with the smaller number again and again until all that is left is a prime number.

To write 72 as the product of its prime factors, look for the smallest prime factor of 72
That is 2

	72
2	36
2	18
2	9
3	3
3	1

Divide 72 by 2
$72 \div 2 = 36$

Repeat with the new number (36).
$36 \div 2 = 18$

Repeat until a number is reached which does not have 2 as a factor.
$18 \div 2 = 9$ 2 is not a factor of 9

Pick the next prime number (3) to see if it is a factor of 9
$9 \div 3 = 3$

Repeat with the new number (3).
$3 \div 3 = 1$ so the process is complete

Then the final answer is $72 = 2 \times 2 \times 2 \times 3 \times 3$

Example 26

Write 120 as a product of its prime factors

Solution 26

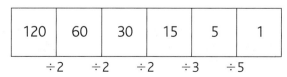

120	60	30	15	5	1
	$\div 2$	$\div 2$	$\div 2$	$\div 3$	$\div 5$

$120 = 2 \times 2 \times 2 \times 3 \times 5$

6.10 Highest common factors and lowest common multiples

The **highest common factor** (HCF) of two numbers is the largest number which is a factor of both of the numbers.

The highest common factor (HCF) of 8 and 12 is 4 as it is the biggest number that is a factor of 8 and of 12

For larger numbers, it is useful to list the factors of each number and pick out the highest number.

Example 27

Find the highest common factor (HCF) of 24 and 36

Solution 27

The factors of 24 are 1, 2, 3, 4, 6, 8, 12 and 24
The factors of 36 are 1, 2, 3, 4, 6, 9, 12, 18 and 36

The numbers which appear in both lists are 1, 2, 3, 4, 6 and 12
So the highest common factor of 24 and 36 is 12.

The **lowest common multiple** (LCM) of two numbers is the smallest number which is a multiple of both numbers.

The lowest common multiple of 8 and 12 is 24, as it is the smallest number which has 8 and 12 as factors.

For larger numbers, it is useful to list the multiples of each number and then to pick out the smallest number that appears in both lists.

Example 28

Find the lowest common multiple (LCM) of 15 and 20

Solution 28

The first few multiples of 15 are   15, 30, 45, 60, 75 and so on.
The first few multiples of 20 are   20, 40, 60, 80, 100 and so on.

The lowest number which appears in both lists is 60

So the lowest common multiple of 15 and 20 is 60

Exercise 6O

1 Find the two prime numbers between 30 and 40

2 Find two prime numbers which have a sum of 7

3 Find two prime numbers which have a product of 14

4 Find two prime numbers which are factors of 20

5 Find two prime numbers which are factors of 24

6 Find two prime numbers which are factors of 33

7 Write the following numbers as a product of two prime factors.
    a 10   **b** 15   **c** 21   **d** 22   **e** 33   **f** 39

8 Which of the following show a number written correctly as a product of prime factors?
    a $12 = 2 \times 2 \times 3$ **b** $19 = 2 \times 9$ **c** $20 = 2 + 2 + 5$
    d $16 = 2 \times 2 \times 2 \times 2$ **e** $54 = 2 \times 2 \times 2 \times 7$

9 Write the following numbers as a products of their prime factors.
    a 30   **b** 42   **c** 48   **d** 36   **e** 60   **f** 63
    g 54   **h** 80   **i** 76   **j** 88   **k** 68   **l** 66

10 Find the highest common factor (HCF) of the following pairs of numbers.
    a 12 and 14   **b** 6 and 9   **c** 6 and 8   **d** 8 and 10   **e** 6 and 10

11 Find the highest common factor (HCF) of the following pairs of numbers.
    a 12 and 18   **b** 10 and 15   **c** 16 and 20   **d** 18 and 24   **e** 24 and 30

12 Find the lowest common multiple (LCM) of the following pairs of numbers.
    a 6 and 8   **b** 6 and 9   **c** 6 and 10   **d** 9 and 12   **e** 10 and 15

13 Find the lowest common multiple (LCM) of the following pairs of numbers
    a 12 and 15   **b** 12 and 24   **c** 12 and 18   **d** 18 and 24   **e** 20 and 24

14 **a** Find the number of multiples of 3 that are less than 100
    b Find the number of multiples of 5 that are less than 100

15 Fred has two flashing lamps. The first lamp flashes every 4 seconds. The second lamp flashes every 6 seconds. Both lamps start flashing together.
    a After how many seconds will they flash together again?
    b How many times in a minute will they flash together?

16 As a product of its prime factors, $360 = 2 \times 2 \times 2 \times 3 \times 3 \times 5$
    Write 720 as a product of its prime factors.

17 2, 3, 5, 7, 21, 22, 24 Which of the numbers in the list are
    a factors of 288   **b** factors of 550?

18 Write each of the numbers below as a product of its prime factors.
    a 105   **b** 539   **c** 231   **d** 847   **e** 1001

19 Find the lowest common multiple of the following pairs of numbers.
    a 24 and 30   **b** 27 and 36   **c** 28 and 35   **d** 36 and 42   **e** 54 and 72

Chapter summary

You should know

★ How to write numbers using figures and words

★ The **place value** of figures in a number

★ How to read and write numbers on a number line

★ How to add and subtract numbers on a number line

★ How to round numbers to the nearest 10, 100 or 1000

★ How to use mental methods to add, subtract, multiply and divide whole numbers

★ The terms **sum, difference** and **product**

★ How to use suitable non-calculator methods to add, subtract, multiply and divide whole numbers

★ How to use suitable methods to check calculations

★ How to use a calculator to add, subtract, multiply and divide whole numbers

★ The terms **factor** and **multiple**

★ The terms **square number** and **cube number**

★ How to work out the value of an expression which may contain brackets and more than one type of operation

★ How to write a number as a product of its **prime factors**

★ How to find the **highest common factor (HCF)** of two numbers

★ How to find the **lowest common multiple(LCM)** of two numbers

Chapter 6 review questions

1   Write these numbers in figures

    a   one thousand, eight hundred and twenty four

    b   three thousand, six hundred and fifty two   **c**   three hundred and two

    d   eight thousand and fifty two   **e**   Four thousand and seven

2   Write these numbers in words

    a   452   **b**   6372   **c**   4056   **d**   7003   **e**   12 053

3   What numbers are displayed on these dials?

4   Copy the number line. Mark the numbers shown below on the number line with an arrow

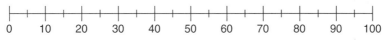

   a   60   **b**   85   **c**   5

5   What numbers are
shown by arrows
a, **b** and **c** on the
number line?

6   Work out the answers to these mentally

   a   25 + 35   **b**   38 + 62   **c**   99 − 67   **d**   100 − 45
   e   48 + 34   **f**   36 + 49   **g**   65 − 38   **h**   67 − 59
   i   36 + 85   **j**   25 + 15 + 16   **k**   36 + 95   **l**   56 − 29
   m   36 + 88   **n**   59 + 85   **o**   90 − 64   **p**   180 − 56
   q   90 − 48   **r**   360 − 248   **s**   180 − 34   **t**   90 − 57

7   Work out the answers to these using pen and paper

   a   687 + 115 + 2401   **b**   345 − 86   **c**   67 × 7   **d**   347 × 8
   e   64 ÷ 4   **f**   248 ÷ 5   **g**   46 × 46   **h**   34 × 56
   i   47 × 34   **j**   256 ÷ 23   **k**   879 ÷ 35

8   **a**   Round each of these numbers to the nearest 10
           i 439   **ii** 599   **iii** 945   **iv** 749   **v** 4145
           vi 996   **vii** 7478   **viii** 3256   **ix** 1004   **x** 10 005
       b   Round each of these numbers to the nearest 100
           i 439   **ii** 599   **iii** 945   **iv** 749   **v** 4145
           vi 996   **vii** 7478   **viii** 3256   **ix** 1004   **x** 10 005
       c   Round off each of these numbers to the nearest 1000
           i 3987   **ii** 599   **iii** 945   **iv** 749   **v** 4145
           vi 996   **vii** 7478   **viii** 3256   **ix** 1004   **x** 10 005

9   Check whether the following calculations are correct using rounding.
   a   36 × 32 = 1152   **b**   24 × 39 = 2232   **c**   64 × 128 = 8192
   d   54 × 219 = 15 714   **e**   The twenty ninth square number is 58

10 Check whether the following calculations are correct using the inverse operations.
   a   1728 ÷ 72 = 24   **b**   5280 ÷ 88 = 60   **c**   48 × 54 = 4536
   d   128 × 66 = 8484   **e**   127 × 81 = 10287

11 **a**   Fred earns £84 for each car he sells. In January he sold 17 cars. How much did he
           earn in January?
       b   A crate holds 36 bottles. How many crates are needed to hold 1950 bottles?
       c   1284 people watched a football match. They each paid £18. How much did they
           pay altogether?
       d   56 adults and 68 children went to a concert. Each adult paid £7 and each child
           paid £4. Find the total amount paid.

e A lorry holds 485 crates. Each crate holds 48 bottles. What is the total number of bottles that the lorry can hold?

f A school has 48 classrooms. Each classroom has 32 chairs. How many chairs are in the school?

12 From the numbers in the oval

a Write down a factor of 20

b Write down a multiple of 9

c Write down a square number.

d Write down a cube number.

e Write down two numbers which have a difference of 6

13 Work out

a $6 + 4 \times 3$ **b** $17 - 2 \times 2$ **c** $64 \div (2 + 6)$

d $(5 + 6) \times (10 - 2)$ **e** $63 - 48 - 15$

14 Use a calculator to work out the following

a $128 + 56 \times 48$ **b** $(47 + 58) \times 125$ **c** $\dfrac{36 \times 55}{45}$

d $\dfrac{3456}{12 \times 16}$ **e** $\dfrac{9408}{14 \times 12}$

15 Chocolates are packed into boxes of 32.
How many boxes can be packed using 2500 chocolates?

16 Here is a menu.
Jo buys one tea, two coffees,
two sandwiches and three cakes.
Work out the total cost.

The Café in the Park

Tea	£1.05
Coffee	£1.89
Soft drink	£1.59
Sandwich	£2.65
Cake	£2.79

17 It costs 38p to make a colour photocopy.
Work out the cost of 345 colour photocopies. Give your answer in pounds.

18 54 327 people watched a football match.

a Write 54 327 to the nearest thousand

b Write down the value of the 5 in the number 54 327   (1387 June 2003)

19 Lisa has £10 to buy some stamps. Each stamp costs 28p
Lisa buys the greatest number of stamps she can with the £10

a Work out how many stamps Lisa buys.

b Work out how much change she should get.   (1385 June 2001)

20 a Write the number thirteen thousand, five hundred and ninety one in figures.

b Write down the value of the 7 in 547 682

c Write down 8183 correct to the nearest hundred.   (5540 June 2005)

21 a Express the following numbers as products of their prime factors   **i** 60   **ii** 96

b Find the highest common factor of 60 and 96

c Work out the lowest common multiple of 60 and 96   (1387 June 2003)

Angles 1

London Eye

Tower Bridge

Big Ben

All these photographs show examples of **turning**.
The amount of turn is called an **angle**.

7.1 Fractions of a turn and degrees

The angle turned by the London Eye when it goes all the way round once and the angle turned by the minute hand of Big Ben in one hour are the same. It is a **full turn**.

A full turn is divided into 360 degrees, which is written as 360°.

360°

So, in a half turn, there are 180° .

180°

In a quarter turn, there are 90°, which is called a **right angle**.

90°

A right angle is often marked on diagrams with a small square.

7.2 What is an angle?

An angle is formed where two straight lines meet.

Angle

The lengths of the lines do not affect the size of the angle. All these angles are equal.

Example 1

For each clock, write down the size of the angle shown between the hands.

a   b   c   d

Solution 1

a   The angle shown is a quarter turn. It is a right angle, which is **90°**.
b   This is a half turn. It is **180°**.
c   This is a right angle, which is **90°**.   **d**   This is $\frac{1}{3}$ of a right angle, which is **30°**.

7.3 Special types of angles

An angle which is less than 90° is called an **acute** angle.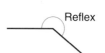

An angle which is between 90° and 180° is called an **obtuse** angle.

An angle which is between 180° and 360° is
called a **reflex** angle.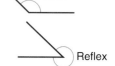

7.4 Naming sides and angles

A line is named using the letters of its end points.
In the diagram the blue line is AB (or BA) and the red line is BC (or CB).

There are three ways of naming angles.

● Use a small letter inside the angle. The letter x is used here.

● Use the name of the corner where the two lines meet to
  form an angle. Here this is called angle B.

● Use the names of the two lines that form the angle.
  This angle is called angle ABC or angle CBA.
  Note that the middle letter of the three letters is always the corner.

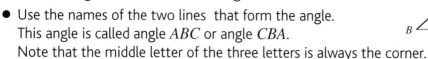

Example 2

a   Name angle a in two different ways.
     Give the special name of this type of angle.
b   Name the horizontal side of the triangle.

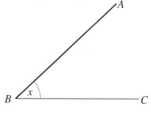

Solution 2

a   Angle a could be called angle R or angle PRQ (or angle QRP).
     It is between 90° and 180° and so it is an **obtuse** angle.
b   The horizontal side is PQ (or QP).

7.5 Perpendicular lines and parallel lines

Two lines are **perpendicular** if the angle between them is a right angle.
DE is **perpendicular** to *FG*.

Lines are **parallel** if they are always the same distance apart. **Parallel** lines never meet, no matter how far they are extended. Straight railway lines, for example, are parallel.

In diagrams, arrows are used to show that lines are **parallel**.

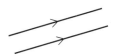

The lines in the diagram are straight.

a Mark with arrows, (>>), a pair of parallel lines.
b Mark with the letter *r* a right angle.
c Name the line which is perpendicular to *AB*.

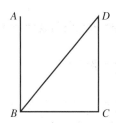

Solution 3

a , b

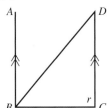

c *BC* is perpendicular to *AB*.

Exercise 7A

1 Which of these angles are the same size as angle *a*?

2 For each clock, write down the size of the angle shown between the hands.

a

b

c

d

e

f

3 Find the size of the angle between the hands of a clock at 5 o'clock.

4 Find the size of the angle shown on each compass.

a
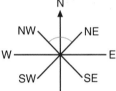

b
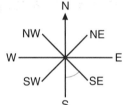

c
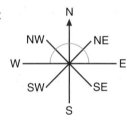

5 **a** Write these angles in order of size. Start with the smallest.

   b Write down the special name of each type of angle.

6 **a** Name the right angle in two different ways.

   b Name the vertical side.

7 **a** Copy the diagram and mark with arrows a pair of parallel lines.

   b What type of angle is angle x?

8 **a** Name the acute angle.

   b Name the pair of parallel sides.

   c Name the side which is perpendicular to EF.

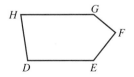

9 Work out the size of the angle the minute hand of a clock turns in

   a 5 minutes   **b** 20 minutes   **c** 35 minutes.

10 Work out the size of the obtuse angle between the hands of a clock at 8 o'clock.

11 For each clock, find the size of the reflex angle shown between the hands.

a

b

12 Work out the size of the reflex angle between the hands of a clock at 10 o'clock.

7.6 Estimating angles

It is useful if you can estimate the sizes of angles, as this will prevent you from giving answers which are not sensible, when you measure angles with a protractor.

Example 4

Estimate the size of this angle.

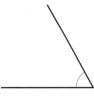

Solution 4
The angle is an acute angle.
It is more than $\frac{1}{2}$ a right angle (45°) but less than 90°.
So a reasonable estimate is 60°.

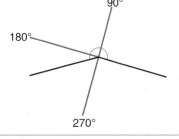

Example 5

Estimate the size of this angle.

Solution 5
The angle is a reflex angle. It is between 180° and 270°.
So a reasonable estimate is 220°.
An alternative method is to estimate the size of the obtuse angle (140°) and to take this away from 360°.
360° − 140° = 220°

Exercise 7B
Estimate the size of each of these angles.

1   **2**   **3**

4   **5**   **6**

7 Estimate the size of
   a angle ABC **b** angle ACB **c** angle BAC.

8 Estimate the size of
   a angle PQR **b** angle PRQ.

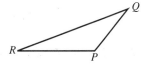

7.7 Measuring angles and lines

*also assessed in
Modules 2 and 4*

To measure and draw angles, you use a protractor.
You will probably use a semi-circular protractor like this.
The outer scale goes clockwise from 0° to 180° and
the inner scale goes anticlockwise from 0° to 180°.
When you measure an angle, you always start from 0
Before you measure an angle, estimate its size.

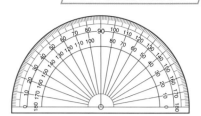

Example 6

Use a protractor to measure the size
of this angle.

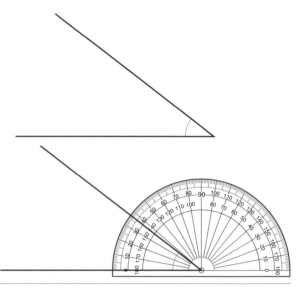

Solution 6

An estimate for the size of the angle is 40°.
Place the centre of the protractor over the
corner with the base line of the protractor
along one side of the angle and then read
from 0 on the outer scale.
The angle is 37°.

Example 7

Use a protractor to measure the size of
this angle.

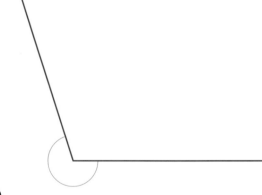

Solution 7

This reflex angle is just under 3 right angles (270°)
and so an estimate for the size of the angle is 260°.

If you are using a semi-circular protractor,
measure the obtuse angle first and take
it away from 360°.

Reading from the inner scale, the obtuse
angle is 108°.

$$360° - 108° = 252°$$

The required angle is 252°.

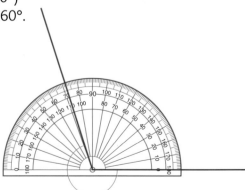

To measure the length of a line, you use a ruler.

Example 8

Measure the length of
a *AB*
b *AC*.

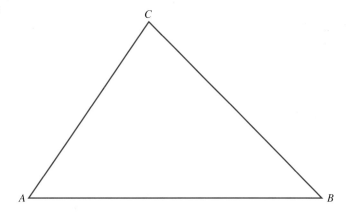

Solution 8

a *AB* = 8 cm
b *AC* = 5.7 cm.

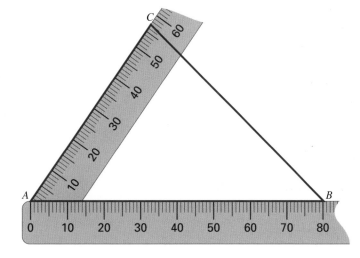

Exercise 7C

In Questions 1–8, estimate the size of these angles and then measure them with a protractor.

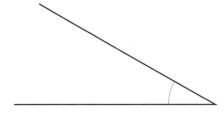

1

2

3

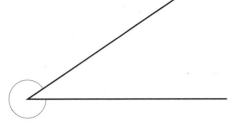

4

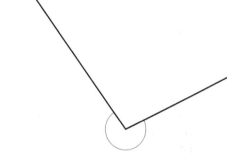

5

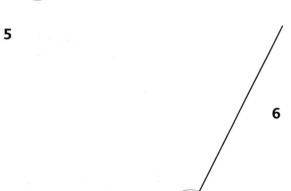

6

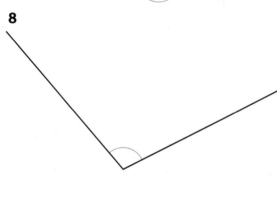

7

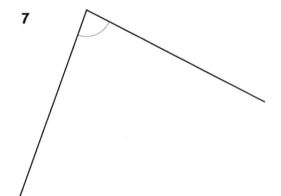

8

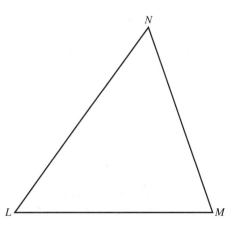

9 **a** For each of these angles, estimate its
size and then measure it with a protractor.
   i angle *LMN*
   ii angle *LNM*
   iii angle *MLN*.
   b Measure the length of each of these lines.
      i *LM*
      ii *LN*
      iii *MN*.

10 a For each of these angles, estimate its
size and then measure it with a protractor.

    i angle *EDF*

    ii angle *DEF*

    iii angle *DFE*.

  b Measure the length of each of these lines.

    i *DE*   **ii** *DF*   **iii** *EF*.

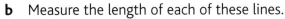

7.8 Drawing angles

also assessed in Modules 2 and 4

Using a protractor, you can draw angles of any size.
In the exam, you will be expected to draw angles to an accuracy of 2°.

Example 9

Draw an angle of 54°.

Solution 9

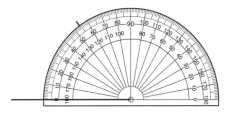

Draw a base line and put the centre of the protractor
on one end of the base line.
Reading from the outer scale, make a mark at 54°.

Join the mark to the end of the base line to complete the angle.

54°

Exercise 7D

In questions 1–15, use a protractor to draw the angles.

1 60°	**2** 130°	**3** 200°	**4** 310°	**5** 45°
6 235°	**7** 105°	**8** 345°	**9** 32°	**10** 158°
11 253°	**12** 81°	**13** 122°	**14** 13°	**15** 309°

16 a Draw a line *AB*.

  b Angle *ABC* = 28°.
Draw angle *ABC*.

17 a Draw a line *PQ*.

  b Angle *QPR* = 136°.
Draw angle *QPR*.

18 a Draw a line *AB* 6.2 cm long.

    A ——————— *B*
        6.2 cm

  b With *AB* as base, draw triangle

    ABC where angle *ABC* = 69°
and angle *BAC* = 41°.

19 a Draw a line *DE* 5.7 cm long.

    D ——————— *E*
        5.7 cm

  b With *DE* as base, draw triangle

    DEF where angle *DEF* = 27°
and angle *EDF* = 134°.

20 Draw triangle *LMN* with *LM* = 7.2 cm, angle *MLN* = 32° and angle *LMN* = 106°.

21 Draw a square with sides 5.3 cm long.

22 Draw a rectangle with length 7.6 cm and width 4.7 cm.

23 Here is a sketch of a quadrilateral (four-sided shape) *ABCD*.

Make an accurate drawing of *ABCD*.

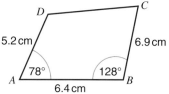

7.9 Angle facts

Right angles

There are 90° in a right angle.

Example 10

Work out the size of angle *x*.

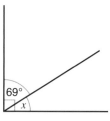

Solution 10

$90° - 69° = 21°$ | Take 69° away from 90°.

$x = 21°$ | State the size of angle *x*.

Angles on a straight line

The angle made on a straight line is 180°. If there are two or more angles on a straight line, they must add up to 180°.

The angles on a straight line add up to 180°.

Example 11

Work out the size of angle *y*.

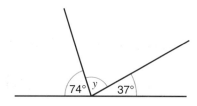

Solution 11

$74° + 37° = 111°$

$180° - 111° = 69°$

$y = 69°$

| Add 74° and 37°. |
| Take your result away from 180°. |
| State the size of angle y. |

Example 12

The diagram is wrong.
Explain why.

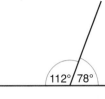

Diagram NOT
accurately drawn

Solution 12

The angles add up to 190°. They should add up to 180°.

Angles at a point

Angles a, b and c are called **angles at a point**.
When you add angles a, b and c, you get a full turn.
There are 360° in a full turn.

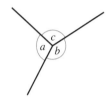

The angles at a point add up to 360°.

Example 13

Work out the size of angle p.

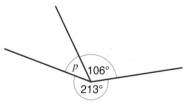

Solution 13

$213° + 106° = 319°$

$360° - 319° = 41°$

$p = 41°$

| Add 213° and 106°. |
| Take your result away from 360°. |
| State the size of angle p. |

Opposite angles

When two straight lines cross, the
opposite angles are equal.

$a = b$

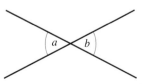

The two unmarked angles are also equal to each other.

When two straight lines cross, the opposite angles are equal.

Example 14

Find the size of   **a** angle x **b** angle y.
Give a reason for each answer.

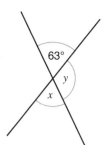

Solution 14

a $x = 63°$ Opposite angles are equal.

b $y = 180° - 63° = 117°$

The angles on a straight line add up to 180°.

Exercise 7E

The diagrams in this exercise are not accurately drawn.
In Questions 1–10, find the size of each angle marked with a letter.

1

2

3
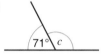

4
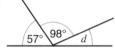

5
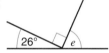

6

7

8

9

10
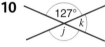

11 In the diagram, DEF is a straight line.
   a Work out the size of angle FEG.
   b Give a reason for your answer.

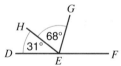

12 **a** Work out the value of x.
     b Give a reason for your answer.

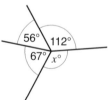

13 In the diagram, three lines meet at a point.
   a Find the value of   **i** x **ii** y.
   b Give a reason for each answer.

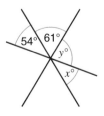

14 In the diagram, is *XYZ* a straight line?
Explain your answer.

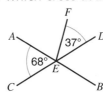

15 In the diagram, *AB* and *CD* are straight lines which cross at *E*.
EF is a straight line.

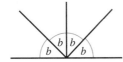

    a Find the size of
       i angle *DEB*
      ii angle *BEC*
     iii angle *AEF*.
    b Give a reason for each answer.

In Questions **16–20**, find the size of each of the angles marked with a letter.

16

17

18

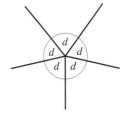

19

20

Chapter summary

You should now be able to

★ estimate the size of an angle

★ measure an angle using a protractor

★ draw an angle using a protractor

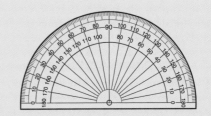

You should now know and use these facts

★ There are 360° in a full turn.

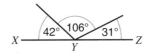

★ There are 90° in a right angle.

★ An acute angle is less than 90°.

★ An obtuse angle is between 90° and 180°.

★ A reflex angle is between 180° and 360°.

★ Perpendicular lines are at right angles to each other.

★ Parallel lines are always the same distance apart.

★ The angles on a straight line add up to 180°.

★ The angles at a point add up to 360°.

★ When two straight lines cross, opposite angles are equal.

Chapter 7 review questions

1 How many degrees are there in:
  a a full turn   **b** a quarter turn   **c** a half turn   **d** a right angle?

2 a Write down the special name for this type of angle.

  b Write down the special name for this type of angle.

(1387 June 2004)

3 Find the angle between
  a North east and South east,   **b** West and South west.

4 a Name the horizontal line.
  b Name the obtuse angle.
  c Name a pair of perpendicular sides.
  d Use the resource sheet to draw a line through A parallel to BC.

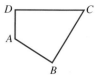

5 Estimate the size of these angles and then measure them with a protractor.
  a   **b**

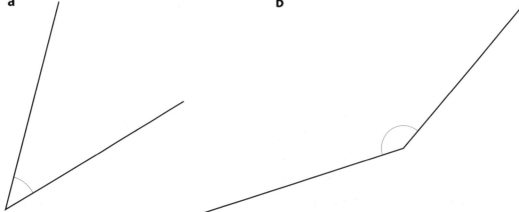

c   **d**

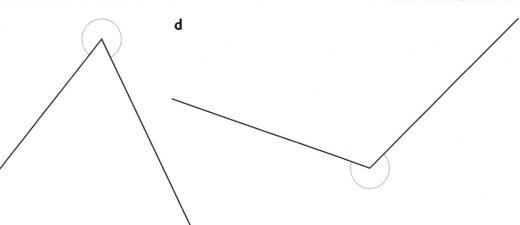

6   **a**   Measure the length of *FG*.

     b   Measure the size of angle *H*.

     c   Measure the size of angle *FGH*.

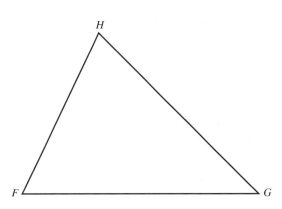

7   Use a protractor to draw these angles.

     a   78°   **b**   261°   **c**   113°   **d**   327°.

     In Questions **8–11**,   **a**   find the size of each of the angles marked with a letter

                              b   give a reason for your answer.

8   **9**

                            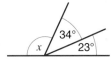

10   **11**

12   Helen is standing at *H*. She is facing North.
      She turns anticlockwise through 1 right angle.

     a   In what direction is she now facing?

     Later, Harry stands at *H*. He faces South.
     He turns clockwise through $1\frac{1}{2}$ right angles.

     b   In what direction will he then be facing?   (1387 June 1997)

13 PQ is a horizontal line.

On the diagram, mark

    a   a different horizontal line with a letter H

    b   an acute angle with a letter A

    c   an obtuse angle with a letter O.

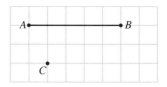

(1387 June 1996)

14   On the grid, draw a line from the point C
which is perpendicular to the line AB.

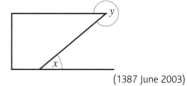

(1387 June 2004)

15   The lines in the diagram are straight.

    a   Mark with arrows, (>>), a pair of parallel lines.

    b   Mark with the letter R a right angle.

    c   What type of angle is shown by the letter **i** x **ii** y?

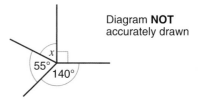

(1387 June 2003)

16   The angle marked x is less than a right angle.

    a   Write down the mathematical name for x.

    b   Work out the size of the angle marked x.

Diagram **NOT**
accurately drawn

17   The diagram is wrong.

Explain why.

Diagram **NOT**
accurately drawn

(1387 June 2004)

Factsheet

Names of parts of a circle

Here is a **circle**.
The **centre** of this circle is the point O.
The distance from O to any point on the circle is 2 cm.
So the **radius** of the circle is 2 cm.

The radius of a circle is the distance from the centre of the circle to any point on the circle.

A **radius** of a circle is any straight line drawn from the centre of the circle to a point on the circle. The plural of radius is **radii**.

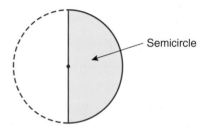

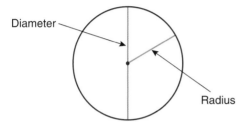

A **diameter** of a circle is any straight line drawn through the centre of the circle from a point on the circle to another point on the circle.
The length of a diameter is twice the radius of the circle.
A diameter of a circle divides the circle into two **semicircles**.

The distance around a circle is the **circumference** of the circle.
An **arc** of a circle is part of the circumference of the circle.

A **chord** of a circle is a straight line joining any two points on the circle.
This means that a diameter of a circle is a chord that passes through the centre of the circle.

A **tangent** to a circle is a line that touches the circle at only one point.

A **sector** of a circle is a region between two radii and an arc.

A **segment** of a circle is a region between a chord and an arc.

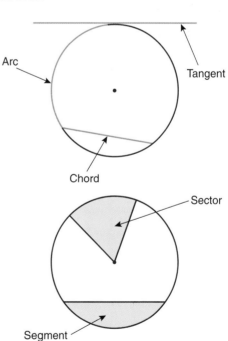

Fractions and decimals

8.1 What is a fraction?

$\frac{2}{7}$ of this circle is shaded.

$\frac{2}{7}$ is a **fraction**.

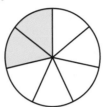

The top number shows that 2 parts of the circle are shaded.		The top number of the fraction is called the **numerator**.

$\frac{2}{7}$

The bottom number shows that the circle is divided into 7 equal parts.		The bottom number of the fraction is called the **denominator**.

Example 1

Write down the fraction of the shape that is shaded.

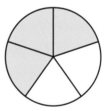

Solution 1

3 parts are shaded.
So the top number (numerator) of the fraction is 3

The circle is divided into **5** equal parts.
So the bottom number (denominator) of the fraction is 5

$\frac{3}{5}$ of the shape is shaded.

Example 2

There are 30 students in a class.
17 of the students walk to school.
Write down the fraction of the students that

a walk to school **b** do **not** walk to school.

Solution 2

a There are **17** students **out of 30** that walk to school.
The fraction of students that walk to school is $\frac{17}{30}$

b $30 - 17 = 13$
13 students **out of 30** do **not** walk to school.
The fraction of students that do not walk to school is $\frac{13}{30}$

Exercise 8A

In questions **1** to **8**, write down the fraction of the shape that is shaded.

1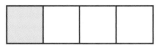

2

3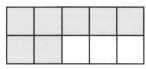

4

5

6

7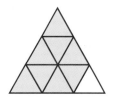

8

9 Write down the fraction of the shape that is
    a shaded   **b** unshaded.

10 Write down the fraction of the shape that is
    a shaded   **b** unshaded.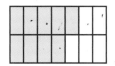

11 On the diagrams on the resource sheet shade in the fraction given next to each diagram.

    a 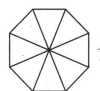 $\frac{1}{5}$ **b** $\frac{3}{8}$ **c** $\frac{3}{4}$

12 There are 29 students in a class. 13 of the students are girls.
    What fraction of the class are girls?

13 In a family of five people, two people are left handed. What fraction of the family are
    a left handed   **b** not left handed?

14 There are two red, three blue and six black beads in a box.
    What fraction of the beads are
    a blue   **b** black?

15 There are 75 cars in a car park. 32 of the cars are white.
    Write down the fraction of the cars that are
    a white   **b** not white.

16 Lesley has one geography, three history and five science books.
    What fraction of her books are
    a geography books   **b** geography or history books?

17 Amy says that $\frac{1}{3}$ of this flag is white.
    Is Amy correct?
    Give a reason for your answer.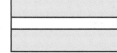

18   Lee chooses some tiles. He wants $\frac{3}{5}$ of each tile he chooses to be blue.

Which of these tiles could Lee choose?

     A   B   C   D   E

 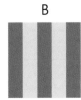 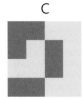 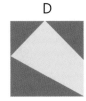 

8.2 Equivalent fractions

Equivalent fractions are fractions that are equal.

These rectangles are all the same size.

One half of each rectangle is shaded.

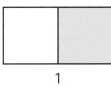

$\frac{1}{2}$ $\frac{2}{4}$ $\frac{4}{8}$

The diagrams show that

$\frac{1}{2}$ is equal to $\frac{2}{4}$ and $\frac{4}{8}$

$\frac{1}{2}, \frac{2}{4}$ and $\frac{4}{8}$ are equivalent fractions.

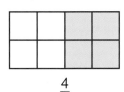

$$\frac{1}{2} = \frac{2}{4} \qquad \frac{1}{2} = \frac{4}{8}$$

To find an equivalent fraction, multiply the numerator and the denominator by the same number.

Example 3

Use the diagrams to write down a fraction that is equivalent to $\frac{3}{4}$.

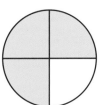

Solution 3

Shade the same area of the second circle as is shaded in the first. 6 parts will be shaded.

This shows that $\frac{3}{4} = \frac{6}{8}$

$\frac{6}{8}$ is equivalent to $\frac{3}{4}$

Example 4

Complete $\dfrac{2}{3} = \dfrac{}{12}$

Solution 4

$$\overset{\times 4}{\dfrac{2}{3}} = \underset{\times 4}{\dfrac{8}{12}}$$

Example 5

Shade $\dfrac{1}{3}$ of the circle.

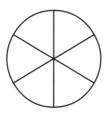

Solution 5

The circle has six equal parts so change $\dfrac{1}{3}$ to sixths.

$$\overset{\times 2}{\dfrac{1}{3}} = \underset{\times 2}{\dfrac{2}{6}}$$

$\dfrac{1}{3}$ is the same as $\dfrac{2}{6}$ so shade **two** of the six parts of the circle.

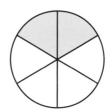

Exercise 8B

In questions **1** to **15**, copy the fractions and fill in the missing number to make the fractions equivalent.

1 $\dfrac{1}{3} = \dfrac{}{9}$ 2 $\dfrac{1}{5} = \dfrac{}{10}$ 3 $\dfrac{1}{7} = \dfrac{2}{}$ 4 $\dfrac{2}{3} = \dfrac{}{9}$

5 $\dfrac{3}{4} = \dfrac{}{8}$ 6 $\dfrac{4}{7} = \dfrac{}{14}$ 7 $\dfrac{5}{6} = \dfrac{15}{}$ 8 $\dfrac{3}{5} = \dfrac{12}{}$

9 $\dfrac{3}{8} = \dfrac{}{32}$ 10 $\dfrac{4}{9} = \dfrac{}{45}$ 11 $\dfrac{7}{8} = \dfrac{28}{}$ 12 $\dfrac{7}{10} = \dfrac{}{100}$

13 $\dfrac{5}{12} = \dfrac{15}{}$ 14 $\dfrac{9}{20} = \dfrac{}{60}$ 15 $\dfrac{8}{15} = \dfrac{40}{}$

In questions **16** to **21** shade the given fraction on the diagrams on the resource sheet.

16    $\dfrac{1}{6}$ 17 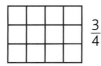 $\dfrac{3}{4}$ 18 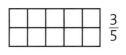 $\dfrac{3}{5}$

19 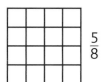 $\dfrac{5}{8}$ 20 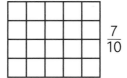 $\dfrac{7}{10}$ 21 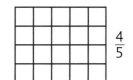 $\dfrac{4}{5}$

8.3 Simplifying fractions

also assessed in Module 2

A fraction can be simplified if the numerator and denominator can be divided by the same number.

This process is called **cancelling**.

When a fraction cannot be simplified, it is in its **simplest form** or in its **lowest terms**.

Example 6

Find the simplest form of the fractions   **a** $\frac{5}{10}$ **b** $\frac{18}{30}$

Solution 6

a Divide both 5 and 10 by 5

$\frac{1}{2}$ cannot be simplified.

The simplest form of $\frac{5}{10}$ is $\frac{1}{2}$

$\frac{5}{10} = \frac{1}{2}$ ($\div 5$)

b Method 1

Divide both 18 and 30 by 2

Then divide both 9 and 15 by 3

There is no number that will divide exactly into both 3 and 5 so the simplest form of $\frac{18}{30}$ is $\frac{3}{5}$

$\frac{18}{30} = \frac{9}{15}$ ($\div 2$) $\frac{9}{15} = \frac{3}{5}$ ($\div 3$)

Method 2

6 is the largest number that goes exactly into both 18 and 30 (in other words, 6 is the HCF of 18 and 30)

If the HCF is used, then only one step is needed to simplify the fraction.

The simplest form of $\frac{18}{30}$ is $\frac{3}{5}$

$\frac{18}{30} = \frac{3}{5}$ ($\div 6$)

Example 7

Prateek has 24 toy cars. 10 of these cars are blue.

What fraction of Prateek's toy cars are blue? Give your fraction in its simplest form.

Solution 7

Prateek has **10** blue cars out of **24** toy cars.

$\frac{10}{24}$ of the toy cars are blue.

Both 10 and 24 are even numbers so divide both numbers by 2

$\frac{10}{24} = \frac{5}{12}$

$\frac{10}{24} = \frac{5}{12}$ ($\div 2$)

$\frac{5}{12}$ cannot be simplified further so $\frac{5}{12}$ of the toy cars are blue.

Exercise 8C

In questions **1** to **15** write each fraction in its simplest form.

1 $\frac{3}{6}$ 2 $\frac{5}{15}$ 3 $\frac{6}{8}$ 4 $\frac{7}{21}$ 5 $\frac{10}{40}$

6 $\frac{20}{25}$ 7 $\frac{12}{16}$ 8 $\frac{16}{20}$ 9 $\frac{25}{100}$ 10 $\frac{30}{90}$

11 $\frac{24}{50}$ 12 $\frac{42}{48}$ 13 $\frac{100}{150}$ 14 $\frac{80}{120}$ 15 $\frac{75}{200}$

In questions **16** to **20** write down the fraction of the shape that is shaded.
Give each fraction in its simplest form.

16 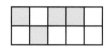   17   18

19 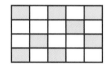   20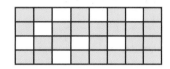

In questions **21** to **25** give each fraction in its simplest form.

21   A class contains 30 students. 12 of these students are girls.
Write down the fraction of the class that are girls.

22   Jack has 40 model farm animals. Eight of the animals are horses.
Write down the fraction of the model farm animals that are horses.

23   There are four red, three blue and five yellow counters in a bag.
Write down the fraction of the counters that are blue.

24   In a car park there are 20 silver, 16 blue, nine red and three green cars.
Write down the fraction of the cars that are

   a   silver   **b**   blue   **c**   red or green

25   There are 30 cakes in a shop. Five of the cakes are chocolate.
Write down the fraction of the cakes that are **not** chocolate.

8.4 Ordering fractions

Here are two rectangles which are the same size.

The second rectangle has more parts shaded than
the first rectangle.

This shows that $\frac{7}{10}$ is bigger than $\frac{3}{10}$

When fractions have the same denominator,
you can compare the numerators to put the
fractions in order.

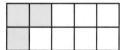

$\frac{3}{10}$ of this rectangle is shaded

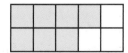

$\frac{7}{10}$ of this rectangle is shaded

Example 8

Put the fractions $\frac{7}{9}$, $\frac{4}{9}$, $\frac{8}{9}$ and $\frac{2}{9}$ in order of size.

Start with the smallest fraction.

Solution 8

All the fractions have the same denominator so compare the numerators to put the fractions in order of size.

$$\frac{2}{9}, \quad \frac{4}{9}, \quad \frac{7}{9}, \quad \frac{8}{9}$$

Example 9

Ben shades $\frac{3}{4}$ of a rectangle. Lucy shades $\frac{4}{5}$ of an identical rectangle.

Who has shaded in more of their rectangle? Give a reason for your answer.

Solution 9

Compare the fractions by writing them with a **common denominator**.

The denominators 4 and 5 both divide exactly into 20

Find a fraction equivalent to $\frac{3}{4}$ that has a denominator of 20

Find a fraction equivalent to $\frac{4}{5}$ that has a denominator of 20

$\frac{16}{20}$ is bigger than $\frac{15}{20}$ so $\frac{4}{5}$ is bigger than $\frac{3}{4}$

As $\frac{4}{5}$ is bigger than $\frac{3}{4}$, Lucy shaded in more than Ben.

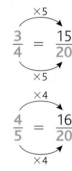

$$\overset{\times 5}{\frac{3}{4}} = \underset{\times 5}{\frac{15}{20}}$$

$$\overset{\times 4}{\frac{4}{5}} = \underset{\times 4}{\frac{16}{20}}$$

Example 10

Which fraction is bigger $\frac{1}{3}$ or $\frac{2}{5}$?

Solution 10

The smallest number that the denominators 3 and 5 both divide exactly into is 15

$$\overset{\times 5}{\frac{1}{3}} = \underset{\times 5}{\frac{5}{15}} \qquad \overset{\times 3}{\frac{2}{5}} = \underset{\times 3}{\frac{6}{15}} \qquad \frac{6}{15} \text{ is bigger than } \frac{5}{15}$$

So $\frac{2}{5}$ is bigger than $\frac{1}{3}$

Example 11

Write the fractions $\frac{1}{4}$, $\frac{2}{10}$ and $\frac{3}{5}$ in order of size. Start with the smallest fraction.

Solution 11

The smallest number that the denominators 4, 10 and 5 all divide exactly into is 20

Find an equivalent fraction for each of $\frac{1}{4}$, $\frac{2}{10}$ and $\frac{3}{5}$ with a denominator of 20

$$\overset{\times 5}{\underset{\times 5}{\frac{1}{4} = \frac{5}{20}}} \qquad \overset{\times 2}{\underset{\times 2}{\frac{2}{10} = \frac{4}{20}}} \qquad \overset{\times 4}{\underset{\times 4}{\frac{3}{5} = \frac{12}{20}}}$$

Starting with the smallest fraction, the order is $\quad \dfrac{4}{20}, \quad \dfrac{5}{20}, \quad \dfrac{12}{20}$

that is $\quad \dfrac{2}{10}, \quad \dfrac{1}{4}, \quad \dfrac{3}{5}$

Exercise 8D

In questions **1** to **10** write the fractions in order of size. Start with the smallest fraction.

1 $\frac{3}{5}$, $\frac{7}{10}$

2 $\frac{5}{8}$, $\frac{3}{4}$

3 $\frac{3}{4}$, $\frac{2}{3}$

4 $\frac{5}{6}$, $\frac{3}{4}$

5 $\frac{2}{3}$, $\frac{5}{6}$, $\frac{7}{12}$

6 $\frac{9}{20}$, $\frac{4}{5}$, $\frac{3}{4}$

7 $\frac{4}{15}$, $\frac{1}{3}$, $\frac{3}{10}$

8 $\frac{3}{4}$, $\frac{9}{16}$, $\frac{5}{8}$

9 $\frac{23}{40}$, $\frac{7}{10}$, $\frac{3}{5}$, $\frac{13}{20}$

10 $\frac{1}{2}$, $\frac{3}{5}$, $\frac{5}{12}$, $\frac{11}{30}$, $\frac{7}{15}$

11 Julie and Susan have identical chocolate bars.

Julie eats $\frac{3}{4}$ of her chocolate bar. Susan eats $\frac{7}{8}$ of her chocolate bar.

Who eats more chocolate? You must give a reason for your answer.

12 Ahmid says that $\frac{7}{12}$ is bigger than $\frac{5}{6}$ because 7 is bigger than 5

Is Ahmid correct? You must give a reason for your answer.

8.5 Improper fractions and mixed numbers

An **improper fraction** is one in which the numerator is greater than the denominator.

$\frac{5}{4}$, $\frac{12}{5}$ and $\frac{14}{8}$ and are all improper fractions.

The improper fraction $\frac{5}{4}$ can be thought of as '5 over 4', or as '5 quarters'.

Similarly, the improper fraction $\frac{12}{5}$ can be thought of as '12 over 5', or as '12 fifths'.

A **mixed number** is a number which has a whole number part and a fractional part.

$2\frac{3}{4}$, $3\frac{1}{5}$ and $6\frac{7}{8}$ are mixed numbers.

Mixed numbers can be changed to improper fractions and vice versa.

To change $2\frac{3}{4}$ to an improper fraction, work out how many quarters there are in $2\frac{3}{4}$.

There are 4 quarters in 1 and so there are (2×4) quarters in 2.
Add the extra 3 quarters to get 11 quarters.

So $2\frac{3}{4} = \frac{11}{4}$

> A good way of setting this out is $2\frac{3}{4} = \dfrac{(2 \times 4) + 3}{4} = \dfrac{11}{4}$

Example 12

Change these mixed numbers to improper fractions.
a $3\frac{1}{2}$ **b** $4\frac{3}{5}$

Solution 12

a There are 2 halves in 1, so there are 6 halves in 6
  Add the extra 1 half to make 7 halves.

  $3\frac{1}{2} = \frac{7}{2}$

b There are 5 fifths in 1, so there are $4 \times 5 = 20$ fifths in 4
  Add the extra 3 fifths to make 23 fifths

  $4\frac{3}{5} = \frac{23}{5}$

To change an improper fraction to a mixed number, reverse the above process.

To change the improper fraction $\frac{17}{6}$ to a mixed number, firstly work out how many whole ones there are.

6 sixths is 1; 12 sixths is 2 and so in 17 sixths there are 2 whole ones and 5 sixths.

  $\frac{17}{6} = 2\frac{5}{6}$

A good way of setting this out is $17 \div 6 = 2$ remainder 5
2 is the whole number. $\frac{5}{6}$ is the fraction.

Example 13

Change these improper fractions to mixed numbers.
a $\frac{5}{2}$ **b** $\frac{15}{4}$

Solution 13

a 2 halves is 1; 4 halves is 2 and so in 5 halves there are 2 whole ones and 1 half.

  $\frac{5}{2} = 2\frac{1}{2}$

b 4 quarters is 1; 12 quarters is 3 and so in 15 quarters there are 3 whole ones and 3 quarters.

  $\frac{15}{4} = 3\frac{3}{4}$

Exercise 8E

1 Change these mixed numbers to improper fractions.

   a $1\frac{1}{2}$ **b** $1\frac{1}{3}$ **c** $1\frac{3}{5}$ **d** $1\frac{1}{6}$ **e** $1\frac{7}{8}$

2 Change these mixed numbers to improper fractions.

   a $4\frac{1}{2}$ **b** $2\frac{1}{4}$ **c** $4\frac{3}{4}$ **d** $2\frac{2}{3}$ **e** $4\frac{2}{5}$

3 Change these improper fractions to mixed numbers.

   a $\frac{7}{5}$ **b** $\frac{4}{3}$ **c** $\frac{7}{6}$ **d** $\frac{11}{8}$ **e** $\frac{5}{4}$

4 Change these improper fractions to mixed numbers.

   a $\frac{17}{4}$ **b** $\frac{14}{5}$ **c** $\frac{27}{5}$ **d** $\frac{38}{5}$ **e** $\frac{25}{4}$

8.6 Reading and writing decimals

The lengths of two pencils are measured.

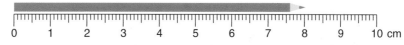

The length of the red pencil is exactly 8 cm. This can also be written as 8.0 cm.

The length of the blue pencil is not a whole number of centimetres.

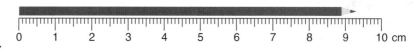

Look at the diagram. Each centimetre is divided into ten equal parts called tenths of a centimetre, also known as millimetres.

A decimal point is used to separate the whole number of centimetres from the number of tenths of a centimetre.
The length of the blue pencil is 9.3 cm.

Example 14

Write down the length of the key.

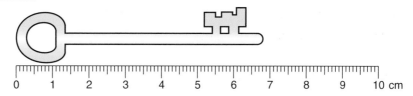

Solution 14

The length of the key is 6 whole centimetres and 8 tenths of a centimetre.
The length of the key is 6.8 cm.

Example 15

Write down the weight of the parcel.

Solution 15

The scale measures weight in kilograms.
Each kilogram is divided into tenths.
The parcel weighs 1.7 kg.

Exercise 8F

In questions **1** to **5** write down the length of each pencil.

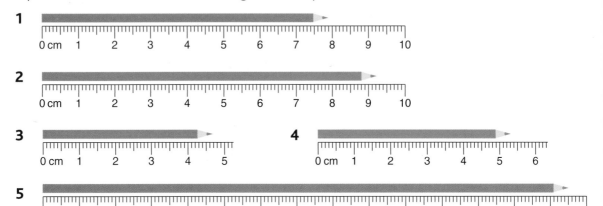

In questions **6** to **8** write down the weight of each parcel.

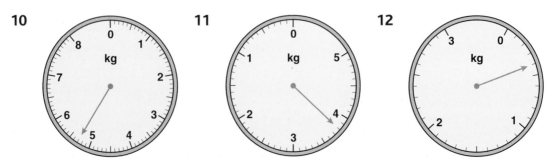

9   Write down the number that each arrow is pointing to on the scales.

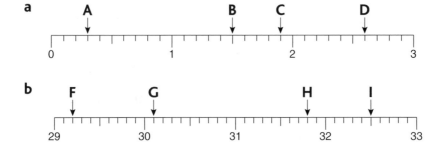

In questions **10** to **12** write down the weight shown on each scale.

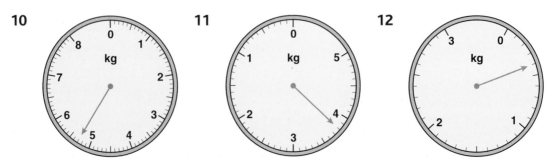

8.7 Understanding place value

The decimal point separates the whole number part from the part that is less than 1

Look at the table. The first number on the right of the decimal point tells us how many tenths there are.

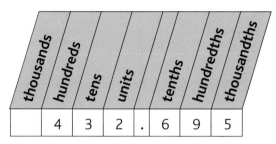

thousands	hundreds	tens	units	.	tenths	hundredths	thousandths
	4	3	2	.	6	9	5

There can be more numbers after the decimal point.

The column headings tell us the **place value** of each figure.

This number in the table is read as 'four hundred and thirty two point six nine five'.

The column headings tell us that

- the 4 has a value of four hundreds
- the 3 has a value of three tens
- the 2 has a value of two units
- the 6 has a value of six tenths
- the 9 has a value of nine hundredths
- the 5 has a value of five thousandths

Example 16

Write down the value of the 2 in the number 34.72

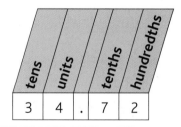

tens	units	.	tenths	hundredths
3	4	.	7	2

Solution 16
The 2 has a value of two hundredths.

Example 17

Write down the number that each arrow is pointing to on the scale.

Solution 17

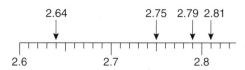

Exercise 8G

1 Write down the value of the 6 in each number.

	thousands	hundreds	tens	units	.	tenths	hundredths	thousandths
a		6	5	2	.	8	1	
b			8	7	.	6	3	4
c			1	3	5	.	4	2	6
d	7	5	8	9	.	0	6	
e				6	.	5	2	

2 Write down the value of the 4 in each number.

   a 56.43   **b** 4521.8   **c** 98.243   **d** 0.814   **e** 342.1

3 Write down the value of the 9 in each number.

   a 3.19   **b** 792.3   **c** 0.039   **d** 79.3   **e** 1.9

4 Write down the number that each arrow is pointing to on the scales.

a 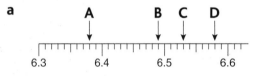 **b**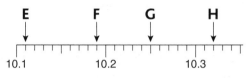

c 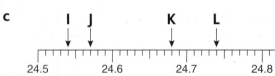 **d**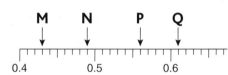

8.8 Ordering decimals

Five boys took part in a long jump competition. The table shows the distance each boy jumped.

Adam	4.3 m
Brian	4.2 m
Colin	4.39 m
Daneep	4.4 m
Elliot	4.33 m

To decide who jumped the furthest, put the distances in order. To put decimals in order, look at the place values.

Use column headings to show the value of each figure.

Write a **0** in each empty box.

units	.	tenths	hundredths
4	.	3	0
4	.	2	0
4	.	3	9
4	.	4	0
4	.	3	3

All the numbers have a 4 in the units column.

In the tenths column, the smallest number is 2 and the largest number is 4

So, 4.2 is the smallest number and 4.4 is the largest number.

units	tenths	hundredths
4 .	3	0
4 .	3	9
4 .	3	3

Three of the numbers have a 3 in the tenths column.
To order these numbers use the hundredths column.

The numbers in the hundredths column are 0, 9 and 3
In order, these are **0**, **3**, **9**

So the three numbers in order are 4.3**0**, 4.3**3**, 4.3**9**.
That is 4.3, 4.33, 4.39

In order of size, the five numbers are 4.2, 4.3, 4.33, 4.39, 4.4.

Putting the boys' distances in order gives:

So Daneep jumped the furthest.

Brian	4.2 m
Adam	4.3 m
Elliot	4.33 m
Colin	4.39 m
Daneep	4.4 m

Example 18

Write the numbers 7.53, 7.5, 7.6, 7.65, 7.56 in order of size
starting with the biggest.

Solution 18
Use column headings to show the value of each figure.
Write a **0** in each empty box.
As all the numbers have a 7 in the units column, look at the tenths.
7.6 and 7.65 both have a 6 in the tenths column but 7.65 has
a 5 in the hundredths column so 7.65 is bigger than 7.60
7.53, 7.50 and 7.56 all have a 5 in the tenths column.
To order these numbers use the hundredths column.
Starting with the biggest, the order of the numbers is

    7.65,   7.6,   7.56,   7.53,   7.5

units	tenths	hundredths
7 .	5	3
7 .	5	0
7 .	6	0
7 .	6	5
7 .	5	6

Exercise 8H

In questions **1** to **12** write the numbers in order of size.
Start with the smallest number each time.

1

tens	units	tenths	hundredths	thousandths
6	8 .	3	8	3
6	8 .	3	8	7
6	8 .	3	7	

2

units	tenths	hundredths
5 .	7	7
5 .	0	7
5 .	7	

3   6.76, 6.66, 6.67   **4**   8.11, 8, 8.1, 8.01

5   0.09, 0.9, 0.92, 0.2   **6**   73.24, 73.2, 73.42, 73.4

7   2.314, 2.413, 2.134, 2.341, 2.431   **8**   0.373, 0.37, 0.73, 0.333, 0.733

9   15.8, 15.38, 15.3, 15.833, 15.803   **10**   0.045, 0.05, 0.0545, 0.055, 0.0454

11   6.067, 6.006, 6.07, 6.06, 6.077, 6.076   **12**   8.092, 8.9, 8.02, 8.09, 8.2, 8.29, 8.92

13   The table shows the heights, in metres, of five children.
Write down the children in order of height. Start with the tallest child.

Linda	1.34m
Anthony	1.4m
Chris	1.43m
Ian	1.33m
Julie	1.3m

14   The table shows the time, in seconds, in which five runners ran 100 m
Write down the order in which the runners finished the race.

Linford	10.2
Dwain	10.02
Roger	10.23
Steve	10.12
Maurice	10.21

8.9 Converting decimals to fractions

Using place values, some decimals can be converted to fractions

$$0.7 = \frac{7}{10} \qquad\qquad 0.06 = \frac{6}{100}$$

$$0.76 = \frac{7}{10} + \frac{6}{100}$$

$$= \frac{70}{100} + \frac{6}{100}$$

$$= \frac{76}{100}$$

To convert decimals to fractions, use the place values of the figures.

Example 19

Write 0.13 as a fraction.

Solution 19

$$0.13 = \frac{13}{100}$$

The heading of the last column with a figure in it gives the denominator.

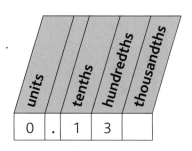

Example 20

Write 0.024 as a fraction.
Give your fraction in its simplest form.

Solution 20

$0.024 = \dfrac{24}{1000}$

The heading of the last column with a figure in it is
thousandths, so the denominator is 1000

$$\dfrac{24}{1000} = \dfrac{12}{500} = \dfrac{6}{250} = \dfrac{3}{125}$$

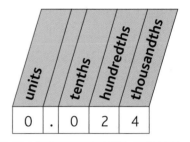

units		tenths	hundredths	thousandths
0	.	0	2	4

Example 21

Write 3.7 as a fraction.

Solution 21

$3.7 = 3\frac{7}{10}$

The 3 is the whole number part, the .7 is $\frac{7}{10}$

units		tenths	hundredths	thousandths
3	.	7		

Exercise 8I

1 Write the decimals
   as fractions

	units		tenths	hundredths	thousandths
a	0	.	3		
b	0	.	0	7	
c	0	.	1	9	
d	0	.	2	5	3
e	0	.	0	8	9

In questions **2** to **15** write each of the decimals as a fraction in its simplest form.

2 0.7

3 0.14

4 0.123

5 0.08

6 0.093

7 0.006

8 0.72

9 0.2

10 0.242

11 2.5

12 25.06

13 12.8

14 6.17

15 2.84

8.10 Converting fractions to decimals

also assessed in
Module 4

All fractions can be written as decimals.

The fractions and decimals in the table are ones that are used frequently and should be learnt.

Other fractions can be changed into decimals.

Decimal	Fraction
0.01	$\frac{1}{100}$
0.1	$\frac{1}{10}$
0.25	$\frac{1}{4}$
0.5	$\frac{1}{2}$
0.75	$\frac{3}{4}$

Example 22

Write the following fractions as decimals

a $\frac{9}{10}$ b $\frac{23}{100}$

Solution 22

a $\frac{9}{10} = 0.9$ b $\frac{23}{100} = 0.23$

Example 23

Write the following fractions as decimals.   a $\frac{2}{5}$ b $\frac{11}{25}$

Solution 23

Method 1 – using equivalent fractions

a $\frac{2}{5} = \frac{4}{10} = 0.4$ b $\frac{11}{25} = \frac{44}{100} = 0.44$

Method 2 – using a calculator

a $\frac{2}{5}$ means $2 \div 5$ b $\frac{11}{25}$ means $11 \div 25$

Using a calculator,   Using a calculator,

2 ÷ 5 = 0.4   11 ÷ 25 = 0.44

$\frac{2}{5} = 0.4$ $\frac{11}{25} = 0.44$

Short division is suitable for changing $\frac{2}{5}$ to a decimal because the denominator is small.

$\frac{2}{5}$ means $2 \div 5$

$\begin{array}{r} 0.4 \\ 5\overline{)2.^20} \end{array}$

| 2.0 is the same as 2 so divide 2.0 by 5 |

| 5 does not divide into 2 so put down a zero and carry 2 |

$\frac{2}{5} = 0.4$

| 5 divides into 20 four times |

Not all fractions can be written as exact decimals.

$\frac{1}{3} = 1 \div 3 = 0.33333....$

In this decimal, the 3 keeps repeating.

When a decimal has repeating figures, it is called a **recurring decimal.**

To show that a figure recurs, put a dot above the figure.

So   0.33333... is written as $0.\dot{3}$ and $\frac{1}{3} = 0.\dot{3}$

Sometimes, more than one figure recurs,

$$\frac{3}{11} = 3 \div 11 = 0.272727....$$

Put a dot above each recurring figure.

So $\frac{3}{11} = 0.\dot{2}\dot{7}$

Example 24

Write the following fractions as decimals

a $\frac{7}{9}$ **b** $\frac{13}{22}$ **c** $\frac{5}{7}$

Solution 24

a $\frac{7}{9}$ means $7 \div 9$ | Work out $7 \div 9$ on a calculator. |

Using a calculator, 7 $\boxed{\div}$ 9 $\boxed{=}$

0.777777... = $0.\dot{7}$ | The 7 recurs so put a dot above the 7 |

b $\frac{13}{22}$ means $13 \div 22$ | Work out $13 \div 22$ on a calculator. |

Using a calculator, 13 $\boxed{\div}$ 22 $\boxed{=}$ | The 90 recurs so put a dot above each of these figures. |

0.5909090... = $0.5\dot{9}\dot{0}$ | Do not put a dot above the 5, as it does not recur. |

c $\frac{5}{7}$ means $5 \div 7$ | Work out $5 \div 7$ on a calculator. |

Using a calculator, 5 $\boxed{\div}$ 7 $\boxed{=}$ | A group of six figures recurs. There isn't enough room to see all the figures recurring but you can see that the same pattern of figures is starting again. |

0.714285714... = $0.\dot{7}14285\dot{5}$ | When more than two figures recur, just two dots are used, one above the first figure in the recurring group and one above the last figure in the group. |

Exercise 8J

1 Write the following fractions as decimals.

a $\frac{9}{10}$ **b** $\frac{37}{100}$ **c** $\frac{3}{100}$ **d** $\frac{561}{1000}$ **e** $\frac{8}{1000}$

2 Write the following as equivalent fractions and then as decimals.

   a $\dfrac{4}{5} = \dfrac{}{10}$ **b** $\dfrac{7}{50} = \dfrac{}{100}$ **c** $\dfrac{8}{25} = \dfrac{}{100}$ **d** $\dfrac{9}{500} = \dfrac{}{1000}$ **e** $\dfrac{3}{20} = \dfrac{}{100}$

3 Write down the following fractions as decimals.

   a $\dfrac{1}{2}$ **b** $\dfrac{1}{4}$ **c** $\dfrac{1}{10}$ **d** $\dfrac{1}{100}$ **e** $\dfrac{3}{4}$

4 Use short division to change these fractions to decimals.

   a $\dfrac{3}{5}$ **b** $\dfrac{3}{8}$

5 Use a calculator to change these fractions to decimals.

   a $\dfrac{1}{8}$ **b** $\dfrac{9}{40}$ **c** $\dfrac{23}{25}$ **d** $\dfrac{7}{8}$ **e** $\dfrac{11}{16}$

6 Use a calculator to change these fractions to decimals.

   a $\dfrac{2}{3}$ **b** $\dfrac{8}{9}$ **c** $\dfrac{5}{11}$ **d** $\dfrac{7}{12}$ **e** $\dfrac{1}{7}$

Chapter summary

You should know and be able to use these facts
★ The top number of a fraction is called the **numerator**.
★ The bottom number of a fraction is called the **denominator**.
★ **Equivalent fractions** are fractions that are equal.
★ A fraction can be simplified if the numerator and denominator can both be divided by the same number. This process is called **cancelling**.
★ A fraction that cannot be simplified is in its **simplest form**.
★ To compare fractions, first write them with the same denominator.
★ In a decimal the decimal point separates the whole number part from the part that is less than one.
★ Decimals can be put in order by looking at the place value of each number. First compare the whole number part, then the tenths, then the hundredths, then the thousandths.
★ Decimals can be converted to fractions by using their place value.
★ Fractions can be converted to decimals by using equivalent fractions or division.
★ Some fractions convert to recurring decimals.
★ change an **improper fraction** to a **mixed number** and vice versa

Chapter 8 review questions

1 Write down the fraction of each shape that is shaded.
   Give each fraction in its simplest form.

   a **b** **c** **d**

2 Write down the fraction of
   this shape that is shaded.
   Give your fraction in its
   simplest form.

   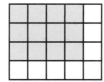

3 **a** Write down the fraction of this shape that is shaded.
       Write your fraction in its simplest form.

   b Shade $\frac{2}{3}$ of this shape

       on the resource sheet.

   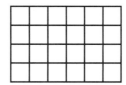

   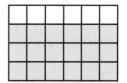

   (1387 June 2003)

4 There are 60 cars in a car park. 35 of the cars are silver.
   Write down the fraction of cars in the car park that are silver.
   Give your fraction in its simplest possible form.

5 Copy the fractions and fill in the missing number to make a pair of equivalent fractions.
   a $\frac{4}{5} = \frac{}{15}$ **b** $\frac{3}{8} = \frac{6}{}$ **c** $\frac{9}{10} = \frac{}{50}$ **d** $\frac{5}{8} = \frac{20}{}$

6 **a** Shade $\frac{1}{4}$ of this shape.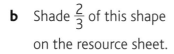

   b Copy the fractions and write a number on the
       dotted line so that the two fractions are equivalent

       $\frac{1}{4} = \frac{...}{12}$

7 Give each fraction in its simplest form.
   a $\frac{4}{8}$ **b** $\frac{5}{15}$ **c** $\frac{10}{40}$ **d** $\frac{75}{100}$

8 Write down the reading on each of these scales.

   a   A   B   C   **b**   **c**

   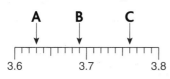

   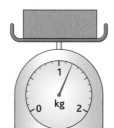   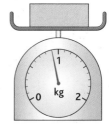

9 Write down the value of the 6 in each of the following numbers.
   a 56.3   **b** 9.62   **c** 0.916   **d** 45.16

10 Five girls each threw a ball in a competition.
The table shows the distance, in metres,
each girl threw the ball.
Write down the distances in order of size.
Start with the longest distance.

Anna	20.4
Bianca	19.96
Chaya	19.9
Debbie	20.34
Eloise	20.04

11 Write each fraction as a decimal. You may **not** use your calculator.

a $\frac{7}{10}$ **b** $\frac{9}{100}$ **c** $\frac{43}{100}$ **d** $\frac{67}{1000}$ **e** $\frac{2}{5}$ **f** $\frac{7}{20}$

12 Write 0.45 as a fraction. Give your fraction in its simplest form.

13 Write 0.028 as a fraction. Give your fraction in its simplest form.

14 Here are two fractions $\frac{3}{5}$ and $\frac{2}{3}$
Explain which is the larger fraction.
You may use the grids to help with
your explanation.

(1387 June 2003)

15 Change $\frac{7}{8}$ to a decimal.

16 Amanda and Mary each had the same size of chocolate bar.
Amanda ate $\frac{2}{3}$ of her bar of chocolate. Mary ate $\frac{5}{8}$ of her bar of chocolate. Work out
which girl had eaten the most chocolate. You must give a reason for your answer.

17 Write these five numbers in order of size. Start with the smallest number

     2.5,   0.5,   0.52,   2.2,   0.25   (1388 Jan 2003)

18 $\frac{7}{12},$ $\frac{5}{6},$ $\frac{2}{3}$

Write these fractions in order of size. Start with the smallest fraction.

(1388 Mar 2002)

19 Write these five fractions in order of size. Start with the smallest fraction.

     $\frac{2}{5},$ $\frac{1}{3},$ $\frac{1}{2},$ $\frac{3}{8},$ $\frac{4}{11}$

20 a Write 0.35 as a fraction. Give your answer in its simplest form.

     b Write $\frac{3}{8}$ as a decimal.   (1387 June 2002)

21 Use your calculator to write each fraction as a decimal.

a $\frac{23}{40}$ **b** $\frac{5}{6}$ **c** $\frac{11}{16}$ **d** $\frac{4}{11}$ **e** $\frac{7}{90}$

22 Change to improper fractions.

a $2\frac{2}{3}$ **b** $8\frac{4}{5}$

Directed numbers

9.1 What is a directed number?

also assessed in Module 4

A **directed number** is a number together with a + or a − sign.

Examples of directed numbers are

+4   −6   +3.2   −560

One use of directed numbers is for temperature in degrees Celsius.

+3° means 3 degrees above 0°

−5° means 5 degrees below 0°

Temperature can be shown on a thermometer scale.

Usually, temperatures above 0° do not have the + sign.

Temperatures below 0° must have the − sign.

Example 1

Put these temperatures in order.

Start with the smallest.

−2° C   4° C   −3° C   3° C   0° C

Solution 1

The correct order is

−3° C
−2° C
0° C
3° C
4° C

This is shown on the thermometer.

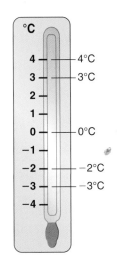

Example 2

At 6 o'clock the temperature was 2°C.

By midnight the temperature had fallen by 5°C.

Work out the temperature at midnight.

Solution 2

Start at 2 and count down 5

The temperature at midnight was −3°C.

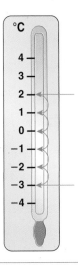

A rise in temperature means moving up the scale; a fall means moving down the scale.

Example 3

The temperature falls from 3 °C to −1 °C.

By how much has the temperature changed?

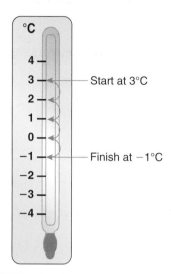

Solution 3

The temperature has fallen by 4°C.

Another possible answer is to write that the change in temperature is −4°C.

Directed numbers can also be shown on a horizontal scale.

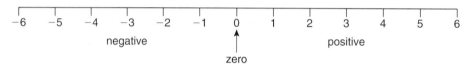

On this scale think of addition as moving to the right (→)
and subtraction as moving to the left (←).

Numbers to the right of 0 are called **positive numbers**.
Numbers to the left of 0 are called **negative numbers**.

Example 4

Use the horizontal scale to work out   **a** $-6 + 5$ **b** $5 - 8$

Solution 4

a   Start at −6 and move 5 to the right. You finish on −1   So $-6 + 5 = -1$

b   Start at 5 and move 8 to the left. You finish on −3   So $5 - 8 = -3$

Exercise 9A

1   Put these temperatures in order. Start with the lowest temperature.

      −3° C   2° C   −4° C   1° C   4° C

2   Put these directed numbers in order. Start with the smallest directed number.

      2   1   −4   −2   0

3   At midnight the temperature was −5°C. By 9 o'clock the following morning the temperature had risen by 3 °C. Find the temperature at 9 o'clock.

4 The temperature inside a freezer is $-3°C$. The temperature outside the freezer is 7°C higher. Find the temperature outside the freezer.

5 On Monday the temperature was 4°C. By Tuesday, the temperature had fallen by 7°C. Find the temperature on Tuesday.

6 On Friday the temperature was $-3\,°C$. By Saturday, the temperature had fallen by $3\,°C$. Find the temperature on Saturday.

7 At 6 o'clock the temperature was 4°C. By midnight the temperature was $-5°C$. By how much had the temperature changed between 6 o'clock and midnight?

8 Copy and complete the table.

Temperature (°C) at at midnight	Temperature (°C) at 9 o'clock the next morning	Change (°C)
4	1	-3
6	4	
5	8	
-4	-2	
-5	-7	
-4	3	
-4	4	

9 Copy and complete the table.

Temperature (°C) at at midnight	Temperature (°C) at 9 o'clock the next morning	Change (°C)
4	-1	-5
6		2
	3	3
-4		2
-6	-1	
-4		-1
	4	-5
-3	-2	
5		8

10 Use a number line to work out

a	$-5+2$	**b**	$-3+3$	**c**	$-6+7$	**d**	$-6+10$
e	$-5+7$	**f**	$8-5$	**g**	$-1-3$	**h**	$-2-2$
i	$0-5$	**j**	$-3-3$	**k**	$4-7$	**l**	$6-10$

11　Copy and complete the following by using a number line to find the missing numbers.

　　a　$-4 + ? = -2$　　**b**　$-4 + ? = 1$　　**c**　$-4 + ? = 2$　　**d**　$-3 - ? = -5$

　　e　$-4 - ? = -7$　**f**　$3 - ? = -1$　　**g**　$5 - ? = -2$　　**h**　$3 - ? = -3$

12　Copy and complete the following by using a number line to find the missing numbers.

　　a　$? - 3 = 4$　　　　　**b**　$? - 4 = -2$　　　　　**c**　$? + 3 = 2$

　　d　$? + 2 = -4$　　　　**e**　$? + 3 = -7$　　　　**f**　$? - 2 = -3$

　　g　$? - 4 = 4$　　　　　**h**　$? - 2 = -2$

9.2 Addition and subtraction of directed numbers

also assessed in
Module 4

Positive numbers are shown with a $+$, for example $+5$,

and negative numbers are shown with a $-$, for example -4.

When adding or subtracting directed numbers, it is useful to put them in brackets.

Addition

The sum $(-3) + (+2)$ means add the positive number $+2$ to the negative number -3

Using a number line the first directed number (-3) is the start position.

The $+$ sign between two directed numbers means 'followed by'.

The second directed number means 'move up' if it is a positive number or 'move down' if it is a negative number.

So $(-3) + (+2)$　means 'start at -3', followed by 'move up 2'.

　　$(-3) + (+2) = (-1)$

The sum $(+3) + (-3)$ means 'start at $+3$' followed by 'move down 3'

So　　$(+3) + (-3) = 0$

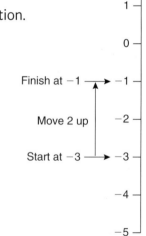

Subtraction

Subtracting any number from itself always gives the answer 0, for example

　　$3 - 3 = 0$

The subtraction $3 - 3 = 0$ written with directed numbers is

　　$(+3) - (+3) = 0$

Compare this with the addition　　　　　　$(+3) + (-3) = 0$

Subtracting $(+3)$ is the same as adding (-3)

Subtracting -3 from itself gives 0　　　　$(-3) - (-3) = 0$

Compare this with the addition　　　　　　$(-3) + (+3) = 0$

So subtracting (-3) is the same as adding $(+3)$

Example 5

Work out   **a** $(-6) + (-5)$ **b**   Work out $(+5) - (-8)$

Solution 5

a   Start at -6 and move down 5. You finish on -11.

So $(-6) + (-5) = (-11)$ or -11

b   Subtracting (-8) is the same as adding $(+8)$

$(+5) - (-8) = (+5) + (+8)$

Start at $(+5)$ and move up 8. You finish on $+13$

So $(+5) - (-8) = (+13)$ or 13

Directed numbers can also be written without the brackets.

Example 6

a   Work out $5 - 8$ **b**   Work out $-7 + 8$

Solution 6

a   Start at 5 and move down 8. You finish on -3 So $5 - 8 = -3$

b   Start at -7 and move up 8. You finish on 1   So $-7 + 8 = 1$

Exercise 9B

1   Work out

   a $(-3) + (+1)$ **b** $(+1) + (-5)$ **c** $(-5) + (+2)$ **d** $(-2) + (-4)$

   e $(+3) + (+6)$ **f** $(-4) + (-5)$ **g** $(-5) + (+5)$ **h** $(-4) + (+7)$

   i $(+2) + (-5)$ **j** $(-3) + (+7)$ **k** $(-6) + (+10)$ **l** $(+4) + (-11)$

2   Work out

   a $(+8) - (+4)$ **b** $(+2) - (+5)$ **c** $(+3) - (+7)$ **d** $(-2) - (+2)$

   e $(-5) - (-4)$ **f** $(-4) - (+2)$ **g** $(-5) - (-3)$ **h** $(+3) - (-3)$

   i $(-7) - (+2)$ **j** $(-2) - (-2)$ **k** $(-4) - (-6)$ **l** $(-9) - (-5)$

3   Fill in the missing directed number.

   a $(+3) + (\ ) = (+5)$ **b** $(+4) + (\ ) = (+3)$ **c** $(-7) + (\ ) = (-3)$

   d $(-6) + (\ ) = (-8)$ **e** $(+3) - (\ ) = 0$ **f** $(+8) - (\ ) = (+3)$

   g $(+4) - (\ ) = (+7)$ **h** $(-3) - (\ ) = (-7)$ **i** $(-6) - (\ ) = (-2)$

   j $(-3) - (\ ) = (+4)$

4   Fill in the missing directed number.

   a $(\ ) + (+3) = (+2)$ **b** $(\ ) + (-3) = (-4)$ **c** $(\ ) + (+4) = (+5)$

   d $(\ ) + (-5) = 0$ **e** $(\ ) + (+4) = (-2)$ **f** $(\ ) - (+3) = (+2)$

   g $(\ ) - (-4) = (+5)$ **h** $(\ ) - (-3) = (+4)$ **i** $(\ ) - (+4) = (-2)$

5 Work out

    a $-4 - 3$ **b** $5 - 8$ **c** $-6 + 4$ **d** $-4 - 4$ **e** $-3 + 7$

    f $-4 + 4$ **g** $-8 - 1 - 3$ **h** $-5 + 7 - 2$ **i** $2 - 6 + 5$

6 Work out

    a $-14 - 24$ **b** $-16 + 25$ **c** $25 - 38$ **d** $-23 - 45$

    e $-34 + 48$ **f** $34 - 58$ **g** $-23 - 45$ **h** $32 - 38$

7 Work out the sum of

    a (-4) and (-2) **b** $(+5)$ and (-3) **c** (-4) and $(+3)$

    d 3 and -4 **e** 6 and -8 **f** 4 and -4

9.3 Multiplication and division of directed numbers

Multiplication

also assessed in Module 4

$(+3)$ is the same as 3 $(+2)$ is the same as 2

so $(+3) \times (+2)$ is the same as $3 \times 2 = 6$

3×2 also means $2 + 2 + 2$ $3 \times (-2)$ means $(-2) + (-2) + (-2)$

so $3 \times (-2)$ or $(+3) \times (-2) = (-6)$

Look at the patterns in the multiplications on the right.

The blue numbers are decreasing by 1

The orange numbers are increasing by 2

The pattern continues like this

The rules are

$$(+3) \times (-2) = (-6)$$
$$(+2) \times (-2) = (-4)$$
$$(+1) \times (-2) = (-2)$$
$$0 \times (-2) = 0$$

$$(-1) \times (-2) = (+2)$$
$$(-2) \times (-2) = (+4)$$
$$(-3) \times (-2) = (+6)$$

$(+) \times (+) = (+)$ positive $\times$ positive $=$ positive

$(+) \times (-) = (-)$ positive $\times$ negative $=$ negative

$(-) \times (+) = (-)$ negative $\times$ positive $=$ negative

$(-) \times (-) = (+)$ negative $\times$ negative $=$ positive

Division

$3 \times 2 = 6$ $6 \div 3 = 2$ and $6 \div 2 = 3$

$(+3) \times (-2) = (-6)$,   so $(-6) \div (+3) = (-2)$ and $(-6) \div (-2) = (+3)$

The rules are

$(+) \div (+) = (+)$ positive $\div$ positive $=$ positive

$(+) \div (-) = (-)$ positive $\div$ negative $=$ negative

$(-) \div (+) = (-)$ negative $\div$ positive $=$ negative

$(-) \div (-) = (+)$ negative $\div$ negative $=$ positive

When multiplying or dividing two directed numbers you can remember the rules by the following

if the signs are the **same**, the answer is **positive**;

if the signs are **different**, the answer is **negative**.

Example 7

a Work out $(+5) \times (-3)$

b Work out $(-16) \div (-2)$

Solution 7

a $(+5) \times (-3) = (-15)$

(-15) is also written as -15

> the signs are different so the answer is negative and $5 \times 3 = 15$

b $(-16) \div (-2) = (+8)$

$(+8)$ is also written as 8

> the signs are the same so the answer is positive and $16 \div 2 = 8$

Exercise 9C

1 Work out

a $(+2) \times (-4)$ **b** $(-3) \times (-5)$ **c** $(-4) \times (-6)$

d $(+3) \times (+5)$ **e** $(-2) \times (+5)$ **f** $(-4) \times (+5)$

g $(-3) \times (+8)$ **h** $(-1) \times (+9)$ **i** $(-4) \times (-4)$

2 Work out

a $(+6) \div (+3)$ **b** $(-8) \div (+4)$ **c** $(+10) \div (-5)$

d $(-12) \div (-3)$ **e** $(-8) \div (+4)$ **f** $(-12) \div (-12)$

g $(-14) \div (+2)$ **h** $(+12) \div (+4)$

3 Find the missing directed number.

a $(+10) \div (\ ) = (-2)$ **b** $(-8) \div (\ ) = (+2)$ **c** $(-3) \times (\ ) = (+12)$

d $(-5) \times (\ ) = (+20)$ **e** $(+5) \times (\ ) = (-25)$ **f** $(\ ) \times (-4) = (+20)$

g $(\ ) \div (+3) = (+4)$ **h** $(\ ) \div (-4) = (-5)$ **i** $(+16) \div (\ ) = (-2)$

4 Work out the product of

a (-6) and $(+3)$ **b** (-5) and $(+4)$ **c** $(+3)$ and (-5)

d (-6) and (-6) **e** $(+3)$ and $(+4)$ **f** (-4) and $(+9)$

g (-5) and (-4) **h** $(+3)$ and (-2)

9.4 Using a calculator

> *also assessed in Module 4*

The negative sign for directed numbers and the subtraction sign look very similar.

Different calculators have different buttons for these two signs.

Basic calculators have a 'change sign' key usually marked $\boxed{+/-}$.

To enter a negative number such as (-4), press 4 and then press the $\boxed{+/-}$ key.

Scientific calculators have the negative sign shown by $\boxed{(-)}$.

To enter a negative number such as (-4), press the $\boxed{(-)}$ key and then press 4

Example 8

a Work out $(+5.2) - (-17.8)$ **b** Work out $(-6.3) \times (-7.5)$

Show how to input these calculations into both basic and scientific calculators.

Solution 8

a 23   **b** 47.25

On a scientific calculator

a Press $[\,(\,][\,+\,]$ 5.2 $[\,)\,][\,-\,][\,(\,][\,-\,]$ 17.8 $[\,)\,][\,=\,]$

b Press $[\,(\,][\,-\,]$ 6.3 $[\,)\,][\,\times\,][\,(\,][\,-\,]$ 7.5 $[\,)\,][\,=\,]$

On a basic calculator

a Press $[\,+\,]$ 5.2 $[\,-\,]$ 17.8 $[\,+/-\,][\,=\,]$

b Press 6.3 $[\,+/-\,][\,\times\,]$ 7.5 $[\,+/-\,][\,=\,]$

More complicated expressions can also be worked out using a calculator.

Example 9

Work out $\dfrac{6.25 \times (-12.3)}{(-7.5)}$ showing how you would use a basic and a scientific calculator to do this.

Solution 9

On a scientific calculator

10.25   Press 6.25 $[\,\times\,][\,(\,][\,-\,]$ 12.3 $[\,)\,][\,\div\,][\,(\,][\,-\,]$ 7.5 $[\,)\,][\,=\,]$

On a basic calculator

10.25   Press 6.25 $[\,\times\,]$ 12.3 $[\,+/-\,][\,\div\,]$ 7.5 $[\,+/-\,][\,=\,]$

Exercise 9D

1 Use a calculator to work out

a $(+3.6) \times (+4.8)$	**b** $(-3.5) \times (+2.4)$	**c** $(-2.8) \times (+1.5)$
d $(+13.5) - (-17.7)$	**e** $(+12.4) \div (-2.5)$	**f** $(-28.7) \div (-3.5)$
g $(-16.4) \div (-12.5)$	**h** $(-23.8) + (-34.9)$	**i** $(-45.8) - (+34.7)$

2 Use a calculator to find the missing directed number.

a $(+2.5) \div (\ ) = (-5)$

b $(-15.3) \div (\ ) = (+4.5)$

c $(+5.2) \times (\ ) = (+19.76)$

d $(\ ) \times (+2.3) = (-12.88)$

e $(\ ) \times (-5.5) = (+48.4)$

f $(\ ) \div (-8.4) = (+5.6)$

g $(\ ) \div (+4.9) = (-122.5)$

h $(+34.56) + (\ ) = (+25.7)$

i $(-23.8) + (\ ) = (+16.8)$

j $(-34.56) - (\ ) = (-17.86)$

k $(\ ) - (+26.8) = (-16.9)$

l $(\ ) - (-34.44) = (+13.89)$

3 Work out

a $\dfrac{3.75 \times (+12.4)}{(-2.5)}$

b $\dfrac{(-3.6) \times (-13.5)}{(+3.75)}$

c $\dfrac{(+18.4) \times (-9.6)}{(-1.2)}$

d $\dfrac{(+4.5)}{(-3.6)} - 1.9$

e $\dfrac{(-37.8)}{(-4.5)} - 15.6$

Chapter summary

> **You should know and be able to use these facts**
>
> ★ Solve problems which involve changes of temperature
>
> ★ Put directed numbers in order, smallest first
>
> ★ Use non-calculator and calculator methods to
>   - Add and subtract directed numbers
>   - Multiply and divide directed numbers

Chapter 9 review questions

1 The map shows four cities and their temperatures.

    a Put the temperatures in order.
Start with the lowest.

    b Work out the difference in
temperature between

        i London and Cardiff

        ii Belfast and Edinburgh

        iii Edinburgh and London

(Source of UK Outline map is **www.georesources.co.uk**)

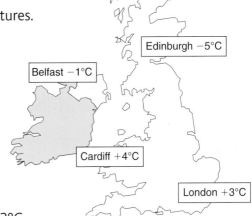

2 At 6 pm on Monday, the temperature was $-2°C$.
By midnight the temperature had fallen by $4°C$.

    a Work out the temperature at midnight.

At midnight on Wednesday the temperature was $-5°C$.
By 9 o'clock the next day the temperature was $6°C$.

    b Work out the increase in temperature from midnight to 9 o'clock.

3 The table shows the temperatures in a garden taken every 4 hours.

Time	Temperature °C
Midnight	−1
4 am	−6
8 am	−3
Noon	+1
4 pm	+4
8 pm	0

  a Write down the lowest temperature in the table.

  b Write down the highest temperature in the table.

  c Work out the increase in temperature from 8 am to noon.

  d Work out the biggest difference in temperature in the table.

4 Put these numbers in order. Start with the smallest.

$$-3 \quad 0 \quad 2 \quad -4 \quad 6 \quad -1$$

5 Work out

  a $(+2) + (+3)$ **b** $(-5) + (+3)$ **c** $(-6) + (-4)$

  d $(+4) + (-4)$ **e** $(+6) - (+4)$ **f** $(+8) - (+9)$

  g $(-3) - (+5)$ **h** $(-6) - (+4)$ **i** $(+4) - (-3)$

  j $(-6) - (-4)$ **k** $(-3) - (-7)$

6 Work out

  a $(+3) \times (+5)$ **b** $(+6) \times (+6)$ **c** $(+5) \times (-4)$

  d $(+4) \times (-7)$ **e** $(-5) \times (+2)$ **f** $(-6) \times (+3)$

  g $(-7) \times (-1)$ **h** $(-4) \times (-3)$ **i** $(-5) \times (-6)$

7 Work out

  a $(+6) \div (+3)$ **b** $(+30) \div (+5)$ **c** $(-30) \div (+5)$

  d $(+25) \div (-5)$ **e** $(-28) \div (+2)$ **f** $(-60) \div (-2)$

  g $(-40) \div (-4)$

8 Work out

  a $\dfrac{(-5) \times (+4)}{(+2)}$ **b** $\dfrac{(-4) \times (-5)}{(+2)}$ **c** $\dfrac{(+6) \times (-4)}{(-3)}$

  d $\dfrac{(-5) \times (-8)}{(-4)}$ **e** $\dfrac{(-6)}{(+2)} + (-2)$ **f** $(-3) - \dfrac{(-6)}{(+2)}$

9 Find the missing directed number.

  a $(-5) + \, ? = (-3)$ **b** $(+4) - \, ? = (-3)$ **c** $? - (-5) = (+2)$

  d $? + (-3) = (+1)$ **e** $(+3) - \, ? = 0$ **f** $(-3) + \, ? = (-8)$

10 Find the missing directed number.

  a $-3 + \, ? = 5$ **b** $4 - \, ? = -3$ **c** $? + (-3) = 5$

  d $-5 - \, ? = -2$ **e** $4 - 9 = \, ?$ **f** $-5 - \, ? = -2$

11 The table shows the lowest temperatures during five months in 2004 in a town in Scotland.

Month	Temperature
January	$-16°C$
March	$-6°C$
May	$-1°C$
July	$4°C$
September	$7°C$

a Work out the difference in lowest temperature between January and March.

b Work out the difference in lowest temperature between March and July.

c In which month was the lowest temperature 5°C higher than the lowest temperature in May?

The lowest temperature in November was 10°C lower than the lowest temperature in May.

d Work out the lowest temperature in November.

(5540 June 2005)

12 The table shows the temperature on the surface of each of five planets.

Planet	Temperature
Venus	$480°C$
Mars	$-60°C$
Jupiter	$-150°C$
Saturn	$-180°C$
Uranus	$-210°C$

a Work out the difference in temperature between Mars and Jupiter.

b Work out the difference in temperature between Venus and Mars.

c Which planet has a temperature 30°C higher than the temperature on Saturn?

The temperature on Pluto is 20°C lower than the temperature on Uranus.

d Work out the temperature on Pluto.

(1387 June 2005)

13 Work out

a $(+3.4) \times (-2.4)$ b $(-2.5) \times (-3.6)$ c $6.3 \times (-12.8)$

d $(+4.8) \times (+5.5)$ e $(+409) \times (-4.8)$

14 Work out

a $240 \div (-1.2)$ b $(-340) \div (-2.5)$ c $(-3.88) \div (+12.5)$

d $(-208) \div 1.25$ e $\dfrac{1.25 \times (+12.4)}{(-2.5)}$ f $\dfrac{(-3.6) \times (-4.5)}{(+3.75)}$

g $\dfrac{(+18.375) \times (-9.8)}{(-1.2)}$ h $\dfrac{(+4.5)}{(-2.4)} - 1.8$ i $\dfrac{(-18.9)}{(-4.5)} - 5.6$

j $6.4 - \dfrac{(-5.6)}{(-0.7)}$ k $(+25.5) - \dfrac{(16.4)}{(-2.5)}$

Decimals

10.1 Rounding decimals

The answer on a calculator often has more decimal places than are needed. When this happens, the answer can be **rounded** to the nearest whole number.

Example 1

Round to the nearest whole number

a   6.3   **b**   6.8   **c**   6.5

Solution 1

a   6.3 is between 6 and 7
        6.3 is closer to 6 than 7
        6.3 rounds to 6, to the nearest whole number.

b   6.8 is closer to 7 than 6
        6.8 rounds to 7, to the nearest whole number.

c

   6.5 is halfway between 6 and 7
   If a number is exactly halfway between two
   numbers, the rule is to round up.
   6.5 rounds to 7, to the nearest whole number.

> A number can be rounded without
> using a number line.
> Just look at the number of tenths.
> If this figure is less than 5, do not
> change the whole number part.
> If it is equal to 5 or greater than 5 then
> add one to the whole number part.

Example 2

Round to the nearest whole number

a   2.4   **b**   2.7   **c**   2.5

Solution 2

a   The 4 in 2.4 is less than 5, so do not change the
        whole number part, 2
        To the nearest whole number, 2.4 rounds to 2

b   In 2.7, the 7 is greater than 5, so increase the
        whole number part by 1
        This means 2.7 rounds to 3

c   In 2.5, the 5 is equal to 5, so increase the whole number
        part by 1
        2.5 also rounds to 3

tens	units		tenths	hundredths	thousandths
	2	.	4		
	2	.	7		
	2	.	5		

Example 3

Round these to the nearest kilogram.

a 4.091 kg   **b** 17.562 kg

Solution 3

a The number 4.091 has a **0** in the tenths column.
0 is less than 5 so do not change the whole
number part.
4.091 kg rounds to 4 kg.

b The number 17.562 has a **5** in the tenths column
so increase the whole number part by 1
17.562 kg rounds to 18 kg.

tens	units	.	tenths	hundredths	thousandths
	4	.	0	9	1
1	7	.	5	6	2

Exercise 10A

1 Round these to the nearest whole number.

a	4.8	**b**	7.2	**c**	12.6	**d**	6.9	**e**	14.1	**f**	5.7
g	0.6	**h**	23.5	**i**	132.2	**j**	86.7	**k**	9.5	**l**	49.9

2 Round these to the nearest whole number.

a	2.67	**b**	4.29	**c**	6.34	**d**	1.78	**e**	2.51	**f**	3.08
g	16.712	**h**	25.129	**i**	0.834	**j**	9.671	**k**	79.519	**l**	7.092

3 Round these to the nearest pound (£).

a	£4.95	**b**	£6.04	**c**	£45.56	**d**	£17.09
e	£2.50	**f**	£8.99	**g**	£103.27	**h**	£19.99

4 Round these to the nearest metre (m).

a	8.7 m	**b**	2.1 m	**c**	9.48 m	**d**	12.91 m
e	0.76 m	**f**	3.09 m	**g**	19.5 m	**h**	1.49 m

5 Round these to the nearest kilometre (km).

a	5.67 km	**b**	2.124 km	**c**	29.562 km	**d**	1.095 km
e	7.843 km	**f**	84.19 km	**g**	109.98 km	**h**	0.87 km

6 Round these to the nearest kilogram (kg).

a	8.5 kg	**b**	63.14 kg	**c**	3.199 kg	**d**	8.499 kg
e	39.901 kg	**f**	2.08 kg	**g**	6.995 kg	**h**	12.3 kg

10.2 Estimating

It is often useful to work out an estimate to an answer rather than work out the exact
answer.
Estimates can be worked out by rounding the numbers in the calculation to the nearest
whole number.

Example 4

Work out an estimate for

a 6.7 × 3.1

b the total cost of 5 CDs at £8.99 each.

Solution 4

a 6.7 × 3.1
6.7 rounds to 7
3.1 rounds to 3

> Round each number to the nearest whole number.

7 × 3 = 21
An estimate is 21

b 5 × 8.99

> To work out the total cost, multiply the price of one CD by the number of CDs.
>
> Round 8.99 to the nearest whole number.

8.99 rounds to 9
5 × 9 = 45
An estimate for total cost is £45

Exercise 10B

1 Work out an estimate for
    a 4.3 × 2.9   **b** 10.1 × 5.2   **c** 8.1 ÷ 1.9   **d** 29.5 ÷ 5.4   **e** 9.1 × 2.85
    f 19.8 × 2.4   **g** 40.12 ÷ 3.76   **h** 9.78 × 0.6   **i** 4.95 × 2.1   **j** 12.09 ÷ 1.98

2 Work out an estimate for the total cost of
    a three Easter eggs at £2.99 each
    b four magazines at £1.89 each
    c six pens at £0.99 each
    d two CDs at £9.79 each
    e three packets of biscuits at £0.89 each and two bottles of cola at £1.23 each.

3 Emily bought
    three magazines at £1.99 each
    two pens at £0.86 each
    one box of chocolates at £3.87
    Work out an estimate for the total amount of money that Emily spent.

4 A group of eight people go to the cinema. Tickets cost £4.95 each. Work out an estimate for the total cost of the tickets.

5 Books cost £2.89 each. Work out an estimate of the number of books that can be bought for £15

6 Sets of stickers cost £1.99 each. Work out an estimate of the number of sets of stickers that can be bought for £12

7 Jack wants to buy three CDs that cost £9.87 each. He has £30
    Does he have enough money to buy the three CDs? Give a reason for your answer.

8 A family of two adults and three children go to the cinema. Adult tickets cost £6.95 and child tickets cost £4.50. Work out an estimate for the total cost of all five tickets.

10.3 Adding and subtracting decimals

When adding or subtracting decimals, line up the decimal points first.

Example 5

Add 4.56 and 12.7

Solution 5

```
      4 . 5 6
+   1 2 . 7 0
```

Write the numbers underneath each other.
Make sure that the decimal points line up.
Write a 0 here to show there are no hundredths.

```
      4 . 5 6
+   1 2 . 7 0
    1 7 . 2 6
        1
```

The decimal point in the answer goes underneath the decimal points in the question.

Add the numbers.

Example 6

Add 8, 6.72 and 9.03

Solution 6

```
      8 . 0 0
      6 . 7 2
+     9 . 0 3
```

8 has no tenths and no hundredths. It is the same as 8.00
Write the numbers underneath each other.
Make sure that the decimal points line up.

```
      8 . 0 0
      6 . 7 2
+     9 . 0 3
    2 3 . 7 5
      2
```

The decimal point in the answer goes underneath the decimal points in the question.

Add the numbers.

Example 7

Subtract 7.23 from 19.8

Solution 7

```
    1 9 . 8 0
−       7 . 2 3
```

Write a zero here to show there are no hundredths.

The decimal point in the answer goes underneath the decimal points in the question.

```
    1 9 . ⁷8̸ ¹0
−       7 . 2 3
    1 2 . 5 7
```

Subtract the numbers. 3 cannot be subtracted from 0 so borrow 1 from the 8.

Example 8

Mandy buys a magazine costing £2.60 and a book costing £4.95

Mandy pays with a £10 note.

Work out how much change Mandy should get.

Solution 8

$$
\begin{array}{r}
2\,.\,6\;0 \\
+\quad 4\,.\,9\;5 \\
\hline
7\,.\,5\;5 \\
\end{array}
$$

> First add 2.60 and 4.95 to work out the total amount Mandy spends.

$$
\begin{array}{r}
{}^{1}\!0\,.\,{}^{1}\!0\;{}^{1}0 \\
-\quad 7\,.\,5\;5 \\
\hline
2\,.\,4\;5 \\
\end{array}
$$

> Next subtract 7.55 from 10
> Write two zeros after the decimal point

Mandy should get £2.45 change.

Exercise 10C

1   Work out

    a   8.2 + 9.7   **b**   5.67 + 0.94   **c**   12.45 + 3.49   **d**   76.29 + 64.67

    e   13.1 + 5.69   **f**   87.34 + 45.9   **g**   345.06 + 24.8   **h**   15.2 + 8.953

    i   4 + 6.2 + 8.77   **j**   23 + 15.6 + 3.45

2   Work out

    a   8.57 − 3.21   **b**   19.31 − 7.16   **c**   56.43 − 12.56   **d**   67.65 − 45.8

    e   8.6 − 3.42   **f**   14.6 − 4.31   **g**   9 − 3.4   **h**   17 − 5.43

    i   8.72 − 6.04   **j**   7.34 − 3.286

3   A plank of wood measures 4.5 m. Ben cuts 1.85 m from the plank of wood. Work out the length of wood left.

4   Craig buys a newspaper costing £1.30 and a magazine costing £3.85. He pays with a £10 note. Work out how much change Craig gets.

5   James is 1.9 m tall. Sarah is 1.52 m tall. How much taller than Sarah is James?

6   Two teams took part in a relay race. The times, in seconds, for each runner are shown in the tables. Which team won the race? You must give a reason for your answer.

Team A	Times (s)
Runner 1	10.54
Runner 2	10.2
Runner 3	10.11
Runner 4	9.87

Team B	Times (s)
Runner 1	10.6
Runner 2	10.27
Runner 3	9.98
Runner 4	9.89

10.4 Multiplying decimals

Multiplication of whole numbers by 10, 100, 1000 was covered in Chapter 6.
Here is a reminder.

- When a number is multiplied by *ten* each figure moves *one* place to the left.
- When a number is multiplied by *one hundred* each figure moves *two* places to the left.
- When a number is multiplied by *one thousand* each figure moves *three* places to the left.

The same method can be used to multiply decimals by 10, 100 or 1000

ten thousands	thousands	hundreds	tens	units		
			3	4		
		3	4	0		34 × 10 = 340
	3	4	0	0		34 × 100 = 3400
3	4	0	0	0		34 × 1000 = 34 000

Example 9

Work out
a 4.56 × 10   **b** 3.29 × 100   **c** 0.58 × 1000

Solution 9

	hundreds	tens	units	.	tenths	hundredths	
a			4	.	5	6	
		4	5	.	6		To multiply by 10, move the figures *one* place to the left. 4.56 × 10 = 45.6
b			3	.	2	9	
	3	2	9				To multiply by 100, move the figures *two* places to the left. 3.29 × 100 = 329
c			0	.	5	8	
	5	8		.			To multiply by 1000, move the figures *three* places to the left.
	5	8	0				Write a zero in the units column. 0.58 × 1000 = 580 A decimal point is not needed as 580.0 is the same as 580

Example 10

Jerry buys 10 bottles of cola at £1.24 each.
Work out the total cost.

Solution 10

$1.24 \times 10 = 12.4$

The total cost is £12.40

> As the answer is a sum of money, there must be two figures after the decimal point to show the 40 pence.

Exercise 10D

1 Work out

    a 4.5×10 **b** 6.32×10 **c** 15.46×10

    d 0.54×10 **e** 0.013×10 **f** 2.008×10

2 Work out

    a 9.92×100 **b** 3.231×100 **c** 7.4×100

    d $0.006\,51 \times 100$ **e** 0.2×100 **f** 0.0035×100

3 Work out

    a 6.254×1000 **b** 8.62×1000 **c** 0.65×1000

    d 1.8×1000 **e** 0.03×1000 **f** 0.3408×1000

4 Work out

    a 9.62×10 **b** 67.231×100 **c** 0.83×10

    d 0.0065×1000 **e** 8.2×100 **f** 0.9×100

    g 8.41×100 **h** 43.2×1000 **i** 0.21×1000

    j 6.08×100 **k** 0.0134×10 **l** 56.1×100

5 Work out the missing number

    a $3.45 \times ? = 345$ **b** $67.8 \times ? = 678$ **c** $0.07 \times ? = 0.7$

    d $0.056 \times ? = 5.6$ **e** $8.2 \times ? = 820$ **f** $7.8 \times ? = 7800$

    g $1.04 \times ? = 10.4$ **h** $0.003 \times ? = 3$ **i** $0.09 \times ? = 9$

    j $0.8 \times ? = 8$ **k** $0.04 \times ? = 40$ **l** $0.5006 \times ? = 50.06$

6 Work out the cost of

    a 10 magazines at £1.59 each   **b** 100 bars of chocolate at £0.36 each

    c 10 packets of biscuits at £1.06 each   **d** 10 cushions at £4.56 each

    e 100 pencils at £0.18 each

Another way of doing calculations with decimals is to do the calculation as if the decimal point was not there. An estimate of the answer can then be used to postion the decimal point.

Example 11

A game costs £3.65
Kris buys four of these games.

a Work out an estimate for the total cost.

b Work out the exact total cost.

Solution 11

a 3.65×4

| To find the total cost, multiply £3.65 by 4 |

$4 \times 4 = 16$

| Round 3.65 to the nearest whole number. |

An estimate for the total cost is £16

b
```
      3  6  5
×     ₂  ₂  4
   ─────────────
   1  4  6  0
```

| Ignore the decimal point and do the multiplication with whole numbers. |
| The estimate in **a** is £16 |
| This means that the decimal point will go between the 4 and the 6 because 14.60 is close to 16 (1.460 would be too small and 146.0 would be too big). |

The total cost is £14.60

Example 12

Multiply 5.12 by 4.6

Solution 12

```
         5  1  2
×           4  6
   ──────────────
      3  0 ₁7  2
+  2  0  4  8  0
   ──────────────
   2  3  5  5  2
            1
```

| Ignore the decimal points and do multiplication with whole numbers. |

Estimate $= 5 \times 5$
        $= 25$

| Round 5.12 to 5 and round 4.5 to 5 |
| An estimate for the answer is 5×5 |

$5.12 \times 4.6 = 23.552$

| This means that the decimal point will go between the 3 and the 5 because 23.552 is close to 25 |

| 5.12 has 2 decimal places and 4.6 has 1 decimal place, so there are $2 + 1 = 3$ decimal places in the question. There are also 3 decimal places in the answer. |

The number of decimal places in the answer is the same as the total number of decimal places in the question.

This rule is another way of finding the position of the decimal point in the answer.

Example 13

Multiply 3.4 by 0.2

Solution 13

$$\begin{array}{r} 3\ \ 4 \\ \times \quad\ 2 \\ \hline 6\ \ 8 \end{array}$$

> Do the multiplicataion with whole numbers.

$3.4 \times 0.2 = 0.68$

> The total number of decimal places in the question is 2 so there must be 2 decimal places in the answer.

Exercise 10E

1 Work out

    a 3.2×3 **b** 4.6×2 **c** 7.3×4 **d** 12.4×3

    e 24.6×4 **f** 3.7×5 **g** 72.4×5 **h** 92.1×4

2 Work out the total cost of

    a four CDs at £9.45 each   **b** three magazines at £2.65 each

    c five pillows at £3.75 each   **d** six mugs at £1.28 each

3 A toy costs £2.35
    Nasreen buys three of these toys.
    a Work out an estimate for the total cost.
    b Work out the exact total cost.

4 A CD costs £9.65
    James buys six of these CDs.
    a Work out an estimate for the total cost.
    b Work out the exact total cost.

5 Work out

    a 6.34×0.4 **b** 4.21×0.3 **c** 0.02×0.4 **d** 0.08×0.3

    e 2.16×0.3 **f** 0.54×0.8 **g** 0.723×0.06 **h** 3.15×0.8

6 Work out

    a 3.1×4.2 **b** 0.36×1.4 **c** 3.6×2.3 **d** 7.4×0.53

    e 8.6×2.4 **f** 9.2×0.15 **g** 0.064×0.73 **h** 0.095×3.4

7 Work out the cost of 0.6 kg of carrots at £0.25 per kilogram.

8 Work out the cost of 1.6 m of material at £4.20 per metre.

10.5 Dividing decimals

Division as the inverse of mutiplication was covered in Chapter 6.
Here is a reminder.

- When a number is divided
  by *ten* each figure moves *one*
  place to the right.
- When a number is divided
  by *one hundred* each figure
  moves *two* places to the right.
- When a number is divided
  by *one thousand* each figure
  moves *three* places to the right.

ten thousands	thousands	hundreds	tens	units	
3	4	0	0	0	
	3	4	0	0	$34\,000 \div 10 = 3400$
		3	4	0	$34\,000 \div 100 = 340$
			3	4	$34\,000 \div 1000 = 34$

The same method can be used to divide decimals by 10, 100 or 1000

Example 14

Work out

a $43.6 \div 10$ **b** $50.3 \div 100$ **c** $58 \div 1000$

Solution 14

	tens	units	.	tenths	hundredths	
a	4	3	.	6		
		4	.	3	6	To divide by 10, move the figures *one* place to the right. $43.6 \div 10 = 4.36$
b	5	0	.	3		
		0	.	5	0	3	To divide by 100, move the figures *two* places to the right. $50.3 \div 100 = 0.503$
c	5	8				
		0	.	0	5	8	To divide by 1000, move the figures *three* places to the right. Write a zero in the tenths column. $58 \div 1000 = 0.058$

Exercise 10F

1   Work out

    a $87.2 \div 10$ **b** $342 \div 10$ **c** $0.54 \div 10$ **d** $0.0428 \div 10$

2   Work out

    a $782.3 \div 100$ **b** $452 \div 100$ **c** $28.4 \div 100$ **d** $0.62 \div 100$

3   Work out

    a $2578.2 \div 1000$ **b** $5627 \div 1000$ **c** $98.1 \div 1000$

    d $45 \div 1000$ **e** $5.2 \div 1000$ **f** $0.6 \div 1000$

4   Work out

    a $456 \div 100$ **b** $72.3 \div 10$ **c** $0.76 \div 10$ **d** $53 \div 100$

    e $0.9 \div 10$ **f** $67.2 \div 100$ **g** $7 \div 1000$ **h** $4 \div 100$

    i $0.054 \div 10$ **j** $2.31 \div 100$ **k** $45 \div 1000$ **l** $6.01 \div 100$

5   Write down the missing number.

    a $78 \div ? = 7.8$ **b** $0.987 \div ? = 0.009\,87$ **c** $231 \div ? = 0.231$

    d $45.2 \div ? = 0.452$ **e** $4 \div ? = 0.4$ **f** $8 \div ? = 0.008$

    g $5 \div ? = 0.05$ **h** $9.7 \div ? = 0.097$ **i** $234 \div ? = 2.34$

    j $613 \div ? = 0.613$ **k** $568 \div ? = 56.8$ **l** $98.2 \div ? = 0.0982$

6   Work out

    a 4.5×100 **b** 0.083×1000 **c** $3.45 \div 10$

    d 0.6×100 **e** $85 \div 100$ **f** $23.4 \div 1000$

    g 0.803×100 **h** $65 \div 100$ **i** 1.2×10

    j $0.007\,03 \times 1000$ **k** $8.04 \div 100$ **l** $4.2 \div 10$

    m $3.78 \div 100$ **n** $64 \div 100$ **o** 0.23×1000

When dividing a decimal by a whole number, the decimal point in the answer goes above the decimal point in the original number.

Example 15

a   Divide 35.4 by 2   **b**   Divide 84.2 by 4

Solution 15

a
$$
\begin{array}{r}
1\,7\,.\,7 \\
2\overline{)3\,{}^{1}5\,.\,{}^{1}4}
\end{array}
$$

b
$$
\begin{array}{r}
2\,1\,.\,0\,\,5 \\
4\overline{)8\,4\,.\,2\,\,{}^{2}0}
\end{array}
$$

Sometimes you need to write an extra zero.

To divide a number by a decimal, multiply *both* the number and the decimal by a power of 10 (10, 100, 1000...) to make the decimal a whole number. It is much easier to divide by a whole number than by a decimal.

Example 16

Divide 20 by 0.4

Solution 16

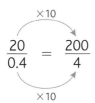

$\times 10$

$$\frac{20}{0.4} = \frac{200}{4}$$

$\times 10$

To make 0.4 a whole number, multiply it by 10
So multiply both 20 and 0.4 by 10

Then divide in the usual way

$$\begin{array}{r} 5\,0 \\ 4\overline{)2\,0\,0} \end{array}$$

Example 17

Divide 58.2 by 0.03

Solution 17

$\times 100$

$$\frac{58.2}{0.03} = \frac{5820}{3}$$

$\times 100$

To make 0.03 a whole number, multiply it by 100
So multiply both 58.2 and 0.03 by 100

Then divide in the usual way

$$\begin{array}{r} 1\ 9\ 4\ 0 \\ 3\overline{)5\ ^28\ ^12\ 0} \end{array}$$

Exercise 10G

1 Work out

a	68.2 ÷ 2	**b**	3.65 ÷ 5	**c**	82.2 ÷ 3	**d**	0.312 ÷ 2
e	42.6 ÷ 6	**f**	5.13 ÷ 3	**g**	0.275 ÷ 5	**h**	5.3 ÷ 2
i	0.84 ÷ 5	**j**	78 ÷ 0.06	**k**	7.08 ÷ 3	**l**	37 ÷ 4

2 Work out

a	12 ÷ 0.2	**b**	4.2 ÷ 0.3	**c**	0.145 ÷ 0.5	**d**	19.2 ÷ 0.03
e	0.72 ÷ 0.03	**f**	26 ÷ 0.4	**g**	5 ÷ 0.2	**h**	9 ÷ 0.04
i	6.12 ÷ 0.003	**j**	0.035 ÷ 0.7	**k**	0.048 ÷ 0.6	**l**	0.008 28 ÷ 0.09

3 Five people share £130.65 equally. Work out how much each person will get.

4 Four cups of coffee cost £5.40. Work out the price of one cup of coffee.

5 Amin has a plank of wood that measures 3.4 m
He cuts it up into 4 equal pieces.
Work out the length of each piece.

6 A bottle of lemonade holds 1.5 litres. A glass will hold 0.3 litres.
How many glasses can be filled from the bottle of lemonade?

10.6 Further estimates

How you round can make a difference to an estimate.

Look at these estimates for the calculation 20×0.51

$20 \times 1 = 20$

> By rounding 0.51 to the nearest whole number (1), the estimate for the calculation is 20

$20 \times 0.5 = 10$

> By rounding 0.51 to the nearest tenth (0.5), the estimate for the calculation is 10

Numbers can be rounded to, for example, the nearest hundredth, tenth, whole number, ten, hundred or thousand.

0.041 rounded to the nearest hundredth or to two decimal places, is 0.04

0.76 rounded to the nearest tenth or one decimal place, is 0.8

1.2 rounded to the nearest whole number is 1

58 rounded to the nearest 10 is 60

328 rounded to the nearest 100 is 300

6574 rounded to the nearest 1000 is 7000

Example 18

a Round 59 to the nearest 10
b Round 0.36 to one decimal place.
c Use your answers to parts **a** and **b** to estimate the value of 59×0.36

Solution 18

a 59 rounds to 60
b 0.36 rounds to 0.4
c $60 \times 4 = 240$ $\boxed{59 \times 0.36 \text{ rounds to } 60 \times 0.4}$
    so $60 \times 0.4 = 24.0$
                $= 24$

Example 19

Work out an estimate for

$$\frac{5.63 \times 0.24}{3.04}$$

Solution 19

5.63 rounds to 6

0.24 rounds to 0.2

3.04 rounds to 3

> Round 5.63 to the nearest whole number.
> Round 0.24 to one decimal place.
> Round 3.04 to the nearest whole number.

$$\frac{5.63 \times 0.24}{3.04} \text{ rounds to } \frac{6 \times 0.2}{3} = \frac{1.2}{3} = 0.4$$

Exercise 10H

1 Work out an estimate for the cost of

    a 28 books at £4.95 each   **b** 190 pencils at £0.39 each

    c 22 pens at £1.68 each   **d** 56 cinema tickets at £6.95 each

    e 34 text books at £8.99 each

2 **a** Round 38.4 to the nearest ten

    b round 0.68 to one decimal place

    c use your answers to **a** and **b** to work out an estimate for 38.4×0.68

3 Work out an estimate for

    a 78.2×0.32 **b** 108×4.6 **c** $78.4 \div 0.19$

    d 3982×0.034 **e** $64.2 \div 0.059$

4 Work out an estimate for $\dfrac{9.27 \times 0.39}{2.01}$

5 Work out an estimate for $\dfrac{78.4}{1.9 \times 4.87}$

6 Work out an estimate for the cost of 43 litres of petrol costing 84.8p per litre.

10.7 Rounding to decimal places

Answers obtained using a calculator often fill the calculator screen and are more accurate than necessary.

When this happens, round the final answer to a number of decimal places.

- You will be told how many decimal places to round to.
- Count that number of places after the decimal point and look at the next figure.
- If the next figure is less than 5 do not change the previous figure.
- If the next figure is 5 or more, increase the previous figure by 1

Example 20

Round
a 3.762 to one decimal place
b 0.06412 to two decimal places
c 56.9178 to three decimal places.

Solution 20

a 3.**76**2 to *one* decimal place
3.762 rounds to 3.**8** to one
decimal place

> The figure in the *first* decimal place is 7
> The figure in the next decimal place is 6
> 6 is bigger than 5 so increase the 7 to 8

b 0.0**64**12 to *two* decimal places
0.06412 rounds to 0.06 to
two decimal places

> The figure in the *second* decimal place is 6
> The figure in the next decimal place is 4 so
> the 6 does not change.

c 56.91**78** to *three* decimal places
56.9178 rounds to 56.91**8** to three
decimal places

> The figure in the *third* decimal place is 7
> The figure in the next decimal place is 8 so
> round the 7 to 8

Exercise 10I

1 Round these numbers to one decimal place
    a 34.63   **b** 7.827   **c** 3.4962   **d** 0.854
    e 0.283   **f** 0.071 32   **g** 0.209   **h** 5.98

2 Round these numbers to two decimal places
    a 73.124   **b** 8.9572   **c** 3.4209   **d** 7.5613
    e 0.9184   **f** 0.0763   **g** 0.9127   **h** 0.0762

3 Round these numbers to three decimal places
    a 6.2463   **b** 0.8762   **c** 0.7347   **d** 0.786 21
    e 0.030 56   **f** 8.6745   **g** 0.056 43   **h** 0.006 271

4 Round these to the number of decimal places given in the brackets
    a 45.56 (1)   **b** 3.2517 (3)   **c** 23.724 (2)   **d** 4.569 (2)
    e 0.035 25 (3)   **f** 5.6592 (3)   **g** 0.426 (1)   **h** 0.234 51 (2)
    i 7.6029 (3)   **j** 8.795 (2)   **k** 50.8342 (3)   **l** 0.000 981 6 (3)

5 Use your calculator to work out the value of the following.
Give each answer correct to one decimal place.
    a $35.4 \div 0.7$ **b** 23.8×1.78

    c $(4.98 + 3.57) \div 1.3$ **d** $\dfrac{6.7}{12.1 - 8.3}$

10.8 Rounding to significant figures

A number rounded to **one significant figure** has only one figure that is not zero.

5937 rounded to one significant figure is 6000
0.006 183 rounded to one significant figure is 0.006

A number rounded to two significant figures is more accurate than a number rounded to one significant figure.

To round 5937 to *two* significant figures look at the *third* figure (3). As this is less than 5, do not change the previous figure (9) and write zeros in the tens column and the units column.

So 5937 rounded to two significant figures is 5900

To round 0.006 183 to *two* significant figures, look at the *third* figure (8) after the zeros at the beginning. As this is more than 5, increase the previous figure (1) by 1. Remember to include the zeros at the beginning in your answer.

So 0.006 183 rounded to two significant figures is 0.006 2

To round whole numbers greater than one to *three* significant figures, look at the *fourth* figure.

To round decimals to *three* significant figures, look at the *fourth* figure *after the zeros* at the beginning.

5937 rounded to three significant figures is 5940
0.006 183 rounded to three significant figures is 0.006 18

Example 21

Round

a 3462 to one significant figure

b 7.38 to two significant figures

c 0.3469 to three significant figures

d 0.0201 to two significant figures

Solution 21

a 3462
3462 rounds to 3000 to one significant figure

> The *second* figure is 4. As this is less than 5, the 3 stays as it is and a zero goes in all the other places.

b 7.38
7.38 rounds to 7.4 to two significant figures

> The *third* figure is 8
> As this is more than 5, increase the 3 by 1

c 0.3469
0.3469 rounds to 0.347 to three significant figures

> The *fourth* figure after the zero at the beginning is 9
> As this is more than 5, increase the 6 by 1

d 0.0201
0.0201 rounds to 0.020 to two significant figures

> The *third* figure after the zeros at the beginning is 1
> As this is less than 5, the zero before the 1 stays as it is.
> The zero at the end is needed as it is the second significant figure.

Example 22

Use your calculator to work out the value of $\dfrac{6.73 + 4.5}{12.03 - 9.73}$

Give your answer correct to two significant figures.

Solution 22

$6.73 + 4.5 = 11.23$ | Use a calculator to work out the value of the numerator. |

$12.03 - 9.73 = 2.3$ | Use a calculator to work out the value of the denominator. |

$11.23 \div 2.3 = 4.882\ 608\ 696...$ | The line in a fraction means divide.
Now use a calculator to work out $11.23 \div 2.3$
Write down all the figures shown on your calculator. |

$4.\mathbf{8}82\ 608\ 696 = 4.9$ correct to two significant figures | To give the answer to two significant figures, look at the third figure (**8**). As this is more than 5, increase the figure before it by 1 |

Exercise 10J

1 Round these numbers to one significant figure

     a 8234   **b** 76 420   **c** 453   **d** 72

     e 0.381   **f** 0.004 56   **g** 0.109   **h** 532.4

2 Round these numbers to two significant figures

     a 4263   **b** 8719   **c** 685   **d** 3.84

     e 798   **f** 0.005 62   **g** 703   **h** 0.4032

3 Round these numbers to three significant figures

     a 8736   **b** 56.24   **c** 27.839   **d** 0.786 21

     e 0.030 56   **f** 87.98   **g** 6 735 412   **h** 907.189

4 Round these to the number of significant figures given in the brackets

     a 6712 (1)   **b** 8614 (3)   **c** 6926 (2)   **d** 82.14 (2)

     e 876.3 (3)   **f** 12.52 (3)   **g** 0.0426 (1)   **h** 0.002 345 1 (2)

     i 7.6024 (3)   **j** 8.795 (2)   **k** 508 342 (3)   **l** 0.000 481 6 (3)

5 Use your calculator to work out the value of the following.
Give each answer correct to three significant figures.

     a $5421 \div 23$ **b** 423×871 **c** 0.0562×0.041

     d $\dfrac{3250 \times 720}{0.32}$ **e** $\dfrac{9.6}{13.21 - 9.1}$ **f** $\dfrac{27.31 - 8.96}{4.56 + 9.8}$

10.9 Problems with decimals

There are many types of problems with decimals – some of these involve money.

Example 23

Ribbon costs 39p per metre.
Lesley bought 6.25 m of ribbon.
Work out the total cost of the ribbon.

Solution 23

39×6.25

= 243.75 pence

| This gives the total cost of the ribbon in pence. |
| Use a calculator to work out the answer. |

243.75 rounds to 244

Total cost = 244p = £2.44

| Round the number of pence to the nearest whole number. |
| Give the answer in pounds. |

Example 24

Mrs. Manners buys

3 packets of biscuits at 63p each	
2 tins of beans at 35p each	
1 box of washing powder at £4.78	
Total	

a Copy and complete the shopping bill.

b Mrs Manners pays with a £10 note.
Work out how much change Mrs Manners should get.

Solution 24

a 3×63
= 189p
= £1.89

| This gives the total cost of the biscuits in pence. |

| Divide by 100 to change pence to pounds. |

2×35
= 70p
= £0.70

| This gives the total cost of the beans in pence. As the answer is a sum of money, there must be two figures after the decimal point to show the 70 pence. |

£4.78

| This is the cost of the washing powder. |

1.89 + 0.70 + 4.78
= £7.37

| This gives the total cost in pounds. |

3 packets of biscuits at 63p each	£1.89
2 tins of beans at 35p each	£0.70
1 box of washing powder at £4.78	£4.78
Total	£7.37

b 10 − 7.37 = 2.63

| This gives the change in pounds from £10 |

She should get £2.63 change.

Exercise 10K

1 Petrol costs 89.4p a litre. Jim bought 36 litres of petrol.
Work out the total cost of the petrol.

2 Jeremy buys four pens at 58p each, two pads of paper at 95p each and one book at £3.95
He pays with a £10 note.
Work out how much change Jeremy should get from £10

3 Anita buys a packet of biscuits at 78p, a packet of crisps at 35p, three bottles of water
at 43p each and a ready meal at £4.56. She pays with a £20 note.
Work out how much change she should get.

4 Mr. Shah hires a sander. The cost of hiring the sander is £5.60 for the first hour then
£3.50 for each extra hour.
Work out how much it will cost Mr. Shah to hire the sander for 7 hours.

5

Adults	£12.60
Children	half price

The price of entry to a zoo is £12.60 for each adult. Children's tickets are half the
adult price. A family of two adults and three children go to the zoo.
Work out the total cost of their tickets.

6 Andrew works for 37 hours in one week. He is paid £6.40 per hour.
Work out Andrew's pay for the week.

7 Julie works for 12 hours. She is paid £9.60 per hour for the first 8 hours.
For the remaining hours she is paid £14.40 per hour.
Work out the total amount Julie is paid.

8 Mr. Jones is buying a television. He can buy the television in cash for £420 or by using
a credit plan. For the credit plan he has to pay six monthly payments of £73.40
Work out the difference between using the credit plan and paying cash.

9 Amanda has £10 to buy some stamps. Each stamp costs 29p.
Work out the greatest number of stamps that Amanda can buy.

10 Tom has a mobile phone. Each month he pays 14.2p for each minute he uses his
mobile phone plus a monthly charge of £14.65.
In April, Tom uses his mobile phone for 326 minutes.
Work out the total amount that Tom pays.

Chapter summary

You should now be able to:

★ **Round** a decimal number to the nearest whole number.

★ Use non-calculator methods to:
- add decimals
- subtract decimals
- multiply decimals
- divide a decimal by a whole number
- divide a decimal by another decimal
- work out an estimate to problems involving decimals by rounding, for example to the nearest tenth (1 decimal place)
- round to a given number of **decimal places**
- round to a given number of **significant figures**.

★ Use a calculator to solve problems involving decimals.

Chapter 10 review questions

1 Round the following to the nearest whole number

    a 7.8   **b** 3.5   **c** 16.2   **d** 5.432   **e** 79.942

2 Round the following to the number of significant figures given in the brackets

    a 3546 (1)   **b** 3546 (2)   **c** 0.005 62 (1)

    d 23.76 (2)   **e** 2.4387 (3)   **f** 696 213 (2)

3 Round 17.49 to the nearest integer.   (1388 March 2002)

4 Work out

    a $5 + 3.6 + 8.21$ **b** $26.574 + 8.79$

    c $29.54 - 6.79$ **d** $34.7 - 8.92$

5 Work out

    a 5.6×10 **b** $76.2 \div 100$ **c** $9 \div 100$

    d 0.0062×100 **e** 0.87×1000

6 Work out

    a 8.1×2 **b** 3.45×5 **c** 0.2×0.3

    d 0.4×0.08 **e** 6.1×4.2 **f** 0.32×5.6

7 Work out

    a $6.25 \div 5$ **b** $75.6 \div 3$ **c** $47.7 \div 9$

    d $56 \div 0.2$ **e** $46.2 \div 0.03$ **f** $0.84 \div 0.004$

8 Work out an estimate for the cost of

    a   six books at £6.99 each   **b**   five plants at £3.87 each

    c   18 meals at £3.15 each   **d**   182 calculators at £4.85 each

9 Work out an estimate for

    a 9.8×3.2 **b** $28.3 \div 10.4$ **c** $\dfrac{62.1 + 39.52}{1.87}$ **d** $\dfrac{5.6 + 6.34}{2.69}$

10 Carla buys the following items from a post office.

          five envelopes at 30p each
          one pen at £1.40

    She pays with a £5 note.

    Work out how much change Carla should receive from the £5

11 **a**   Estimate the value of 198×3.1

    Books are sold for £3.95 each.

    b   Estimate the number of these books that can be bought for £20

12 **a**   Round 67 to the nearest 10

    b   Write down an estimate for the value of 67×4.2 (1388 Jan 2002)

13 **a**   0.3   0.06   0.058   0.26

        Write these four decimals in order of size.
        Start with the smallest decimal.

    b   Write 0.3 as a fraction.

    c   Work out $0.3 - 0.26$

    d   Work out 0.058×100 (1388 Jan 2002)

14 **a**   Work out 41.3×100

    b   Work out 0.4×0.6

    c   Work out $5.2 - 1.37$ (1388 March 2003)

15 Henry bought

          two pencils at 28p each,
          four pads of paper at £1.20 each and
          one magazine at £2.95 each.

    He paid with a £10 note.
    How much change should Henry get from £10?   (1385 June 2000)

16 Work out an estimate for the value of $\dfrac{296}{1.84 \times 0.32}$

17 Work out an estimate for $\dfrac{39.0201}{0.2107}$ (1385 Nov 2002)

18 **a**   Work out $\dfrac{11}{12} - \dfrac{5}{6}$

    b   Estimate the value of $\dfrac{68 \times 401}{198}$ (1387 June 2004)

19 Use your calculator to work out

a $(2.8 + 1.5) \times 0.72$

b $\dfrac{5.6 \times 2.7}{0.3}$

c $\dfrac{8.4}{12.1 - 7.3}$

d $\dfrac{29.4 - 15.24}{0.19 + 0.21}$

20 Work out the value of the following. Give each answer correct to two significant figures.

a $\dfrac{6.7 + 3.8}{8.3 - 1.9}$

b $(19.32 - 6.8) \times 1.2$

c $5.6 \div 0.08 - 5.4 \times 2.1$

21 Fred buys his lunch.
He buys

      a can of drink costing 60 pence

      a sandwich costing £1.19

      a packet of crisps costing 41p

He pays with a £10 note.

Work out how much change he should get from the £10

22 Crisps cost 34p per packet.
A bottle of orange juice costs £1.28

Michelle buys three packets of crisps and one bottle of orange juice.
She pays with a £5 note.
Work out how much change she should get. (1388 Jan 2002)

23 Petrol costs 89.3p per litre. Mr. Peters buys 32.7 litres of petrol. Work out the total cost of the petrol. Give your answer in pounds.

24 A badge costs 78p.
Sam has £5.
He buys as many badges as he can.
Work out the amount of change Sam should get from £5.
Give your answer in pence. (1388 March 2003)

Algebra 1

11.1 Using letters to represent numbers

Algebra is a part of mathematics that uses letters in place of numbers.

Some students are going to have their photograph taken.

The number of students cannot be counted because the photographer is in the way.

A letter can be used in place of the number of students. We will use the letter n.

There are n students in the row.

Example 1

There are n students in the row.
Two more students join the row.

How many students are now in the row?

Solution 1
Since two more students are added to the row there are now

$n + 2$ students.

Example 2

There are n students in the row.
One student is taken away from the row.

How many students are now in the row?

Solution 2
Since one student is taken away from the row there are now

$n - 1$ students.

A second row of n students is added.
There are now two rows of students.

The total number of students is $n + n$.
This can also be written as $2 \times n$ or as $n \times 2$
The simplest way to write this is $2n$.

Example 3

There are now four rows. Each row has n students.

What is the total number of students?

Solution 3
Since there are now four rows, the total number of
students is $n + n + n + n$.
This can be written as $4 \times n$, which is the same as $4n$ students.

Example 4

There are three rows here. Each row has n students.
Five students are added.

What is the total number of students?

Solution 4
The number of students in the three rows is $3n$.
Since five more students are now added, the total
number of students is $3n + 5$ students.

Example 5

Sam buys six apples. Each apple costs x pence.
Find, in terms of x, the total cost of the six apples.

Solution 5
Since there are six apples, each one costing x pence,
the total cost

$$= x + x + x + x + x + x$$
$$= 6 \times x$$
$$= 6x \text{ pence.}$$

Exercise 11A

1   Write these in the simplest way

    a $2 \times n$ **b** $x \times 3$ **c** $y + y$

    d $p + p + p$ **e** $a + a + a + a + a + a$

2   There are n people in the back row of a cinema. Three more people join the back row.
How many people are now in the back row?

3   There are n people on a bus. Five more people get on the bus.
How many people are now on the bus?

4   There are n people on a bus. Two people get off the bus.
How many people are now on the bus?

5   There are six coaches. Each coach has n passengers.
What is the total number of passengers?

6   Stuart buys 12 red roses. Each red rose costs r pence.
Find, in terms of r, the total cost of the 12 red roses.

7   Georgina buys three bags of sweets.
Each bag contains q sweets.

    a Write down the total number of sweets in the three bags.

    The shopkeeper puts two more sweets into one of the bags.

    b Find, in terms of q, the total number of sweets that Georgina now has.

8   Jessica has five CD cases.
Each CD case contains y CDs.
Jessica also has three CDs not in cases.
Find, in terms of y, the total number of CDs that Jessica has.

9   The students in a class line up in two rows.
In each row there are x students.
One student is taken away from one of the rows.
Find, in terms of x, the number of students left.

10   Mrs. Edwards buys five packs of crayons.
There are c crayons in each pack.
After using them with her class, Mrs. Edwards finds that one pack has two crayons missing.
Find, in terms of c, the total number of crayons that are now in the packs.

11.2 Expressions and terms

$3n + 5$ is called an **algebraic expression.**
An algebraic expression must contain at least one letter.
Each part of an expression is called a **term** of the expression.
For the expression $3n + 5$ the terms are $3n$ and $+5$
An expression can contain more than one letter.

Example 6

Write down the four terms of the expression $3x - y + 2z - 6$

Solution 6

The four terms are $3x$ and $-y$ and $+2z$ and -6

Example 7

A box of chocolates contains p plain chocolates and q milk chocolates only.
Write down an expression, in terms of p and q, for the total number of chocolates in the box.

Solution 7

The total number of chocolates in the box is $p + q$

Example 8

There are b large nails in each box and c small nails in each packet.
Bob buys three boxes of large nails.

a   Write down an expression, in terms of b, for the total number of large nails Bob buys.

Bob also buys two packets of small nails.
He uses seven large nails and five small nails.

b   Write down an expression, in terms of b and c, for the total number of nails left.

Solution 8

a   In the three boxes the total number of large nails is $3b$

b   In the two packets there is a total of $2c$ nails.

   Bob buys a total of $3b + 2c$ nails.
   He uses a total of $7 + 5 = 12$ nails.
   The total number of nails left is $3b + 2c - 12$

The value of an expression can be worked out if the value of each letter is known.

Example 9

Work out the value of the expression $3n + 5$ when $n = 10$

Solution 9

$3n + 5 = 3 \times n + 5$

When $n = 10$, $3n + 5 = 3 \times 10 + 5$
$$= 30 + 5$$
$$= 35$$

Exercise 11B

1 A class has x boys and y girls.
Write down an expression, in terms of x and y, for the total number of students in the class.

2 Bill runs x metres and Jane runs y metres. Bill runs further than Jane.
Write down an expression, in terms of x and y, for the number of metres Bill has run further than Jane.

3 Jo buys b fruit cakes. She then eats c of them.
Write down an expression, in terms of b and c, for the total number of fruit cakes Jo has left.

4 Marbles are sold in packets and boxes. There are p marbles in each packet and q marbles in each box. Tim buys four packets and three boxes.

  a Write down an expression, in terms of p and q, for the total number of marbles Tim buys.

  b Tim then gives 10 marbles to each of his two sisters. Write down an expression, in terms of p and q, for the total number of marbles Tim has left.

5 Each bicycle needs two wheels. Each tricycle needs three wheels. Each car needs five wheels.

  a What is the total number of wheels needed to make
    i four bicycles,
    ii four bicycles and two tricycles
    iii four bicycles and two tricycles and three cars?

  b Write down an expression for the total number of wheels needed to make
    i m bicycles, two tricycles and three cars
    ii m bicycles, n tricycles and three cars
    iii four bicycles, n tricycles and p cars
    iv m bicycles, two tricycles and p cars
    v m bicycles, n tricycles and p cars.

6 Work out the value of each of these expressions when $x = 2$

  a $2x$ **b** $x + 3$ **c** $x - 1$

  d $2x + 3$ **e** $4x - 1$ **f** $2x - 2$

7 Work out the value of each of these expressions, when $x = 5$ and $y = 4$

  a $x + y$ **b** $y + x$ **c** $x + y + 3$

  d $x - y$ **e** $y - x$ **f** $2x + y$

  g $2x + 2y + 6$ **h** $2x - 3y + 2$

8 Work out the value of each of these expressions, when $x = 10$, $y = 4$ and $z = 3$

  a $x + y + z$ **b** $x + y - z$ **c** $x - y - z$

  d $x - 2y - 3z$ **e** $2x - 2y - 2z$ **f** $2x - 3y - 3z - 1$

11.3 Collecting like terms

In the expression $3x + 2x + 6$, the terms $3x$ and $+2x$ are called **like terms**.
Like terms are terms which use the same letter.

Since $3x$ is $x + x + x$ and $2x$ is $x + x$, the like terms $3x$ and $+2x$ can be combined to become $x + x + x + x + x$, which is written as $5x$.

A shorter method is to work out $3 + 2 = 5$ to find the number in front of the x.
So the expression $3x + 2x + 6$ can be simplified to $5x + 6$
$5x$ and $+6$ are not like terms so $5x$ and $+6$ cannot be combined.

Example 10

Simplify the expression $2p + 4q + 5p$

Solution 10
Since $2p$ and $+5p$ are like terms they can be combined.
$2p + 5p = 7p$
So $2p + 5p + 4q = 7p + 4q$
($7p$ and $+4q$ are not like terms so cannot be combined)

Example 11

Simplify the expression $4x - 3x + 2$

Solution 11
Since $4x$ and $-3x$ are like terms they can be combined.
$4x - 3x = 1x$ since $4 - 3 = 1$
A simpler way to write $1x$ is just to write x
So $4x - 3x + 2 = x + 2$

Example 12

Simplify $3x + 2y - 3y + 5x$

Solution 12
Collect like terms together to write
$3x + 2y - 3y + 5x = 3x + 5x + 2y - 3y$
$3x + 5x = 8x$

and

$+2y - 3y = -1y = -y$

so

$3x + 2y - 3y + 5x = 8x - y$

Exercise 11C

1 Simplify these expressions by collecting like terms.

   a $3x + x$ **b** $y + 2y$ **c** $5p - p$

2 Simplify these expressions by collecting like terms.

   a $2a + 4a$ **b** $5b + 2b$

   c $c + 3c$ **d** $7d + d$

   e $6m - 4m$ **f** $3y - 4y$

3 Write down which two of these four expressions **cannot** be simplified.

   a $p + p + q$ **b** $2p + q$

   c $p + 2q$ **d** $p + q + q$

4 Write down which of these four expressions **cannot** be simplified.

   a $2x + 3x - 4$ **b** $3x + 4y - 2x$

   c $4x - 3 + 2y$ **d** $2x + 4y - 3$

5 Simplify these expressions by collecting like terms.

   a $2p + 3p + 5 - 1$ **b** $3 + 7b + 2 + 2b$

   c $2c + 1 + 4c - 2$ **d** $3d - 6 + 7d + 3$

   e $4 - 2m + 4m + 1$ **f** $3y - 2y + 3 - y + 5$

6 Simplify

   a $3x + x + 4y + 2y$ **b** $6x - x + 5y - 2y$

   c $4x + 5x - 3x + 2y$ **d** $x + 2x + 5x - 4x + 7y - 2y$

   e $5x + 3y - y + 2x$ **f** $x + 6y + 4x - 2y - 3x$

   g $4p + 2q - 3p - 3q$ **h** $8m - n - n + 2m$

   i $2w + v - 3w + 4v + 2w$ **j** $3c + 2d - 5d + c + 4d - 2c$

   k $5e + 3f - 2 + 5f - e + 1$ **l** $4s - 3t - 7s + 2t$

11.4 Multiplying with numbers and letters

also assessed in Module 4

The simplest way to write $4 \times n$ is $4n$.

In the same way the simplest way to write $a \times b$ is ab, leaving out the multiplication sign as before.

So mn is the same as $m \times n$.

The simplest way to write $a \times a$ is a^2.

a^2 is read as 'a squared'.

Do not write $a \times a$ as aa.

The simplest way to write $a \times b \times c$ is abc.

The simplest way to write $a \times a \times a$ is a^3.

a^3 is read as 'a cubed'.

Example 13

Multiply $4x$ by 2

Solution 13

$$4x \times 2 = 4 \times x \times 2$$
$$= 4 \times 2 \times x$$
$$= 8 \times x$$
$$4x \times 2 = 8x$$

Example 14

Multiply $3x$ by $4y$.

Solution 14

$$3x \times 4y = 3 \times x \times 4 \times y$$
$$= 3 \times 4 \times x \times y$$
$$= 12 \times xy$$
$$3x \times 4y = 12xy$$

Example 15

Simplify $5x \times y \times 4z$.

Solution 15

$$5x \times y \times 4z = 5 \times x \times y \times 4 \times z$$
$$= 5 \times 4 \times x \times y \times z$$
$$= 20 \times xyz$$
$$5x \times y \times 4z = 20xyz$$

Example 16

Simplify $3p \times 2p \times 4p$.

Solution 16

$$3p \times 2p \times 4p = 3 \times p \times 2 \times p \times 4 \times p$$
$$= 3 \times 2 \times 4 \times p \times p \times p$$
$$3p \times 2p \times 4p = 24p^3$$

Example 17

Work out the value of the expression $3b^3$ when $b = 2$.

Solution 17

$$3b^3 = 3 \times b \times b \times b$$
$$= 3 \times 2 \times 2 \times 2$$
$$= 3 \times 8$$
$$= 24$$

Example 18

Work out the value of the expression xy^2 when $x = 5, y = 3$

Solution 18

$$xy^2 = x \times y^2$$
$$= x \times y \times y$$
$$= 5 \times 3 \times 3$$
$$= 5 \times 9$$
$$= 45$$

Exercise 11D

1 Write these expressions in the simplest way.

   a $r \times s$ **b** $x \times y \times z$ **c** $m \times m$

   d $12 \times s \times t \times u$ **e** $6x \times y \times z$ **f** $a \times 24 \times b \times c$

   g $w \times w \times w$ **h** $3 \times x \times x$ **i** $a \times 4 \times a \times a$

2 Simplify

   a $3 \times 2b$ **b** $3x \times 2$ **c** $5p \times x$ **d** $x \times 4q$

   e $3a \times 5b$ **f** $6y \times 4x$ **g** $3 \times 2p \times 2q$ **h** $4m \times 2p \times 2$

   i $2a \times 3a$ **j** $3c \times 2d \times 5e$ **k** $2a \times 3b \times 4c$ **l** $5a \times a \times 4a$

   m $2a \times 4b \times 3a$ **n** $2ef \times 3e$

3 Work out the value of each of these expressions when $x = 10$

    a x^2 **b** x^3 **c** $2x^2$

4 Work out the value of each of these expressions when $a = 2, b = 3$ and $c = 1$

    a abc **b** $4ab + c$ **c** $5bc - ac$

5 Work out the value of each of these expressions when $p = 2, q = 3$ and $r = 5$

    a pq^2 **b** $4rp^2 - 10q^2$ **c** $p^3 - q^3$

11.5 Multiplying out brackets

There are three rows. Each row has n students.

The number of students is $3 \times n = 3n$
Two students are added to each of the three
rows, so $3 \times 2 = 6$ students are added.
There are now $n + 2$ students in each row.

$$n + 2$$
$$n + 2$$
$$\underline{n + 2}$$
$$3(n + 2)$$

Total number of students $= 3(n + 2) = 3 \times n + 3 \times 2 = 3n + 6$

The simplest way of writing this is $3(n + 2) = 3n + 6$
Writing $3(n + 2)$ as $3n + 6$ is called multiplying out brackets.

Example 19

Multiply out $5(n + 1)$.

Solution 19
$$\begin{aligned} 5(n + 1) &= 5 \times (n + 1) \\ &= 5 \times n + 5 \times 1 \\ &= 5n + 5 \end{aligned}$$

Example 20

Multiply out $5(2x + 3)$.

Solution 20
$$\begin{aligned} 5(2x + 3) &= 5 \times 2x + 5 \times 3 \\ &= 10x + 15 \end{aligned}$$

Example 21

Multiply out $4(2a - 5b + 1)$.

Solution 21
$$\begin{aligned} 4(2a - 5b + 1) &= 4 \times 2a + 4 \times -5b + 4 \times 1 \\ &= 8a - 20b + 4 \end{aligned}$$

positive times negative is negative

Example 22

Simplify $3(2a + 3) + 2(a - 2)$.

Solution 22
$$\begin{aligned} 3(2a + 3) + 2(a - 2) &= 3 \times 2a + 3 \times 3 + 2 \times a + 2 \times -2 \\ &= 6a + 9 + 2a - 4 \\ &= 8a + 5 \end{aligned}$$

Example 23

Simplify $2(2x + y) + 5(3x - 2y)$.

Solution 23

$$2(2x + y) + 5(3x - 2y) = 2 \times 2x + 2 \times y + 5 \times 3x + 5 \times -2y$$
$$= 4x + 2y + 15x - 10y$$
$$= 4x + 15x + 2y - 10y$$
$$= 19x - 8y$$

Exercise 11E

1 Multiply out
  a $2(n + 1)$ b $3(a + 2)$ c $4(p + 3)$ d $2(2 + n)$
  e $2(n - 1)$ f $3(a - 4)$ g $4(p - 2)$ h $2(3 - n)$

2 Multiply out
  a $5(c + d)$ b $3(m + n)$ c $2(c - d)$ d $4(m - n)$

3 Multiply out
  a $2(2x + 3y)$ b $3(3a - 1)$ c $5(3g - 4)$
  d $3(3x + 4y)$ e $4(2a - b)$ f $2(3g - 4h)$
  g $7(x + 2y + 3)$ h $2(a + 4b - 1)$ i $3(2p - 2q - 1)$

4 Simplify
  a $2(p + 1) + 5$ b $2(q + 1) + 3q$ c $2(r + 4) - 5$
  d $2(t + 3) - t$ e $3(a + 1) + 1(a + 2)$ f $2(n + 1) + 3(n + 2)$
  g $2(m + 1) + 3(2m + 1)$ h $2(2c + 1) + 3(3c + 2)$ i $2(m + 3) + 3(2m - 1)$
  j $2(c + 5) + 5(3c - 2)$ k $2(3d + 4) + 3(1 - 2d)$ l $3(m + 3n) + 3(2m - n)$
  m $2(2c + d) + 5(c - 2d)$ n $2(2p - 3q) + 2(2p - q)$

11.6 Factorising

Factorising is the opposite operation to multiplying out brackets.
The factors of 4 are 1, 2 and 4
The factors of 6 are 1, 2, 3 and 6
The **common factors** of 4 and 6 are 1 and 2
The **highest common factor** of 4 and 6 is 2

Example 24

Factorise $4c + 6s$.

Solution 24

The highest common factor of 4 and 6 is **2**
$$4c + 6s = 2 \times 2c + 2 \times 3s$$
$$= 2(2c + 3s)$$

Example 25

Factorise $8c - 12s$.

Solution 25

The highest common factor of 8 and 12 is **4**
$$8c - 12s = 4 \times 2c - 4 \times 3s$$
$$= 4(2c - 3s)$$

Example 26

Factorise $6b + 9$

Solution 26

The highest common factor of 6 and 9 is **3**

$6b + 9 = \mathbf{3} \times 2b + \mathbf{3} \times 3$

$\qquad = \mathbf{3}(2b + 3)$

Example 27

Factorise $6a - 12b + 3$

Solution 27

The highest common factor of 6 and 12 and 3 is **3**

$6a - 12b + 3 = \mathbf{3} \times 2a - \mathbf{3} \times 4b + \mathbf{3} \times 1$

$\qquad\qquad = \mathbf{3}(2a - 4b + 1)$

Exercise 11F

1 Copy and complete the following.

  a $4x + 4 = 4 \times x + 4 \times 1 = 4(\ldots + \ldots)$

  b $2a + 4 = 2 \times a + 2 \times 2 = 2(\ldots + \ldots)$

  c $3a + 3b = 3 \times a + 3 \times b = 3(\ldots + \ldots)$

  d $12p + 4q = 4 \times 3p + 4 \times q = 4(\ldots + \ldots)$

  e $10x - 6y = 2 \times 5x - 2 \times 3y = 2(\ldots - \ldots)$

  f $12p + 18q = 6 \times 2p + 6 \times 3q = 6(\ldots + \ldots)$

  g $3r + 6s + 9t = 3 \times r + 3 \times 2s + 3 \times 3t = 3(\ldots + \ldots + \ldots)$

  h $4x + 6y - 8z = 2 \times 2x + 2 \times 3y - 2 \times 4z = 2(\ldots + \ldots - \ldots)$

2 Factorise

  a $2x + 2$ **b** $3y + 6$ **c** $5p - 10$ **d** $3d + 6e$

  e $6x + 2y$ **f** $3a - 12b$ **g** $12p - 6q$ **h** $4d + 6e$

  i $10c - 6d$ **j** $8x + 12y$ **k** $10m - 15n + 5$ **l** $8p - 6q + 4$

  m $9d - 6e - 12f$

Chapter summary

You should now know that:

★ An **algebraic expression** must contain at least one letter. For example, $3n + 5$, $6 - x$, $8p$, y, $4(k - 3)$ and $3ab + c$ are all algebraic expressions.

★ The $3n$ and the $+5$ are called **terms** of the expression $3n + 5$

★ To **collect like terms**, for example, $2a + 3b + a - 4b$, combine the terms which contain the same letter to give $3a - b$.

★ To simplify expressions which have a multiplication sign, remove the multiplication sign, for example, $4 \times a = 4a$, $a \times b = ab$, $a \times b \times c = abc$. When the same letter is multiplied, use indices, for example, $a \times a = a^2$, $a \times a \times a = a^3$

★ To find the value of an expression, replace each letter by its given value and work out the result.

★ To **multiply out brackets**, multiply each term inside the bracket by the number outside the bracket. For example, $3(n + 2) = 3n + 6$

★ **Factorising** is the opposite process to multiplying out brackets. Factorise by using the common factor, for example, $4c + 6cs = 2c(2 + 3s)$.

Chapter 11 review questions

1 Eggs are sold in boxes. There are six eggs in each box. Mrs. Smith buys p boxes of eggs.
  a Write down an expression, in terms of p, for the number of eggs that Mrs. Smith buys.
  She uses five of these eggs.
  b Write down an expression, in terms of p, for the number of eggs left.

2 Yasmin buys some flowers. She buys ten daffodils at r pence each.
  a Write down an expression, in terms of r, for the cost of the ten daffodils.
  She also buys seven tulips at t pence each.
  b Write down an expression, in terms of r and t, for the total cost of the ten
    daffodils and seven tulips.

3 Simplify
  a $m + m + m + m + m$ **b** $n \times n$ **c** $4x + 3x$
  d $a^2 + a^2 + a^2$ **e** $2p \times 7q$

4 Work out the value of the expression $2y + 7z$ when $y = 1$ and $z = 10$

5 Simplify
  a $5x + y + 4x + 3y$ **b** $6a - b - 2a - 2b$

6 **a** Multiply out $4(3x + 2)$ **b** Simplify $2(3x + 1) + 3(x - 2)$

7 Factorise
  a $2r + 6$ **b** $4s - 10t$

8 **a** Simplify $3r \times 2p$ **b** Simplify $7x - 3 + 4x - 5$

9 Simplify
  a $3(a + 2) - 5$ **b** $4(b - 3) - 3b$ **c** $2(3c + d) + 3(c + d)$

10 A bicycle has two wheels.
   A tricycle has three wheels.
   In a shop there are p bicycles and q tricycles.
   Write down an expression, in terms of p and q, for the total number of wheels on the
   bicycles and the tricycles in the shop.

11 Factorise
   a $6a - 12b + 30$ **b** $8x + 12y - 16z$

12 **a** Simplify $x^2 + 2x^2 + 3x^2$.
   b Work out the value of these expressions when $x = 2$
     i x^2 **ii** $x^2 + 2x^2 + 3x^2$

13 Simplify
   a $5(2n + 3m) + 3(n - 4m)$ **b** $4(2n + 2m + 1) + 3(2n - 4p - 3)$

14 Work out the value of the expression mn^2 when $m = 2, n = 3$

15 $P = a + bc$
   Work out the value of P when $a = -5, b = 6$ and $c = 2$

Perimeter and area of 2-D shapes

12

CHAPTER

12.1 Perimeter

Here is a diagram of a garden.
How much fencing is needed to go around the edge of the garden?

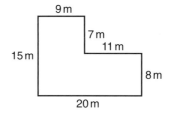

The distance around the edge is the sum of the lengths of all the edges.

Distance around the edge $= 15\,m + 9\,m + 7\,m + 11\,m + 8\,m + 20\,m$
$= 15\,m + 9\,m + 7\,m + 11\,m + 8\,m + 20\,m$

This distance is called the **perimeter** of the shape.

The perimeter of a two-dimensional shape is the total distance around the edge or boundary of the shape.

As perimeter is a distance, the units of perimeter are the units of length. So perimeters can be measured in millimetres (mm), centimetres (cm), metres (m) or kilometres (km) for example.

Example 1

Work out the perimeter of this rectangle.

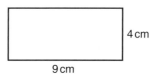

Solution 1
Perimeter $= 9 + 4 + 9 + 4$
So perimeter $= 26\,cm$

| Add the four lengths to find the perimeter. |

Example 2

The diagram shows a shaded shape on a centimetre grid.

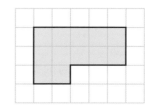

Work out the perimeter of the shape.

Solution 2

Write the lengths of each of the six sides
on the diagram.

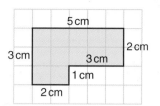

Perimeter = 3 + 5 + 2 + 3 + 1 + 2
= 16 cm

Example 3

Work out the perimeter of this shape.
All the corners are right angles.

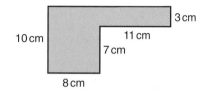

Solution 3

Missing length = 8 cm + 11 cm
= 19 cm

> The length of one of the six sides is not given in the diagram.
> Work out the length of this side first

Perimeter = 19 + 3 + 11 + 7 + 8 + 10
= 58 cm

Example 4

Here is a regular octagon.
Each side of the octagon has a length of 5 cm.
Work out the perimeter of the octagon.

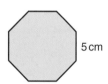

Solution 4

Perimeter = 8 × 5
= 40 cm

> A regular octagon has 8 equal sides.

Exercise 12A

1   The diagram shows four coloured shapes,
    A, *B*, *C* and *D*, drawn on a centimetre grid.
    Work out the perimeter of each shape.

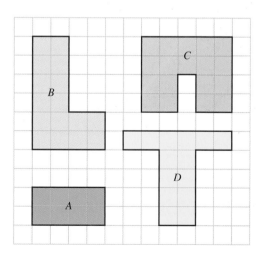

2 Work out the perimeters of these rectangles.

a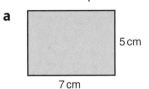
5 cm
7 cm

b
9 m
4 m

c
6 cm
12 cm

3 Work out the perimeter of this triangle.
8 cm   7 cm
11 cm

4 Work out the perimeters of these shapes. All the corners are right angles.

a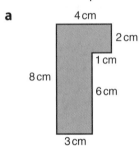
4 cm
2 cm
1 cm
8 cm
6 cm
3 cm

b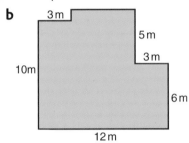
3 m
5 m
3 m
10 m
6 m
12 m

c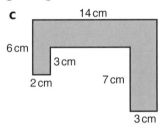
14 cm
6 cm
3 cm
2 cm
7 cm
3 cm

5 Work out the perimeter of this shape.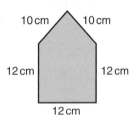
10 cm   10 cm
12 cm   12 cm
12 cm

6 A square has sides of length 6 cm.
Work out the perimeter of the square.

7 An equilateral triangle has a perimeter of 24 cm.
Work out the length of each side of the triangle.

8 The diagram shows a rectangle.
The length of the rectangle is 9 cm.
The perimeter of the rectangle is 28 cm.
Work out the width of the rectangle.

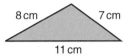
9 cm
9 cm

 9 Work out the perimeters of these rectangles.

a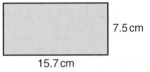
7.5 cm
15.7 cm

b
19.7 mm
9.8 mm

10 The diagram shows a trapezium.
Work out the perimeter of the
trapezium.

11 Work out the perimeter of this shape.

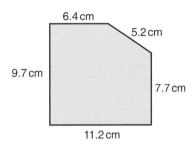

12 An isosceles triangle has two sides of length 15.7 cm and one side of length 11.4 cm.
Work out the perimeter of this triangle.

13 Here is a regular hexagon.
Each side of the hexagon has a length of 8.6 cm.
Work out the perimeter of the hexagon.

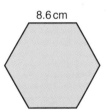

14 Here is a regular octagon.
The perimeter of the octagon is 56 cm.
Work out the length of each side of the octagon.

15

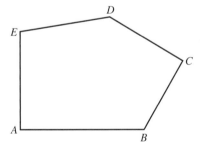

ABCDE is a pentagon. Measure as accurately as possible the length of each side of
the pentagon. Work out the perimeter of the pentagon *ABCDE*.

12.2 Area

Here is a square with sides of length 1 cm.
It is called a centimetre square.

The **area** of a two-dimensional shape is a measure of
the amount of space inside the shape.
The area of a centimetre square is 1 square centimetre. This is written as 1 cm².
The area of a square with sides of length 1 m (a metre square) is 1 square metre or 1 m².

Shape A is drawn on a centimetre grid.
Shape A is a rectangle.

The area of the rectangle is the number of centimetre squares inside the rectangle.
This is 15

So the area of rectangle A is 15 cm².

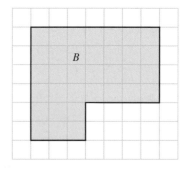

Example 5

Shape B is shown on a centimetre grid.
Find the area of shape B and give the units of your answer.

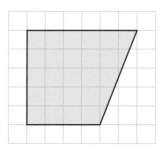

Solution 5

Number of squares = 34
Area of shape = 34 cm²

| Count the number of squares inside the shape. |
| Each square is a centimetre square, with an area of 1 cm². |

Example 6

Find an estimate for the area of the shape shown on a centimetre grid.

Solution 6

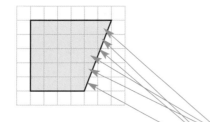

Number of whole squares = 22
Total of part squares = 3 squares
The area of the shape is about
(22 + 3) cm² that is, about 25 cm²

The shape does not fit exactly into whole squares. This is why the question asks for an *estimate*.

Each part of a square which is a half a square or more is counted as a whole square.

Each part of a square which is less than half a square is ignored.

Each of these is counted as 1 square.

Each of these is ignored.

The part squares are counted as 3 squares in total.

Example 7

The diagram shows a shaded shape
drawn on a centimetre grid.
Find an estimate for the area of the shape.

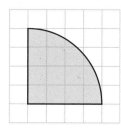

Solution 7

	This shape has a curved edge.
Number of whole squares = 8	Count the number of whole squares.
Number of part squares counted = 5	Count the number of part squares which are a half square or more.
The area is about (8 + 5) = 13 cm²	Ignore the part squares that are less than a half square.

Exercise 12B

1 Find the area of this shape shown on a centimetre grid.
Give the units of your answer.

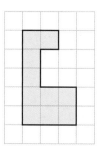

2 The diagram shows four shapes, *A*, *B*, *C* and *D* drawn on a centimetre grid.
Find the area of each shape.

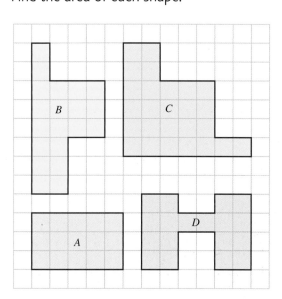

3 The diagram shows three shapes, A, B, and C drawn on a centimetre grid. Find an estimate for the area of each shape.

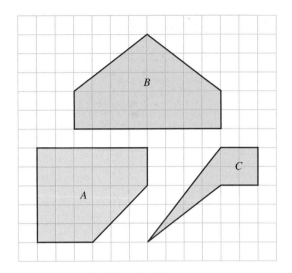

4 A shape is shown on a centimetre grid. Find an estimate for the area of the shape.

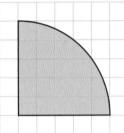

5 A shape is shown on a centimetre grid. Find an estimate for the area of the shape.

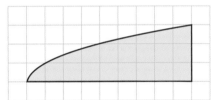

6 Find an estimate for the area of this shape drawn on a centimetre grid.

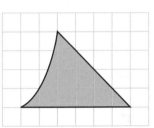

7 Find an estimate for the area of this circle drawn on a centimetre grid.

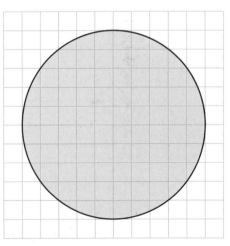

12.3 Areas of rectangles, squares, triangles and parallelograms

Rectangles and squares

The length of this rectangle is 4 cm and its width is 3 cm.
The rectangle is divided up into centimetre squares.
There are 12 centimetre squares inside the rectangle,
so the area of the rectangle is 12 cm²
The number of squares inside the rectangle is $4 \times 3 = 12$

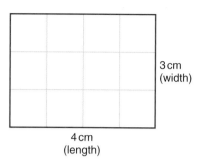

3 cm
(width)

4 cm
(length)

So to find the area of a rectangle,
multiply its length by its width.

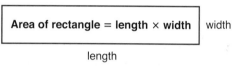

| **Area of rectangle = length × width** | width |

length

For a square, the width is equal to the length.
So the area of a square = length × length.

**Area of square =
length × length**

length

length

Triangles

The diagram shows a triangle *ABC*.
A rectangle has been drawn around the triangle.
The inside of the rectangle has been split into
four triangles.

Triangles 1 and 2 are congruent, so area of triangle 1 = area of triangle 2
Also, area of triangle 3 = area of triangle 4
This means that the area of triangle *ABC* is half the area of the rectangle.

The length of the rectangle is the base of the triangle
and the width of the rectangle is the height of the
triangle.

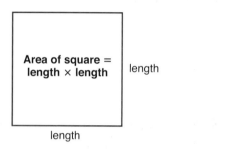

height *h*

base *b*

Area of the rectangle = base × height

So, to find the area of a triangle, work out a half
of its base × its height.

The 'height' of the triangle is the
vertical or *perpendicular* height.

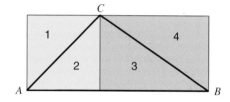

height *h*

**Area of triangle =
$\frac{1}{2}$ × base × height**

base *b*

Parallelograms

Here are two congruent triangles.

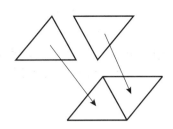

The triangles can be put together to form a parallelogram.

Congruent triangles have equal areas, so the area of the parallelogram is twice the area of one of the triangles.

The area of one triangle is $\frac{1}{2} \times$ base $\times$ height. So the area of two congruent triangles is ($\frac{1}{2} \times$ base $\times$ height) + ($\frac{1}{2} \times$ base $\times$ height) = base $\times$ height.

To find the area of a parallelogram, multiply its base by its height.

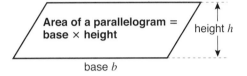

Area of a parallelogram = base × height
height h
base b

Example 8

Work out the area of **a** the rectangle, **b** the square.

a

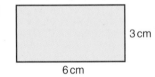

3 cm

6 cm

b

4.6 m

4.6 m

Solution 8

a Area = 6 × 3
= 18 cm²

> Area of a rectangle = length × width
> Remember to put the units of the answer.

b Area = 4.6 × 4.6
= 21.16 m²

> Area of a square = length × length
> As the lengths are in metres, the units of the area are m².

Example 9

Work out the area of **a** the triangle, **b** the parallelogram.

a

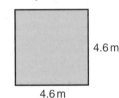

4 cm

7 cm

b

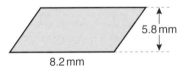

5.8 mm

8.2 mm

Solution 9

a Area = $\frac{1}{2} \times 7 \times 4$
= 14 cm²

> Area of a triangle = $\frac{1}{2} \times$ base × height
> 7 × 4 = 28
> $\frac{1}{2} \times 28 = 14$

b Area = 8.2 × 5.8
= 47.56 mm²

> Area of a parallelogram = base × height
> As the lengths are in millimetres, the units of the area are mm².

Example 10

Work out the areas of the shapes shown on a centimetre grid.

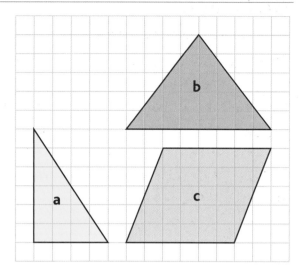

Solution 10

a Area $= \frac{1}{2} \times 4 \times 6 = 12$ cm²   The triangle has a base of 4 cm and a height of 6 cm.

b Area $= \frac{1}{2} \times 8 \times 5 = 20$ cm²   The triangle has a base of 8 cm and a height of 5 cm.

c Area $= 6 \times 5 = 30$ cm²   The parallelogram has a base of 6 cm and a height of 5 cm.

Exercise 12C

1 Work out the areas of these rectangles and squares.

a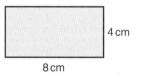
8 cm, 4 cm

b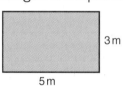
5 m, 3 m

c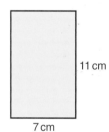
7 cm, 11 cm

d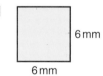
6 mm, 6 mm

e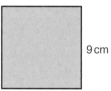
9 cm, 9 cm

2 Work out the areas of these triangles and parallelograms.

a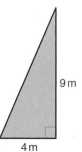
8 cm, 10 cm

b 9 m, 4 m

c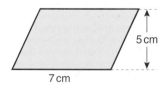
7 cm, 5 cm

d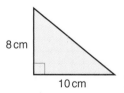
6 mm, 9 mm

e
12 cm, 5 cm

3 Work out the area of each of these shapes drawn on a centimetre grid

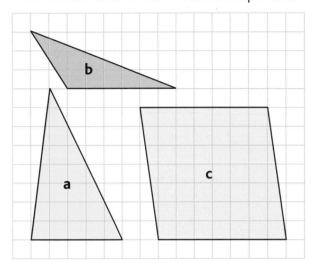

4 Copy and complete this table.

Shape	Length	Width	Area
Rectangle	4 cm	3 cm	
Rectangle	7 cm	9 cm	
Rectangle	10 cm		40 cm²
Rectangle	9 cm		27 cm²
Rectangle		5 cm	30 cm²

5 Copy and complete this table.

Shape	Base	Height	Area
Triangle	6 cm	5 cm	
Triangle	5 cm	10 cm	
Parallelogram	8 cm	4 cm	
Parallelogram	7 cm		56 cm²
Triangle		8 cm	24 cm²

6 Work out the areas of these rectangles and squares.
Give your answers correct to the nearest whole number.

a
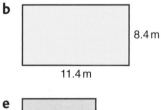

5.3 cm
9.6 cm

b

8.4 m
11.4 m

c
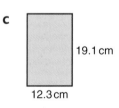

19.1 cm
12.3 cm

d

6.3 mm
6.3 mm

e
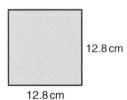

12.8 cm
12.8 cm

7 Work out the areas of these triangles and parallelograms.
Give your answers correct to the nearest whole number.

a

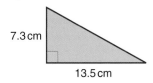

7.3 cm

13.5 cm

b

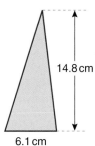

14.8 cm

6.1 cm

c

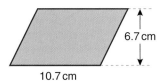

6.7 cm

10.7 cm

d

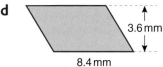

3.6 mm

8.4 mm

12.4 Problems involving areas

The areas of rectangles, squares, triangles and parallelograms can be used to work out the areas of other shapes.

Example 11

Work out the area of the trapezium.

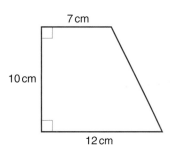

7 cm

10 cm

12 cm

Solution 11

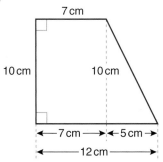

7 cm

10 cm   10 cm

←—7 cm—→←—5 cm—→

←———12 cm———→

| The trapezium can be split into a triangle and a rectangle as shown. |
| The rectangle is 7 cm by 10 cm. |
| The triangle has a base of $(12 - 7)$ cm or 5 cm and a height of 10 cm. |

Area of rectangle $= 7 \times 10$
$\qquad\qquad\qquad = 70 \text{ cm}^2$

| Area of rectangle = length $\times$ width. |

Area of triangle $= \frac{1}{2} \times 5 \times 10$
$\qquad\qquad\quad = 25 \text{ cm}^2$

| Area of a triangle $= \frac{1}{2} \times$ base $\times$ height. |

Area of trapezium $= 70 + 25$
$\qquad\qquad\qquad\quad = 95 \text{ cm}^2$

| Remember to give the units of the answer. |

Example 12

A piece of card is in the shape of a rectangle.

The length of the rectangle is 10 cm.

The width of the rectangle is 8 cm.

A rectangular hole is cut from the card as shown in the diagram.

The hole is 4 cm by 2 cm.

Work out the area of the card that is left.

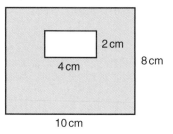

Solution 12

To find the area of card that is left, take the area of the small rectangle away from the area of the large rectangle.

Area of large rectangle = $10 \times 8 = 80$ cm²

Area of small rectangle = $4 \times 2 = 8$ cm²

Area of card left = $(80 - 8)$ cm² = 72 cm²

Example 13

A rectangular wall is 450 cm long and 300 cm high. The wall is to be tiled.

The tiles are squares of side 50 cm. How many tiles are needed?

Solution 13

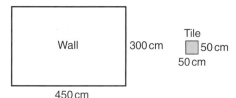

There is no diagram given with this question so it is a good idea to draw one.

Method 1

Number of tiles needed for the length $= \dfrac{450}{50} = 9$

One way to answer questions like this is to work out how many tiles are needed for the length and how many are needed for the height.

Number of tiles needed for the height $= \dfrac{300}{50} = 6$

Number of tiles needed = 9×6

Number of tiles needed = 54

So there are 6 rows, each with 9 tiles.

Multiply 9 by 6 to get the total number of tiles.

Method 2

Area of wall = $450 \times 300 = 135\,000$ cm²

Area of a tile = $50 \times 50 = 2500$ cm²

Number of tiles needed = $\dfrac{135\,000}{2500} = 54$

The other method is to divide the area of the wall by the area of one tile.

Exercise 12D

1 Work out the area of this trapezium.

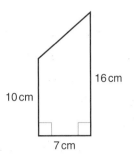

2 Work out the area of this shape.

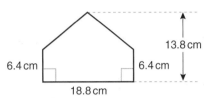

3 The diagram shows the floor plan of a room.

Work out the area of the floor.
Give the units of your answer.

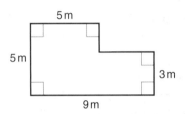

4 The diagram shows a rectangular piece of **green** paper with a corner removed.

Work out the area of the **green** paper that is left.

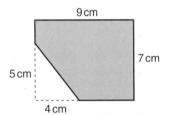

5 The floor of a room is a 5 metre by 3 metre rectangle. The carpet used to cover the floor completely costs £8.95 a square metre. Work out the cost of the carpet used.

6 Karl wants to make a rectangular lawn in his garden. He wants the lawn to be 30 m by 10 m. Karl buys rectangular strips of turf 5 m long and 1 m wide. Work out how many strips of turf Karl needs to buy.

7 Work out the area of the shaded region in this diagram.

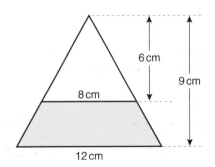

8 A wall is a 300 cm by 250 cm rectangle. Tiles, which are squares of side 50 cm, are used to tile the wall. Work out how many tiles are needed.

9 Trevor is going to paint some doors in his house. Each door is a 2 m by 0.85 m rectangle and he is going to paint both sides of each door.
Each tin of paint that he is going to use covers 8 m². Trevor wants to paint 20 doors. How many tins of paint does he need to buy?

10 A rectangle is 9 cm by 4 cm. A square has the same area as the rectangle. Work out the length of each side of the square.

Chapter summary

You should now know:

★ How to find the perimeter of a shape by adding the lengths of its sides

★ How to work out the perimeter of a rectangle

★ How to find the area of a shape by counting squares

★ How to find the area of a rectangle using

area of a rectangle = length × width

★ How to find the area of a triangle using

area of a triangle = $\frac{1}{2}$ × base × height

★ How to find the area of a parallelogram using

area of a parallelogram = base × height

★ How to find the area of a shape made from triangles and rectangles

★ How to solve problems involving areas

Chapter 12 review questions

1 A shaded shape is shown on the grid of centimetre squares.
   a Find the area of the shaded shape.
   b Find the perimeter of the shaded shape.

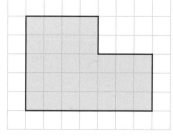

(1388 March 2003)

2 This is a grid of centimetre squares. Write down the perimeter of the shaded shape.

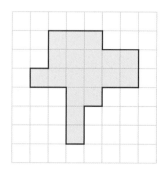

(1388 March 2003)

3 Work out the area, in square centimetres, of the shaded shape.

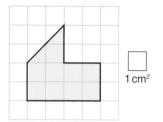

1 cm²

(1387 June 2004)

4 a Find the area of the shaded shape.
  b Find the perimeter of the shaded shape.

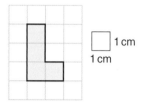

1 cm
1 cm

(1388 May 2002)

5 Here is a rectangle.
  The length of the rectangle is 4 cm.
  The width of the rectangle is 3 cm.

  a Work out the area of the rectangle.

  b Work out the perimeter of the rectangle.

4 cm
3 cm

Diagram **NOT** accurately drawn

(1387 June 2003)

6 This diagram shows the plan of a floor.

  a Work out the perimeter of the floor.

  b Work out the area of the floor.

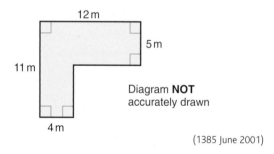

12 m
5 m
11 m
4 m

Diagram **NOT** accurately drawn

(1385 June 2001)

7 a Work out the perimeter of the shape.

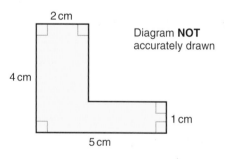

2 cm
4 cm
5 cm
1 cm

Diagram **NOT** accurately drawn

  b Work out the area of the triangle. State the units with your answer.

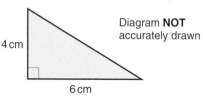

4 cm
6 cm

Diagram **NOT** accurately drawn

(1385 Nov 2000)

8

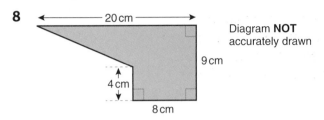

Diagram **NOT** accurately drawn

The diagram shows a shape.
Work out the area of the shape.   (1387 Nov 2003)

9

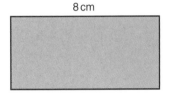

Diagram **NOT** accurately drawn

The perimeter of this rectangle is 22 cm.
The length of the rectangle is 8 cm.
Work out the area of the rectangle.   (1385 Nov 2001)

10 a Work out the perimeter of the whole shape *ABCD*.

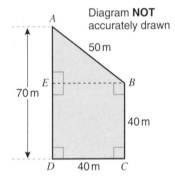

Diagram **NOT** accurately drawn

In part **b** you must write down the units with your answer.
b Work out the area of
   i the square *EBCD*
   ii the triangle *ABE*.   (1384 June 1997)

11 The diagram shows a wall with a door in it.
Work out the shaded area.

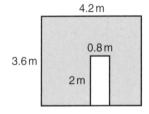

12 Mary's floor is a rectangle 8 m long and 5 m wide.
She wants to cover the floor completely with carpet tiles.
Each carpet tile is square with sides of length 50 cm.
Each carpet tile costs £4.19
Work out the cost of covering Mary's floor completely with carpet tiles.

(1387 Nov 2004)

13   Three different rectangles each have an area of 28 cm².
         The lengths of all the sides are whole numbers of centimetres.
         For each rectangle work out the length of the two sides.
         Copy the diagrams and write your answers next to them.

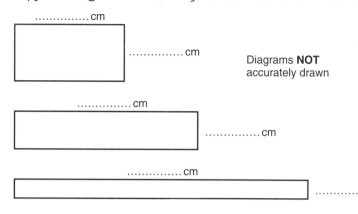

Diagrams **NOT**
accurately drawn

(1387 June 2000)

14   Here is a right-angled triangle.
         a   Make an accurate drawing of this triangle.
         b   Find, by measurement, the perimeter of the
                 triangle.
                 Give your answer in cm.
         c   Find, by calculation, the area of the triangle.
                 Give the units of your answer.

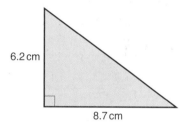

Sequences

13.1 Sequences

A **sequence** is a pattern of shapes or numbers which follow a rule.

Here is a sequence of *shapes* using triangles:

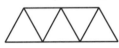

Pattern 1   Pattern 2   Pattern 3   Pattern 4
1 triangle   2 triangles   3 triangles   4 triangles

The **rule** to find the next pattern is 'Add an extra triangle' to the previous pattern.

Pattern 5 is formed by adding a triangle to Pattern 4.

Pattern 5 is   There are 5 triangles in Pattern 5.

Here is a sequence of *numbers*.

   3, 5, 7, 9, ...

The numbers in the sequence are called **terms of the sequence**.

   3 is the **1st term**
   5 is the 2nd term
   7 is the 3rd term
   9 is the 4th term

The **rule** to find the next term is 'Add 2' to the previous term.

The 5th term is $9 + 2 = 11$
The 6th term is 13, and so on.

Example 1

Here is a sequence of patterns
made up of crosses.

   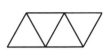

Pattern 1   Pattern 2   Pattern 3   Pattern 4

a   Write down the rule for this sequence.

b   Draw Pattern 5.

c   Complete the table

Pattern number	1	2	3	4	5	6
Number of crosses	2	4	6	8		

Solution 1

a The rule is 'Add a column of 2 crosses'

b ✗ ✗ ✗ ✗ ✗
     ✗ ✗ ✗ ✗

c

Pattern number	1	2	3	4	5	6
Number of crosses	2	4	6	8	10	12

+2 +2

Example 2

Here is a sequence of numbers:

2, 5, 8, 11, ...

a Write down the 3rd term.

b Write down the rule for this sequence.

c Write down the next two terms of this sequence.

d Work out the 10th term of this sequence.

Solution 2

a 8   **b** Add 3

c 5th term is 11 + 3 = **14**
      6th term is 14 + 3 = **17**

d Adding 3 each time, the 7th term is 20,
                          the 8th term is 23,
                          the 9th term is 26,
                          the 10th term is **29**

Example 3

Here is a sequence of numbers:

61, 55, 49, ... , ... , 31, 25

a Write down the rule for this sequence.

b Write down the 4th and 5th terms.

c Write down the 8th term.

Solution 3

a Subtract 6

b 4th term is 49 − 6 = **43**
      5th term is 43 − 6 = **37**

c 8th term is 25 − 6 = **19**

Example 4

Here is a sequence of patterns made up of yellow and blue triangles.

                     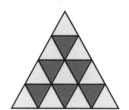

Pattern 1   Pattern 2   Pattern 3   Pattern 4

a Draw Pattern 5.

b Copy and complete the table.

c Write down the total number of triangles in Pattern 8.

Pattern number	1	2	3	4	5	6
Number of yellow triangles	1	3	6	10		
Number of blue triangles	0	1	3	6		
Total number of triangles	1	4	9	16		

Solution 4

a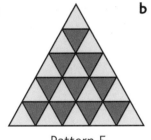

Pattern 5

b

Pattern number	1	2	3	4	5	6
Number of yellow triangles	1	3	6	10	**15**	**21**
		+2	+3	+4	+5	+6
Number of blue triangles	0	1	3	6	**10**	15
		+1	+2	+3	+4	+5
Total number of triangles	1	4	9	16	**25**	36

c 1, 4, 9, 16, **25** and **36** are square numbers.
$1 = 1^2, 4 = 2^2, 9 = 3^2, 16 = 4^2, 25 = 5^2$ and $36 = 6^2$.
So for Pattern 8, the total number of triangles is $8^2 = 8 \times 8 = 64$

Example 5

Here is a sequence of numbers:

   1, 10, 100, 1000, ...

a Write down the rule for this sequence.   **b** Write down the 5th and 6th terms.

Solution 5

a Multiply by 10

b 5th term is $1000 \times 10 = \mathbf{10\ 000}$
6th term is $10\ 000 \times 10 = \mathbf{100\ 000}$

 Exercise 13A

1 Here is a sequence of patterns made up of hexagons.

　　　　　　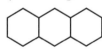　　　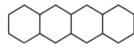

   Pattern 1　　　Pattern 2　　　Pattern 3　　　Pattern 4

   a Write down the rule for this sequence.

   b Draw Pattern 5

2 Here is a sequence of patterns made up of crosses.

   Pattern 1　　　Pattern 2　　　Pattern 3　　　Pattern 4

   a Write down the rule for this sequence.

   b Draw Pattern 5

   c Copy and complete the table.

Pattern number	1	2	3	4	5	6
Number of crosses	1	5	9	13		

3 Here is a sequence of patterns made up of hexagons.

Pattern 1   Pattern 2   Pattern 3   Pattern 4

a Write down the rule for this sequence.   **b** Draw Pattern 5

c Copy and complete the table.

Pattern number	1	2	3	4	5	6
Number of hexagons	1	3	5	7		

d Write down the number of hexagons in Pattern 9

4 Here is a sequence of patterns made up of dots and squares.

Pattern 1   Pattern 2   Pattern 3   Pattern 4

a Write down the rule for the sequence of dots.

b Write down the rule for the sequence of squares.

c Draw Pattern 5

d Copy and complete the table.

Pattern number	1	2	3	4	5	6
Number of dots	3	6	9	12		
Number of squares	1	2	3	4		

5 Here is a sequence of patterns made up of blue and yellow dots.

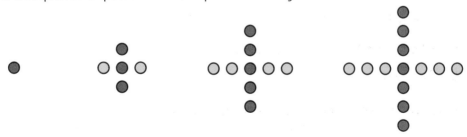

Pattern 1   Pattern 2   Pattern 3   Pattern 4

a Copy and complete the table.

Pattern number	1	2	3	4	5	6
Number of blue dots	1	3	5	7		
Number of yellow dots	0	2	4	6		
Total number of dots	1	5	9	13		

b Write down the total number of dots in Pattern 10

6 Here is a sequence of numbers.

   5, 7, 9, 11, …

   a Write down the third term

   b Write down the rule for this sequence.

   c Write down the next two terms of this sequence.

   d Work out the ninth term of this sequence.

7 Here is a sequence of numbers.

   24, 21, 18, 15, …

   a Write down the rule for this sequence.

   b Write down the next two terms of this sequence.

   c Work out the eighth term of this sequence.

   d Which term in this sequence is 0?

8 Write down the third and fourth terms of each of these sequences.

   a 2, 4, … , …, 10, 12, …   **b** 2, 4, … , …, 32, 64, …

9 Here is a sequence of numbers.

   41, 37, 33, …, …, 21, 17, …

   a Write down the rule for this sequence.

   b Write down the fourth and fifth terms.

   c Work out the tenth term.

10 a Write down the next two terms in each of these sequences.

   i 1, 2, 3, 4, …   **ii** 2, 3, 5, 8, …

   b Use the sequences in part **a** to work out the next two terms in the sequence

   3, 5, 8, 12, …

11 a Write down the next two terms in each of these sequences.

   i 1, 3, 5, 7, …   **ii** 1, 2, 4, 8, …

   b Use the sequences in part **a** to work out the next two terms in the sequence

   2, 5, 9, 15, …

12 a Write down the next two terms in each of these sequences.

   i 1, 4, 7, 10, …   **ii** 1, 3, 9, 27, …

   b Use the sequences in part **a** to work out the next two terms in the sequence

   2, 7, 16, 37, …

13 The first three terms in a sequence of numbers are 2, 4, 8
   Ann says that the next number is 16
   Bill says that the next number is 14

   a Write down the rule Ann has used.

   b Explain why both Ann and Bill could be correct.

14 Here are the first five terms of a sequence of numbers.

     7, 12, 17, 22, 27

  a Write down the next two terms of the sequence.

  b Write down the rule for the sequence.

  c John says that 196 is not a term of the sequence. Explain why John is correct.

15 Here are the first five terms of a sequence of numbers.

     7, 9, 11, 13, 15

  a Work out the 10th term of the sequence.

  b Explain how you found your answer.

  c Explain why 256 is not a term of the sequence.

13.2 Input and output machines

One-stage input and output machine

Input and output machines are ways of showing the operations within a calculation.

This machine shows the operation $\times 3$

Since the machine shows only one operation it is called a **one-stage input and output machine**. It is sometimes called a one-stage number machine.

The arrows show the direction through the machine.

For an input of 5, the output is $5 \times 3 = 15$

For an input of 7, the output is 21

For an input of 10, the output is 30

Here is a table to show this information.

When the input is 6, the output is **18** since $6 \times 3 = 18$

To find the input, when the output is 24,
work backwards through the machine.

The inverse of $\times 3$ is $\div 3$ See Section 1.6

  Inverse operation machine

When the output is 24, the input is $24 \div 3 = 8$

When the input is n, the output is $3n$ since $n \times 3 = 3n$.

$\times 3$	
Input	Output
5	15
6	18
7	21
8	24
10	30
n	$3n$

Example 6

Here is a table for an input and output machine.
It adds 4
Complete the table.

+ 4	
Input	Output
1	5
2	**a** ......
4	**b** ......
c	10
d	16
n	**e** ......

Solution 6

a   When the input is 2, the output is $2 + 4 = 6$

b   When the input is 4, the output is $4 + 4 = 8$

c   The inverse of $+ 4$ is $- 4$

$$6 \xleftarrow{10 - 4} \boxed{- 4} \leftarrow 10$$

When the output is 10, the input is $10 - 4 = 6$

d   When the output is 16, the input is $16 - 4 = 12$

e
$$n \longrightarrow \boxed{+ 4} \longrightarrow n + 4$$

When the input is n, the output is $n + 4$

Example 7

Here is a table for an input and output machine.
It adds q.
Complete the table.

+ q	
Input	Output
1	$1 + q$
2	**a** ......
5	**b** ......
c	$7 + q$
n	**d** ......
e	$5q$

Solution 7

a   When the input is 2, the output is $2 + q$

b   When the input is 5, the output is $5 + q$

c   The inverse of $+ q$ is $- q$.

When the output is $7 + q$, the input is $7 + q - q = 7$

d   When the input is n, the output is $n + q$

$$n \longrightarrow \boxed{+ q} \longrightarrow n + q$$

e
$$4q \xleftarrow{5q - q} \boxed{- q} \leftarrow 5q$$

When the output is $5q$, the input is $5q - q = 4q$

Exercise 13B

1   **a**   Write down the inverse of $+ 5$

     b   Write down the inverse of $\times 6$

     c   Write down the inverse of $- 2$

     d   Write down the inverse of $\div 7$

Questions **2–7** show a table for an input and output machine.

For each question, copy and complete the table.

2

+ 8	
Input	Output
1	9
2	......
3	......
4	......
5	......
n	......

3

+ 5	
Input	Output
1	6
2	......
3	......
......	10
......	16
n	......

4

× 4	
Input	Output
1	......
2	......
4	......
......	20
......	44
n	......

5

− 3	
Input	Output
3	......
4	......
5	......
......	4
......	10
n	......

6

÷ 2	
Input	Output
2	......
4	......
8	......
......	8
......	12
......	n

7

− p	
Input	Output
1	......
2	......
3	......
n	......
......	$8 - p$
......	$2p$

Two-stage input and output machine

This machine shows the operation × 3 followed by the operation + 2
This is called a **two-stage input and output machine.** It is sometimes called a two-stage number machine.

Input $\longrightarrow$ ×3 $\longrightarrow$ +2 $\longrightarrow$ Output

The arrows show the direction through the machine.

For an input of 0, the output is $0 \times 3 + 2 = 0 + 2 = 2$

0 $\longrightarrow$ ×3 $\longrightarrow$ $0 \times 3 = 0$ $\longrightarrow$ +2 $\longrightarrow$ $0 + 2$ $\longrightarrow$ 2

For an input of 1, the output is $1 \times 3 + 2 = 3 + 2 = 5$

1 $\longrightarrow$ ×3 $\longrightarrow$ $1 \times 3 = 3$ $\longrightarrow$ +2 $\longrightarrow$ $3 + 2$ $\longrightarrow$ 5

For an input of 2, the output is $2 \times 3 + 2 = 6 + 2 = 8$
For an input of 3, the output is $3 \times 3 + 2 = 11$

Here is a table to show this information.

When the input is 4, the output is $4 \times 3 + 2 = 14$

To find the input, when the output is 20, work backwards through the machine.

$? \rightarrow \boxed{\times 3} \leftarrow \boxed{+2} \rightarrow 20$

The inverse of $+ 2$ is $- 2$

The inverse of $\times 3$ is $\div 3$

Inverse operation machine

$6 \xleftarrow{18 \div 3} \boxed{\div 3} \xleftarrow{(20-2)=18} \boxed{-2} \leftarrow 20$

× 3 + 2	
Input	Output
0	2
1	5
2	8
3	11
4	14
6	20
n	$3n + 2$

When the output is 20, the input is $(20 - 2) \div 3 = 18 \div 3 = 6$

To find the output, when the input is n, work forwards through the machine.

$n \rightarrow \boxed{\times 3} \xrightarrow{n \times 3 = 3n} \boxed{+2} \rightarrow 3n + 2$

The output is $3n + 2$ since $n \times 3 + 2 = 3n + 2$

Example 8

Here is a table for a two-stage input and output machine. Complete the table.

− 1 × 2	
Input	Output
1	0
2	a ......
4	b ......
c	8
d	20
n	e ......

Solution 8

a When the input is 2, the output is
$(2 - 1) \times 2 = 1 \times 2 = \mathbf{2}$

b When the input is 4, the output is
$(4 - 1) \times 2 = 3 \times 2 = \mathbf{6}$

c $5 \xleftarrow{4+1} \boxed{+1} \xleftarrow{(8 \div 2) = 4} \boxed{\div 2} \leftarrow 8$

When the output is 8, the input is $(8 \div 2) + 1 = \mathbf{5}$

d $11 \xleftarrow{10+1} \boxed{+1} \xleftarrow{(20 \div 2) = 10} \boxed{\div 2} \leftarrow 20$

When the output is 20, the input is $(20 \div 2) + 1 = \mathbf{11}$

The inverse of $\times 2$ is $\div 2$ and the inverse of $- 1$ is $+ 1$. These give the inverse operation machine

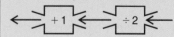

e $n \rightarrow \boxed{-1} \xrightarrow{(n-1) = 10} \boxed{\times 2} \xrightarrow{(n-1) \times 2} 2(n - 1)$

When the input is n, the output is $(n - 1) \times 2 = \mathbf{2(n - 1)}$

Example 9

Here is a table for an input and output machine.
Complete the table, giving your answers
in their simplest form.

$-x + y$	
Input	Output
1	$1 - x + y$
3	**a** ......
$2x$	**b** ......
$x - y$	**c** ......
d	$5y$

Solution 9

a When the input is 3, the output is
$(3 - x) + y = \mathbf{3 - x + y}$

b When the input is $2x$, the output is
$(2x - x) + y = \mathbf{x + y}$

c
$$x - y \longrightarrow \boxed{-x} \xleftarrow{-y} \boxed{+y} \longrightarrow 0$$

When the input is $x - y$, the output is $(x - y - x) + y = \mathbf{0}$

d
$$4y + x \longleftarrow \boxed{+x} \xleftarrow{4y} \boxed{-y} \longleftarrow 5y$$

When the output is $5y$, the input is $(5y - y) + x = \mathbf{4y + x}$

Exercise 13C

Questions **1–10** show tables for input and output machines.
The tables are incomplete. Copy and complete each table.

1

$\times 3 - 2$	
Input	Output
1	1
2	4
3	......
4	......
5	......
n	......

2

$\times 4 + 3$	
Input	Output
1	7
2	......
3	......
4	......
5	......
n	......

3

$\times 2 - 1$	
Input	Output
1	......
2	......
3	......
4	......
5	......
n	......

4

$\times (-1) + 6$	
Input	Output
1	5
2	4
3	......
4	......
5	......
n	......

5

$\times (-2) + 11$	
Input	Output
1	9
2	......
3	......
4	......
5	......
n	......

6

$- 1 \times 3$	
Input	Output
1	0
2	......
4	......
......	21
......	30
n	......

7

× 3 − 1	
Input	Output
1	......
2	......
4	......
......	20
......	29
n	......

8

+ 3 × 2	
Input	Output
1	......
2	......
4	......
......	20
......	24
n	......

9

× 5 + 2	
Input	Output
1	......
2	......
4	......
......	37
......	52
n	......

10

− 2 × 4	
Input	Output
1	−4
3	......
4	......
......	16
......	32
n	......

11 Here is a table for an input and output machine.
Copy and complete the table, giving your answers in their simplest form.

+ r − t	
Input	Output
1	$1 + r - t$
6	......
r	......
t	......
......	1

13.3 Finding an expression for the nth term of an arithmetic sequence

Here are some examples of arithmetic sequences.

  i   9, 10, 11, 12, 13, ...
  ii 1, 4, 7, 10, 13, ...
  iii 20, 18, 16, 14, 12, ...

An **arithmetic sequence** is a sequence of numbers with a rule 'Add a fixed number'.
The fixed number is the difference, or step, between consecutive terms.
In **i** the first term of the sequence is 9 and the second term is 10.

So the difference is 1 since $10 - 9 = 1$ and also $11 - 10 = 1$ and so on.
In **ii** the difference is 3 since $4 - 1 = 3$ and $7 - 4 = 3$ and so on.
In **iii**, the terms go downwards. The difference is -2 since
$18 - 20 = -2$ and $16 - 18 = -2$ and so on.

Here is a completed table for an input and output machine.

× 3 − 2		
Input	Output	
0	−2	zero term
1	1	1st term
2	4	2nd term
3	7	3rd term
4	10	4th term
5	13	5th term
n	$3n - 2$	*n*th term

The output numbers 1, 4, 7, 10, 13 are the first five terms of an arithmetic sequence.
The input numbers give the position of each term.
The 1st term is 1, the 2nd term is 4, the 3rd term is 7 and so on.
The *n*th term is the output when the input is *n*.

The *n*th term of the arithmetic sequence 1, 4, 7, 10, 13, ... is $3n - 2$

The 3 in $3n - 2$ is the **difference** between consecutive terms.
The −2 in $3n - 2$ is the term before the 1st term, sometimes called the **zero term**, since
$1 - 3 = -2$. The zero term is the output when the input is 0.

In general, for an arithmetic sequence, the *n*th term is the

    difference $\times n +$ **zero term**

Example 10

Here are the first five terms of an arithmetic sequence 7, 11, 15, 19, 23
Write down
a the difference between consecutive terms,
b the zero term,
c an expression, in terms of *n*, for the *n*th term of this sequence.

Solution 10

a The difference between consecutive terms is 4, since $11 - 7 = 4$

b The zero term is $7 - 4 = \mathbf{3}$

c The *n*th term is $4n + \mathbf{3}$

Input	Output	
0		zero term
1	7	1st term
2	11	2nd term
3	15	3rd term
4	19	4th term
5	23	5th term
n		*n*th term

Example 11

Here are the first five terms of an arithmetic sequence 9, 7, 5, 3, 1
Write down, in terms of n, an expression for the nth term of this sequence.

Solution 11

The difference between consecutive terms is -2, since $7 - 9 = -2$

The zero term is **11**

The nth term is $-2n + 11$

Input	Output	
0		zero term
1	9	1st term
2	7	2nd term
3	5	3rd term
4	3	4th term
5	1	5th term
n		nth term

Example 12

Here are the first four terms of an arithmetic sequence 2, 6, 10, 14
a Write down, in terms of n, an expression for the nth term of this sequence.
b Find the 100th term of the sequence.

Solution 12

a The difference between consecutive terms is 4, since $6 - 2 = 4$
The zero term is $2 - 4 = -2$
The nth term is $4n - 2$

b nth term is $4n - 2$
  100th term $= 4 \times 100 - 2$
       $= 400 - 2$
       $= 398$

Exercise 13D

Questions **1–5** each show an **arithmetic sequence**.

For each arithmetic sequence
a write down the difference between consecutive terms.
b write down the zero term.
c write down, in terms of n, an expression for the nth term of the sequence.

1 5, 6, 7, 8, ...   **2** 5, 9, 13, 17, 21, ...   **3** 2, 5, 8, 11, 14, ...

4 22, 19, 16, 13, 10, ...   **5** −4, 0, 4, 8, 12, ...

6 Here are the first five terms of an arithmetic sequence 6, 11, 16, 21, 26

    a Write down, in terms of n, an expression for the nth term of this sequence.

    b Find the 100th term of the sequence.

7 Here are the first five terms of an arithmetic sequence 1, 7, 13, 19, 25

    a Write down, in terms of n, an expression for the nth term of this sequence.

    b Find the 50th term of the sequence.

8 Here are the first five terms of an arithmetic sequence $-4, -1, 2, 5, 8$

    a Write down, in terms of n, an expression for the nth term of this sequence.

    b Find the 1000th term of the sequence.

9 Here are the first five terms of an arithmetic sequence $20, 10, 0, -10, -20$

    a Write down, in terms of n, an expression for the nth term of this sequence.

    b Find the 20th term of the sequence.

10 **a** Write down, in terms of n, an expression for the nth term of the arithmetic sequence 1, 3, 5, 7, ...

    b Write down, in terms of n, an expression for the nth term of the arithmetic sequence 2, 4, 6, 8, ...

    c Use your answers to parts **a** and **b** to find, in terms of n, an expression for the nth term of the arithmetic sequence 3, 7, 11, 15, ...

Chapter summary

You should know and be able to use these facts

★ A **sequence** is a pattern of shapes or numbers which follow a rule.
The **terms of a sequence** are the numbers in the sequence.
Know how to give the **rule** of a sequence, for example, the rule of the sequence 5, 7, 9, 11, ... is 'Add 2'
Know how to use the rule to find later terms in a sequence.

★ **Input and output machines** show the operations and the order of operations within a calculation. For example it might show 'add 4' or it might show 'subtract 2 then multiply by 3'

★ Inverse operations are used to find inputs when the outputs are given.

★ An **arithmetic sequence** is a sequence of numbers with a rule, 'Add a fixed number', for example, 1, 4, 7, 10, 13, ... is an arithmetic sequence with the rule, 'Add 3'
The **difference** between consecutive terms in an arithmetic sequence is the increase or decrease in value from one term to the next.
The **zero term** of a sequence is the output when the input is 0
To find the nth term of an arithmetic sequence, use

     nth term is the **difference** $\times n +$ **zero term.**

Chapter 13 review questions

1 **a** Here are the first four terms of a number sequence.

3,   7,   11,   15

Write down the next two terms of the sequence.

b Explain how you found your answer. (1388 March 2005)

2 Here are the first five terms of a number sequence.

16,   12,   8,   4,   0

a Write down the next two terms of the sequence.

Here are the first six terms of a different number sequence

7,   12,   17,   22,   27,   32

b Write down an expression, in terms of n, for the nth term of this sequence.

(1385 Nov 2001)

3 Here is a sequence of numbers 5, 9, 13, 17, 21, ...

a   **i** Write down the next term of this sequence.

ii Explain how you found your answer.

b Write down the 10th term of this sequence.

4 Here are the first six terms of a number sequence.

100,   96,   92,   88,   84,   80

a Write down the next term of the number sequence.

b Explain how you found your answer.

Sam said that 5 is a term of this number sequence.
Sam is wrong.

c Explain why.

5 Here is a table for a two-stage number machine.
It multiplies by 2 then subtracts 1.
Copy and complete the missing numbers in the table.

× 2 − 1	
Input	Output
1	1
2	3
3	......
5	......
......	15

(1387 June 2003)

6 The nth term of an arithmetic sequence is $5n - 6$
Find the value of

a   the 1st term of this sequence   **b**   the 2nd term of this sequence

c   the 3rd term of this sequence   **d**   the 10th term of this sequence.

7   Here is a table for an input and output machine.
Copy and complete the table.

+ 1 × 3	
Input	Output
1	......
2	......
4	......
......	21
......	30
n	......

8   Here are the first five terms of an arithmetic sequence

   7,   10,   13,   16,   19

Find an expression, in terms of n, for the nth term of this sequence.

9   Here is a table for an input and output machine.
Complete the table,
giving your answers in their simplest form.

+ 4p	
Input	Output
1	$1 + 4p$
n	......
$p + q$	......
......	$9p$
......	$p + 1$

10   Here are some patterns made out of tiles.

   Pattern   Pattern   Pattern
   number 1   number 2   number 3

a   Draw pattern number 4 and pattern number 5.

b   Copy and complete the table.

Pattern number	1	2	3	4	5	6	7
Number of tiles	1	3	6				

c   **i**   How many tiles are needed for pattern number 12?

   ii   Explain how you found this answer.

(1385 June 1999)

11   Here are the first four terms of an arithmetic sequence.

   3,   7,   11,   15

Write down, in terms of n, an expression for the nth term of the sequence.

(1388 Jan 2005)

12 Here is a table for an input and output machine.
Copy and complete the table, giving your
answers in their simplest form.

$+3-p$	
Input	Output
1	$4-p$
5	......
p	......
......	$1-p$
......	5

13 Here are the first five terms of an arithmetic sequence.

24,   20,   16,   12,   8

    a Write down, in terms of n, an expression for the nth term of this sequence.

    b Find the 20th term of the sequence.

14 Here are the first five terms of an arithmetic sequence.

8,   11,   14,   17,   20

    a Find an expression, in terms of n, for the nth term of this sequence.

    b John says the number 100 is a term of this sequence. John is wrong.
Explain why.

Angles 2

14.1 Triangles

also assessed in
Module 4

Draw a triangle on paper and label its angles a, b and c. 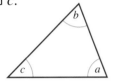	Tear off its corners.	Fit angles a, b and c together. They make a straight line.

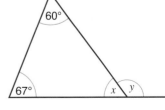

This *shows* that the angles in this triangle add up to 180° but it is not a **proof**. That comes later in this chapter.

The angles on a straight line add up to 180° and so the angles in this triangle add up to 180°.

The angle sum of a triangle is 180°.

Example 1

Work out the size of angle x.

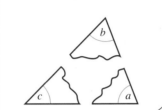

Solution 1

$72° + 57° = 129°$	Add 72° and 57°
$180° - 129° = 51°$	Take the result away from 180°, as the angle sum of a triangle is 180°.
$x = 51°$	State the size of angle x.

Sometimes both the fact that the angle sum of a triangle is 180° and the angle facts from Chapter 7 are needed.

Example 2

Work out the size of   **a**   angle x **b**   angle y.
Give reasons for your answers.

Solution 2

a $67° + 60° = 127°$ **b** $180° - 53° = 127°$
   $180° - 127° = 53°$ $y = 127°$
        $x = 53°$

Angle sum of triangle is 180°.	Sum of angles on a straight line is 180°.

Exercise 14A

In this exercise, the triangles are not accurately drawn.

In Questions **1–12**, find the size of each of the angles marked with letters and show your working.

1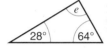

2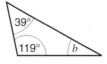

3

4

5

6

7

8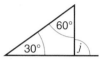

9

10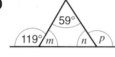

11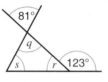

12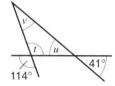

In Questions **13–15**, find the size of each of the angles marked with letters and show your working.
Give reasons for your answers.

13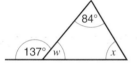

14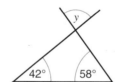

15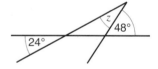

14.2 Equilateral triangles and isosceles triangles

also assessed in Module 4

An **equilateral** triangle has three equal sides and three equal angles.
As the angle sum of a triangle is 180°, the size of each angle is
180 ÷ 3 = 60°.

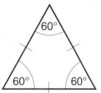

An **isosceles** triangle has two equal sides and the angles opposite the equal sides are equal.

A triangle whose sides are all different lengths is called a **scalene** triangle.

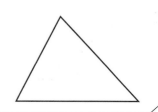

Example 3

Work out the size of   **a** angle x **b** angle y.
Give reasons for your answers.

Solution 3

a $x = 41°$ | Isosceles triangle with equal angles opposite equal sides. |

b $41° + 41° = 82°$

   $180° - 82° = 98°$ | Angle sum of triangle is 180°. |

                $y = 98°$

Example 4

Work out the size of angle x.
Give reasons for your answer.

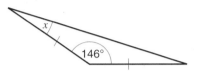

Solution 4

$180° - 146° = 34°$ | Angle sum of triangle is 180°. |

   $34° \div 2 = 17°$ | Isosceles triangle with equal angles opposite equal sides. |

        $x = 17°$

Exercise 14B

In this exercise, the triangles are not accurately drawn.

In Questions **1–12**, find the size of each of the angles marked with letters and show your working.

1
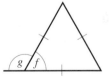

2
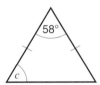

3
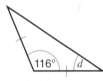

4
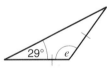

5

6

7
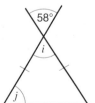

8
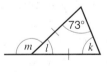

9
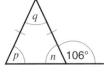

10

11
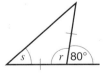

12
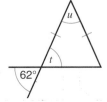

In Questions **13–15**, find the size of each of the angles marked with letters and show your working.
Give reasons for your answers.

13

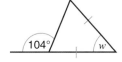

14

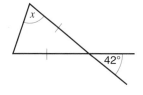

15

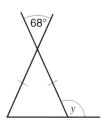

14.3 Corresponding angles and alternate angles

Parallel lines are always the same distance apart. They never meet. (Section 7.5)
In diagrams, arrows are used to show that lines are parallel.

In the diagram, a straight line crosses two parallel lines. The shaded angles are called **corresponding angles** and are equal to each other.

The F shape formed by corresponding angles can be helpful in recognising them.

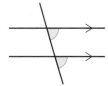

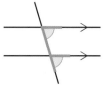

Other pairs of corresponding angles have been shaded in the diagrams below.

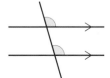

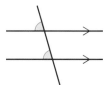

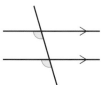

In the diagram, a straight line crosses two parallel lines.

The shaded angles are called **alternate angles** and are equal to each other.

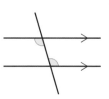

The Z shape formed by alternate angles can be helpful in recognising them.

Another pair of alternate angles has been shaded in this diagram.

Example 5

Write down the letter of the angle which is

a corresponding to the shaded angle,

b alternate to the shaded angle.

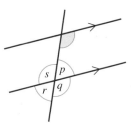

Solution 5

a Angle q is the corresponding angle to the shaded angle.

b Angle s is the alternate angle to the shaded angle.

> Notice that they form an F shape.

> Notice that they form a Z shape.

Example 6

a Find the size of angle x.

b Give a reason for your answer.

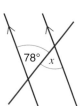

Solution 6

a $x = 78°$ **b** Alternate angles.

Example 7

a Find the size of angle p.

b Give a reason for your answer.

c Find the size of angle q.

d Give a reason for your answer.

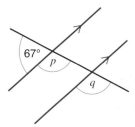

Solution 7

a $180° - 67° = 113°$
$p = 113°$

b The sum of the angles on a straight line is 180°.

c $q = 113°$

d Corresponding angles.

Exercise 14C

In this exercise, the diagrams are not accurately drawn.

1 Write down the letter of the angle which is

   a corresponding to the shaded angle,

   b alternate to the shaded angle.

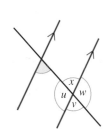

2 Write down the letter of the angle which is
  a corresponding to the shaded angle,
  b alternate to the shaded angle.

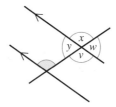

In Questions **3–5**, find the sizes of the angles marked with letters and state whether the pairs of angles are corresponding or alternate.

3

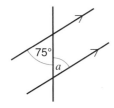

4

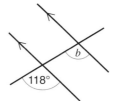

5

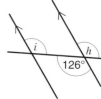

In Questions **6–20**, find the sizes of the angles marked with letters.
Give reasons for your answers.

6

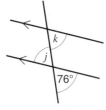

7

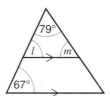

8

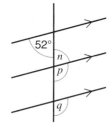

9

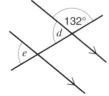

10

11

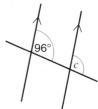

12

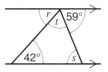

13

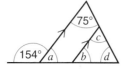

14

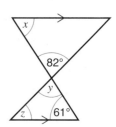

15

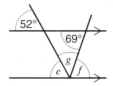

16

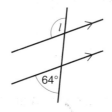

17

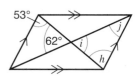

18

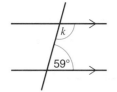

19

20

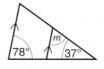

14.4 Proofs

In mathematics, a proof is a reasoned argument to show that a statement is always true. The proofs which follow make use of corresponding and alternate angles.

Proof 1

An exterior angle of a triangle is equal to the sum of the interior angles at the other two vertices

The diagram shows a triangle PQR.

Extend the side PQ to S.

At Q draw a line QT parallel to PR.

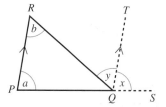

Then angle x = angle a (corresponding angles)

and   angle y = angle b (alternate angles)

Adding, $x + y = a + b$

$x + y$ is the exterior angle of the triangle and $a + b$ is the sum of the interior angles at the other two vertices and so the statement is true.

Proof 2

The angle sum of a triangle is 180°

This proof starts in the same way as Proof 1.

The diagram shows a triangle PQR.

Extend the side PQ to S.

At Q draw a line QT parallel to PR.

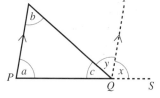

Then angle x = angle a (corresponding angles)

and   angle y = angle b (alternate angles)

Adding, $x + y = a + b$

As x, y and c are angles on a straight line, their angle sum is 180°, that is

   $x + y + c = 180°$

So $a + b + c = 180°$ which proves that the statement is true.

Proof 3

The opposite angles of a parallelogram are equal

Draw a diagonal of the parallelogram.

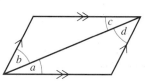

angle a = angle c (alternate angles)

angle b = angle d (alternate angles)

Adding, $a + b = c + d$ which proves that the statement is true.

Example 8

a Find the size of angle w.

b Give a reason for your answer.

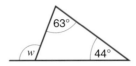

Solution 8

a $63° + 44° = 107°$

$w = 107°$

b Exterior angle of a triangle.

(As the full reason is long, it may be shortened to this.)

Exercise 14D

In this exercise, the diagrams are not accurately drawn.
Find the size of each of the angles marked with letters.

Give reasons for your answers.

1

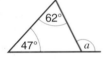

2

3

4

5

6

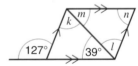

7

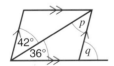

8

14.5 Bearings

also assessed in Module 4

Bearings are used to describe directions.

Bearings are measured **clockwise** ◯ from **North**.

When the angle is less than 100°, one or two zeros are written in front of the angle, so that the bearing still has three figures.

Example 9

Measure the bearing of B from A.

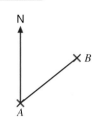

Solution 9

From North, measure the angle clockwise.

The angle is 52°.

So the bearing is 052°.

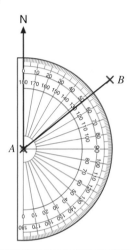

Example 10

Measure the bearing of Q from P.

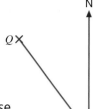

Solution 10

To find the angle clockwise from North with a semi-circular protractor measure the shaded anticlockwise angle (38°) and subtract it from 360°.

$$360° - 38° = 342°$$

The bearing of Q from P is 342°.

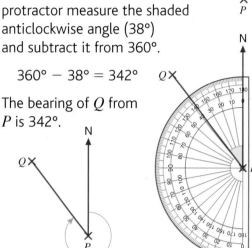

Example 11

Folkestone and Dover are shown on the map.
The bearing of a ship from Folkestone is 117°.
The bearing of the ship from Dover is 209°.

Draw an accurate diagram to show the position of the ship.

Mark the position with a cross X. Label it S.

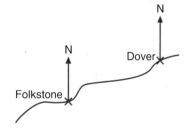

Solution 11

Draw a line on a bearing of 117° from Folkestone.
Draw a line on a bearing of 209° from Dover by measuring an angle of 151° (360° − 209°) anticlockwise from North.

(Alternatively, measure an angle of 29° clockwise from *South*.)

Put a X where the lines cross.

Label the position S.

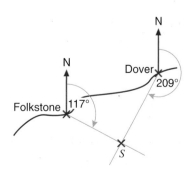

Sometimes, answers to questions have to be worked out, not found using a protractor.

Example 12

The bearing of B from A is 061°.

Work out the bearing of A from B.

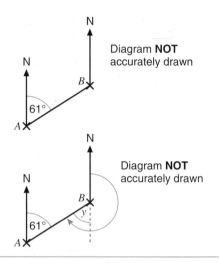

Diagram **NOT** accurately drawn

Solution 12

The bearing of A from B is the reflex angle at B.

$y = 61°$ (alternate angles)

Bearing $= 180° + 61°$

$\quad\quad = 241°$

Diagram **NOT** accurately drawn

Exercise 14E

In Questions **1–4**, measure the bearing of Q from P.

1

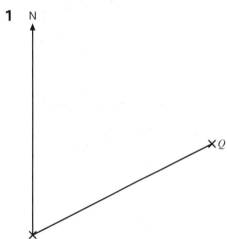

2

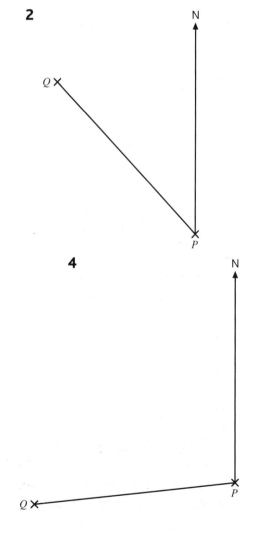

3

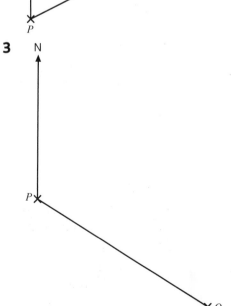

4

5 Draw diagrams similar to those in Questions **1–4** to show the bearings

   a 026°   **b** 217°   **c** 109°   **d** 334°.

6 The diagram shows two points, A and B.
The bearing of a point L from A is 048°.
The bearing of L from B is 292°.
On the diagram on the resource sheet find the
position of L by making an accurate drawing.

7 The diagram shows two points, P and Q.
The bearing of a point M from P is 114°.
The bearing of M from Q is 213°.
On the diagram on the resource sheet find the
position of M by making an accurate drawing.

8 Cromer and Great Yarmouth are shown on the map.
The bearing of a ship from Cromer is 052°.
The bearing of the ship from Great Yarmouth is 348°.
On the diagram on the resource sheet find the position
of the ship by making an accurate drawing.
Mark the position of the ship with a cross X.
Label it S.

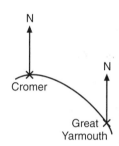

9 The bearing of Q from P is 038°.
Work out the bearing of P from Q.

10 The bearing of T from S is 146°.
Work out the bearing of S from T.

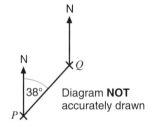

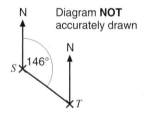

11 The bearing of B from A is 074°.
The bearing of C from B is 180°.
$AB = AC$.
Work out the bearing of C from A.

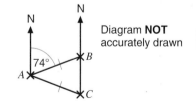

12 The diagram shows the positions of
York, Scarborough and Hull.
The bearing of Scarborough from
York is 052°.
The bearing of Hull from York is 118°.
The distance between York and Scarborough is
the same as the distance between York and Hull.
Work out the bearing of Hull from Scarborough.

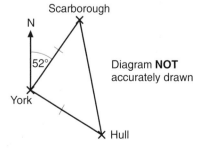

Chapter summary

> ### You should know and be able to use these facts
>
> ★ The angle sum of a triangle is 180°.
>
> ★ An **equilateral** triangle has three equal angles and three equal sides.
>
>
>
> ★ An **isosceles** triangle has two equal sides and the angles opposite the equal sides are equal.
>
> ★ A triangle whose sides are all different lengths is called a **scalene** triangle.
>
> ★ Where a straight line crosses two parallel lines, the **corresponding angles** are equal.
>
> ★ Where a straight line crosses two parallel lines, the **alternate angles** are equal.
>
> ★ Opposite angles of a parallelogram are equal.
>
> ★ **Bearings** are measured **clockwise** ⌒ from **North**.
>
> ### You should also know these proofs
>
> ★ An exterior angle of a triangle is equal to the sum of the interior angles at the other two vertices.
>
> ★ The angle sum of a triangle is 180°.

Chapter 14 review questions

In Questions **1–8**, find the size of each of the angles marked with a letter.
The diagrams are not accurately drawn.

1

2

3

4

5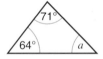

6

7

8

9 In triangle ABC, $AB = AC$ and angle $C = 50°$.

    a Write down the special name of triangle ABC.

    b Work out the value of y.

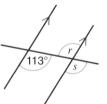

Diagram **NOT** accurately drawn

(1385 June 1999)

10 a i Write down the size of the
          angle marked x.
     ii Give a reason for your answer.

   b i Write down the size of the
          angle marked y.
     ii Give a reason for your answer.

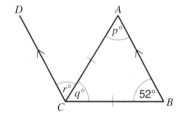

Diagram **NOT**
accurately drawn

(1384 Nov 1996)

11 $AC = BC$
    AB is parallel to DC
    Angle $ABC = 52°$

   a Work out the value of   **i** p **ii** q

   The angles marked $p°$ and $r°$ are equal.

   b What geometrical name is given to
          this type of equal angles?

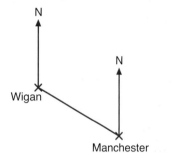

(1384 Nov 1997)

12 The diagram represents the positions
    of Wigan and Manchester.

   a Measure and write down the
          bearing of Manchester
          from Wigan.

   b Find the bearing of Wigan
          from Manchester.

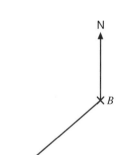

(1385 June 1998)

13 Measure the bearing of A from B.

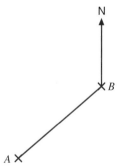

(1387 March 2004)

14 Work out the bearing of
    i B from P,   **ii** P from A.

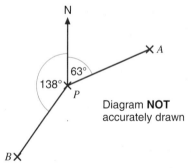

Diagram **NOT**
accurately drawn

(1387 Nov 2004)

15 The diagram shows the position of each
    of three buildings in a town.

    The bearing of the Hospital from the
    Art Gallery is 072°.
    The Cinema is due East of the Hospital.
    The distance from the Hospital to the
    Art Gallery is equal to the distance
    from the Hospital to the Cinema.

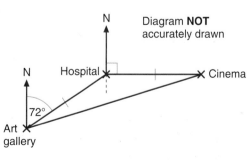

Diagram **NOT**
accurately drawn

    Work out the bearing of the Cinema from the Art Gallery.   (1387 Nov 2003)

Graphs 1

15.1 Coordinates in the first quadrant

Coordinates are used to describe the position of a point on a grid.

The **x-axis** and the **y-axis** cross at the point O, called the origin.
The x-axis measures the horizontal distance from the origin.
The y-axis measures the vertical distance from the origin.
The number of units **across** is always written **first** in the brackets.
The number of units **up** is always written **second** in the brackets.

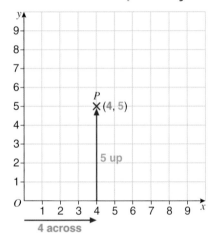

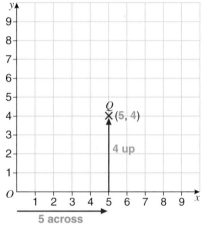

The point P is **4** units across from O
and **5** units up from O.

The point Q has coordinates (**5**, **4**).

The coordinates of point P are written as (**4**, **5**).

y-coordinate

x-coordinate

Example 1

Write down
a the name of the capital city at
the point (3, 6).
b the coordinates of Prague.
c the name of the capital city which
is closest to the point (2, 3).

Solution 1

a London

b (6, 5)

c Madrid

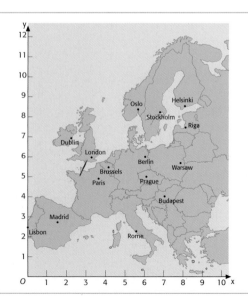

Exercise 15A

1   Use the diagram in Example 1 to answer questions **a–j**
   a   Write down the name of the capital city at the point (2, 7)
   b   Write down the name of the capital city at the point (6, 6)
   c   Write down the coordinates of Budapest.
   d   Write down the name of the capital city which is closest to the point (6, 2)
   e   Write down the the the name of the country which has a city at the point (3, 4)
   f   Write down the names of the two capital cities which have an x-coordinate of 8
   g   Write down the names of the two capital cities that have a y-coordinate of 5
   h   Write down the name of the capital city which is about halfway between the points (4, 4) and (4, 7)
   i   Write down the name of the capital city which is about halfway between the points (4, 7) and (7, 10)
   j   Write down the name of the capital city which has an x-coordinate of 0

2   On the resource sheet, plot and label the following points on the grid.
   a   The point P which has coordinates (2, 2)
   b   The point Q which has coordinates (3, 2)
   c   The point R which has coordinates (1, 5)
   d   The point S which has coordinates (5, 1)
   e   The point T which has coordinates (4, 6)

3   Write down the name given to the point with coordinates (0, 0)

15.2 Coordinates in all four quadrants

All points on the x-axis have a y-coordinate equal to 0
The point A is **4** units across from O and is **on** the x-axis.
A has coordinates (4, 0).

The point B is **2** units across from O and **2** units *down* from O.
The coordinates of point B are written as (2, -2).

The point C is **4** units across from O in the negative direction and **6** units up.
The coordinates of point C are written as (-4, 6).

The point D is **3** units across from O in the negative direction and **4** units down.
The coordinates of point D are written as (-3, -4).

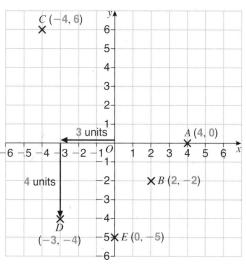

All points on the y-axis have x-coordinate equal to 0
The point E is **on** the y-axis and is **5** units down.
E has coordinates (0, -5).

Exercise 15B

1 a Write down the coordinates of the point A.
   b Write down the coordinates of the point B.
   c Write down the coordinates of the point C.
   d Write down the coordinates of the point D.
   e Write down the coordinates of the point E.

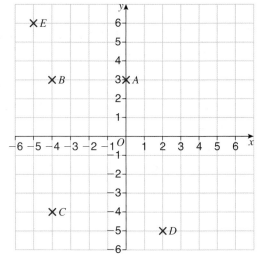

2 In this question, use the resource sheet to plot and label the following points.
   a The point Q which has coordinates $(3, 0)$
   b The point R which has coordinates $(4, -2)$
   c The point S which has coordinates $(-1, 3)$
   d The point T which has coordinates $(0, -1)$
   e The point U which has coordinates $(-5, -6)$

3 Use the resource sheet to answer these questions.
   a Write down the coordinates of the points **i** J **ii** K **iii** L.
   b $JKLM$ is a rectangle. On the grid, mark the position of the point M and write down the coordinates of the point M.
   c P is the point with coordinates $(5, -5)$. $JKLP$ is a quadrilateral. Write down the mathematical name of this quadrilateral.
   d $JKNL$ is a parallelogram. Write down the coordinates of the point N.

15.3 Finding the coordinates of the midpoint of a line

The **midpoint** of a line is a point on the line which is the same distance from one end of the line as it is from the other.

The points and lines on this grid will be used in the examples that follow.

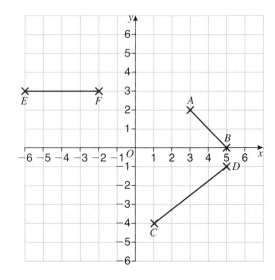

Example 2

On the grid a line joins the point E $(-6, 3)$ to the point F $(-2, 3)$.
Find the coordinates of the midpoint of this line.

Solution 2

The distance from E to F is 4 units across.

The distance from E to the midpoint, M,
is half of $4 = 2$ units across.

The point M has coordinates $(-4, 3)$.

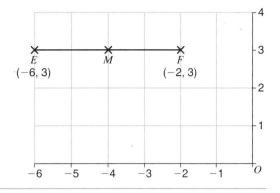

Example 3

On the grid a line joins the point A $(3, 2)$ to the point B $(5, 0)$.
Find the coordinates of the midpoint of this line.

Solution 3

The distance from A to B is the length of the
diagonals of two grid squares.

The distance from A to the midpoint, M, is half
of 2 diagonals $= 1$ diagonal.

The midpoint has coordinates $(4, 1)$

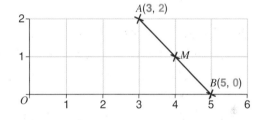

Another method of finding the coordinates of the midpoint of the line joining $(3, 2)$ to
$(5, 0)$ is to write the x-coordinate of the midpoint as $\frac{1}{2}$ of $(3 + 5) = 4$,
and the y-coordinate of the midpoint as $\frac{1}{2}$ of $(2 + 0) = 1$
The midpoint has coordinates $(4, 1)$.

Example 4

On the grid a line joins the point C $(1, -4)$
to the point D $(5, -1)$.
Find the coordinates of the midpoint of this line.

Solution 4

M is the midpoint of the line CD.

The x-coordinate of M is $\frac{1}{2}$ of $(1 + 5) = 3$,

The y-coordinate of M is $\frac{1}{2}$ of $(-4 + (-1)) = -2.5$

The midpoint has coordinates $(3, -2.5)$.

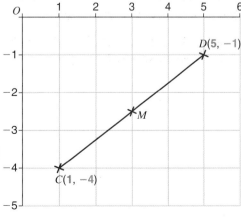

Exercise 15C

1   Using the resource sheet, find the coordinates of the midpoint of the following lines.

a AB b CD c AK d JK e CI f AD

g KB h EG i AJ j DI k AH l FK

Use the resource sheet for Questions **2–4**

2   Find the coordinates of the midpoints of the lines joining the following points.

a $(1, 2)$ and $(5, 2)$ b $(-3, -2)$ and $(-3, 4)$ c $(0, 0)$ and $(4, 6)$

d $(3, -2)$ and $(-5, 2)$ e $(-2, 0)$ and $(3, 2)$ f $(-3, -4)$ and $(2, -1)$

3   The point $(3, 2)$ is the midpoint of the line PQ. The coordinates of P are $(0, 1)$
    Find the coordinates of the point Q.

4   The point $(-1, -2)$ is the midpoint of the line ST. The coordinates of S are $(-4, 2)$
    Find the coordinates of the point T.

Chapter summary

> **You should now know:**
>
> ★   That the **origin** is the point on a coordinate grid at which the x-axis and y-axis cross.
>
> **You should also be able to:**
>
> ★   Plot and write down **coordinates** in all four quadrants. For example, the point with coordinates $(3, -4)$ is 3 units to the right of the origin $(0, 0)$ in the x-direction and 4 units down in the y-direction.
>
> ★   Find the coordinates of the **midpoint** of a line joining two given points. For example for the line joining $(1, 6)$ and $(3, 4)$, $\dfrac{1+3}{2} = 2$ and $\dfrac{6+4}{2} = 5$ so the midpoint of the line is $(2, 5)$.

Chapter 15 review questions

1   Use the resource sheet to answer this question.

a   Write down the coordinates of the point

    i A ii B.

b   On the grid, mark with a cross (x) the midpoint of the line AB.

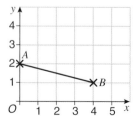

(1387 June 2005)

2 **a** Write down the coordinates of the points
     i P **ii** Q **iii** R.

  b **i** On the resource sheet, join the points
     to form triangle PQR.
     ii Write down the mathematical name
     of triangle PQR.

  c Write down the coordinates of the
     midpoint of
     i the side QR **ii** the side PQ
     iii the side PR.

  d $PQRS$ is a rectangle. Write down the
     coordinates of the point S.

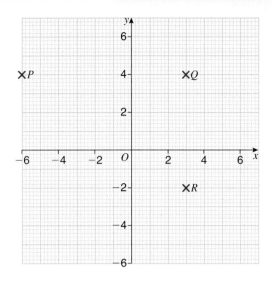

Graphs 2

16.1 Equations of vertical and horizontal lines

The diagram shows a vertical line drawn through the points $A(2, 6)$, $B(2, 2)$, $C(2, -1)$ and $D(2, -5)$.

The x-coordinate of each of these four points on the line is 2

All other points on this line also have an x-coordinate $= 2$

$x = 2$ is called the **equation of the line**.

Similarly, the x-coordinate of all points on the y-axis is 0

$x = 0$ is the equation of the y-axis.

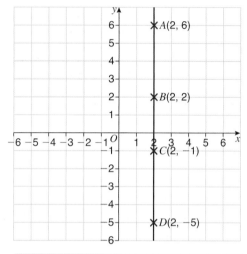

This diagram shows a horizontal line drawn through the points $P(-5, 3)$, $Q(-2, 3)$, $R(1, 3)$ and $S(4, 3)$.

The y-coordinate of all points on this horizontal line is 3
The equation of the line is $y = 3$

Similarly, the y-coordinate of all points on the x-axis is 0
$y = 0$ is the equation of the x-axis.

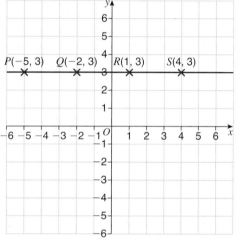

Example 1

From the grid:

a Write down the equation of the line EF

b Write down the equation of the line GH

c The point T is $(3, -2)$.
   i Write down the equation of the vertical line through T.
   ii Write down the equation of the horizontal line through T.

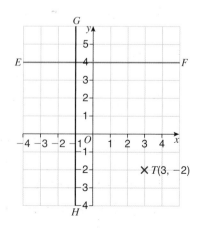

Solution 1

a $y = 4$

> The y-coordinate of all points on the line EF is 4

b $x = -1$

> The x-coordinate of all points on the line GH is -1

c i $x = 3$

> Draw the vertical blue line through T
> The x-coordinate of all points on this vertical line is 3

 ii $y = -2$

> Draw the horizontal red line through T
> The y-coordinate of all points on this horizontal line is -2

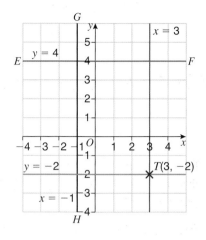

Exercise 16A

1 The diagram shows a square $ABCD$ and a rectangle $PQRS$.

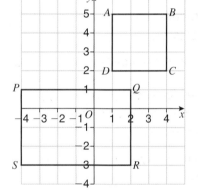

   a Write down the equation of the line
   - **i** AB **ii** BC **iii** CD
   - **iv** AD **v** QR **vi** RS
   - **vii** SP **viii** QP

   b For the rectangle $PQRS$, write down the equation of
   - **i** the horizontal line of symmetry,
   - **ii** the vertical line of symmetry.

   c For the square $ABCD$, write down the equation of
   - **i** the horizontal line of symmetry,
   - **ii** the vertical line of symmetry.

2 The point T is $(1, -1)$.

   a Write down the equation of the vertical line through T.

   b Write down the equation of the horizontal line through T.

3 The point U is $(-7, -9)$.

   a Write down the equation of the horizontal line through U.

   b Write down the equation of the vertical line through U.

4 Write down the equation of the line through the points

   a $(-4, -3)$ and $(-4, 1)$

   b $(0, -8)$ and $(0, 3)$

   c $(-1, -8)$ and $(7, -8)$.

16.2 Straight line graphs

The diagram shows a line drawn through the points $A(4, 4)$, $B(1, 1)$, $C(-2, -2)$, $D(-5, -5)$ and the origin O $(0, 0)$.

For each of these five points the y-coordinate is equal to the x-coordinate.

All other points on this line also have y-coordinate equal to the x-coordinate.

The equation of this line is $y = x$

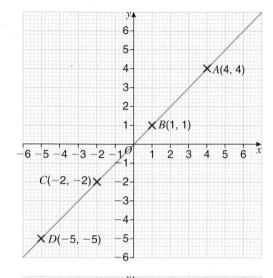

This diagram shows a line drawn through the points and $P(-5, 5)$, $Q(-3, 3)$, $R(1, -1)$, $S(4, -4)$ and the origin O $(0, 0)$.

For each of these five points the y-coordinate is equal to minus the x-coordinate. For example, for the point $P(-5, 5)$, the y-coordinate is $5 = -(-5)$.

All other points on this line also have a y-coordinate equal to minus the x-coordinate.

The equation of this line is $y = -x$

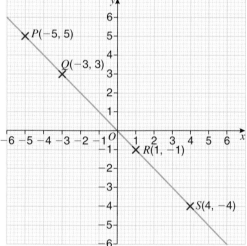

Example 2

a Find the equation of the line which passes through the points $E(3, 6)$, $F(1, 2)$, and $H(-2, -4)$.

b Find the equation of the line which passes through the points $T(3, 9)$, $U(2, 6)$, $V(-1, -3)$ and $W(-3, -9)$.

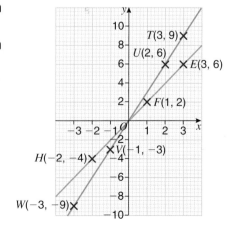

Solution 2

a   ×2
      E(3, 6)   ×2
                   F(1, 2)   ×2
                                H(−2, −4)

For all points on this line the *y*-coordinate is twice the *x*-coordinate, so the equation of this line is $y = 2x$

b   ×3
      T(3, 9)   ×3
                   U(2, 6)   ×3
                                V(−1, −3)   ×3
                                               W(−3, −9)

For all points on this line the *y*-coordinate is three times the *x*-coordinate, so the equation of this line is $y = 3x$

Tables of values

When drawing graphs, the coordinates of the points to be plotted are often shown in a **table of values**.

The straight line, with equation $y = 2x + 3$ passes through the point (3, 9), since $9 = 2 \times 3 + 3$. It also passes through the points (2, 7), (1, 5), (0, 3), (−1, 1), (−2, −1) and (−3, −3).

The table of values for these points is

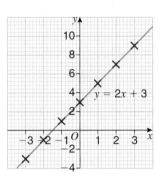

x	−3	−2	−1	0	1	2	3
y	−3	−1	1	3	5	7	9

The graph of $y = 2x + 3$ is shown on the grid.

Equations of the form $y = mx + c$, where *m* and *c* are numbers, always give straight line graphs.

Example 3

a   Complete this table of values for $y = 3x - 1$

x	−2	−1	0	1	2	3	4
y	−7			2	5		11

b   On the grid, draw the graph of $y = 3x - 1$

c   Use your graph to estimate the value of *x* when $y = 4$

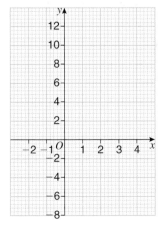

Solution 3

a
$$y = 3x - 1$$
When $x = 3$, $\quad y = 3 \times 3 - 1 = 8$
When $x = 0$, $\quad y = 3 \times 0 - 1 = -1$
When $x = -1$, $\quad y = 3 \times (-1) - 1 = -4$

x	−2	−1	0	1	2	3	4
y	−7	−4	−1	2	5	8	11

c When $y = 4$, $x = 1.7$

b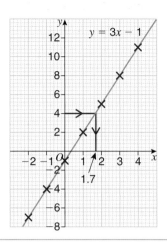

Example 4

a Draw the graph of $y = 5x - 4$. Use values of x from $x = -1$ to $x = 4$
b The point with coordinates $(k, 8)$ lies on the graph of $y = 5x - 4$

Use your graph to find the value of k.

Solution 4

a
$$y = 5x - 4$$
When $x = 4$, $\quad y = 5 \times 4 - 4 = 16$
When $x = 3$, $\quad y = 5 \times 3 - 4 = 11$
When $x = 2$, $\quad y = 5 \times 2 - 4 = 6$
When $x = 1$, $\quad y = 5 \times 1 - 4 = 1$
When $x = 0$, $\quad y = 5 \times 0 - 4 = -4$
When $x = -1$, $\quad y = 5 \times (-1) - 4 = -9$

x	−1	0	1	2	3	4
y	−9	−4	1	6	11	16

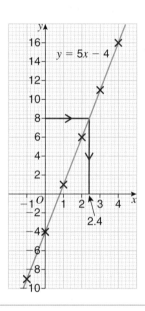

b At the point $(k, 8)$, $y = 8$
From the graph, when $y = 8$, $x = 2.4$ So $k = 2.4$

Exercise 16B

1 a i On the resource sheet, plot the points $(-1, 0)$, $(0, 1)$, $(2, 3)$, $(4, 5)$. Join the points with a straight line.
ii By comparing the x-coordinate and the y-coordinate of each point, find the equation of your line.
b i On the resource sheet, plot the points $(-2, 4)$, $(0, 0)$, $(1, -2)$, $(3, -6)$. Join the points with a straight line.
ii Find the equation of the line.

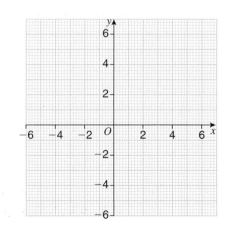

2 Here is a table of values for $y = 5 - 2x$

x	-2	-1	0	1	2	3	4
y	9	7	5	3	1	-1	-3

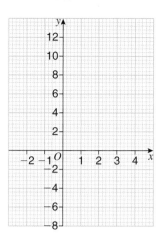

a On the resource sheet draw the graph of $y = 5 - 2x$

b Write down the coordinates of the points where your graph crosses

    i the y-axis   **ii** the x-axis.

c Use your graph to find the value of x when $y = 6$

3 a Copy and complete this table of values for $y = 4x - 7$

x	0	1	2	3	4	5
y		-3			9	

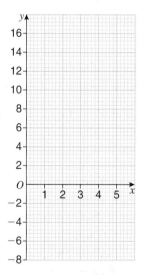

b On the resource sheet draw the graph of $y = 4x - 7$.

c Write down the coordinates of the point where your graph crosses the y-axis.

d Write down an estimate for the x-coordinate of the point where your graph crosses the x-axis.

e   **i** On the same axes, draw the graph of $x = 2.5$

    ii Write down the coordinates of the point where the two graphs cross.

f   **i** On the same axes, draw the graph of $y = -5$

    ii Write down the coordinates of the point where the graph of $y = -5$ crosses the graph of $y = 4x - 7$.

4 a Copy and complete this table of values for $y = 3x - 4$

x	-3	-2	-1	0	1	2	3
y			-7		-1		5

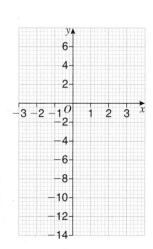

b On the resource sheet draw the graph of $y = 3x - 4$

c Write down the coordinates of the point where your graph crosses the y-axis.

d   **i** On the same axes, draw the graph of $y = x$.

    ii Write down the coordinates of the point where the two graphs cross.

e Find the coordinates of the point where the graph of $y = -x$ crosses the graph of $y = 3x - 4$

5 **a** On the resource sheet draw the graph of $y = 4x - 2$
Use values of x from $x = -2$ to $x = 3$

b The point with coordinates $(1.5, k)$ lies on the graph of
$y = 4x - 2$
Use your graph to find the value of k.

c On the same grid, draw the graph of
   i $y = 4x$ **ii** $y = 4x + 2$ **iii** $y = 4x - 4$

d What do you notice about the lines you have drawn?

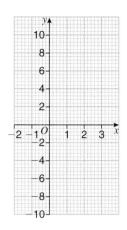

6 **a** Draw the graph of $y = 2 - x$. Use values of x from
$x = -3$ to $x = 4$.

b The point with coordinates $(k, 3.5)$ lies on the graph of $y = 2 - x$.
Use your graph to find the value of k.

16.3 Graph of $x + y = k$

Equations of the form $x + y = k$, where k is a number, always give straight line graphs.
To draw these straight line graphs, tables of values are not needed.

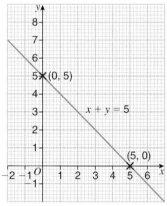

Consider the equation $x + y = 5$
When $x = 0$, $y = 5$ so $(0, 5)$ is a point on the graph of $x + y = 5$
When $y = 0$, $x = 5$ so $(5, 0)$ is a point on the graph of $x + y = 5$

The graph of $x + y = 5$ is shown here.

The line $x + y = 5$ crosses the axes at the points $(0, 5)$ and $(5, 0)$.

Example 5

a Find the coordinates of the points where the graph of $x + y = 6$ crosses the axes.
b Draw the graph of $x + y = 6$
c Find the coordinates of the point where the graphs of $y = x$ and $x + y = 6$ cross.

Solution 5

a On the x-axis, $y = 0$
When $y = 0$, $x = 6$
The graph crosses the x-axis at the point $(6, 0)$.

On the y-axis, $x = 0$
When $x = 0$, $y = 6$
The graph crosses the y-axis at the point $(0, 6)$.

c The graph of $y = x$ crosses the graph of
$x + y = 6$ at the point $(3, 3)$.

b

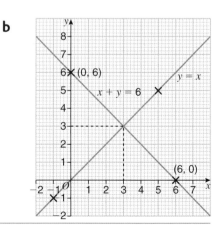

Exercise 16C

1 Find the coordinates of the points where the graphs of the following equations cross the axes:

   a $x + y = 2$ **b** $x + y = 7$ **c** $x + y = 11$

   d $x + y = 15$ **e** $x + y = -4$ **f** $x + y = -3$

2 **a** On the same axes, draw the graphs of:

       i $x + y = 2$ **ii** $x + y = 7$ **iii** $x + y = 10$

       iv $x + y = 13$ **v** $x + y = -10$ **vi** $x + y = -8$

   b What do you notice about the six graphs you have drawn?

Chapter summary

You should now be able to:

★ Recognise the equations of vertical and horizontal lines. For example you should know that:
  - $x = 5$ is the equation of the **vertical line** passing through the point (5, 3)
  - $y = 3$ is the equation of the **horizontal line** passing through the point (5, 3)

★ Recognise the graphs with equations $y = x$ and $y = -x$.

★ Draw a **straight line graph** from a given linear equation and given values of x where the equation is of the form $y = mx + c$, where m and c are numbers by:
  - drawing a **table of values** for calculated values of y
  - plotting the points from the table of values
  - joining the points with a straight line.

★ Draw a straight line graph from a given equation in the form $x + y = k$, where k is a number, plot the points where the line crosses the x-axis and the y-axis and join the points with a straight line. For example $x + y = 2$ crosses the axes at (0, 2) and (2, 0).

Chapter 16 review questions

1 The point T is (2, −3)

   a Write down the equation of the horizontal line through T.

   b Write down the equation of the vertical line through T.

2 Write down the equation of the line through the points

   a (−4, 0) and (4, 0)

   b (−7, −8) and (−7, 8).

3 Copy and complete this table of values for $y = 5x + 13$

x	−4	−3	−2	−1	0	1	2
y							

4　**a**　Copy and complete the table of values for $y = 3x + 1$

x	−2	−1	0	1	2	3
y	−5			4		10

　　b　On the resource sheet draw the graph of $y = 3x + 1$

　　c　Use your graph to find the value of x when $y = 6$ 　　　　(1385 Nov 2002)

5　**a**　Copy and complete the table of values for $y = 2x + 3$

x	−2	−1	0	1	2	3
y		1	3			

　　b　On the resource sheet, draw the graph of $y = 2x + 3$

　　c　Use your graph to find　**i** the value of y when $x = -1.3$
　　　　　　　　　　　　　　ii the value of x when $y = 5.4$ 　　　　(1387 June 2004)

6　**a**　Copy and complete the table of values for $y = 3 - 2x$

x	−2	−1	0	1	2	3
y	7		3			−3

　　b　On the resource sheet draw the graph of $y = 3 - 2x$

　　c　Use your graph to find the value of y when $x = 2.2$

　　The point with coordinates $(k, 4)$ lies on the graph of $y = 3 - 2x$

　　d　Use your graph to find the value of k.

7　**a**　On the same axes, draw the graphs of
　　　　i $x + y = 6$　　**ii** $y = x$

　　b　Write down the coordinates of the point where the two graphs cross.

　　c　Write down
　　　　i the gradient　**ii** the y-intercept of the straight line $y = -5x + 9$

8　**a**　On the same axes, draw the graphs of
　　　　i $x + y = 10$　　**ii** $y = 3x$

　　b　Write down the coordinates of the point where the two graphs cross.

Measure

17.1 Reading scales

This is a speedometer in a car

and this is the knob on an oven.

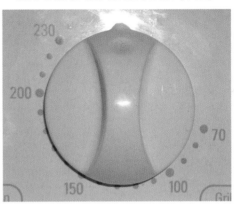

It is important to be able to read and use different types of scales.
Here are some common scales.

This ruler measures the
length of the line.

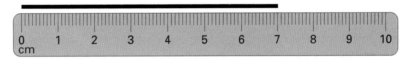

The units shown on the ruler are centimetres (cm). The line is 7 cm long.

This measuring cylinder measures the
volume of liquid.
There are 90 cm^3 of liquid in the cylinder.

These scales measure the
weight of potatoes.
The weight of potatoes is 2 kg.

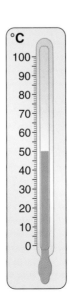

This thermometer measures
temperature.
The temperature is 50°C.

This clock shows the time.
The time is 1 o'clock.

Example 1

Write down the number marked by

a   arrow A

b   arrow B

c   arrow C.

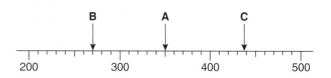

Solution 1

It is first necessary to work out what each small division on the scale represents. There are 10 small divisions for each 100, so each small division is 10

a   The number marked by A is 350

> The arrow A is halfway between 300 and 400

b   The number marked by B is 270

> The arrow B is between 200 and 300.
> The arrow is on the seventh small division from 200 so is 70 more than 200

c   The number marked by C is 438

> The arrow C is between 400 and 500
> The arrow is between the third and fourth small division from 400, so the arrow is between 430 and 440
> The arrow is a little more than halfway between 430 and 440 so it is necessary to estimate the number marked by the arrow.

Example 2

Find the number 4.8 on this number line. Mark it with an arrow (↓).

Solution 2

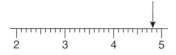

> 4.8 is between 4 and 5
> There are 10 small divisions between 4 and 5 so 10 small divisions is 1, and each small division is 0.1
> 4.8 is 0.8 more than 4 and this means 8 small divisions after 4

Example 3

What time is shown on this clock?

Solution 3

The time shown on the clock is 9.30 or half past 9

> The clock has no numbers on it but it has 12 divisions. Each division marks an hour for the hour hand, and 5 minutes for the minute hand. The hour hand is pointing between 9 and 10
> The minute hand is pointing to 6, which is 6 × 5 = 30 minutes after the hour.

1 Write down the readings on these scales. State the units of each answer

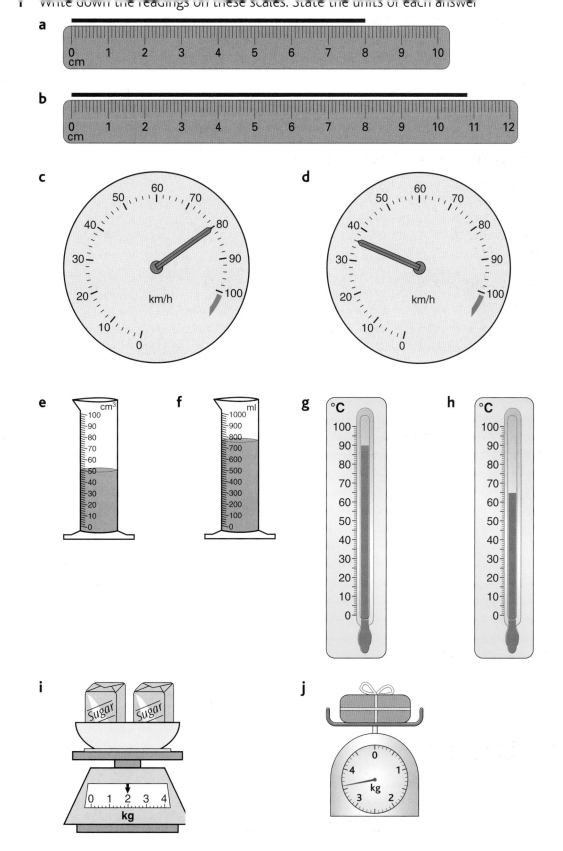

a

b

c

d

e

f

g

h

i

j

a

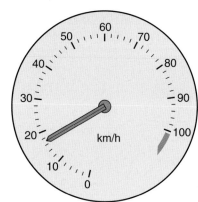

1 2 3 4 5 6 7 8 9 10 11 12 13 14 15 16 17 18 19 20 21 22 23 24 25 26 27 28 29 30
cm

b

cm³
100
90
80
70
60
50
40
30
20
10
0

c

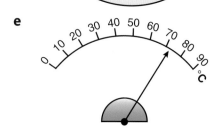

60
50 · · · | · · · 70
40 · · · · · · · · 80
30 · · · · · · · · 90
20 · · · · · · · 100
10 · · · · ·
0
km/h

d

0

40   10

l

30   20

e

0 10 20 30 40 50 60 70 80 90
°C

---

3 Write down the number marked by
i arrow A, **ii** arrow B, **iii** arrow C.
Be as accurate as possible.

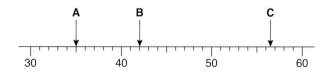

A   B   C
↓   ↓   ↓
500   600   700   800

---

4 Write down the number marked by
i arrow A, **ii** arrow B, **iii** arrow C.
Be as accurate as possible.

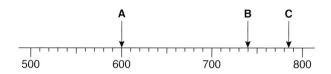

A   B   C
↓   ↓   ↓
30   40   50   60

---

5 Write down the number marked by
i arrow A, **ii** arrow B, **iii** arrow C.
Be as accurate as possible.

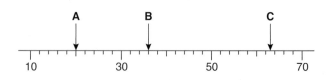

A   B   C
↓   ↓   ↓
10   30   50   70

---

6 **i** Use the resource sheet to answer this question. Find the number 280 on the number line. Mark it with an arrow (↓A)

ii Find the number 365 on the number line. Mark it with an arrow (↓B)

7 Write down the times shown on the clocks.

a

b

c

d

8 John sets his alarm for the time shown on this digital clock.
On the resource sheet draw the hands on the clock face to show the same time as the digital clock.

9 John has to catch a bus at the time shown on this digital clock.
On the resource sheet draw the hands on the clock face to show the same time as the digital clock.

10 The diagram shows a temperature scale marked in degrees Celsius (°C) and in degrees Fahrenheit (°F).

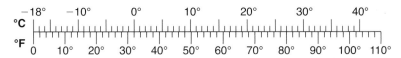

a What is the temperature in °C when the temperature is 50°F?

b What is the temperature in °F when the temperature is 40°C?

c What is the temperature in °F when the temperature is 25°C?

d What is the temperature in °C when the temperature is 42°F?

17.2 Time

It is important to be able to tell the time from clocks. There were some questions on telling the time in the last section.

A **digital** clock or watch has a number display.

Other clocks and watches are **analogue**.

An analogue clock or watch has hands.

This analogue clock shows the time as quarter to four. It does not say whether this is in the morning or in the afternoon. Analogue clocks only show 12-hour clock times.

To show whether a time on a 12-hour clock is in the morning, afternoon or evening we use **am** for times before noon (midday) and **pm** for times after noon.

24-hour clock times number the hours in a day from 00 to 24
In the 24-hour clock, times always have 4 figures.

Here are some examples of times on 12-hour and 24-hour clocks.

Times	12-hour clock	24-hour clock
3 minutes past midnight	12 03 am	00 03
4 o'clock early morning	4 am	04 00
Half past 11 late morning	11 30 am	11 30
4 o'clock in the afternoon	4 pm	16 00
Quarter past 7 in the evening	7 15 pm	19 15
3 minutes to midnight	11 57 pm	23 57

16 00 is read as sixteen hundred or sixteen hundred hours.

19 15 is read as nineteen fifteen.

At half past 3 in the morning (3 30 am),

a digital clock shows  an analogue clock shows

At half past 3 in the afternoon (3 30 pm),

a digital clock shows an analogue clock shows

Example 4

Change these times from 12-hour clock times to 24-hour clock times

a 10 15 am **b** 7 50 am **c** 5 pm

Solution 4

a 10 15

10 15 **am** is **before** noon and already has four figures.
So 10 15 stays the same.

b 07 50

7 50 **am** is **before** noon so 7 50 stays the same but there must be four figures in the 24-hour clock so write a 0 before the 7

c 17 00

5 **pm** is 5 hours **after** noon. Noon is 12 00 so add 5 to the 12 and write 00 as the number of minutes.

Example 5

Change these times from 24-hour clock times to 12-hour clock times.

a 09 05 **b** 23 00 **c** 21 40

Solution 5

a   9 05 am

> 9 is less than 12 so 09 05 is before noon.
> 09 05 stays the same, but write '09' as 9 and write **am** to show that
> 09 05 is **before** noon.

b   11 00 pm or 11 pm

> 23 is more than 12 so 23 00 is 11 hours (23 − 12 = 11) **after** noon so
> write **pm** and then 00 as the number of minutes. 11 00 pm is often
> shortened to 11 pm.

c   9 40 pm

> 21 is more than 12 so 21 40 is **after** noon so write **pm**.
> Subtract 12 from 21 to get the hours, (21 − 12 = 9)
> The number of minutes, 40, stays the same.

Exercise 17B

1   Change these times from 12-hour clock times to 24-hour clock times.

   a   9 am   **b**   9 pm   **c**   4 20 am   **d**   4 20 pm

   e   11 35 am   **f**   10 07 pm   **g**   12 18 pm   **h**   11 15 pm

2   Change these times from 24-hour clock times to 12-hour clock times, using am or pm.

   a   07 00   **b**   09 45   **c**   15 40   **d**   22 30

   e   10 58   **f**   01 56   **g**   18 00   **h**   12 40

3   Look at the time on this clock.

   a   If it is the morning, write the time in

      i   the 12-hour clock

      ii   the 24 hour clock.

   b   If it is the evening, write the time in

      i   the 12-hour clock

      ii   the 24 hour clock.

4   Write each of these times in **i** the 12-hour clock **ii** the 24-hour clock.

   a   half past 6 in the morning   **b**   twenty past ten at night

   c   5 past 1 in the morning   **d**   quarter to 8 in the evening

   e   twenty to seven in the morning   **f**   10 to 3 in the afternoon.

The following facts to do with time should be learnt.   60 seconds = 1 minute

                                          60 minutes = 1 hour

                                          24 hours = 1 day

                                          7 days = 1 week

Example 6

How many minutes are there in

a   2 hours   **b**   13 hours 40 minutes?

Solution 6

As there are 60 minutes in 1 hour, to change hours to minutes, multiply by 60

a   2 hours = 2 × 60 minutes

  = 120 minutes

> Work this out as
> 2 × 6 = 12 so 2 × 60 = 120

b   13 hours = 13 × 60 minutes

  = 780 minutes

> Use a calculator to work out 13 × 60

13 hours 40 minutes = 780 + 40

  = 820 minutes

> Then add on the 40 minutes.

Example 7

Change   **a** 180 seconds   **b** 255 seconds to minutes and seconds.

Solution 7

As there are 60 seconds in 1 minute, to change seconds to minutes, divide by 60

a   180 seconds = 180 ÷ 60 minutes

  = 3 minutes

> Work this out as 180 ÷ 60 = 18 ÷ 6 = 3

b   255 seconds = 255 ÷ 60 minutes

  = 4.25 minutes

  = 4 minutes 15 seconds

> Use a calculator to work out 255 ÷ 60
>
> A common mistake is to think that 4.25 minutes is 4 minutes 25 seconds.
>
> 0.25 minutes = 0.25 × 60 = 15 seconds so 4.25 minutes is 4 minutes 15 seconds.
>
> (Another way of finding the number of seconds above 4 minutes is to work out the number of seconds in 4 minutes (4 × 60 = 240) and then subtract it from 255)

Example 8

A painter takes 2 hours 48 minutes to paint the walls of a room and 1 hour 26 minutes to paint the window and the door. How long does she take in total?

Solution 8

Total time = 2 h 48 minutes + 1 h 26 minutes

> To find the total time add the two times.

2 + 1 = 3 hours

> Add the hours first.

48 + 26 = 74 minutes

> Then add the minutes.

74 minutes = 60 minutes + 14 minutes

  = 1 h 14 minutes

> Now change the minutes to hours and minutes. (60 minutes = 1 hour)

3 h + 1 h 14 minutes = 4 h 14 minutes

> Add these two answers.

Time taken = 4 hours 14 minutes

Example 9

One day, Sally spends 5 hours 20 minutes revising for her mathematics and science examinations. She spends 3 hours 45 minutes revising for mathematics. Work out how long she spends revising for science.

Solution 9

Science time = 5 h 20 minutes − 3 h 45 minutes

5 h 20 minutes = 4 h + 1 h + 20 minutes

$\qquad\qquad$ = 4 h + 60 minutes + 20 minutes

$\qquad\qquad$ = 4 h 80 minutes

Science time = 4 h 80 minutes − 3 h 45 minutes

$\qquad\qquad$ = 1 hour 35 minutes

> To find the time spent on science, find the difference between the two times.

> Look at the minutes first. You cannot take 45 from 20.

> Write 5 h as 4 h + 60 minutes

> 4 − 3 = 1 and 80 − 45 = 35

Example 10

A car journey starts at 10.35 am and finishes at 3.50 pm.
How long does the journey take?

Solution 10

Method 1

10.35 am to 11 am is 25 minutes

11 am to 3 pm is 4 hours

3 pm to 3.50 pm is 50 minutes

25 minutes + 4 hours + 50 minutes
$\quad$ = 4 hours 75 minutes
$\quad$ = 4 hours + 60 minutes + 15 minutes

Journey time = 5 hours 15 minutes

> Find the time from 10.35 am, the start.

> First, find the time to the next hour, in this case, 11 am
> 60 − 35 = 25 minutes.

> Next, find the time to the nearest hour before the finish, that is, 11 am to 3 pm.

> Then find the number of minutes to the finishing time, 3.50 pm.

> Finally, add all the times.

Method 2

$\quad$ 10.35 am = 10 35

$\quad\quad$ 3.50 pm = 15 50

15 h 50 minutes − 10 h 35 minutes
$\qquad\qquad$ = 5 h 15 minutes

> Using the 24-hour clock.

> Change both times to the 24-hour clock.

> 15 − 10 = 5 and 50 − 35 = 15

Using timetables

Times in a timetable are always given using the 24-hour clock.

Example 11

Here is part of a railway timetable.

Faversham	06 36		06 53	06 58		07 11
Sittingbourne	06 47		07 02	07 07		07 22
Gillingham	07 02	07 06	07 16	07 20	07 28	07 39
Chatham	07 06	07 10	07 20	07 24	07 31	07 43
Rochester		07 13	–		07 33	–
Swanley		07 40	–		07 58	–
St Mary Cray		07 45	–		08 03	–
Bromley South		07 52	07 50		08 11	08 14
London		08 17	08 15		08 35	08 38

a   A train leaves Gillingham at 07 28. At what time is this train at Bromley South?

b   Another train leaves Faversham at 06 53. How long does it take this train to get to London?

c   Michael is travelling from Sittingbourne to Chatham. He needs to be in Chatham *before* 07 35. Write down the time of the latest train he can catch in Sittingbourne.

Solution 11

In the timetable, each column gives the times at which a train is at each station.

a   The train is at Bromley South at 08 11

07 28
07 31
07 33
07 58
08 03
08 11
08 35

Find 07 28 in the table in the row for Gillingham and go down the column to the row for Bromley South.

b   The time taken is the time from 06 53 to 08 15

Find the 06 53 train in the Faversham row and find the time this train gets to London. This is 08 15

06 53 to 07 00 is 7 minutes
07 00 to 08 00 is 1 hour
08 00 to 08 15 is 15 minutes

Find the time from 06 53 to 08 15 as in Example 10 Method 1.

Time taken = 7 minutes + 1 h + 15 minutes
           = 1 hour 22 minutes

c   07 07

Look along the row for Chatham to find the latest time before 07 35. This is 07 31, but this train is not from Sittingbourne. The train before it arrives at 07 24 so find the time at which this train leaves Sittingbourne.

Exercise 17C

1 Change these times to minutes.

a 4 hours	**b** 11 hours	**c** 2 hours 50 minutes
d $1\frac{1}{4}$ hours	**e** 360 seconds	**f** 900 seconds

2 Change these times to hours.

a 2 days   **b** 1 week   **c** 480 minutes   **d** 7200 seconds

3 How many minutes are there in a day?

4 Change these times to minutes and seconds.

a 570 seconds   **b** 430 seconds   **c** 235 seconds

5 Change these times to hours and minutes.

a 340 minutes   **b** 294 minutes

6 A train leaves Dartford at 14 46 and arrives in London at 15 28
How long does the journey take?

7 A train leaves London at 12 03 and arrives in Ramsgate at 13 55
How long does the journey take?

8 Lance goes for a cycle ride. He leaves home at 12 15 and cycles for
5 hours 55 minutes. At what time does he finish his ride?

9 On Saturday Tony works in his garden for 5 hours 25 minutes. On Sunday he works in his garden for 3 hours 10 minutes. How long in total does he work in his garden on these two days?

10 A school's day starts at 8.35 am. The school's day ends at 3.20 pm.
How long does the school's day last?

11 A coach journey starts at 11 25 and is due to end at 16 10
    a How long should the journey take?
The coach actually arrives at its destination 20 minutes early.
    b How long does the journey take?

12 Stuart takes 5 hours 20 minutes to run a marathon. Michael takes 3 hours 30 minutes to run the same marathon. How much longer does Stuart take to run the marathon?

Here is part of a bus timetable.

Gravesend, Garrick Street	06 03		07 03	07 28	07 54
Chalk Post Office	06 13		07 13	07 40	
Higham	06 20		07 20	07 47	
Strood	06 27		07 27	08 00	08 16
Chatham, Rail Station	06 33		07 33	08 11	08 27
Medway Hospital	06 54	07 25		08 36	
Parkwood	07 13	07 44		08 55	09 09
Hempstead Valley	07 20	07 52	08 10	09 03	09 16

Here is part of a railway timetable.

Faversham	06 36		06 53	06 58		07 11
Sittingbourne	06 47		07 02	07 07		07 22
Gillingham	07 02	07 06	07 16	07 20	07 28	07 39
Chatham	07 06	07 10	07 20	07 24	07 31	07 43
Rochester		07 13	–		07 33	–
Swanley		07 40	–		07 58	–
St Mary Cray		07 45	–		08 03	–
Bromley South		07 52	07 50		08 11	08 14
London		08 17	08 15		08 35	08 38

Use these timetables to answer the following questions.

13 Rohit catches the 07 47 bus from Higham.
   a At what time should he arrive at Hempstead Valley?
   b How long should this bus journey take?

14 How many minutes does it take the 06 03 bus from Gravesend to reach Parkwood?

15 Karl is travelling from Chatham to London. He needs to arrive in London *before* 08 20
   Write down the time of the latest train he can catch from Chatham.

16 Chris wants to be in London by 08 40. He has to take a bus from Chalk Post Office to
   Chatham Rail Station, and then a train to London.
   a What is the time of the latest bus he can catch?
   b How long will the bus and train journeys take in total?
   c How long will he have to wait at the rail station?

17 When the 07 25 bus from Medway Hospital reaches Hempstead Valley, it waits
   25 minutes before returning to the hospital. At what time does this bus leave
   Hempstead Valley for its return journey to the hospital?

18 A train leaves Chatham at 07 20
   a At what time should this train reach London?
   b How long should this train take to reach London?

   Another train is due to leave Chatham at 07 31. This train takes longer to reach
   London than the 07 20 from Chatham.
   c Work out how many minutes longer the 07 31 train should take than the 07 20

19 The 06 36 train from Faversham starts at Ramsgate. The journey from Ramsgate to
   Faversham takes 51 minutes. At what time does this train leave Ramsgate?

20 Natasha travels by train from Sittingbourne to London. She leaves her home at 05 55
   Her journey to Sittingbourne station takes 65 minutes. Her train was on time. How
   long did Natasha wait for her train at Sittingbourne?

17.3 Units

Since 1971, the units used in the UK are supposed to be **metric** units, like metres, kilograms and litres. However miles, pounds and pints are still used. These are called **imperial** units.

The table shows some important metric units and imperial units.

	Length	Area	Capacity/volume	Weight
Metric	kilometre (km) metre (m) centimetre (cm) millimetre (mm)	hectare m² cm²	litre (*l*) millilitre (m*l*) m² cm³	tonne kilogram (kg) gram (g)
Imperial	mile yard foot inch	acre	gallon pint	ton pound ounce

Example 12

Write down a sensible metric unit that should be used to measure

a   the height of a house

b   the weight of an elephant

c   the amount of petrol in a car tank.

Solution 12

The question asks for metric units.

a   The height of a house can be measured in metres.

> A house is not 1 km in height and centimetres are too small.

b   The weight of an elephant can be measured in kilograms.

> An elephant is heavy so the expected answer is kilograms, but tonnes would be accepted.

c   The amount of petrol in a car tank can be measured in litres.

> Petrol is bought in litres.

Example 13

Decide whether each of these sentences is sensible. If a sentence is not sensible, change the unit so that it is.

a   My teacher is 1.8 mm tall.

b   A television programme lasted 30 minutes.

c   Lisa went to the supermarket and bought 3 tonnes of potatoes.

Solution 13

a My teacher is 1.8 m tall.

> 1.8 mm is clearly too short. The unit should be metres.

b This is a sensible sentence.

c Lisa went to the supermarket and bought 3 kg of potatoes.

> 3 tonnes is a lot of potatoes and Lisa could not carry 3 tonnes. The unit should be kg.

Example 14

The picture shows a man standing next to a tree. The man and the tree are drawn to the same scale.

Write down an estimate for the height in metres of

a the man   **b** the tree.

Solution 14

a The height of the man is 2 m

> A reasonable estimate for the height of a man is 1.5 m to 2 m.

b Height of tree = 4 × height of man

> In the scale drawing the height of the tree is 4 times the height of the man.

Height of tree = 4 × 2 m = 8 m

> Multiply the height of the man by 4

Exercise 17D

1 Write down both the metric and the imperial units that are sensible for measuring each of the following.

  a The distance from London to York

  b The length of a pencil

  c The height of Blackpool Tower

  d The weight of a train

  e The weight of new-born baby

  f The weight of a packet of sweets

  g The volume of water in a swimming pool

  h The volume of drink in a large bottle of cola.

2 The following sentences do not make sense because the wrong unit has been used. Write the sentences using the correct unit for each.

  a The weight of a packet of biscuits is 150 kg

  b The thickness of a book is 3 m

  c The height of a giraffe is 5 km

  d A tea cup can hold 300 *l* of tea.

3 The picture shows Sean standing beside a wall. Sean and the wall are drawn to the same scale.

Estimate the height and the length of the wall.

17.4 Converting between metric units

To change from one metric unit to another metric unit it is necessary to know the results in this table.

Length	Weight	Capacity/volume
10 mm = 1 cm	1000 mg = 1 g	100 c*l* = 1 litre
100 cm = 1 m	1000 g = 1 kg	1000 m*l* = 1 litre
1000 mm = 1 m	1000 kg = 1 tonne	1000 cm³ = 1 litre
1000 m = 1 km		1000 *l* = 1 m³

You only need to multiply or divide by 10, 100 or 1000

- **When you change from a unit to a larger unit you divide.**
- **When you change from a unit to a smaller unit you multiply.**

For example, to convert lengths

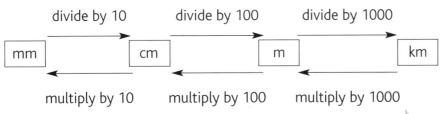

Example 15

a   Change 12 m to centimetres.   **b**   Change 2670 g to kg.

Solution 15

a   12 m = 12 × 100 cm
          = 1200 cm

> Centimetres are smaller than metres so there are more of them. As 100 cm = 1 m, multiply by 100

b   2670 g = 2670 ÷ 1000
            = 2.67 kg

> Kilograms are larger than grams so there are fewer of them. As 1000 g = 1 kg, divide by 1000

Exercise 17E

1   Change these lengths to millimetres.

    a 5 cm   **b** 13 cm   **c** 8.4 cm   **d** 28.9 cm   **e** 8.27 cm

2   Change these lengths to centimetres.

    a 6 m   **b** 210 mm   **c** 5.1 m   **d** 0.84 m

    e 59 mm   **f** 483 mm   **g** 3 km   **h** 0.067 km

3   Change these lengths to metres.

    a 4 km   **b** 500 cm   **c** 9.2 km   **d** 230 cm   **e** 0.62 km

4   Change these lengths to kilometres.

    a 6000 m   **b** 2600 m   **c** 640 m

5   Change these weights to kilograms.

    a 3 tonnes   **b** 8.2 tonnes   **c** 6000 g

    d 900 g   **e** 430 g   **f** 4700 g

6   Change these weights to grams.

    a 7 kg   **b** 48 kg   **c** 2.3 kg

    d 9000 mg   **e** 830 mg   **f** 1 tonne

7   Change these weights to tonnes.

    a 7000 kg   **b** 800 kg   **c** 700 g   **d** 320 g

8   Change these volumes to litres.

    a 2000 m*l*   **b** 700 c*l*   **c** 5900 m*l*   **d** 45 000 m*l*

9   Change these volumes to millilitres

    a 3 *l*   **b** 7.2 *l*   **c** 2 c*l*

10   A bottle of drink contains 70 cl. How many litres of drink are there in ten of these bottles?

17.5 Converting between metric and imperial units

When converting between the metric and imperial
systems, methods of proportion can be used.
These approximate conversions should be learnt.

Metric	Imperial
2.5 cm	1 inch
8 km	5 miles
1 m	39 inches
30 cm	1 foot
1 kg	2.2 pounds
4.5 litres	1 gallon
1 litre	1.75 pints

Example 16

a Change 6 litres to pints.

b Change 11 pounds to kilograms.

Solution 16

a 1 litre is approximately $1\frac{3}{4}$ pints,
or 1.75 pints

There will be more pints than litres so *multiply* the number of litres by the number of pints in 1 litre.

$6 \times 1.75 = 10.5$

6 litres is approximately 10.5 pints

b 1 kg is approximately 2.2 pounds

$11 \div 2.2 = 5$

There will be fewer kg than pounds so *divide* the number of pounds by 2.2

11 pounds is approximately 5 kg

Exercise 17F

1 Change 10 miles to kilometres.

2 Change 3 kilograms to pounds.

3 Change 7 pints to litres.

4 Change 6 gallons to litres.

5 Change 8 inches to centimetres.

6 Change 32 kilometres to miles.

7 Change 90 centimetres to feet.

8 Change 22 pounds to kilograms.

9 Change 2 litres to pints.

10 Change 36 litres to gallons.

11 Changes 25 centimetres to inches.

12 Alan fills his car up with petrol. He buys 45 litres. Change 45 litres to gallons.

13 Oliver buys 4 pounds of apples. Change 4 pounds to kilograms.

14 The distance between two towns is 300 miles. Change 300 miles to kilometres.

15 A car is travelling at a speed of 80 kilometres per hour.
Change 80 kilometres per hour to miles per hour.

17.6 Compound measures – speed and density

Speed

A car travels 90 kilometres in 3 hours. If it travels the 90 km at the same speed for the whole 3 hours, then the car would travel $\dfrac{90}{3} = 30$ km each hour. This means that 30 kilometres per hour is the **average speed** of the car.

The word 'per' here means 'each' or 'for every'.

Notice that the distance travelled is divided by the time taken so

$$\text{average speed} = \frac{\text{total distance travelled}}{\text{total time taken}}$$

Speed is called a **compound measure** because it involves a unit of length *and* a unit of time. Speed is often measured in kilometres per hour, miles per hour or metres per second.

We write 30 kilometres per hour as 30 km/h – the '/' is a sort of division sign showing that speed is distance divided by time.

If a car travels at an average speed of 40 km/h,

the car travels 40 km in 1 hour,

$40 \times 2 = 80$ km in 2 hours,

$40 \times 3 = 120$ km in 3 hours and so on.

So $\qquad$ **distance = average speed × time**

The time the car takes to travel 120 km at 40 km/h is $\dfrac{120}{40} = 3$ hours.

So $\qquad$ $\text{time} = \dfrac{\text{distance}}{\text{average speed}}$

Using D to stand for distance, S to stand for average speed and T to stand for time, this diagram shows a way to remember these results.

Just cover the thing you want to work out with your thumb. What's left shows you what do do.

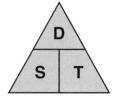

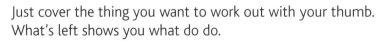

distance $\quad$ = speed × time

speed $\quad = \dfrac{\text{distance}}{\text{time}}$

time $\quad = \dfrac{\text{distance}}{\text{speed}}$

Example 17

The distance from London to Nottingham is 195 km. Nitesh drives from London to Nottingham in 3 hours. Work out Nitesh's average speed for this journey.

Solution 17

average speed $= \dfrac{195}{3} = 65$ km/h

average speed $= \dfrac{\text{total distance travelled}}{\text{total time taken}}$

The distance is in km and the time is in hours, so the speed is in km/h.

Example 18

Michael goes for a cycle ride. He rides for 3 hours at an average speed of 15 miles per hour.
Work out the distance he rode.

Solution 18

distance $= 15 \times 3 = 45$ miles

distance = average speed × time.
The speed is in miles per hour and the time is in hours, so the distance is in miles.

Example 19

Here is a distance chart, which shows the distances in kilometres between some cities.

a Use the chart to find the distance from Glasgow to Liverpool.

Susan drives from Glasgow to Liverpool at an average speed of 40 km/h.

b Work out the time, in hours and minutes, her journey takes.

Cardiff

600	Edinburgh					
602	72	Glasgow				
362	362	401	Hull			
335	311	340	90	Leeds		
266	344	348	206	117	Liverpool	
304	612	613	383	359	304	Swansea

Solution 19

a The distance between Glasgow and Liverpool is 348 km.

Read down from Glasgow and across from Liverpool.

Cardiff

600	Edinburgh					
602	72	Glasgow				
362	362	401	Hull			
335	311	340	90	Leeds		
266	344	348	206	117	Liverpool	
304	612	613	383	359	304	Swansea

b   Time $= \dfrac{348}{40}$

$\qquad\quad = 8.7$ h

$0.7 \times 60 = 42$

Time $= 8$ h 42 minutes

time $= \dfrac{\text{distance}}{\text{average speed}}$

Speed is in km/h and distance is in km so the time is in hours.

8.7 h $= 8$ h $+ 0.7$ h

To change 0.7 h to minutes, multiply 0.7 by 60, as there are 60 minutes in an hour.

Exercise 17G

1 Paul goes for a walk. He walks 12 km in 2 hours. Work out his average speed on the walk.

2 Greg goes for a cycle ride. He rides for 4 hours at an average speed of 20 km/h. Work out the distance that Greg rides.

3 The distances in the chart are in kilometres.

Bristol						
330	Hull					
187	143	Leicester				
269	71	82	Lincoln			
183	275	156	214	London		
261	154	142	135	296	Manchester	
349	65	169	119	312	105	York

   a Use the distance chart to find the distance between Hull and London.

   Kim drives from Hull to London at an average speed of 50 km/h.

   b Work out the time her journey takes.

4 Tim sets off from his home at 11 am and goes for a 20 km run. He arrives back at his home at 1 pm. Work out Tim's average speed.

5 How far does Stuart travel in 30 minutes if his average speed is 50 miles per hour?

6 A horse runs 12 km at an average speed of 10 km/h. How long, in hours and minutes, does this take?

7 A racing car travels at 85 m/s. Work out the distance the car travels in 0.4 seconds.

8 Change a speed of 85 m/s to km/h.

9 John drives from his home to visit a friend.
John drives the first 3 hours at an average speed of 40 km/h.
   a Work out the distance he drives in the 3 hours.

   John then drives the remaining 60 km to his friend's house at an average speed of 30 km/h.
   b Work out the time John takes to drive the 60 km.
   c Work out
      i the total distance that John drives to his friend's house
      ii the total time he takes to drive from his home to his friend's house.
   d Work out John's average speed for his journey from his home to his friend's house.

10 In an athletics match the 100 m was won in a time of 9.91 s and the 200 m was won in a time of 19.79 s. Which race was won with the faster average speed? You must give a reason for your answer.

Use this chart to answer questions **11** and **12**.

The distances in the chart are in kilometres.

Bristol						
330	Hull					
187	143	Leicester				
269	71	82	Lincoln			
183	275	156	214	London		
261	154	142	135	296	Manchester	
349	65	169	119	312	105	York

11 One morning James drives from his home in Hull to Lincoln and then from Lincoln to York.

    a   **i** Find the total distance he drives.

        ii How much further is this than the direct route from Hull to York?

In the afternoon James returns home by the direct route from York to Hull.
His average speed is 50 km/h in both the morning and the afternoon.

    b Work out how many minutes less his afternoon journey takes than his morning journey.

12 On Monday Jane drives from Bristol to Lincoln, and then from Lincoln to Hull.
On Tuesday she returns by the direct route from Hull to Bristol.
Her average speed is 50 km/h on both days.
Work out how many minutes less her journey took on Tuesday than on Monday.

Density

To work out the density of a substance, divide its mass by its volume

$$\text{density} = \frac{\text{mass}}{\text{volume}}$$

Density is also a compound measure. It involves a unit of mass and a unit of volume.

In the diagram M stands for mass, D stands for density and V stands for volume.

$$\text{mass} = \text{density} \times \text{volume}$$
$$\text{density} = \frac{\text{mass}}{\text{volume}}$$
$$\text{volume} = \frac{\text{mass}}{\text{density}}$$

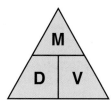

When the mass is measured in kg and the volume in cubic metres (m^3), then density is measured in kg per m^3 or kg/m^3. Density can also be measured in g/cm^3.

Example 20

A piece of silver has a mass of 42 g and a volume of 4 cm^3. Work out the density of silver.

Solution 20

$\text{Density} = \dfrac{\text{mass}}{\text{volume}}$

      $= \dfrac{42}{4}$

      $= 10.5$ g/cm^3

> Divide the mass by the volume.

> As the mass is in g and the volume is in cm^3, the density is in g/cm^3.

Example 21

The density of steel is 7700 kg/m³.

a   A steel bar has a volume of 2.5 m³. Work out the mass of the bar.

b   A block of steel has a mass of 1540 kg. Work out the volume of the block.

Solution 21

a   Mass = density × volume | Multiply the density by the volume. |

$\qquad$ = 7700 × 2.5

$\qquad$ = 19 250 kg | As the density is in kg/m³ and the volume is in m³, the mass is in kg. |

b   Volume = $\dfrac{\text{mass}}{\text{density}}$ | Divide the mass by the density. |

$\qquad = \dfrac{1540}{7700}$ | As the mass is in kg and the density is in kg/m³ the volume is in m³. |

$\qquad = 0.2$ m³

Exercise 17H

1   The density of iron is 7.86 g/cm³. The volume of an iron block is 100 cm³. Work out the mass of the iron block.

2   A slab of concrete has a volume of 60 cm³ and a mass of 15 000 g. Work out the density of the concrete.

3   Gold has a density of 19.3 g/cm³. The gold in a ring has a mass of 15 g. Work out the volume of the gold in the ring.

4   The density of balsa wood is 0.2 g/cm³. The volume of a model made of balsa wood is 150 cm³. Work out the mass of the model.

5   14.7 g of sulphur has a volume of 7.5 cm³. Work out the density of sulphur.

Chapter summary

You should now be able to

★   Read and interpret scales on a range of measuring instruments

★   Tell the time on digital and analogue clocks

★   Read and use times on the 12-hour and 24-hour clocks

★   Solve problems involving time, including changing units

★   Read timetables and distance charts

★   Choose a suitable unit for a measurement

★   Estimate lengths from scale drawings

★   Convert between metric units

★   Convert between metric and imperial units

★   Understand and use speed and density

Chapter 17 review questions

1 Write down the **metric** unit you would use to measure:

  a the length of a person's hand

  b the weight of a mouse

  c the distance from Manchester to London

  d a teaspoon of medicine. *(1384 June 1998)*

2 The picture shows the scale on the side of a kettle.

  How many litres of water are needed to fill 5 cups?

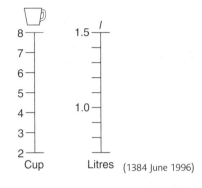

(1384 June 1996)

3 Hamish arrived at the train station at the time shown on the clock.

  a Write down the time shown.

  The train arrived 30 minutes later.

  b Use the resource sheet to draw the hands on the clock face to show the time when the train arrived.

  c Write this time as it would be shown on a 24-hour clock

    i in the morning   **ii** in the evening.

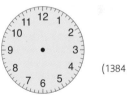

(1384 June 1997)

4 Write down the reading shown on this scale.

  Be as accurate as you can.

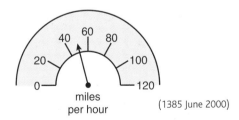

(1385 June 2000)

5 Write down the name of a unit which is used to measure:

  a the length of a garden

  b the amount of petrol in a car's petrol tank

  c the area of a school playing field

  d the weight of a calculator. *(1385 June 2000)*

6 Copy and complete this table with sensible units for each measurement.

	Metric	Imperial
The distance from Leeds to Liverpool	....	miles
The weight of a small packet of crisps	grams	....
The amount of petrol in a car's petrol tank	....	....

(1385 June 2001)

7 a

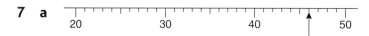

Write down the number marked with an arrow.

b

Write down the number marked with an arrow.

c

Find the number 430 on the number line.
Mark it with an arrow (↑) on the resource sheet.

d

Find the number 3.7 on the number line.
Mark it with an arrow (↑) on the resource sheet.

(1387 June 2003)

8 Copy and complete this table.
Write a sensible unit for each measurement.

	Metric	Imperial
The weight of a turkey	....	pounds
The volume of water in a swimming pool	....	gallons
The width of this page	centimetres	....

(1387 June 2003)

9   Write down the reading on each of these scales.

    a   Thermometer

    b   Speedometer

    c   Weighing scales

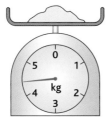

(1388 March 2002)

10   **a**   What is the reading on Scale A?

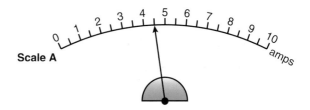

    b   What is the reading on Scale B?

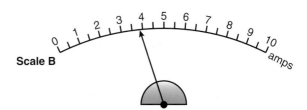

    c   On the resource sheet draw an arrow on Scale C to show a reading of 6.2 amps. Be as accurate as you can.

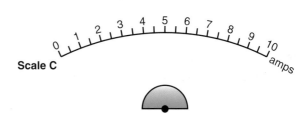

    d   The diagram can be used to convert between temperatures in °C and temperatures in °F.

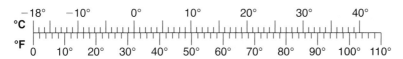

      Use the diagram to convert

       i   10°C to °F   **ii**   14°F to °C.   (1385 May 2002)

11 Here is part of a train timetable from Crewe to London.

Station	Time of Leaving
Crewe	08 00
Wolverhampton	08 40
Birmingham	09 00
Coventry	09 30
Rugby	09 40
Milton Keynes	10 10

a At what time should the train leave Coventry?

The train should arrive in London at 10 45

b How long should the train take to travel from Crewe to London?

Verity arrived at Milton Keynes at 09 53

c How many minutes should she have to wait before the 10 10 train leaves?

(1387 June 2003)

12 Here is part of a bus timetable.

Bolton – Walkden – Manchester								
Mondays to Fridays								
Bolton, Bus Station						07 05		
Farnworth, King Street			06 30		06 54	07 24	07 39	
New Bury, Tennyson Road			06 36		07 00	07 30	07 45	
Little Hulton, Spa Hotel			06 42		07 06	07 36	07 51	
Little Hulton, Cleggs Ln			06 46		07 11	07 41	07 56	
Walkden Centre		06 35	06 52	07 02	07 17	07 47	08 02	
Worsley, Court House	06 12	06 42	06 59	07 11	07 26	07 56	08 11	
Monton Green	06 18	06 48	07 07	07 19	07 34	08 04	08 19	
Eccless, College Croft	06 25	06 55	07 15	07 27	07 42	08 12	08 27	
Manchester, Cannon St	06 46	07 22	07 42	07 54	08 09	08 39	08 54	

A bus is due to arrive at Manchester, Cannon St at 08 09

a At what time should this bus leave Farnworth, King Street?

Only one bus starts from Worsley Court House.

b At what time should this bus arrive at Manchester, Cannon St?

A bus leaves Bolton Bus Station at 07 05

c How long should it take to travel to Worsley Court House on this bus?

(1384 June 1999)

13 Here is part of a bus timetable.

Wigan – Atherton – Eccles – Manchester					
Wigan, Bus Station	05 30	05 55	06 20		06 40
Castle Hill	05 45	06 10	06 35		06 55
Hindley Green	05 52	06 17	06 42		07 02
Atherton	05 58	06 23	06 48	07 00	07 10
Tyldesley	06 04	06 29	06 54	07 06	07 16
Monton Green	06 25	06 50	07 15	07 29	07 39
Eccles	06 31	06 56	07 22	07 36	07 46
Weaste	06 33	06 58	07 25	07 39	07 49
Trafford Road	06 36	07 01	07 30	07 44	07 54
Manchester, Bus Station	06 50	07 17	07 46	08 00	08 10

a At what time should the 06 20 from Wigan arrive at Monton Green?

b How long should it take the 06 29 bus from Tyldesley to travel to Trafford Road?

Susan catches a bus in Atherton.
She needs to be in Eccles by 07 00.

c What is the time of the latest bus she could catch from Atherton?

(1385 June 2000)

14 The diagram shows a man standing
next to a tram.
The man is of average height.

a Write down an estimate for the
height of the man.
Give your answer in metres.

b Estimate the length of the tram.
Give your answer in metres.

(1384 June 1999)

15 The diagram shows a man standing next to a radio mast.
The man is of average height.

a Write down an estimate for the height of the man.
Give your answer in metres.

b Estimate the height of the radio mast.
Give your answer in metres.

(1385 June 2001)

16 a Write down the name of a **metric** unit which is used to measure:

    i the distance from London to Brighton

    ii the weight of a bar of soap.

  b **i** Change 240 millimetres to centimetres.

    ii Change 3.8 litres to millilitres.

(1388 March 2003)

17 **a** Write down a sensible **metric** unit that should be used to measure
   i the height of a school hall
   ii the weight of a pencil.

b Write down a sensible **imperial** unit that should be used to measure
the distance between London and Manchester.

(1387 June 2004)

18 Change 4 kg to pounds.

19 Change 28 miles to kilometres.

20 The mass of 5 m³ of copper is 44 800 kg.

a Work out the density of copper.

The density of zinc is 7130 kg/m³.

b Work out the mass of 5 m³ of zinc.

(1387 Nov 2003)

21 Daniel leaves his home at 07 00.
He drives 87 miles to work.
He drives at an average speed of 36 miles per hour.

At what time does Daniel arrive at work?

(1387 Nov 2003)

22 These two metal blocks each have a
volume of 0.5 m³.
The density of the copper block is
8900 kg per m³.
The density of the nickel block is 8800 kg per m³.

Calculate the difference in the masses of the blocks.

(1385 June 2001)

23 This dial shows how much petrol is in the
petrol tank of a car.

The full petrol tank holds 40 litres.
Estimate how many litres are left in the
petrol tank.

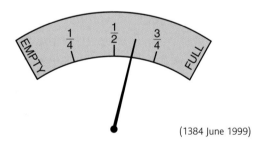

(1384 June 1999)

Percentages 1

18.1 Introduction

... all salaries will increase by 6% ...

The pictures show examples of the use of **percentages**.

Per cent means 'out of 100'.
35 per cent means 35 out of 100 or, as a fraction, $\frac{35}{100}$
35 per cent is written as 35%.

Learn these percentages with their fraction and decimal equivalents.

Percentage	Fraction	Decimal
1%	$\frac{1}{100}$	$\frac{1}{100} = 0.01$
10%	$\frac{10}{100} = \frac{1}{10}$	$\frac{10}{100} = 0.1$
20%	$\frac{20}{100} = \frac{1}{5}$	$\frac{20}{100} = 0.2$
25%	$\frac{25}{100} = \frac{1}{4}$	$\frac{25}{100} = 0.25$
50%	$\frac{50}{100} = \frac{1}{2}$	$\frac{50}{100} = 0.5$
75%	$\frac{75}{100} = \frac{3}{4}$	$\frac{75}{100} = 0.75$
100%	$\frac{100}{100} = 1$	$\frac{100}{100} = 1$

Example 1

Shade 30% of this diagram.

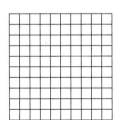

Solution 1

The large square is divided into 100 small squares.

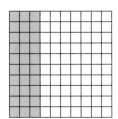

> 30% means 30 out of 100 or $\frac{30}{100}$ so shade 30 of the 100 small squares.

Example 2

Write each of these percentages as: **i** a fraction in its simplest form   **ii** a decimal.

a   45%   **b**   3%   **c** $17\frac{1}{2}\%$

Solution 2

a   **i** $45\% = \dfrac{45}{100}$

> Write 45% as a fraction with a denominator of 100

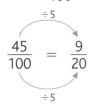

$$\frac{45}{100} = \frac{9}{20}$$

> 5 is a common factor of 45 and 100
> Divide both 45 and 100 by 5 to get $\frac{9}{20}$
> 9 and 20 do not have a common factor and so $\frac{9}{20}$ is in its simplest form.

   ii $45\% = \dfrac{45}{100}$

> Write the percentage as a fraction with a denominator of 100

$$\frac{45}{100} = 0.45$$

> Change the fraction into a decimal.

b   **i** $3\% = \dfrac{3}{100}$

> $\frac{3}{100}$ cannot be simplified as there is no number that divides exactly into both 3 and 100

   ii $3\% = \dfrac{3}{100} = 0.03$

> Write the 3 in the hundredths column and a 0 in the tenths column.

c   **i** $17\frac{1}{2}\% = \dfrac{17\frac{1}{2}}{100}$

> $17\frac{1}{2}\%$ means $17\frac{1}{2}$ out of 100

$$\frac{17\frac{1}{2}}{100} \overset{\times 2}{\underset{\times 2}{=}} \frac{35}{200}$$

> Multiply both $17\frac{1}{2}$ and 100 by 2 to change the $17\frac{1}{2}$ to a whole number.

$$\frac{35}{200} \overset{\div 5}{\underset{\div 5}{=}} \frac{7}{40}$$

> 5 is a common factor of 35 and 200
> Divide both 35 and 200 by 5 to get $\frac{7}{40}$
> 7 and 40 do not have a common factor and so $\frac{7}{40}$ is in its simplest form.

   ii   **(1)** $17\frac{1}{2}\% = 17.5\% = \dfrac{17.5}{100}$

> $\frac{1}{2}$ is the same as 0.5

$$\frac{17.5}{100} = 17.5 \div 100$$

> To work out $17.5 \div 100$ without a calculator move each figure of the 17.5 two places to the right as described in Section 7.5

$$17\frac{1}{2}\% = 0.175$$

   (2) $\dfrac{17.5}{100} = \dfrac{175}{1000}$

> Alternatively, multiply both 17.5 and 100 by 10 and then write $\frac{175}{1000}$ as a decimal.

$$17\frac{1}{2}\% = 0.175$$

   (3) $\dfrac{17.5}{100} = 0.175$

> With a calculator, work this out by keying in
> 17.5 [÷] 100 [=]

Example 3

What percentage of the shape is shaded?

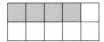

Solution 3

$\frac{4}{10}$ is shaded

> The shape is made up of 10 equal sized squares.
> 4 of the 10 squares are shaded.

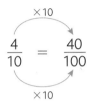

$$\frac{4}{10} = \frac{40}{100}$$

> A percentage is a fraction with a denominator of 100
> As $10 \times 10 = 100$, to get a denominator of 100, multiply both 10 and 4 by 10

$\frac{40}{100} = 40\%$

40% of the shape is shaded.

Exercise 18A

1 Write each percentage as a fraction.

    a 79%   **b** 9%   **c** 57%   **d** 1%   **e** 7%

2 Write each percentage as a fraction in its simplest form.

    a 50%   **b** 25%   **c** 75%   **d** 30%

    e 2%   **f** 84%   **g** 95%   **h** 32%

3 Write each percentage as a decimal.

    a 63%   **b** 98%   **c** 7%

    d 25%   **e** 60%   **f** 23.5%

4 28% of children walk to school.
What fraction of children walk to school? Give your fraction in its simplest form.

5 78% of the houses on a street have double glazing.
Write down the fraction of the houses that have double glazing.
Give your fraction in its simplest form.

6 60% of office workers go to work by train.
Write down the fraction of office workers who go to work by train.
Give your fraction in its simplest form.

7 92% of students in a class have a mobile telephone.
Work out the fraction of students that do **not** have a mobile telephone.
Give your fraction in its simplest form.

8 What percentage of each of the following shapes is shaded?

a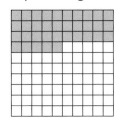

b

c

d

9 Write each percentage as: **i** a fraction in its simplest form **ii** a decimal.

a $12\tfrac{1}{2}\%$ **b** $7\tfrac{1}{2}\%$ **c** $2\tfrac{1}{2}\%$ **d** $6\tfrac{1}{4}\%$

Writing numbers in order of size

Example 4

Write these numbers in order of size.
Start with the smallest number.

$\tfrac{1}{2}$ 0.54 $\tfrac{11}{20}$ 53%

Solution 4
Change all the numbers to decimals so they can be compared.

$\tfrac{1}{2} = 0.5$

> This is a fact you should know.

0.54

> 0.54 is already a decimal.

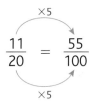

$\dfrac{11}{20} = \dfrac{55}{100}$

> Change $\tfrac{11}{20}$ into a fraction with a denominator of 100

$\dfrac{55}{100} = 0.55$

> Change $\tfrac{55}{100}$ to a decimal.

So $\dfrac{11}{20} = 0.55$

$53\% = \dfrac{53}{100} = 0.53$

0.50   0.53   0.54   0.55

> Write 0.5 as 0.50 so that all numbers have two decimal places. Then write the decimals in order of size.

$\tfrac{1}{2}$ 53%   0.54 $\tfrac{11}{20}$

> Write the numbers in their original forms.

Example 5

Use a calculator to write these numbers in order of size.
Start with the smallest number.

$0.38 \quad \frac{3}{8} \quad 42\% \quad \frac{13}{40}$

Solution 5

Change all the numbers into decimals so they can be compared.

0.38

| 0.38 is already a decimal. |

$\frac{3}{8} = 0.375$

| To change $\frac{3}{8}$ to a decimal using a calculator, key in [3] [÷] [8] [=] |

$42\% = 0.42$

| $42\% = 42 \div 100$ |

$\frac{13}{40} = 0.325$

| To change $\frac{13}{40}$ to a decimal using a calculator, key in [13] [÷] [40] [=] |

0.325   0.375   0.380   0.420

| Write 0.38 and 0.42 with three decimal places and then write the decimals in order of size. |

$\frac{13}{40} \quad \frac{3}{8} \quad 0.38 \quad 42\%$

| Write the numbers in their original forms. |

Exercise 18B

1 **a** Write 32% as a decimal.   **b** Write $\frac{3}{10}$ as a decimal.
   c Which is bigger 32% or $\frac{3}{10}$?

2 **a** Write $\frac{3}{4}$ as a decimal.   **b** Write 72% as a decimal.
   c Which is bigger $\frac{3}{4}$ or 72%?

3 In each part, write the numbers in order of size. Start with the **smallest** number.
   a $\frac{1}{2}$ 53%   0.48   **b** 0.73 $\frac{3}{4}$ $\frac{7}{10}$ 72%
   c $\frac{1}{4}$ 0.2   23%   **d** 0.44 $\frac{4}{10}$ 48% $\frac{9}{20}$

4 **a** Write $\frac{9}{40}$ as a decimal.   **b** Write 24% as a decimal.
   c Which is bigger $\frac{9}{40}$ or 24%?

5 **a** Write 38% as a decimal.   **b** Write $\frac{7}{16}$ as a decimal.
   c Which is bigger 38% or $\frac{7}{16}$?

6 In each part, write the numbers in order of size. Start with the **largest** number.
   a 57% $\frac{11}{20}$ 0.58 $\frac{5}{8}$
   b $\frac{3}{20}$ 0.14   17% $\frac{1}{8}$
   c $\frac{27}{40}$ 68%   0.7 $\frac{5}{8}$

18.2 Percentages of quantities

also assessed in
Module 4

To find a percentage of a quantity, the percentage should first be written as a fraction or a decimal.

Example 6

a Find 25% of 60   **b** Find 16% of 75

Solution 6

a If a percentage can be written as a simple fraction then this is the easiest way to work out a percentage of a quantity.

$25\% = \frac{1}{4}$ This is a fact you should know.

$60 \div 4 = 15$ To find $\frac{1}{4}$ of 60, divide 60 by 4

25% of $60 = 15$

$\frac{1}{4}$ of 60 is 15 and $\frac{1}{4} \times 60$ is also 15

In maths, 'of' means multiply.

b   **Non-calculator**

$\dfrac{16}{\overset{}{\underset{4}{\cancel{100}}}} \times \overset{3}{\cancel{75}}$ Divide both 75 and 100 by 25

$= \dfrac{\overset{4}{\cancel{16}}}{\underset{1}{\cancel{4}}} \times 3$ Divide both 16 and 4 by 4

$= 4 \times 3 = 12$

16% of $75 = 12$

Calculator

$16\% = 0.16$

So work out 0.16×75 Key in

16% of $75 = 12$ [0.16] [×] [75] [=]

Example 7

David earns £300. He gets a bonus of 12%.
Without using a calculator, work out David's bonus.

Solution 7

12% of 300

$= \dfrac{12}{100} \times 300$ Write 12% as a fraction and remember that 'of' means multiply.

$= \dfrac{12}{\underset{1}{\cancel{100}}} \times \overset{3}{\cancel{300}}$ Divide both 100 and 300 by 100

$= 12 \times 3 = 36$

David's bonus is £36

Example 8

Colin invests £1850.
The interest rate is 5.2% per year.
Use a calculator to work out how much interest Colin receives after one year.

Solution 8

5.2% of 1850

$$= \frac{5.2}{100} \times 1850$$

$$= 96.2$$

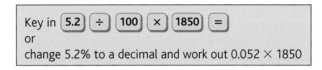

Key in 5.2   ÷   100   ×   1850   =

or

change 5.2% to a decimal and work out 0.052 × 1850

Colin receives £96.20 interest after one year.

As the answer is an amount of money, there must be two figures after the decimal point.

Exercise 18C

1 Work out

a	50% of 300	**b**	25% of 40	**c**	50% of 84	**d**	10% of 70
e	25% of 12	**f**	20% of 30	**g**	50% of 18	**h**	10% of 15
i	20% of 50	**j**	75% of 40				

2 Work out

a	20% of £300	**b**	25% of 60 g	**c**	20% of 80 cm	**d**	75% of 400 m
e	80% of £30	**f**	4% of 700 g	**g**	12% of 300 kg	**h**	65% of 300 km
i	24% of £400	**j**	16% of $200				

3 Tony earns £400. He gets a bonus of 15%. Work out Tony's bonus.

4 There are 150 shop assistants in a large store. 8% of the shop assistants are male. How many of the shop assistants are male?

5 Danya invests £250. The interest rate is 4% per year. How much interest will she receive after one year?

6 Work out:

a	34% of 50 m	**b**	12% of £36	**c**	5% of £32.40	**d**	8% of 62 kg
e	95% of £23 000	**f**	14% of 90 m	**g**	4.2% of 60 km	**h**	3.2% of £14 000
i	$17\frac{1}{2}$% of £300	**j**	$6\frac{1}{4}$% of 40 cm				

7 Anna scored 65% in a test. The test was out of 40 marks. How many marks did Anna score?

8 There are 2400 students in a school. 17% of the students in the school wear glasses. How many of the students wear glasses.

9 A shop has 4600 DVDs. 23% of the DVDs are thrillers. How many of the DVDs in the shop are thrillers?

10 The price of a washing machine is £520. Ahmid pays a deposit of 35% of the price. Work out his deposit.

11 Martin invests £3500. The interest rate is 4.3% per year.
How much interest will he receive at the end of one year?

12 There are 2400 trees in a forest. 18% of the trees are oak trees.
How many oak trees are in the forest?

Chapter summary

> **You should know**
>
> ★ **'Per cent'** means 'out of 100'
>
> ★ 35 per cent means 35 out of 100 or, as a fraction, $\frac{35}{100}$
>
> ★ 35 per cent is written as 35%
>
> **You should be able to**
>
> ★ Order a list of percentages, fractions and decimals and change all the quantities into decimals
>
> ★ Work out a percentage of a quantity

Chapter 18 review questions

1 Write 80% as a fraction in its simplest form.

2 Write 2% as a decimal.

3 78% of the houses in a street have broadband. What percentage of the houses in the street do not have broadband?

4 a Write down the fraction of the shape that is shaded.
Give your fraction in its simplest form.

   b Write down the percentage of this shape that is shaded.

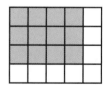

5 a Write 0.45 as a percentage.

   b Write $\frac{3}{4}$ as a percentage.

   c Write 30% as a fraction in its simplest form.   (1388 Jan 2003)

6 **a** Work out 50% of £24

A school trip costs £24 per pupil.
85 pupils go on the school trip.

b Work out the total amount of money paid by the 85 pupils.

7 Work out 20% of 6500

8 **a** Change $\frac{7}{8}$ to a decimal.

b Use your answer to part **a** to write $\frac{7}{8}$ as a percentage.

9 Write these numbers in order of size. Start with the largest number.

  0.8   70% $\frac{7}{8}$ $\frac{3}{4}$ (1385 Nov 2000)

10 Work out 34% of 1500

11 Lisa had £10.50
She gave 8% to charity and kept the rest of the money.
Work out how much money she kept.   (1385 Jan 2002)

12 30% $\frac{1}{4}$ 0.35 $\frac{1}{3}$ $\frac{2}{5}$ 0.299
Write this list of six numbers in order of size.
Start with the smallest number.   (1385 June 2001)

Powers and roots

19.1 Powers and roots

Powers and indices

Square numbers and cube numbers were introduced in Section 1.7

The first four square numbers are 1, 4, 9, 16 because they are 1×1, 2×2, 3×3 and 4×4

The first four cube numbers are 1, 8, 27, 64 because they are $1 \times 1 \times 1$, $2 \times 2 \times 2$, $3 \times 3 \times 3$ and $4 \times 4 \times 4$

Expressions like 3×3 can be written in the shorter form of 3^2. The '2' is called the **power** or **index** and gives the number of 3s which are multiplied together.

$2 \times 2 \times 2$ can be written as 2^3, where 3 is the power or index.

$5 \times 5 \times 5 \times 5$ can be written as 5^4, where 4 is the power or index (5^4 is read as 5 to the power 4, or 5 raised to the power 4).

Example 1

Work out

a 6^2 **b** 10^3 **c** 2^4

Solution 1

a $6^2 = 6 \times 6 = 36$ **b** $10^3 = 10 \times 10 \times 10 = 1000$

c $2^4 = 2 \times 2 \times 2 \times 2 = 16$

Section 1.9 showed how to write any number as the product of its prime factors. Powers can be used to make these expressions shorter.

For example, 40 as the product of its prime factors is $40 = 2 \times 2 \times 2 \times 5$
and 40 as the product of powers of its prime factors is $40 = 2^3 \times 5$

Example 2

a Express 240 as the product of its prime factors.

b Express your answer as the product of powers of its prime factors.

Solution 2

a $240 = 2 \times 120$
$ = 2 \times 2 \times 60$
$ = 2 \times 2 \times 2 \times 30$
$ = 2 \times 2 \times 2 \times 2 \times 15$
$ = 2 \times 2 \times 2 \times 2 \times 3 \times 5$

b $240 = 2^4 \times 3 \times 5$

Square roots and cube roots

The **square root** of 36 is 6 because $6^2 = 36$
(6 is the number which when multiplied by itself gives 36.)

The sign for the square root of a number is $\sqrt{}$, so $\sqrt{36} = 6$.

Example 3

Work out

a $\sqrt{9}$ **b** $\sqrt{16} + \sqrt{100}$

Solution 3

a $\sqrt{9} = 3$

b $\sqrt{16} + \sqrt{100} = 4 + 10 = 14$ | Work out each square root and then add them. |

$6 \times 6 = 36$ and also $(-6) \times (-6) = 36$

So the square root of 36 has two possible values, 6 and -6
-6 is called the **negative** square root of 36
(So 6 could be called the positive square root of 36)

The **cube root** of 64 is 4 because $4^3 = 64$ that is $4 \times 4 \times 4 = 64$
-4 is *not* a cube root of 64 because $(-4)^3 = -64$

The sign for the cube root of a number is $\sqrt[3]{}$, so $\sqrt[3]{64} = 4$

Example 4

a Find the positive square root and the negative square root of 100
b Find **i** $\sqrt[3]{8}$ **ii** $\sqrt[3]{-27}$

Solution 4

a The positive square root is 10 and the negative square root is -10

b **i** $\sqrt[3]{8} = 2$ because $2^3 = 8$

   ii $\sqrt[3]{-27} = -3$ because $(-3)^3 = (-3) \times (-3) \times (-3) = -27$

Exercise 19A

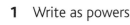

1 Write as powers

   a $9 \times 9 \times 9 \times 9$ **b** $7 \times 7 \times 7 \times 7 \times 7 \times 7$ **c** $8 \times 8 \times 8 \times 8 \times 8$

2 Work out

   a 5^2 **b** 4^2 **c** 7^2 **d** 10^2 **e** 1^2 **f** 8^2

3 Work out

   a 2^3 **b** 5^3 **c** 1^3 **d** 3^3

   e 2^5 **f** 10^4 **g** 3^4 **h** 9^3

4   Work out

    a $\sqrt{4}$ **b** $\sqrt{16}$ **c** $\sqrt{100}$ **d** $\sqrt{64}$ **e** $\sqrt{81}$

5   Work out

    a $2^2 + 2^3$ **b** $1 + 3 + 3^2$ **c** $4^3 - 4^2$ **d** $5^3 - 5^2$ **e** $10^3 - 10^2$

    f $5^3 - 4^2$ **g** $4^3 + 4^2$ **h** $3^3 - 4^2$ **i** $5^3 + 5^2$ **j** $2^3 - 3^2$

6   Work out

    a $\sqrt{4} + \sqrt{9}$ **b** $\sqrt{1} + \sqrt{16}$ **c** $\sqrt{25} + \sqrt{4}$ **d** $\sqrt{25} - \sqrt{9}$

    e $\sqrt{4} \times \sqrt{9}$ **f** $\sqrt{16} \times \sqrt{9}$ **g** $\sqrt{4} \times \sqrt{16}$ **h** $\sqrt{25} \times \sqrt{9}$

    i $\sqrt{36} \div \sqrt{9}$ **j** $\sqrt{100} \div \sqrt{4}$ **k** $\sqrt{64} + \sqrt{16}$ **l** $\sqrt{81} \div \sqrt{9}$

    m $\sqrt{9} \times \sqrt{9}$ **n** $\sqrt{5^2}$ **o** $\sqrt{8} \times \sqrt{8}$ **p** $\sqrt{13^2}$

7   Work out

    a $\sqrt[3]{8}$ **b** $\sqrt[3]{27}$ **c** $\sqrt[3]{125}$ **d** $\sqrt[3]{1000}$

8   Find the negative square root of the following numbers.

    a 9   **b** 64   **c** 100   **d** 4   **e** 1

9   Write each of these numbers as a product of powers of its prime factors.

    a 48   **b** 50   **c** 98   **d** 300   **e** 72

19.2 Order of operations

When dealing with expressions which involve powers and other operations use **BIDMAS**. BIDMAS was covered in Section 1.8

Remember that BIDMAS stands for

    Brackets, **I**ndices, **D**ivision, **M**ultiplication, **A**ddition and **S**ubtraction.

Indices is another name for powers, and so work out powers after brackets but before the other four operations. Powers include square roots and cube roots.

Example 5

Work out

a 2×6^2 **b** $10^2 + 10^3$ **c** $16 \div 2^4$

Solution 5

a $6^2 = 6 \times 6 = 36$ | Squaring is done before the multiplication by 2 |

       $2 \times 6^2 = 72$

b $10^2 + 10^3 = 100 + 1000 = 1100$ | Squaring and cubing are carried out before addition. |

c $16 \div 2^4 = 16 \div 16 = 1$ | Work out the 2^4 first, followed by the division. |

Brackets can alter the usual order of working out an expression.

Example 6

Work out

a $(2 \times 5)^2$

b $(3 + 4)^2$

Solution 6

a $2 \times 5 = 10$
$10^2 = 100$

> Work out the bracket first.
> Then square the answer.

b $(3 + 4)^2 = 7^2 = 49$

> Addition inside the bracket is carried out first, followed by squaring.

Exercise 19B

1 Work out

    a 2×5^2
    b 2×4^2
    c 3×2^2
    d 5×10^2

    e 4×3^2
    f 6×2^2
    g 8×1^2
    h 5×2^2

2 Work out

    a $(2 + 5)^2$
    b $(7 - 3)^2$
    c $(5 + 5)^2$
    d $(12 - 5)^2$

    e $(4 + 4)^2$
    f $(8 - 5)^2$
    g $(20 - 10)^2$
    h $(18 - 9)^2$

3 Work out

    a $20 - 3^2$
    b $17 + 4^2$
    c $17 - 4^2$
    d $27 - 4^2$

    e $36 + 4^2$
    f $25 - 5^2$
    g $14 - 4^2$
    h $22 - 5^2$

4 Work out

    a $24 \div 2^2$
    b $44 \div 2^2$
    c $50 \div 5^2$

    d $100 \div 5^2$
    e $36 \div 3^2$
    f $(10 \div 2)^2$

    g $(12 \div 2)^2$
    h $(15 \div 5)^2$
    i $(21 \div 3)^2$

5 Work out

    a $4^2 - 3^2$
    b $4^2 + 3^2$
    c $5^2 - 4^2$

    d $6^2 - 3^2$
    e $10^2 - 3^2$
    f $6^2 + 1^2$

    g $6^2 - 4^2$
    h $7^2 - 3^2$
    i $6^2 + 8^2$

6 Work out

    a $2 \times \sqrt{9}$
    b $4 \times \sqrt{4}$
    c $5 \times \sqrt{100}$

    d $\sqrt{9} \times \sqrt{4}$
    e $\sqrt{4} \times 2$
    f $\sqrt{9} \times 5$

    g $\sqrt{25} \times 6$
    h $\sqrt{36} \times 5$
    i $\sqrt{100} \times 7$

19.3 Index laws for multiplication and division

Look at this calculation.

also assessed in
Module 4

$$2^3 \times 2^4 = 2 \times 2 \times 2 \times 2 \times 2 \times 2 \times 2 = 2^7$$

Notice that $7 = 3 + 4$

So to work out one number raised to a power **multiplied** by the *same* number to a second power, **add** the powers.

$$3^6 \div 3^2 = \frac{3 \times 3 \times 3 \times 3 \times 3 \times 3}{3 \times 3} = 3 \times 3 \times 3 \times 3 = 3^4$$

Notice that $4 = 6 - 2$

So to work out one number raised to a power **divided** by the *same* number to a second power, **subtract** the powers.

Example 7

Write as a power of 4

a $4^5 \times 4^3$ **b** $4^9 \div 4^2$ **c** $\dfrac{4^6 \times 4^7}{4^3}$

Solution 7

a $4^5 \times 4^3 = 4^8$ | Add the powers $5 + 3 = 8$ |

b $4^9 \div 4^2 = 4^7$ | Subtract the powers $9 - 2 = 7$ |

c $\dfrac{4^6 \times 4^7}{4^3} = \dfrac{4^{13}}{4^3} = 4^{13-3} = 4^{10}$

Reciprocals

The **reciprocal** of a number is what it has to be multiplied by to get 1 as the answer.

$2 \times \frac{1}{2} = 1$, so the reciprocal of 2 is $\frac{1}{2}$ and the reciprocal of $\frac{1}{2}$ is 2

The reciprocal of 3 is $\frac{1}{3}$ and the reciprocal of $\frac{1}{3}$ is 3 because $3 \times \frac{1}{3} = 1$

$\frac{2}{3} \times \frac{3}{2} = 1$, so the reciprocal of $\frac{2}{3}$ is $\frac{3}{2}$ and the reciprocal of $\frac{3}{2}$ is $\frac{2}{3}$

To find the reciprocal of a fraction, turn it upside down (invert it).

The reciprocal of $\frac{4}{5}$ is $\frac{5}{4}$ (or $1\frac{1}{4}$)

Example 8

Find the reciprocal of $1\frac{2}{3}$

Solution 8

Write the mixed number $1\frac{2}{3}$ as the improper fraction $\frac{5}{3}$

Turn $\frac{5}{3}$ upside down to get $\frac{3}{5}$

The reciprocal of $1\frac{2}{3}$ is $\frac{3}{5}$

Exercise 19C

1 Write as powers of 2

  a $2^4 \times 2^5$ **b** $2^3 \times 2^4$ **c** $2^2 \times 2^6$ **d** $2^4 \times 2^3$ **e** $2^4 \times 2^6$

2 Write as powers of 3

  a $3^4 \div 3^2$ **b** $3^5 \div 3^2$ **c** $3^4 \div 3$ **d** $3^6 \div 3^2$ **e** $3^{10} \div 3^4$

3 Write as a power of a single number

  a $4^4 \div 4^2$ **b** $5^7 \div 5^2$ **c** $3^4 \times 3^2$ **d** $6^4 \times 6^3$ **e** $10^4 \div 10^2$

4 Work out the following. Give each answer as a power of 3

  a $\dfrac{3^3 \times 3^5}{3^4}$ **b** $\dfrac{3 \times 3^7}{3^4}$ **c** $\dfrac{3^9}{3^4 \times 3^3}$ **d** $\dfrac{3^2 \times 3^{10}}{3^2 \times 3^5}$

5 Work out the value of the following.

  a $3^4 \div 3^2$ **b** $4^5 \div 4^3$ **c** $2^5 \div 2^2$ **d** $10^4 \div 10^2$

6 Find the reciprocals of these whole numbers.

  a 5   **b** 7   **c** 10   **d** 8

7 Find the reciprocals of these numbers.

  a $\frac{1}{3}$ **b** $\frac{2}{3}$ **c** $\frac{4}{3}$ **d** $\frac{1}{4}$ **e** $\frac{2}{5}$

  f $\frac{1}{10}$ **g** $1\frac{1}{2}$ **h** $3\frac{1}{2}$ **i** $3\frac{2}{3}$ **j** 2.5

8 Work out each value of n

  a $40 = 5 \times 2^n$ **b** $32 = 2^n$ **c** $50 = 5^n \times 2$

  d $48 = 3 \times 2^n$ **e** $54 = 2 \times 3^n$ **f** $120 = 15 \times 2^n$

9 $96 = 2^m \times 3^n$ where m and n are whole numbers. Find the value of m and the value of n.

10 $180 = 2^p \times 3^q \times 5$ where p and q are whole numbers. Find the value of p and the value of q.

19.4 Using a calculator

There are two methods of working out powers on a calculator.
The first method is to carry out the calculation using multiplication.

6.4^2 is worked out by keying in 6.4 $\boxed{\times}$ 6.4 $\boxed{=}$ which gives the answer 40.96

1.1^3 is worked out by keying in 1.1 $\boxed{\times}$ 1.1 $\boxed{\times}$ 1.1 $\boxed{=}$ which gives the answer 1.331

The second method can be used on a scientific calculator.

For working out squares on a scientific calculator, use the $\boxed{x^2}$ key.

Key in 6.4 $\boxed{x^2}$ and the display shows 40.96

For working out cubes, some scientific calculators have a cube key $\boxed{x^3}$.

So 1.1^3 is worked out by keying in 1.1 $\boxed{x^3}$ and the display shows 1.331

All scientific calculators have a power or index key. This comes in two forms.

The first form is $\boxed{y^x}$ – to work out 1.1^3, key in 1.1 $\boxed{y^x}$ 3 $\boxed{=}$ and the display shows 1.331

The second form is $\boxed{\wedge}$ – to work out 1.1^3 , key in 1.1 $\boxed{\wedge}$ 3 $\boxed{=}$ and the display shows 1.331

Make sure you know how to work out powers on your own calculator.

Example 9

Use a calculator to work out

a 4.5^2 **b** $2.3^2 + 3.1^3$

Solution 9

a $4.5^2 = 20.25$ | Either key in 4.5 $\boxed{\times}$ 4.5 $\boxed{=}$ or key in 4.5 $\boxed{x^2}$ |

b $2.3^2 = 5.29$
Write down the result 5.29
$3.1^3 = 29.791$
Write down the result 29.791
$5.29 + 29.791 = 35.081$

| Either key in 2.3 $\boxed{\times}$ 2.3 $\boxed{=}$ or key in 2.3 $\boxed{x^2}$ |
| Key in 3.1 $\boxed{\times}$ 3.1 $\boxed{\times}$ 3.1 $\boxed{=}$ or key in 3.1 $\boxed{x^3}$ |
| Add the two results for the answer. |

To find a square root on a calculator, use the $\boxed{\sqrt{}}$ key.

Example 10

Work out

a $\sqrt{6.25}$ **b** $\sqrt{12.96} + \sqrt{12.25}$

Solution 10

a $\sqrt{6.25} = 2.5$ | Key in $\boxed{\sqrt{}}$ 6.25 $\boxed{=}$ |

b $\sqrt{12.96} = 3.6$
Write down the result 3.6
$\sqrt{12.25} = 3.5$
Write down the result 3.5
$3.6 + 3.5 = 7.1$

| Key in $\boxed{\sqrt{}}$ 12.96 $\boxed{=}$ |
| Key in $\boxed{\sqrt{}}$ 12.25 $\boxed{=}$ |
| Add the two results for the answer. |

Not all numbers have exact square roots. For example $\sqrt{12} = 3.464\ 101\ 6...$, where the dots are used to show that the decimal answer never stops.

In cases such as this, it is a good idea to write down all the figures on the calculator display first, and then the answer can be rounded if necessary. For example, $\sqrt{12}$ correct to one decimal place is 3.5

Calculators always give the positive square root of a number, never the negative square root.

Exercise 19D

1 Work out

   a 8.4^2 **b** 9.2^2 **c** 3.6^2 **d** 24^2 **e** 15.4^2

2 Work out

   a $134 + 21^2$ **b** $231 + 31^2$ **c** $37 + 23^2$ **d** $502 + 35^2$

3 Work out

   a $23^2 + 31^2$ **b** $25^2 + 23^2$ **c** $19^2 + 22^2$ **d** $35^2 + 45^2$

4 Work out

   a $200 - 14^2$ **b** $20 - 1.4^2$ **c** $356 - 17^2$ **d** $366 - 16^2$

5 Work out

   a 2.3^3 **b** 7^3 **c** 21^3 **d** 2.5^3

6 Work out

   a $\sqrt{576}$ **b** $\sqrt{1024}$ **c** $\sqrt{625}$ **d** $\sqrt{1296}$

7 Work out, giving your answers correct to one decimal place

   a $\sqrt{200}$ **b** $\sqrt{300}$ **c** $\sqrt{80}$ **d** $\sqrt{128}$ **e** $\sqrt{125}$

8 Work out

   a $\sqrt{31.36} + \sqrt{12.96}$ **b** $\sqrt{13.69} + \sqrt{20.25}$

   c $\sqrt{70.56} - \sqrt{33.64}$ **d** $\sqrt{14.44} - \sqrt{6.76}$

9 Work out, giving your answers correct to one decimal place

   a $2.4^2 + \sqrt{10}$ **b** $\sqrt{30.5} + \sqrt{13.1}$

   c $\sqrt{30} - \sqrt{18}$ **d** $\sqrt{305} - \sqrt{140}$

10 Work out, giving your answers to one decimal place

   a $1.5^2 + 1.5$ **b** $2.5^3 + 2.5$ **c** $3.4^3 + 3.4^2$ **d** $8^3 - 6.5^2$

Chapter summary

You should now know that:

★ in 3^2 the '2' is called the **power** or **index**. It gives the number of 3s which are multiplied together

★ in $\sqrt{36}$ the $\sqrt{}$ means the **square root**. $\sqrt{36} = 6$ because $6 \times 6 = 36$ that is 6 is the number which, when multiplied by itself, gives 36

★ the square root of a number has two possible values, the positive square root and the negative square root. For example the square roots of 36 are 6 and -6

★ in $\sqrt[3]{64}$ the $\sqrt[3]{}$ means the **cube root**. $\sqrt[3]{64} = 4$ because $4 \times 4 \times 4 = 64$

★ when dealing with expresssions which involve powers and other operations use **BIDMAS** to carry the calculations out in the right order
  - **B**rackets
  - **I**ndices (powers)
  - **D**ivision
  - **M**ultiplication
  - **A**ddition
  - **S**ubtraction

★ the **reciprocal** of a number is what it has to be multiplied by to get 1 as the answer. For example, the reciprocal of 2 is $\frac{1}{2}$

★ to find the reciprocal of fraction, turn it upside down. For example, the reciprocal of $\frac{4}{5}$ is $\frac{5}{4}$

You should now know how to:

★ use index laws
  - to work out a number raised to a power multiplied by the same number raised to a power, add the powers
  - to work out a number raised to a power divided by the same number raised to a power, subtract the powers

★ write a whole number as a product of powers of its prime fctors

★ use a calculator to work out powers of a number

★ use a calculator to work out the square root of a number

Chapter 19 review questions

1 Work out

    a 3^2 **b** 4^2 **c** 10^2 **d** 7^2 **e** 5^2

2 Work out

    a 9^2 **b** 1^2 **c** 0^2 **d** 20^2 **e** 100^2

3 Work out

    a 8^2 **b** 80^2 **c** 800^2 **d** 8000^2

4 Work out

    a 6^2 **b** 60^2 **c** 600^2 **d** 6000^2

5 Write down the values of

    a $\sqrt{100}$ **b** $\sqrt{25}$ **c** $\sqrt{16}$ **d** $\sqrt{9}$ **e** $\sqrt{49}$

6 Work out

    a 2^3 **b** 3^3 **c** 5^3 **d** 1^3 **e** 10^3

7 Work out

a $4^2 + \sqrt{25}$ b $2^3 + 2^3$ c $3^3 + 2^3$ d $5^3 + 10^3$

8 Work out

a $5^2 + \sqrt{36}$ b $2^2 + 2^3$ c $3^2 + 2^3$ d $5^3 + 10^2$

9 Work out

a $3 \times \sqrt{25}$ b $4 \times \sqrt{36}$ c $10 \times \sqrt{9}$ d $8 \times \sqrt{49}$

10 Work out

a $4 \times \sqrt{25}$ b $\sqrt{4} \times \sqrt{36}$ c $\sqrt{100} \times \sqrt{16}$ d $\sqrt{81} \times \sqrt{49}$

11 Work out

a $4^2 \div 8$ b $4^3 \div 8^2$ c $10^3 \div 10^2$ d $3^3 \div 3$

12 Work out

a $\sqrt{5^2}$ b $\sqrt{10^2}$ c $(\sqrt{9})^2$ d $(\sqrt{81})^2$

13 Work out

a $(2 + 3)^2$ b $(5 - 1)^2$ c $2 + 3^3$ d $10^3 - \sqrt{100}$

14 Write as powers of 2

a $2^3 \times 2^4$ b $2^6 \div 2^4$ c $(2^3)^2$

15 Express 120 as a product of powers of its prime factors.   (1387 Nov 2003)

16 Work out

a 1.3^2 b 2.4^2 c $\sqrt{625}$ d $\sqrt{13.69}$ e 12^3

17 Work out

a 1.4^2 b 2.5×1.4^2

18 Use your calculator to work out the value of $\sqrt{(15 + 27.25)}$ (1387 June 2004)

19 Work out the following. Give your answer correct to one decimal place.

a $\sqrt{14}$ b $\sqrt{20}$ c $\sqrt{1000}$ d $\sqrt{3.5}$

20 The perimeter of a square is 50 cm. Work out the area of the square.

21 a Work out the value of $3.8^2 - \sqrt{75}$
Write down all the figures on your calculator display.

b Write your answer to part **a** correct to one significant figure.

(1387 June 2005)

22 a Factorise $y^2 + 3y$ b Solve   **i** $\dfrac{x}{2} = 7$ **ii** $4y + 3 = 2y - 4$

Three-dimensional shapes

Dorling Kindersley

All these photographs show examples of **three-dimensional shapes**.

Three-dimensional shapes have length, breadth and height. They are not flat, like squares and circles.

Three-dimensional is often written as '**3-D**'.

20.1 Types of three-dimensional shapes

The **cube** and the **cuboid** (rectangular box) are two of the most familiar 3-D shapes.

A 3-D shape which is the same shape all along its length is called a **prism**. When you cut through a prism so that the cut is parallel to an end, you always get the same shape, called the **cross-section** of the prism.

Cube   Cuboid

Both cubes and cuboids are prisms. A cube has a square cross-section and a cuboid has a rectangular cross-section.

Triangular prism   Hexagonal prism

The shape of a prism's cross-section is used to describe the prism but a prism with a circular cross-section has a special name – a **cylinder**.

Cylinder

The name **pyramid** brings to mind the square-based pyramids of ancient Egypt but the base may be any shape. A pyramid with a circular base is called a **cone**.

Triangle-based pyramid

Square-based pyramid

Cone

The **sphere** is a very familiar 3-D shape. Like a ball, it is circular in every direction.

Sphere

20.2 Faces, vertices and edges

The diagram shows a cube with one *face* shaded. A cube has 6 faces, all of them squares.

The line where two faces meet is an *edge*, shown in green. A cube has 12 edges.

Edges meet at a *vertex* or corner. A cube has 8 vertices.

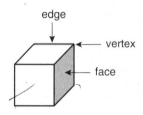
edge
vertex
face

Example 1

a For a pentagonal prism, write down
   i the number of faces   **ii** the number of edges
  iii the number of vertices.

b What shapes are its faces?

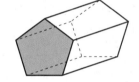

Solution 1

a The prism has
   i 7 faces   **ii** 15 edges   **iii** 10 vertices.

b Two of its faces are pentagons and five are rectangles.

Exercise 20A

1 Copy and complete the table.

3-D shape	Number of faces	Number of edges	Number of vertices
Cube	6	12	8
Cuboid			
Triangular prism			
Pentagonal prism	7	15	10
Hexagonal prism			
Triangle-based pyramid			
Square-based pyramid			

2 What shapes are the faces of

    a a triangular prism   **b** a hexagonal prism   **c** a square-based pyramid?

20.3 Nets

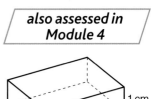

also assessed in Module 4

A **net** of a 3-D shape is a flat (two-dimensional) shape which can be cut out and folded to make the 3-D shape.

The sketch shows a cuboid and here is a net of the cuboid. (It is not the only possible one.)

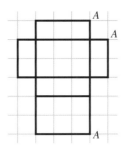

Diagram **NOT** accurately drawn

When the net is folded to make the cuboid, the three points labelled A meet at a vertex.

Example 2

Draw an accurate, full-size net of a cube of side 2 cm.

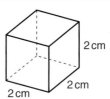

Solution 2

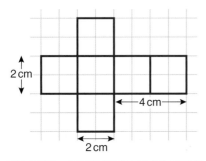

Diagram **NOT** accurately drawn

Example 3

The diagram is a sketch of a net of a 3-D shape.

a On a copy of the sketch, label the points which meet at P when the net is folded to make the 3-D shape.

b Sketch the 3-D shape and write down its name.

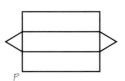

Solution 3

a

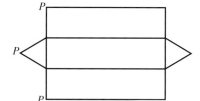

b

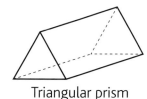

Triangular prism

Exercise 20B

1 On centimetre squared paper draw two accurate, full-size nets of a cube of side 2 cm, which are different from the net in Example 2.

2 On centimetre squared paper draw an accurate, full-size net of a cuboid which is 2 cm by 2 cm by 3 cm.

3 Here is a sketch of the net of a 3-D shape.
Sketch the 3-D shape and write down its name.

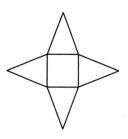

4 Each face of a triangle-based pyramid is an equilateral triangle of side 3 cm.
Draw an accurate, full-size net of the pyramid.

5 Here is a sketch of the net of a 3-D shape.
Sketch the 3-D shape and write down its name.

6 The diagram is a sketch of a net of a triangular prism.
On a copy of the sketch, label the point which meets at Q, when the net is folded to make the triangular prism.

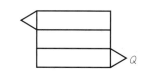

7 The diagram is a sketch of a triangular prism.
Make an accurate, full-size drawing of a net of the triangular prism.

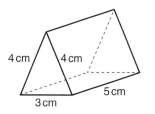

8 The diagram is a sketch of a net of a 3-D shape.
  a Write down its name.
  b How many
    i faces
    ii edges
    iii vertices has the 3-D shape got?

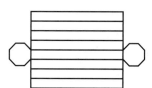

9   The diagram is a sketch of a 3-D shape.

   a   Write down its name.

   b   Sketch a net of the 3-D shape.

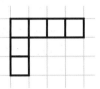

10   The diagram has six 1 cm squares joined edge to edge.

   a   Explain why it is *not* the net of a centimetre cube.

   b   Draw a different diagram with six 1 cm squares joined edge to edge that is not the net of a centimetre cube.

20.4 Isometric paper

also assessed in Module 4

Isometric paper is a grid of equilateral triangles. It can be lines or dots.
Isometric paper is useful for showing 3-D shapes.

Example 4

A cuboid is 3 cm by 2 cm by 1 cm.
On an isometric grid, make an accurate, full size drawing of the cuboid.

Solution 4

Diagram **NOT** accurately drawn

Example 5

The diagram shows the cross-section of a prism, which is 2 cm long.
On an isometric grid, make an accurate, full size drawing of the prism.

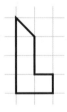

Solution 5

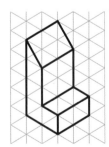

Diagram **NOT** accurately drawn

Exercise 20C

1   On isometric grids make accurate, full-size drawings of these 3-D shapes.

    a   A cube of side 1 cm.   **b**   A cube of side 3 cm.

    c   A cuboid which is 4 cm by 3 cm by 2 cm.

    d   A cuboid which is 2 cm by 2 cm by 5 cm.

2   On isometric grids make accurate full-size drawings of these 3-D shapes.
They are all prisms with the cross-sections and lengths as shown.

a

Length 4 cm

b
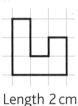

Length 2 cm

c

Length 3 cm

d
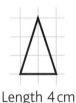

Length 4 cm

e
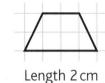

Length 2 cm

f

Length 3 cm

20.5 Volume

also assessed in Module 4

The **volume** of a 3-D shape is the amount of space it takes up.

The diagram shows a cube with edges 1 cm long.
It is called a centimetre cube and its volume is 1 cubic centimetre
(written 1 cm^3).

The volume of a 3-D shape is the number of centimetre cubes
it contains.

The solid prism shown in this diagram is made from centimetre
cubes.
There are 9 centimetre cubes and so the volume of the prism
is 9 cm^3.

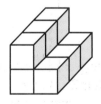

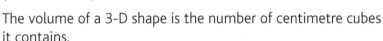

Example 6

The diagram shows a cuboid made from
centimetre cubes.

Find the volume of the cuboid.

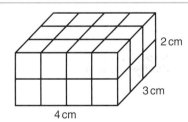

2 cm

3 cm

4 cm

Solution 6

There are 12 centimetre cubes in each layer and there are two layers.
So the number of centimetre cubes is 12 × 2 = 24

The volume of the cuboid is 24 cm^3.

Volume of a cuboid

In Example 6, multiplying the length by the width (4 × 3) gives the number of centimetre cubes (12) in each layer.

Multiplying this by the height (12 × 2) gives the number of centimetre cubes altogether (24).

So the number of centimetre cubes is 4 × 3 × 2 = 24

This shows that   **volume of a cuboid = length × width × height**

The volume, V, of a cuboid with length l, width w and

height h is given by the formula   **$V = lwh$**

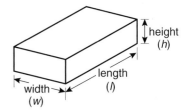

When the length, width and height are measured in centimetres, the volume is in cm³. When they are measured in metres, the volume is in m³, and so on.
When this formula is used, the length, width and height must *all* be measured in the *same* units.

Example 7

Work out the volume of the cuboid shown in the diagram.

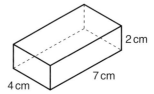

Solution 7

Volume $= 7 \times 4 \times 2 = 56$ cm³

Exercise 20D

1   The diagrams show solid prisms made from centimetre cubes.
Find the volume of each prism.

a 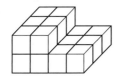   **b** 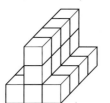   **c** 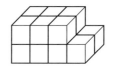   **d**

2   Work out the volumes of the cuboids shown.
Give the units of your answers.

a 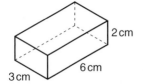   **b** 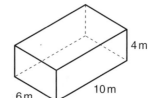   **c**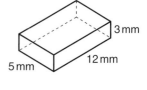

3   Work out the volume of a cuboid which is 40 cm by 30 cm by 20 cm.

4   Work out the volume of a cuboid which is 20 m by 7 m by 5 m.

5 Work out the volume of a cuboid which is 25 mm by 10 mm by 8 mm.

6 A cuboid measures 4 m by 2 m by 50 cm.
 a Explain why its volume is *not* 400 m³.
 b Work out its volume in m³.

7 Work out the volume, in m³, of a cuboid which is 5 m by 2 m by 40 cm.

8 A cuboid measures 10 cm by 4 cm by 5 mm.
 Work out its volume
 a in cm³   **b** in mm³.

Problems involving the volume of cuboids

In some examination questions, more than just working out the volume of a cuboid is required. For example, the volume of the cuboid might be given and one of its dimensions has to be found.

Example 8

The volume of a cuboid is 216 cm³. Its length is 9 cm and its width is 6 cm.
Work out its height.

Solution 8

Let the height of the cuboid be h cm. | Use a letter to stand for the height. |

$216 = 9 \times 6 \times h$ | Substitute the given values for V, l and w in $V = lwh$. |

$54h = 216$ | Simplify $9 \times 6 \times h$ as $54h$ and write it on the left-hand side. |

$h = \dfrac{216}{54} = 4$ | Divide both sides by 54 to find the value of h. |

The height of the cuboid is 4 cm. | State the answer. |

In some questions, the number of small cuboids which fit inside a large cuboid has to be found.

Example 9

A packet is a cuboid which is 10 cm by 5 cm by 4 cm.
A box is a cuboid which is 80 cm by 60 cm by 40 cm.

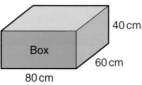

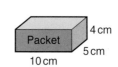

Work out how many packets will fit exactly into the box.

Solution 9

Method 1

$$\frac{80}{10} = 8$$

| Work out how many times the length of the packet (10 cm) will fit into the length of the box (80 cm). |

$$\frac{60}{5} = 12$$

| Work out how many times the width of the packet will fit into the width of the box. |

$$\frac{40}{4} = 10$$

| Work out how many times the height of the packet will fit into the height of the box. |

$$8 \times 12 \times 10 = 960$$

| *Multiply* the three results to find the number of packets which will fit exactly into the box. |

Method 2

$$80 \times 60 \times 40 = 192\,000 \text{ cm}^3$$

| Work out the volume of the box. |

$$10 \times 5 \times 4 = 200 \text{ cm}^3$$

| Work out the volume of a packet. |

$$\frac{192\,000}{200} = 960$$

| *Divide* the volume of the box by the volume of the packet to find the number of packets which will fit exactly into the box. |

Exercise 20E

1 The volume of a cuboid is 400 cm³. Its length is 10 cm and its width is 8 cm. Work out its height.

2 The volume of a cuboid is 600 cm³. Its length is 20 cm and its height is 5 cm. Work out its width.

3 The volume of a cuboid is 180 cm³. Its width is 6 cm and its height is 2 cm. Work out its length.

4 The volume of a cuboid is 120 m³. Its length is 8 m and its width is 6 m. Work out its height.

5 Copy and complete the table.

Length (cm)	Width (cm)	Height (cm)	Volume (cm³)
10		4	280
50	20		7000
	6	5	270
5	4		70
25		4	650

6 A packet is a cuboid which is
5 cm by 3 cm by 2 cm.
A box is a cuboid which is 20 cm
by 18 cm by 10 cm.
Work out how many packets will
fit exactly into the box.

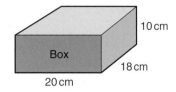

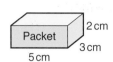

7 A box of chocolates measures 20 cm by 20 cm by 5 cm.
A container is a cuboid which measures 80 cm by 60 cm by 30 cm.
Work out the greatest number of boxes which can be packed in the container.

8 A crate is full of boxes.
The crate is a cuboid with side 1 m.
A box is a cuboid which is 25 cm by 20 cm by 10 cm.
Work out the number of boxes in the crate.

9 A packet of butter measures 11 cm by 6.5 cm by 4 cm.
A box measures 55 cm by 26 cm by 24 cm.
How many packets of butter are needed to fill the box?

10 Kate fills a container with boxes. Each box is a cube of side 0.5 m.
The container is a cuboid of length 6 m, width 5 m and height 3 m.
Work out how many boxes will fit exactly into the container.

Volume of a prism

The diagram shows a cuboid.
A cuboid is a prism with a rectangle as its cross-section.

Volume of the cuboid = **5 × 2 × 8**
$$= 80 \text{ cm}^3$$

The area of cross-section of the prism is **5 × 2** = 10 cm².
8 cm is its length.

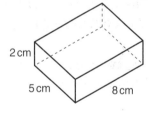

This shows that ┃ **volume of a prism = area of cross-section × length** ┃

Example 10

The diagram shows a prism with a right-angled triangle
as its cross-section.

Work out the volume of the prism.

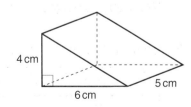

Solution 10

Area of cross-section = $\frac{1}{2}$ × 6 × 4
$$= 12 \text{ cm}^2$$

Volume = 12 × 5 = 60 cm³

┃ Work out the area of the triangular cross-section using
area = $\frac{1}{2}$ × base × vertical height. ┃

┃ Multiply the area of the cross-section by the length to
get the volume of the prism. ┃

Example 11

The diagram shows a trapezium.
The trapezium is the cross-section of a prism.
The length of the prism is 8 cm.

Work out the volume of the prism.

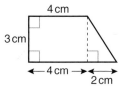

Solution 11
Method 1

Split the trapezium into a rectangle and a triangle.

Area of rectangle = $4 \times 3 = 12$ cm²
Area of triangle = $\frac{1}{2} \times 2 \times 3 = 3$ cm²

Work out the area of the rectangle and the area of the triangle.

Area of cross-section = 12 + 3
                     = 15 cm²

Add the area of the rectangle and the area of the triangle to get the area of the trapezium cross-section.

Volume = $15 \times 8 = 120$ cm³

Multiply the area of the cross-section by the length to get the volume of the prism.

Method 2
Area of cross-section = $\frac{1}{2} \times (6 + 4) \times 3$
                     = $\frac{1}{2} \times 10 \times 3$
                     = 15 cm²

Work out the area of the trapezium cross-section using area = $\frac{1}{2} \times$ sum of parallel sides $\times$ distance between them.

Volume = $15 \times 8 = 120$ cm³

Multiply the area of the cross-section by the length to get the volume of the prism.

Exercise 20F

1   The area of cross-section of a prism is 14 cm². The length of the prism is 6 cm.
    Work out the volume of the prism.

2   The volume of a prism is 63 cm³. Its area of cross-section is 9 cm².
    Work out the length of the prism.

3   The diagram shows a prism with a right-angled
    triangle as its cross-section.
    Work out the volume of the prism.

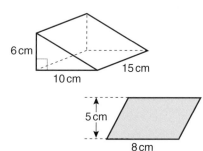

4   The diagram shows a parallelogram.
    The parallelogram is the cross-section of a prism.
    The length of the prism is 7 cm.
    Work out the volume of the prism.

5 The diagram shows a trapezium.
The trapezium is the cross-section of a prism.
The length of the prism is 5 cm.
Work out the volume of the prism.

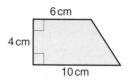

6 The diagram shows a prism. The cross-section of the prism is a trapezium.
The lengths of the parallel sides of the trapezium are
12 cm and 8 cm. The distance between the parallel
sides of the trapezium is 6 cm.
The length of the prism is 9 cm.
Work out the volume of the prism.

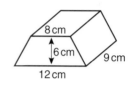

7 The diagram shows the cross-section of a prism.
All the corners are right angles.
The length of the prism is 8 cm.
Work out the volume of the prism.

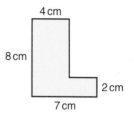

8 The diagram shows the cross-section of a barn.
The length of the barn is 15 m.
Find the volume of the barn.

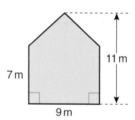

9 The diagram shows a prism with a right-angled triangle
as its cross-section. The volume of the prism is 126 cm³.
Work out the length of the prism.

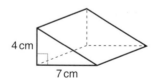

20.6 Surface area

The diagram shows a cube of side 2 cm.
Each of its six faces is a square.
The area of each square face is $2 \times 2 = 4$ cm².
So the surface area of the cube is $6 \times 4 = 24$ cm².

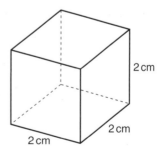

The surface area of the cube could be found by
drawing an accurate, full-size net of the cube
(see Example 2) and counting the number of
centimetre squares inside it.

Nets are helpful in finding the surface areas of 3-D shapes, but a sketch of a net of the 3-D
shape with lengths shown on it is usually used.

Example 12

The diagram shows a prism with a right-angled triangle as its cross-section.

Work out the surface area of the prism.

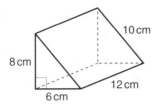

Solution 12

Draw a sketch of a net of the prism. There is no need to show the length of every edge but show all those which will be used in the working.

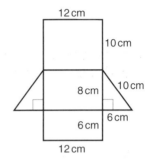

Method 1

$12 \times 10 + 12 \times 8 + 12 \times 6$
$= 120 + 96 + 72 = 288$

> Work out the areas of the three rectangles.

$\frac{1}{2} \times 6 \times 8 + \frac{1}{2} \times 6 \times 8$
$= 24 + 24 = 48$

> Work out the areas of the two triangles.

$288 + 48 = 336 \text{ cm}^2$

> Add the two results to find the surface area.

Method 2

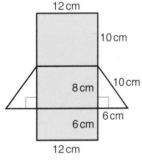

> Work out the total area of the three rectangles in one step by treating them as a single rectangle which is 12 cm by $(10 + 8 + 6)$ cm, that is 12 cm by 24 cm.
>
> Total area of the three rectangles $= 12 \times 24$
> $= 288 \text{ cm}^2$.

> The two triangles are congruent. So find the area of one triangle and multiply it by 2
>
> Total area of the two triangles $= 2 \times \frac{1}{2} \times 6 \times 8$
> $= 48 \text{ cm}^2$.

$288 + 48 = 336 \text{ cm}^2$

> Add the two results to find the surface area.

Exercise 20G

1   Work out the surface area of each of these 3-D shapes.
    For each shape, draw a sketch of the net.

    a   A cube of side 5 cm.

    b   A cuboid which is 4 cm by 4 cm by 8 cm.

    c   A cuboid which is 7 cm by 3 cm by 10 cm.

2   Work out the surface area of this prism with a
    right-angled triangle as its cross-section.

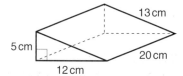

3   Work out the surface area of this prism with
    an isosceles triangle as its cross-section.

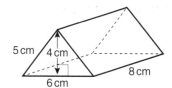

4   Calculate the surface area of this
    square-based pyramid.
    The *vertical* height, v, of each of the
    triangular faces is 10 cm.

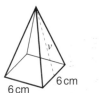

5   What is the surface area of a prism of length
    20 cm with this trapezium as its cross-section?

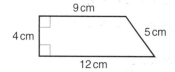

6   What is the surface area of a prism of length 15 cm
    with this isosceles trapezium as its cross-section?

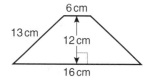

20.7 Dimensions

The perimeter of a rectangle is given by the expression $2l + 2w$. The circumference of a
circle is given by πd. Perimeter and circumference are both *lengths*.
Each term in the expression $2l + 2w$ and πd consists of 'a number × a length'.
Therefore, we say that the expressions have the **dimension** *length*.
(Numbers, such as 2 and π, have no dimensions.)

The area of a rectangle is given by the expression lw. The area of a circle is given by πr^2.
Each term consists of 'a number × a length × a length'.
The expressions have the dimensions length × length.

The volume of a cuboid is given by the expression lwh. The volume of a cylinder is given by
$\pi r^2 h$.

Each term consists of 'a number $\times$ a length $\times$ a length $\times$ a length'.
The expressions have the dimensions *length $\times$ length $\times$ length*.

So, for example, if a, b and c represent lengths,

$a + b$, $2a + 3b$, $\pi(b + c)$ and $\frac{1}{2}b + c$ represent lengths because each expression has
dimension length.

$ab + bc$, $a(b + c)$, πab, $\dfrac{b^2c}{b + c}$ and $\frac{1}{2}bc$ represent areas because each expression has
dimension *length $\times$ length*.

abc, $\frac{1}{3}b^2c$, $4a(ab + bc)$ and $\pi a^2(b + c)$ represent volumes because each expression has
dimension *length $\times$ length $\times$ length*.

Example 13

x, y and z represent lengths.
For each of these expressions, state whether it could represent a length, an area, a volume
of none of these.

a $5xy$ **b** $\pi y(x^2 + z^2)$ **c** $2x(y + 3)$ **d** $\dfrac{3xy}{(x + y)}$

Solution 13

a an area | The expression has dimensions *length $\times$ length*. |

b a volume | The dimensions of πy is length. Inside the brackets, both x^2 and z^2 have dimensions *length $\times$ length*. So the dimensions of the expression are *length $\times$ length $\times$ length*. |

c none of these | Multiply out the brackets, obtaining $2xy + 6x$. The first term has the dimensions *length $\times$ length* but the second term has the dimension length. |

d a length | The top term has the dimensions *length $\times$ length*. The bottom term has the dimension length. $\dfrac{length \times length}{length} = length$ |

Exercise 20H

Throughout this exercise, the letters b, h and r represent lengths.
Numbers such as 3, $\frac{1}{2}$ and π are numbers which have no dimensions.

1 Here are some expressions.

$\frac{1}{2}bh$ $4h + 3r$ $\pi(r + h)$ bhr $5h^2$ bh^2

   a Write down the expressions which could represent a length.

   b Write down the expressions which could represent an area.

2 Here are some expressions.

$$2bh \qquad r^2h \qquad 3b + 2r \qquad b(h + r) \qquad \pi r^2b \qquad \frac{r^3}{b + h}$$

   a Write down the expressions which could represent an area.

   b Write down the expressions which could represent a volume.

3 Here are some expressions.

$$b + rh \qquad b(3 + r) \qquad \pi b^3 + 4h^2 \qquad bh + \pi r^2 \qquad \frac{3b + r^2}{h}$$

   Write down the **one** expression which could represent an area.

4 Here are some expressions.

$$4b^2h \qquad \pi r^2(h + 2) \qquad \frac{5h^4}{b + r} \qquad (h + 2r)^3 \qquad \tfrac{1}{3}b^2h$$

   Write down the **one** expression which could **not** represent a volume.

5 Copy the table and complete it by putting a tick (✓) in the correct column to show whether the expression could be used for length, area, volume or none of these.

Expression	Length	Area	Volume	None of these
$2rh$				
$\pi r + 4h$				
$\dfrac{(r + h)^2}{3b}$				
$b^3 + rh$				
$\pi r^2(h + r)$				
$\dfrac{bhr}{(b + h)}$				

20.8 Coordinates in three dimensions

To locate a point in two dimensions, two perpendicular axes are used (the x-axis and the y-axis) and two coordinates are given (the x-coordinate and the y-coordinate).

In three dimensions, an extra axis is needed (the z-axis), the three axes being perpendicular to each other.
The position of a point is given by three coordinates –
the x-coordinate, the y-coordinate and the z-coordinate.

For example,
the coordinates of P are $(0, 1, 0)$
the coordinates of Q are $(0, 3, 2)$
and the coordinates of R are $(1, 3, 2)$.

As with coordinates in two dimensions, negative coordinates are needed to locate some points.

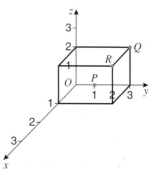

Example 14

Write down the coordinates of S, T and U.

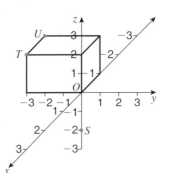

Solution 14

The coordinates are

S $(0, 0, -2)$, T $(0, -3, 2)$ and U $(-1, -3, 2)$

Exercise 20I

1   Write down the coordinates of P, Q and R.

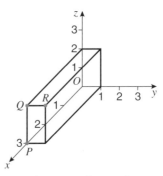

2   Draw a diagram to show the points A $(1, 0, 0)$, B $(1, 0, 3)$ and C $(1, 2, 3)$.

3   Write down the coordinates of A, B and C.

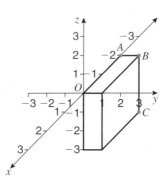

4   Draw a diagram to show the points
    D $(0, 0, -1)$, E $(3, 0, -1)$ and F $(3, -2, -1)$.

5   The coordinates of five of the corners of a cuboid are $(1, 0, 0)$, $(1, -3, 0)$, $(1, -3, -1)$, $(1, 0, -1)$ and $(-2, 0, 0)$. Find the coordinates of the other three corners.

Chapter summary

★   **You should now know:**

★   **Three-dimensional (3-D)** shapes have length, breadth and height

★   The names of common 3-D shapes – **cube, cuboid, prism, cylinder, pyramid, cone** and **sphere**

★ A prism's **cross-section** is the same all along its length

★ The meaning of **face**, **vertex** and **edge** in relation to 3-D shapes

★ How to draw a **net**

★ How to use **isometric grids** to make drawings of 3-D shapes

★ How to find the **volume** of a cuboid and solve related problems
volume of a cuboid = length × width × height

★ How to find the volume of a prism
volume of a prism = area of cross-section × length

★ How to use dimensions to find whether an expression could represent a length, an area or a volume

★ How to use coordinates in three dimensions

Chapter 20 review questions

Where necessary, give answers correct to 3 significant figures.
If your calculator does not have a π button take the value of π to be 3.142, unless the question instructs otherwise.

1 Write down the mathematical name for each of these 3-D shapes.

a

b

(4400 Nov 2004)

2 Use the resource sheet to answer this question.
The diagrams show some solids and their nets.
An arrow has been drawn from one solid to its net.
Draw an arrow from each of the other solids to its net.

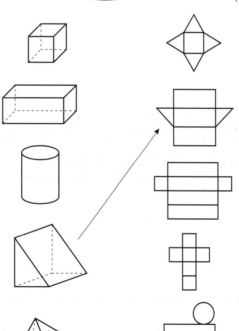

(1387 June 2003)

3 The diagram shows a cuboid.

   a For the cuboid, write down
     i the number of faces
     ii the number of vertices.

   b Work out the volume of the cuboid.

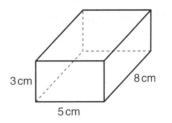

Diagram **NOT** accurately drawn

3 cm   8 cm

5 cm

(4400 May 2004)

4 The measurements of the cuboid on the grid are 3 cm by 2 cm by 1 cm.
On an isometric grid, draw a cuboid with measurements which are **double** the measurements of the above cuboid.

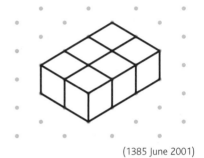

(1385 June 2001)

5 Here is a solid prism made from centimetre cubes.

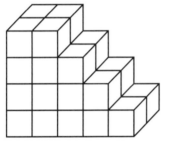

 1 cm³

Find the volume of the solid prism.

(1387 June 2004)

6 The diagram represents a large tank in the shape of a cuboid.
The tank has a base.
It does not have a top.
The width of the tank is 2.8 metres.
The length of the tank is 3.2 metres.
The height of the tank is 4.5 metres.

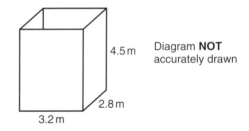

4.5 m   Diagram **NOT** accurately drawn

2.8 m

3.2 m

The outside of the tank is going to be painted. 1 litre of paint will cover 2.5 m² of the tank. The cost of paint is £2.99 per litre.

Calculate the cost of paint needed to paint the outside of the tank.   (1387 June 2003)

7 Here are three expressions.

Expression	Length	Area	Volume	None of these
$\pi a^2 b$				
$\pi b^2 + 2h$				
$2ah$				

a, b and h are lengths. π and 2 are numbers which have no dimensions.
Put a tick (✓) in the correct column to show whether the expression can be used for length, area, volume or none of these.   (1385 May 2002)

8 The table shows six expressions.
a, b and c are lengths.
2 and 3 are numbers and have no dimension.

$2a + 3a$	$3ab$	$a + b + c$	$2a^2c$	$2a^2 + bc$	$ab(b + 2c)$

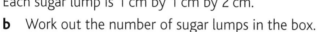

   i Put the letter A in the box underneath each of the **two** expressions that could represent an **area**.

  ii Put the letter V in the box underneath each of the **two** expressions that could represent a **volume**.

(1385 Nov 2002)

9 The diagram shows a box in the shape of a cuboid.

  a Work out the volume of the box.

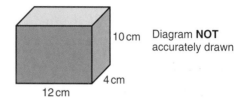

The box is full of sugar lumps.
Each sugar lump is in the shape of a cuboid.
Each sugar lump is 1 cm by 1 cm by 2 cm.

  b Work out the number of sugar lumps in the box.

(1388 Mar 2003)

Algebra 2

21.1 Multiplying out brackets

In section 11.5, brackets are multiplied by positive whole numbers.
To multiply out brackets, multiply each term inside the bracket by the term outside the bracket, for example, $4(2a - 5b + 1) = 8a - 20b + 4$

Brackets can be multiplied by negative numbers or terms involving letters.
'**Expand** $-a(2a - 5)$' is another way of saying 'multiply out $-a(2a - 5)$' so multiply each term inside the bracket by $-a$.

Example 1

Expand $2y(y^2 + 3)$

Solution 1
$2y(y + 3) = 2y \times y + 2y \times 3$
$2y(y + 3) = 2y^2 + 6y$

Example 2

Expand and simplify $5p - 3(p - q)$

Solution 2
$5p - 3(p - q) = 5p - 3 \times p - 3 \times -q$
$\qquad\qquad\quad = 5p - 3p + 3q$
$5p - 3(p - q) = 2p + 3q$

negative × negative is positive

Example 3

Expand and simplify $x(x + 2) + 4(x + 2)$

Solution 3
$x(x + 2) + 4(x + 2) = x \times x + x \times 2 + 4 \times x + 4 \times (+2)$
$\qquad\qquad\qquad\qquad = x^2 + 2x + 4x + 8$
$x(x + 2) + 4(x + 2) = x^2 + 6x + 8$

The expressions in Example 3 could be linked to the areas of these 2 rectangles.

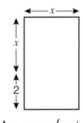

Area $= x(x + 2)$

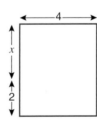

Area $= 4(x + 2)$

Combining these two rectangles gives a single rectangle with length $(x + 4)$ and width $(x + 2)$

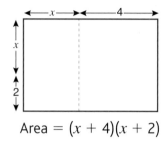

Area $= (x + 4)(x + 2)$

The area of the large rectangle is equal to the sum of the areas of the two smaller rectangles so

$$(x + 4)(x + 2) = x(x + 2) + 4(x + 2)$$

To expand two brackets, multiply each term in the first bracket by the second bracket so

$$(x + a)(x + b) = x(x + b) + a(x + b)$$
$$= x^2 + bx + ax + ab$$

Example 4

Expand and simplify $(x + 2)(x - 3)$

Solution 4

$$(x + 2)(x - 3) = x(x - 3) + 2(x - 3)$$
$$= x^2 - 3x + 2x - 6$$
$$(x + 2)(x - 3) = x^2 - x - 6$$

Example 5

Expand and simplify $(n - 2)^2$

Solution 5

$$(n - 2)^2 = (n - 2)(n - 2)$$
$$= n(n - 2) - 2(n - 2)$$
$$= n^2 - 2n - 2n + 4$$
$$(n - 2)^2 = n^2 - 4n + 4$$

Exercise 21A

1   Multiply out

   a $n(n + 1)$ **b** $c(c + 4)$ **c** $a(3a + 2)$ **d** $b(5 + 7b)$

   e $2n(n - 1)$ **f** $a(4 - a)$ **g** $2p(p - 3)$ **h** $4y(2y - 1)$

2   Multiply out

   a $-2(a + 1)$ **b** $-3(n + 4)$ **c** $-(b + 1)$ **d** $-2(c^2 + 3c)$

   e $-3(a - 1)$ **f** $-2(n - 4)$ **g** $-(y - 1)$ **h** $-5(d^2 - d)$

3   Expand $a(b + c)$

4   Expand and simplify

   a $4p - 2(p + 1)$ **b** $5q - 3(q + 3)$ **c** $5y - 3(2y + 1)$

   d $3 - (n + 3)$ **e** $2q - 3(q - 1)$ **f** $4 - 3(r - 1)$

   g $4x - 3(2x - 1)$ **h** $2b + 1 - 3(b - 3)$

5   Expand and simplify $x(x + 1) + 1(x + 1)$

6   Expand and simplify
   a $x(x + 2) + 1(x + 2)$ b $q(q + 1) + 3(q + 1)$
   c $r(r - 3) + (r - 3)$ d $s(s + 4) - 2(s + 1)$
   e $t(t - 3) - (t + 1)$ f $m(m - 4) - (m - 1)$
   g $a(a - 3) - 2(a - 1)$ h $n(n + 2) - 4(n - 2)$

7   Expand and simplify
   a $(x + 1)(x + 2)$ b $(q + 3)(q + 1)$ c $(r + 1)(r - 3)$
   d $(x + 4)(x + 3)$ e $(x + 2)(x - 1)$ f $(x + 3)(x - 3)$
   g $(r - 1)(r + 3)$ h $(x - 2)(x + 4)$ i $(x - 2)(x - 1)$
   j $(x - 3)(x - 4)$

8   Expand and simplify
   a $(x + 1)^2$ b $(x + 2)^2$ c $(x + 3)^2$
   d $(x - 1)^2$ e $(x - 2)^2$ f $(x - 3)^2$

21.2 Further factorising

also assessed in
Module 4

In section 11.6, expressions are factorised by taking out a number which is a common factor, for example, $4c + 6s = 2(2c + 3s)$.

Expressions can also be factorised by taking out a letter which is a common factor.

Example 6

Factorise $ab + ac$

Solution 6
$ab + ac = a \times b + a \times c$
$\qquad\quad = a(b + c)$
$ab + ac = a(b + c)$

Example 7

Factorise $y^2 - y$

Solution 7
$y^2 - y = y \times y - 1 \times y$
$\qquad\quad = y \times y - y \times 1$
$\qquad\quad = y(y - 1)$
$y^2 - y = y(y - 1)$

Exercise 21B

Factorise

1   $pq + pr$ 2 $xy + zy$ 3 $ab - 7b$

4   $db - b$ 5 $pq + py + p$ 6 $y^2 + yz$

7   $y^2 + 5y$ 8 $y^2 + y$ 9 $4y^2 - 3y$

10   $y^3 + 2y$ 11 $y^3 + y$ 12 $y^3 - 5y$

13   $p^2 + pq + pr$ 14 $y^3 + y^2 + y$ 15 $ay^3 - by^2 + cy$

Chapter summary

> **You should know and be able to use these facts**
>
> ★ **Expanding** brackets means multiplying out brackets. To expand two brackets, multiply each term in the first bracket by the second bracket so
> $(x + a)(x + b) = x(x + b) + a(x + b) = x^2 + bx + ax + ab$ and then simplify if possible, for example,
>
> $$(x - 2)(x + 5) = x(x + 5) - 2(x + 5) = x^2 + 5x - 2x - 10 = x^2 + 3x - 10$$
>
> ★ Factorising an expression involving terms which have a common letter, means taking out the letter as a factor, for example, $c^2 + 6c = c(c + 6)$

Chapter 21 review questions

1 Simplify

    a $q + q + q + q$ **b** Simplify $d \times 3 \times e$ **c** Expand $p(p - 5)$

2 Factorise   **a** $ab + 2bc$ **b** $2x + 3ax^3$

3 Expand and simplify

    a $3b + 1 - 4(b - 2)$ **b** $y(2y - 7)$

    c $(x + 2)(x + 7)$ **d** $4 + (m + 1)^2$

4 **a** Factorise $y^2 + 3y$

5 $P = a + bc$

    Work out the value of P when $a = -5$, $b = 6$ and $c = 2$

6 Expand $5y(3 - 5y)$

7 Factorise $k^2 + k$

Estimating and accuracy

22.1 Rounding

In the diagram, 6.8 is closer to the integer 7 than it is to the integer 6, so the value of 6.8 rounded to the nearest integer is 7

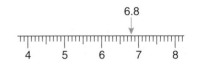

Similarly, the value of 16.24 rounded to the nearest integer is 16 as it is closer to the integer 16 than it is to the integer 17

When rounding a number to the nearest integer,

● the whole number part is **increased by 1** if the first figure after the decimal point is **5 or more**

● the whole number part **does not change** if the first figure after the decimal point is **less than 5**

Example 1

Round these numbers to the nearest integer

a 7.4 **b** 56.7 **c** 132. 07 **d** 7.5

Solution 1

	Number	Rounded to the nearest integer	
a	7.4	7	4 is less than 5 so do not change the whole number part.
b	56.7	57	7 is more than 5 so increase the 56 by 1
c	132.07	132	0 is less than 5 and so do not change the whole number part.
d	7.5	8	The first figure after the decimal point is 5 and so increase the 7 by 1

Rounding numbers has appeared in earlier chapters.

Rounding whole numbers to the nearest 10, 100 and 1000 was covered in section 6.3

Rounding numbers to one significant figure was covered in section 10.8

Example 2

Round these numbers to one significant figure.

a 78   **b** 52   **c** 349   **d** 132.07   **e** 7.5

Solution 2

a 80   **b** 50   **c** 300   **d** 100   **e** 8

In a decimal less than 1, the most significant figure in the number is the first non-zero figure after the decimal point.

0.078

In the number 0.078, the most significant figure is the 7
Rounded to one significant figure, 0.078 is 0.08, because the figure after the 7 is more than 5

0.506

In the number 0.506, the most significant figure is the 5
Rounded to one significant figure, 0.506 becomes 0.5, because the figure after the 5 is less than 5

Example 3

Write these numbers correct to one significant figure.

a 0.78   **b** 0.0547   **c** 0.0074

d 0.854   **e** 0.98

> Writing a number **correct to** one significant figure means the same as rounding it to one significant figure.

Solution 3

a 0.8   **b** 0.05   **c** 0.007   **d** 0.9   **e** 1

Numbers correct to one significant figure can be used to work out an approximate, or rough, value of an expression. An approximate value is called an **estimate**.

Example 4

Work out an estimate for the value of each of these expressions.

a 17.2×52.3 **b** $18.3 \div 3.9$ **c** $\dfrac{6.4 \times 179.8}{0.52}$

Solution 4

a   20 × 50

| Write each number correct to one significant figure. |

= 1000

| 1000 is an estimate for the value of 17.2 × 52.3 |

b   20 ÷ 4

| Write each number correct to one significant figure. |

= 5

| 5 is an estimate for the value of 18.3 ÷ 3.9 |

c $\dfrac{6 \times 200}{0.5}$

| Write each number correct to one significant figure. |

$= \dfrac{1200}{0.5}$

| Multiply 6 by 200 |

= 2400

| $0.5 = \frac{1}{2}$ and dividing by $\frac{1}{2}$ is the same as multiplying by 2
 2400 is an estimate for the value of $\dfrac{6.4 \times 179.8}{0.52}$ |

Exercise 22A

1   Write these numbers to the nearest integer.

    a   3.4   **b**   4.7   **c**   12.9   **d**   23.4   **e**   7.7

2   Write these numbers to the nearest integer.

    a   4.0   **b**   6.5   **c**   10.5   **d**   3.05   **e**   9.9

3   Write these numbers to the nearest integer.

    a   3.7   **b**   4.47   **c**   123. 7   **d**   0.3   **e**   2.38

4   Round these numbers to one significant figure.

    a   56   **b**   74   **c**   138   **d**   456   **e**   1205

5   Round these numbers to one significant figure.

    a   12   **b**   45   **c**   199   **d**   698   **e**   999

6   Write these numbers correct to one significant figure.

    a   16.3   **b**   4.7   **c**   24.9   **d**   7.7   **e**   8.5

7   Round these numbers to one significant figure.

    a   13.44   **b**   6.88   **c**   4.65   **d**   7.07   **e**   9.54

8   Write these numbers correct to one significant figure.

    a   0.61   **b**   0.77   **c**   0.45   **d**   0.056   **e**   0.0079

9   Work out an estimate for the value of each of these expressions by first rounding the numbers correct to one significant figure.

    a   3.4 × 4.9   **b**   5.4 × 3.8   **c**   9.4 × 9.9   **d**   13.4 × 3.9   **e**   24.4 × 4.7

    f   8.4 × 14.9   **g**   19.6 × 11.2   **h**   22.6 × 8.8   **i**   14.6 × 37.2 **j**   29.6 × 31.2

10 Work out an estimate for the value of each of these expressions.

    a 22×37 **b** 41×27 **c** 39×42 **d** 122×18

    e 102×97 **f** 203×58 **g** 199×312 **h** 212×387

    i 999×99 **j** 3124×48

11 Work out an estimate for the value of each of these expressions.

    a $6.4 \div 2.9$ **b** $16.4 \div 1.9$ **c** $26.9 \div 2.9$ **d** $38.4 \div 9.8$

    e $106 \div 11.2$ **f** $211 \div 12$ **g** $346 \div 3.2$ **h** $985 \div 478$

    i $377 \div 48$ **j** $2334 \div 12.9$

12 Work out an estimate for

    a $\dfrac{5.4 \times 4.9}{10.1}$ **b** $\dfrac{9.8 \times 4.9}{5.1}$ **c** $\dfrac{16.4 \times 9.9}{16.8}$

    d $\dfrac{6.8 \times 19.9}{12.1}$ **e** $\dfrac{17.4 \times 20.3}{38.7}$

13 Work out an estimate for

    a $\dfrac{12.2}{5.9} + 8.1$ **b** $\dfrac{21.2}{4.88} - 3.2$ **c** $\dfrac{111}{5.2} - \dfrac{23.3}{11.2}$ **d** $\dfrac{209}{51.2} + \dfrac{33.1}{10.8}$

22.2 Solving problems using approximations

Estimates are used to check whether the size of an answer to a problem is sensible.

Example 5

Work out an estimate for the total cost of 112 televisions at £198 each.

Solution 5

100×200 | Write each number correct to one significant figure. |

         $= 20\,000$ | $20\,000$ is an estimate for the value of 112×198 |

£20 000 is an estimate for the total cost.

Example 6

One of the following answers is the correct answer to

    $\dfrac{82 \times 47}{3.76}$

  a 272.6 **b** 1025 **c** 0.464 **d** $14\,491$

Use estimates to decide which answer is correct.

Solution 6

Rounding each number to one significant figure gives

$$\frac{80 \times 50}{4} = \frac{4000}{4} = 1000$$

The nearest value to 1000 is answer **b**, 1025

Exercise 22B

1   The weight of a can of beans is 424.5 grams. Estimate for the weight of 18 cans of beans.

2   The cost of a cinema ticket is £4.55. Find the approximate cost of 13 tickets.

3   There are 58 classrooms in a school. There are 32 chairs in each room. Work out an estimate for the total number of chairs in all of these rooms.

4   212 students went on a school trip. The total cost was £425. Work out the approximate cost for each student.

5   Work out an estimate for the number of minutes in   **a** a day   **b** a year.

6   Bill says that the number of hours in a year is 87 600. Use rounding to show that Bill is wrong.

7   Jessica earns £5.95 for each hour she works. Find an estimate for the amount of money Jessica earns when she works for 22 hours.

8   John works 18 days each month. He travels to work by train. The train fare is £3.35 per day. Work out an estimate for the total cost of John's train journeys for the month.

9   Becky earns £82.50 for $7\frac{1}{2}$ hours work. Work out an estimate for the amount of money that she earns each hour.

10   A rectangular field has a length of 61.2 metres and a width of 48.6 metres.

   a   Work out an estimate for the area of the field.

   22 grams of fertilizer is spread on each square metre of the field.

   b   Work out an estimate for the total weight of fertilizer spread on the field. Give your answer in kilograms.

11   A parcel weighs 512.5 grams. Find an estimate for the total weight of 19 of these parcels. Give your answer in kilograms.

12   The length of a rectangular picture is 19.6 cm. The area of the picture is 186.2 cm². Find an estimate for the width of the picture.

13   One of the following answers is the correct answer to

$$\frac{58.5 \times 21.5}{2.4}$$

   a   110.25   **b**   14.875   **c**   526.75   **d**   1575.5

   Use estimates to decide which answer is correct.

14 Decide which one of the following answers is the correct answer to

$$\frac{234.3}{1.32} + \frac{159.6}{11.4}$$

    a   403.3   **b**   309.7   **c**   28.4   **d**   191.5

15 At a football match all adults pay £17.50 each and all children pay £12.25 each. There were 8748 adults and 3458 children at the football match. Work out an estimate for the total amount of money paid.

22.3 Interpreting calculator displays

Take care when writing down the answer from a calculator display, especially when the problem involves money. Answers which are in pounds and pence should always be written with two figures after the decimal point. Calculators will not give two figures after the decimal point if the number of pence is a multiple of 10

£5 ÷ 2 = £2.50 but, using a calculator, 5 ÷ 2 = gives 2.5

When it is an amount of money, the calculator display 2.5 means £2.50 (two pounds fifty pence) while 2.05 means £2.05 (two pounds five pence)

Sometimes, the answer to a money calculation must be rounded to the nearest penny, because the number of pence is not a whole number.

Example 7

The price of a litre of petrol is 96.9p. Liz buys 14.5 litres of petrol. Calculate how much Liz has to pay. Give your answer in pounds and pence.

Solution 7
On the calculator 96.9 × 14.5 = 1405.05

This is the answer in pence, so to change 1405.05 pence to pounds, divide it by 100 to get 14.0505

£14.0505 = £14.05 to the nearest penny.

Example 8

A jar holds 128 ml of water. How many of these jars can be completely filled using 2000 ml of water?

Solution 8
On the calculator 2000 ÷ 128 = gives 15.625

> To the nearest whole number 15.625 is 16 but 16 jars cannot be completely filled.

So 15 jars can be completely filled.

Example 9

A car travels at an average speed of 50 km/h. How long will it take the car to travel 120 km? Give your answer in hours and minutes.

Solution 9

$$\text{time} = \frac{120}{50}$$

| $\text{time} = \dfrac{\text{distance}}{\text{average speed}}$ (see section 17.5) |

$$= 2.4\,\text{h}$$

| Speed is in km/h and distance is in km so the time is in hours. |

| 2.4h = 2h + 0.4h |

$$0.4 \times 60 = 24$$

| To change 0.4 h to minutes, multiply 0.4 by 60, as there are 60 minutes in an hour. |

$$\text{Time} = 2 \text{ hours } 24 \text{ minutes}$$

Exercise 22C

1 The cost of a litre of petrol is 97.9p. Work out the cost of 18.6 litres of petrol.

2 A credit card company charges 1.7% of the balance each month. Work out the charge on a balance of   **a** £422   **b** £568.23

3 The cost of electricity is 11.623p for each unit. Work out the cost of 1125 units.

4 A glass holds 125 ml of wine. How many of these glasses can be completely filled from a box holding 2800 ml of wine?

5 1330 passengers are going on a coach trip. Each coach holds 58 passengers. Work out the smallest number of coaches needed.

6 It takes 22 minutes to fill a tank. How many tanks can be completely filled in 10 hours?

7 A consultant receives 43.4p for each mile that he drives his car. How much money should he receive when he drives 237 miles?

8 3.6 metres of gold wire costs £5.22. Work out the cost of 4.75 metres of gold wire.

9 A rectangular carpet is 6.3 m long and 5.8 m wide.
   a Work out the area of the carpet.

   The carpet costs £11.99 per square metre.
   b Work out the cost of the carpet.

10 A car travels at an average speed of 50 miles per hour. Work out the time it takes the car to travel   **a** 125 miles   **b** 160 miles. Give your answers in hours and minutes.

11 A train travels at an average speed of 108 km/h. Work out the distance the train travels in   **a** 2 hours 30 minutes   **b** 3 hours 10 minutes.

22.4 Problem solving using a calculator

There are some problems in mathematics where the exact answer is hard to find.
Sometimes the method of **trial and improvement** can be used.
In this method, start with an estimate of the answer and then do trials to improve the
estimate.

Here is a rectangle. The length of the rectangle
is 2 metres more than the width.
The area of the rectangle is 29.25 m².

Length

Area = 29.25 m² Width

A sensible first estimate is 5 m for the width, giving the length as 5 m + 2 m = 7 m
This gives an area of 7 × 5 = 35 m², which is too big as 35 > 29.25
The second estimate for the width must be less than 5 m, so try 4 m.

Show the trials in a table and use area = length × width.

Width (m)	Length (m)	Area (m²)
5	7	35 (>29.25) too big
4	6	24 (<29.25) too small

The width is between 4 m and 5 m, so try 4.5 m, which is halfway between.

Width (m)	Length (m)	Area (m²)
4.5	6.5	29.25 correct

So the width of the rectangle is 4.5 m and its length is 6.5 m.

Example 10

The product of two numbers is 768. One number is 8 more than the other number. Find
the two numbers.

Solution 10
Use trial and improvement. Record the results in a table.

First number	Second number	Product	Too big or too small?
10	18	180	Too small as 180 < 768
20	28	560	Too small
30	38	1140	Too large
25	33	825	Too large
24	32	768	Correct

The two numbers are 24 and 32

Not all problems should be done using trial and improvement. In many cases it can be solved more simply.

Example 11

Jim's house uses 1378 units of electricity. Each unit costs 42.8p. VAT is charged on the cost of the electricity at 5%.
Work out the total amount that Jim must pay.

Solution 11
Cost of 1378 units = 1378 × 42.8 = 58978.4 pence   = £589.784
VAT   = 5% of £589.784 = 0.05 × 589.784 = £29.4892
Total   = £619.2732
£619.2732 = £619.27 to the nearest penny

Jim must pay £619.27

Exercise 22D

1 The length of the rectangle is 4 metres more than the width. Use trial and improvement to work out the width.

Length

Area = 192 m²   Width

2 The product of two numbers is 572. One number is 4 more than the other. Use trial and improvement to find the two numbers.

3 The product of two numbers is 924. One number is 5 less than the other. Use trial and improvement to find the two numbers.

4 The length of a rectangle is twice the width. The area of the rectangle is 578 m². Use trial and improvement to work out the width of the rectangle.

5 Owen's house uses 1346 units of electricity. Each unit of electricity costs 44.5 pence. VAT is charged at 5%. Work out the amount that Owen has to pay.

6 Liz buys a car. The list price of the car is £6995. The total price is the list price plus VAT at 17.5%. She decides to pay a deposit of 20% of the total price. Work out how much she pays as a deposit.

7 Steve's house uses 745 units of gas. Each unit of gas costs 23.756 pence. VAT at 5% is charged on the cost of the gas. Work out how much Steve has to pay.

8 Jamal thinks of a number. He squares the number and then doubles his answer. He gets 1352. Use trial and improvement to find the number.

9 Louise's pay increased by 8% to £243. Use trial and improvement to find Louise's pay before she had the pay rise.

10 A graphical calculator costs £53.12. If Bob buys more than 30 graphical calculators he gets a $3\frac{1}{2}$% discount of the total cost. Bob buys 35 graphical calculators and gets the discount. How much should Bob pay?

22.5 Accuracy of measurements

With a centimetre stick, lengths can be measured correct to the nearest centimetre.
Measured with a centimetre stick, the length of a piece of A4 paper is 30 cm.

This does not mean that the length of the A4 paper is exactly 30 centimetres.
It is 30 centimetres correct to the nearest centimetre.

The exact length of the piece of
A4 paper is somewhere between
29.5 cm and 30.5 cm.

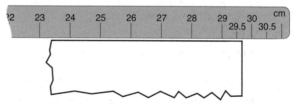

So 30 cm to the nearest centimetre means that the minimum (least) possible length is
29.5 cm and the maximum (greatest) possible length is 30.5 cm.

With a ruler, lengths can be measured correct to the nearest millimetre.
Measured with a ruler, the length of a piece of A4 paper is 298 mm.

The exact length of the piece of A4 paper
is between 297.5 mm and 298.5 mm.
So 298 mm to the nearest millimetre
means that the minimum (least) possible
length is 297.5 mm and the maximum
(greatest) possible length is 298.5 mm.

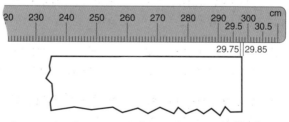

Measurements given to the nearest whole unit may be inaccurate by up to one half of a
unit below and one half of a unit above.
For example, '8 kg to the nearest kilogram' means that the least possible weight is 7.5 kg
and the greatest possible weight is 8.5 kg.

Example 12

Write down   **i** the smallest possible volume   **ii** the greatest possible volume of

a   a large tank which holds 52 litres of water correct to the nearest litre,

b   a small bowl which holds 124 millilitres of water correct to the nearest millilitre.

Solution 12

		Smallest possible volume	Greatest possible volume
a	52 litres correct to the nearest litre	51.5 litres	52.5 litres
b	124 millilitres correct to the nearest millilitre	123.5 millilitres	124.5 millilitres

Example 13

The length of a calculator is 12.8 cm correct to the nearest **millimetre**.
Write down

a   the minimum possible length it could be,

b   the maximum possible length it could be.

Solution 13
Write 12.8 cm as 128 mm, as the measurement is accurate to the nearest millimetre.

	Minimum possible length	Maximum possible length
128 mm correct to the nearest millimetre	127.5 mm or 12.75 cm	128.5 mm or 12.85 cm

Exercise 22E

1   The length of a pencil is 12 cm correct to the nearest cm. Write down the maximum length it could be.

2   The weight of an envelope is 45 grams correct to the nearest gram. Write down the minimum weight it could be.

3   The capacity of a jug is 4 litres correct to the nearest litre. Write down the minimum capacity of the jug.

4   The radius of a plate is 9.7 cm correct to the nearest millimetre. Write down
    a   the least possible length it could be,   **b**   the greatest possible length it could be.

5   Magda's height is 1.59 m correct to the nearest centimetre. Write down in **metres**
    a   the minimum possible height she could be,
    b   the maximum possible height she could be.

6 The length of a pencil is 10 cm correct to the nearest cm. The length of a pencil case is 102 mm correct to the nearest mm. Explain why the pen might **not** fit in the case.

7 The width of a cupboard is measured to be 82 cm correct to the nearest cm. There is a gap of 822 mm correct to the nearest mm in the wall. Explain how the cupboard might fit in the wall.

Chapter summary

You should now be able to:

★ Round numbers correct to 1 significant figure.

★ Use rounding to estimate and check answers to problems.

★ Carry out correct calculations on a calculator and interpret the display.

★ Solve problems by using trial and improvement.

★ Recognise that measurements given to the nearest whole unit may be inaccurate by up to one half of a unit in either direction.

Chapter 22 review questions

1 Round these numbers to the nearest integer.
   a 13.8   **b** 47.22   **c** 22.56   **d** 4.63

2 Round these numbers to one significant figure.
   a 3.56   **b** 0.079   **c** 234   **d** 34.89   **e** 20.055

3 Work out the approximate value of the following expressions by rounding the values to one significant figure.
   a 4.2×7.8 **b** 19.2×31.8 **c** 42×78 **d** 231×47.8

4 Work out the approximate value of the following expressions by rounding the values to one significant figure.
   a $\dfrac{101}{9.9}$ **b** $\dfrac{10.3}{9.9}$ **c** $\dfrac{51.2}{4.9}$ **d** $\dfrac{205.5}{10.4}$ **e** $\dfrac{798}{19.9}$

5 Work out the approximate value of the following expressions by rounding the values to one significant figure.
   a $\dfrac{41.8 \times 31.2}{11.2}$ **b** $\dfrac{91.5 \times 29.9}{10.3}$ **c** $\dfrac{101.8 \times 39.6}{21.3}$ **d** $\dfrac{503}{11.2 \times 9.8}$

6 Work out an estimate for the cost of
   a 99 radios at £19.90 each   **b** 49 tins of paint at £3.99 each
   c 112 pounds of potatoes at 39 pence for each pound

7 Books are sold for £3.95 each. Estimate the number of these books that can be bought for £20

8 Estimate the value of $\dfrac{68 \times 401}{198}$

(1387 June 2004)

9 The length of a field is 45 metres correct to the nearest metre.

  a Write down the maximum length it could be

  b Write down the minimum length it could be.

10 Work out an estimate for the value of $\dfrac{637}{3.2 \times 9.8}$

(1387 June 2005)

11 Alison travels by car to her meetings.
Alison's company pays her 32p for each mile she travels.

One day Alison writes down the distance readings from her car.

Start of the day: 2430 miles
End of the day: 2658 miles

  a Work out how much the company pays Alison for her day's travel.

The next day Alison travelled a total of 145 miles.

She travelled $\frac{2}{5}$ of this distance in the morning.

  b How many miles did she travel during the rest of the day?

(1387 June 2005)

12 Petrol costs 107.9 pence per litre. Sarfraz buys 21.6 litres of petrol. How much should Sarfraz pay?

13 A car travels at an average speed of 96 kilometres per hour. Work out the distance the car travels in 2 hours 20 minutes.

14 The time it takes to fill a water tank is 7 minutes to the nearest minute.

  a Write down the shortest time it could be.

  b Write down the longest time it could be.

15 a Work out the value of $3.8^2 - \sqrt{75}$
Write down all the figures on your calculator display

  b Round your answer to part **a** correct to 1 significant figure.

(1387 June 2005)

16 The length of a rectangle is 4 metres more than its width. The area of the rectangle is 837 square metres. Use the method of trial and improvement to work out the length and the width of the rectangle.

17 Nina started a new job. After six months she was given a 15% pay rise. Her new pay was £368. Use the method of trial and improvement to work out her pay when she started the new job.

Two-dimensional shapes 23

This chapter is about two-dimensional shapes. Two-dimensional shapes are flat. Two-dimensional is often written as 2-D.

23.1 Symmetry

Symmetry is often seen in buildings, in art and in nature.

The picture of the Taj Mahal has a type of symmetry called **line symmetry**.
A shape has line symmetry if it can be folded so that one part of the shape fits exactly on top of the other part.
The fold line is called the **line of symmetry** or the **axis of symmetry**.

Taj Mahal

This arrow has one line of symmetry.
Put a mirror on the line of symmetry and look into the mirror.
The arrow looks the same.
This is why line symmetry is sometimes called **reflection symmetry** and the line of symmetry is sometimes called the **mirror line**.

Notice that corner A of the arrow is the same distance away from the mirror line as corner B. This is also true for the other corners as well.

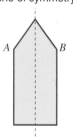
Line of symmetry

Tracing paper can be used to see if a shape has line symmetry. Trace the shape. Then fold the tracing and see if one part fits exactly over the other part.

A shape has **rotational symmetry** if a tracing of the shape fits exactly on top of the shape in more than one position.

This hub cap has rotational symmetry.

The number of positions that the tracing fits exactly on top of the shape is called its **order of rotational symmetry.**

To find the order of rotational symmetry of this star start by making a tracing of it.

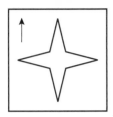

Mark the tracing with an arrow to show
which side of the paper was at the top
at the start.

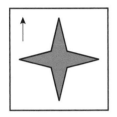

Place the tracing over the star.
Turn the tracing paper through a quarter turn
clockwise.
The tracing of the star fits exactly on top of
the star.

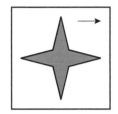

Keep turning the tracing paper through a quarter turn clockwise, until you get back to
the starting position. After each quarter turn, the tracing of the star fits exactly on top
of the star.

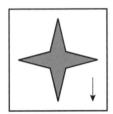 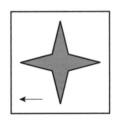 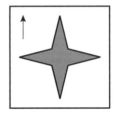

The tracing of the star fits exactly on top of the star in *four* ways. So the star has
rotational symmetry of order 4.

Look at the picture of the hub cap on the previous page. What is its order of rotational
symmetry?

The star has four lines of symmetry as well as having rotational symmetry. The arrow used
earlier has one line of symmetry but does not have rotational symmetry.

Some shapes do not have any symmetry.
Here is a shape that does not have line symmetry and does not have rotational   **?**
symmetry.

Example 1

Draw in all the lines of symmetry on this flag.

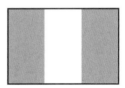

Solution 1

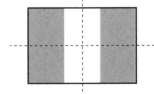

"*All* the lines" suggests that there
is more than one line of symmetry.

Example 2

Find the order of rotational symmetry of this shape.

Solution 2

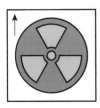

Trace the shape.

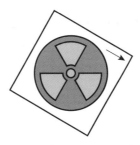

Turn the tracing paper through $\frac{1}{3}$ of a turn. The tracing fits exactly on top of the shape.

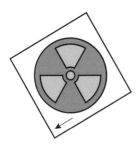

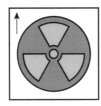

Turn the tracing paper through another $\frac{1}{3}$ of a turn.

The tracing again fits exactly on top of the shape.

Turn the tracing paper through another $\frac{1}{3}$ of a turn.

The tracing paper is back in its starting position.

There are three different ways the tracing will fit exactly on top of the shape. So the shape has rotational symmetry of order 3

Example 3

Complete the drawing of the shape so that it has line symmetry.

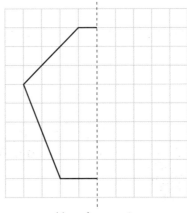

Line of symmetry

Solution 3

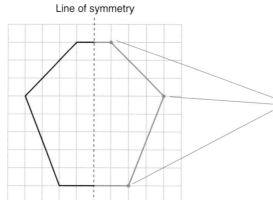

Line of symmetry

Mark the mirror images of the corners, on the other side of the line of symmetry.
For each corner, mark its mirror image so that the corner and its image are the same distance from the line of symmetry.
Then complete the shape.

Example 4

Shade four more squares in the pattern so that the dotted line is a line of symmetry.

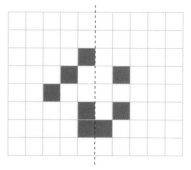

Solution 4

Compare the two sides of the pattern.
Shade four squares so that each shaded square has an image on the other side of the line of symmetry.

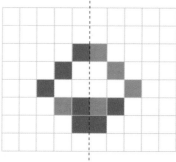

Example 5

The diagram shows part of a shape. Complete the shape so that it has no lines of symmetry and has rotational symmetry of order 2

Solution 5

Rotational symmetry of order 2 means that the completed shape must look the same when it is rotated through a half turn.

Make a tracing of the shape and rotate it through a half turn to make the completed shape.

Make a tracing of the completed shape and check that it has no lines of symmetry and rotational symmetry of order 2

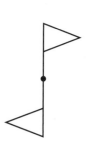

Exercise 23A

1 For each shape, write down if it has line symmetry or not.

a   b   c   d

e   f  g

h   i   j

2 Each of the following shapes has line symmetry. Draw all the lines of symmetry on the diagrams on the resource sheet.

a  b   c

d   e   f

3 One of the shapes in Question **2** does not have rotational symmetry. Write down the letter of this shape.

4 Using tracing paper, if necessary, write down which of the following shapes have rotational symmetry and which do not have rotational symmetry.
For the shapes that have rotational symmetry, write down the order.

a   b   c   d   e

f   g   h   i   j

5 a Complete the shape on the resource sheet so that it has line symmetry.

   b Write down the name of the complete shape.

Line of symmetry

6 Complete each of these shapes on the resource sheet so that it has line symmetry.

a   Line of symmetry   **b**   Line of symmetry

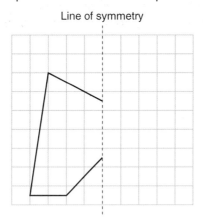   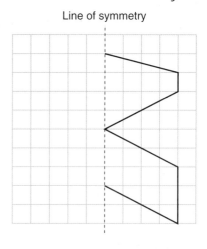

7 Each diagram shows an incomplete pattern.
   On the diagrams **a** and **b** shade four more squares in each diagram so that the dotted line is a line of symmetry of each complete pattern.

a   **b**

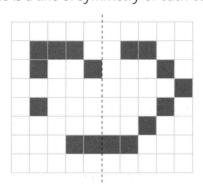   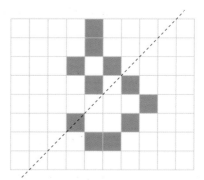

   c On the diagram on the resource sheet shade six more squares so that both dotted lines are lines of symmetry of the complete pattern.

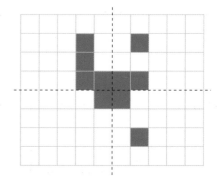

8 The diagram shows an incomplete pattern.

On the diagram shade three more squares so that
the complete pattern has rotational symmetry of order 4.

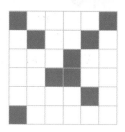

9 a Draw a shape that has two lines of symmetry and rotational symmetry of order 2.
b Draw a shape with one line of symmetry and no rotational symmetry.
c Draw a shape that has no lines of symmetry and rotational symmetry of order 4.

23.2 Triangles

Here is a **right-angled** triangle.
It has one angle of 90°.

Here is an **isosceles** triangle.
It has two sides the same length.

Here is an **equilateral** triangle.
All its sides are the same length.

An isosceles triangle has one line of symmetry.

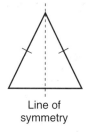

Line of
symmetry

23.3 Symmetry of quadrilaterals

A **quadrilateral** has four sides. Some quadrilaterals have special names.
Here are some of the properties of special quadrilaterals.

Square

All sides equal in length
All angles are 90°

Rectangle

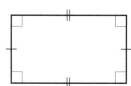

Opposite sides equal in length
All angles are 90°

Rhombus

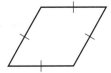

All sides equal in length
Opposite sides parallel
Opposite angles equal

Parallelogram

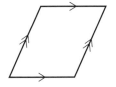

Opposite sides equal in length and parallel
Opposite angles equal

Trapezium

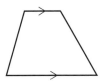

One pair of parallel sides

Isosceles Trapezium

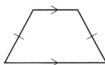

One pair of parallel sides
Non-parallel sides equal in length

Kite

Two pairs of adjacent sides equal in length
(**adjacent** means 'next to')

Exercise 23B

1 a Draw an equilateral triangle. Draw all its lines of symmetry.

   b Find the order of rotational symmetry of an equilateral triangle.

2 a On squared paper, draw a right-angled triangle that has one line of symmetry. Draw the line of symmetry on your triangle.

   b Write down what is special about this right-angled triangle.

3 There are two quadrilaterals described above that do not have any lines of symmetry. Give the names of these quadrilaterals.

4 Draw each of the following quadrilaterals and show all the lines of symmetry. Write down how many lines of symmetry each shape has:

   a rectangle   **b** kite   **c** square

   d rhombus   **e** isosceles trapezium.

5 There are three quadrilaterals described before this exercise that do not have rotational symmetry. Give the names of these quadrilaterals.

6 Find the order of rotational symmetry of:

   a a square   **b** a rectangle   **c** a parallelogram **d** a rhombus.

7 The diagram shows an arrowhead and its one line of symmetry.

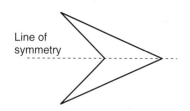

Line of symmetry

  a On the diagram of the arrowhead mark clearly any pairs of lines that have the same length.

  b State whether an arrowhead has rotational symmetry or not.

  c Which other quadrilateral has these same properties?

23.4 Symmetry of regular polygons

A **polygon** is a closed, flat shape with straight sides.

A triangle is a polygon with three sides.
A quadrilateral is a polygon with four sides.

A regular polygon is a polygon with all its sides the same length and all its angles equal.

An equilateral triangle is a regular polygon with three sides.
It has three lines of symmetry and rotational symmetry of order 3.

A square is a regular polygon with four sides. It has four lines of symmetry and rotational symmetry of order 4.
Other polygons have special names. Here are some of them.

Pentagon	Hexagon	Heptagon	Octagon	Decagon
5 sides	6 sides	7 sides	8 sides	10 sides

Exercise 23C

1 a How many lines of symmetry does a regular pentagon have?

  b On a sketch of a regular pentagon draw the lines of symmetry.

2 a How many lines of symmetry does a regular hexagon have?

  b On a sketch of a regular hexagon draw the lines of symmetry.

3 a How many lines of symmetry does a regular octagon have?

  b On a sketch of a regular octagon draw the lines of symmetry.

4 Find the order of rotational symmetry of:

  a a regular pentagon   **b** a regular hexagon

  c a regular heptagon   **d** a regular octagon.

5 For a regular polygon, what is the link between the number of sides it has and

   a the number of lines of symmetry it has?

   b its order of rotational symmetry?

6 Here is a regular nonagon.

   a How many sides has a nonagon?

   b How many lines of symmetry does a regular nonagon have?

   c What is the order of rotational symmetry of a regular nonagon?

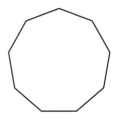

7 A regular polygon has 20 lines of symmetry.

   a How many sides has this polygon?

   b What is the order of rotational symmetry of this polygon?

8 A regular polygon has rotational symmetry of order 16
How many lines of symmetry does this polygon have?

23.5 Drawing shapes

Here are some more examples of making accurate drawings of shapes. Those in section 7.8 needed only a ruler and a protractor but some of these require compasses.

Example 6

Here is a sketch of a triangle.

Make an accurate drawing of the triangle.

Solution 6

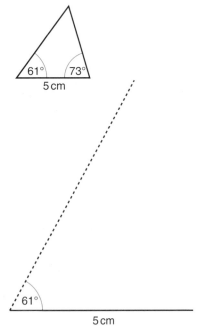

Step 1 – Use a ruler to draw a line 5 cm long.

Step 2 – Use a protractor to draw an angle of 61°.

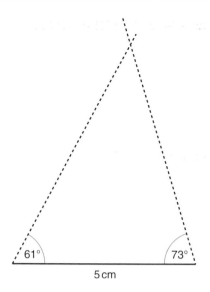

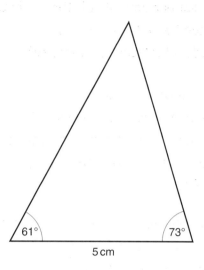

Step 3 – Use a protractor to draw an angle of 73°.

Step 4 – Complete the triangle.

Exercise 23D

In questions **1–5**, sketches of triangles are shown.
Make an accurate drawing of each of these triangles.

1

2

3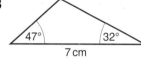

4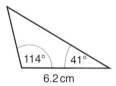

5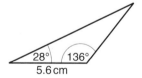

Example 7

Here is a sketch of a triangle.
Make an accurate drawing of the triangle.

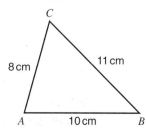

An accurate drawing made with a ruler and compasses but not a protractor is called a construction. So Example 6 is a construction.

Solution 7

Step 1
Draw a line 10 cm long using a ruler.
This is the base, AB, of the triangle.
Sometimes in exam questions, this base line
will be drawn on the question paper.

Step 2
Using a ruler, set your compasses to 8 cm.
Put the point of the compasses on A and draw an
arc of a circle.

Step 3
Using a ruler, set your compasses to 11 cm.
Put the point of the compasses on B and draw an
arc of a circle.

Step 4
The point where the two arcs cross is the third vertex,
(corner) C, of the triangle.
CB is 11 cm long and CA is 8 cm long, so join C to A
and C to B to complete triangle ABC.

It is important that all construction lines can be seen.
They should not be rubbed out when you have finished
drawing the shape.

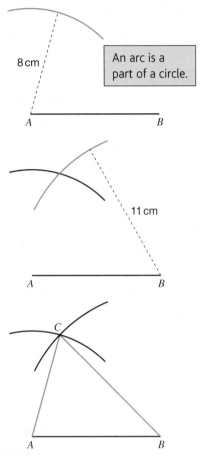

An arc is a part of a circle.

Example 8

$ABCD$ is a parallelogram where $AB = DC = 9$ cm, and $AD = BC = 6$ cm.
Angle $DAC = 50°$.

Make an accurate drawing of the parallelogram.

Solution 8

Step 1
In most exam questions, there will be a sketch
of the shape to be drawn – usually with the
statement 'Diagram **NOT** accurately drawn'.
If there is not, it is useful to draw a sketch
and mark in the information from the question.

Sketch

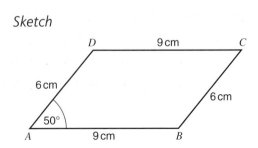

Step 2
Draw a line 9 cm long using a ruler.
This is the base, *AB*, of the parallelogram.

A   9 cm   B

Step 3
Using a protractor, measure an angle of 50°
and draw a line at 50° to *AB*.
Using compasses, mark off a length of 6 cm
on this line. This will be the point *D*.

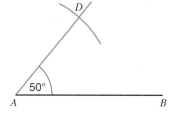

Step 4
The point *C* is 6 cm from *B* and 9 cm from *D*.

Draw an arc with centre *B* and radius 6 cm.

Draw an arc with centre *D* and radius 9 cm.

The point *C* is where these two arcs cross.

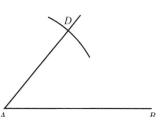

Step 5
Parallelogram *ABCD* can now be completed by
joining *C* to *B* and to *D*.

Notice that it was necessary to measure only
one angle.

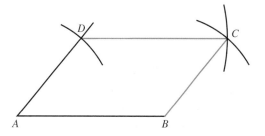

Exercise 23E

1 Here is a sketch of triangle *ABC*.
Use a ruler and compasses to construct the triangle when

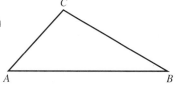

  a *AB* = 10 cm, *CA* = 8 cm and *CB* = 9 cm

  b *AB* = 8.7 cm, *CA* = 9.4 cm and *CB* = 8.1 cm

  c *AB* = 4.6 cm, *CA* = 10.4 cm and *CB* = 7.9 cm

  d *AB* = 3.5 cm, *CA* = 12 cm and *CB* = 12.5 cm.

In each case measure the size of the largest angle of the triangle.

2 Use a ruler and compasses to construct an equilateral triangle with sides of length 8 cm.

3 Here is a sketch of triangle *LMN*.

  a Make an accurate drawing of triangle *LMN*.

  b Measure the length of the side *LN*.

Give your answer to the nearest 0.1 cm.

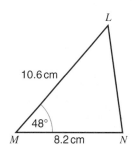

4 Here is a sketch of a rhombus.
Make an accurate drawing of the rhombus.

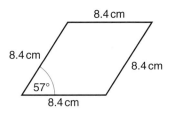

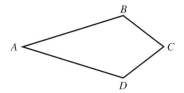

5 Here is a sketch of a kite *ABCD*.
AC = 10.8 cm, *AB* = *AD* = 8.2 cm,
BC = *DC* = 4.7 cm
Use a ruler and compasses to construct the kite.

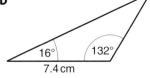

6 Here are sketches of three triangles.
Make an accurate drawing of each triangle.

a

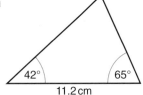

b

c

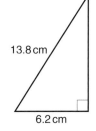

7 Triangle *ABC* is isosceles. The sides *AB* and *AC* are both 9.6 cm long. The angles at *B* and *C* are both 38°.

   a Draw a sketch of triangle *ABC*, showing the lengths of sides *AB* and *AC* and the size of the angles at *B* and *C*.

   b Make an accurate drawing of triangle *ABC*.

   c Measure the length of *BC*. Give your answer to the nearest 0.1 cm.

8 In triangle *PQR*, the side *PQ* is 5.8 cm long, the side *QR* is 6.4 cm long and the size of the angle *PQR* is 106°.

   a Draw a sketch of triangle *PQR*, showing the lengths of sides *PQ* and *QR* and the size of angle *PQR*.

   b Make an accurate drawing of triangle *PQR*.

   c Measure the length of *PR*. Give your answer to the nearest 0.1 cm.

9 The diagram is a sketch of triangle *ABC*.

When the length of the side *AC* is 7.6 cm, it
is possible to draw two different triangles.
Make accurate drawings of the two
possible triangles.

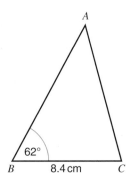

23.6 Congruent shapes

Look at these three shapes.

A tracing of any one of the shapes will fit exactly over the other two shapes. These shapes are called **congruent** shapes, because they are exactly the same shape and exactly the same size.

Example 9

In this diagram, there are two pairs of congruent shapes. Write down the letters of these pairs.

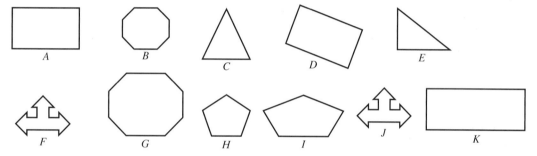

Solution 9

Shape A and shape D are congruent.

Shape F and shape J are congruent.

You can use tracing paper to check.

Exercise 23F

1   Here are eight shapes. There are two pairs of congruent shapes.
    Write down the letters of the shapes that are congruent.

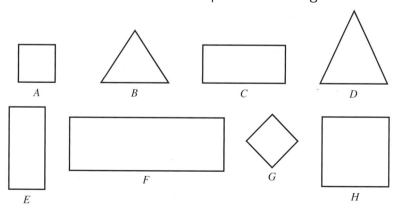

2 Here are nine shapes. There are two pairs of congruent shapes.

Write down the letters of these pairs.

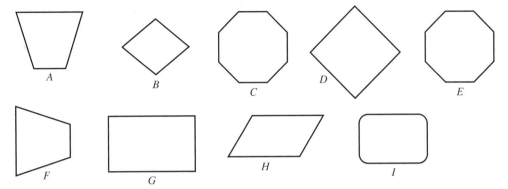

3 Give the letters of all congruent triangles from the nine triangles below.

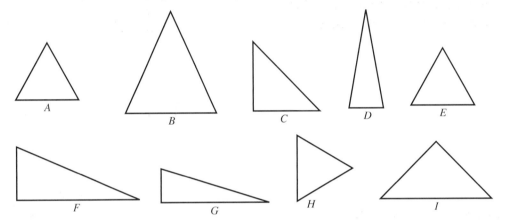

4 In each part of question **4**, there is a pair of congruent shapes. Write down the letters of this pair.

a

b

c

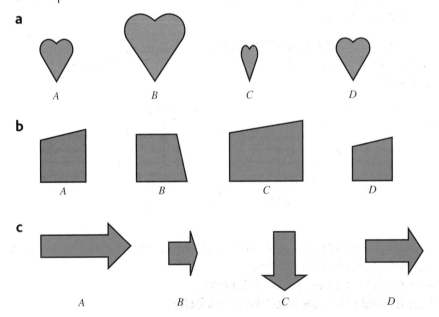

d

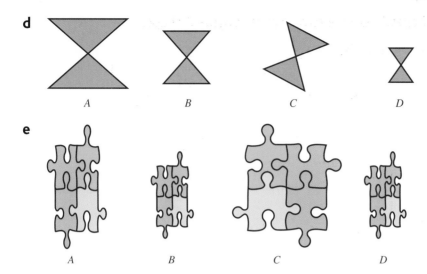

A   B   C   D

e

A   B   C   D

5 On the diagram, draw a shape that is congruent to the shaded shape.

23.7 Circles

Here is a **circle**.
The **centre** of this circle is the point O.
The distance from O to any point on the circle is 2 cm.
So the **radius** of the circle is 2 cm.

The radius of a circle is the distance from the centre of the circle to any point on the circle.

A radius of a circle is any straight line drawn from the centre of the circle to a point on the circle.
The plural of radius is **radii**.

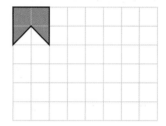

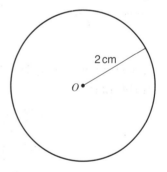

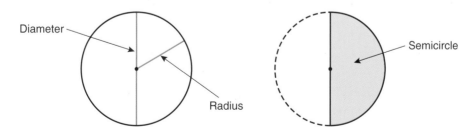

A diameter of a circle is any straight line drawn through the centre of the circle from a point on the circle to another point on the circle.
The length of a diameter is twice the radius of the circle.
A diameter of a circle divides the circle into two **semicircles**.

The distance around a circle is the **circumference** of the circle.
An **arc** of a circle is part of the circumference of the circle.

A **chord** of a circle is a straight line joining any two points on the circle.
This means that a diameter of a circle is a chord that passes through the centre of the circle.

A **tangent** to a circle is a line that touches the circle at only one point.

A **sector** of a circle is a region between two radii and an arc.

A **segment** of a circle is a region between a chord and an arc.

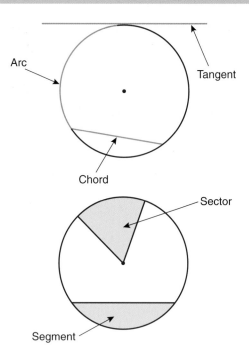

Arc · Tangent · Chord · Sector · Segment

Example 10

Draw a circle with a diameter of 10 cm.

Solution 10

The radius is half the diameter.
$\frac{1}{2}$ of 10 cm = 5 cm
So the radius is 5 cm.

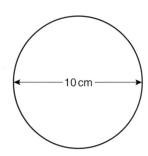

10 cm

Use compasses to draw the circle.
Open the compasses to the radius, in this case 5 cm.

5 cm

Exercise 23G

1 a Draw a circle of radius 7 cm.

   b Draw a circle of diameter 16 cm.

2 a Draw a circle of radius 6 cm.

   b On your drawing, draw and label
      i a radius   **ii** a diameter   **iii** a chord   **iv** an arc.

3 The diagram shows a circle, centre O and a chord, AB.
The radius of the circle is 5 cm.

  a Draw the circle.

  The length of the chord AB is 6 cm.

  b Mark and label a point A on the circle you have drawn.
Accurately find and label the point B on the circle.

  c Draw the chord AB.

  d Measure and write down the size of the angle AOB.

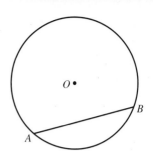

4 The diagram shows a circle, centre O, a chord AB and
two radii OA and OB. The radius of the circle is 8 cm and
angle $AOB = 80°$.

  a Make an accurate drawing of the circle, the chord
and the two radii.

  b Measure and write down the length of AB.

  c Draw the line of symmetry on your drawing.

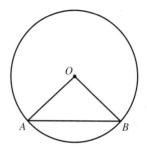

23.8 Tessellations

Look at this pattern.

This type of pattern is called a **tessellation**.
The pattern is made by using the same shape
without overlapping or leaving gaps.

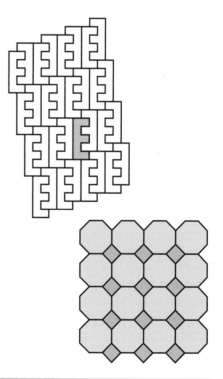

Tessellations can also be made using more than
one shape. Here is a tessellation made from
squares and regular octagons.

Tessellating is like tiling a flat surface so that
there are no gaps between the tiles and so that
the tiles do not overlap.

Example 11

On the grid show how the shaded shape
will tessellate.
You should draw six more shapes.

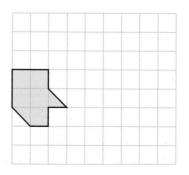

Solution 11

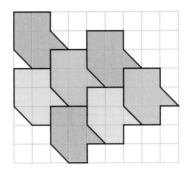

Exercise 23H

1 Draw a diagram to show how a rectangle tessellates.
You should draw at least six congruent rectangles.

2 Complete the diagram on the resource
sheet to show how the shape will
tessellate.
You should draw six more shapes.

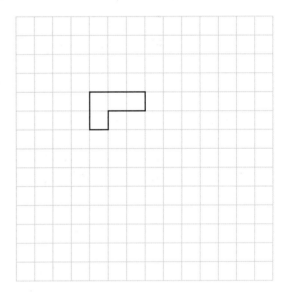

3 Complete the diagram to show how the
shaded shape will tessellate.
You should draw at least five more shapes.

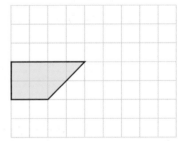

4 Complete the diagram to show how this
shape will tessellate.
You should draw at least six more shapes.

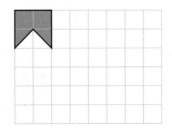

5 Use the squared paper on the resource sheet to show how this shape will tessellate.

6 Draw a diagram to show that congruent circles do not tessellate.

Chapter summary

You should now be able to:

★ Recognise when a shape has line symmetry

★ Draw the lines of symmetry on a shape

★ Recognise when a shape has rotational symmetry

★ Find the order of rotational symmetry of a shape

★ Complete drawings so that they have line symmetry and/or rotational symmetry

★ Know and use the symmetry of right-angled triangles, isosceles triangles, equilateral triangles, special quadrilaterals and regular polygons

★ Draw triangles and quadrilaterals accurately using a ruler, protractor and compasses

★ Recognise congruent shapes

★ Draw circles using compasses

★ Recognise and name the parts of a circle

★ Show how a shape tessellates.

Chapter 23 review questions

1 Write down which signs have line symmetry.

a   b   c   d

e   f  g   h

(1384 June 1996)

2   Draw in all the lines of symmetry on the shapes on the resource sheet.

a    **b**

(1385 June 1996)

3   Draw each of the shapes that have rotational symmetry.

a   **b**   **c**   **d**   **e**

(1384 June 1997)

4   **a**   On the shapes on the resource sheet draw in all the lines of symmetry.

i    **ii**

b   Write down the order of rotational symmetry for these shapes.

i    **ii**

c   Use squared paper to draw a shape with two lines of symmetry **and** rotational symmetry of order 2

(1385 June 2000)

5   **a**   Draw in all the lines of symmetry on the shapes on the resource sheet.

Rectangle   Parallelogram

b   Write down the order of rotational symmetry for the
  i rectangle
  ii parallelogram.

(1384 June 1995)

6 a Complete the drawing of the shape so that it has line symmetry, with AB as the line of symmetry.

b Write down the name of the complete shape.

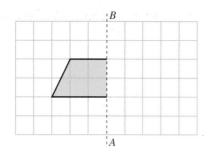

7

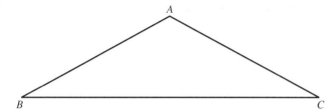

a Measure the length of BC.

b **i** Measure the size of angle B.

  ii Write down the special name given to this type of triangle.

In the triangle ABC, $AB = AC$.

c Draw the line of symmetry of the triangle.

(1388 Jan 2003)

8 Here is an accurate drawing of a shape.

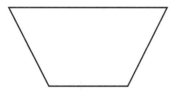

a Draw the line of symmetry on the shape.

b Write down the special name for this shape.

(1388 March 2002)

9 a On the diagram on the resource sheet shade **one** square so that the shape has exactly **one** line of symmetry.

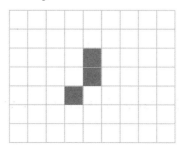

b On the diagram shade **one** square so that the shape has rotational symmetry of order 2.

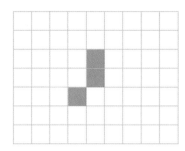

(1387 June 2004)

10 Here are nine shapes.

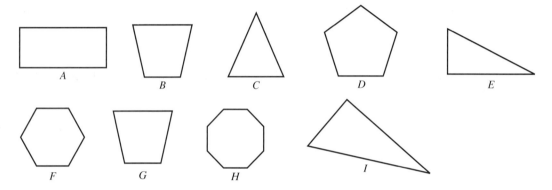

a Write down the letter of the shape that is
  i a pentagon
  ii an isosceles triangle.
b Write down the letters of the pair of congruent shapes.

11 Use ruler and compasses to construct this triangle accurately.
You must show all your construction lines.

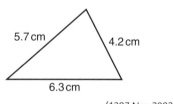

(1387 Nov 2003)

12 a Measure the length of the line.

The line is to be the diameter of a circle.
  b Mark the centre of the circle with a cross.
  c Draw the circle.

(1387 June 2003)

13 Make an accurate drawing of a rectangle 8 cm long and 4.5 cm wide.

(1385 June 1996)

14 The diagram shows a sketch of triangle *ABC*.

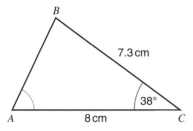

Diagram **NOT**
accurately drawn

BC = 7.3 cm.
AC = 8 cm.
Angle *C* = 38°.

a Make an accurate drawing of triangle *ABC*.

b Measure the size of angle *A* on your diagram.

(1387 June 2004)

15 Use a ruler and compasses to construct an equilateral triangle with sides of length 4 centimetres.
You must show all construction lines.

(1387 June 2004)

16 *ABCD* is a quadrilateral.
AB = 6 cm
AC = 9 cm
BC = 5 cm
Angle *BAD* = 66°
AD = 3.5 cm.

Make an accurate drawing of the quadrilateral *ABCD*.

(1387 Nov 2001)

17 a What special name is given to this polygon?

One of the polygons below is congruent to the polygon shown in part **a**.

b Write down the letter of this polygon.

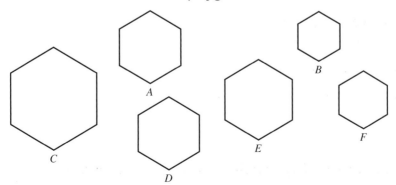

c Use isometric paper to show how this shape will tessellate. You should draw at least eight shapes.

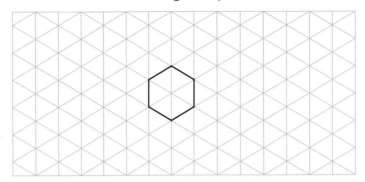

(1387 June 2004)

18 a Draw a rectangle and draw in all the lines of symmetry.

b Write down the name of a four-sided shape that has rotational symmetry of order 4

c On the grid show how this kite will tessellate. You should draw at least six kites.

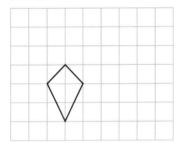

(1385 June 1998)

19 a Each angle of an equilateral triangle is 60°. A tessellation is made using congruent equilateral triangles. How many triangles meet at any vertex?

b Each angle of a regular hexagon is 120°. A tessellation is made using congruent regular hexagons. How many hexagons meet at any vertex?

c Explain why it is possible to make a tessellation using **both** congruent equilateral triangles **and** congruent regular hexagons.

20 The diagram shows part of a shape. The shape has rotational symmetry of order 4 about the point P.

a On the grid on the resource sheet complete the shape.

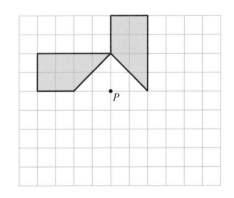

  b On the grid on the resource sheet show how the shaded shape will tessellate. You should draw at least five shapes.

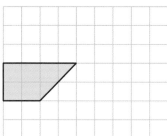

(1387 May 2002)

21 The diagram shows a sketch of triangle XYZ.

    a Make an accurate drawing of triangle XYZ.

    b On your drawing, measure
        i the length of XZ **ii** the size of angle Z.

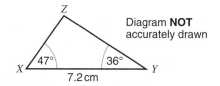

Diagram **NOT** accurately drawn

22 The diagram shows a sketch of triangle PQR.

    a Make an accurate drawing of triangle PQR.

    b Measure the size of angle Q on your drawing.

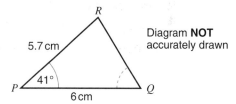

Diagram **NOT** accurately drawn

Angles 3

24.1 Quadrilaterals

A **quadrilateral** is a shape with four straight sides and four angles. To find the angle sum of a quadrilateral, draw a quadrilateral on paper and label its angles a, b, c and d.

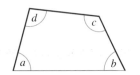

Tear off its corners.

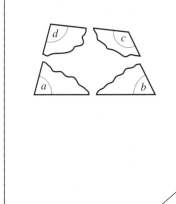

Fit angles a, b, c and d together at a point.

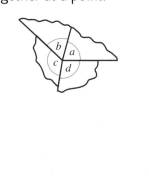

The angles at a point add up to 360° and so this shows that the angles in this quadrilateral add up to 360°.

> **The angle sum of a quadrilateral is 360°.**

To *prove* this result, draw a **diagonal** of the quadrilateral.
The diagonal splits the quadrilateral into two triangles.
The angle sum of each triangle is 180°.
So the angle sum of the quadrilateral is $2 \times 180° = 360°$.

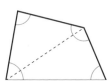

Example 1

Work out the size of angle x.

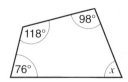

Solution 1

$76° + 118° + 98° = 292°$ Add 76, 118 and 98

$360° - 292° = 68°$ Take the result away from 360, as the angle sum of a quadrilateral is 360°.

$x = 68°$ State the size of angle x.

Example 2

a   Write down the size of angle x.

b   Work out the size of angle y.   **Give reasons for your answer.**

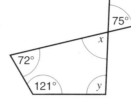

Solution 2

a $x = 75°$

$\boxed{\text{Where two straight lines cross, the opposite angles are equal.}}$

b $121° + 72° + 75° = 268°$

$\quad 360° - 268° = 92°$ $\boxed{\text{Angle sum of a quadrilateral is 360°}}$

$\quad y = 92°$

Example 3

The diagram shows a kite.

a   Write down the size of angle x.

b   Work out the size of angle y.   **Give reasons for your answer.**

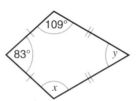

Solution 3

a $x = 109°$

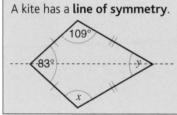

A kite has a **line of symmetry**.

Angle x is a reflection of the 109° angle and so the two angles are equal.

b $83° + 109° + 109° = 301°$

$\quad 360° - 301° = 59°$

$\quad y = 59°$

$\boxed{\text{Angle sum of a quadrilateral is 360°.}}$

Example 4

a   Find the size of angle x.

b   Give a reason for your answer.

c   Find the size of angle y.

d   Give reasons for your answer.

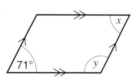

Solution 4

a $x = 71°$

b   Opposite angles of a parallelogram are equal.

c $2 \times 71° = 142°$

$\quad 360° - 142° = 218°$

$\quad 218° \div 2 = 109°$

$\quad y = 109°$

d   Angle sum of a quadrilateral is 360°.

$\quad$ Opposite angles of a parallelogram are equal.

Exercise 24A

In this exercise, the quadrilaterals are not accurately drawn.

In Questions **1–12**, find the size of each of the angles marked with letters and show your working.

1

2

3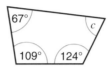

4

5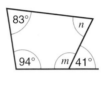

6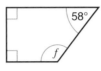

7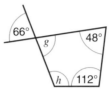

8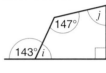

9

10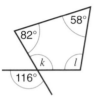

11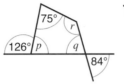

12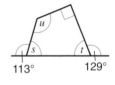

13 The diagram shows a kite.

   a Write down the size of angle v.

   b Work out the size of angle w.

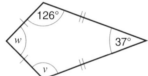

14 The diagram shows a kite.

   Work out the value of x.

15 The diagram shows an isosceles trapezium.

   a Write down the value of a.

   b Work out the value of b.

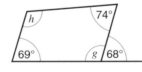

In Questions **16–22**, find the sizes of the angles marked with letters and show your working. **Give reasons for your answers.**

16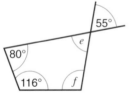

17

18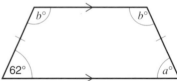

19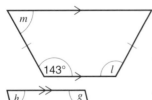

20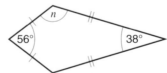

21

22

24.2 Polygons

A **polygon** is a shape with three or more straight sides.

Some polygons have special names.

A 3-sided polygon is called a **triangle**.
A 4-sided polygon is called a **quadrilateral**.
A 5-sided polygon is called a **pentagon**.
A 6-sided polygon is called a **hexagon**.
An 8-sided polygon is called an **octagon**.
A 10-sided polygon is called a **decagon**.

To find the sum of the angles of a polygon, split it into triangles.

For example, for this hexagon, draw as many diagonals as possible from one corner.

This splits the hexagon into four triangles.
The angle sum of a triangle is 180° and so the
sum of the angles of a hexagon is 4 × 180° = 720°.

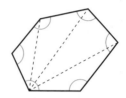

Sometimes, these angles are called **interior angles** to
emphasise that they are *inside* the polygon.

Using this method, the sum of the interior angles of any polygon can be found.

Number of sides	Number of triangles	Sum of the interior angles
4	2	360°
5	3	540°
6	4	720°
7	5	900°
8	6	1080°
9	7	1260°
10	8	1440°

The number of triangles into which the polygon can be split up is always two less than the
number of sides.

Example 5

Find the sum of the angles of a 12-sided polygon (**dodecagon**).

Solution 5

$$12 - 2 = 10$$ Subtract 2 from the number of sides to find the number of triangles.

$$10 \times 180 = 1800$$ Multiply the number of triangles by 180.

The sum of the angles = 1800° State the sum of the angles in degrees.

A polygon with all its sides the same length and all its angles the same size is called a
regular polygon.

So a square *is* a regular polygon, because all its sides are
the same length and all its angles are 90°, but a rhombus
is *not* a regular polygon.

Although its sides are all the same length, its angles are not all the same size.

Here are three more regular polygons.

a regular pentagon

a regular hexagon

a regular octagon

The Pentagon in Washington DC
is the headquarters of the
US Department of Defence.

Bees' honeycomb is made
up of regular hexagons.

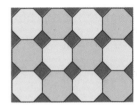

Regular octagons tessellate
with squares.

Example 6

Find the size of each interior angle of a regular decagon.

Solution 6

$10 - 2 = 8$ | Subtract 2 from the number of sides to find the number of triangles.

$8 \times 180 = 1440$ | Multiply the number of triangles by 180 to find the sum of all 10 interior angles.

$1440 \div 10 = 144$ | All 10 interior angles are the same size. So divide 1440 by 10

Each interior angle is 144° | State the size of each interior angle.

Example 7

The diagram shows a regular 9-sided polygon
(nonagon) with centre O.

a Work out the size of **i** angle x **ii** angle y.

b Use your answer to part **a ii** to work out the
size of each interior angle of the polygon.

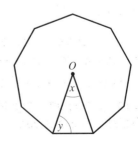

Solution 7

a i $x = 360° \div 9$

> Each corner of the polygon could be joined to the centre O to make 9 equal angles at O. The total of all 9 angles is 360°, as altogether they make a complete turn.

       $x = 40°$

> State the size of angle x.

       (40° is the angle at the centre of a regular 9-sided polygon.)

ii $180° - 40° = 140$

> The angle sum of a triangle is 180° and so the sum of the two base angles is 140°.

         $140° \div 2 = 70°$

> The triangle is isosceles and so the two base angles are equal.

             $y = 70°$

> State the size of angle y.

b $2 \times 70° = 140°$

> Because the polygon is regular, it has nine lines of symmetry and each interior angle is twice the size of each base angle of the triangle.

     Each interior angle is 140°.

> State the size of each interior angle.

Exercise 24B

In this exercise, the polygons are not accurately drawn.

1   Find the sum of the angles of a 15-sided polygon.

2   Find the sum of the angles of a 20-sided polygon.

3   A polygon can be split into 17 triangles by drawing diagonals from one corner. How many sides has the polygon?

In Questions **4–9**, find the size of each of the angles marked with letters and show your working.

4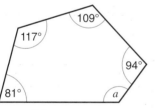

5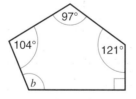

6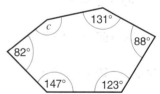

7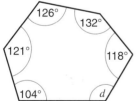

8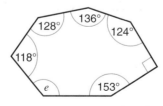

9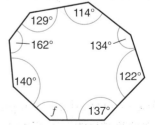

10   The diagram shows a pentagon. All its sides are the same length.

     a   Work out the value of g.

     b   Is the pentagon a regular polygon? Explain your answer.

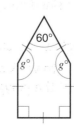

11   Work out the size of each interior angle of

    a a regular pentagon   **b** a regular hexagon   **c** a regular octagon.

12   Work out the size of each interior angle of a regular 15-sided polygon.

13   Work out the size of each interior angle of a regular 20-sided polygon.

14   Work out the size of the angle at the centre of a regular pentagon.

15   Work out the size of the angle at the centre of a regular 12-sided polygon.

Australia's 50 cent coin is a regular 12-sided polygon (dodecagon)

16   The angle at the centre of a regular polygon is 60°.
    How many sides has the polygon?

17   The angle at the centre of a regular polygon is 20°.

    a How many sides has the polygon?

    b Work out the size of each interior angle of the polygon.

18 **a** Work out the angle at the centre of a regular octagon.

    b Draw a circle with a radius of 5 cm and, using your answer to part **a** , draw a regular octagon inside the circle.

19 **a** Work out the angle at the centre of a regular 10-sided polygon.

    b Draw a circle with a radius of 5 cm and, using your answer to part **a** , draw a regular 10-sided polygon inside the circle.

20   The diagram shows a pentagon.
Work out the size of

    a angle h **b** angle i.

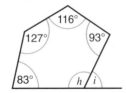

21   The diagram shows a hexagon.
Work out the size of

    a angle j **b** angle k.

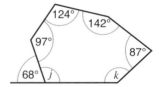

22   Craig says, 'The sum of the interior angles of this polygon is 1000°'.
    Explain why he must be wrong.

23   The diagram shows a quadrilateral.

    a Work out the size of each of the angles marked with letters.

    b Work out $l + m + n + p$

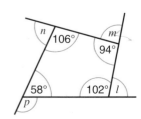

24 The diagram shows a pentagon.

    a Work out the size of each of the angles marked with letters.

    b Work out $q + r + s + t + u$

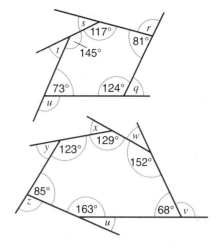

25 The diagram shows a hexagon.

    a Work out the size of each of the angles marked with letters.

    b Work out $u + v + w + x + y + z$

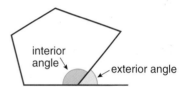

24.3 Exterior angles

A polygon's interior angles are the angles *inside* the polygon.

Extend a side to make an **exterior angle**, which is *outside* the polygon.

At each **vertex** (corner), the interior angle and the exterior angle are on a straight line and so their sum is 180°.

    interior angle + exterior angle = 180°

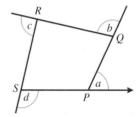

> **The sum of the exterior angles of any polygon is 360°.**

To show this, imagine someone standing at P on this quadrilateral, facing in the direction of the arrow.

They turn through angle a, so that they are facing in the direction PQ, and then walk to Q.

At Q, they turn through angle b, so that they are facing in the direction QR, and then walk to R.

At R, they turn through angle c, so that they are facing in the direction RS, and then walk to S.

At S, they turn through angle d.

They are now facing in the direction of the arrow again and so they have turned through 360°.

The total angle they have turned through is also the sum of the exterior angles of the quadrilateral.

So $a + b + c + d = 360°$

The same argument can be used with *any* polygon, not just a quadrilateral.

Example 8

The sizes of four of the exterior angles of a pentagon are 67°, 114°, 58° and 73°. Work out the size of the other exterior angle.

Solution 8

$67° + 114° + 58° + 73° = 312°$ | Add the four given exterior angles. |

$360° - 312° = 48°$ | Subtract the result from 360. |

Exterior angle = 48° | State the size of the exterior angle. |

Example 9

For a regular 18-sided polygon, work out

a the size of each exterior angle, **b** the size of each interior angle.

Solution 9

a $360° \div 18 = 20°$

> Because the polygon is regular, all 18 exterior angles are equal. Their sum is 360° and so divide 360° by 18.

b $180° - 20° = 160°$

> At a corner, the sum of the interior angle and the exterior angle is 180°. So subtract 20° from 180°.

Example 10

The size of each interior angle of a regular polygon is 150°. Work out

a the size of each exterior angle, **b** the number of sides the polygon has.

Solution 10

a $180° - 150° = 30°$

> At a corner, the sum of the interior angle and the exterior angle is 180°. So subtract 150° from 180°.

b $360° \div 30 = 12$

> Because the polygon is regular, all the exterior angles are 30°. Their sum is 360° and so divide 360 by 30.

Exercise 24C

1 At a vertex (corner) of a polygon, the size of the interior angle is 134°.
Work out the size of the exterior angle.

2 At a vertex of a polygon, the size of the exterior angle is 67°.
Work out the size of the interior angle.

3 The sizes of three of the exterior angles of a quadrilateral are 72°, 119° and 107°.
Work out the size of the other exterior angle.

4 The sizes of five of the exterior angles of a hexagon are 43°, 109°, 58°, 74° and 49°.
Work out the size of the other exterior angle.

5 Work out the size of each exterior angle of a regular octagon.

6 Work out the size of each exterior angle of a regular 9-sided polygon.

7 For a regular 24-sided polygon, work out
   a the size of each exterior angle, **b** the size of each interior angle.

8 For a regular 40-sided polygon, work out
   a the size of each exterior angle, **b** the size of each interior angle.

9 The size of each interior angle of a regular polygon is 168°. Work out
   a the size of each exterior angle, **b** the number of sides the polygon has.

10 The size of each interior angle of a regular polygon is 170°.
Work out the number of sides the polygon has.

Chapter summary

You should know and be able to use these facts

★ A **quadrilateral** is a shape with four straight sides and four angles.

★ The angle sum of a quadrilateral is 360°.

★ A **polygon** is a shape with three or more straight sides.

A 5-sided polygon is called a **pentagon**.

★ A 6-sided polygon is called a **hexagon**.

★ An 8-sided polygon is called an **octagon**.

★ A 10-sided polygon is called a **decagon**.

★ The angle sum of a polygon can be found by subtracting 2 from the number of sides and multiplying the result by 180°.

★ A polygon with all its sides the same length and all its angles the same size is called a **regular** polygon.

★ At a vertex, interior angle + exterior angle = 180°.

★ The sum of the exterior angles of any polygon is 360°. To find the size of each exterior angle of a regular polygon, divide 360° by the number of sides.

Chapter 24 review questions

In questions **1–4**, find the size of each of the angles marked with a letter. The diagrams are not accurately drawn.

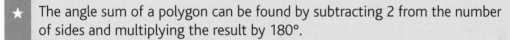

1 109° i 64° 84°

2 112° k 94° j

3 141° l 92° 114° 117° 128°

4 m 57° n

5 Calculate the value of x.

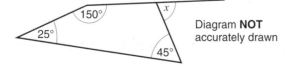

150° x 25° 45°

Diagram **NOT** accurately drawn

(4400 Nov 2004)

6 Work out the value of a.

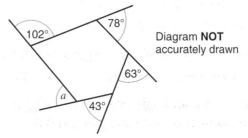

102° 78° 63° a 43°

Diagram **NOT** accurately drawn

(1388 March 2002)

7 Work out the size of each exterior angle of a regular 10-sided polygon.

8 **a** Work out the sum of the interior angles of a 9-sided polygon.
The size of each exterior angle of a regular polygon is 20°.
b Work out how many sides the polygon has.

9 The diagram shows a regular hexagon.
a Work out the value of x.
b Work out the value of y.

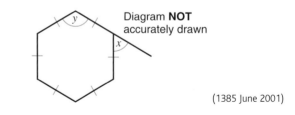

Diagram **NOT**
accurately drawn

(1385 June 2001)

10 *ABCDE* is a regular pentagon.
AEF and *CDF* are straight lines.
Work out the size of angle *DFE*.
Give reasons for your answer.

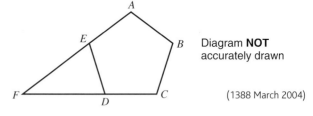

Diagram **NOT**
accurately drawn

(1388 March 2004)

Practical graphs

25.1 Real-life graphs

Graphs can be used to show the relationship between two quantities in real-life situations.

This graph shows the relationship between the number of litres of petrol and the total cost of the petrol. The graph can be used to find the approximate cost of a given number of litres of petrol. It can also be used to estimate the number of litres of petrol that can be bought for a given amount of money.

The graph is a straight line. Straight line graphs are called **linear graphs.**

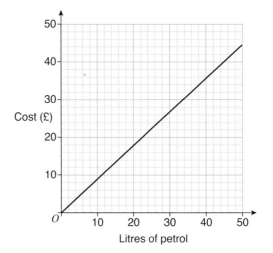

Example 1

Use the graph above to estimate
a the cost of 18 litres of petrol
b the number of litres of petrol that can be bought for £40
c the number of litres of petrol that can be bought for £56

Solution 1
a For **18** litres of petrol the cost is £16
b For **£40** approximately **45** litres of petrol can be bought.
c The graph does not show £56 so the number of litres must be calculated from what is known.

> **£56 = £40 + £16**
> so **45 litres + 18 litres** = 63 litres.

So £56 buys 63 litres of petrol.

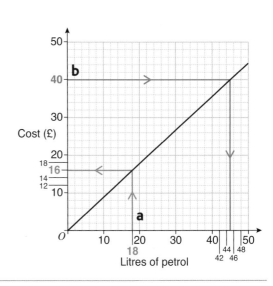

Example 2

Arthur and Bruce are two male chimpanzees.
Their weights and heights are measured.

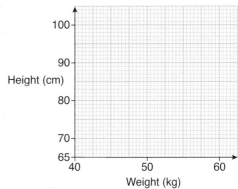

	Weight (kg)	Height (cm)
Arthur	43	70
Bruce	60	100

a On the grid, plot this information.
   Join the points with a straight line to form a linear graph.

b Charles is another male chimpanzee. His weight is 55 kg.
   Use your graph to estimate the height of Charles.

Solution 2

a

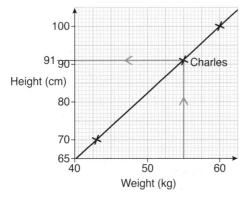

b Charles' height = 91 cm.

Example 3

The diagram shows a rectangular tank filling up with water.

The diagonal of the surface of the water is of length d when
the height of the water is h.

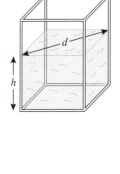

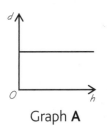

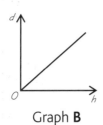

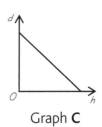

Graph **A**   Graph **B**   Graph **C**

a Which of the three graphs shows the relationship between d and h?

The water then leaks, at a constant rate, from a hole in the bottom.

b Sketch a graph which shows the relationship between the height h and the time t.

Solution 3

a Graph **A**

> *d* does not change as the height, *h*, of the water increases.

b

> Water leaks out at a constant rate so after each second the height decreases by the same amount.
>
>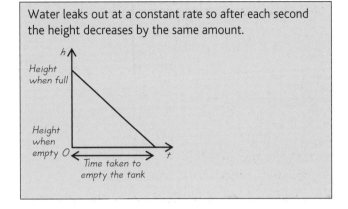

Example 4

Tracey fires a pellet into the air. The pellet stays in the air for four seconds.
The graph shows the height, in metres, of the pellet during part of its flight.

Use the graph to estimate

a the greatest height reached by the pellet

b the height of the pellet after three seconds

c the two times at which the pellet is at a height of 18 metres.

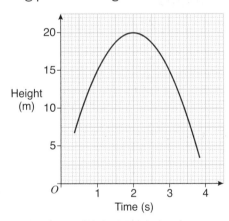

Solution 4

a The greatest height = 20 metres.

b **15 metres**

c **1.4 seconds** and **2.6 seconds**

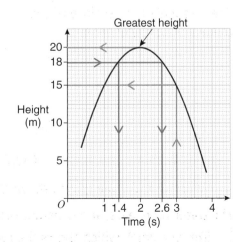

Exercise 25A

1 Malcolm buys a DVD player.
He pays a deposit of £50 and
12 equal monthly instalments.
The graph shows the amount he
has paid at the end of each month.

Using the graph, estimate

a the amount Malcolm has paid
after 8 months

b after how many months he
has paid £100

c the amount that Malcolm has
paid after 6 months.

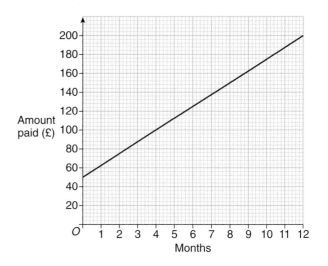

2 This linear graph shows the relationship
between the circumference of a circle
and its diameter.

Use the graph to estimate

a the circumference of a circle
of diameter 2 cm

b the diameter of a circle with a
circumference of 14 cm

c the circumference of a circle of
diameter 12 cm.

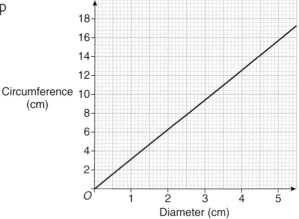

3 Julie invests £100 in a bank account.
The graph shows the amount, in £, that is
in this account during the first five years.

Using the graph estimate

a the amount in this account after
  i 2 years
  ii 3 years 6 months

b After how many years there
is £131 in this account.

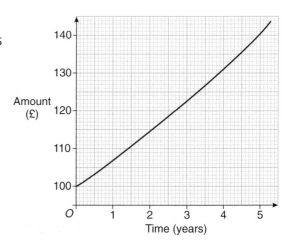

Answer Question **4** on the resource sheet

4 Alex repairs washing machines.
He charges a fixed amount plus an extra
amount for each hour that he works.
The table shows his charges for three repairs.

Time (hours)	1	2	6
Charge (£)	45	70	170

a Plot this information on the grid. Join the points with a straight line to form a
linear graph.

Use your graph to estimate

b the cost of a repair taking   **i** 4 hours   **ii** $2\frac{1}{2}$ hours.

c the fixed amount that Alex charges.

Use the resource sheet to answer Question 5.

5 Peter measures the distance from his elbow to his fingertips and then measures the
distance from his shoulder to his fingertips. Peter then takes similar measurements
from two of his friends.

The table shows these measurements, given to the nearest millimetre.

Distance from elbow to fingertips (cm)	40	46	50
Distance from shoulder to fingertips (cm)	64.7	74.4	80.9

a Plot this information on a grid. Join the points with a straight line to form a linear
graph.

Use your graph to estimate

b the distance from the shoulder to the fingertips of a person whose distance from
elbow to fingertips is 42.5 cm

c the distance from the elbow to the fingertips of a person whose distance from
shoulder to fingertips is 78 cm.

6 The diagrams show three containers filling up with water.

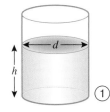
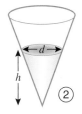

d is the diameter of the surface of the water when the height of the water is h.
These graphs each show a relationship between d and h.

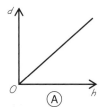
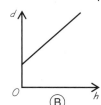
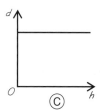

a Match the graphs with the containers.

Water then leaks, at a constant rate, from a hole in the bottom of **one** of the containers. The graph shows the relationship between the height of water h and the time t.

b Which container is leaking?

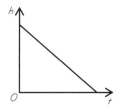

25.2 Conversion graphs

A graph can be used to change from one unit of measure to another. This type of graph is called a **conversion graph**.

Here is a conversion graph which can be used to change speeds from miles per hour to kilometres per hour.

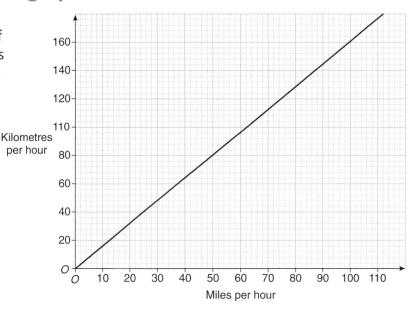

Kilometres per hour

Miles per hour

Example 5

Use the graph above to change
a 50 miles per hour to kilometres per hour
b 140 kilometres per hour to miles per hour
c 320 kilometres per hour to miles per hour.

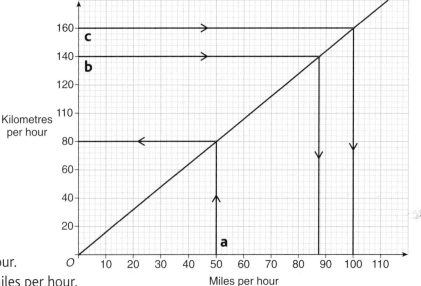

Solution 5

a 80 kilometres per hour.
b Approximately 88 miles per hour.
c 320 kilometres per hour = 2×160 kilometres per hour
$= 2 \times 100$ miles per hour
$= 200$ miles per hour.

Exercise 25B

1 The diagram shows a conversion graph from pounds (£) to Jordanian dinars.

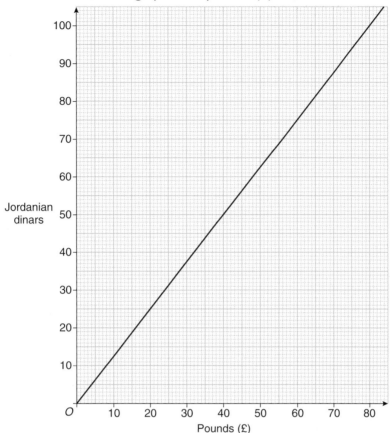

Use the graph to change
a £40 to Jordanian dinars
b 75 Jordanian dinars to pounds
c 80 Jordanian dinars to pounds
d £52 to Jordanian dinars.

2 The diagram shows a conversion graph from degrees Celsius (°C) to degrees Fahrenheit (°F).

a Use the graph to change
   i 40°C to degrees Fahrenheit
   ii 176°F to degrees Celsius.

b There is one point on the conversion graph at which the degrees Fahrenheit is the same as the degrees Celsius. Write down the coordinates of this point.

c The difference in temperature between two towns is 12 degrees Celsius. Use the graph to estimate this difference in degrees Fahrenheit.

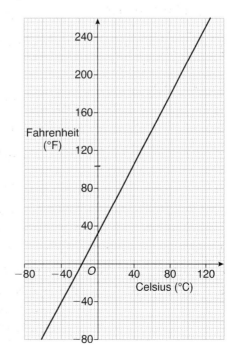

Answer Question 3 on the resource sheet.

3   A group of students visit Australia.
     The exchange rate is £1 = 2.4 Australian dollars.

Pounds (£)	1	2	10
Australian dollars	2.4		

   a   Complete the table on the resource sheet.

   b   On the grid, plot the information from part **a**. Join the points with a straight
          line to form a linear graph.

   c   Use your graph to convert
          i £6.50 into Australian dollars
          ii 10 Australian dollars into pounds.

4   The diagram shows a conversion graph
     between ounces and grams.

     Use the graph to change

   a   **i** 6 ounces to grams
          ii 15 ounces to grams

   b   **i** 100 grams to ounces
          ii 320 grams to ounces.

     One kilogram is equal to 1000 grams.

   c   Use the graph to estimate the
          number of ounces in 2 kilograms.

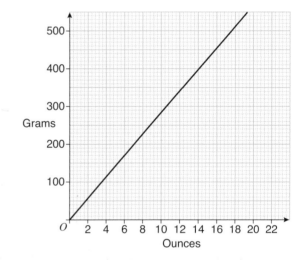

5   The conversion graph can be used
     for changing between inches
     and centimetres.

     1 foot = 12 inches.

   a   Use the graph to change
          i 1 foot to centimetres
          ii 15 inches to centimetres
          iii 23 centimetres to inches.

   b   Lisa is 5 feet 10 inches tall.
          Use the graph to estimate Lisa's
          height in centimetres.

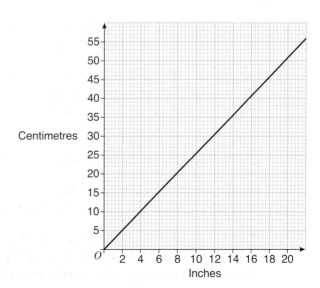

6 The first diagram shows a conversion graph from euros (€) to pounds (£).

The second diagram shows a conversion graph from pounds (£) to American dollars ($)

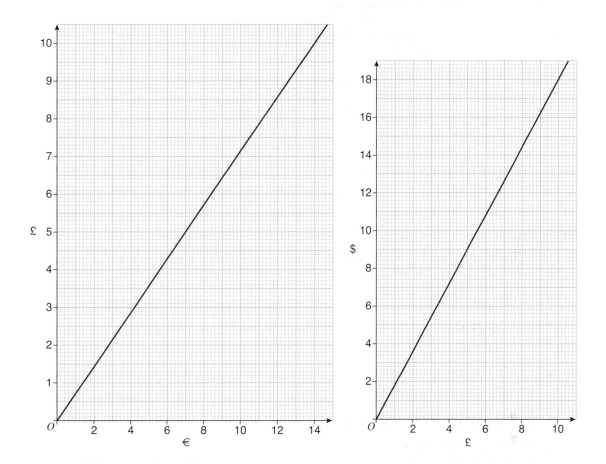

In the summer of 2005, the Smith family and the Jones family go overseas for their holidays.

a The Smith family goes to Spain. Mrs. Smith changes £500 into euros. Use the conversion graph to change £500 into euros.

b The Jones family goes to America. Mr. Jones changes £680 into American dollars. Use the conversion graph to change £680 into American dollars. Give your answer to the nearest $10

c A meal in Spain costs €12.60 Use both conversion graphs to change €12.60 into American dollars.

d Mrs. Jones buys a T-shirt for $13. Use both conversion graphs to estimate the cost of this T-shirt in euros.

e While in Spain Mr. Smith sees a villa for sale at €420 000. The same villa is advertised in an American newspaper for $530 000. Use the conversion graphs to work out the difference in price.

25.3 Distance–time graphs

These are sometimes called **'travel graphs'**.
Yakub cycled from his home to his cousin's house. On his way he waited for his sister before continuing the journey.
He and his sister stayed at his cousin's house and then they returned home.
Here is a distance–time graph showing the complete journey.

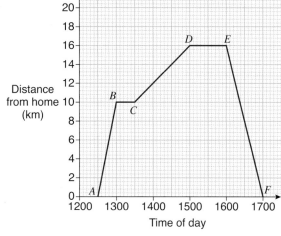

The point A shows that Yakub left home at 1230.

The straight line AB shows that Yakub first cycles at a **constant speed**. He cycles 10 km in half an hour (from 1230 to 1300).

This is the same speed as cycling 20 km in 1 hour.
Yakub's speed for the first half hour of his journey is 20 kilometres per hour.

The horizontal line BC shows that, for the second half hour of his journey, (from 1300 to 1330) Yakub is not moving. He is still 10 km from home, waiting for his sister.

The line CD shows Yakub continuing his journey to his cousin's house. His cousin's house is 16 km from home. He cycles the remaining 6 km ($16 - 10$) in 1.5 hours (from 1330 to 1500). During this part of the journey, Yakub cycles at a constant speed. His speed is 4 kilometres per hour ($6 \div 1.5 = 4$).

The horizontal line DE shows that for one hour (from 1500 to 1600) Yakub is not moving and is still 16 km from home, at his cousin's house.

The line EF shows the return journey home. He arrives back home at 1700 having cycled 16 km in 1 hour at a constant speed. His speed on this final part of his journey is 16 kilometres per hour.

Example 6

Peter and Jane go to the seaside, a distance of 30 kilometres from their home.
Peter leaves home at 12.30 pm on his bicycle.
Jane leaves later on her scooter.
The distance-time graphs show some information about their journeys.

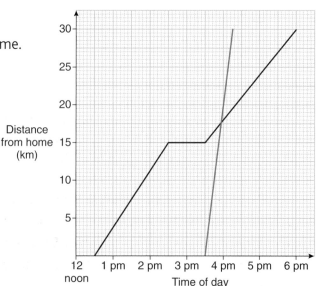

a Peter takes a break on his journey.
  i For how long does Peter take a break?
  ii How far from the seaside is he when he takes his break?

b Peter cycles more quickly before the break than after it. Explain how the graph shows this.

c At what time does Jane leave home?

d Estimate the time at which Jane passes Peter.

e By how many minutes does Jane arrive at the seaside before Peter?

Solution 6

a   **i** Break from 2.30 pm to 3.30 pm = 1 hour.
  ii 30 − 15 = 15 kilometres.

b The line before the break is steeper than the line after the break.

c 3.30 pm

d The two graphs cross at about 3.55 pm

e From 4.15 pm to 6.00 pm = 1hour 45 minutes = 105 minutes.

Exercise 25C

1 The travel graph shows some information about the flight of an aeroplane from London to Rome and back again.

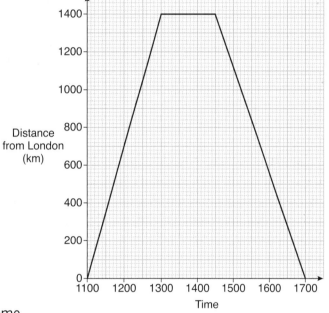

   a At what time did the flight leave London?

   b How many kilometres is Rome from London?

   c At what time did the aeroplane arrive in Rome?

   d How long did the aeroplane remain in Rome?

   e How many hours did the flight back take?

   f Work out the average speed, in kilometres per hour, of the aeroplane from London to Rome.

   g Estimate the distance of the aeroplane from Rome
      i at 1230   **ii** at 1512.

Use the resource sheet to answer Question 2.

2 Sangita cycles from Bury to the airport, a distance of 24 miles.
   The distance–time graph shows some information about her journey.

   a At what time does Sangita leave Bury?

   b   **i** How many miles is Sangita from Bury at 1200?
      ii How many miles is Sangita from the airport at 1200?

   c Sangita stops for lunch. How many minutes does she stop for lunch?

   d Explain how the graph shows that Sangita cycles more slowly after lunch.

   e Work out the speed, in miles per hour, of Sangita for the part of her journey before lunch.

Simon leaves the airport at 1300 and travels at a steady speed to Bury. He arrives in Bury at 1345.

f On the grid, draw a distance–time graph for Simon's journey.

g Use your graph to work out Simon's speed.

h Use your graph to estimate the time at which Simon and Sangita are at the same distance from the airport.

Answer Question 3 on the resource sheet.

3 Mr Jacobs leaves home at 1015 and drives 90 kilometres to see a customer. He drives at 90 km/h. Mr Jacobs stays with the customer for 45 minutes and then travels back home at 60 km/h.

a Show this information on the grid.

b At what time did Mr Jacobs arrive back home?

4 Ken sets off from home to go to his office but on his way he remembers that he has left his keys in the front door. He returns home to collect them and sets off for work again. The distance–time graph shows information about his journey to the office.

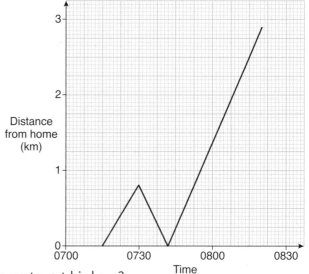

a At what time did Ken first set off to work?

b How far is Ken's office from his home?

c How far had he gone before he turned back?

d At what time did he arrive back home to get his keys?

e How long did the total journey take him?

f Ken travelled more quickly after he picked up his keys than before he turned back. Explain how the graph shows this.

g Work out the speed of Ken's journey back home to get his keys. Give your answer in km/h.

Chapter summary

You should now know:

★ How to use graphs showing relationships in real-life situations, for example converting between currencies, by plotting and reading coordinates of points on a **conversion graph**.

★ How to draw and interpret **distance-time graphs**, recognising that:
- straight lines represent constant speed
- horizontal lines represent no movement
- the steeper the graph the greater the speed.

Chapter 25 review questions

Use the resource sheet to answer this question.

1 A man left home at 12 noon to go for a cycle ride. The travel graph represents part of the man's journey.

At 12.45 pm the man stopped for a rest.

a For how many minutes did he rest?

b Find his distance from home at 1.30 pm.

The man stopped for another rest at 2 pm. He rested for one hour. Then he cycled home at a steady speed. It took him 2 hours.

c Complete the travel graph.

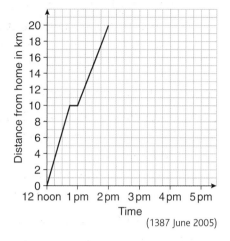

(1387 June 2005)

2 The diagram shows a conversion graph between kilometres and miles.

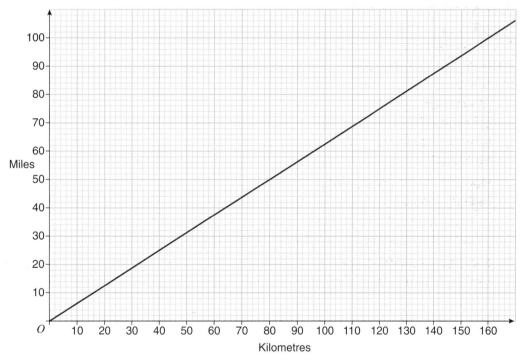

Salim travels from Manchester to Blackpool, a distance of 50 miles.

a Use the graph to change 50 miles into kilometres.

He then travels 144 kilometres to Leeds.

b Use the graph to change 144 kilometres into miles.

Susan travels by train from London to Birmingham, a distance of 120 miles.

c Change 120 miles into kilometres.

Pat and Sam are travelling home from work. Pat's average speed is 45 miles per hour. Sam's average speed is 70 kilometres per hour.

d Use the graph to find whose average speed is greater.

Use the resource sheet to answer Question 3.

3 A mobile telephone bill is made up of a standing charge and a charge for each unit of calls made. The table shows some information about the total charge for units used.

Number of units used	50	100	150	200	250
Total charge (£)	12.00	16.00	20.00	24.00	28.00

a Use this information to draw a straight line graph on the resource sheet.

b Use your graph to estimate:

   i the total charge for 175 units

   ii the total charge for 115 units

   iii the number of units used when the total charge is £26

   iv the number of units used when the total charge is £12.50

c Use your graph to write down the standing charge.

4 Linford runs in a 100 metres race.

The graph shows his speed, in metres per second, during the race.

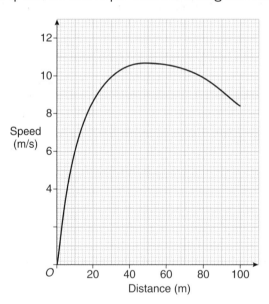

a Write down Linford's speed after he has covered a distance of 10 m.

b Write down Linford's greatest speed.

c Write down the distance Linford has covered when his speed is 7.4 m/s.

There are **two** times when Linford's speed is 9 m/s.

d Find the distance he covers between these two times.   (1385 June 2002)

5 Anil cycled from his home to the park.
Anil waited in the park.
Then he cycled back home.
Here is a distance–time graph for Anil's complete journey.

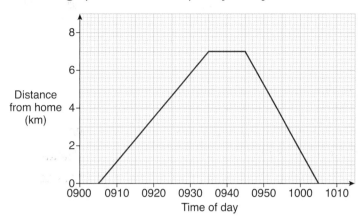

a At what time did Anil leave home?

b What is the distance from Anil's home to the park?

c How many minutes did Anil wait in the park?

d Work out Anil's average speed on his journey home. Give your answer
in kilometres per hour.

(1387 June 2004)

6 The graph shows the rate of rainfall, in mm per hour, one afternoon last year.

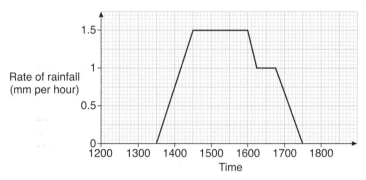

a At what time did it start to rain?

b What was the rate of rainfall at 1700?

c What happened to the rate of rainfall between 1600 and 1615?

(1388 January 2004)

Further fractions

26.1 Fractions of an amount

To find a fraction of an amount where the numerator of the fraction is 1, think of that amount divided into equal parts.

Example 1

Find $\frac{1}{4}$ of £24

Solution 1

$24 \div 4 = 6$ Finding $\frac{1}{4}$ of an amount is the same as dividing the amount into 4 equal parts.

$\frac{1}{4}$ of £24 = £6

To find a fraction of an amount where the numerator is more than 1, think of the calculation in two stages. First, divide the amount by the denominator. Then multiply the result by the numerator.

Example 2

Find $\frac{2}{3}$ of £24

Solution 2

$24 \div 3 = 8$ Divide 24 by 3. The result is 8

$8 \times 2 = 16$ Multiply 8 by 2

$\frac{2}{3}$ of £24 = £16

Exercise 26A

1 Find $\frac{1}{2}$ of

a £8	**b** £20	**c** £12	**d** £16	**e** £24
f £44	**g** £80	**h** £60	**i** £1000	**j** £320

2 Find $\frac{1}{5}$ of

a £10	**b** £25	**c** £30	**d** £50	**e** £65
f £80	**g** £95	**h** £125	**i** £220	**j** £240

3 Find $\frac{1}{3}$ of

a	£6	**b**	£12	**c**	£15	**d**	£21	**e**	£30
f	£60	**g**	£45	**h**	£75	**i**	£96	**j**	£105

4 Find $\frac{1}{6}$ of

a	£18	**b**	£24	**c**	£30	**d**	£66	**e**	£42
f	£60	**g**	£54	**h**	£72	**i**	£96	**j**	£114

Find:

5
a **i** $\frac{1}{4}$ of £8   **ii** $\frac{3}{4}$ of £8
b **i** $\frac{1}{4}$ of £40   **ii** $\frac{3}{4}$ of £40
c **i** $\frac{1}{4}$ of 28 cm   **ii** $\frac{3}{4}$ of 28 cm
d **i** $\frac{1}{4}$ of 44 kg   **ii** $\frac{3}{4}$ of 44 kg
e **i** $\frac{1}{4}$ of 100 cm   **ii** $\frac{3}{4}$ of 100 cm

6
a **i** $\frac{1}{10}$ of £20   **ii** $\frac{3}{10}$ of £20
b **i** $\frac{1}{10}$ of £40   **ii** $\frac{7}{10}$ of £40
c **i** $\frac{1}{10}$ of 30 cm   **ii** $\frac{3}{10}$ of 30 cm
d **i** $\frac{1}{10}$ of 440 kg   **ii** $\frac{3}{10}$ of 440 kg
e **i** $\frac{1}{10}$ of 120 cm   **ii** $\frac{7}{10}$ of 120 cm

7
a **i** $\frac{1}{5}$ of £20   **ii** $\frac{2}{5}$ of £20
b **i** $\frac{1}{5}$ of £15   **ii** $\frac{3}{5}$ of £15
c **i** $\frac{1}{6}$ of £12   **ii** $\frac{5}{6}$ of £12
d **i** $\frac{1}{3}$ of 18 kg   **ii** $\frac{2}{3}$ of 18 kg
e **i** $\frac{1}{4}$ of 20 cm   **ii** $\frac{3}{4}$ of 20 cm

8
a $\frac{3}{4}$ of 12 cm   **b** $\frac{3}{4}$ of £32   **c** $\frac{2}{3}$ of 15 cm   **d** $\frac{3}{5}$ of 30 kg   **e** $\frac{2}{5}$ of £35
f $\frac{4}{5}$ of 60 cm   **g** $\frac{5}{6}$ of 120 g   **h** $\frac{5}{8}$ of 32 m   **i** $\frac{3}{10}$ of 1300 km

9 Fred gets £30 pocket money each month. He saves of $\frac{2}{3}$ his pocket money.
How many pounds does he save?

10 There are 800 students in a school. $\frac{3}{5}$ of the students are boys.
Work out the number of boys in the school.

11 $\frac{8}{9}$ of an iceberg lies below the surface of the water. The total volume of an iceberg is 990 m³. What volume of the iceberg is below water?

12 There are 36 students in a class. Javed says that $\frac{3}{8}$ of the students are boys.
Explain why Javed cannot be right.

13 **a** Find of $\frac{3}{4}$ £184   **b** Find $\frac{3}{4}$ of £224   **c** Find $\frac{3}{4}$ of £576

14 **a** Find $\frac{5}{8}$ of £496   **b** Find $\frac{5}{8}$ of 78.4 miles   **c** Find $\frac{5}{8}$ of £35.28

15 **a** Find $\frac{5}{6}$ of £318   **b** Find $\frac{5}{6}$ of 345 km   **c** Find $\frac{5}{6}$ of 21 litres

16 **a** Find $\frac{17}{20}$ of £460   **b** Find $\frac{15}{16}$ of 336 m   **c** Find $\frac{7}{40}$ of 660 kg

17 In a school $\frac{11}{20}$ of the students are girls. There are 1140 students in the school. Work out the number of girls.

18 In a train $\frac{7}{9}$ of the seats are standard class. There are 882 seats on the train. Work out the number of standard class seats.

26.2 Expressing one amount as a fraction of another

To express one amount as a fraction of another amount, write them as a fraction with the first amount as the numerator and the second amount as the denominator.

The two amounts must be in the same units.

Simplify the fraction if possible.

Example 3

John earns £40. He saves £15 of this. Write £15 as a fraction of £40
Give your fraction in its simplest form.

Solution 3

$\frac{15}{40}$

The two amounts are both in pounds and so write a fraction with 15 as the numerator and 40 as the denominator.

$\frac{15}{40} = \frac{3}{8}$

Divide the numerator and the denominator by 5 to get the fraction in its simplest form.

Example 4

One day, a baby sleeps for 10 hours. Write 10 hours as a fraction of 1 day.

Solution 4

The two times must have the same units. There are 24 hours in 1 day.

$\frac{10}{24}$

Write a fraction with 10 as the numerator and 24 as the denominator.

$\frac{10}{25} = \frac{5}{12}$

Divide the numerator and the denominator by 2 to get the fraction in its simplest form.

Exercise 26B

1 Express the first number as a fraction of the second number.
Give your answer in its simplest form.

    a 5 and 20　　　**b** 6 and 10　　　**c** 8 and 16　　　**d** 4 and 12

    e 10 and 15　　　**f** 6 and 9　　　　**g** 5 and 15　　　**h** 8 and 10

    i 8 and 12　　　　**j** 12 and 16

2 Express the first amount as a fraction of the second amount.
Give your fraction in its simplest form.

    a £20 and £50　　　　　　　**b** 25p and 40p

    c 18 kg and 20 kg　　　　　　**d** 40 cm and 60 cm

    e 24 mm and 30 mm

3 Express the first amount as a fraction of the second amount.
Give your answer in its simplest form.

    a 60p and £2　　　　　　　　**b** 6 hours and 1 day

    c 36 minutes and 3 hours　　　**d** £1.40 and £6

    e 27 seconds and 2 minutes

4 Mijan earns £20. He spends £6 on bus fares. Write £6 as a fraction of £20
Give your answer in its simplest form.

5 In a school there are 400 boys and 600 girls. Write the number of boys as a fraction of
the number of students in the school.
Give your fraction in its simplest form.

6 Will earns £240 each week. He pays £72 each week in rent. Write the amount Will
pays in rent as a fraction of the amount he earns.
Give your fraction in its simplest form.

7 Amy makes pink paint by mixing 6 litres of red paint with 9 litres of white paint.
Write the volume of red paint as a fraction of the volume of pink paint.
Give your fraction in its simplest form.

8 The price of a bottle of squash increased from £1.60 by 8 pence.
Write 8 pence as a fraction of £1.60

9 Dosha claims that she spends $\frac{3}{8}$ of her allowance on clothes.
Her allowance is £32. She spends £12 on clothes. Is she correct?

26.3 Addition and subtraction of fractions

$\frac{3}{5}$ of the rectangle is shaded red and

$\frac{1}{5}$ of the rectangle is shaded green.

$\frac{4}{5}$ of the rectangle is shaded altogether.

So $\frac{3}{5} + \frac{1}{5} = \frac{4}{5}$

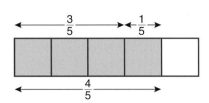

To add fractions with the same denominator, add the numerators but do not change the denominator.

To add fractions with different denominators, first find the smallest number that the denominators all divide exactly into (the **lowest common denominator**). Then change the fractions to equivalent fractions with this denominator. Equivalent fractions were covered in chapter 8.

Example 5

Work out $\frac{2}{3} + \frac{1}{5}$

Solution 5

The lowest common denominator is 15
Change each fraction to an equivalent fraction with a denominator of 15

$$\overset{\times 5}{\frac{2}{3}} = \frac{10}{15} \underset{\times 5}{} \quad \text{and} \quad \overset{\times 3}{\frac{1}{5}} = \frac{3}{15} \underset{\times 3}{}$$

So $\frac{2}{3} + \frac{1}{5} = \frac{10}{15} + \frac{3}{15}$

$\frac{2}{3} + \frac{1}{5} = \frac{13}{15}$ Add the numerators but do not change the denominator.

Example 6

Work out $\frac{7}{8} + \frac{1}{2}$ Give your answer as a mixed number.

Solution 6

The lowest common denominator is 8
Change $\frac{1}{2}$ to an equivalent fraction with a denominator of 8

$\frac{7}{8} + \frac{1}{2} = \frac{7}{8} + \frac{4}{8}$

$\frac{7}{8} + \frac{1}{2} = \frac{11}{8}$ Add the numerators but do not change the denominator.

$\frac{11}{8} = 1\frac{3}{8}$ Change the improper fraction to a mixed number.

$\frac{7}{8} + \frac{1}{2} = 1\frac{3}{8}$

Fractions can be subtracted in a similar way.

Example 7

Work out $\frac{4}{5} - \frac{3}{4}$

Solution 7

The lowest common denominator is 20

$\frac{4}{5} = \frac{16}{20}$ and $\frac{3}{4} = \frac{15}{20}$ | Change each fraction to an equivalent fraction with a denominator of 20

$\frac{4}{5} - \frac{3}{4} = \frac{16}{20} - \frac{15}{20}$

$\frac{4}{5} - \frac{3}{4} = \frac{1}{20}$ | Subtract the numerators but do not change the denominator.

Example 8

Some students each chose one PE activity.

$\frac{2}{5}$ of the students chose soccer.

$\frac{1}{8}$ of the students chose hockey.

All the other students chose swimming.
What fraction of the students chose swimming?

Solution 8

Add $\frac{2}{5}$ and $\frac{1}{8}$ to find the fraction of the students whose chose soccer or hockey.

$\frac{2}{5} + \frac{1}{8} = \frac{16}{40} + \frac{5}{40} = \frac{21}{40}$

Subtract $\frac{21}{40}$ from 1 (that's all of the students) to find the fraction of the students who chose swimming.

$1 - \frac{21}{40} = \frac{40}{40} - \frac{21}{40} = \frac{19}{40}$

$\frac{19}{40}$ of the students chose swimming.

Exercise 26C

Give each answer in its simplest form.

1 **a** $\frac{1}{7} + \frac{2}{7}$ **b** $\frac{1}{4} + \frac{1}{4}$ **c** $\frac{1}{3} + \frac{2}{3}$ **d** $\frac{1}{8} + \frac{3}{8}$

    e $\frac{1}{6} + \frac{1}{6}$ **f** $\frac{8}{15} + \frac{2}{15}$ **g** $\frac{4}{7} - \frac{2}{7}$ **h** $\frac{7}{8} - \frac{1}{8}$

    i $\frac{8}{9} - \frac{2}{9}$ **j** $\frac{7}{10} - \frac{2}{10}$ **k** $\frac{7}{12} + \frac{3}{12} - \frac{1}{12}$

2 **a** $\frac{1}{3} + \frac{1}{2}$ **b** $\frac{1}{3} + \frac{1}{4}$ **c** $\frac{2}{3} + \frac{1}{4}$ **d** $\frac{1}{2} + \frac{2}{5}$ **e** $\frac{1}{5} + \frac{2}{3}$

3 **a** $\frac{1}{2} - \frac{1}{4}$ **b** $\frac{1}{3} - \frac{1}{4}$ **c** $\frac{3}{4} - \frac{1}{2}$ **d** $\frac{2}{3} - \frac{1}{4}$ **e** $\frac{1}{2} - \frac{2}{5}$

4 Uzma went on a journey. She travelled $\frac{1}{2}$ of the distance by bus, $\frac{1}{4}$ of the distance by taxi and she walked the rest. What fraction of the distance did she walk?

5 Simon spends $\frac{1}{2}$ of his money on rent $\frac{1}{3}$ and of his money on transport.

    a What fraction of his money does he spend on rent and transport altogether?

    b What fraction of his money is left?

6 Bill makes a lemon and lime drink. $\frac{1}{2}$ of the drink is water, $\frac{1}{6}$ of the drink is lemon squash and the rest of the drink is lime squash. What fraction of the drink is lime squash?

7 Last season, Pearson Athletic won $\frac{7}{10}$ of its matches, drew $\frac{1}{5}$ and lost the rest. What fraction of its matches did it lose?

8 $\frac{1}{2}$ of a garden is lawn. $\frac{2}{5}$ of the garden is a vegetable patch. The rest of the garden is a flower bed. What fraction of the garden is a flower bed?

26.4 Addition and subtraction of mixed numbers

When adding mixed numbers together, work out the whole number parts and the fraction parts separately.

For example, to work out $2\frac{1}{3} + 4\frac{1}{2}$

    $2 + 4 = 6$ Add the whole number parts.

    $\frac{1}{3} + \frac{1}{2} = \frac{2}{6} + \frac{3}{6} = \frac{5}{6}$ Add the fraction parts.

$2\frac{1}{3} + 4\frac{1}{2} = 6 + \frac{5}{6} = 6\frac{5}{6}$ Combine the two results.

Sometimes adding the fraction parts gives an improper fraction.

For example, adding the fraction parts of $2\frac{2}{3}$ and $4\frac{1}{2}$ gives $\frac{2}{3} + \frac{1}{2} = \frac{4}{6} + \frac{3}{6} = \frac{7}{6}$

$\frac{7}{6}$ is an improper fraction. As a mixed number, this is $1\frac{1}{6}$

So $2\frac{2}{3} + 4\frac{1}{2} = 6 + 1\frac{1}{6} = 7\frac{1}{6}$

Example 9

One piece of tape is $1\frac{3}{4}$ metres long. A second piece of tape is $2\frac{3}{5}$ metres long.

Work out the total length in metres of the two pieces of tape. Give your answer as a mixed number.

Solution 9

$1\frac{3}{4} + 2\frac{3}{5}$

            $1 + 2 = 3$

$\frac{3}{4} + \frac{3}{5} = \frac{15}{20} + \frac{12}{20} = \frac{27}{20}$

               $\frac{27}{20} = 1\frac{7}{20}$

        $3 + 1\frac{7}{20} = 4\frac{7}{20}$

   Total length $= 4\frac{7}{20}$ m

The total length is the sum of the two lengths.
Add the whole number parts.
Add the fraction parts.
Convert the improper fraction to a mixed number.
Combine the two parts and give the answer as a mixed number.

Mixed numbers can be subtracted in a similar way.

Example 10

Work out $3\frac{2}{3} - 1\frac{1}{2}$

Solution 10

$3 - 1 = 2$

$\frac{2}{3} - \frac{1}{2} = \frac{4}{6} - \frac{3}{6} = \frac{1}{6}$

$2 + \frac{1}{6} = 2\frac{1}{6}$

$3\frac{2}{3} - 1\frac{1}{2} = 2\frac{1}{6}$

Subtract the whole number parts.

Subtract the fraction parts.

Combine the two parts.

Example 11

Work out $4\frac{1}{4} - 2\frac{7}{10}$

Solution 11
Method 1

$4\frac{1}{4} = \frac{17}{4}$ and $2\frac{7}{10} = \frac{27}{10}$

Change mixed numbers to improper fractions.

The lowest common denominator is 20

Change each fraction to an equivalent fraction with a denominator of 20

$$\overset{\times 5}{\frac{17}{4}} = \frac{85}{20} \quad \text{and} \quad \overset{\times 2}{\frac{27}{10}} = \frac{54}{20}$$
$$\underset{\times 5}{\phantom{\frac{17}{4}}} \qquad\qquad \underset{\times 2}{\phantom{\frac{27}{10}}}$$

$\frac{17}{4} - \frac{27}{10} = \frac{85}{20} - \frac{54}{20} = \frac{31}{20}$

Subtract the numerators but do not change the denominator.

$\frac{31}{20} = 1\frac{11}{20}$

Give the answer as a mixed number.

$4\frac{1}{4} - 2\frac{7}{10} = 1\frac{11}{20}$

Method 2

$4 - 2 = 2$

Subtract the whole number parts.

$\frac{1}{4} - \frac{7}{10} = \frac{5}{20} - \frac{14}{20} = -\frac{9}{20}$

Subtract the fraction parts.

$2 - \frac{9}{20} = 1 + 1 - \frac{9}{20} = 1 + \frac{20}{20} - \frac{9}{20} = 1 + \frac{11}{20} = 1\frac{11}{20}$

Combine the two results.

$4\frac{1}{4} - 2\frac{7}{10} = 1\frac{11}{20}$

Exercise 26D

Work out each answer as a mixed number or a fraction in its simplest form in questions **1** to **8**.

1　**a** $2\frac{1}{2} + \frac{1}{4}$　　**b** $3\frac{1}{3} + \frac{1}{3}$　　**c** $12\frac{1}{4} + \frac{1}{4}$　　**d** $\frac{1}{6} + 2\frac{1}{4}$　　**e** $\frac{1}{4} + 1\frac{1}{3}$

2　**a** $2\frac{1}{2} + 1\frac{1}{4}$　　**b** $3\frac{1}{5} + \frac{2}{5}$　　**c** $3\frac{1}{2} + \frac{1}{2}$　　**d** $3\frac{2}{3} + \frac{1}{6}$　　**e** $\frac{3}{8} + 2\frac{1}{4}$

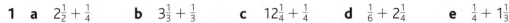

3 **a** $2\frac{1}{4} + \frac{3}{4}$ **b** $2\frac{1}{5} + 1\frac{3}{5}$ **c** $2\frac{1}{6} + 3\frac{5}{6}$ **d** $2\frac{1}{9} + 4\frac{4}{9}$ **e** $6\frac{3}{8} + 1\frac{5}{8}$

4 **a** $2\frac{4}{5} + 1\frac{3}{5}$ **b** $3\frac{5}{9} + 1\frac{8}{9}$ **c** $6\frac{3}{4} + 1\frac{1}{2}$ **d** $4\frac{4}{5} + 1\frac{1}{2}$

5 **a** $2\frac{3}{4} - \frac{1}{2}$ **b** $3\frac{3}{5} - \frac{1}{2}$ **c** $2\frac{3}{4} - \frac{1}{3}$ **d** $4\frac{4}{5} - \frac{1}{4}$ **e** $3\frac{7}{8} - \frac{1}{2}$

6 **a** $2\frac{1}{2} - 1\frac{1}{4}$ **b** $4\frac{3}{4} - 2\frac{1}{2}$ **c** $4\frac{1}{2} - 2\frac{3}{4}$ **d** $3\frac{1}{6} - 1\frac{1}{2}$ **e** $5\frac{1}{3} - 1\frac{3}{4}$

7 **a** $1 - \frac{1}{3}$ **b** $3 - \frac{2}{5}$ **c** $4 - \frac{5}{8}$ **d** $6 - 5\frac{1}{4}$ **e** $8 - 4\frac{2}{3}$

8 Work out the total length of the rods.

$1\frac{5}{8}$ cm $1\frac{3}{4}$ cm

9 John walks $2\frac{1}{2}$ miles to the next village. He then walks a further $2\frac{2}{3}$ miles to the river. How far has he walked altogether?

10 Tammy watches two films. The first film is $1\frac{3}{4}$ hours long and the second one is $2\frac{1}{3}$ hours long. Work out the total length of the two films.

11 Two sticks are $2\frac{1}{2}$ metres and $1\frac{1}{3}$ metres long. Work out the difference between the lengths of the two sticks.

26.5 Multiplication of a fraction by an integer

Multiplication by an integer (a whole number) is the same as repeated addition.

So $2 \times \frac{4}{9}$ is the same as $\frac{4}{9} + \frac{4}{9} = \frac{8}{9}$

To multiply a fraction by an integer, multiply the numerator of the fraction by the integer. Do not change the denominator of the fraction.

Example 12

Work out $6 \times \frac{2}{3}$

Solution 12

$6 \times \frac{2}{3} = \frac{12}{3}$

| Multiply the numerator of the fraction by the integer. Do not change the denominator. |

$6 \times \frac{2}{3} = 4$

| The answer is an integer in this case. |

Exercise 26E

Give each answer in its simplest form.

1 **a** $2 \times \frac{1}{3}$ **b** $3 \times \frac{1}{4}$ **c** $3 \times \frac{1}{5}$ **d** $2 \times \frac{2}{5}$ **e** $3 \times \frac{2}{7}$ **f** $5 \times \frac{2}{11}$

2 **a** $2 \times \frac{1}{6}$ **b** $2 \times \frac{1}{4}$ **c** $4 \times \frac{1}{10}$ **d** $5 \times \frac{1}{10}$ **e** $5 \times \frac{2}{15}$ **f** $3 \times \frac{2}{9}$

3 a $\frac{1}{5} \times 3$ b $\frac{3}{7} \times 2$ c $\frac{1}{6} \times 3$ d $\frac{3}{8} \times 2$ e $\frac{1}{8} \times 4$ f $2 \times \frac{2}{9}$

    g $3 \times \frac{1}{9}$ h $4 \times \frac{1}{8}$ i $\frac{3}{10} \times 2$ j $\frac{3}{6} \times 2$ k $\frac{5}{12} \times 2$

4 James drinks $\frac{1}{6}$ of a litre of milk each day. What fraction of a litre of milk does James drink in 3 days?

5 Mary eats $\frac{1}{8}$ of a tin of sweets each day. What fraction of the tin of sweets does Mary eat in 6 days?

26.6 Division of a fraction by an integer

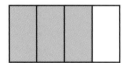 Divide the red area by 2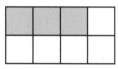

$\frac{3}{4}$ of this rectangle is shaded red.   Now $\frac{3}{8}$ of the rectangle is shaded.

$$\text{So } \frac{3}{4} \div 2 = \frac{3}{8}$$

To divide a fraction by an integer, multiply the denominator of the fraction by the integer to get the new denominator. Do not change the numerator of the fraction.

Example 13

Work out $= \frac{4}{5} \div 3$

Solution 13

$\frac{4}{5} \div 3 = \frac{4}{5 \times 3}$ Multiply the denominator of the fraction by the integer to get the new denominator. Do not change the numerator of the fraction.

$\frac{4}{5} \div 3 = \frac{4}{15}$ $\frac{4}{15}$ is in its simplest form.

Exercise 26F

Give each answer in its simplest form.

1 a $\frac{1}{2} \div 2$ b $\frac{1}{3} \div 2$ c $\frac{1}{5} \div 2$ d $\frac{1}{7} \div 2$ e $\frac{1}{10} \div 2$

2 a $\frac{2}{3} \div 2$ b $\frac{4}{5} \div 2$ c $\frac{6}{7} \div 2$ d $\frac{8}{9} \div 2$ e $\frac{4}{9} \div 2$

3 a $\frac{3}{4} \div 2$ b $\frac{5}{6} \div 2$ c $\frac{3}{8} \div 2$ d $\frac{5}{6} \div 3$ e $\frac{5}{6} \div 4$

4 a $\frac{3}{8} \div 6$ b $\frac{2}{5} \div 4$ c $\frac{5}{8} \div 10$ d $\frac{3}{5} \div 6$ e $\frac{3}{4} \div 6$

5 Hassan has a chocolate bar. He keeps half for himself and shares the rest equally between his three friends. What fraction of the full bar does each friend get?

6 Three friends Jenna, Alex and Jo, share the driving on a car journey. Jenna drives for one quarter of the journey. Alex and Jo share the rest of the driving equally. What fraction of the journey did Alex drive?

26.7 Multiplication of a fraction by a unit fraction

A **unit fraction** has a numerator of 1 and the denominator is a whole number.

Examples of unit fractions are and $\frac{1}{2}$ $\frac{1}{4}$ $\frac{1}{5}$ and $\frac{1}{10}$

$\frac{2}{4}$ is not a unit fraction but can be cancelled to give the unit fraction $\frac{1}{2}$

$\frac{3}{4}$ is not a unit fraction and cannot be cancelled to give a unit fraction.

In the diagram the area of the rectangle is $\frac{3}{4} \times \frac{1}{2}$

To multiply $\frac{3}{4}$ by $\frac{1}{2}$

● Multiply the numerators $3 \times 1 = 3$

● Multiply the denominators $4 \times 2 = 8$

So $\frac{3}{4} \times \frac{1}{2} = \frac{3}{8}$

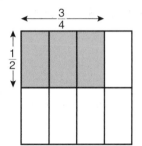

Example 14

Work out $\frac{1}{4} \times \frac{2}{5}$. Give your answer as a fraction in its simplest form.

Solution 14

$\frac{1}{4} \times \frac{2}{5} = \frac{2}{20}$ Multiply the numerators.
                   Multiply the denominators.

$\frac{2}{20} = \frac{1}{10}$

$\frac{1}{4} \times \frac{2}{5} = \frac{1}{10}$

Example 15

$\frac{3}{5}$ of the students in a class are girls. $\frac{1}{6}$ of these girls have blue eyes.
What fraction of the class are blue-eyed girls?
Give your fraction in its simplest form.

Solution 15

$\frac{1}{6}$ of $\frac{3}{5} = \frac{1}{6} \times \frac{3}{5}$ 'of' means the same as 'multiply'

$\frac{1}{6} \times \frac{3}{5} = \frac{3}{30}$ Multiply the numerators.
                   Multiply the denominators.

$\frac{3}{30} = \frac{1}{10}$

$\frac{1}{10}$ of the class are blue-eyed girls.

Exercise 26G

Work out each answer in its simplest form

1   **a** $\frac{3}{5} \times \frac{1}{2}$ **b** $\frac{1}{4} \times \frac{3}{5}$ **c** $\frac{1}{4} \times \frac{1}{5}$ **d** $\frac{1}{2} \times \frac{1}{5}$ **e** $\frac{1}{2} \times \frac{3}{7}$

2   **a** $\frac{1}{5} \times \frac{2}{3}$ **b** $\frac{1}{4} \times \frac{1}{3}$ **c** $\frac{1}{3} \times \frac{2}{3}$ **d** $\frac{1}{4} \times \frac{3}{4}$ **e** $\frac{1}{6} \times \frac{5}{7}$

3   **a** $\frac{4}{5} \times \frac{1}{2}$ **b** $\frac{1}{4} \times \frac{4}{5}$ **c** $\frac{1}{4} \times \frac{8}{9}$ **d** $\frac{1}{2} \times \frac{2}{5}$ **e** $\frac{1}{2} \times \frac{2}{3}$

4   **a** $\frac{4}{7} \times \frac{1}{4}$ **b** $\frac{3}{4} \times \frac{1}{9}$ **c** $\frac{1}{5} \times \frac{5}{8}$ **d** $\frac{1}{3} \times \frac{3}{5}$ **e** $\frac{1}{2} \times \frac{4}{5}$

5   **a** $\frac{1}{4}$ of $\frac{4}{5}$ **b** $\frac{1}{2}$ of $\frac{2}{3}$ **c** $\frac{1}{3}$ of $\frac{3}{8}$ **d** $\frac{1}{4}$ of $\frac{8}{9}$ **e** $\frac{1}{5}$ of $\frac{5}{6}$

6   **a** $\frac{1}{4}$ of $\frac{2}{5}$ **b** $\frac{1}{4}$ of $\frac{2}{3}$ **c** $\frac{1}{3}$ of $\frac{6}{7}$ **d** $\frac{1}{5}$ of $\frac{10}{11}$ **e** $\frac{1}{4}$ of $\frac{6}{7}$

7 In a box of chocolates, $\frac{1}{2}$ are plain. $\frac{1}{3}$ of the plain chocolates have nut centres. What fraction of the chocolates are plain with nut centres?

8 Bill has a video collection. $\frac{3}{4}$ of his video collection are football matches. $\frac{1}{2}$ of these football matches are Premier League. What fraction of Bill's video collection are Premier League football matches?

9 Becky is an athlete. She spends $\frac{2}{3}$ of her training time running. She spends $\frac{1}{4}$ of her running time on the track. What fraction of her training time does she spend running on the track?

10 In a car park, $\frac{2}{5}$ of the cars are estate cars. $\frac{1}{4}$ of these estate cars are red. What fraction of the cars in the car park are red estate cars?

26.8 Multiplication of fractions

To multiply two fractions, multiply the numerators and then multiply the denominators, just like you did in Section 26.7.

Example 16

Work out $\frac{2}{3} \times \frac{2}{5}$

Solution 16

$\frac{2}{3} \times \frac{2}{5} = \frac{4}{15}$

Multiply the numerators $2 \times 2 = 4$

Multiply the denominators $3 \times 5 = 15$

$\frac{4}{15}$ is in its simplest form.

Example 17

Find $1\frac{2}{3} \times \frac{3}{8}$. Give your answer in its simplest form.

Solution 17

$1\frac{2}{3} \times \frac{3}{8} = \frac{5}{3} \times \frac{3}{8}$

$\frac{5}{3} \times \frac{3}{8} = \frac{5 \times 3}{3 \times 8} = \frac{15}{24} = \frac{5}{8}$

$1\frac{2}{3} \times \frac{3}{8} = \frac{5}{8}$

Exercise 26H

Work out

1 a $\frac{2}{3} \times \frac{2}{7}$ **b** $\frac{2}{3} \times \frac{4}{5}$ **c** $\frac{3}{4} \times \frac{3}{5}$ **d** $\frac{2}{3} \times \frac{2}{3}$ **e** $\frac{3}{4} \times \frac{3}{4}$

2 a $\frac{3}{10} \times \frac{3}{5}$ **b** $\frac{7}{10} \times \frac{3}{5}$ **c** $\frac{2}{9} \times \frac{2}{3}$ **d** $\frac{2}{3} \times \frac{4}{7}$ **e** $\frac{3}{5} \times \frac{6}{7}$

Work out the following. Give each answer in its simplest form.

3 a $\frac{2}{3} \times \frac{3}{4}$ **b** $\frac{2}{3} \times \frac{5}{6}$ **c** $\frac{2}{3} \times \frac{3}{5}$ **d** $\frac{2}{5} \times \frac{5}{6}$ **e** $\frac{3}{5} \times \frac{5}{6}$

4 a $\frac{3}{4} \times \frac{2}{5}$ **b** $\frac{2}{3} \times \frac{3}{8}$ **c** $\frac{10}{11} \times \frac{3}{5}$ **d** $\frac{5}{6} \times \frac{4}{5}$ **e** $\frac{3}{10} \times \frac{5}{6}$

5 a $\frac{5}{6} \times \frac{7}{10}$ **b** $\frac{5}{8} \times \frac{3}{10}$ **c** $\frac{5}{7} \times \frac{7}{10}$ **d** $\frac{3}{7} \times \frac{7}{10}$ **e** $\frac{4}{5} \times \frac{5}{8}$

6 a $\frac{2}{3}$ of $\frac{5}{12}$ **b** $\frac{3}{4}$ of $\frac{4}{9}$ **c** $\frac{5}{8}$ of $\frac{4}{9}$ **d** $\frac{7}{8}$ of $\frac{4}{7}$ **e** $\frac{4}{5}$ of $\frac{5}{6}$

7 $\frac{2}{3}$ of a square is shaded. $\frac{3}{4}$ of the shaded part is shaded blue. What fraction of the whole square is shaded blue?

8 Camilla spends $\frac{3}{4}$ of Saturday morning doing homework. She spends $\frac{3}{5}$ of this homework time doing maths. What fraction of Saturday morning does Camilla spend doing maths homework?

9 A carpet covers $\frac{4}{5}$ of a floor. $\frac{4}{5}$ of the carpet is red. What fraction of the floor is covered with red carpet?

10 In a crowd, $\frac{2}{5}$ of the people are female. $\frac{7}{10}$ of the females are girls. What fraction of the crowd is girls?

11 Work out

a $1\frac{3}{4} \times \frac{3}{7}$ **b** $2\frac{1}{2} \times \frac{4}{5}$ **c** $1\frac{2}{3} \times \frac{3}{10}$ **d** $2\frac{1}{4} \times \frac{7}{9}$ **e** $1\frac{4}{5} \times 2\frac{2}{3}$

26.9 Calculations with fractions

When multiplying fractions, it is sometimes possible to simplify the multiplication by cancelling.

Example 18

Work out $\frac{5}{14} \times \frac{7}{10}$

Solution 18

$$\frac{5}{14} \times \frac{7}{10} = \frac{5 \times 7}{14 \times 10}$$

$$\frac{\overset{1}{5} \times 7}{14 \times \underset{2}{10}} = \frac{1 \times 7}{14 \times 2}$$ Cancel the 5 and the 10

$$\frac{1 \times \overset{1}{7}}{\underset{2}{14} \times 2} = \frac{1 \times 1}{2 \times 2}$$ Cancel the 7 and the 14

$$\frac{1 \times 1}{2 \times 2} = \frac{1}{4}$$

$$\frac{5}{14} \times \frac{7}{10} = \frac{1}{4}$$

Division of fractions and mixed numbers

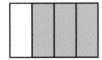

$\frac{3}{4}$ of this rectangle is shaded red.

Divide the red area by 2

Now $\frac{3}{8}$ of the rectangle is shaded.

So $\frac{3}{4} \div 2 = \frac{3}{8}$ also $\frac{3}{4} \times \frac{1}{2} = \frac{3}{8}$

So dividing by 2 is the same as multiplying by $\frac{1}{2}$

To work out $3 \div \frac{3}{4}$
consider how many times $\frac{3}{4}$ goes into 3

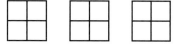

There are $\frac{12}{4}$ in 3 whole
squares, this is 4 lots of $\frac{3}{4}$

So $3 \div \frac{3}{4} = 4$ also $3 \times \frac{4}{3} = 4$

So dividing by $\frac{3}{4}$ is the same as multiplying by $\frac{4}{3}$

$\frac{4}{3}$ is $\frac{3}{4}$ turned upside down.

To divide by a fraction
- do not change the first fraction
- change the division sign into a multiplication sign
- turn the second fraction upside down
- multiply the fractions.

When dividing mixed numbers, first write the mixed numbers as improper fractions.

Example 19

a   Work out $\frac{5}{8} \div \frac{3}{4}$. Give your fraction in its simplest form.

b   Work out $3\frac{3}{4} \div \frac{5}{6}$

Solution 19

a $\frac{5}{8} \div \frac{3}{4} = \frac{5}{8} \times \frac{4}{3}$

                Do not change the $\frac{5}{8}$

                Change $\div$ to $\times$

                Turn $\frac{3}{4}$ upside down to get $\frac{4}{3}$

$\frac{5}{8} \times \frac{4}{3} = \dfrac{5 \times \overset{1}{\cancel{4}}}{\underset{2}{\cancel{8}} \times 3} = \dfrac{5 \times 1}{2 \times 3} = \dfrac{5}{6}$ Cancel the 4 and the 8 then multiply

$\frac{5}{8} \div \frac{3}{4} = \frac{5}{6}$

b $3\frac{3}{4} \div \frac{5}{6} = \frac{15}{4} \div \frac{5}{6}$ Write the mixed number as an improper fraction.

$\frac{15}{4} \div \frac{5}{6} = \frac{15}{4} \times \frac{6}{5}$ Do not change the $\frac{15}{4}$

                Change $\div$ to $\times$

                Turn $\frac{5}{6}$ upside down to get $\frac{6}{5}$

$\frac{15}{4} \times \frac{6}{5} = \dfrac{\overset{3}{\cancel{15}} \times \overset{3}{\cancel{6}}}{\underset{2}{\cancel{4}} \times \underset{1}{\cancel{5}}} = \dfrac{3 \times 3}{2 \times 1} = \dfrac{9}{2}$ Cancel then multiply.

$3\frac{3}{4} \div \frac{5}{6} = 4\frac{1}{2}$ Write $\frac{9}{2}$ as a mixed number.

Exercise 26I

Give each answer in its simplest form.

1 **a** $\frac{5}{6} \times \frac{3}{10}$ **b** $\frac{3}{14} \times \frac{7}{9}$ **c** $\frac{5}{7} \times \frac{7}{15}$ **d** $\frac{5}{6} \times \frac{9}{10}$ **e** $\frac{5}{9} \times \frac{6}{25}$

2 **a** $\frac{5}{8} \times \frac{4}{15}$ **b** $\frac{3}{8} \times \frac{4}{9}$ **c** $\frac{5}{12} \times \frac{18}{25}$ **d** $\frac{5}{9} \times \frac{9}{10}$ **e** $\frac{5}{14} \times \frac{7}{25}$

3 **a** $\frac{1}{4} \div \frac{1}{3}$ **b** $\frac{3}{5} \div \frac{1}{2}$ **c** $\frac{4}{5} \div \frac{3}{10}$ **d** $\frac{9}{16} \div \frac{3}{8}$

4 **a** $2\frac{4}{5} \div \frac{1}{10}$ **b** $2\frac{1}{3} \div \frac{1}{9}$ **c** $3\frac{3}{4} \div 1\frac{4}{5}$ **d** $6\frac{2}{3} \div 2\frac{8}{9}$

Chapter summary

> **You should now be able to:**
>
> ★ find a fraction of an amount
>
> ★ write one amount as a fraction of another
>
> ★ add and subtract fractions and mixed numbers
>
> ★ multiply any fraction by an integer
>
> ★ divide any fraction by an integer
>
> ★ multiply one fraction by another fraction
>
> ★ divide one fraction by another fraction

Chapter 26 review questions

1 Work out

   a $\frac{1}{4}$ of £48   **b** $\frac{1}{5}$ of £50   **c** $\frac{1}{3}$ of £60   **d** $\frac{1}{4}$ of £60   **e** $\frac{1}{8}$ of 48 km

2 Work out

   a $\frac{3}{4}$ of £44   **b** $\frac{2}{3}$ of £18   **c** $\frac{3}{4}$ of £2   **d** $\frac{4}{5}$ of £4   **e** $\frac{4}{5}$ of £45

3 Express the first number as a fraction of the second number. Give your fraction in its simplest form.

   a 2 and 6   **b** 3 and 12   **c** 6 and 8   **d** 8 and 12
   e 16 and 20   **f** 24 and 60   **g** 16 and 48

4 Work out

   a $\frac{2}{7} + \frac{2}{7}$ **b** $\frac{2}{5} + \frac{1}{5}$ **c** $\frac{1}{7} + \frac{4}{7}$ **d** $\frac{2}{9} + \frac{7}{9}$ **e** $\frac{3}{11} + \frac{2}{11}$

5 Work out

   a $\frac{1}{2} - \frac{1}{3}$ **b** $\frac{2}{3} - \frac{1}{4}$ **c** $\frac{1}{3} + \frac{1}{4}$ **d** $\frac{1}{4} + \frac{3}{5}$ **e** $\frac{4}{5} - \frac{2}{3}$

6 A school has 1200 pupils. 575 of these are girls. $\frac{2}{5}$ of the girls like sport. $\frac{3}{5}$ of the boys like sport. Work out the total number of pupils in the school who like sport.

(1387 November 2003)

7 Change to improper fractions   **a** $3\frac{4}{5}$ **b** $9\frac{2}{3}$

8 **a** Work out $\frac{2}{5} + \frac{3}{8}$ **b** Work out $5\frac{2}{3} - 2\frac{3}{4}$ (1387 November 2003)

9 Work out and simplify where possible

   a $\frac{1}{7} \times 4$ **b** $\frac{5}{12} \times 2$ **c** $\frac{1}{8} \times 4$ **d** $\frac{2}{5} \div 2$ **e** $\frac{8}{9} \div 3$ **f** $\frac{4}{9} \div 5$

10 Mary uses $\frac{3}{4}$ of a carton of milk each day. Work out the number of cartons of milk Mary will need for 7 days.

11 Work out and simplify where possible

   a $\frac{4}{5} \times \frac{1}{4}$ **b** $\frac{1}{3} \times \frac{4}{5}$ **c** $\frac{1}{3}$ of $\frac{3}{5}$ **d** $\frac{1}{4}$ of $\frac{8}{11}$ **e** $\frac{6}{11} \times \frac{1}{3}$

12 Owen spends $\frac{2}{3}$ of his income on household expenses. He spends $\frac{1}{4}$ of his household expenses on food. What fraction of his income does he spend on food?

13 Work out, giving each answer in its simplest form

   a $\frac{3}{8} \times \frac{2}{5}$ **b** $\frac{2}{3} \times \frac{5}{8}$ **c** $\frac{5}{9} \times \frac{4}{5}$ **d** $\frac{7}{9} \times \frac{9}{14}$ **e** $\frac{5}{18} \times \frac{9}{20}$

14 The average person spends $\frac{2}{3}$ of the day at home. The average person sleeps for $\frac{3}{8}$ of the time spent at home. What fraction of the day does the average person sleep at home?

15 Work out $1 - \left(\frac{1}{2} + \frac{1}{6}\right)$ (1387 November 2004)

16 Simon spent $\frac{1}{3}$ of his pocket money on a computer game.

He spent $\frac{1}{4}$ of his pocket money on a ticket for a football match.

Work out the fraction of his pocket money that he had left.   (1387 June 2003)

17 Work out the value of $\frac{2}{3} \times \frac{3}{4}$

Give your answer as a fraction in its simplest form.   (1387 June 2005)

Graphs 3

27.1 Graphs of $y = mx + c$

The diagram shows the lines with equations

$y = x$
$y = x + 1$
$y = x + 3$
$y = x - 2$

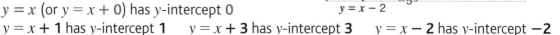

The four lines are parallel; they cross the y-axis at different points (called **y-intercepts**).

The y-intercept of a line is the value of y when $x = 0$

$y = x$ (or $y = x + 0$) has y-intercept **0**

$y = x + 1$ has y-intercept **1**　　$y = x + 3$ has y-intercept **3**　　$y = x - 2$ has y-intercept **−2**

In general, the line $y = x + c$ has y-intercept c since it crosses the y-axis at $(0, c)$

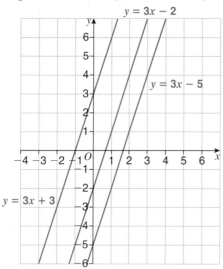

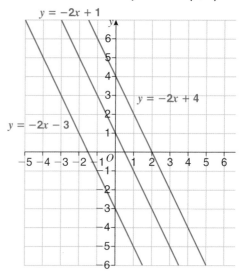

The diagram shows the line with
equations　　$y = 3x + 3$
　　　　　　　$y = 3x - 2$
　　and　　　$y = 3x - 5$

The intercepts on the y-axis are
3, −2 and −5

The three lines are **parallel**.
In the equation of each line,
the x-term includes the number **3**

$y = 3x + 3$　$y = 3x - 2$　$y = 3x - 5$

The diagram shows the line with
equations;　　$y = -2x - 3$
　　　　　　　$y = -2x + 1$
　　and　　　$y = -2x + 4$

The intercepts on the y-axis are
−3, +1 and +4

The three lines are **parallel**.
In the equation of each line,
the x-term includes the number **−2**

$y = -2x - 3$　$y = -2x + 1$　$y = -2x + 4$

For different numbers in the x-term, the slope of the lines are different.

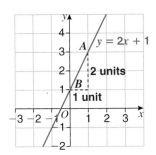

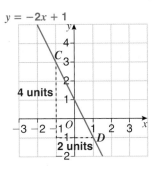

The diagram shows the line $y = 2x + 1$
A and B are two points on the line.
The steepness of the slope of this line can be measured by dividing the vertical distance by the horizontal distance,

The diagram shows the line $y = -2x + 1$
C and D are two points on the line.
The steepness of the slope of this line can be measured by dividing the vertical distance by the horizontal distance,

$$\frac{\text{vertical distance}}{\text{horizontal distance}} = \frac{2 \text{ units}}{1 \text{ unit}} = 2$$

$$\frac{\text{vertical distance}}{\text{horizontal distance}} = \frac{4 \text{ units}}{2 \text{ units}} = 2$$

The steepness of the two lines appears to be the same ($=2$) but the slopes of the two lines clearly look different; from the bottom point on the line, the first line slopes to the right and the second slopes to the left.

A line that slopes to the right, /, is said to have a positive slope.

A line that slopes to the left, \, is said to have a negative slope.

So, the slope of the line $y = 2x + 1$ is **2**
and the slope of the line $y = -2x + 1$ is **−2**.

The slope of a line is called the **gradient** of the line.

The gradient of the line $y = 2x + 1$ is **2**

The gradient of the line $y = -2x + 1$ is **−2**

In general,

for a line with equation $y = mx + c$, the gradient of the line is the value of m.

Example 1

For each of the lines write down
i the gradient   **ii** the y-intercept

a $y = 5x - 7$

b $y = -4x + 3$

Solution 1

a   **i**   gradient $m = 5$

     ii y-intercept $c = -7$

> Compare $y = 5x - 7$
> with $y = mx + c$

b   **i**   gradient $m = -4$

     ii y-intercept $c = 3$

> Compare $y = -4x + 3$
> with $y = mx + c$

Example 2

The diagram shows a straight line graph.

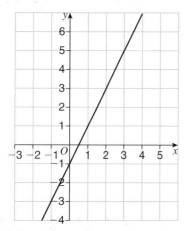

a   Write down the y-intercept of the line.

b   Find the gradient of the line.

c   Write down the equation of the line in the form $y = mx + c$

Solution 2

a y-intercept $= -1$

> The line crosses the y-axis at -1

b

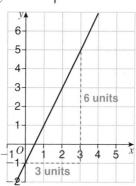

> Choose any two points on the line. From the two points draw a vertical line and a horizontal line to form a right-angle triangle

The gradient of the line is positive.

> The line slopes to the right, /

$$\text{Gradient} = +\frac{6 \text{ units}}{3 \text{ units}} = +2$$

> $\text{Gradient} = \dfrac{\text{vertical distance}}{\text{horizontal distance}}$

c $m = 2$ and $c = -1$ so

     $y = 2x - 1$

> $y = mx + c$ where $m =$ the gradient and $c =$ the y-intercept

Using straight line graphs

The diagram shows the graph of $y = x$ and the graph of $x + y = 6$.

The graph of $y = x$ crosses the graph of $x + y = 6$ at the point $(3, 3)$

$x = 3$, $y = 3$ is the solution of the simultaneous equations

$y = x$ and $x + y = 6$ since

$3 = 3$ and $3 + 3 = 6$

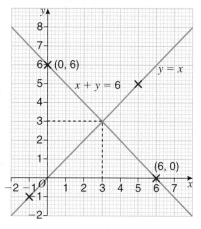

Exercise 27A

1 The grid shows the graphs of three straight lines.

   a Write down the equation of the line

      i AB **ii** CD **iii** EF

   b Find the gradient of each of these lines.

2 **a** On the resource sheet draw the graph of $y = x + 2$ and the graph of $x + y = 4$

   b **i** Write down the coordinates of the point where these two graphs cross.

     ii Write down the solution of the simultaneous equations $y = x + 2$ and $x + y = 4$

3 For each of the lines write down **i** the gradient **ii** the y-intercept

   a $y = 2x + 3$ **b** $y = x - 5$ **c** $y = -3x$

   d $y = \frac{2}{3}x + 1$ **e** $y = 8 - 3x$

27.2 Graphs of quadratic functions

All these expressions contain a letter squared.

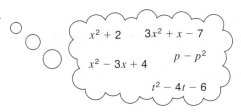

$x^2 + 2$ $3x^2 + x - 7$

$x^2 - 3x + 4$ $p - p^2$

$t^2 - 4t - 6$

They are called **quadratic** expressions or **quadratic functions**.

To draw the graph of a quadratic function a table of values can be used.

Example 3

Draw the graph of $y = x^2$. Use values of x from $x = -3$ to $x = 3$

Solution 3

$$y = x^2$$

When $x = 3$, $y = 3 \times 3 = 9$ When $x = -1$, $y = -1 \times -1 = 1$
When $x = 2$, $y = 2 \times 2 = 4$ When $x = -2$, $y = -2 \times -2 = 4$
When $x = 1$, $y = 1 \times 1 = 1$ When $x = -3$, $y = -3 \times -3 = 9$
When $x = 0$, $y = 0 \times 0 = 0$

x	-3	-2	-1	0	1	2	3
y	9	4	1	0	1	4	9

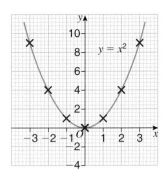

The lowest point of this graph is where the graph turns. It is the origin $(0, 0)$.

It is called the **minimum point**.

Graphs of quadratic functions always look like $\smile$ or $\frown$.

Example 4

a Complete this table of values for $y = 4 - x^2$

x	-3	-2	-1	0	1	2	3
y	-5		3		3		

b Draw the graph of $y = 4 - x^2$ from $x = -3$ to $x = 3$

c Write down the values of x where the graph crosses the x-axis.

Solution 4

a
$$y = 4 - x^2$$
When $x = 3$, $y = 4 - 3 \times 3 = 4 - 9 = -5$
When $x = 2$, $y = 4 - 2 \times 2 = 4 - 4 = 0$
When $x = 0$, $y = 4 - 0 \times 0 = 4$
When $x = -2$, $y = 4 - (-2) \times (-2) = 4 - 4 = 0$

x	-3	-2	-1	0	1	2	3
y	-5	0	3	4	3	0	-5

b

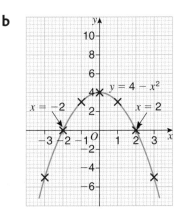

c $x = -2$ and $x = 2$.

The highest point on this graph is where the graph turns. It is the point $(0, 4)$.

It is called the **maximum point**.

Example 5

a Complete this table of values for $y = x^2 + x - 6$

x	-4	-3	-2	-1	0	1	2	3
y	6	0	-4		-6			6

b Draw the graph of $y = x^2 + x - 6$ from $x = -4$ to $x = 3$

c Write down the values of x where the graph crosses the x-axis.

d **i** Draw the line of symmetry of your graph.
   ii Write down the equation of this line of symmetry.

e Use your graph to find an estimate for the minimum value of y.

Solution 5

a
$$y = x^2 + x - 6$$
When $x = 2$, $y = 2 \times 2 + 2 - 6 = 4 + 2 - 6 = 0$
When $x = 1$, $y = 1 \times 1 + 1 - 6 = 1 + 1 - 6 = -4$
When $x = -1$, $y = (-1) \times (-1) + (-1) - 6 = 1 - 1 - 6 = -6$

x	-4	-3	-2	-1	0	1	2	3
y	6	0	-4	-6	-6	-4	0	6

b

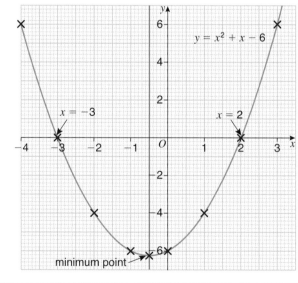

c $x = -3$ and $x = 2$

d **i** The **green** line is the line of symmetry of the graph.
   ii $x = -0.5$

e Minimum value of $y = -6.3$

Exercise 27B

1 Here is a table of values for
$y = x^2 - 1$

x	-3	-2	-1	0	1	2	3
y	8	3	0	-1	0	3	8

  a Draw the graph of $y = x^2 - 1$

  b On the same grid draw the graph of $y = x^2 - 5$

2 a Copy and complete this table of values for $y = 2 - x^2$

x	-3	-2	-1	0	1	2	3
y	-7	-2	1			-2	

  b Draw the graph of $y = 2 - x^2$

  c Write down the coordinates of the maximum point.

  d Estimate the values of x where the graph crosses the x-axis.

3 a Copy and complete this table of values for $y = 2x^2$

x	-3	-2	-1	0	1	2	3
y	18	8		0		8	

  b Draw the graph of $y = 2x^2$ from $x = -3$ to $x = 3$

4 a Copy and complete this table of values for $y = x^2 - x$

x	-3	-2	-1	0	1	2	3
y	12		2	0			6

  b Draw the graph of $y = x^2 - x$ from $x = -3$ to $x = 3$.

  c Write down the values of x where the graph crosses the x-axis.

  d i Draw the line of symmetry of your graph.
    ii Write down the equation of this line of symmetry.

  e Use your graph to find an estimate for the minimum value of y.

5 a Copy and complete this table of values for $y = x^2 + 2x - 3$

x	-4	-3	-2	-1	0	1	2
y	5	0	-3		-3		

  b Draw the graph of $y = x^2 + 2x - 3$ from $x = -4$ to $x = 2$

  c Write down the values of x where the graph crosses the x-axis.

  d Write down the coordinates of the minimum point.

27.3 Using graphs of quadratic functions to solve equations

The grid shows the graph of
$y = x^2 + x - 6$
The solutions of the equation
$0 = x^2 + x - 6$ are the x-values where
$y = 0$
From the graph, $y = 0$ when $x = -3$
and $x = 2$

$x = -3$ and $x = 2$ are the **solutions** of
the equation $x^2 + x - 6 = 0$

$x^2 + x - 6 = 0$ is an example of a
quadratic equation.

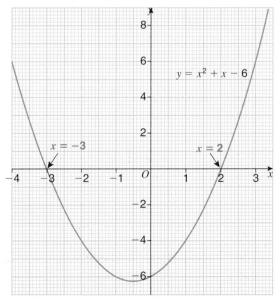

Example 6

The grid shows the graph of $y = x^2 - 5x - 3$

Use the graph to find estimates of the solutions
to the equation $x^2 - 5x - 3 = 0$

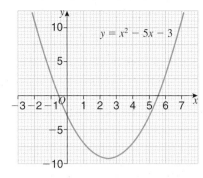

Solution 6

$$\underbrace{x^2 - 5x - 3}_{y} = 0$$

Using the graph of $y = x^2 - 5x - 3$,
when $y = 0$, the solutions are $x = -0.5$
and $x = 5.5$

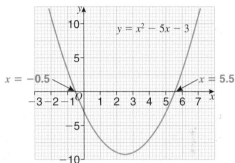

Example 7

The grid shows the graph of $y = 6 - x^2$

a Use the graph to find estimates of the
solutions to the equation $6 - x^2 = 0$

b i On the grid draw the graph of $y = 2$
   ii Write down the values of the
   x-coordinates of the points where the
   two graphs cross.

c Use the graph of $y = 6 - x^2$ to find estimates
of the solutions to the equation $6 - x^2 = -2$

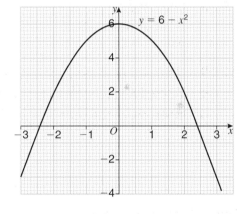

Solution 7

a $$\underbrace{6 - x^2}_{y} = 0$$

Using the graph of $y = 6 - x^2$,
when $y = 0$ the solutions are
$x = -2.4$ and $x = 2.4$

b i The **orange** line shows the
   graph of $y = 2$.
   ii $x = -2$ and $x = 2$

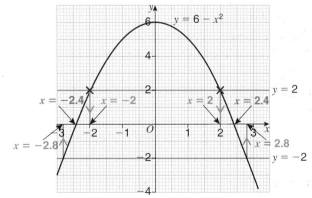

c Comparing $6 - x^2 = -2$ with $y = 6 - x^2$ gives $y = -2$

The **blue** line shows the graph of $y = -2$. From the graph, when $y = -2$, the solutions
are $x = -2.8$ and $x = 2.8$

Exercise 27C

1 **a** Draw the graph of $y = x^2$ from $x = -3$ to $x = 3$

   b **i** On the same axes, draw the graph of $y = 4$

     ii Write down the values of the x-coordinates of the points where the two graphs cross.

   c Use the graph of $y = x^2$ to find estimates of the solutions to the equation $x^2 = 7$

2 The grid shows the graph of $y = 2x^2 - 3x$

   a Use the graph to find the solutions of the equation $2x^2 - 3x = 0$

   b Use the graph to find the solutions of the equation $2x^2 - 3x = 5$

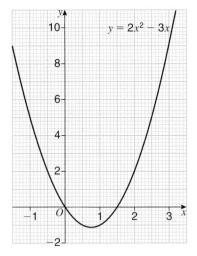

3 The grid shows the graph of $y = 8 + 3x - 2x^2$

   a Use the graph to find estimates of the solutions to the equation $8 + 3x - 2x^2 = 0$

   b Use the graph to find the solutions to the equation $8 + 3x - 2x^2 = 3$

   c Use the graph to find the solutions to the equation $8 + 3x - 2x^2 = 6$

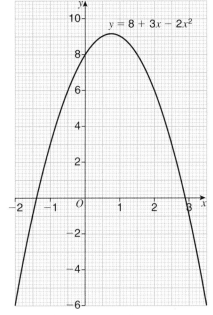

4 **a** On the resource sheet, draw the graph of $y = 3 + x - x^2$

    Use values of x between -2 and 3

   b Use your graph to write down an estimate for

    i the maximum value of y

    ii the solutions of $3 + x - x^2 = 0$

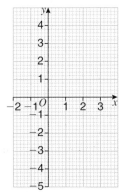

Chapter summary

You should now be able to:

★ Recognise that equations in the form $y = mx + c$, where m and c are numbers, are straight lines of **gradient** $= m$ and **y-intercept** $= c$. For example, $y = 6x - 7$ is the equation of a straight line with gradient $= 6$ and y-intercept $= -7$. The line crosses the y-axis at the point $(0, -7)$.

★ Write down the solution of a pair of simultaneous equations, given the straight line graph of each equation, using the coordinates of the point where the two lines cross.

★ Find the gradient of a line drawn on a grid.

★ Recognise that a **quadratic function** contains a term with a letter squared, for example, $x^2 + 5x - 7$

★ Draw the graph of a quadratic function from a given equation and given values of x by:
  • drawing a **table of values** for calculated values of y
  • plotting the points from the table of values
  • joining the points with a smooth curve.

★ Recognise that the **minimum point** on the graph of a quadratic function is the lowest point where the graph turns, and that the **maximum point** on the graph is the highest point where the graph turns.

★ Recognise that $x^2 + 5x - 7 = 0$ is an example of a **quadratic equation**. It can be solved from the graph of $y = x^2 + 5x - 7$ by finding the values of x at the points where $y = 0$, that is where the graph crosses the x-axis.

Chapter 27 review questions

1 a Use the graphs to find the gradient of
  i $y = 2x$ **ii** $x + y = 3$
  b Write down the solution of the simultaneous equations $y = 2x$ and $x + y = 3$

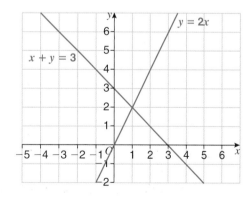

2 Write down **i** the gradient **ii** the y-intercept of each of the straight lines
  a $y = 4x - 7$
  b $y = -5x + 9$

3 a On a grid plot the points $(2, 9)$ and $(-1, -3)$
  b Find the gradient of the straight line passing through the points $(2, 9)$ and $(-1, -3)$
  c Find the equation of this straight line.

4 Copy and complete this table of values for $y = x^2 - 10$

x	-3	-2	-1	0	1	2	3
y							

5 a Copy and complete this table of values for $y = 7 - x^2$

x	-3	-2	-1	0	1	2	3
y	-2			7		3	

b Draw the graph of $y = 7 - x^2$ from $x = -3$ to $x = 3$

c Write down the coordinates of the maximum point.

d Estimate the values of x where the graph crosses the x-axis.

6 a Copy and complete this table of values for $y = x^2 - 2x$

x	-2	-1	0	1	2	3
y		3				3

b Draw the graph of $y = x^2 - 2x$ from $x = -2$ to $x = 3$

c Write down the values of x where the graph crosses the x-axis.

d **i** Draw the line of symmetry of your graph.
ii Write down the equation of this line of symmetry.

e Use your graph to find an estimate for the minimum value of y.

7 a Copy and complete this table of values for $y = x^2 - 3x - 1$

x	-2	-1	0	1	2	3	4
y		3	-1	-3			3

b On the resource sheet draw the graph of $y = x^2 - 3x - 1$

c Use your graph to find an estimate for the minimum value of y.   (1388 March 2003)

8 a On the resource sheet draw the graph of $y = x^2 - x - 4$
Use values of x between -2 and $+3$

b Use your graph to write down an estimate for
i the minimum value of y
ii the solutions of the equation $x^2 - x - 4 = 0$ (1385 June 1998)

9 By drawing the graph of $y = x^2 + x - 6$, using values of x from -4 to $+3$

a write down the solutions of the equation $x^2 + x - 6 = 0$

b write down an estimate for the solutions of the equation $x^2 + x - 6 = 1$

Percentages 2

CHAPTER

28.1 Using percentages

These examples show how to increase and decrease quantities by a given percentage.

Example 1

In a sale, normal prices are reduced by 15%.
The normal price of a DVD player is £80
Work out the sale price.

Solution 1

Method 1

15% of 80

> First work out the reduction in the normal price.

$$= \frac{15}{100} \times 80$$

> Write the percentage as a fraction.
> Work out the multiplication.

$$= \frac{15}{\cancel{100}_{10}} \times \cancel{80}^{8}$$

$$= \frac{\cancel{15}^{3}}{\cancel{10}_{2}} \times 8$$

$$= \frac{3}{\cancel{2}_{1}} \times \cancel{8}^{4}$$

$$= 3 \times 4 = 12$$

> The reduction in the normal price is £12

$$80 - 12 = 68$$

> Subtract to work out the sale price.

Sale price = £68

Method 2

$$100\% - 15\% = 85\%$$

$$85\% = 0.85$$

$$0.85 \times 80$$

$$= 68$$

Sale price = £68

> The normal price is reduced by 15%.
> Subtract 15% from 100%.
> The sale price is 85% of the normal price.
> 0.85 is called the multiplier.
> Find 85% of 80. (This reduces 80 by 15%.)
> With this method, the actual reduction in the normal price is not found.

Example 2

Hugh's salary is £25 000 a year.
His salary is increased by 4%.
Work out his new salary.

Solution 2

Method 1

4% of 25 000

| Work out the increase in Hugh's salary. |

$$= \frac{4}{100} \times 25\,000$$

$$= \frac{4}{\overset{1}{\cancel{100}}} \times \overset{250}{\cancel{25\,000}}$$

$$= 4 \times 250 = 1000$$

| His increase in salary is £1000 |

25 000 + 1000 = 26 000

| Add to work out his new salary. |

Hugh's new salary is £26 000

Method 2

100% + 4% = 104%

| Hugh's salary is increased by 4%.
Add 4% to 100%.
His new salary is 104% of £25 000
1.04 is called the multiplier. |

104% = 1.04

1.04 × 25 000

$$= 26\,000$$

| Find 104% of 25 000
(This increases 25 000 by 4%.) |

Hugh's new salary is £26 000

Example 3

The value of a car depreciates by 10% each year.
The value of a car when new is £4000
Work out the value of the car after

a   one year   **b**   three years.

Solution 3

a $\frac{10}{100} \times 4000 = 400$

| Work out 10% of £4000 |

4000 − 400 = 3600

| 'Depreciates' means that the value of the car decreases.
Subtract £400 from the value of the car when new. |

The value of the car after
one year is £3600

b $\frac{10}{100} \times 3600 = 360$

| Work out 10% of £3600 (the value of the car after one year).
Subtract £360 from the value of the car after one year to find
the value of the car after two years.
Work out 10% of £3240 (the value of the car after two years).
Subtract £324 from the value of the car after two years to find
the value of the car after three years. |

3600 − 360 = 3240

$\frac{10}{100} \times 3240 = 324$

3240 − 324 = 2916

The value of the car after three years is £2916

Exercise 28A

1. Jeevan earns £200 per week. He gets a wage rise of 10%.
   How much does Jeevan earn per week after his rise?

2. In a sale all prices are reduced by 15%.
   Work out the sale price of each of the following:

15% OFF

Computer normally £1200

Television normally £300

CD Player normally £40

   a. a television set that normally costs £300
   b. a CD player that normally costs £40
   c. a computer that normally costs £1200

3. The table shows the salaries of three workers.
   Each of these workers receives a 5% salary increase.
   Work out the new salary of each worker.

Helen	£12 000
Tom	£24 000
Sandeep	£32 000

4. Hanni invests £3000. The interest rate is 4% per year.
   How much will Hanni have in his bank account at the end of one year?

5. The price of a computer is £450. Its price is reduced by 15% in a sale.
   Work out the sale price of the computer.

6. Jenny puts £600 into a bank account. At the end of one year 3.5% interest is added.
   How much is in her account at the end of one year?

7. A holiday normally costs £850. It is reduced by 12%.
   How much will the holiday now cost?

8. A year ago, the value of Richard's house was £85 000. Its value has now increased by 9%. Work out the value of his house now.

9. Ria buys a car for £2300. The value of the car depreciates by 20% each year.
   Work out the value of the car at the end of
   a. one year
   b. three years.

10. Value Added Tax (VAT) is charged at a rate of $17\frac{1}{2}$%. A builder's bill is £962 before VAT is added. What will the bill be after VAT has been added?

11 Pat normally pays £45 for her train fare. All train fares are increased by 9%.
How much will Pat now have to pay?

12 The total price of a radio is £46.80 plus VAT at 17.5%.
Work out the total price of the radio.

28.2 One quantity as a percentage of another quantity

To write one quantity as a percentage of another quantity:

● write down the first quantity as a fraction of the second quantity
● change the fraction to a percentage.

Example 4

a Change 11 out of 20 to a percentage. Do not use a calculator.
b Change 23 out of 40 to a percentage. You may use a calculator.

Solution 4

a $\dfrac{11}{20}$

| Write the first number as a fraction of the second number. |

$$\overset{\times 5}{\underset{\times 5}{\dfrac{11}{20} = \dfrac{55}{100}}}$$

| Change $\frac{11}{20}$ to a fraction with a denominator of 100 |

$$\dfrac{55}{100} = 55\%$$

| Per cent means 'out of a hundred' so $\frac{55}{100} = 55\%$. |

11 out of 20 = 55%

b $\dfrac{23}{40}$

| Write the first number as a fraction of the second number. |

| Change the fraction to a decimal. |

$$\dfrac{23}{40} = 0.575$$

$$0.575 = \dfrac{57.5}{100}$$

$$\dfrac{57.5}{100} = 57.5\%$$

| Per cent means 'out of a hundred' so $\frac{57.5}{100} = 57.5\%$. |

23 out of 40 = 57.5%

In **a**, $\frac{11}{20} \times 100 = 55$ and, in **b** $\frac{23}{40} \times 100 = 57.5$

So, to change a fraction to a percentage, multiply the fraction by 100

Example 5

Write 45 cm out of 2 m as a percentage.

Solution 5

There are two different types of units in the question – centimetres and metres.
Quantities must have the same units before the percentage is found.
In this case, express both lengths in centimetres.

2 m = 200 cm

$\frac{45}{200}$

> Remember 1 m = 100 cm.
> Write 45 as fraction of 200
> Multiply $\frac{45}{200}$ by 100 to change it to a percentage.

$\frac{45}{200} \times 100 = 22.5\%$

45 cm is 22.5% of 2 m.

Example 6

Patrick bought 24 oranges. 3 of the oranges were bad.
What percentage of the oranges were bad?

Solution 6

$\frac{3}{24}$

> Write 3 out of 24 as a fraction.
> Multiply $\frac{3}{24}$ by 100 to change it to a percentage.

$\frac{3}{24} \times 100 = 12.5\%$

12.5% of the oranges were bad.

Exercise 28B

1 Write

   a £3 out of £6 as a percentage   **b** 2 kg out of 8 kg as a percentage

   c 4p out of 10p as a percentage   **d** 8 cm out of 40 cm as a percentage

   e £80 out of £400 as a percentage   **f** £3 out of £30 as a percentage

   g 7 kg out of 35 kg as a percentage   **h** 3 m out of 20 m as a percentage

   i 90 km out of 100 km as a percentage   **j** £36 out of £48 as a percentage

2 Write

   a 20p out of £2 as a percentage   **b** 25 cm out of 1 m as a percentage

   c 600 g out of 1 kg as a percentage   **d** 800 m out of 1 km as a percentage

   e 60p out of £2.40 as a percentage   **f** 15 mm out of 6 cm as a percentage

   g 36 minutes out of 1 hour as a percentage   **h** 50 cm out of 4 m as a percentage

3 Janet scored 36 out of 40 in a German test. Work out her score as a percentage.

4 There are 240 students in Year 10. 150 of the students in Year 10 are boys.

   a What percentage of Year 10 students are boys?

   b What percentage of Year 10 students are girls?

5 Jerry took 60 bottles to a bottle bank.
27 of the bottles were green. What percentage of the bottles were green?

6 There are 80 pages in a book. 30 of the pages have pictures on them.
What percentage of the pages in the book have pictures on them?

7 In a survey, 1440 out of 2500 people say that they are going on holiday in the summer.

   a What percentage are going on holiday?

   b What percentage are **not** going on holiday?

8 A box of cereal weighs 750 g. It contains 210 g of dried fruit. What percentage of the cereal is dried fruit?

9 A 40 g serving of cereal contains 8 g of protein, 24 g of carbohydrates, 4.5 g of fat and 3.5 g of fibre. What percentage of the serving is

   a protein   **b** carbohydrates

   c fat   **d** fibre?

Chapter summary

You should be able to:

★ Increase or decrease a quantity by a given percentage

★ Express one quantity as apercentage of another quantity

★ Change a fraction to a percentage by multiplying the fraction by 100

Chapter 28 review questions

1 **a** Write 45 cm out of 1 m as a percentage

   b Write 300 g out of 2 kg as a percentage

2 Jo did a maths test. There was a total of 40 marks for the test.
Jo got 65% of the marks.

   a Work out 65% of 40

Jo got 36 out of 80 in an English test.

   b Work out 36 out of 80 as a percentage.   (1385 June 2000)

3 There are 800 students at Prestfield School.
144 of these students were absent from school on Wednesday.

   a Work out how many students were **not** absent on Wednesday.

Trudy says that more than 25% of the 800 students were absent on Wednesday.

   b Is Trudy correct? Explain your answer.

45% of these 800 students are girls.

   c Work out 45% of 800

There are 176 students in Year 10

   d Write 176 out of 800 as a percentage.   (1387 June 2004)

4 Lisa had £10.50
   She gave 8% to charity and kept the rest of the money.
   Work out how much money she kept.   (1385 Jan 2002)

5 In a sale, all the normal prices are reduced by 15%.
   The normal price of a jacket is £42
   Syreeta buys the jacket in the sale.
   Work out the sale price of the jacket.   (1385 June 2001)

6 The price of a telephone is £36.40 plus VAT.
   VAT is charged at 17.5%.

   a Work out the amount of VAT charged.

   In a sale, normal prices are reduced by 12%.
   The normal price of a camera is £79

   b Work out the sale price of the camera.   (1385 June 2002)

7 The depreciation of a car is 20% each year.
   The value of the car is £8500
   Work out the value of the car at the end of three years.

Equations and inequalities

29

CHAPTER

29.1 Equations

An equation must always have an equals sign '='.
The expression before the equals sign is called the
left-hand side of the **equation**.
The expression after the equals sign is called the
right-hand side of the **equation**.

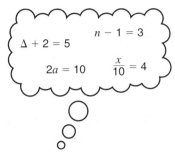

$$n - 1 = 3$$

left-hand side   right-hand side

These are four examples of
equations

The two sides of the equation $n - 1 = 3$ can be swapped over and written as $3 = n - 1$

The **solution** of an equation is the value of the symbol or letter that makes the equation true.

To **solve** the equation $\Delta + 2 = 5$, find the value of Δ so that $\Delta + 2 = 5$ is true.

To solve the equation $n - 1 = 3$, find the value of n so that $n - 1 = 3$ is true.

To solve the equation $2a = 10$, find the value of a so that $2 \times a = 10$ is true.

To solve the equation $\dfrac{x}{10} = 4$, find the value of x so that $x \div 10 = 4$ is true.

In algebra, $x \div 10$ is written as $\dfrac{x}{10}$.

The four equations in the bubble can be solved mentally.

Example 1

Solve the equation $\Delta + 2 = 5$

Solution 1
$\Delta = 3$ since $3 + 2 = 5$

Example 2

Solve the equation $n - 1 = 3$

Solution 2
$n = 4$ since $4 - 1 = 3$

Example 3

Solve the equation $2a = 10$

Solution 3
$2 \times a = 10$
$a = 5$ since $2 \times 5 = 10$

Example 4

Solve the equation $\dfrac{x}{10} = 4$

Solution 4
$x = 40$ since $40 \div 10 = 4$

Exercise 29A

1 What number must Δ be equal to?

    a $\Delta + 1 = 3$ **b** $\Delta - 2 = 5$ **c** $3 + \Delta = 15$

    d $\Delta - 4 = 0$ **e** $20 - \Delta = 18$

2 Solve these equations.

    a $x + 2 = 8$ **b** $a - 10 = 5$ **c** $4 + p = 8$

    d $8 - q = 1$ **e** $x - 3 = 0$ **f** $2 + c = 2$

    g $20 - r = 11$ **h** $6 = t + 2$ **i** $10 = u - 2$

    j $13 = 8 + y$

3 What number must Δ be equal to?

    a $3 \times \Delta = 15$ **b** $4 \times \Delta = 24$ **c** $\Delta \div 4 = 6$

    d $\Delta \times 2 = 18$ **e** $30 \div \Delta = 10$

4 Solve these equations.

    a $2x = 20$ **b** $3a = 9$ **c** $4t = 20$

    d $5p = 35$ **e** $12 = 2d$ **f** $\dfrac{x}{2} = 8$

    g $\dfrac{a}{2} = 5$ **h** $\dfrac{t}{3} = 3$ **i** $\dfrac{y}{5} = 5$

    j $3 = \dfrac{c}{4}$ **k** $\dfrac{10}{x} = 5$ **l** $3 = \dfrac{15}{y}$

29.2 The balance method for solving equations

Some equations can be solved mentally.
To solve more complicated equations the **balance method** is used.
The left-hand side of the equation must balance with the right-hand side of the equation.

$$3x + 5 = 17$$

          left-hand side   right-hand side
         of the equation   of the equation

To keep the balance, do the same to the left-hand side and the right-hand side of the equation.

Balance	Explanation	Step
$3x + 5$ 17 LHS RHS	The scales balance because both sides are equal.	$3x + 5 = 17$

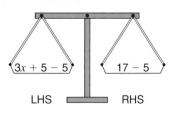

LHS RHS

To keep the balance

> Subtract 5 from **both** sides.

$3x + 5 - 5 = 17 - 5$

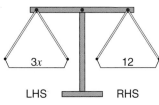

LHS RHS

The scales still balance and show that $3x = 12$

$3x = 12$

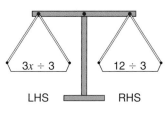

LHS RHS

To keep the balance

> Divide **both** sides by 3

$3x \div 3 = 12 \div 3$

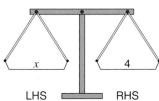

LHS RHS

to get the solution

$x = 4$

The solution of the equation $3x + 5 = 17$ is $x = 4$

Check: When $x = 4$, $3 \times 4 + 5 = 17$ since $12 + 5 = 17$ ✓

The balance method can also be used to solve this equation,

$$28 = 5p - 2$$

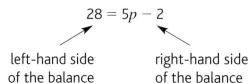

left-hand side of the balance

right-hand side of the balance

Balance	**Explanation**	**Step**

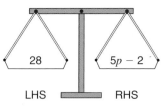

LHS RHS

Starting with

$28 = 5p - 2$

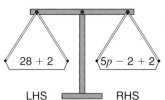

LHS RHS

To keep the balance

> Add 2 to **both** sides.

$28 + 2 = 5p - 2 + 2$

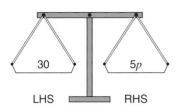

The scales still balance and show that $30 = 5p$

$$30 = 5p$$

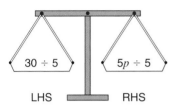

To keep the balance

Divide **both** sides by 5

$$30 \div 5 = 5p \div 5$$

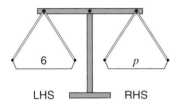

to get the solution $6 = p$

The solution of the equation $28 = 5p - 2$ is $p = 6$
Check: When $p = 6$, $28 = 5 \times 6 - 2$ since $28 = 30 - 2$ ✓

Example 5

Use the balance method to solve the equation $a - 7 = 19$

Solution 5

$$a - 7 = 19$$
$$a - 7 + 7 = 19 + 7 \quad \boxed{\text{Add 7 to \textbf{both} sides.}}$$
$$a = 26$$

Check: When $a = 26$, $26 - 7 = 19$ ✓

Example 6

Use the balance method to solve the equation $6y = 72$

Solution 6

$$6y = 72$$
$$6y \div 6 = 72 \div 6 \quad \boxed{\text{Divide \textbf{both} sides by 6}}$$
$$y = 12$$

Check: When $y = 12$, $6 \times 12 = 72$ ✓

Example 7

Use the balance method to solve the equation $4x + 3 = 31$

Solution 7

$$4x + 3 = 31$$
$$4x + 3 - 3 = 31 - 3 \quad \boxed{\text{Subtract 3 from \textbf{both} sides.}}$$
$$4x = 28$$
$$4x \div 4 = 28 \div 4 \quad \boxed{\text{Divide \textbf{both} sides by 4}}$$
$$x = 7$$

Check: When $x = 7$, $4 \times 7 + 3 = 28 + 3 = 31$ ✓

Example 8

Solve the equation $\dfrac{q + 5}{2} = 6$

Solution 8

$$\dfrac{q + 5}{2} = 6$$

$$\dfrac{q + 5}{2} \times 2 = 6 \times 2 \qquad \boxed{\text{Multiply \textbf{both} sides by 2}}$$

$$q + 5 = 12$$

$$q + 5 - 5 = 12 - 5 \qquad \boxed{\text{Subtract 5 from \textbf{both} sides.}}$$

$$q = 7$$

Check: When $q = 7$, $\dfrac{7 + 5}{2} = \dfrac{12}{2} = 6$ ✓

Exercise 29B

Use the balance method to solve these equations.

1 $a + 7 = 19$ **2** $3b = 39$ **3** $5 = c - 6$ **4** $2d + 1 = 19$

5 $3e - 4 = 23$ **6** $5f + 9 = 44$ **7** $7g + 4 = 4$ **8** $6h + 23 = 29$

9 $4p - 3 = 17$ **10** $8 + 2q = 22$ **11** $15 + 2r = 37$ **12** $13 = 2t - 5$

13 $23 = 2u + 5$ **14** $26 = 6 + 2x$ **15** $41 = 5 + 6y$ **16** $13 = 3a - 5$

17 $23 = 4d - 5$ **18** $27 = 4k - 9$ **19** $3 + 8x = 67$ **20** $14 + 9y + 1 = 42$

21 $\dfrac{x + 1}{3} = 2$ **22** $\dfrac{y - 2}{4} = 1$ **23** $\dfrac{x}{3} + 2 = 5$ **24** $2 = \dfrac{p - 1}{6}$

25 $5 = \dfrac{2q - 1}{3}$

The next example shows that solutions of equations are not always whole numbers.

Example 9

Solve the equation $4 = 7x - 1$

Solution 9

$$4 = 7x - 1$$

$$4 + 1 = 7x - 1 + 1 \qquad \boxed{\text{Add 1 to \textbf{both} sides.}}$$

$$5 = 7x$$

$$5 \div 7 = 7x \div 7 \qquad \boxed{\text{Divide \textbf{both} sides by 7}}$$

$$x = \tfrac{5}{7} \qquad \boxed{\text{Write the answer as a fraction.}}$$

Check: When $x = \tfrac{5}{7}$, $4 = 7 \times \tfrac{5}{7} - 1$ since $4 = 5 - 1$ ✓

Exercise 29C

Solve these equations.

1 $4a = 1$ **2** $5x = 3$ **3** $3y + 1 = 2$ **4** $2b + 11 = 14$

5 $4c - 1 = 2$ **6** $5d + 2 = 5$ **7** $7e + 5 = 11$ **8** $6f + 24 = 29$

9 $4g - 6 = 1$ **10** $18 + 3h = 22$ **11** $6 + 2k = 11$ **12** $0 = 4m - 5$

13 $8 = 5n + 4$ **14** $8 = 6 + 3p$ **15** $8 = 5 + 6q$ **16** $1 = 3r - 4$

17 $2 = 10t - 1$ **18** $12 = 7u + 9$ **19** $5 + 8x = 14$ **20** $12 + 10y = 32 - 5$

21 $\dfrac{2p + 7}{2} = 5$ **22** $\dfrac{3x - 1}{2} = 2$ **23** $\dfrac{2x}{5} - 1 = 4$ **24** $\dfrac{1 + 5y}{2} = 6$

The next examples show that solutions of equations are not always positive.

Example 10

Solve the equation $2y + 15 = 3$

Solution 10

$$2y + 15 = 3$$
$$2y + 15 - 15 = 3 - 15 \qquad \boxed{\text{Subtract 15 from } \textbf{both} \text{ sides.}}$$
$$2y = -12$$
$$2y \div 2 = -12 \div 2 \qquad \boxed{\text{Divide } \textbf{both} \text{ sides by 2}}$$
$$y = -6$$

Check: When $y = -6$, $2 \times (-6) + 15 = 3$ since $-12 + 15 = 3$ ✓

Example 11

Solve the equation $6 - 7x = 11$

Solution 11

$$6 - 7x = 11$$
$$6 - 7x + 7x = 11 + 7x \qquad \boxed{\text{Add } 7x \text{ to } \textbf{both} \text{ sides so that the sign of the term in } x \text{ is positive.}}$$
$$6 = 11 + 7x$$
$$6 - 11 = 11 + 7x - 11 \qquad \boxed{\text{Subtract 11 from } \textbf{both} \text{ sides.}}$$
$$-5 = 7x$$
$$-5 \div 7 = 7x \div 7 \qquad \boxed{\begin{array}{l}\text{Divide } \textbf{both} \text{ sides by 7} \\ \text{Write the answer as a fraction.}\end{array}}$$
$$\frac{-5}{7} = x$$
$$x = -\frac{5}{7}$$

Check: When $x = -\dfrac{5}{7}$, $6 - 7 \times \left(-\dfrac{5}{7}\right) = 11$ since $6 + 5 = 11$ ✓

Exercise 29D

Solve these equations.

1 $4a = -8$ **2** $5b + 6 = 1$ **3** $3c + 8 = 2$ **4** $11 - 2d = 17$

5 $4e + 30 = 2$ **6** $11 = 4f + 27$ **7** $13 = 5h + 18$ **8** $27 = 36 + 3k$

9 $8 = 15 + 2m$ **10** $2n + 12 = 9$ **11** $3p + 5 = 3$ **12** $6q + 20 = 19$

13 $4 - 6r = 13$ **14** $8 + 3t = 0$ **15** $5 - 2u = 36$ **16** $12 = 5x + 20$

17 $20 = 11 - 4y$ **18** $5 + \dfrac{x}{4} = 1$ **19** $\dfrac{1 - y}{4} = 1$ **20** $\dfrac{4p + 9}{2} = 1$

29.3 Setting up equations

Equations can be used to solve problems.

Example 12

Kevin thinks of a number. He doubles the number and then adds 7. His answer is 19
Work out the number that Kevin thinks of.

Solution 12

Let n be the number Kevin is thinking of.

$2n$ Double the number, n; $2 \times n = 2n$

$2n + 7$ Add 7

$2n + 7 = 19$ Form the equation by writing, $2n + 7$ equal to Kevin's answer of 19

$2n = 12$ Solve the equation by subtracting 7 from both sides and dividing both sides by 2

$n = 6$

The number Kevin thinks of is 6

Example 13

All the angles are measured in degrees.

a Write down an expression, in terms of x, for the sum of
the angles of this triangle.

b By forming an equation, work out
  i the value of x,   **ii** the size of the largest angle of this triangle.

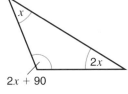

Solution 13

a Sum of the angles $= x + 2x + 90 + 2x$ Add the three angles and collect like terms.

$= 5x + 90$ The sum of the angles of a triangle $= 180°$

b **i** $5x + 90 = 180$

$5x = 90$ Subtract 90 from both sides.

$x = 18$ Divide both sides by 5

  ii Substitute $x = 18$, $2x + 90 = 2 \times 18 + 90 = 126°$ The largest angle is $2x + 90$

Exercise 29E

1 Cath thinks of a number. She multiplies the number by 4 then subtracts 5. Her answer is 27. Work out the number that Cath thinks of.

2 Bill pays 96 pence for a pen and a pencil. The pen costs five times as much as the pencil. The pencil costs x pence.
   a Write down an expression, in terms of x, for the cost of the pen.
   b By forming an equation, work out
      i the value of x **ii** the cost of the pen.

3 All angles are measured in degrees.
   a Write down an expression, in terms of x, for the sum of the angles of this quadrilateral. Simplify your answer.
   The sum of the angles in a quadrilateral is 360°.
   b By forming an equation, work out
      i the value of x
      ii the size of the largest angle of this quadrilateral.

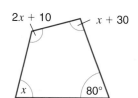

4 Eggs are sold in cartons, each containing y eggs.
   Viv buys 3 of these cartons of eggs.
   One carton has 4 broken eggs in it.
   Viv has now just 23 good eggs.
   How many eggs does each carton contain?

5 The lengths, in centimetres, of the sides of a triangle are $2s + 1$, $3s$ and $5s - 3$
   The perimeter of the triangle is 38 cm.
   Find the length of the smallest side of this triangle.

6 Mansoor is p years of age.
   Mansoor's father is three times as old as Mansoor.
   a Write down an expression, in terms of p, for the age of Mansoor's father.
   In 5 years time Mansoor's father will be 47 years of age.
   b Write down an equation in p, to show this information.
   c Solve your equation to find Mansoor's present age.

7 A bag contains b yellow balls, $3b + 2$ red balls and $b + 8$ blue balls.
   a Write an expression, in terms of b, for the total number of balls in the bag.
   b The total number of balls in the bag is 45.
      i By forming an equation, find the value of b.
      ii How many blue balls are in the bag?
      iii How many more red balls are there than blue balls in the bag?

8 A bag contains red sweets, yellow sweets and green sweets only.
   There are $2t$ red sweets, $4t - 5$ yellow sweets and $14 - 3t$ green sweets.
   There is a total of 21 sweets in a bag.
   a By forming an equation, work out the number of red sweets in the bag.
   b Work out the number of yellow sweets in the bag.

9 Samantha works for x hours each week for 3 weeks.
   In the fourth week she works for an extra 10 hours.
   She works a total of 150 hours during these 4 weeks.
   By forming an equation, work out

   a the value of x

   b the number of hours that Samantha works in the fourth week.

10 Four of the angles in a pentagon are each $(x + 70)°$.
    The fifth angle is $(x + 100)°$.

    a Write down an equation, in terms of x, using this information. Give your answer in
       its simplest form.

    b By solving your equation in part **a**, work out the value of x.

29.4 Solving equations that have brackets

To solve equations that have brackets:

- Step 1: multiply out the brackets
- Step 2: collect any like terms
- Step 3: use the balance method to solve the equation.

Example 14

Solve the equation $2(a + 3) = 18$

Solution 14

$$2(a + 3) = 18$$
$$2a + 6 = 18$$
$$2a + 6 - 6 = 18 - 6$$
$$2a = 12$$
$$2a ÷ 2 = 12 ÷ 2$$
$$a = 6$$

Multiply out the brackets by multiplying the number
outside with each symbol or number inside the brackets.

Use the balance method to solve the equation.

Example 15

Solve the equation $2(2x - 1) + x = 20$

Solution 15

$$2(2x - 1) + x = 20$$
$$4x - 2 + x = 20$$
$$5x - 2 = 20$$
$$5x - 2 + 2 = 20 + 2$$
$$5x = 22$$
$$5x ÷ 5 = 22 ÷ 5$$
$$x = \frac{22}{5} = 4.4$$

Multiply out the brackets.

Collect like terms in x

Use the balance method to solve the equation.

Example 16

Georgina is x years old.
Jessica is 4 years younger than Georgina.

a Write down, in terms of x, an expression for Jessica's age.

Angela is 3 times as old as Jessica.
The sum of the ages of Angela and Georgina is 40

b Work out the ages of Georgina and Jessica.

Solution 16

a Jessica's age is $x - 4$

b Angela's age is $3(x - 4)$ | Multiply Jessica's age by 3

$3(x - 4) + x = 40$ | Form the equation using 'The sum of the ages of Angela and Georgina is 40' Solve the equation

$3x - 12 + x = 40$ | Multiply out the brackets

$4x - 12 = 40$ | Collect like terms in x

$4x = 52$ | Add 12 to both sides.

$x = 13$ | Divide both sides by 4

Georgina's age is 13 | Georgina is 13 years old and Jessica is 9 years old since she is 4 years younger than Georgina.

Jessica's age is $x - 4 = 13 - 4 = 9$

Exercise 29F

Solve these equations.

1 $2(a + 1) = 4$ **2** $3(b + 2) = 15$ **3** $4(c + 3) = 28$

4 $2(d - 1) = 8$ **5** $4(e - 3) = 20$ **6** $5(g - 6) = 20$

7 $2(2h + 1) = 22$ **8** $2(3k + 1) = 26$ **9** $3(4m - 3) = 27$

10 $2(n + 3) = 11$ **11** $4(p + 3) = 18$ **12** $2(2q + 3) = 16$

13 $3(r + 2) = 0$ **14** $3(1 - t) = 6$ **15** $5(1 - 2u) = 35$

16 $12 = 2(4w + 1)$ **17** $20 = 11 + 4(x + 1)$ **18** $4(3y + 2) - 10y = 16$

19 $6(x + 5) + x = 23$ **20** $7 = 2(1 + 6y) - 9y$

21 The width of a rectangle is x cm. The length of the rectangle is 6 cm longer than its width.

     a Write down an expression, in terms of x, for the length of the rectangle.

     The perimeter of the rectangle is 40 cm

     b By forming an equation, work out
         i the value of x **ii** the length of the rectangle.

22 The diagram shows an L-shape.

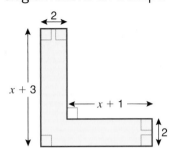

The lengths of the edges are given in centimetres. The area of the shape is 44 cm².

a Write down an equation, in terms of x, using this information.

b By solving your answer to part **a** work out
    i the value of x
    ii the perimeter of the shape.

29.5 Solving equations that have letters on both sides

Example 17

Solve the equation $5d + 1 = 4 - d$

Solution 17

$5d + 1 = 4 - d$	Use the balance method.
$5d + 1 + d = 4 - d + d$	Add d to both sides.
$6d + 1 = 4$	Collect like terms.
$6d = 3$	Subtract 1 from both sides.
$d = 3 \div 6$	Divide both sides by 6
$d = 0.5$	

Example 18

Solve the equation $5(3y + 2) = 13y + 4$

Solution 18

$5(3y + 2) = 13y + 4$	Multiply out the brackets.
$15y + 10 = 13y + 4$	
$2y + 10 = 4$	Subtract $13y$ form both sides.
$2y = 4 - 10$	Subtract 10 from both sides.
$2y = -6$	
$y = -3$	Divide both sides by 2

Example 19

The diagram shows a square and a rectangle.
The lengths of the edges are given in centimetres.
The perimeter of the square is equal to the
perimeter of the rectangle.

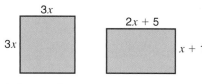

a   Write down an equation, in terms of x, using this information.
b   By solving your equation, work out the area of the square.

Solution 19

a   Perimeter of the square $= 4 \times 3x = 12x$

Perimeter of the rectangle $= 2 \times (2x + 5) + 2 \times (x + 1)$

$$= 4x + 10 + 2x + 2$$

$$= 6x + 12$$

$$12x = 6x + 12 \qquad \boxed{\text{Both perimeters are equal.}}$$

b $\qquad 12x = 6x + 12 \qquad \boxed{\text{Solve the equation.}}$

$\qquad\quad 6x = 12 \qquad \boxed{\text{Subtract } 6x \text{ from both sides.}}$

$\qquad\quad\; x = 2 \qquad \boxed{\text{Divide both sides by 6}}$

The length of each side of the square is $3x$ cm $= 6$ cm $\boxed{\text{Substitute } x = 2 \text{ into } 3x}$
The area of the square $= 6$ cm $\times 6$ cm $= 36$ cm²

Exercise 29G

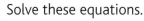

Solve these equations.

1   $3x = 2x + 1$

2   $5y = 2y + 9$

3   $3p = p + 6$

4   $2x = 8 - 2x$

5   $y = 8 - y$

6   $3x = 4 - 2x$

7   $3x + 1 = 2x + 4$

8   $2a + 4 = a + 7$

9   $8x + 4 = 3x + 8$

10   $4(x + 1) = x + 10$

11   $5(c + 3) = 3c + 1$

12   $6(x - 1) = 2x + 8$

13   $3(2d - 1) = 4d - 7$

14   $4(x - 1) = 3(x + 1)$

15   $5(3x - 1) = 7(x + 1)$

16   $2(2g - 5) = 4(1 - g)$

17   $5(2x + 3) = 2(3 - x) + 3$

18   $\dfrac{x}{2} = x - 3$

19   $\dfrac{5y}{2} = y - 6$

20   $4 + \dfrac{3x}{5} = x$

21   The diagram shows an equilateral triangle and
a square.
The lengths of the edges are given in centimetres.
The perimeter of the equilateral triangle is equal
to the perimeter of the square.

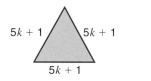

a   Write down an equation, in terms of k, using this information.
b   By solving your equation, work out the area of the square.

22 Brian, Clare and Daniel share a sum of money.
Brian's share is £4w.
Clare's share is £(2w − 1).
Daniel's share is £(8w − 8).
Daniel's share is the same as the sum of Brian's share and Clare's share.

a Write down an equation, in terms of w, using this information.

b Work out, in £, the total sum of money shared by Brian, Clare and Daniel.

23 The diagram shows a rectangle.
Work out the value of x.

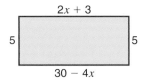

$2x + 3$

5   5

$30 − 4x$

29.6 Inequality signs

In this section these signs are used

● < means less than, for example 3 < 4
● > means greater than , for example 5 > 4
● ≤ means less than or equal to
● ≥ means greater than or equal to.

The number of 20p coins > the number of 50p coins.
The number of 50p coins < the number of 20p coins.

Four coins are chosen from these coins.

The number of 50p coins that can be chosen ≤ 2
The number of 20p coins that can be chosen ≤ 4

The number of 20p coins that can be chosen ≥ 2
The number of 50p coins that can be chosen ≥ 0

Exercise 29H

Copy these statements and state whether each of them is TRUE or FALSE.

1 7 > 4

2 3 > 5

3 6 < 4

4 5 > 3

5 4 > 6

6 4 ≥ 2

7 1 ≥ 1

8 0 ≤ 4

9 3 ≤ 3

10 $7 ≤ 6\frac{1}{2}$

11 1 + 3 ≤ 6

12 7 ≤ 4 + 5

13 3 ≥ 6 − 2

14 $−2 > −3 + \frac{1}{4}$

15 −2 > −1

16 5 + 2 ≥ 7

17 15 − 7 ≥ 8.5

18 5.5 − 7 ≤ −5 + 4

19 3 − 7 < −5 + 1

20 3 − 7 ≥ −5 + 1

29.7 Inequalities on a number line

The inequality $x > 1$ is shown on a number line.
The open circle shows that $x = 1$ is not included.

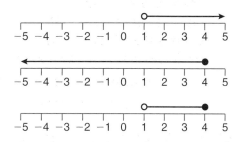

The inequality $x \leqslant 4$ is shown on a number line.
The filled circle shows that $x = 4$ is included.

This number line shows the values of x which
satisfy **both** $x > 1$ and $x \leqslant 4$
We write this as $1 < x \leqslant 4$

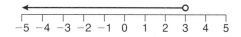

Example 20

Write down the inequality shown on the number line.

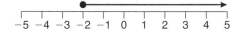

Solution 20
$x < 3$

Example 21

Show the inequality $x \geqslant -2$ on a
number line.

Solution 21

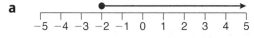

Example 22

Write down the inequality shown on the
number line.

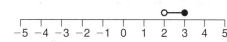

Solution 22
$0 < x \leqslant 4$

Exercise 29I

1 Write down the inequality shown on the number line:

a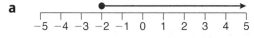

b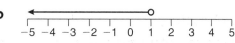

c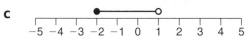

d

e

f

Answer questions **2** to **4** on the resource sheet.

2 On a number line, show the inequality

  a $x > 2$ **b** $x < 5$ **c** $x \geqslant 0$ **d** $x \leqslant -1$

3 Show on a number line the values of x which satisfy **both** these inequalities.

  a $x > 1$ and $x < 3$ **b** $x > -1$ and $x \leqslant 0$ **c** $x \geqslant -4$ and $x \leqslant -1$

4 On a number line, show the inequality

  a $-1 < x \leqslant 3$ **b** $-4 \leqslant x < 0$ **c** $-5 < x \leqslant -2$

29.8 Solving inequalities

Inequalities can be solved in a similar way to equations. The inequality sign must be kept throughout and the solution is an inequality with the letter on its own.

Example 23

Solve the inequality $2x - 1 < 7$

Solution 23

$$2x - 1 < 7$$
$$2x - 1 + 1 < 7 + 1 \qquad \boxed{\text{Add 1 to both sides}}$$
$$2x < 8$$
$$x < 4 \qquad \boxed{\text{Divide both sides by 2}}$$

Example 24

a   Solve the inequality $5x + 3 \leqslant x + 9$

b   Show your solution on a number line.

Solution 24

a
$$5x + 3 \leqslant x + 9$$
$$5x + 3 - x \leqslant x + 9 - x \qquad \boxed{\text{Subtract } x \text{ from both sides}}$$
$$4x + 3 \leqslant 9$$
$$4x \leqslant 6 \qquad \boxed{\text{Subtract 3 from both sides}}$$
$$x \leqslant 1.5 \qquad \boxed{\text{Divide both sides by 4 } (6 \div 4 = 1.5)}$$

b

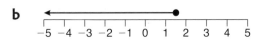

Exercise 29J

1   Solve these inequalities.

    a $x + 1 < 5$ **b** $x - 2 > 7$ **c** $2x < 8$

    d $3x \geqslant 6$ **e** $4x \leqslant 3$

2   Solve these inequalities.

    a $2x + 1 < 9$ **b** $3x - 1 > 8$ **c** $4x + 3 < 15$

    d $5x + 12 \geqslant 2$ **e** $6x - 3 \leqslant 0$

3   **a**   Solve the inequality $10x + 1 > 16$.

    b   Show your solution on a number line.

4   Solve these inequalities.

    a $3x < 2x + 10$ **b** $5x > x + 12$ **c** $4x \leqslant x - 6$

    d $7x \geqslant 2x + 35$ **e** $9x \geqslant 5x - 18$

5 a Solve the inequality $3x \leqslant 2 - x$

b Show your solution on a number line.

6 Solve the inequality $5x + 7 \leqslant 19 - x$.

29.9 Integer solutions to inequalities

The inequality $-4 < x \leqslant 2$ is shown on the number line below.

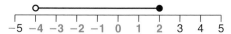

$$-5 \quad -4 \quad -3 \quad -2 \quad -1 \quad 0 \quad 1 \quad 2 \quad 3 \quad 4 \quad 5$$

Integers are whole numbers. They can be positive or negative or zero.

So the integer values which satisfy the inequality $-4 < x \leqslant 2$ are $-3, -2, -1, 0, 1$ and 2

Example 25

$-5 < y < 3$
y is an integer.

Write down all the possible values of y.

Solution 25
$-4, -3, -2, -1, 0, 1$ and 2

Example 26

$2p + 1 < 12$
p is a positive integer.
Write down all the possible values of p.

Solution 26
$$2p + 1 < 12$$
$$2p + 1 - 1 < 12 - 1$$
$$2p < 11$$
$$p < 5.5$$

p is a **positive** integer so the possible values of p are $1, 2, 3, 4$ and 5

Example 27

$-4 < 2n \leqslant 3$
n is an integer.
Find all the possible values of n.

Solution 27

$-4 < 2n \leqslant 3$	Split $-4 < 2n \leqslant 3$	
$-4 < 2n$ AND $2n \leqslant 3$	Solve both inequalities	
$-2 < n$ AND $n \leqslant 1.5$	Combine both the inequalities	
$-2 < n \leqslant 1.5$	Write down the integer values satisfying $-2 < n \leqslant 1.5$	

The possible values of n are $-1, 0$ and 1

Exercise 29K

1   **a**   Show the inequality $1 \leqslant x \leqslant 4$ on a number line.

    b   If x is an integer, use your number line to write down all the possible values of x.

2   **a**   Show the inequality $2 \leqslant y \leqslant 4$ on a number line.

    b   If y is an integer, use your number line to write down all the possible values of y.

3   **a**   Show the inequality $-4 < n < -1$ on a number line.

    b   If n is an integer, use your number line to write down all the possible values of n.

4   **a**   Show the inequality $-3 \leqslant p < 2$ on a number line.

    b   If p is an integer, use your number line to write down all the possible values of p.

5   $-1 < x \leqslant 3$
    x is an integer. Write down all the possible values of x.

6   $-8 < y < -5$
    y is an integer. Write down all the possible values of y.

7   $0 \leqslant p < 7$
    p is an integer. Write down all the possible values of p.

8   $-6 < 2x < 4$
    x is an integer. Write down all the possible values of x.

9   $-3 < 2q \leqslant 8$
    q is an integer. Write down all the possible values of q.

10 $-3 < 2r < 9$
    r is an integer. Write down all the possible values of r.

11 $-5 < 3m \leqslant 9$
    m is an integer. Write down all the possible values of m.

12 $-6 < 5x < 7$
    x is an integer. Write down all the possible values of x.

13 $-3 < 4w \leqslant 13$
    w is an integer. Write down all the possible values of w.

14 $-4 < x + 2 \leqslant 6$
    x is an integer. Write down all the possible values of x.

15 $-3 < x - 1 \leqslant 5$
    x is an integer. Write down all the possible values of x.

16 $2p \leqslant 9$
    p is a positive integer. Write down all the possible values of p.

17 $5q - 1 < 19$
    q is a positive integer. Write down all the possible values of q.

18 $2x + 10 > 1$
    x is a negative integer. Write down all the possible values of x.

Chapter summary

You should now know how to:

★ **Solve an equation** by finding the value of the unknown symbol or letter that makes the equation true. For example $x = 2$ is the solution of the equation $x + 3 = 5$

★ Solve equations by doing the same to the right-hand side of the equation as to the left-hand side of the equation – this is called the **balance method**

★ Solve equations which have brackets by multiplying out the brackets, collecting any like terms and then using the balance method.

You should also know that:

★ The **signs** used for **inequalities** are $<$, $>$, $\leqslant$ and $\geqslant$
   $<$ means less than $>$ means greater than
   $\leqslant$ means less than or equal to $\geqslant$ means greater than or equal to.

★ To **show an inequality** on a number line, you use a ($\circ$) together with a line for $<$ and $>$, and use a ($\bullet$) together with a line for $\leqslant$ and $\geqslant$. For example $x > 1$ is shown as

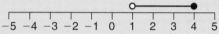

and $1 < x \leqslant 4$ is shown as

★ Inequalities can be solved in a similar way to equations. The inequality sign must be kept throughout and the solution is an inequality with the letters on its own.

★ To find **integer solutions** to inequalities a number line can be used. The integer solutions to the inequality $-2 < p \leqslant 1$ are $-1, 0$ and 1

Chapter 29 review questions

1 **a** Solve $2x = 8$ **b** Solve $y - 3 = 9$

2 **a** Solve $3y + 2 = 17$ **b** Solve $\dfrac{x}{3} = 5$

3 $-6 < y < -3$
     y is an integer.
     Write down all the possible values of y.

4 Solve
     a $2x + 9 = 4x + 6$ **b** $5(x - 2) = 20$ **c** $21 = 3(2x + 11)$

5 Solve $5x + 3 > 19$

(1388 March 2005)

6 **a** Solve $6(2x + 3) = 2(4x + 7)$ **b** Solve $\dfrac{x}{4} + 2 = 7$

     c Solve $\dfrac{3x}{5} = x - 3$

7 $5p \leq 17$

p is a **positive** integer. Write down all the possible values of p.

8 The diagram shows the lengths, in centimetres, of each side of the rectangle.

a Work out the value of x.

The perimeter of the rectangle is P cm.

b Work out the value of P.

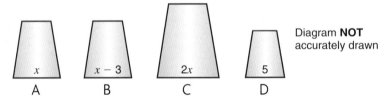

9 Solve $5(x - 2) = 8 - 7x$

10 **a** Solve the inequality $3x \leq 7 - x$

b Show your answer to part **a** on a number line.

11 These four blocks, A, B, C and D have a total mass of 62 grams.
The mass, in grams, of each block is shown on the diagram.

Diagram **NOT** accurately drawn

A x B $x - 3$ C $2x$ D   5

i Express this information as an equation in terms of x.

ii Solve your equation and write down the masses of blocks A, B and C.

(1385 November 2001)

12 $-5 < 2m \leq 9$

m is an integer. Write down all the possible values of m.

13 Fred is x years old. His sister, Mary, is 4 years older than Fred.

a   **i** Write down an expression, in terms of x, for Mary's age.

Sarfraz is twice as old as Fred.

     ii Write down an expression, in terms of x, for the total of Fred's age, Mary's age and Sarfraz's age.

The total of Fred's age, Mary's age and Sarfraz's age is 64 years.

b Form an equation and solve it to find Fred's age.

14 $3x + 20 > 3$

x is a **negative** integer. Write down all the possible values of x.

15 $ABCD$ is a quadrilateral.
Work out the size of the largest angle in the quadrilateral.

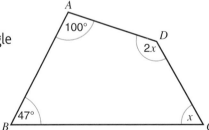

(1387 June 2004)

16 $2 < 6y + 19$

y is a **negative** integer.

Write down all the possible values of y.

17 The diagram represents a garden in the shape of a rectangle.

All measurements are given in metres.

The garden has a flowerbed in one corner.

The flowerbed is a square of side x.

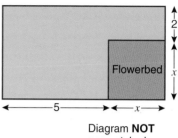

a Write down an expression, in terms of x, for the shortest side of the garden.

Diagram **NOT** accurately drawn

b Find an expression, in terms of x, for the perimeter of the garden. Give your answer in its simplest form.

The perimeter of the garden is 20 metres.

c Find the value of x.

(1387 June 2003)

18 **a** Solve the inequality $4x - 3 < 7$.

An inequality is shown on the number line.

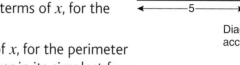

b Write down the inequality.

19 $ABCDE$ is a pentagon.

Work out the size of the largest angle of the pentagon.

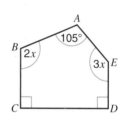

20 The diagram shows the lengths, in centimetres, of each side of an isosceles triangle.

a Work out the value of x.

The perimeter of the triangle is P cm.

b Work out the value of P.

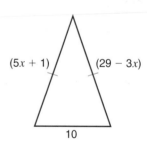

Formulae

A **formula** is a way of describing a fact or a rule. A formula can be written in words or using algebraic expressions.

30.1 Using a word formula

> **distance = average speed × time**

This is a **word formula** which can be used to work out the distance travelled when the average speed and time of a journey are known. It is sometimes called a rule.

For example, a car has an average speed of 50 km/h and travels for 3 hours. The word formula can be used to work out the distance travelled.

The value for the average speed and the value for the time are **substituted** into the word formula and the answer is then calculated, giving

> **distance = 50 × 3 = 150 km**

So the distance travelled by the car is 150 km.

Example 1

Melissa is cooking a turkey. She uses the following rule to work out, in minutes, the cooking time:

> **cooking time = weight of turkey, in kg × 40 + 30**

Work out the cooking time for Melissa to cook a turkey of weight 3 kg.

Solution 1
Substituting the weight of the turkey into the rule (or word formula) gives

cooking time = 3 × 40 + 30
= 150 minutes.

Example 2

Here is a formula for working out how much it costs to do some printing:

| printing cost | = | cost of one sheet of paper | × | number of sheets of paper | + | fixed charge |

The cost of one sheet of paper is £0.05
2000 sheets of paper are used.
The fixed charge is £40

Work out the printing cost.

Solution 2

Substituting into the formula gives

$$\text{printing cost} = £0.05 \times 2000 + £40$$
$$= £100 + £40$$
$$= £140$$

Exercise 30A

1 Packets of crisps cost 40p each.
Use the rule

> **cost = number of packets of crisps × 40**

to work out the cost of 5 packets of crisps.

2 Sunita works for 20 hours at a rate of pay of £6 an hour. The rule is

> **pay = rate of pay × hours worked.**

Use this rule to work out Sunita's pay.

3 Use the formula

> **distance = average speed × time**

to work out
  a the distance travelled by a bicycle travelling for 2 hours at an average speed of 18 km per hour
  b the distance travelled by a car moving at an average speed of 100 km per hour for 1.5 hours.

4 To work out the area of a rectangle, in cm², Marc uses the formula

> **area = length in cm × width in cm.**

Using this formula, work out the area of a rectangle of length 8 cm and width 3 cm.

5 This formula gives the number of heat units a plant gains in a day

> **number of heat units = (highest temperature + lowest temperature) ÷ 2 − 10.**

On Friday, the highest temperature was 19°C and the lowest temperature was 11°C. Use this formula to work out the number of heat units that a plant gained on Friday.

6 A sum of money is shared equally between three friends.
A rule to work out the amount of money, in £, that each friend gets is

> **amount = sum of money ÷ 3.**

Use this rule to work out the amount of money each friend gets when the sum of money is £12.60

7   The total cost of cartons of milk is given by the formula

> **total cost = price for one carton of milk × number of cartons**

The price of one carton of milk is £1.30
Use this formula to work out
   a   the total cost of 8 cartons of milk   **b**   the total cost of 20 cartons of milk.

8   The cost of using gas is given by the formula

> **cost of using gas = number of units used × cost of one unit + fixed charge**

The cost of one unit of gas is £0.60 and the fixed charge is £28
Bill uses 480 units of gas.
Use this formula to work out the cost, in £, of the gas used by Bill.

30.2 Writing a word formula

Example 3

Daniel buys some chocolate bars at 30p each.
Write down a word formula that Daniel could use to work out the total cost of the chocolate bars that he buys.

Solution 3
Total cost, in pence = number of chocolate bars × 30

Example 4

Helen is paid a rate of pay for each hour she works. In addition she is paid a bonus.
a   Write down a word formula that can be used to work out Helen's total pay.
Helen works for 35 hours at a rate of pay of £8 for each hour and is paid a bonus of £20
b   Use your formula to work out Helen's total pay.

Solution 4
a   Total pay = rate of pay × number of hours worked + bonus.
b   Total pay = £8 × 35 + £20
                  = £280 + £20 = £300

Exercise 30B

1   Georgina buys some packets of crisps at 42p each. Write down a word formula that Georgina can use to work out the total cost of the crisps.

2   Hawksworth Rovers play football matches. 3 points are awarded for each win. Write down a word formula that can be used to work out the total number of points that Hawksworth Rovers are awarded for the matches they win.

3 Jo is paid a rate of pay for each hour that she works. Write down a word formula that Jo can use to work out her total pay.

4 The chocolates in a box are shared equally between four people. Write down a word formula that can be used to work out the number of chocolates that each person gets.

5 A taxi driver charges a fixed charge plus a rate of £1.50 for each mile of a journey. Write down a word formula that can be used to work out the total cost of a journey in this taxi.

6 Jessica buys some sweets costing 3p each.
   a Write down a word formula that could be used to work out the total cost of the sweets.
   b If Jessica buys five sweets, use your formula to work out the total cost of the sweets.

7 Karim sells computers. He is paid a bonus of £5 for each computer that he sells.
   a Write down a word formula which could be used to work out Karim's total bonus.
   b Use your formula to work out Karim's total bonus when he sells 8 computers.

8 Alec pays a fixed charge of £12 each month for his mobile phone. In addition, calls are charged at 8 p for each minute that he uses his phone.
   a Write down a word formula which could be used to work out Alec's phone bill.

   In May, Alec uses his mobile phone for 140 minutes.
   b Use your formula to work out Alec's phone bill in May.

9 Boxes of screws cost £1.20 each. Bags of nails cost £1.10 each.
   Peter buys some boxes of screws and some bags of nails.
   a Write down a word formula that Peter could use to work out the total cost of the screws and the nails.

   Peter buys three boxes of screws and four bags of nails.
   b Use your formula to work out the total cost of the screws and the nails that Peter buys.

10 In a chess competition, 2 points are awarded for a win, 1 point is awarded for a draw and no points are awarded for a loss.
   a Write down a word formula which could be used to work out the total number of points that are awarded.

   Trevor plays 10 games of chess. He wins 5 games, draws 3 games and loses 2 games.
   b Use your formula to work out the total number of points that Trevor is awarded.

30.3 Using an algebraic formula

In Section 12.3 the area of a rectangle was found using the word formula

area = length × width

If the letter l represents the length of a rectangle and the letter w represents the width of the rectangle, the area (A) of the rectangle can be found using the formula

$$A = lw$$

This is called an **algebraic formula**.

A appears on its own and only on the left-hand side of the formula.

A is called the **subject of the formula**, and lw is the expression used to work out the value of this subject.

Example 5

Use the formula

$$A = lw$$

to work out the area (A) of a rectangle, when $l = 5$ cm and $w = 3$ cm.

Solution 5

Substituting the values of l and w into the formula $A = lw$, gives

$$A = 5 \times 3$$
$$= 15 \text{ cm}^2$$

Example 6

A box of chocolates contains p plain chocolates and q milk chocolates only.
The formula $T = p + q$ is used to work out the total number (T) of chocolates in the box.
Work out the value of T when $p = 12$ and $q = 16$

Solution 6

$$T = 12 + 16 = 28$$

Example 7

$$P = ma + F$$

Use this formula to work out the value of P

a   when $m = 4$, $a = 10$ and $F = 15$ **b**   when $m = 3$, $a = -2$ and $F = 8$

Solution 7

a $P = ma + F$
$$= 4 \times 10 + 15$$
$$= 40 + 15$$
$$= 55$$

b $P = ma + F$
$$= 3 \times -2 + 8$$
$$= -6 + 8$$
$$= 2$$

Exercise 30C

1 Sunita's pay is worked out using the formula

$P = rh$

$P =$ pay, $r =$ rate of pay for each hour worked and $h =$ number of hours worked. Use this formula to work out Sunita's pay when she works for 5 hours at a rate of £8 an hour.

2 $T = c + d$

    a $c = 12, d = 9$ **b** $c = 10, d = -6$

       Work out the value of T.   Work out the value of T.

3 The formula $m = \dfrac{y - c}{x}$ can be used to work out the gradient of a straight line.

    a Use this formula to work out the value of m when $x = 2, y = 11$ and $c = 4$

    b Use this formula to work out the value of m when $x = 3, y = 1$ and $c = 10$

4 The formula $v = u + at$ is used to work out velocity, v.
Use this formula to work out the value of v when

    a $u = 5, a = 10$ and $t = 3$ **b** $u = 4, a = -5$ and $t = 2$

    c $u = -20, a = -2$ and $t = 8$

5 Robert wishes to change degrees Celsius (C) to degrees Fahrenheit (F).
He uses the formula $F = \frac{9}{5}C + 32$
Use this formula to find the value of F when

    a $C = 30$ **b** $C = 0$ **c** $C = -40$

6 The cooking time, T minutes, to cook a joint of meat is given by the formula

$T = 20w + 30$

where w kg is the weight of the joint of meat.
Use this formula to work out the cooking time when

    a $w = 4$ **b** $w = 2.5$

7 The formula $d = st$ is used to work out the distance d travelled, when the time taken is t and the average speed is s.
Use this formula to work out the value of d

    a when $s = 30$ and $t = 2$ **b** when $s = 5.5$ and $t = 6$

    c when $s = 20$ and $t = 3.4$

8 A formula to find the area, A, of a trapezium is $A = \frac{1}{2}(a + b)h$

    a Use this formula to work out the value of A when $a = 5, b = 11$ and $h = 3$

    b Use this formula to work out the value of A when $a = 3.6, b = 7.4$ and $h = 4$

30.4 Writing an algebraic formula

The diagram shows a rectangle.
a = the length of the rectangle.
b = the width of the rectangle.
The perimeter of a shape is the total distance around the edges of the shape.

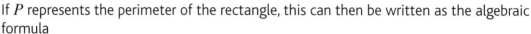

The perimeter of the rectangle $= a + b + a + b$
Collecting the like terms together gives the
perimeter $= 2a + 2b$
If P represents the perimeter of the rectangle, this can then be written as the algebraic formula

$$P = 2a + 2b$$

When writing an algebraic formula it is important to define what each letter stands for.

Example 8

In some football matches 3 points are awarded for a win, 1 point is awarded for a draw and no points are awarded for a loss.

Write down an algebraic formula that can be used to work out the total points awarded to a football team. You must define the letters used.

Solution 8
Let P = the total number of points awarded to each team.
Let w = the number of matches won.
Let d = the number of matches drawn.

The number of points awarded for wins $= 3 \times$ the number of matches won $= 3 \times w = 3w$
The number of points awarded for draws $= 1 \times$ the number of matches drawn $= 1 \times d = d$

The formula for the total number of points awarded to each team is $P = 3w + d$

Exercise 30D

1 A florist sells t tulips at 40 p each and d daffodils at 30 p each. If C is the total cost, in pence, of the flowers sold, write down, in terms of t and d, a formula for C.

2 A shop sells eating apples and baking apples.
Write down an algebraic formula that can be used to work out the total number of apples that the shop sells each day. You must define the letters used.

3 Dan hires a car for his holidays. He pays a fixed charge of £75 plus £30 for each day that he has the car.

    a Write down a formula that Dan can use to work out the total cost to hire the car. You must define the letters used.

    b Use your formula to work out the cost of hiring this car for 7 days.

4   a   Write down a formula that can be used to work out the perimeter of an equilateral triangle. You must define the letters used.

    b   Use your formula to work out the perimeter of an equilateral triangle of side 5 m.

5   Andrew earns p pounds per hour. He works for t hours. He earns a bonus of b pounds.

    a   Write down a formula for the total amount he earns, T pounds.

    b   Use your formula to work out the value of T when $p = 5$, $t = 38$ and $b = 20$

6   A box of nails costs £1.50. A box of screws costs £2
   Bob buys n boxes of nails and s boxes of screws. The total cost is C pounds.

    a   Write a formula for C in terms of n and s.

    b   Work out the value of C when $n = 4$ and $s = 3$

7   Jean sits a mathematics exam, an English exam and a science exam. Her mean mark is x%.
   Write down a formula that can be used to work out the value of x. You must define the letters used.

8   A bus can seat p passengers, and eight more passengers are allowed to stand.

    a   Write down a formula that can be used to work out the total number, T, of passengers that can travel on b buses.

   Six identical buses, each seating 60 passengers, take supporters to a football match.

    b   Use your formula to work out the total number of passengers when each bus is full.

30.5 Using a formula inversely

In using algebraic formulae so far, information has been given so that the subject of each formula can be worked out.

An algebraic formula can also be used to work out the value of a letter other than the subject. To do this the balance method, described in Section 29.2, is often used.

Example 9

Use the formula $A = lw$ to work out the value of w when $A = 24$ and $l = 8$.

Solution 9

$A = l \times w$

Substituting $A = 24$ and $l = 8$ into the formula gives

$24 = 8 \times w$

Using the balance method,

$24 \div 8 = 8 \times w \div 8$ | Divide both sides by 8 |

    $w = 3$

Example 10

$v = u + at$

a Work out the value of t when $v = 24$, $u = 10$ and $a = 7$
b Work out the value of u when $v = 15$, $a = -10$ and $t = 3$.

Solution 10

$v = u + at$

a Substituting $v = 24$, $u = 10$ and $a = 7$ into the formula gives

$$24 = 10 + 7t$$
$$24 - 10 = 10 + 7t - 10 \qquad \boxed{\text{Subtract 10 from both sides.}}$$
$$14 = 7t$$
$$14 \div 7 = 7t \div 7 \qquad \boxed{\text{Divide both sides by 7}}$$
$$t = 2$$

b Substituting $v = 15$, $a = -10$ and $t = 3$ into the formula gives

$$15 = u + (-10) \times 3$$
$$15 = u - 30$$
$$15 + 30 = u - 30 + 30 \qquad \boxed{\text{Add 30 to both sides.}}$$
$$u = 45$$

Exercise 30E

1 $T = p + q$
    a Work out the value of p when $T = 20$ and $q = 7$
    b Work out the value of p when $T = 12$ and $q = -5$

2 $V = IR$ is a formula used in physics.
    a Work out the value of I when $V = 20$ and $R = 2$
    b Work out the value of R when $V = 10$ and $I = 4$

3 $P = 2a + 2b$ is a formula used to work out the perimeter P, of a rectangle of length a and width b.
    a If $P = 18$ and $b = 4$ Work out the value of a.
    b If $P = 7$ and $a = 2$ Work out the value of b.

4 $v = u + at$
    a $v = 15$, $a = 3$ and $t = 4$ Work out the value of u.
    b $v = 20$, $u = 60$ and $a = -10$ Work out the value of t.
    c Work out the value of a when $v = 6$, $u = 12$ and $t = 2$

5 $y = mx + c$
    a Work out the value of c when $y = 5$, $m = 3$ and $x = 2$
    b Work out the value of m when $y = 3$, $x = 2$ and $c = -4$
    c Work out the value of x when $y = 1$, $m = -4$ and $c = 3$

6   The cooking time, T minutes, to cook a joint of meat is given by the formula

$T = 20w + 30$

where w kg is the weight of the joint of meat.

a   The cooking time for a joint of meat is 90 minutes. Work out the weight, in kg, of this joint of meat.

b   Explain why a cooking time of 25 minutes is not possible.

7 $P = \dfrac{s(t-1)}{3}$

a   Work out the value of s when $P = 8$ and $t = 7$

b   Work out the value of t when $P = 1$ and $s = 6$

c   Work out the value of s when $P = 4$ and $t = -5$

30.6 Changing the subject of a formula

p is the subject of the formula

$p = 2q + 3$

> The subject of the formula appears just once and only on the left-hand side of the formula.

The formula can be rearranged using the balance method, as follows

$$p - 3 = 2q + 3 - 3$$ Subtract 3 from both sides.

$$p - 3 = 2q$$

$$\frac{p-3}{2} = \frac{2q}{2}$$ Divide **both** sides by 2

$$\frac{p-3}{2} = q$$

This is written as $q = \dfrac{p-3}{2}$

The subject of the formula $p = 2q + 3$ has now been changed to make q the subject of the formula.

Example 11

Make R the subject of the formula $V = IR$.

Solution 11

$V = IR$

$\dfrac{V}{I} = \dfrac{IR}{I}$ Divide both sides by I.

$R = \dfrac{V}{I}$

Example 12

The formula $P = 2(a + b)$ can be used to work out the perimeter, P, of a rectangle of length a and width b.

Make b the subject of the formula.

Solution 12

$P = 2(a + b)$

Multiplying out the brackets first gives

$$P = 2a + 2b$$
$$P - 2a = 2a + 2b - 2a$$
$$P - 2a = 2b$$
$$\frac{P - 2a}{2} = \frac{2b}{2}$$
$$b = \frac{P - 2a}{2}$$

Example 13

Rearrange the formula $W = ut + at^2$ to make u the subject.

Solution 13

$$W = ut + at^2$$
$$W - at^2 = ut + at^2 - at^2$$
$$W - at^2 = ut$$
$$\frac{W - at^2}{t} = \frac{ut}{t}$$
$$u = \frac{W - at^2}{t}$$

Example 14

Make x the subject of the formula $y = 3 - 4x$.

Solution 14

$$y = 3 - 4x$$
$$y + 4x = 3 - 4x + 4x$$
$$y + 4x = 3$$
$$y + 4x - y = 3 - y$$
$$4x = 3 - y$$
$$\frac{4x}{4} = \frac{3 - y}{4}$$
$$x = \frac{3 - y}{4}$$

Exercise 30F

1 Make x the subject of the formula

   a $y = x + 7$ **b** $y = 4x$ **c** $y = 2x + 1$

   d $y = 3x - 5$ **e** $y = 1 - x$ **f** $y = 6 - 2x$

2 Make w the subject of the formula $A = lw$.

3 Make t the subject of the formula $s = 5t + 2u$.

4   Make m the subject of the formula $W = 3n - 2m$.

5   A formula to find velocity is given by $v = u + at$.
Rearrange this formula to make
  a u the subject of the formula
  b a the subject of the formula
  c t the subject of the formula

6   Make P the subject of the formula
  a $D = 3(P + Q)$ **b** $D = 4(2P - 3Q)$ **c** $D = 2(5Q - P)$

7   Make a the subject of the formula $c = \dfrac{a - b}{3}$.

8   Make f the subject of the formula $g = \dfrac{e + 3f}{2}$.

30.7 Expressions, identities, equations and formulae

We know from Section 11.2 that $3x - 6$ is called an **expression**.

The expression $3x - 6$ can be factorised to give $3x - 6 = 3(x - 2)$.
$3x - 6 = 3(x - 2)$ is called an **identity** because the left-hand side, $3x - 6$, says the same as the right-hand side, $3(x - 2)$. Another example of an identity is $5x = x + 4x$.

From Section 29.1, we know that $3x - 6 = 0$ is called an **equation**, which can be solved to find the value of x.

$P = 3x - 6$ is called a **formula**. The value of P can be worked out if the value of x is known. A formula has at least two letters.

Exercise 30G

1   Write down whether each of the following is an *expression*, or an *identity*, or an *equation*, or a *formula*.

  a $4x = x + x + x + x$ **b** $y = Ax$
  c $3m + 2m = 5m$ **d** $y - 3 = 2$
  e $5s + t$ **f** $A = \dfrac{bh}{2}$
  g $p + q = 3$ **h** $p^3 + q^2$
  i $C = 3r - 2s$ **j** $6(y + 4) = 6y + 24$
  k $\dfrac{x}{3} = 4$ **l** $y = mx + c$
  m $c + c + d + d + d = 2c + 3d$ **n** $q^2 + q - 3 = 0$

  o $7r^2 + 3s$

2 Here is a mixture of some terms and some signs.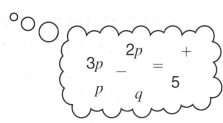

Using these, but not necessarily all of them, write down an example of

a an expression   **b** an identity

c an equation   **d** a formula

$$3p \quad \begin{array}{c} 2p \\ - \end{array} \quad \begin{array}{c} + \\ = \\ 5 \end{array}$$

$$p \qquad q$$

Chapter summary

You should now know:

★ That a **formula** can be written in words, or written using algebraic expressions to describe a rule or a relationship. For example area = length × width is a **word formula** to find the area of a rectangle. This can also be written as an **algebraic formula**, $A = lw$, where A = area, l = length and w = width

★ That in a formula, for example $A = lw$, A is called the **subject** of the formula

★ The meanings of **expression**, **identity**, **equation** and **formula**.

You should also be able to:

★ Find the value of the **subject** of a formula by **substituting** given values for the letters on the right-hand side

★ Find the value of a letter, in a formula, that is not the subject of the formula by substituting known values into the formula and solving the equation formed

★ **Change the subject** of a formula by rearranging the terms in the formula.

Chapter 30 review questions

1 Tanya picks strawberries to earn some money.
She puts the strawberries in baskets.

This formula can be used to work out her pay.

> Pay = £15 per day + £2 for each full basket.

Tanya worked all day on Monday.
She filled 12 baskets with strawberries.

Work out Tanya's pay on Monday.

(1388 March 2004)

2 You can use this rule to work out the cost of a taxi journey:

cost of taxi journey = cost per kilometre × number of kilometres.

The cost per kilometre of a taxi journey is 40 pence.
Use the rule to work out the cost of a taxi journey of 12 km.

3 The cost, in pounds, of hiring a car can be worked out using this rule.

> Add 3 to the number of days' hire
>
> Multiply your answer by 10

a Work out the cost of hiring a car for 4 days.

Bishen hired a car. The cost was £120

b Work out the number of days for which Bishen hired the car.

The cost of hiring a car for n days is C pounds.

c Write down a formula for C in terms of n.

(1388 June 2005)

4 John tries to hit some tins at a fair.
He is given 6 balls to do this.
He scores 5 points for each hit and loses 3 points for each miss.

a Write down a word formula that can be used to work out the total number of points scored.

John has 4 hits and 2 misses.

b Use your formula to work out the total number of points scored by John.

5 A bicycle has 2 wheels.
A tricycle has 3 wheels.
In a shop there are x bicycles and y tricycles.
The total number of wheels on the bicycles and the tricycles in the shop is given by W.
Write down a formula for W in terms of x and y.

6 Here are some patterns made with crosses.

```
   ×              × ×            × × ×           × × × ×
  × ×            × × ×          × × × ×         × × × × ×
  × ×            × × ×          × × × ×         × × × × ×
Pattern Number 1   Pattern Number 2   Pattern Number 3   Pattern Number 4
```

a Draw Pattern Number 5.

b Copy and complete the table for Pattern Number 5 and Pattern Number 6

Pattern Number (n)	1	2	3	4	5	6
Number of crosses (C)	5	8	11	14		

c Work out the Pattern Number that has 26 crosses.

d Work out the number of crosses in Pattern Number 10

e Write down a formula for the number of crosses, C, in terms of the Pattern Number, n.

(1385 May 2002)

7 Copy and complete the table by writing either **expression** or **equation** or **identity** or **formula** in each space.
The first has been done for you.

$A = \frac{1}{2}bh$	*formula*
$x^2 + 5 = 86$	
$7m + 5n$	
$3p + 2q = p + p + p + q + q$	

(1388 March 2005)

8 $V = 2r + 3t$
Work out the value of r when $V = 20$ and $t = 2$

9 $D = 3s - 7t$
Work out the value of D when $s = -4$ and $t = 2$

10 $M = \dfrac{Q(P + 2)}{6}$
Work out the value of M when $P = -4$ and $Q = 30$

11 A shop sells televisions on credit.
The weekly payment is w pounds.
The total amount paid, C pounds, is given by the formula $C = 10w + 45$
The total amount paid for a particular television is £370
Calculate the weekly payment for the television.

12 A ruler costs 45 pence. A pen costs 30 pence.
Louisa buys x rulers and y pens. The total cost is C pence.
  a Write a formula for C in terms of x and y.
  b Work out the value of y when $C = 240$ and $x = 2$

13 The formula gives the number of Heat Units a plant gains in a day.

$$\text{Number of Heat Units} = \left(\frac{\text{highest temperature} + \text{lowest temperature}}{2} \right) - 10$$

On Monday, the highest temperature was 29 °C and the lowest temperature was 19 °C.
  a Work out the number of Heat Units the plant gained on Monday.

On Tuesday, the highest temperature was 26 °C and the number of Heat Units the plant gained was 11.
  b Work out the lowest temperature on Tuesday.

(1387 November 2003)

14 Make g the subject of the formula $m = 4g - 3$

15 Make k the subject of the formula $p = 9k + n$

16 Jo uses the formula $F = \frac{9}{5}C + 32$ to change degrees Celsius (C) to degrees Fahrenheit (F).

   a Use this formula to find

      i the value of F when $C = 40$

      ii the value of C when $F = 50$

   b Rearrange the formula to make C the subject of the formula.

17 The fraction, p, of an adult's dose of medicine which should be given to a child who weighs w kg is given by the formula

$$p = \frac{3w + 20}{200}$$

A child weighs 35 kg.

   a Work out the fraction of an adult's dose which should be given to this child. Give your answer as a fraction in its simplest form.

   b Use the formula $p = \dfrac{3w + 20}{200}$ to find the weight of a child whose dose is the same as an adult's dose.

(1385 June 2002)

The circle
The cylinder

31.1 Circumference of a circle

The **circumference** is the special name of the perimeter of a circle, that is, the distance all around it.

Measure the circumference and diameter of some circular objects.

For each one, work out the value of $\dfrac{\text{circumference}}{\text{diameter}}$.

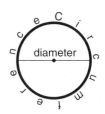

The answer is always just over 3

The value of $\dfrac{\text{circumference}}{\text{diameter}}$ is the same for every circle, 3.142

correct to 3 decimal places.

The actual value cannot be found exactly and the Greek letter π (pi) is used to represent it.

So, for all circles,

$$\frac{\text{circumference}}{\text{diameter}} = \pi \qquad \text{and} \qquad \text{circumference} = \pi \times \text{diameter}$$

Using C to stand for the circumference of a circle with diameter d,

$$\frac{C}{d} = \pi \qquad \text{and} \qquad C = \pi d$$

To find the circumference of a circle, multiply its diameter by π.

Example 1

Work out the circumference of a circle with a diameter of 6.8 cm.
Give your answer correct to 1 decimal place.

Solution 1

$\pi \times 6.8$	Multiply the diameter by π. Use your calculator's π button, if it has one. Otherwise use 3.142
$= 21.3628\ldots$	Write down at least four figures of the calculator display.
Circumference $= 21.4$ cm	Round the circumference to 1 decimal place. The units (cm) are the same as the diameter's.

Sometimes the radius, not the diameter, is given in a question. In that case, one way of finding the circumference is to double the radius to obtain the diameter and then multiply the diameter by π.

Alternatively, use the fact that a circle's diameter d is twice its radius r, that is, $d = 2r$. Replace d by $2r$ in the formula $C = \pi d$ giving $C = \pi \times 2r$ which can be written as

$$C = 2\pi r$$

Example 2

Work out the circumference of a circle with a radius of 8.2 m.
Give your answer correct to 1 decimal place.

Solution 2
Method 1
$8.2 \times 2 = 16.4$

	Double the radius to find the diameter.

$\pi \times 16.4$

$= 51.522...$

Circumference $= 51.5$ m

	Double the radius to find the diameter. Multiply the diameter by π. Write down at least four figures of the calculator display. Round the circumference to 1 decimal place. The units are m.

Method 2
$2 \times \pi \times 8.2$

$= 51.522...$

Circumference $= 51.5$ m

	Substitute 8.2 for r in the formula $C = 2\pi r$. Write down at least four figures of the calculator display. Round the circumference to 1 decimal place. The units are m.

Sometimes the circumference is given and the diameter or radius has to be found.

Example 3

The circumference of a circle is 29.4 cm.
Work out its diameter. Give your answer correct to 2 decimal places.

Solution 3
Method 1
$29.4 = \pi d$
$\pi d \div \pi = 29.4 \div \pi$
$d = 29.4 \div \pi$
$\quad = 9.3583...$
Diameter $= 9.36$ cm

	Substitute 29.4 for C in the formula $C = \pi d$. Divide both sides by π. Divide 29.4 by π and write down at least four figures of the calculator display. Round the diameter to 2 decimal places. The units are cm.

The formula $C = \pi d$ can be rearranged with d as the subject and used to find the diameter of a circle, if its circumference is given.

Dividing both sides of $C = \pi d$ by π gives $\quad d = \dfrac{C}{\pi}$

To find the diameter of a circle, divide its circumference by π.

Method 2
29.4 ÷ π
= 9.3583...
Diameter = 9.36 cm

> Divide the circumference by π.
> Write down at least four figures of the calculator display.
> Round the diameter to 2 decimal places. The units are cm.

Exercise 31A

If your calculator does not have a π button, take the value of π to be 3.142
Give answers correct to 1 decimal place unless stated otherwise.

1 Work out the circumferences of circles with these diameters.

    a   4.2 cm   **b** 9.7 m   **c**   29 cm   **d**   12.7 cm   **e**   17 m

2 Work out the circumferences of circles with these radii. Give your answers correct to 2 decimal places.

    a   3.9 cm   **b**   13 cm   **c**   6.3 m   **d**   29 m   **e**   19.4 cm

3 Work out the diameters of circles with these circumferences.

    a   17 cm   **b**   25 m   **c**   23.8 cm   **d**   32.1 cm   **e**   76.3 m

4 The circumference of a circle is 28.7 cm. Work out its radius. Give your answer correct to 2 decimal places.

5 The diameter of the London Eye is 135 m. Work out its circumference. Give your answer to the nearest metre.

6 The tree with the greatest circumference in the world is a Montezuma cypress tree in Mexico. Its circumference is 35.8 m. Work out its diameter.

7 Taking the Equator as a circle of radius 6370 km, work out the length of the Equator. Give your answer correct to 1 significant figure.

8 The circumference of a football is 70 cm. Work out its radius.

9 A semicircle has a diameter of 25 cm.
Work out its perimeter.
(Hint: the perimeter includes the diameter.)

10 A semicircle has a radius of 19 m.
Work out its perimeter.

11 The diagram shows a running track.
The ends are semicircles of diameter 57.3 m and the straights are 110 m long.
Work out the total perimeter of the track.
Give your answer correct to the nearest metre.

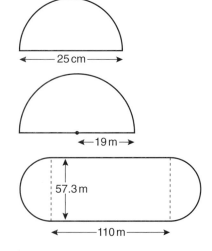

12 A reel of cotton has a radius of 1.3 cm. The cotton is wrapped round it 500 times. Work out the total length of cotton. Give your answer in metres.

13 The radius of a cylindrical tin of soup is 3.8 cm.
Work out the length of the label. (Ignore the overlap.)

14 The diameter of a car wheel is 52 cm.
 a Work out the circumference of the wheel. Give your answer correct to the nearest centimetre.
 b Work out the distance the car travels when the wheel makes 400 complete turns. Give your answer in metres.

15 The big wheel of a 'penny-farthing' bicycle has a radius of 0.75 m.
Work out the number of complete turns the big wheel makes when the bicycle travels 1 kilometre.

31.2 Area of a circle

The diagram shows a circle which has been split up into equal sectors.

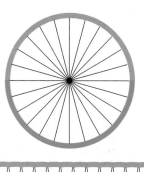

The sectors can be rearranged to make this new shape.

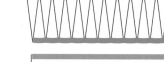

Splitting the circle up into more and more sectors and rearranging them, the new shape becomes very nearly a rectangle.

radius

The length of the rectangle is half the circumference of the circle, and the width of the rectangle is equal to the radius of the circle.

$\frac{1}{2}$ circumference

The area of the rectangle is equal to the area of the circle.

Area of circle $= \frac{1}{2}$ circumference $\times$ radius
Using A to stand for the area of a circle with radius r,

$$A = \frac{1}{2} \times 2\pi r \times r$$

$$A = \pi r^2$$

To find the area of a circle, multiply π by the square of the radius.

This means that the area of a circle is $\pi \times$ radius $\times$ radius.

Example 4

The radius of a circle is 6.7 cm.
Work out its area.
Give your answer correct to the nearest whole number.

Solution 4

$\pi \times 6.7^2$

Press the calculator keys exactly as shown here and then press $=$
or press π $\times$ 6.7 $\times$ 6.7 and then press $=$.

$= 141.026...$

Write down at least four figures of the calculator display.

Area $= 141$ cm^2

Round the area to the nearest whole number. The units are cm^2.

If the diameter, not the radius, is given, the first step is to halve the diameter to get the radius.

Example 5

The diameter of a circle is 9.6 m.
Work out its area.
Give your answer correct to 1 decimal place.

Solution 5

$9.6 \div 2 = 4.8$

Divide the diameter by 2 to get the radius.

$\pi \times 4.8^2$

Square the radius and then multiply by π.

$= 72.3822...$

Write down at least four figures of the calculator display.

Area $= 72.4$ m^2

Round the area to 1 decimal place. The units are m^2.

Exercise 31B

If your calculator does not have a π button, take the value of π to be 3.142
Give answers correct to 1 decimal place, unless the question states otherwise.

1   Work out the areas of circles with these radii.
    a   7.2 cm   **b**   14 m   **c**   1.5 cm   **d**   3.7 m   **e**   2.43 cm

2   Work out the areas of circles with these diameters.
    a   3.8 cm   **b**   5.9 cm   **c**   18 m   **d**   0.47 m   **e**   7.42 cm

3   The radius of a dartboard is 22.86 cm. Work out its area to the nearest cm^2.

4   The diameter of Avebury stone circle is 365 m.
Work out the area enclosed by the circle.
Give your answer correct to 1 significant figure.

5   The radius of a semicircle is 2.7 m.
       Work out its area.

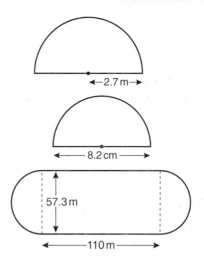

←2.7 m→

6   The diameter of a semicircle is 8.2 cm.
       Work out its area.

←——— 8.2 cm ———→

7   The diagram shows a running track.
       The ends are semicircles of diameter
       57.3 m and the straights are 110 m long.

       Work out the area enclosed by the track.
       Give your answer correct to the nearest m².

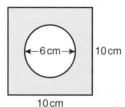

57.3 m

←——————110 m——————→

8   The diagram shows a circle of diameter
       6 cm inside a square of side 10 cm.

       a   Work out the area of the square.

       b   Work out the area of the circle.

       c   By subtraction, work out the area of
              the coloured part of the diagram.

←6 cm→   10 cm

10 cm

9   The diagram shows a circle of radius 7 cm
       inside a circle of radius 9 cm.

       Work out the area of the shaded part of
       the diagram, correct to the nearest cm².

7 cm

9 cm

10 The diagram shows an 8 cm by 6 cm
       rectangle inside a circle of diameter 10 cm.

       Work out the area of the shaded part of
       the diagram.

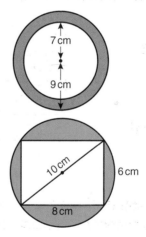

10 cm   6 cm

8 cm

31.3 Circumferences and areas in terms of π

Answers to questions involving the circumference or area of a circle are sometimes given
in terms of π, which is exact, not as a number, which is approximate.

Example 6

The diameter of a circle is 8 cm. Find the circumference of the circle.
Give your answer as a multiple of π.

Solution 6

$\pi \times 8$ | Multiply the diameter by π. |

Circumference $= 8\pi$ cm | Write the 8 before the π. The units are cm. |

Example 7

The radius of a circle is 3 m.
Find the area of the circle.
Give your answer as a multiple of π.

Solution 7

$\pi \times 3^2 = \pi \times 9$

| Square the radius and then multiply by π. |

Area $= 9\pi$ m^2

| Write the 9 before the π. The units are m^2. |

Example 8

The diameter of a semicircle is 12 cm.
Find the perimeter of the semicircle.
Give your answer in terms of π.

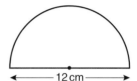

$\longleftarrow$ 12 cm $\longrightarrow$

Solution 8

The perimeter is the sum of the arc length and the diameter.

$$\frac{\pi \times 12}{2} = \frac{12\pi}{2} = 6\pi$$

| The arc length is half the circumference of a circle with a diameter of 12 cm. |

Perimeter $= 6\pi + 12$ cm

| To find the perimeter, add the diameter and the arc length. The units are cm. |

If the circumference of a circle is given as a multiple of π, its diameter can be found.

Example 9

The circumference of a circle is 30π m. Find its radius.

Solution 9

$$d = \frac{30\pi}{\pi} = 30$$

| To find the diameter, divide the circumference by π. |

$$\frac{30}{2} = 15$$

| To find the radius, divide the diameter by 2. The units are m. |

Radius $= 15$ m

Exercise 31C

In Questions 1–4, give the answers as multiples of π.

1 Find the circumference of a circle with a diameter of 7 m.

2 Find the area of a circle with a radius of 5 cm.

3 Find the circumference of a circle with a radius of 8 cm.

4 Find the area of a circle with a diameter of 20 m.

5 The diameter of a semicircle is 18 cm. Find the perimeter of the semicircle. Give your answer in terms of π.

6 The radius of a semicircle is 7 cm. Find the perimeter of the semicircle. Give your answer in terms of π.

7 The radius of a semicircle is 10 cm. Find its area. Give your answer as a multiple of π.

8 The circumference of a circle is 16π cm. Find its diameter.

9 The circumference of a circle is 60π m. Find its radius.

10 The circumference of a circle is 14π cm. Find its area. Give your answer as a multiple of π.

31.4 Volume and surface area of a cylinder

A cylinder is a prism with a circle as its cross-section.

Example 10

The radius of the end of a cylinder is 3 cm. Its length is 10 cm.

Work out the volume of the cylinder. Give your answer correct to the nearest cm².

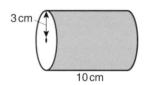

3 cm

10 cm

Solution 10

Area of cross-section $= \pi \times 3^2$

$\qquad\qquad\qquad = \pi \times 9$

$\qquad\qquad\qquad = 28.27433...$ cm²

> Use $A = \pi r^2$ to work out the area of the circular cross-section.
> Use the π button on your calculator, if it has one. Otherwise, take the value of π to be 3.142
> Do not round at this stage. Leave all the figures on your calculator display.

Volume $= 28.27433... \times 10$

$\qquad\quad = 282.7433...$ cm³

> Multiply the area of the cross-section by the length to get the volume of the cylinder.

Volume $= 283$ cm³

> Give the volume correct to the nearest cm³

The volume, V, of a cylinder of radius r and length l is given by the formula

$$V = \pi r^2 l$$

Example 11

The radius of the end of a solid cylinder is 4 cm. Its length is 9 cm.

Work out the total surface area of the cylinder. Give your answer correct to the nearest cm².

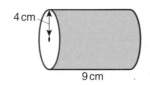

4 cm

9 cm

Solution 11

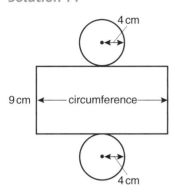

> The total surface area is the sum of the area of the curved surface and the areas of the two circular ends.

> The net of the curved surface of a cylinder is a rectangle. The length of this rectangle is equal to the circumference of the circular end of the cylinder. The two circular ends complete the net.

Total surface area
$$= (2 \times \pi \times 4 \times 9) + (2 \times \pi \times 4^2)$$
$$= 226.19... + 100.53...$$
$$= 327 \text{ cm}^2$$

> The area of the curved surface is the area of the rectangle, $2\pi r \times 9$
> The area of each circular end is πr^2.
> Give the area correct to the nearest cm^2.

The total surface area, S, of a solid cylinder of radius r and length l is given by the formula

$$S = 2\pi rl + 2\pi r^2$$

Exercise 31D

For these questions, use the π button on your calculator, if it has one. Otherwise, take the value of π to be 3.142

1 The radius of the end of a cylinder is 5 cm.
Its length is 15 cm.
Work out the volume of the cylinder.
Give your answer correct to the nearest cm^3.

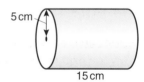

2 The diameter of the end of a cylinder is 8.6 cm.
Its length is 14 cm.
Work out the volume of the cylinder.
Give your answer correct to the nearest cm^3.

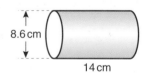

3 The volume of a cylinder is 500 cm^3.
The radius of its end is 7.8 cm.
Work out the length of the cylinder.
Give your answer correct to 2 decimal places.

4 Calculate the surface area of a solid cylinder of radius 4.7 cm and length 6.3 cm.
Give your answer correct to 2 decimal places.

5 Calculate the outside surface area of a hollow cylinder which is open at one end. Its radius is 5.1 cm and its length is 9.4 cm.
Give your answer correct to 1 decimal place.

Chapter summary

> **You should now know:**
>
> ★ how to find the circumference of a circle using
>   circumference of a circle = $\pi \times$ diameter
>   the formulae $C = \pi d$ and $C = 2\pi r$
>
> ★ how to find the diameter (or radius) of a circle if its circumference is known using
>   diameter = $\dfrac{\text{circumference}}{\pi}$ or using the formula $d = \dfrac{C}{\pi}$
>
> ★ how to find the area of a circle using
>   area of a circle = $\pi \times$ radius $\times$ radius
>   the formula $A = \pi r^2$
>
> ★ how to solve problems involving the circumference and area of a circle, including compound shapes and shaded areas
>
> ★ how to express answers to questions involving the circumference or area of a circle in terms of π.
>
> ★ how to find the volum, V, of a cylinder of radius r and length l using the formula $V = \pi r^2 l$
>
> ★ how to find the total surface area, S, of a solid cylinder of radius r and length l using the formula $S = 2\pi r^2 l + 2\pi r^2$

Chapter 31 review questions

If your calculator does not have a π button, take the value of π to be 3.142. Give answers correct to 1 decimal place, unless the question states otherwise.

1   Work out the circumference of a circle with a diameter of 27 cm.

2   Work out the circumference of a circle with a radius of 8.7 m.

3   Work out the diameter of a circle with a circumference of 24.7 cm.

4   Work out the radius of a circle with a circumference of 53.2 cm.

5   Work out the area of a circle with a radius of 7.9 m, correct to the nearest m^2.

6   Work out the area of a circle with a diameter of 3.2 cm.

7   Stonehenge is surrounded by a circular ditch with a diameter of 104 m.
    Work out the total distance round the ditch.
    Give your answer correct to the nearest metre.

8 A discus thrower's circle has a diameter of 2.5 m.
Work out the area of the circle.

9 Work out the perimeter of a semicircle with a diameter of 11 cm.

10 Work out the area of a semicircle with a radius of 7.4 m.

11 Find the circumference of a circle with a diameter of 9 cm.
Give your answer as a multiple of π.

12 Find the area of a circle with a radius of 4 cm. Give your answer as a multiple of π.

13 A table has a top in the shape of a circle with a radius
of 45 centimetres.

  a Calculate the area of the circular table top.
Give your answer correct to the nearest cm².

The base of the table is also in the shape of a circle.
The circumference of this circle is 110 centimetres.

  b Calculate the diameter of the base of the table.

(1384 November 1996)

14 A can of drink is in the shape of a cylinder.
The can has a radius of 4 cm and a height
of 15 cm.

Calculate the volume of the cylinder.
Give your answer correct to the nearest cm³.

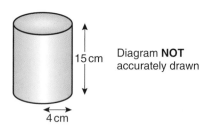

15 cm

Diagram **NOT**
accurately drawn

4 cm

(1387 November 1996)

15 The diagram shows a shape, made
from a semicircle and a rectangle.
The diameter of the semicircle is
12 cm.
The length of the rectangle is 14 cm.

Calculate the **perimeter** of the shape.
Give your answer correct to 1 decimal place.

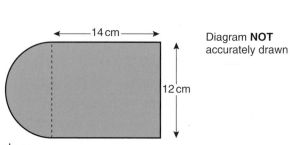

←—— 14 cm ——→

Diagram **NOT**
accurately drawn

12 cm

(1385 June 2002)

16 A mat is made in the shape of a rectangle with a semicircle added at one end.
The width of the mat is 1.52 metres.
The length of the mat is 1.86 metres.

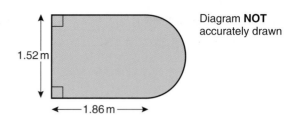

Diagram **NOT** accurately drawn

1.52 m

1.86 m

Calculate the area of the mat.
Give your answer in square metres, correct to 2 decimal places.

(1385 November 1999)

17 The diagram shows a shape.
AB is an arc of a circle, centre O.
Angle $AOB = 90°$.
$OA = OB = 6$ cm.

Calculate

a the area

b the perimeter of the shape.

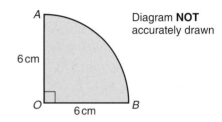

Diagram **NOT** accurately drawn

A

6 cm

O 6 cm B

18 The diagram shows a circle of diameter 70 cm inside a square of side 70 cm.
Work out the area of the shaded part of the diagram.
Give your answer correct to the nearest cm^2.

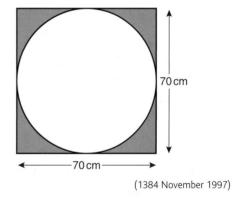

70 cm

70 cm

(1384 November 1997)

19 The diagram shows a right-angled triangle ABC and a circle.
A, B and C are points on the circumference of the circle.
AC is a diameter of the circle.
The radius of the circle is 10 cm.
$AB = 16$ cm and $BC = 12$ cm.

Work out the area of the shaded part of the circle.
Give your answer correct to the nearest cm^2.

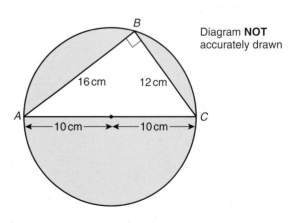

B

Diagram **NOT** accurately drawn

16 cm 12 cm

A 10 cm 10 cm C

(1385 June 1999)

20

Shape A

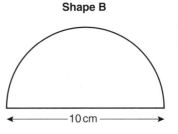

Shape B

Diagrams **NOT** accurately drawn

1 cm

2 cm

1 cm

1 cm

2 cm

4 cm

3 cm

4 cm

10 cm

a   Work out the area of Shape A.

b   **i**   Work out the perimeter of the semicircle, Shape B.
       ii   Work out the area of the semicircle, Shape B.

(1385 June 1998)

21   The diagram shows a rectangle drawn inside a circle.
The centre of the circle is at O.
The rectangle is 15 cm long and 9 cm wide.

Calculate the circumference of the circle.

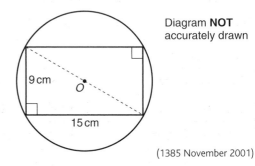

Diagram **NOT** accurately drawn

9 cm

O

15 cm

(1385 November 2001)

22   The diameter of a circle is 12 centimetres.

a   Work out the circumference of the circle.
Give your answer in centimetres correct to one decimal place.

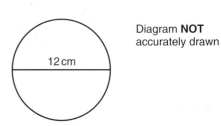

Diagram **NOT** accurately drawn

12 cm

The length of each diagonal of a square is 20 cm.

b   Work out the area of the square.

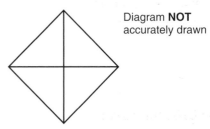

Diagram **NOT** accurately drawn

(1387 November 2004)

Converting units of area and volume

32.1 Converting units of area

Squares A and B are congruent. The sides of square A are measured in metres and the sides of square B are measured in centimetres.

Square A is 1 m by 1 m so the area of square A is $1 \times 1 = 1$ m^2.

100 cm $=$ 1 m, so square B is 100 cm by 100 cm.
The area of square B is $100 \times 100 = 10\,000$ cm^2.

The squares have the same area so $\boxed{\textbf{1 m}^2 = \textbf{100} \times \textbf{100} = \textbf{10 000 cm}^2.}$

There are similar results for other units.

Length	Area
1 cm = 10 mm	1 cm^2 = $\quad$ 10 $\times$ 10 $\quad$ = 100 mm^2
1 m $\;$ = 100 cm	1 m^2 $\;$ = $\quad$ 100 $\times$ 100 $\;$ = 10 000 cm^2
1 km = 1000 m	1 km^2 = 1000 $\times$ 1000 = 1 000 000 m^2

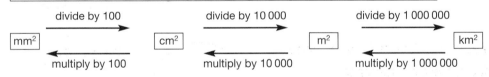

Example 1

Change 4.6 m^2 to cm^2.

Solution 1

4.6 m^2 $= 4.6 \times 10\,000$ cm^2
$\qquad\quad = 46\,000$ cm^2

> 1 m^2 = 10 000 cm^2

> Multiply the number of m^2 by 10 000

Example 2

Change 870 mm^2 to cm^2.

Solution2

870 mm^2 $= \dfrac{870}{100}$ cm^2 $= 8.7$ cm^2

> 1 cm^2 = 100 mm^2
>
> So 1 mm^2 $= \dfrac{1}{100}$ cm^2
>
> Divide the number of mm^2 by 100

Exercise 32A

1 Change to cm²

  a   4 m²   **b**   6.9 m²   **c**   600 mm²   **d**   47 mm²

2 Change to m²

  a   5 km²   **b**   0.3 km²   **c**   40 000 cm²   **d**   560 cm²

3 **a**   How many mm are there in 1 m?   **b**   How many mm² are there in 1 m²?

    c   Change 8.3 m² to mm².

4 Find, in cm², the area of a rectangle which measures

  a   3.2 m by 1.4 m   **b**   45 mm by 8 mm.

5 Work out the area of this triangle in **a** cm², **b** mm².

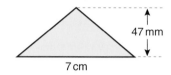

47 mm

7 cm

32.2 Converting units of volume

The units of volume used so far in this chapter have been cm³, m³ and mm³, depending on the units used in a question.

To convert between cm³ and mm³, find the volume of a centimetre cube in both cm³ and in mm³.
Remember that 1 cm = 10 mm.

Volume = 1 cm³   Volume = 10 × 10 × 10
                                               = 1000 mm³

This shows that   **1 cm³ = 1000 mm³**

To change cm³ to mm³, multiply by 1000 and to change mm³ to cm³, divide by 1000

To convert between m³ and cm³, find the volume of a metre cube in both m³ and in cm³.
Remember that 1 m = 100 cm.

                                         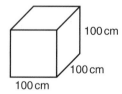

Volume = 1 m³   Volume = 100 × 100 × 100
                                               = 1 000 000 cm³

This shows that   **1 m³ = 1 000 000 cm³**

To change m³ to cm³, multiply by 1 000 000 and to change cm³ to m³, divide by 1 000 000

Example 3

a Change 8 m³ to cm³.

b Change 700 000 cm³ to m³.

Solution 3

a $8 \times 1\,000\,000 = 8\,000\,000$ cm³

Multiply by 1 000 000

b $700\,000 \div 1\,000\,000 = 0.7$ m³

Divide by 1 000 000

Another important unit of volume is the **litre**.

1 litre = 1000 cm³

To change litres to cm³, multiply by 1000 and to change cm³ to litres, divide by 1000

Litres are used to measure the **capacity** of a container – the amount, often of liquid, that a container can hold.

For example, the capacity of a Ford Fiesta's petrol tank is 42 litres.

Example 4

a Change 2.5 litres to cm³.

b Change 12 000 cm³ to litres.

Solution 4

a $2.5 \times 1000 = 2500$ cm³

Multiply by 1000

b $12\,000 \div 1000 = 12$ litres

Divide by 1000

Exercise 32B

1 Change **a** 3 cm³ to mm³ **b** 4500 mm³ to cm³ **c** 0.65 cm³ to mm³.

2 Change **a** 2.8 m³ to cm³ **b** 6 000 000 cm³ to m³ **c** 3 200 000 cm³ to m³.

3 Change **a** 9 litres to cm³ **b** 4.5 litres to cm³ **c** 5600 cm³ to litres.

4 The diagram shows a cuboid.
Work out the volume of the cuboid
  a in cm³ **b** in mm³.

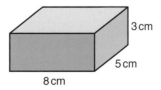

3 cm
5 cm
8 cm

5 The diagram shows a prism.
Work out the volume of the prism
  a in m³ **b** in cm³.

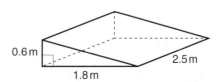

0.6 m
1.8 m
2.5 m

6 A bottle holds 1.5 litres of lemonade. Change 1.5 litres to cm³.

7   A cylindrical bowl has a radius of 15 cm.
It is filled with water to a depth of 12 cm.
Work out the volume of water in the bowl.
Give your answer in litres, correct to 2 decimal places.
(Use the π button on your calculator, if it has one.
Otherwise, take the value of π to be 3.142)

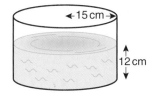

8   The diagram shows a container which is a cuboid.
15.6 litres of water are poured into the container.
Work out the depth of water.

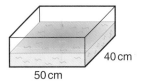

Chapter summary

You should now know:

★   How to convert units of area

★   How to convert units of volume

Chapter 32 review questions

1   Change **a** 8 m² to cm², **b** 420 mm² to cm².

2   Change 2.5 m² to cm².   (1387 June 2003)

3   **a**   Change 8 cm³ to mm³.   **b**   Change 3 m³ to cm³.
  c   Change 5 litres to cm³.   **d**   Change 2500 cm³ to litres.

4   There are 27 wall tiles in a pack.
Only full packs of tiles are sold.
A pack costs £9.72
Barry needs 200 tiles.
  a   **i**   How many full packs of tiles must he buy?
      ii   Work out the total cost of these packs.

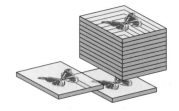

Each tile is a rectangle 20 cm by 15 cm.
  b   Work out the area of one tile.

Navdeep wants to tile a wall. The wall is a rectangle 3 metres by 2.4 metres.
  c   Work out the number of tiles she needs to cover the wall completely.   (1385 June 2000)

Ratio and proportion

CHAPTER

33.1 Introduction to ratio

The pictures show examples of **ratio**. Ratios are used to **compare** quantities.

Ratios are written using a colon (:)
For example, if there are 7 boys and 9 girls in a class, the ratio of the number of boys to the number of girls is 7 : 9
The order of the numbers is important.
The ratio 9 : 7 is the ratio of the number of girls to the number of boys.

Ratios can be simplified like fractions.
The ratio 7 : 9 cannot be simplified, because 7 and 9 have no common factors.
If there are 6 boys and 9 girls, the ratio is 6 : 9
The ratio 6 : 9 can be simplified, because 3 goes exactly into both 6 and 9
Dividing both 6 and 9 by 3 gives the ratio 2 : 3
2 : 3 cannot be simplified and is called the **simplest form** of the ratio.
This means that for every 2 boys in the class there are 3 girls.

Example 1

a Write down the ratio of the number of yellow stars to the number of blue stars.

b Simplify your ratio.

Solution 1

a 9 : 3

b

$$9 : 3$$
$$\div 3 \Big(\quad \Big) \div 3$$
$$3 : 1$$

3 : 1 is the simplest form

> There are 9 yellow stars and 3 blue stars. The 9 must come first as 'yellow stars' is written before 'blue stars'.

> Divide both 9 and 3 by 3

Example 2

A bag contains 15 red counters and 35 black counters.
Write down the ratio of the number of red counters to the number of black counters.
Give your ratio in its simplest form.

Solution 2

15 : 35

÷5 ( ) ÷5

3 : 7

| There are 15 red counters and 35 black counters. The 15 must come first as 'red counters' is written before 'black counters'. |

| Divide both 15 and 35 by 5 |

3 : 7 is the simplest form

| No number goes exactly into both 3 and 7 |

If different units are used for the quantities in a ratio, start by giving the quantities in the same units.

Example 3

Write 8 m to 60 cm as a ratio in its simplest form.

Solution 3

8 m = 8 × 100 cm
= 800 cm

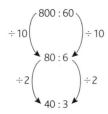

800 : 60

÷10 ( ) ÷10

80 : 6

÷2 ( ) ÷2

40 : 3

| It is easier to change the larger units into the smaller units. So change metres into centimetres. Use 1 m = 100 cm. |

| Write down the ratio. Divide both numbers by 10 Divide both numbers by 2 |

40 : 3 is the simplest form

| No number goes exactly into both 40 and 3 |

Example 4

In a pencil case, there are 4 red, 6 blue and 10 black pencils.
Write down the ratio of the number of red pencils to the number of blue pencils to the number of black pencils.
Give your ratio in its simplest form.

Solution 4

4 : 6 : 10

= 2 : 3 : 5

| Write down the numbers in the same order as the colours appear in the question. Divide all the numbers by 2 |

2 : 3 : 5 is the simplest form.

Exercise 33A

1

Write down the ratio of the number of green hearts to the number of red hearts.

2

Write down the ratio of

a   the number of red stars to the number of blue stars

b   the number of yellow stars to the number of blue stars

c   the number of blue stars to the number of yellow stars

d   the number of yellow stars to the number of blue stars to the number of red stars.

3   For each of the shapes, write down the ratio of the number of grey squares to the number of white squares.

a   b   c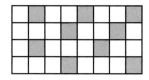

4   Write each ratio in its simplest form.

a	15 : 5	**b**	4 : 12	**c**	25 : 15	**d**	18 : 24	**e**	45 : 30
f	40 : 60	**g**	24 : 40	**h**	48 : 16	**i**	250 : 350	**j**	800 : 200

5   Write each ratio in its simplest form.

a	30 p : £1	**b**	2 m : 50 cm	**c**	20 mm : 5 cm	**d**	600 m : 2 km
e	£2 : 80 p	**f**	4 cm : 35 mm	**g**	£2.50 : £4	**h**	3.5 kg : 500 g

6   A bracelet has 20 yellow beads and 35 orange beads.
Write down the ratio of the number of yellow beads to the number of orange beads.
Give your ratio in its simplest form.

7   In a car park there are 40 silver cars, 32 red cars, and 48 blue cars.
Write down the ratio of the number of silver cars to the number of red cars to the number of blue cars. Give your ratio in its simplest form.

8   A model car has a length of 6 cm. The real car has a length of 3 m.
Write down the ratio of the length of the model car to the length of the real car.
Give your ratio in its simplest form.

9   The weight of a small bag of flour is 500 g. The weight of a large bag of flour is 5 kg.

a   Find, in its simplest form, the ratio of the weight of the small bag of flour to the weight of the large bag of flour.

b   Write down the simplest form of the ratio of the weight of the large bag of flour to the weight of the small bag of flour.

Ratios are sometimes given in the form $1 : n$, where n is a number.

Example 5

Write the ratio $2 : 5$ in the form $1 : n$.

Solution 5

Divide both numbers by 2

Example 6

In school there are 480 boys and 360 girls.
Write down the ratio of the number of boys to the number of girls.
Give your ratio in the form $1 : n$.

Solution 6

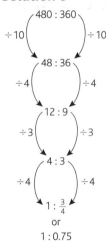

Write down the ratio. The number of boys must go first then the number of girls.

Divide both numbers by 10

Divide both numbers by 4

Divide both numbers by 3

The ratio is now in its simplest form.

Divide both numbers by 4 to put the ratio in the form $1 : n$.

Example 7

In a class, the ratio of the number of boys to the number of girls is $2 : 3$
What fraction of the class are boys?

Solution 7

$2 + 3 = 5$

For every 5 students in the class there are 2 boys and 3 girls.

$\frac{2}{5}$ of the class are boys.

2 of every 5 students are boys.

Exercise 33B

1   Write the following ratios in the form $1 : n$.

   a $4 : 12$ **b** $6 : 24$ **c** $2 : 7$ **d** $2 : 1$ **e** $10 : 3$ **f** $5 : 3$

2   In a school there are 120 computers. In the same school there are 720 pupils.
   Write down the ratio of the number of computers to the number of pupils. Give your
   ratio in the form $1 : n$.

3   In a school assembly there are 160 girls and 200 boys.
   a   Write down the ratio of the number of girls to the number of boys. Give your
   ratio in its simplest form.
   b   Write your answer to part **a** in the form $1 : n$.

4   The length of Amanda's hand is 18 cm. The length of Amanda's foot is 24 cm.
   a   Write down the ratio of the length of Amanda's foot to the length of Amanda's
   hand. Give your ratio in its simplest form.
   b   Write your answer to part **a** in the form $1 : n$.

5   The length of a model car is 12 cm. The length of the real car is 3.6 m.
   Work out the ratio of the length of the model car to the length of the real car. Write
   your answer in the form $1 : n$.

6   A bag contains green beads and purple beads in the ratio $1 : 4$
   What fraction of these beads are green?

7   A box contains red pencils and blue pencils in the ratio $3 : 5$
   What fraction of these pencils are blue?

8   A necklace has gold beads and silver beads in the ratio $5 : 7$
   a   What fraction of the necklace is gold beads?
   b   What fraction of the necklace is silver beads?

9   At a party, the ratio of the number of girls to the number of boys to the number of
   adults is $5 : 4 : 3$
   a   What fraction of the people at the party are girls?
   b   What fraction of the people at the party are adults? Give your fraction in its
   simplest form.

10   In a garden, the ratio of the number of robins to the number of blackbirds to the
   number of sparrows seen in one day is $2 : 4 : 3$
   a   What fraction of the birds seen were robins?
   b   What fraction of the birds seen were sparrows? Give your fraction in its simplest
   form.

33.2 Problems on ratios

If the ratio of two quantities and one of the quantities are known, then the other quantity can be found.

Example 8

To make concrete, 1 part of cement is used to every 5 parts of sand.

a Write down the ratio of cement to sand.

b 2 buckets of cement are used. How many buckets of sand will be needed?

c 20 buckets of sand are used. How many buckets of cement will be needed?

Solution 8

a $1:5$

> 1 bucket of cement is mixed with 5 buckets of sand.

b

> The amount of cement is multiplied by 2 so multiply the amount of sand by 2 as well.

10 buckets of sand will be needed.

> 2 buckets of cement are mixed with 10 buckets of sand.

c $20 \div 5 = 4$

$$\overset{1:5}{\underset{4:20}{\times 4 \Big(\quad \Big) \times 4}}$$

> The amount of sand is multiplied by 4 so multiply the amount of cement by 4 as well.

4 buckets of cement will be needed.

Example 9

The scale of a map is $1 : 100\,000$

Work out the real distance that 6.4 cm on the map represents.

Solution 9

$1 : 100\,000$

> 1 cm on the map represents a real distance of 100 000 cm.

$6.4 \times 100\,000 = 640\,000$

The real distance is 640 000 cm

> To find real distances in centimetres, *multiply* lengths on the map by 100 000

$640\,000 \div 100 = 6400$ m

$6400 \div 1000 = 6.4$ km

> Change 640 000 cm to kilometres using 1 m = 100 cm and 1 km = 1000 m.

6.4 cm on the map represents a real distance of 6.4 km.

Example 10

Tom uses a scale of $1 : 200$ to make a model of an aeroplane.

a The wing length of the model is 7.5 cm.

Work out the wing length of the real aeroplane.

b The length of the real aeroplane is 40 m.

Work out the length of the model.

Solution 10

a 7.5×200

    $= 1500$ cm

> To find lengths on the real aeroplane in centimetres, *multiply* lengths on the model by 200

    $1500 \div 100 = 15$ m
The wing length of the real
aeroplane is 15 m

> Change 1500 cm to metres.

b $40 \times 100 = 4000$ cm

    $4000 \div 200 = 20$ cm

> The model will be smaller than the aeroplane, so change 40 m to centimetres.
> To find lengths on the model, *divide* lengths on the real aeroplane by 200

    The length of the model is 20 cm.

Exercise 33C

1 The ratio of the number of red beads to the number of green beads in a bag is $1 : 3$
Work out the number of green beads if there are

   a   2 red beads   **b**   6 red beads   **c**   15 red beads.

2 In a recipe for pastry, the ratio of the weight of flour to the weight of fat is $2 : 1$
Work out the weight of fat needed for

   a   40 g of flour   **b**   120 g of flour   **c**   1 kg of flour.

3 A bag contains only blue balls and yellow balls. The ratio of the number of blue balls to the number of yellow balls is $3 : 5$
Work out the number of yellow balls in the bag, if there are

   a   6 blue balls   **b**   15 blue balls   **c**   60 blue balls.

4 Orange paint is made by mixing red paint and yellow paint in the ratio $1 : 3$

   a   If 6 litres of red paint are used, how many litres of yellow paint are needed?

   b   If 30 litres of yellow paint are used, how many litres of red paint are needed?

5 Brass is made from copper and zinc in the ratio $5 : 3$ by weight.

   a   If there are 6 kg of zinc, work out the weight of copper.

   b   If there are 25 kg of copper, work out the weight of zinc.

6 In a pet shop, the ratio of the number of rabbits to the number of hamsters is $2 : 5$

   a   Work out the number of hamsters if there are
      i   8 rabbits   **ii**   20 rabbits.

   b   Work out the number of rabbits if there are
      i   15 hamsters   **ii**   40 hamsters.

7 On a map, 1 cm represents 2 km. What distance on the map will represent a real distance of

   a   10 km   **b**   22 km   **c**   7 km?

8 On a map, 1 cm represents 5 km. Work out the real distance between two towns, if their distance apart on the map is

   a   2 cm   **b**   3.1 cm   **c**   8.4 cm.

9   Jim uses a scale of 1 : 100 to draw a plan of a room to scale.
       On the scale drawing the length of the room is 5.6 cm.
       What is the real length of the room?

10   Kylie makes a scale model of a rocking horse. She uses a scale of 1 : 5
       The rocking horse is 125 cm high. How high will her scale model be?

11   The scale of a map is 1 : 100 000
       Work out the distance on the map between two towns if the real distance between
       the towns is
       a   6 km   **b**   10.5 km.

12   The scale of a map is 1 : 50 000
       On the map the distance between two towns is 4.2 cm. Work out the real distance
       between the towns. Give your answer in kilometres.

33.3 Sharing a quantity in a given ratio

There are two methods for sharing a quantity in a given ratio.

Example 11

Pavinder and Salid share £35 in the ratio 4 : 3
Work out how much each boy gets.

Solution 11
Method 1
$4 + 3 = 7$ | Add 4 and 3 to get the total number of shares. |

$35 \div 7 = 5$ | Divide 35 by 7 to work out what each share is worth. |

$5 \times 4 = 20$ | Pavinder gets 4 shares so multiply 5 by 4 |

$5 \times 3 = 15$ | Salid gets 3 shares so multiply 5 by 3 |

Pavinder gets £20
Salid gets £15 | Check that the sum of the two amounts is £35
                         (£20 + £15= £35). |

Method 2
$4 + 3 = 7$ | Add 4 and 3 to get the number of shares. |

Pavinder $\frac{4}{7}$
Salid $\frac{3}{7}$ | Work out the fraction of £35 each person receives. |

$\frac{4}{7} \times 35 = 20$ | Work out $\frac{4}{7}$ of 35 and $\frac{3}{7}$ of 35 |
$\frac{3}{7} \times 35 = 15$

Pavinder gets £20
Salid gets £15 | Check that the sum of the two amounts is £35
                         (£20 + £15= £35). |

Example 12

Anna, Faye and Harriet share 24 sweets in the ratio 1 : 2 : 3
How many sweets does each girl get?

Solution 12

$1 + 2 + 3 = 6$ | Add 1, 2 and 3 to get the total number of shares. |

$24 \div 6 = 4$ | Divide 24 by 6 to work out what each share is worth. |

Anna gets 4 sweets. | Anna gets 1 share. |

Faye gets $4 \times 2 = 8$ sweets. | Faye gets 2 shares so multiply 4 by 2 |

Harriet gets $4 \times 3 = 12$ sweets. | Harriet gets 3 shares so multiply 4 by 3 (check: $4 + 8 + 12 = 24$). |

Exercise 33D

1   **a**   Share £40 in the ratio 1 : 3

    b   Share £15 in the ratio 2 : 3

    c   Share £60 in the ratio 5 : 1

    d   Share £100 in the ratio 3 : 2

2   A bag contains only red beads and blue beads.
    The ratio of the number of red beads to the number of blue beads is 4 : 1
    There are 35 beads in the bag. How many blue beads are there in the bag?

3   In a class, the ratio of the number of girls to the number of boys is 3 : 5
    There are 32 students in the class. Work out the number of girls in the class.

4   Ben and Harry share 50 toy cars in the ratio 2 : 3
    Work out how many toy cars Ben gets.

5   Adam and Bill share £90 in the ratio 1 : 2
    Work out how much each boy gets.

6   Sally is 9 years old. Alex is 11 years old. They share £120 in the ratio of their ages.
    How much money does each girl get?

7   A box contains plain, white and milk chocolates in the ratio 1 : 2 : 3
    There are 36 chocolates in the box. How many of each type of chocolate are there?

8   Ben, Gary and Alan share £80 in the ratio 2 : 3 : 5
    How much money does each boy receive?

9   A recipe for crumble topping uses sugar, fat and flour in the ratio 1 : 2 : 3
    How much of each ingredient is needed to make 900 g of crumble?

10   Share £6 in the ratio 2 : 3 : 5

33.4 Proportion

If 1 pencil costs 15p, then

> **2 pencils cost 30p (2 × 15 p)**
> **3 pencils cost 45p (3 × 15 p)**
> **4 pencils cost 60p (4 × 15 p) and so on.**

The cost depends on the number of pencils.
As the number of pencils increases, the cost increases.

The cost is said to increase in the same **proportion** as the number of pencils, and so the cost is **proportional** to the number of pencils. For example, 4 pencils cost twice as much as 2 pencils, and 18 pencils cost 6 times as much as 3 pencils.

There are many examples of proportion in everyday life. The amount of money a motorist pays for petrol is proportional to how much petrol they put in their tank. The number of dollars a tourist gets in exchange for their pounds is proportional to the number of pounds.

Example 13

5 buns cost £1.50
Work out the cost of 7 of these buns.

Solution 13
This is called the **unitary** method, because it finds the cost of *one* bun first.

$$\begin{array}{r} 30 \\ 5\overline{)150} \end{array}$$

> Work out the cost of 1 bun.
> Divide the cost of five buns by 5

$30 \times 7 = 210$

> Work out the cost of 7 buns.
> Multiply the cost of one bun by 7

7 buns cost £2.10

> As the answer is more than £1, give the answer in pounds.

Example 14

Here is a list of the ingredients needed to make carrot soup for 4 people:

> **200 g carrots**
> **2 onions**
> **40 g butter**
> **300 ml stock**

Work out the amount of each ingredient needed to make carrot soup for 12 people.

Solution 14

12 ÷ 4 = 3

| Carrot soup for 12 people needs 3 times as much of each ingredient as carrot soup for 4 people. So multiply each amount by 3 |

200 × 3 = 600
2 × 3 = 6
40 × 3 = 120
300 × 3 = 900

The amount of each ingredient is 600 g carrots, 6 onions, 120 g butter and 900 ml stock.

Example 15

a Janet went on holiday to France. She changed £200 into euros.
The exchange rate was £1 = 1.62 euros.
Work out the number of euros Janet got.

b Janet came home. She had 62 euros left.
She changed her 62 euros to pounds. The new exchange rate was £1 = 1.55 euros.
Work out how much Janet got, in pounds, for 62 euros.

Solution 15

a 200 × 1.62 = 324

| Janet got 1.62 euros for every £1, so *multiply* the number of pounds by 1.62 |

Janet got 324 euros

b 62 ÷ 1.55 = 40

| Janet got £1 for every 1.55 euros, so *divide* the number of euros by 1.55 |

Janet got £40

Exercise 33E

1 A car travels at a steady speed of 60 miles each hour.
Work out the number of hours it takes to travel
   a   120 miles   **b**   300 miles.

2 3 pencils cost 96 p. Work out the cost of 5 of these pencils.

3 Four 1 litre tins of paint cost a total of £36.60
Work out the cost of seven of the 1 litre tins of paint.

4 One tin of paint contains enough paint to cover 10 square metres.
How many tins of paint will be needed to cover
   a   30 square metres   **b**   70 square metres?

5 This is a recipe for 8 pieces of cornflake crunch:

> **200 g of plain chocolate**
> **4 tablespoons of golden syrup**
> **50 g of margarine**
> **100 g of cornflakes**

Work out the amounts needed to make 16 pieces of cornflake crunch.

6 This is a recipe for 10 cookies.

    a Work out the amount of butter needed to make 20 cookies.

    b Work out the amount of flour needed to make 15 cookies.

> 80 g of butter
> 80 g of sugar
> 2 eggs
> 100 g of flour

7 This is a recipe for chickpea curry for 4 people.

    Work out the amounts needed to make chickpea curry for 10 people.

> 2 onions
> 200 g of sweet potato
> 400 g of chickpeas
> 1 teaspoon curry powder

8 This is a recipe for 12 small cakes:

    a Work out the number of eggs needed to make 36 small cakes.

    b Lesley has 6 eggs. Work out how many small cakes she can make if she uses all 6 eggs. She has plenty of all the other ingredients.

> 150 g self-raising flour
> 150 g margarine
> 150 g sugar
> 3 eggs

9 The exchange rate is £1 = $1.80

    a Change £200 into dollars.

    b Change $270 into pounds.

10 Eric went on holiday to America. He changed £450 into dollars.
The exchange rate was £1 = $1.85
Work out how many dollars Eric got.

11 Susan bought a coat for €116 in France.
The exchange rate was £1 = €1.45
Work out the cost of the coat in pounds.

12 Angela buys a pair of jeans in England for £45. She then goes on holiday to America and sees an identical pair of jeans for $55. The exchange rate is £1 = $1.75
In which country are the jeans cheaper and by how much?

Chapter summary

You should now know that:

★ A ratio **compares** quantities – an example of a **ratio** is 4 : 5

★ To write down a ratio, write down the numbers in the correct order, for example, if there are 6 red and 7 blue cars then
  - the ratio of the number of red cars to the number of blue cars is 6 : 7
  - the ratio of the number of blue cars to the number of red cars is 7 : 6

★ If different units are used for the quantities in a ratio, start by giving the quantities in the same units

★ To **simplify** a ratio divide each number in the ratio by the same number

★ A ratio in its **simplest form** cannot be simplified any further

★ Quantities can be **shared** in a given ratio

★ Map **scales** are often written as ratios

★ Two quantities are in **proportion** if their ratio stays the same as the quantities increase or decrease

Chapter 33 review questions

1 Jane has 3 cats and 7 fish. Write down the ratio of the number of cats to the number of fish.

2 Write the ratio 7 : 14 in its simplest form.

3 Simplify the ratio 6 : 9   *(1388 January 2004)*

4 4 identical notebooks cost 84p.
Work out the cost of 9 of the same notebooks.

5 On a map, 1 cm represents 2 km. What distance on the map will represent a real distance of
  a 8 km   **b** 20 km   **c** 9 km?

6 On a map, 1 cm represents 4 km. Work out the real distance between two towns if their distance apart on the map is
  a 3 cm   **b** 1.2 cm   **c** 12.8 cm.

7 John and Adam share 30 sweets in the ratio 2 : 3
Work out how many sweets Adam gets.

8 The ratio of girls to boys in a school is 2 : 3
  a What fraction of these students are boys?
  In Year 8 the ratio of girls to boys is 1 : 3
  There are 300 students in Year 8.
  b Work out the number of girls in Year 8.   *(1388 January 2004)*

9   This is a recipe for making Tuna Bake for 4 people.

> **Tuna Bake**
>
> Ingredients for 4 people
>
> 400 g of tuna
> 400 g of mushroom soup
> 100 g of grated cheddar cheese
> 4 spring onions
> 250 g of breadcrumbs

Work out the amounts needed to make a Tuna Bake for 10 people.   (1385 June 2001)

10   Here are the ingredients needed to make 500 ml of custard.

> **Custard**
>
> Makes 500 ml
>
> 400 ml of milk
> 3 large egg yolks
> 50 g sugar
> 2 teaspoons of cornflour

     a   Work out the amount of sugar needed to make 2000 ml of custard.

     b   Work out the amount of milk needed to make 750 ml of custard.   (1387 June 2005)

11
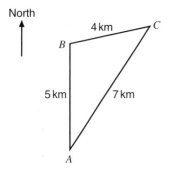

Diagram **NOT** accurately drawn

B is 5 km North of *A*.
C is 4 km from *B*.
C is 7 km from *A*.

     a   Make an accurate scale drawing of triangle *ABC*.
        Use a scale of 1 cm to 1 km.

     b   From your accurate scale drawing, measure the bearing of *C* from *A*.

     c   Find the bearing of *A* from *C*.   (1385 November 2000)

12   Here is a sketch of a triangle.

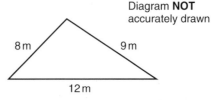

Diagram **NOT** accurately drawn

The lengths of the sides of the triangle are 8 m, 9 m and 12 m.
Use a scale of 1 cm to 2 m to make an accurate scale drawing of the triangle.

(1385 June 2001)

13 The crosses on the diagram show the positions of three places A, B and C.
The scale of the diagram is 1 cm to 5 km.

Tariq cycled in a straight line from A to C.
He left A at 1.30 pm.
He cycled at an average speed of 10 kilometres per hour.
Use a scale of 1 cm to 2 m to make an accurate scale drawing of the triangle.

a Find the time he arrived at C.

b Find the bearing of   **i** B from A **ii** A from C (1385 November 2002)

14 In the diagram, Point A marks the position of Prestwich.
The position of Radcliffe is to be marked on the diagram as point B.

a On the diagram, mark with a cross (✗) the position of B, given that
B is on a bearing of 320° from A and
B is 6 cm from A.

The scale of the diagram is 1 : 50 000

b Work out the real distance 6 cm represents.
Give your answer in kilometres.

(1387 November 2005)

15 Kelly bought 4 identical computer disks for £3.60
Work out the cost of 9 of these computer disks.   (1385 November 2002)

16 A model is made of an aeroplane.

The length of the model is 18 centimetres.
The length of the real aeroplane is 45 metres.

Work out the ratio of the length of the model to the length of the real aeroplane.
Write your answer in the form 1 : n.   (1388 March 2003)

17   Margaret goes on holiday to Switzerland.
The exchange rate is £1 = 2.10 francs.

She changed £450 into francs.
How many francs should she get?   (1387 June 2005)

18   In Portugal, a suitcase costs 23 euros.
In England, an identical suitcase costs £15
The exchange rate is £1 = 1.45 euros.
In which country is the suitcase cheaper and by how much?

19   Here is a list of ingredients needed to make leek soup for 6 people.

> **Ingredients for 6 people**
>
> 600 g leeks
> 30 g butter
> 3 tablespoons of wholemeal flour
> 450 ml milk
> 600 ml water

Work out the amount of each ingredient needed to make leek soup for 4 people.

20   Bill gave his three daughters a total of £32.40
The money was shared in the ratios 4 : 3 : 2
Jane had the largest share.
Work out how much money Bill gave to Jane.   (1385 November 2001)

21   Stephen and Joanne share £210 in the ratio 6 : 1
How much more money does Stephen get than Joanne?   (1385 June 2001)

22   Prendeep bought a necklace in the United States of America.
Prendeep paid 108 dollars ($).
Arthur bought an identical necklace in Germany.
Arthur paid 117 euros (€).

| £1 = $1.44 |
| £1 = €1.6 |

Calculate, in pounds, the difference between the prices paid for the two necklaces.
Show how you worked out your answer.   (1387 November 2003)

Planes of symmetry
Plans and elevations

34.1 Planes of symmetry

When a mirror is placed on a line of symmetry of a two-dimensional shape and looked at from either side, the shape looks the same (see Section 23.1). In other words, each half of the shape is a mirror image of the other half.

In a similar way, when a plane cuts a 3-D shape in two so that each half is a mirror image of the other half, the plane is called a **plane of symmetry**.

These diagrams show all the planes of symmetry of a cuboid.

The diagram shows a prism with an isosceles trapezium as its cross-section. The prism has two planes of symmetry. Draw these planes of symmetry.

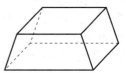

Solution 1

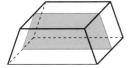 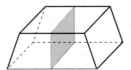

Exercise 34A

Answer this exercise on the resource sheet.

1 Draw *one* plane of symmetry on each of the 3-D shapes.

a

Cube

b

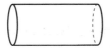

Cylinder

c

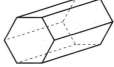

Prism with a regular hexagon cross-section

d

Cone

e

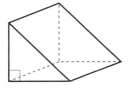

Prism with an isosceles right-angled triangle cross-section

f

Square-based pyramid

2 The diagram shows a prism with an equilateral triangle as its cross-section. It has four planes of symmetry.
On each of the diagrams, on the resource sheet draw a different plane of symmetry.

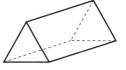

3 The diagram shows a prism.

   a On the diagram on the resource sheet, draw a plane of symmetry.

   b How many planes of symmetry has the prism?

34.2 Plans and elevations

The diagram shows a prism with an isosceles triangle as its cross-section.

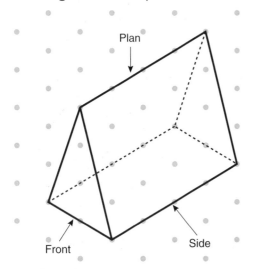

The view from above is called the **plan**.

The view from the front is called the **front elevation**.

The view from the side is called the **side elevation**.

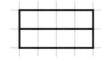

Example 2

The diagram shows a prism.

Draw a sketch of the plan, front elevation and side elevation.

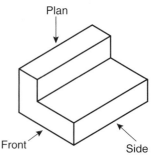

Solution 2

Plan   Front elevation   Side elevation

Exercise 34B

1 On centimetre squared paper draw the plan, front elevation and side elevation for this cuboid.

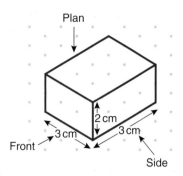

2 On centimetre squared paper draw the plan, front elevation and side elevation for this prism.

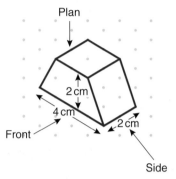

3 Sketch the plan, front elevation and side elevation for each of these 3-D shapes.

  a    **b** 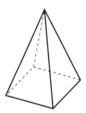   **c**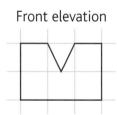

4 Here are the front elevation and side elevation of a prism.
The front elevation shows the cross-section of the prism.

Front elevation   **Side elevation**

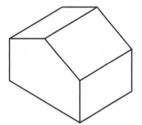
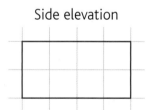

  a On squared paper, draw a plan view of the prism.

  b Draw a 3-D sketch of the prism.

Chapter summary

You should now know:

★ A plane of symmetry cuts a three-dimensional shape in half, so that each half is a mirror image of the other half.

★ How to draw and interpret plans and elevations of 3-D shapes

Chapter 34 review questions

1 Here are the plan and elevation of a prism.
The front elevation shows the cross-section
of the prism.

    a On squared paper, draw a side elevation of
the prism.

    b Draw a 3-D sketch of the prism.

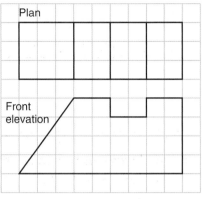

(1387 June 2003)

2 a The diagram represents a solid cube.
Copy the diagram and draw a plane of symmetry on
your diagram.

A different solid cube has one red face and the other faces
are coloured white.
The solid cube is biased.
Sophie rolled the solid cube 200 times.
The solid landed on the red face 46 times.
The solid landed on a white face the other times.
Sophie rolls the solid again.

    b Estimate the probability that the solid will land on a white face.

Each face of a different solid is either rectangular or hexagonal.
When this solid is rolled, the probability that it will land on a rectangular face is 0.85
Billy rolls this solid 1000 times.

    c Estimate the number of times it will land on a rectangular face.

(1385 November 2001)

Transformations

35

CHAPTER

35.1 Introduction

A **transformation** changes the position or size of a shape.

Using the 'Nudge' instruction or the arrow keys, a computer can move a shape to a new position.

This is a **translation**

A computer can also rotate, reflect (flip) and enlarge a shape.

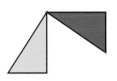

A **rotation**

A **reflection**

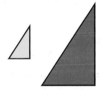

An **enlargement**

In each case, the starting shape is the yellow triangle.
The finishing shape, called the **image**, is the red triangle.
The yellow triangle **maps onto** the red triangle.

Translation, rotation, reflection and enlargement are **transformations**.

35.2 Translations

In the diagram below, shape **A** has been mapped onto shape **B** by a **translation**. In a translation, all points of the shape move the same distance in the same direction. All points of shape **A** move three squares to the right and five squares up.

In a translation

- the lengths of the sides of the shape do not change
- the angles of the shape do not change
- the shape does not turn.

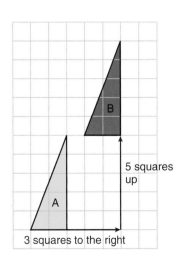

5 squares up

3 squares to the right

Example 1

Describe the translation that maps triangle **P**
onto triangle **Q**.

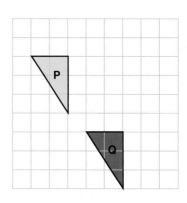

Solution 1

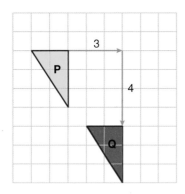

Choose one corner of triangle **P**.

Count the number of squares to the right and
the number of squares down from this corner on
triangle **P** to the same corner on triangle **Q**.

The translation from triangle **P** to triangle **Q** is
three squares to the right and four squares down.

Example 2

Translate shape **A** six squares to the left
and five squares down. Label the new shape **B**.

Solution 2

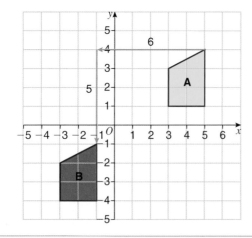

Choose one corner of shape **A**.

Count from this corner six squares to the left
and then count five squares down to find where
this corner has moved to.

The new shape is the same as shape **A**.

Draw the new shape and label it **B**.

The translation 2 squares to the right and 1 square up can be written as $\begin{pmatrix} 2 \\ 1 \end{pmatrix}$. This is a **vector**.

Vectors can be used to describe translations.

The top number shows the number of squares moved to the right or left.
The bottom number shows the number of squares moved up or down.
The rules for which directions are positive and which are negative are the same as for coordinates.
To the right and up are positive.
To the left and down are negative.

Some translations and their vectors are shown on the grid.

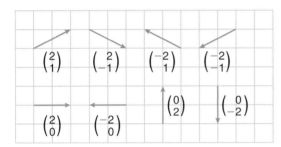

Example 3

a Describe the translation that maps shape **A** onto
   i shape **B**   **ii** shape **C**.

b Translate shape **A** by the vector $\begin{pmatrix} -3 \\ -5 \end{pmatrix}$.

   Label this new shape **D**.

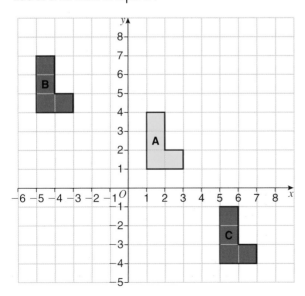

Solution 3

a   **i** From **A** to **B** is the translation
6 to the left and 3 up
or
the translation with vector $\begin{pmatrix} -6 \\ 3 \end{pmatrix}$

> Count the number of squares moved to the left and up from any corner in **A** to the same corner in **B**.

ii From **A** to **C** is the translation 4 to the right and 5 down
or
the translation with vector $\begin{pmatrix} 4 \\ -5 \end{pmatrix}$

> Count the number of squares moved to the right and down from any corner in **A** to the same corner in **C**.

b

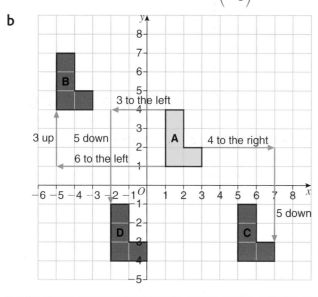

> $\begin{pmatrix} -3 \\ -5 \end{pmatrix}$ means 3 to the left and 5 down.
>
> Choose one corner of shape **A**. Count from this corner three squares to the left and then count five squares down to find to where this corner has moved. The new shape is the same as shape **A**. Draw the new shape and label it **D**.

Exercise 35A

1   Describe the translation that maps shape **P** onto shape **Q**.

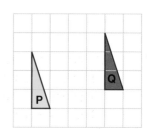

2 Describe the translation that maps triangle **A** onto
  a triangle **B**
  b triangle **C**
  c triangle **D**
  d triangle **E**
  e triangle **F**
  f triangle **G**.

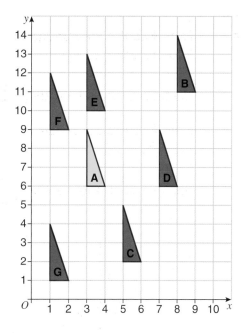

3 On the resource sheet, translate each shape by the translation shown.

a

3 to the right

b

3 up

c

5 to the right
and 2 up

d

6 to the left
and 3 down

4 a Describe the translation that maps
  i shape **A** onto shape **D**
  ii shape **A** onto shape **G**
  iii shape **F** onto shape **B**
  iv shape **C** onto shape **E**

  b The translation that maps shape **C** onto shape **D** is the same as the translation that maps shape **E** onto which shape?

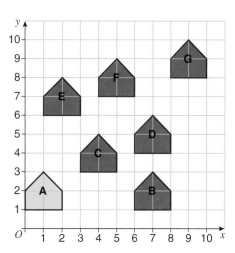

5   On the resource sheet, translate
    triangle **A**
    a   5 to the right and 4 up.
        Label your new triangle **B**.
    b   4 to the right and 6 down.
        Label your new triangle **C**.
    c   7 to the left.
        Label your new triangle **D**.
    d   by the vector $\begin{pmatrix} 3 \\ 2 \end{pmatrix}$.
        Label your new triangle **E**.
    e   by the vector $\begin{pmatrix} -6 \\ -4 \end{pmatrix}$.
        Label your new triangle **F**.
    f   by the vector $\begin{pmatrix} 0 \\ 2 \end{pmatrix}$.
        Label your new triangle **G**.

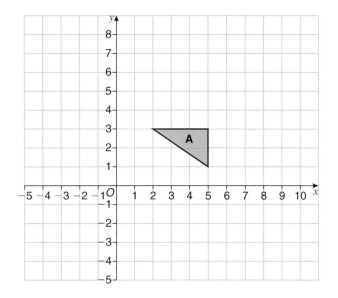

6   The coordinates of the point A of the kite
    are $(-2, 1)$.
    a   The kite is translated so that the point A is
        mapped onto the point $(3, 4)$.

        On the resource sheet, draw the image
        of the kite after this translation.
    b   Describe this translation.

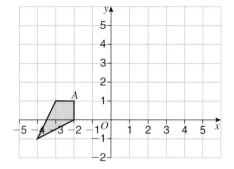

7   a   On the resource sheet, translate the kite **A**
        by the vector $\begin{pmatrix} 4 \\ 7 \end{pmatrix}$. Label this new kite **B**.
    b   On the same diagram, translate kite **B** by
        the vector $\begin{pmatrix} -6 \\ -3 \end{pmatrix}$. Label this new kite **C**.
    c   Describe the translation that maps kite **A**
        onto kite **C**.
    d   Describe the translation that maps kite **C**
        onto kite **A**.

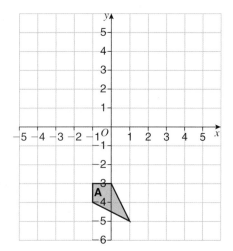

8 The blue rectangle can be used to tessellate the grid completely.

a On the resource sheet, draw eight more rectangles to show how the rectangle can be used to tessellate the grid.

b Use vectors to describe the translations from the blue rectangle to each of the other eight rectangles.

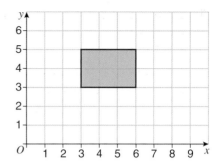

35.3 Rotations

To **rotate** means to turn. A bicycle wheel, the hands of a clock and the drum of a washing machine all turn or rotate.

This face on a stick has rotated 60° **clockwise** (↻) about the point O. The size of the face has not changed.

To describe a rotation give
- the angle of turn
- the direction of turn (**clockwise** or **anticlockwise**)
- the point the shape turns about (the **centre of rotation**).

In a rotation
- the lengths of the sides of the shape do not change
- the angles of the shape do not change
- the shape turns
- the centre of rotation does not move.

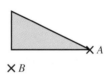

Example 4

Rotate the triangle
a a half turn about the point A
b a quarter turn clockwise about the point B.

Solution 4

a Tracing paper can be used to rotate the shape.
Trace the triangle and mark the point A.
Fix the point A with a pencil or a compass point so that the point A does not move.
Turn the tracing paper about A through a half turn (180°).
For a half turn it does not matter whether the triangle is rotated clockwise or anticlockwise.
Now the position of the image of the triangle can be seen.

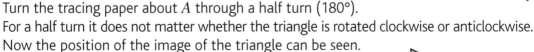

b Tracing paper can be used in a similar way to part **a**.
In this case mark the point B and keep the point B fixed.
Turn the tracing paper about B clockwise through a quarter turn (90°).
Now the position of the image of the triangle can be seen.

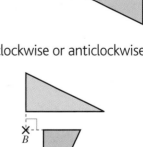

Example 5

Rotate the shaded shape a quarter turn clockwise about the point O.

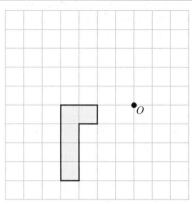

Solution 5

Tracing paper can be used to rotate the shape as before or the lines of the grid can be used as shown.

Notice that each line of the shape has turned through a quarter turn clockwise.

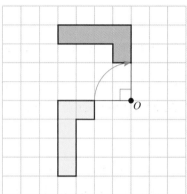

Example 6

Describe the transformation that maps triangle **A** onto triangle **B**.

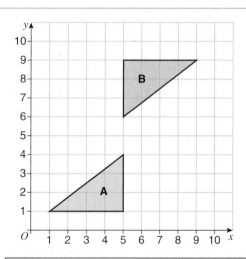

Solution 6

Triangle **A** is mapped onto triangle **B** by a rotation of 180° (a half turn) about the point (5, 5).

Use tracing paper to check that the transformation is a rotation of 180°. Then check that the centre of rotation is the point (5, 5).

Exercise 35B

1   On the resource sheet, rotate each shape a quarter turn clockwise about the point marked with a dot (•).

   a   **b**   **c**

2 On the resource sheet, rotate each shape a quarter turn anticlockwise about the point marked with a dot (•).

a   **b**   **c**

3 On the resource sheet, rotate each shape a half turn about the point marked with a dot (•).

a   **b**   **c**

4 On the resource sheet, rotate the rectangle about the centre of rotation (the dot) through

   a 90° clockwise   **b** 90° anticlockwise   **c** 180°

   Clearly label your answers.

5 On the resource sheet

   a Rotate trapezium **A** a half turn about the origin O.
   Label the new trapezium **B**.

   b Rotate trapezium **A** a quarter turn clockwise about the origin O.
   Label the new trapezium **C**.

   c Rotate trapezium **A** a quarter turn anticlockwise about the origin O.
   Label the new trapezium **D**.

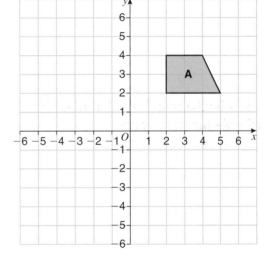

6 Use the resource sheet containing three copies of the diagram showing trapezium **P**.

   a On copy 1 of the diagram, rotate trapezium **P** 180° about the point $(2, 0)$.
   Label the new trapezium **Q**.

   b On copy 2 of the diagram, rotate trapezium **P** 90° clockwise about the point $(-2, 2)$.
   Label the new trapezium **R**.

   c On copy 3 of the diagram, rotate trapezium **P** 90° anticlockwise about the point $(-1, -1)$.
   Label the new trapezium **S**.

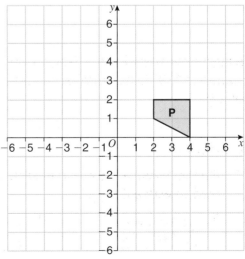

7 a Describe fully the rotation that maps shape **A** onto
>   **i** shape **B**
>   **ii** shape **C**
>   **iii** shape **D**.

b Describe fully the rotation that maps shape **B** onto shape **A**.

c Describe fully the rotation that maps shape **B** onto shape **D**.

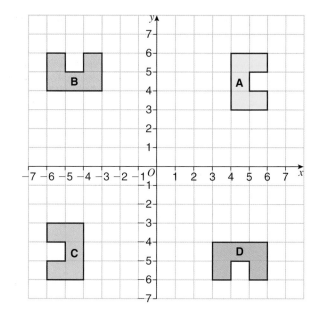

8 a Describe fully the rotation that maps triangle **A** onto
>   **i** triangle **B**   **ii** triangle **C**
>   **iii** triangle **D**   **iv** triangle **E**
>   **v** triangle **F**.

b Describe the transformation that maps triangle **B** onto triangle **E**.

c Describe the transformation that maps
>   **i** triangle **D** onto triangle **B**
>   **ii** triangle **F** onto triangle **E**.

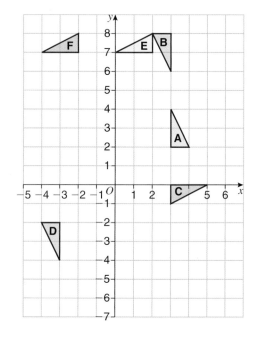

35.4 Reflection

Look in a mirror. You see a reflection.

In the mirror line, the reflection of point A is point B.

● Point B is the same distance behind the mirror line as point A is in front.

● The line joining points A and B is perpendicular (at 90°) to the mirror line.

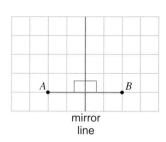

Reflecting each corner of triangle **P** in the mirror line gives the corners of triangle **Q**.

Triangle **Q** is the **reflection** of triangle **P** in the mirror line. Also, triangle **P** is the reflection of triangle **Q** in the mirror line. (In mathematics, mirror lines are like two-way mirrors.)

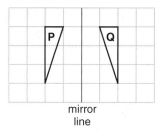

mirror line

In a reflection

- the lengths of the sides of the shape do not change
- the angles of the shape do not change
- the image is as far behind the mirror line as the shape is in front.

To describe a reflection give

- the mirror line.

Example 7

Reflect trapezium **T** in the mirror line. Label the new trapezium **U**.

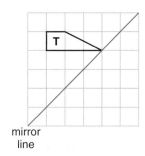

mirror line

Solution 7
Method 1
Reflect each corner in the mirror line so that its image is the same distance behind the mirror line as the corner is in front.

Notice that

- the line joining each corner to its image is perpendicular to the mirror line
- the image of the corner which is on the mirror line is also on the mirror line.

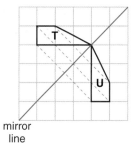

mirror line

Method 2

- Put the edge of a sheet of tracing paper on the mirror line and make a tracing of the trapezium.
- Turn the tracing paper over and put the edge of the tracing paper back on the mirror line.
- Mark the images of the corners with a pencil or compass point.

Method 2 is particularly useful when the shape is not a polygon or not drawn on a grid.

Example 8

Reflect the triangle in the mirror line.

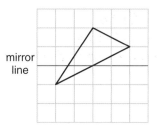

Solution 8

Reflect each corner of the triangle in the mirror line
and join the three images.

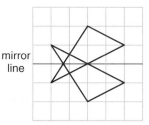

Example 9

The diagram shows a triangle **S** and its image,
triangle **T**, after a reflection.

Draw the mirror line of the reflection.

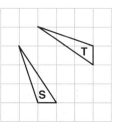

Solution 9
Method 1

Join each corner of triangle **S** to its image on triangle **T**.
The mirror line passes through the midpoints
(marked with crosses) of these lines.

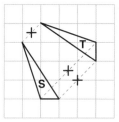

Draw the mirror line by joining the crosses.

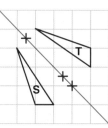

Method 2

Fold the paper so that triangle **S** is exactly on top of triangle **T**.
The fold line is the mirror line.

Example 10

Describe the transformation which maps triangle **A**
onto triangle **B**.

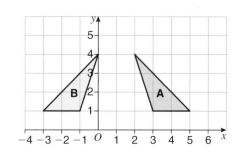

Solution 10

The transformation is a reflection.
The mirror line has the equation $x = 1$
The transformation is **a reflection in the line $x = 1$**

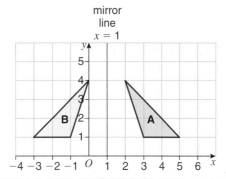

Example 11

Describe fully the transformation which maps
triangle **P** onto triangle **Q**.

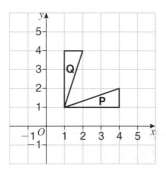

Solution 11

The transformation is a reflection in the line with
equation $y = x$. Equations of lines are covered in
Section 16.2

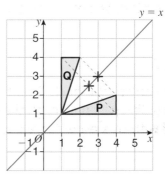

Exercise 35C

1 On the resource sheet, reflect each shape in the mirror line, shown in red.

a

b

c

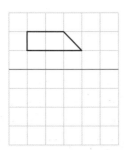

d

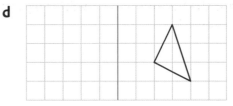

e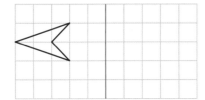

f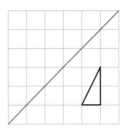

g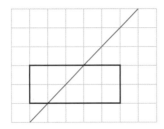

h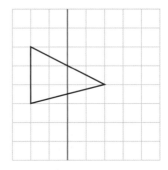

i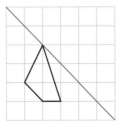

j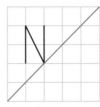

2 In each of the following diagrams, the red line is a mirror line. On the resource sheet, reflect each shape in the mirror line.

a

b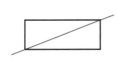

c

d

e

3 Each diagram shows a shape and its image after a reflection. On the resource sheet, draw in the mirror line.

a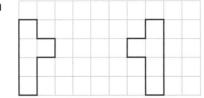

b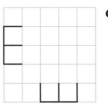

c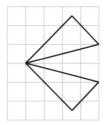

4 On the resource sheet,

  a reflect triangle **A** in the x-axis. Label the new triangle **B**.

  b reflect triangle **A** in the y-axis. Label the new triangle **C**.

  c reflect triangle **C** in the x-axis. Label the new triangle **D**.

  d Describe fully the transformation that maps triangle **A** onto triangle **D**.

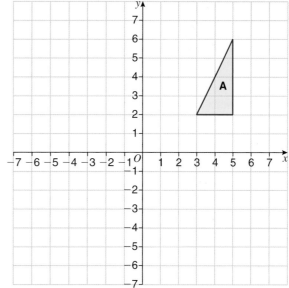

5 The diagram shows triangle **A** and the lines $x = 2$ and $y = 1$

On the resource sheet,

  a reflect triangle **A** in the line $x = 2$ Label this new triangle **B**.

  b reflect triangle **A** in the line $y = 1$ Label this new triangle **C**.

  c reflect triangle **C** in the line $x = 2$ Label this new triangle **D**.

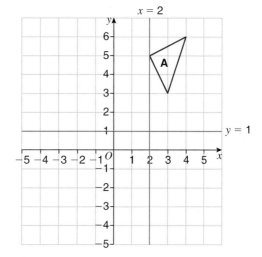

6 On the resource sheet,

  a reflect triangle **P** in the line $x = 1$ Label this new triangle **Q**.

  b reflect triangle **P** in the line $y = 2$ Label this new triangle **R**.

  c describe the reflection that maps triangle **Q** onto triangle **T**.

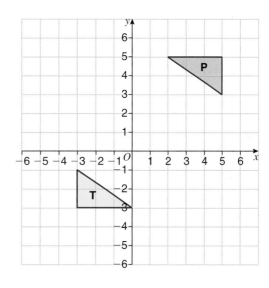

7 Use the resource sheet and

  a reflect triangle **A** in the line $y = x$.
Label this new triangle **B**.

  b reflect triangle **A** in the line $y = -x$.
Label this new triangle **C**.

  c describe fully the transformation that maps triangle **B** onto triangle **A**.

  d describe fully the transformation that maps triangle **B** onto triangle **C**.

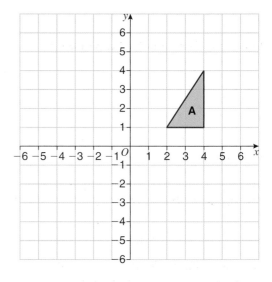

8 The diagram shows eight triangles.

  a Triangle **A** maps onto **four** of the unshaded triangles by a reflection.
Name these four triangles and describe the reflection in each case.

  b Triangle **A** maps onto **three** of the unshaded triangles by a rotation.
Name these three triangles and describe the rotation in each case.

  c How many of the unshaded triangles are congruent to triangle **A**?

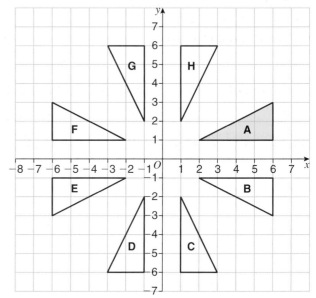

9 **a** On the resource sheet draw the mirror line of the reflection that maps

  i shape **P** onto shape **Q**

  ii shape **P** onto shape **R**.

  b Describe fully the transformation that maps shape **Q** onto shape **P**.

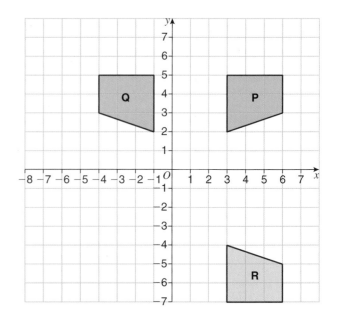

35.5 Enlargement

Here is a photograph of a windmill.

Here is an **enlargement** of the photograph.

The shapes in the two photographs are the same but lengths in the enlargement are 3 times the lengths in the original photograph.

For example, the length of a sail of the windmill in the enlargement is 3 times the length of the sail in the original photograph.

The **scale factor** of an enlargement is the number by which lengths have been multiplied.

So the larger photograph is an enlargement with **scale factor 3** of the smaller photograph.

Here are two shapes drawn on a centimetre grid.

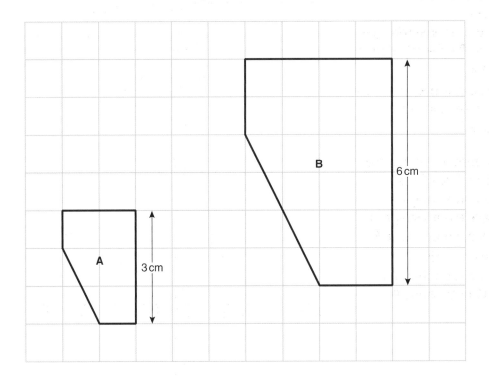

Shape **B** is an enlargement of shape **A**.

The height of shape **A** is 3 cm and the height of shape **B** is 6 cm so the scale factor of the enlargement $= \frac{6}{3} = 2$

Notice that each angle of shape **A** is the same as the corresponding angle of shape **B**.

In an enlargement

- the lengths of the sides of the shape change
- the angles of the shape do not change
- the sides of the shape and the enlargement are parallel.

Example 12

Shape **A** is drawn on a grid of centimetre squares. Draw an enlargement of shape **A** with a scale factor of 3. Label this new shape **B**. One side of shape **B** has already been drawn.

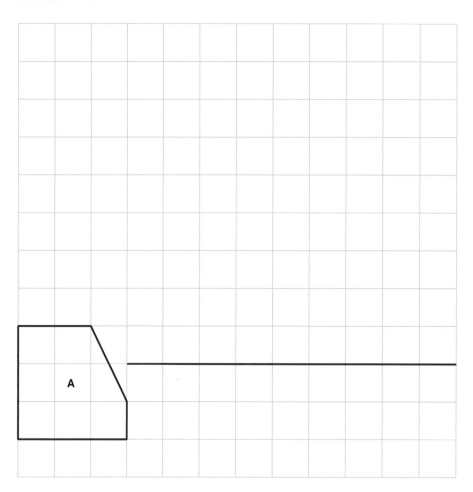

Solution 12

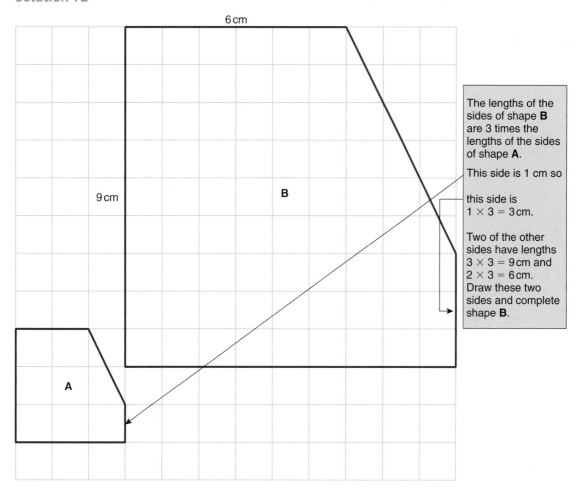

The lengths of the sides of shape **B** are 3 times the lengths of the sides of shape **A**.

This side is 1 cm so this side is $1 \times 3 = 3$ cm.

Two of the other sides have lengths $3 \times 3 = 9$ cm and $2 \times 3 = 6$ cm. Draw these two sides and complete shape **B**.

Example 13

a Find the scale factor of the enlargement that maps shape **A** onto shape **B**.

b Find the scale factor of the enlargement that maps shape **B** onto shape **A**.

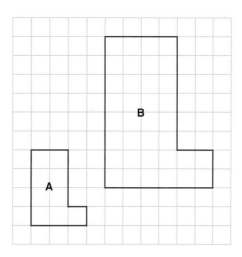

Solution 13

The base of shape **A** is 3 units.
The base of shape **B** is 6 units.

a   Scale factor of the enlargement which
       maps shape **A** onto shape **B** $= \frac{6}{3}$
       Scale factor = 2

The lengths of the sides of shape **B** are twice the
lengths of the sides of shape **A**.

b   Scale factor of the enlargement which
       maps shape **B** onto shape **A** $= \frac{3}{6}$
       Scale factor $= \frac{1}{2}$

In mathematics, the word 'enlargement' is also
used when a shape gets smaller.

This answer means that the lengths of the sides of
shape **A** are $\frac{1}{2}$ the lengths of the sides of shape **B**.

Exercise 35D

1   This rectangle has a length of 4 cm and a width of 3 cm.
       The rectangle is enlarged with a scale factor of 2
       Find the length and the width of the new rectangle.

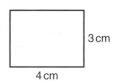

3 cm

4 cm

2   On the resource sheet, draw an enlargement,
       scale factor 2, of the shaded shape.

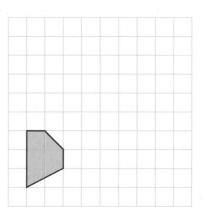

3   The right-angled triangle has a base of 8 cm and a height of 6 cm.
       The triangle is enlarged with a scale factor of $\frac{1}{2}$
       Find the base and the height of the new triangle.

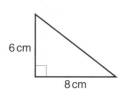

6 cm

8 cm

4   On the resource sheet, draw an enlargement,
       scale factor $\frac{1}{3}$, of the shaded shape.

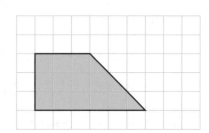

5 On the resource sheet,

    a draw an enlargement of shape **A** with scale factor 3.
Label this enlargement shape **B**.

    b On the same diagram, draw an enlargement of shape **A** with scale factor $\frac{1}{2}$
Label this enlargement shape **C**.

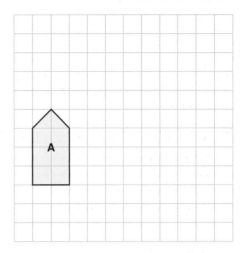

6 The diagram shows four triangles drawn on a grid.

    a Triangle **B** is an enlargement of triangle **A**.
Work out the scale factor.

    b Triangle **C** is an enlargement of triangle **D**.
Work out the scale factor.

    c Triangle **C** is an enlargement of triangle **A**.
Work out the scale factor.

    d Triangle **D** is an enlargement of triangle **A**.
Work out the scale factor.

    e Triangle **D** is an enlargement of triangle **B**.
Work out the scale factor.

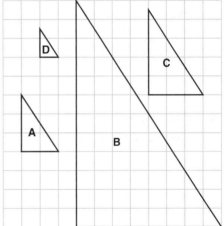

7 Rectangle **Q** is an enlargement of rectangle **P** with a scale factor of 2
Rectangle **R** is an enlargement of rectangle **P** with a scale factor of 3

    a On the resource sheet, draw rectangles **Q** and **R**.

    b Find the perimeter of
        i rectangle **P**   **ii** rectangle **Q**
       iii rectangle **R**.

    c Find the area of
        i rectangle **P**   **ii** rectangle **Q**
       iii rectangle **R**.

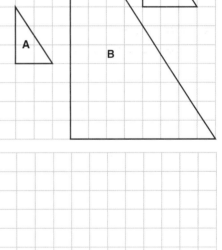

    d Work out the value of   **i** $\dfrac{\text{perimeter of } \mathbf{Q}}{\text{perimeter of } \mathbf{P}}$ **ii** $\dfrac{\text{perimeter of } \mathbf{R}}{\text{perimeter of } \mathbf{P}}$.

    Write down anything that you notice about these values.

    e Work out the value of   **i** $\dfrac{\text{area of } \mathbf{Q}}{\text{area of } \mathbf{P}}$ **ii** $\dfrac{\text{area of } \mathbf{R}}{\text{area of } \mathbf{P}}$.

    Write down anything that you notice about these values.

    f Rectangle **S** is an enlargement of rectangle **P** with a scale factor of 8.
What is the perimeter of rectangle **S**?

35.6 Centre of enlargement

In the diagram, triangle **P** has been enlarged by a scale factor of 2 to give triangle **Q**.

The corner A of triangle **P** is mapped onto the corner A' of triangle **Q**. A line has been drawn through A and A'. Lines have also been drawn joining the other pairs of corners of triangles **P** and **Q**.

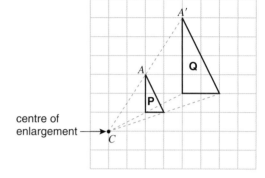

The lines meet at a point C, called the **centre of enlargement**.

C to A is 2 squares across and 3 squares up.
C to A' is 4 squares across and 6 squares up.

So $\dfrac{CA'}{CA} = 2$, the scale factor of the enlargement.

centre of
enlargement

To describe an enlargement give

● the scale factor
● the centre of enlargement.

Example 14

Enlarge the triangle with scale factor 2 and centre O.

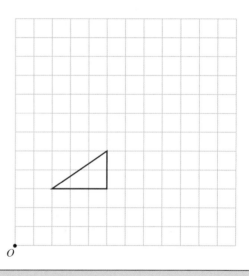

Solution 14

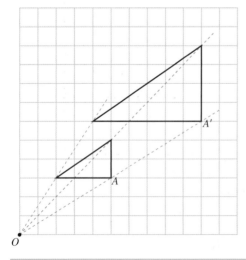

Choose a point A of the triangle.
Join O, the centre of enlargement, to A and extend this line.

O to A is 5 to the right and 3 up.

The scale factor is 2
$2 \times 5 = 10$ and $2 \times 3 = 6$
so
O to A' (A' is the image of A) is 10 to the right and 6 up.

Mark A' on the diagram.

Either repeat this to find the two other corners of the enlarged triangle or draw it using the fact that its sides are twice the length of those of the original triangle.

Always measure from the centre of enlargement.

Example 15

Enlarge triangle **T** by a scale factor $\frac{1}{2}$ with centre $P\,(-4, 3)$.
Label the new triangle **S**.

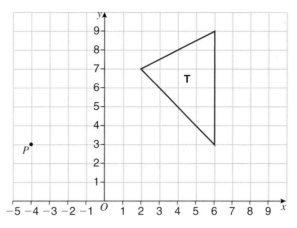

Solution 15

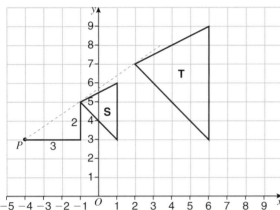

The scale factor is $\frac{1}{2}$ so triangle **S** is smaller than triangle **T**.

Draw a line from P to a point of triangle **T**.

From P to this point is 6 to the right and 4 up. So from P to a point on triangle **S** is 3 to the right and 2 up.

Either repeat this to find the other two corners of the triangle **S** or draw it using the fact that its sides are half the length of those of triangle **T**.

Example 16

Describe fully the transformation that maps triangle **A** onto triangle **B**.

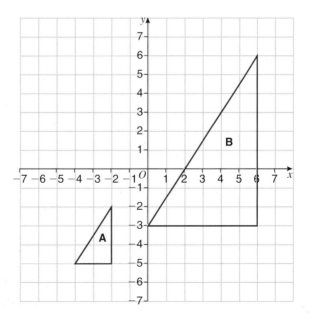

Solution 16

As triangle **B** is the same shape as triangle **A** but is not the same size, an enlargement maps triangle **A** onto triangle **B**.

The length of the base of triangle **B** is 6 squares and the length of the base of triangle **A** is 2 squares.

So scale factor $= \frac{6}{2} = 3$

To find the centre of enlargement, join each corner of triangle **A** to its corresponding corner in triangle **B**. Extend each line until they meet at a point. This point is the centre of enlargement.

The lines meet at the point $(-6, -6)$.

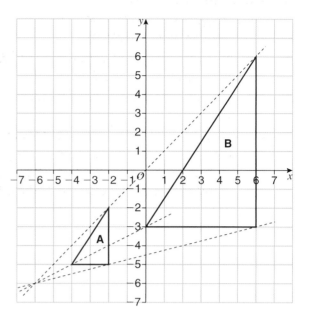

The transformation which maps triangle **A** onto triangle **B** is an enlargement, scale factor 3, centre $(-6, -6)$.

Exercise 35E

1　Copy each diagram onto squared paper and draw the enlargement of the shape with the given scale factor and centre of enlargement marked with a dot (•).

　　a　Scale factor 3　　　　　　　　　　**b**　Scale factor 2

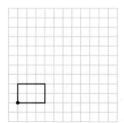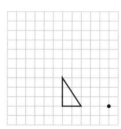

　　c　**i**　Scale factor 2　　　　　　　　**d**　**i**　Scale factor 3
　　　　ii　Scale factor 0.5　　　　　　　　　　**ii**　Scale factor 2
　　　　　　　　　　　　　　　　　　　　　　　　iii　Scale factor $\frac{1}{2}$

　　　　Draw both enlargements　　　　　　　　Draw all three enlargements
　　　　on the same diagram.　　　　　　　　　on the same diagram.

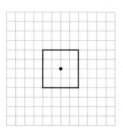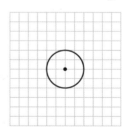

2   On the resource sheet,
   a   Enlarge triangle **A** by a scale factor of 2 with centre of enlargement O (0, 0).
       Label the new triangle **B**.
   b   Enlarge triangle **A** by a scale factor of 3 with centre of enlargement P (5, 5).
       Label the new triangle **C**.
   c   Enlarge triangle **A** by a scale factor of $\frac{1}{2}$ with centre of enlargement Q (4, −5).
       Label the new triangle **D**.
   d   Triangle **C** is an enlargement of triangle **D**.
       i   Find the scale factor of this enlargement.
       ii By drawing lines on your diagram, find the centre of this enlargement. Mark
           this centre with a cross (x) and the letter R.

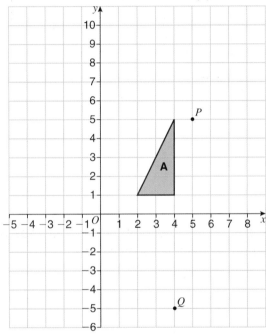

3   Use the resource sheet and
   a   Describe fully the
       transformation that maps
       triangle **P** onto triangle **Q**.
   b   Describe fully the
       transformation that maps
       triangle **P** onto triangle **R**.
   c   Describe fully the
       transformation that maps
       triangle **R** onto triangle **P**.

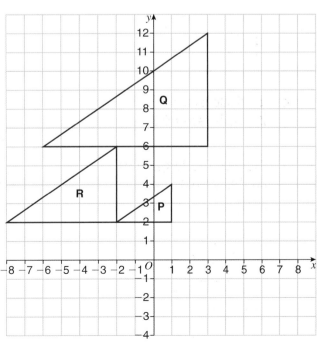

4   On the resource sheet,

   a   Describe fully the transformation that maps quadrilateral **A** onto quadrilateral **B**.

   b   Enlarge quadrilateral **A** by a scale factor of 2 with centre of enlargement (6, 13). Label this image **C**.

   c   Enlarge quadrilateral **B** by a scale factor of $\frac{1}{3}$ with centre of enlargement (4, 3). Label this image **D**.

   d   Describe fully the transformation that maps **A** onto **D**.

   e   Describe fully the transformation that maps **C** onto **D**.

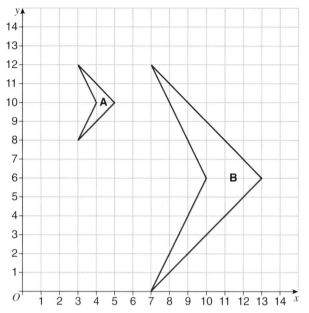

Chapter summary

You should now know and be able to use these facts:

★   A **transformation** of a shape is a change in position or size of the shape. The final shape is the **image**

★   In a **translation** all points of the shape move the same distance in the same direction

★   A translation can be described by how far to the right or left and how far up or down the shape moves

★   A translation can also be described by a vector so that $\begin{pmatrix} 9 \\ -6 \end{pmatrix}$ means 9 to the right and 6 down

★   A **rotation** is described by giving the angle of turn, the direction of turn and the centre of rotation

★   In a **reflection** the image is as far behind the mirror line as the shape is in front

★   A reflection is described by giving the mirror line

★   The scale factor of an **enlargement** is the number by which lengths have been multiplied

★   In an enlargement all lengths are multiplied by the scale factor

★   An enlargement is described by giving the scale factor and the centre of enlargement

★   Translations, rotations and reflections have no effect on lengths and angles

★   Enlargement changes the size of a shape but has no effect on angles.

Chapter 35 review questions

1 Describe fully the transformation which maps shape *A* onto shape *B*.

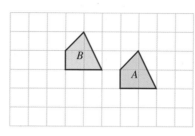

(1388 January 2002)

2 On the resource sheet, rotate triangle **T** a half turn about the point *O*.

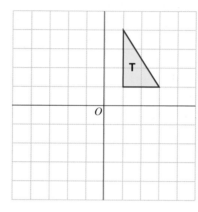

(1388 March 2002)

3 On the resource sheet, reflect these shapes in the mirror lines.

a mirror line

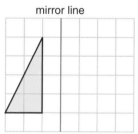

b mirror line

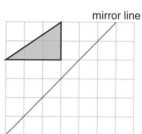

(1384 June 1995)

4 On the grid on the resource sheet, enlarge the shape with a scale factor of 2.

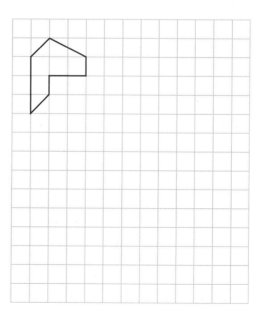

(1387 June 2005)

5 On the resource sheet, rotate the triangle 90° **clockwise** about the point (0, 0).

Draw the triangle in its new position.

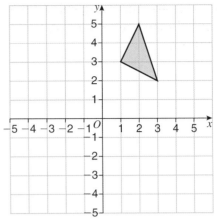

(1385 November 2000)

6

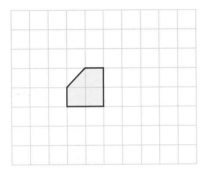

a On the resource sheet, translate the shaded shape 3 squares to the right and 2 squares up.

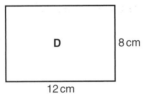

Diagram **NOT** accurately drawn

Rectangle **D** is an enlargement of rectangle **C**.

b Find the scale factor of the enlargement.

(1388 January 2003)

7 **a** On the resource sheet, reflect triangle **P** in the *y*-axis. Label the new shape **Q**.

The line *AB* is drawn on the grid.

b On the same diagram reflect triangle **P** in the line *AB*. Label the new shape **R**.

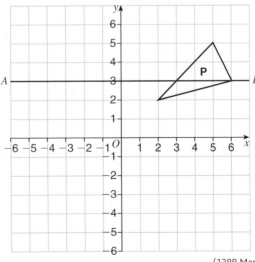

(1388 March 2003)

8 On the resource sheet, enlarge the shaded shape by a scale factor of 2, centre A.

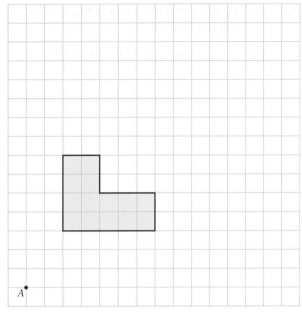

(1388 March 2003)

9 a On the resource sheet, reflect the shape in the y-axis. Label the new shape **T**.

b On the same diagram, rotate the new shape **T** through an angle of 90° anticlockwise using $(0, 0)$ as the centre of rotation. Label the new shape **U**.

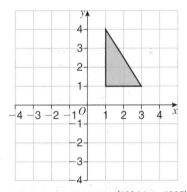

(1384 June 1995)

10 Triangle **B** is a reflection of triangle **A**.

a i On the resource sheet, draw the line of reflection.

ii Write down the equation of the line of reflection.

b Describe fully the single transformation that maps triangle **A** onto triangle **C**.

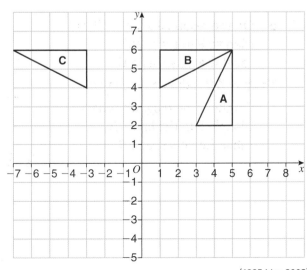

(1385 May 2002)

11 Describe fully the single transformation which takes shape **A** onto shape **B**.

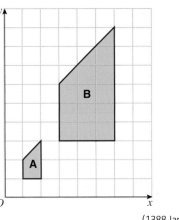

(1388 January 2003)

12

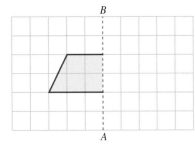

a **i** On the resource sheet, reflect the shaded shape in the line AB.
ii Write down the mathematical name for the shape you have drawn.

b On the resource sheet, rotate the shaded shape $\frac{1}{4}$ **turn anticlockwise**, centre O.

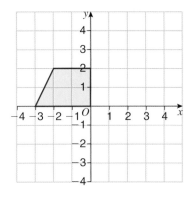

(1388 January 2002)

13 **a** Write down the coordinates of the point
  i A **ii** B

b Write down the mathematical name of the shape $ABCD$.

c On the grid on the resource sheet, enlarge $ABCD$ by a scale factor of 2

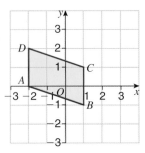

(1384 November 1997)

14 Here is a triangle **T**.

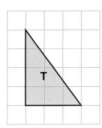

Here are nine more triangles.

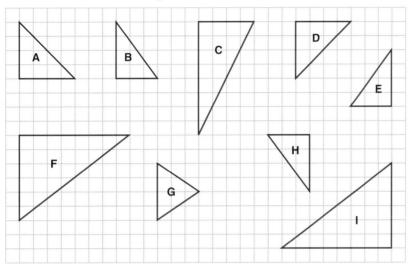

a Write down the letters of the triangles that are congruent to the triangle **T**.

b **i** Write down the letter of a triangle that is an enlargement of triangle **T**.

ii Find the scale factor of the enlargement.

(1385 May 2002)

15 **a** Triangle **P** has a line of symmetry. Write down the equation of this line of symmetry.

b On the resource sheet, reflect triangle **P** in the y-axis. Label your new triangle **Q**.

c On the same diagram on the resource sheet, rotate triangle **P** 90° **clockwise** about (0, 0). Label your new triangle **R**.

d On the same diagram on the resource sheet, translate triangle **P** by the vector $\begin{pmatrix} -5 \\ -4 \end{pmatrix}$.

Label your new triangle **S**.

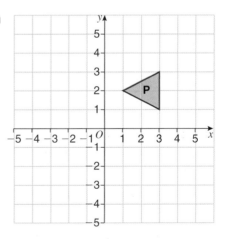

Further algebra

36.1 Index notation

In section 11.4 index notation is used.

$a \times a = a^2$ is read as 'a times a equals a squared'

$a \times a \times a = a^3$ is read as 'a times a times a equals a cubed'.

The number 2 in the expression a^2 is called the **index** or the power.
The index (or power) in the expression a^3 is 3

This can be continued.

$a \times a \times a \times a = a^4$ is read as 'a times a times a times a equals a to the power 4'

$a \times a \times a \times a \times a = a^5$ which is read as 'a to the power 5'

and so on.

Expressions involving powers of the same letter can be multiplied.

$$a^2 \times a^3 = (a \times a) \times (a \times a \times a)$$
$$= a \times a \times a \times a \times a$$
$$a^2 \times a^3 = a^5$$

Note that $a^2 \times a^3 = a^{2+3} = a^5$

In general $x^m \times x^n = x^{m+n}$ (add the indices)

Expressions involving powers of the same letter can be divided.

$$a^5 \div a^2 = \frac{a^5}{a^2} = \frac{a \times a \times a \times a \times a}{a \times a} = a \times a \times a = a^3$$

$$a^5 \div a^2 = a^3$$

Note that $a^5 \div a^2 = a^{5-2} = a^3$

In general $x^m \div x^n = x^{m-n}$ (subtract the indices)

$$x^m \times x^n = x^{m+n}$$

and $x^m \div x^n = x^{m-n}$

are two **laws of indices** which can be used to simplify expressions.

Example 1

Write $a \times a \times a \times a \times a \times a \times a \times a \times a$ using index notation.

Solution 1

$a \times a \times a \times a \times a \times a \times a \times a \times a = a^9$

Example 2

Simplify $3b^4 \times 2b^6$

Solution 2

$3b^4 \times 2b^6 = 3 \times b^4 \times 2 \times b^6$
$\qquad\qquad = 3 \times 2 \times b^4 \times b^6$
$\qquad\qquad = 6 \times b^{4+6}$
$\qquad\qquad = 6 \times b^{10}$
$3b^4 \times 2b^6 = 6b^{10}$

Example 3

Simplify $8p^7 \div 2p^6$

Solution 3

$8p^7 \div 2p^6 = 4 \times p^7 \div p^6$
$\qquad\qquad = 4 \times p^{7-6}$
$8p^7 \div 2p^6 = 4p^1 = 4p \qquad$ (since $p^1 = p$)

Exercise 36A

1 Write using index notation

   a $p \times p \times p$

   b $n \times n \times n \times n \times n \times n \times n \times n$

   c $a \times a \times a \times a \times a \times a$

   d $x \times x \times y \times y \times y$

   e $a \times a \times b \times b \times c \times c$

   f $p \times p \times q \times q \times p$

2 Simplify

   a $x^3 \times x^2$ **b** $y^5 \times y^3$ **c** $n^3 \times n^3$ **d** $p^4 \times p^2$ **e** $p^3 \times p^4$

   f $q^2 \times q^3$ **g** $y^4 \times y^4$ **h** $n \times n^6$ **i** $x^2 \times x$ **j** $q^7 \times q$

3 Simplify

   a $x^5 \div x^3$ **b** $y^7 \div y^3$ **c** $n^6 \div n^2$ **d** $p^6 \div p^3$ **e** $p^5 \div p^4$

   f $q^2 \div q$ **g** $y^6 \div y$ **h** $n^8 \div n^6$ **i** $x^8 \div x^7$ **j** $q^7 \div q$

4 Simplify

   a $3x^2 \times x^5$ **b** $y^3 \times 2y^2$ **c** $3n^5 \times 2n^3$

   d $4p \times 2p^4$ **e** $4p \times 5p$ **f** $3q^6 \times 2q^2$

   g $2y^2 \times 3y^3$ **h** $6n \times 2n^5$ **i** $2 \times 2r^8 \times 4r$

5 Simplify

   a $4x^5 \div x^2$ **b** $6y^6 \div 2y^3$ **c** $8n^7 \div 4n^5$ **d** $12p^8 \div 3p^6$

   e $15p^9 \div 3p^2$ **f** $12q^2 \div 6q$ **g** $24y^4 \div 6y$ **h** $16n^6 \div 8n^5$

   i $8x^9 \div 2x^8$ **j** $4q \div 2q$

6 Simplify

   a $y \times y^4 \times y^3$ **b** $n^3 \times n^3 \times n$ **c** $x \times x^2 \times x^2$ **d** $q^4 \times q \times q^3$

   e $2y^2 \times 3y^3 \times y^3$ **f** $n^4 \times 2n^2 \times 4n$ **g** $2x^4 \times x \times 5x^3$ **h** $3q \times 5q^4 \times 2q^5$

7 Simplify

   a   **i** $x^2 \times x$ **ii** $x^5 \div x^2$ **iii** $(x^2 \times x) + (x^5 \div x^2)$

   b   **i** $2y^2 \times y^2$ **ii** $8y^6 \div 2y^2$ **iii** $(8y^6 \div 2y^2) - (2y^2 \times y^2)$

36.2 Substituting negative numbers into expressions involving powers

Example 4

Work out the value of the expression $4b^3$ when $b = -2$

Solution 4

$4b^3 = 4 \times b \times b \times b$
$= 4 \times (-2) \times (-2) \times (-2)$
$= 4 \times (-8)$
$4b^3 = -32$

Example 5

Work out the value of the expression $5x^2 - 4x$ when $x = -3$

Solution 5

$5x^2 - 4x = 5 \times x^2 - 4 \times x$
$= 5 \times (-3)^2 - 4 \times (-3)$
$= 5 \times (+9) - 4 \times (-3)$
$= 45 + 12$
$5x^2 - 4x = 57$

Example 6

Work out the value of the expression $aq^3 + q^2$ when $a = 2$ and $q = -3$

Solution 6

$aq^3 + q^2 = a \times q^3 + q \times q$
$= 2 \times (-3)^3 + (-3)^2$
$= 2 \times (-27) + 9$
$= -54 + 9$
$aq^3 + q^2 = -45$

Exercise 36B

1 Work out the value of each of these expressions, when $x = -1$
   a x^2 **b** x^3 **c** x^4 **d** x^5 **e** x^6

2 Work out the value of each of these expressions, when $y = -2$
   a y^2 **b** y^3 **c** y^4 **d** y^5 **e** y^6

3 Work out the value of each of these expressions, when $z = -3$
   a z^2 **b** z^3 **c** $2z^2$ **d** $2z^3$ **e** $z^2 + z$

4 Work out the value of each of these expressions, when $a = -2$ and $b = -3$
   a ab **b** ab^2 **c** $a^2 + b^2$ **d** a^2b^2 **e** $a^3 + b^3$ **f** $a^3 - b^3$

5 Work out the value of the expression $2a^2 - a$ when $a = -4$

6 Work out the value of the expression $3a^3 - 2a$ when $a = -2$

7 Work out the value of these expressions when $a = -2$
   a $\dfrac{3a^3}{a^2}$ **b** $3a^2 + 8$ **c** $\dfrac{3a^2 + 8}{a}$ **d** $\dfrac{2a^3 + 6}{a}$

8 Work out the value of the expression $3(x + 1)^2$ when $x = -3$

36.3 Solving equations of the type $ax^2 = b$

In section 9.3, two directed numbers are multiplied. If the answer is positive, the two numbers must either be both positive or both negative.

For example, $(+3) \times (+3) = 9$ and $(-3) \times (-3) = 9$

Using index notation, $(+3)^2 = 9$ and $(-3)^2 = 9$

The equation, $x^2 = 9$ has two solutions, $x = +3$ and $x = -3$, which can be written as $x = \pm 3$

To solve equations of the type $ax^2 = b$, where a and b are numbers, first divide both sides of the equation by a then take the square root, remembering the $\pm$ sign.

> The inverse of squaring is taking the square root.

Example 7

Solve the equation $x^2 = 100$

Solution 7

$x^2 = 100$

> Take the square root of both sides.

$x = \pm\sqrt{100}$

> Remember the $\pm$ sign.

$x = \pm 10$

Check: when $x = +10$,
$(+10) \times (+10) = 100$
when $x = -10$,
$(-10) \times (-10) = 100$

Example 8

Solve the equation $3x^2 = 48$

Solution 8

$3x^2 = 48$

> Divide both sides by 3

$\dfrac{3x^2}{3} = \dfrac{48}{3}$

$x^2 = 16$

> Take the square root of both sides.

$x = \pm\sqrt{16}$

> Remember the $\pm$ sign.

$x = \pm 4$

Check: when $x = +4$,
$3 \times (+4) \times (+4) = 3 \times (+16) = 48$
when $x = -4$,
$3 \times (-4) \times (-4) = 3 \times (+16) = 48$

Example 9

Solve the equation $y^2 + 5 = 14$

Solution 9

$y^2 + 5 = 14$

$y^2 + 5 - 5 = 14 - 5$

> Subtract 5 from both sides.

$y^2 = 9$

$y = \pm\sqrt{9}$

> Take the square root of both sides.

$y = \pm 3$

> Remember the $\pm$ sign.

Check: when $y = +3$, $(+3) \times (+3) + 5 = 9 + 5 = 14$
when $y = -3$, $(-3) \times (-3) + 5 = 9 + 5 = 14$

Exercise 36C

1 By taking the square root of both sides, solve these equations.

    a $x^2 = 1$ **b** $x^2 = 9$ **c** $x^2 = 25$ **d** $x^2 = 64$

    e $y^2 = 100$ **f** $y^2 = 4$ **g** $p^2 = 49$ **h** $q^2 = 81$

2 Which two numbers, when squared, give the answer 16?

3 Solve these equations.

    a $3x^2 = 12$ **b** $2x^2 = 50$ **c** $4x^2 = 64$ **d** $3x^2 = 27$

    e $5y^2 = 20$ **f** $2y^2 = 98$ **g** $3p^2 = 75$ **h** $2q^2 = 72$

4 Solve these equations.

    a $x^2 + 5 = 9$ **b** $x^2 + 6 = 31$ **c** $x^2 + 9 = 25$ **d** $x^2 - 2 = 7$

    e $y^2 - 1 = 0$ **f** $y^2 - 9 = 16$ **g** $p^2 - 7 = 57$ **h** $q^2 + 10 = 59$

5 Solve the equation $4x^2 = 1$

6 Solve the equation $16x^2 = 1$

36.4 Trial and improvement

The equation $x^3 + 2x = 3$ has an exact solution $x = 1$ since $1^3 + 2 \times 1 = 3$

The equation $x^3 + 2x = 12$ has an exact solution $x = 2$ since $2^3 + 2 \times 2 = 12$ but not all equations can be solved exactly, for example $x^3 + 2x = 7$

An approximate solution to the equation $x^3 + 2x = 7$ can be found by first guessing the solution and then using the **method of trial and improvement** to obtain a more accurate answer.

Example 10

a Show that the equation $x^3 + 2x = 7$ has a solution between 1 and 2

b Use a trial and improvement method to find this solution. Give your answer correct to one decimal place.

Solution 10

a

x	LHS $x^3 + 2x$	Compare with RHS 7	
1	$1^3 + 2 \times 1 = 3$	Since $3 < 7$, $x = 1$ is **too small**	
2	$2^3 + 2 \times 2 = 12$	Since $12 > 7$, $x = 2$ is **too big**	Solution is between 1 and 2

b It is not obvious that the solution is closer to 1 or to 2 so as a first trial take the middle value of the interval.

x	$x^3 + 2x$	Compare with RHS 7	
1.5	$1.5^3 + 2 \times 1.5 = 6.375$	Since $6.375 < 7$, $x = 1.5$ is **too small**	Solution is between 1.5 and 2
1.6	$1.6^3 + 2 \times 1.6 = 7.296$	Since $7.296 > 7$, $x = 1.6$ is **too big**	Solution is between 1.5 and 1.6

To decide if the solution is closer to 1.5 or 1.6, try the middle value, 1.55, of the interval

x	$x^3 + 2x$	Compare with RHS 7	
1.55	$1.55^3 + 2 \times 1.55 = 6.823\,875$	Since $6.823\,875 < 7$ $x = 1.55$ is **too small**	Solution is between 1.55 and 1.6

All values between 1.55 and 1.6 are closer to 1.6 than 1.5 so, to one decimal place, the solution of $x^3 + 2x = 7$ which lies between 1 and 2 is $x = 1.6$

Example 11

a Show that $y = -1$ is a solution of the equation $y^2 = \dfrac{1}{y} + 2$

b Use a trial and improvement method to find the solution of $y^2 = \dfrac{1}{y} + 2$ that lies between 1 and 2. Give your answer correct to one decimal place.

Solution 11

a $y = -1$ is a solution of the equation $y^2 = \dfrac{1}{y} + 2$ if $(-1)^2 = \dfrac{1}{(-1)} + 2$ that is

$(+1) = (-1) + 2$ which is true so $y = -1$ is a solution.

b $y^2 = \dfrac{1}{y} + 2$

y	LHS y^2	RHS $\dfrac{1}{y} + 2$	Compare LHS and RHS	
1	$1^2 = 1$	$\dfrac{1}{1} + 2 = 3$	Since $1 < 3$, $y = 1$ is **too small**	
1.5	$1.5^2 = 2.25$	$\dfrac{1}{1.5} + 2 = 2.666...$	Since $2.25 < 2.666...$, $y = 1.5$ is **too small**	
1.7	$1.7^2 = 2.89$	$\dfrac{1}{1.7} + 2 = 2.588...$	Since $2.89 > 2.588...$, $y = 1.7$ is **too big**	Solution is between 1.5 and 1.7
1.6	$1.6^2 = 2.56$	$\dfrac{1}{1.6} + 2 = 2.625$	Since $2.56 < 2.625$, $y = 1.6$ is **too small**	Solution is between 1.6 and 1.7

To decide if the solution is closer to 1.6 or 1.7, try the middle value, 1.65, of the interval

y	LHS y^2	RHS $\dfrac{1}{y} + 2$	Compare LHS and RHS	
1.65	$1.65^2 =$ 2.7225	$\dfrac{1}{1.65} + 2 = 2.6060...$	Since 2.7225 > 2.606..., $x = 1.65$ is too big	Solution is between 1.6 and 1.65

```
   ┌──────────┬──────────┐
  1.6        1.65        1.7
```

All values between 1.6 and 1.65 are closer to 1.6 than 1.7 so, correct to one decimal place, the solution of $y^2 = \dfrac{1}{y} + 2$ which lies between 1 and 2 is $y = 1.6$

Exercise 36D

1 Show that each of these equations has a solution between 0 and 1

    a $x^2 + 4x = 2$ **b** $x^3 + 2x = 1$ **c** $y^3 + 3y^2 = 3$ **d** $x^2(x - 3) + 1 = 0$

2 Use a trial and improvement method to find the solution between 0 and 1 of each of these equations. Give your answers correct to one decimal place.

    a $x^2 + 4x = 2$ **b** $x^3 + 2x = 1$ **c** $y^3 + 3y^2 = 3$ **d** $x^2(x - 3) + 1 = 0$

3 The equation $x^3 + 2x = 9$ has a solution between 1 and 2. Use a trial and improvement method to find this solution. Give your answer correct to two decimal places.

4 The equation $x^3 - 4x = 8$ has a solution between 2 and 3. Use a trial and improvement method to find this solution. Give your answer correct to one decimal place.

5 a Show that the equation $x^3 - 4x = 76$ has a solution between 4 and 5

    b Use a trial and improvement method to find this solution. Give your answer correct to one decimal place.

6 The equation $x^3 = 5x + 6$ has a solution between 2 and 3. Use a trial and improvement method to find this solution. Give your answer correct to one decimal place.

7 a Show that the equation $t^3 = 3(t^2 - 1)$ has a solution between 1 and 2

    b Use a trial and improvement method to find this solution. Give your answer correct to one decimal place.

8 Use a trial and improvement method to find the solution of $x^3 + x = 5$. Give your answer correct to one decimal place.

9 Use a trial and improvement method to find the solution of $x^2 - \dfrac{1}{x} = 4$ that lies between 2 and 3. Give your answer correct to one decimal place.

10 Use a trial and improvement method to find the solution of $x^2 = \dfrac{2}{x} + 7$ that lies between 2 and 3. Give your answer correct to one decimal place.

Chapter summary

You should know and be able to use these facts:

★ $x^m \times x^n = x^{m+n}$ and $x^m \div x^n = x^{m-n}$ are two **laws of indices** which can be used to simplify expressions, for example, $x^2 \times x^3 = x^5$ and $p^8 \div p^3 = p^5$

★ To substitute negative numbers into expressions involving powers remember that $(-) \times (-)$ is $(+)$ and $(-) \times (+)$ is $(-)$, for example, when $x = -3$, $x^2 = 9$ and $x^3 = -27$ and $2x^3 = -54$

★ To solve equations of the type $ax^2 = b$, where a and b are numbers, first divide both sides of the equation by a then take the square root, remembering the $\pm$ sign, for example,

$$2x^2 = 200 \quad 2x^2 \div 2 = 200 \div 2 \quad x^2 = 100 \quad x = \pm\sqrt{100} \quad x = \pm 10$$

★ Approximate solutions to equations which cannot be solved exactly can be found by first guessing the solution and then using the **method of trial and improvement** to obtain a more accurate answer.

Chapter 36 review questions

1 $p = 3, q = -2$
Work out the value of 　　　**a** $p^2 + q^2$ 　　　　　**b** $2p + q^3$

2 Simplify
　a $d^4 \times d^6$ 　　**b** $e^9 \div e^4$ 　　**c** $6p^5 \times 3p^2$ 　　**d** $6q^9 \div 2q^3$

3 Solve 　　　　　**a** $x^2 = 81$ 　　**b** $y^2 - 5 = 31$ 　**c** $4x^2 = 16$

4 **a** Simplify 　**i** $x^4 \times x$ 　**ii** $y^8 \div y^2$ 　　**b** Solve $2x - \dfrac{3}{4} = 2$

5 **a** Factorise $x^2 - 3x$ 　　　　　**b** Simplify $k^5 \div k^2$ 　　　(1387 June 2004)

6 **a** Simplify $5p - 4q + 3p + q$ 　　**b** Simplify $\dfrac{x^7}{x^2}$

　c Factorise $4x + 6$ 　　　　　　**d** Multiply out and simplify $(x + 3)(x - 2)$
　e Simplify $2x^3 \times x^5$ 　　　　　　　　　　　　　　(1386 November 2002)

7 The equation $x^3 - 2x = 67$ has a solution between 4 and 5. Use a trial and improvement method to find this solution. Give your answer correct to one decimal place. You must show **ALL** your working. 　　　(1387 June 2004)

8 The equation $x^3 - 4x = 24$ has a solution between 3 and 4. Use a trial and improvement method to find this solution. Give your answer correct to one decimal place. You must show **ALL** your working. 　　　(1387 June 2005)

9 The equation $x^3 + x = 16$ has a solution between 2 and 3. Use a trial and improvement method to find this solution. Give your answer correct to two decimal places. You must show **ALL** your working. (1385 November 2002)

10 The equation $x^3 + x^2 = 220$ has a solution between 5 and 6. Use a trial and improvement method to find this solution. Give your answer correct to one decimal place. You must show **ALL** your working.

11 Use a trial and improvement method to find the solution of $x^2 = \dfrac{1}{x} + 5$ that lies between 2 and 3. Give your answer correct to one decimal place.

Constructions and loci

37.1 Constructions

The construction of shapes in Chapters 7 and 23 involved the use of rulers for measuring lengths but constructions can also be made in which a ruler may not be used for this purpose. For this reason, they are sometimes called 'straight edge and compasses' constructions. The following examples describe the steps in these constructions.

Example 1

Construct an equilateral triangle with AB as its base.

Solution 1

Draw an arc, centre A, with radius equal to the length of AB.

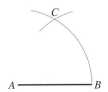

Draw another arc, centre B, with the same radius. The two arcs cross at C.

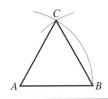

Complete the equilateral triangle ABC.

Each angle of an equilateral triangle is 60° and so the method in Example 1 can be used to construct an angle of 60°.

Example 2

Draw a circle, radius 2 cm, and construct a regular hexagon inside it.

Solution 2

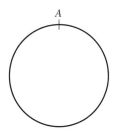

Draw a circle, radius 2 cm, and mark point A on its circumference.

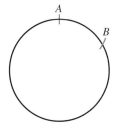

Keeping the compasses set at 2 cm, draw an arc, centre A, which cuts the circle at B. B is the centre of the next arc.

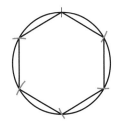

Repeat the process until six points are marked on the circumference.
Join the points to make a regular hexagon.

Example 3

Construct the perpendicular bisector of the line AB.

Solution 3

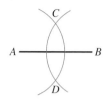

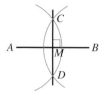

| Draw an arc, centre A, with radius more than half the length of AB. | Draw another arc, centre B, with the same radius. The two arcs cross at C and D. | Draw a line through C and D. The line is the perpendicular bisector of AB and it crosses the line AB at right angles at M, the midpoint of AB. |

Every point on the perpendicular bisector of the line AB is the same distance from A as it is from B. This property will be used later in the chapter.

Example 4

Construct the bisector of angle BAC.

Solution 4

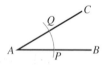

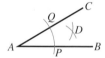

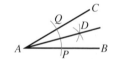

| Draw an arc, centre A, to cross AB at P and AC at Q. | Draw an arc, centre P, and an arc, centre B, with the same radius. The two arcs cross at D. | Draw a line from A through D. This line is the bisector of angle BAC. |

Every point on the bisector of angle BAC is the same distance from the line AB as it is from the line AC. This property will also be used later in the chapter.

Other constructions can be developed from the five basic ones described above. For example, an angle of 120° can be constructed by drawing a further arc, centre C, in Example 1 or an angle of 30° can be constructed by constructing a 60° angle (Example 1) and then bisecting it (Example 4).

Exercise 37A

Answer Questions **1–7** on the resource sheet.

1 Construct an equilateral triangle with PQ as its base. P————————Q

2 Draw a circle with a radius of 3 cm and construct a regular hexagon inside it.

3 Construct the perpendicular bisector of the line RS.   R———————————S

4 Construct the bisector of angle QPR.   **5** Construct the bisector of angle QPR.

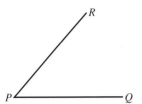

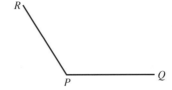

6 Construct the perpendicular bisector of each of the sides of the triangle.

7 Construct the bisector of each of the angles of the triangle.

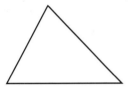

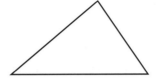

8 Construct an angle of 120°.   **9** Construct an angle of 30°.

37.2 Loci

The **locus** of a point is its path when it obeys given rules or conditions.
Loci is the plural of locus.

The simplest loci, on which many others are based, are the locus of a point which moves so that it is always the same distance from a fixed point and the locus of a point which moves so that it is always the same distance from a fixed line.

Example 5

A point moves so that it is always 2 cm from a fixed point A.
Draw its locus.

Solution 5

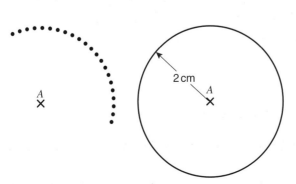

Here are some points which are 2 cm from A.

2 cm

Combining all the points which are 2 cm from A gives a circle, centre A, with a radius of 2 cm.

Example 6

A point moves so that it is always 1 cm from a fixed line AB.
Draw its locus.

Solution 6

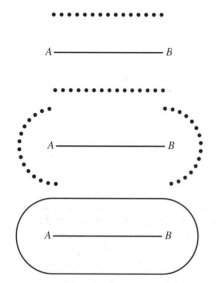

Here are some points which are 1 cm from the line AB. They make lines parallel to AB and 1 cm away from it.

Here are some points which are 1 cm away from point A and 1 cm away from point B. They make semicircles, centres A and B, with a radius of 1 cm.

Combining the two parallel lines and the two semicircles gives the complete locus.

The locus of a point which moves so that it is always an equal distance from two fixed points is the perpendicular bisector of the line joining the two fixed points (Example 2).

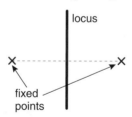

The word **equidistant**, which means 'an equal distance', is sometimes used. So this could also be described as the locus of a point which moves so that it is always equidistant from two fixed points.

The locus of a point which moves so that it is always equidistant from each of two fixed lines is the bisector of the angle between the two fixed lines (Example 4).

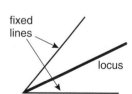

Sometimes a moving point has to satisfy two loci conditions. The position, or positions, of the point are where the loci cross (or intersect).

Example 7

A point P moves so that it is equidistant from A and B.
It is also 2 cm from C.
On the centimetre grid, find the *two* possible positions of P.
Mark them with a cross.

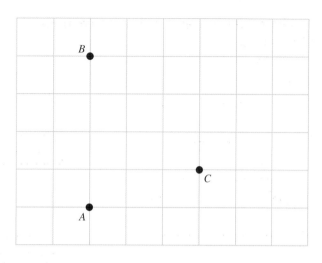

Solution 7

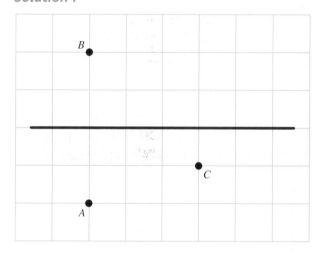

The locus of a point which moves so that it is equidistant from A and B is the perpendicular bisector of the line AB.

Draw this perpendicular bisector.

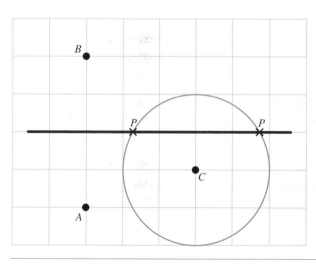

The locus of a point which moves so that it is 2 cm from C is a circle, centre C, with a radius of 2 cm.

The two possible positions of P are where the line and the circle cross.

Exercise 37B

Answer this exercise on the resource sheet.

1 A point moves so that it is always 3 cm away from a fixed point A. Draw its locus.

•A

2 A point moves so that it is always 2 cm away from a fixed line AB. Draw its locus.

A————————B

3 A point moves so that it is always an equal distance from two fixed points A and B. Draw its locus.

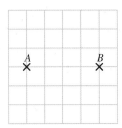

4 A point moves so that it is always an equal distance from two fixed points $A(2, 1)$ and $B(2, 3)$. Draw its locus.

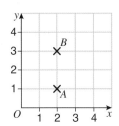

5 A point moves so that it is always an equal distance from two fixed points A and B. Draw its locus.

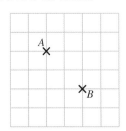

6 A point moves so that it is always an equal distance from two fixed points A and B. Construct its locus.

A✕

✕B

7 A point moves so that it is always the same distance from two fixed lines AB and AC. Construct its locus.

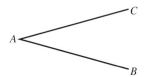

8 A point moves so that it is always the same distance from two fixed lines AB and AC. Draw its locus.

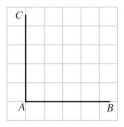

9 A point moves outside this rectangle so that it is always 2 cm from the edges of the rectangle. Draw its locus.

10 A point P moves so that it is 2 cm from A and 3 cm from B. Find the two possible positions of P. Mark them with a cross.

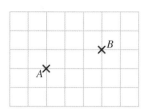

11 A point P moves so that it is equidistant from A and B and 2 cm from C. Find the two possible positions of P. Mark them with a cross.

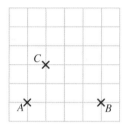

12 The diagram represents Mr. Khan's garden. It is drawn to a scale of 1 cm to 5 metres. He plants a tree which is the same distance from the path as it is from the wall. The tree is also 12 m from the hedge. Find the position of the tree. Mark it with a cross and label it T.

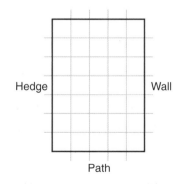

13 A map is drawn to a scale of 1 cm to 10 km. A, B and C are three ports. A ship is 75 km from A. It is also the same distance from B as it is from C. Find the position of the ship. Mark it with a cross and label it S.

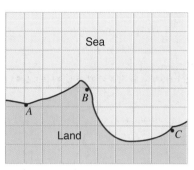

14 AB and AC are two fixed lines. A point P moves so that it is equidistant from A and B and 1 cm from the line AC. Find the two possible position of P. Mark them with crosses.

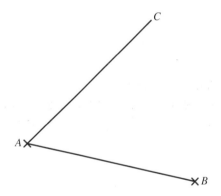

37.3 Regions

Sometimes, when a moving point obeys a rule, the point has to lie inside a **region** rather than on a particular path made up of lines or curves.

Example 8

A point moves so that it is always less than 2 cm from a fixed point A.
Show, by shading, the region which satisfies this condition.

Solution 8

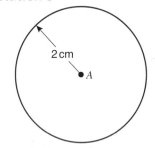 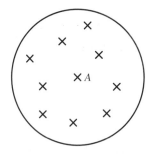 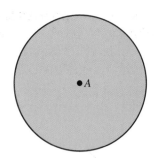

The points on this circle are all 2 cm from A.	Here are some points which are less than 2 cm from A. They are all inside the circle.	Every point inside the shaded region is less than 2 cm from A.

For a point which moves so that it is always *more* than 2 cm from a fixed point A, the point lies in the region *outside* the circle.

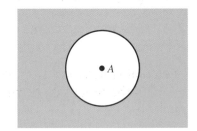

Example 9

A and B are two fixed points.
A point moves so that it is always nearer to A than B.
Show, by shading, the region which satisfies this condition.

$A \times$ $\times B$

Solution 9

Every point on the perpendicular bisector of the line AB is the same distance from A and B.	Here are some points which are nearer A than B.	Every point inside the shaded region is nearer A than B.

For a point which moves so that it is always nearer B
than A, the point lies in the region on the other
side of the line.

Example 10

AB and AC are two fixed lines.
A point moves so that it is always nearer AC than AB.
Show, by shading, the region which satisfies this condition.

Solution 10

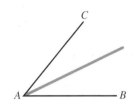

Every point on the bisector
of angle BAC is the same
distance from AB and AC.

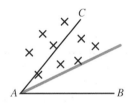

Here are some points which
are nearer AC than AB.

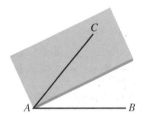

Every point inside the
shaded region is nearer AC
than AB.

For a point which moves so that it is always nearer AB than AC, the point lies in the
region on the other side of the line.

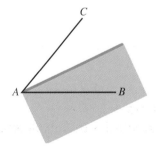

If a moving point has to satisfy two conditions, the region in which both conditions are
satisfied is the overlap (**intersection**) of two regions.

Example 11

A, B and C are three fixed points.
A point moves so that it is always nearer B than A
and less than 2 cm from C.
Show, by shading, the region which satisfies
both these conditions.

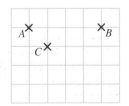

Solution 11 (reduced)

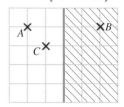

Every point inside this shaded region is nearer B than A.

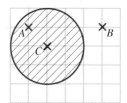

Every point inside this shaded region is less than 2 cm from C.

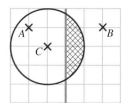

Both conditions are satisfied where the two regions overlap.

Exercise 37C

Answer this exercise on the resource sheets.

1 A point moves so that it is always less than 3 cm away from a fixed point A. Show, by shading, the region which satisfies this condition.

•A

2 A point moves so that it is always less than 2 cm away from a fixed line AB. Show, by shading, the region which satisfies this condition.

A————————B

3 A and B are two fixed points. A point moves so that it is always nearer A than B. Show, by shading, the region which satisfies this condition.

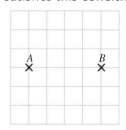

4 $A(2, 1)$ and $B(2, 3)$ are two fixed points. A point moves so that it is always nearer B than A. Show, by shading, the region which satisfies this condition.

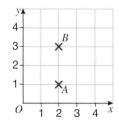

5 A and B are two fixed points. A point moves so that it is always nearer A than B. Show, by shading, the region which satisfies this condition.

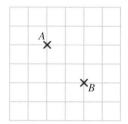

6 A and B are two fixed points. A point moves so that it is always nearer B than A. Show, by shading, the region which satisfies this condition.

A✕

✕B

7 AB and AC are two fixed lines. A point moves so that it is always nearer AB than AC. Show, by shading, the region which satisfies this condition.

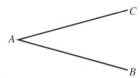

8 AB and AC are two fixed lines.
A point moves so that it is always
nearer AC than AB.
Show, by shading, the region which
satisfies this condition.

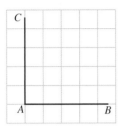

9 A point moves outside this rectangle
so that it is always less than 2 cm from
the edges of the rectangle.
Show, by shading, the region which
satisfies this condition.

10 A point moves so that it is less than
2 cm from A and more than 3 cm
from B. Show, by shading, the region
which satisfies this condition.

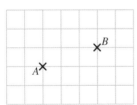

11 A, B and C are three fixed points.
A point moves so that it is always
nearer A than B and less than 2 cm
from C. Show, by shading, the region
which satisfies both these conditions.

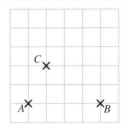

12 $A(0, 2)$ is a fixed point. A point moves
so that its is always less than 2 cm
from A and nearer the x-axis than the
y-axis. Show, by shading, the region
which satisfies this condition.

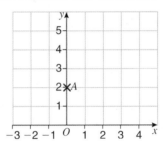

13 The map shows two ports, A and B.
The scale of the map is 1 cm to 10 km.
A ship is less than 25 km from A and
less than 35 km from B. Show, by
shading, the region where the ship is.

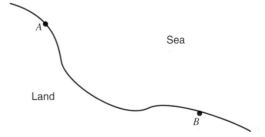

Chapter summary

You should now know:

★ how to construct

- an equilateral triangle with a given base
- a regular hexagon inside a circle
- the perpendicular bisector of a line
- the bisector of an angle

> ★ how to draw the **locus** of a point which moves so that it is
>   - a given distance from a fixed point
>   - a given distance from a fixed line
>   - **equidistant** from two fixed points
>   - equidistant from two fixed lines
>
> ★ how to find points which satisfy two of these conditions.
>
> ★ how to show **regions** which satisfy given conditions, including overlapping regions.

Chapter 37 review questions

Answer these questions on the resource sheets.

1 A point moves so that it is always 1 cm away from a fixed point A. Draw its locus.

2 A point moves so that it is always more than 1 cm away from a fixed point A. Show, by shading, the region which satisfies this condition.

3 P and Q are two points marked on the grid.

Construct accurately the locus of all the points which are equidistant from P and Q.

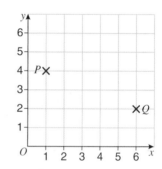

(1384 June 1996)

4 Draw the locus of all points which are 3 cm away from the line AB.

(1385 November 2002)

5 On the diagram, draw the locus of the points, **outside the rectangle**, that are 3 cm from the outside of this rectangle.

(1385 June 2000)

6 A, B and C represent three radio masts on a plan.

Signals from a mast A can be received 300 km away, from mast B 350 km away and from mast C 200 km away. Show, by shading, the region in which signals can be received from all 3 masts.

$\bullet$ B

$\bullet$ A

$\bullet$ C

(1384 November 1994)

7 A treasure chest is buried on an island. P and Q are two trees on this island.

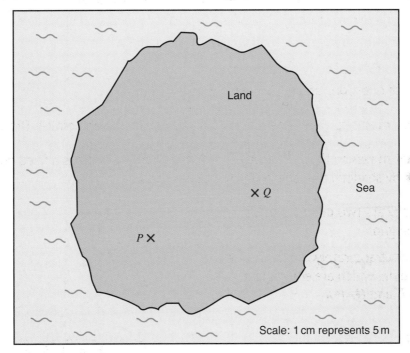

Land

$\times Q$

Sea

$P \times$

Scale: 1 cm represents 5 m

The treasure chest is buried the same distance from P as it is from Q.

a On the diagram, draw accurately the locus of points which are the same distance from P as they are from Q.

On the diagram, 1 centimetre represents 5 metres.
The treasure chest is buried 20 metres from P.

b On the diagram, draw accurately the locus which represents all the points which are 20 metres from P.

c Find the point where the chest is buried.

On the diagram, mark the point clearly with a T.   (1385 November 1998)

8 The grid represents part of a map.

a On the grid, draw a line on a bearing of 037° from the point marked A.

The point C is on a bearing of 300° from the point marked B. C is also 3 cm from B.

b Mark the position of the point C and label it with a letter C.

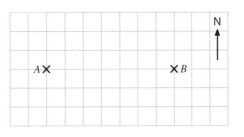

(1385 May 2002)

9 The map shows part of a coastline
and a coastguard station.
1 cm on the map represents 2 km.
A ship is 12 km from the coastguard station
on a bearing of 160°.

Coastguard
Station

N

a Plot the position of the ship from the
coastguard station, using a scale of 1 cm
to represent 2 km.

It is not safe for ships to come within 6 km
of the coastguard station.

b Shade the area on the map which is less than 6 km from the coastguard station.

The distance of a buoy from the coastguard station is 14 km to the nearest km.

c **i** Write down the maximum distance it could be.
  ii Write down the minimum distance it could be.   (1384 June 1994)

10 The scale drawing below shows the positions of an airport tower, T, and a radio mast, M.

1 cm on the diagram represents 20 km.

North

$\times$
T

$\times$
M

a **i** Measure, in centimetres, the distance TM.
  ii Work out the distance in km of the airport tower from the radio mast.
b **i** Measure and write down the bearing of the airport tower from the radio mast.
  ii Write down the bearing of the radio mast from the airport tower.

A plane is 80 km from the radio mast on a bearing of 220°.

c Plot the position of the plane, using a scale of 1 cm to 20 km.

Signals from the radio mast can be received up to a distance of 100 km.

d Shade the region on the scale diagram in which signals from the radio mast can
be received.

The distance of a helicopter from the radio mast is 70 km correct to the nearest
kilometre.

e Write down
  i the maximum distance the helicopter could be from the mast,
  ii the minimum distance the helicopter could be from the mast.   (1384 June 1997)

Pythagoras' theorem

38.1 Pythagoras' theorem

Pythagoras was a famous mathematician in Ancient Greece. The theorem which is named after him is an important result about **right-angled triangles**.

Here is a right-angled triangle ABC.

The angle at C is the right angle.
The side, AB, opposite the right angle is called the **hypotenuse**. It is the longest side in the triangle.

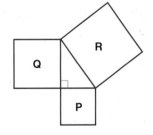

The right-angled triangle in the diagram has sides of length 3 cm, 4 cm and 5 cm.

Squares have been drawn on each side of the triangle and each square has been divided up into squares of side 1 cm.

The area of the square on the side of length 3 cm is 9 cm².
The area of the square on the side of length 4 cm is 16 cm².
The area of the square on the side of length 5 cm (the hypotenuse) is 25 cm².

Notice that $25 = 9 + 16$, that is $5^2 = 3^2 + 4^2$

In other words, 5^2 (the area of the square on the hypotenuse) is equal to the sum of 3^2 and 4^2 (the areas of the squares on the other two sides added together).

This is an example of Pythagoras' theorem, which is only true for right-angled triangles.

> **Pythagoras' theorem states:**
> **In a right-angled triangle, the area of the square on the hypotenuse is equal to the sum of the areas of the squares on the other two sides.**

Area of square **R** = Area of square **P** + Area of square **Q**

Pythagoras' theorem is used to find the length of the third side of a right-angled triangle, when the lengths of the other two sides are known. For this, the theorem is usually stated in terms of the lengths of the sides of the triangle.

That is $c^2 = a^2 + b^2$

In triangle *DEF*, Pythagoras' theorem gives

$$DE^2 = EF^2 + DF^2$$

(*DE*² means that the length of the side *DE* is squared.)

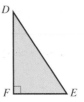

38.2 Finding the length of a hypotenuse

Use Pythagoras' theorem to work out the length of the hypotenuse of a right-angled triangle when the lengths of the two shorter sides are given.

Example 1

Work out the length of the hypotenuse in this triangle

Solution 1

$c^2 = a^2 + b^2$ | State Pythagoras' theorem. |

$c^2 = 8^2 + 15^2$ | Substitute the given lengths. |

$c^2 = 64 + 225$ | Work out 8^2 and 15^2 and add the results. |

$c^2 = 289$ | c is a number which, when squared, gives 289. In other words, c is the square root of 289 |

$c = \sqrt{289} = 17$ | Find $\sqrt{289}$ on a calculator. |

Length of hypotenuse = 17 cm | The answer is sensible, because the hypotenuse is longer than the other two sides. |

15 cm   *c* cm

8 cm

Example 2

Work out the length of the side marked *x* in this triangle.
Give your answer correct to 1 decimal place.

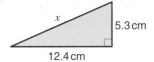

x   5.3 cm

12.4 cm

Solution 2

$c^2 = a^2 + b^2$ | State Pythagoras' theorem. |

$x^2 = 5.3^2 + 12.4^2$ | Substitute the given lengths. |

$x^2 = 28.09 + 153.76$
$x^2 = 181.85$ | Work out 5.3^2 and 12.4^2 and add the results. |

$x = \sqrt{181.85} = 13.48...$ | Use a calculator to find the square root. Write down at least four figures. |

$x = 13.5$ cm (to 1 d.p.) | Give the final answer correct to 1 decimal place. |

It is important to be able to apply Pythagoras' theorem when the triangle is in a different position.

Example 3

In triangle XYZ, angle $X = 90°$, $XY = 8.6$ cm and $XZ = 13.9$ cm. Work out the length of YZ.

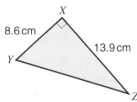

Give your answer correct to 1 decimal place.

Solution 3

	The hypotenuse is the side opposite the right angle. Angle X is the right angle so the hypotenuse is YZ.
$YZ^2 = XY^2 + XZ^2$	State Pythagoras' theorem.
$YZ^2 = 8.6^2 + 13.9^2$	Substitute the given lengths.
$YZ^2 = 73.96 + 193.21$	Work out 8.6^2 and 13.9^2 and add the results.
$YZ^2 = 267.17$	
$YZ = \sqrt{267.17} = 16.34...$	Use a calculator to find the square root. Write down at least four figures.
$YZ = 16.3$ cm (to 1 d.p.)	Give the final answer correct to 1 decimal place.

Exercise 38A

1 Work out the length of the sides marked with letters in these triangles.

a

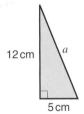

12 cm a 5 cm

b

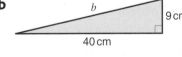

b 9 cm   40 cm

c

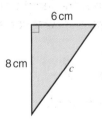

6 cm   8 cm c

2 Work out the length of the sides marked with letters in these triangles.
Give each answer correct to 1 decimal place.

a

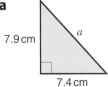

7.9 cm a 7.4 cm

b

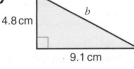

4.8 cm b 9.1 cm

c

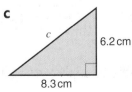

c 6.2 cm   8.3 cm

d

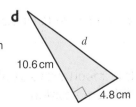

d 10.6 cm   4.8 cm

3 **a** In triangle ABC, angle $A = 90°$, $AB = 3.4$ cm and
$AC = 12.1$ cm.
Work out the length of BC.
Give your answer correct to 1 decimal place.

b In triangle DEF, angle $E = 90°$,
$DE = 6.3$ cm and $EF = 9.8$ cm.
Work out the length of DF.
Give your answer correct to 1 decimal place.

c In triangle PQR, angle $R = 90°$,
$PR = 5.9$ cm and $QR = 13.1$ cm.
Work out the length of PQ.
Give your answer correct to 1 decimal place.

d In triangle XYZ, angle $X = 90°$,
$XY = 12.6$ cm and $XZ = 16.5$ cm.
Work out the length of YZ.
Give your answer correct to 1 decimal place.

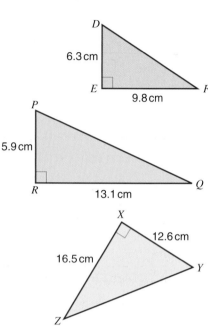

38.3 Finding the length of one of the shorter sides of a right-angled triangle

So far, the lengths of the two shorter sides of a right-angled triangle have been given and the length of the hypotenuse has been worked out.

Pythagoras' theorem can also be used to work out the length of one of the shorter sides in a right-angled triangle when the lengths of the other two sides are known.

Example 4

Work out the length of the side marked a in this triangle.
Give your answer correct to 2 decimal places.

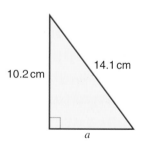

Solution 4

$$c^2 = a^2 + b^2$$ State Pythagoras' theorem.

$$14.1^2 = 10.2^2 + a^2$$ Substitute the given lengths.

$$198.81 = 104.04 + a^2$$ Work out 14.1^2 and 10.2^2.

$$198.81 - 104.04 = a^2$$ Subtract 104.04 from both sides.

$$94.77 = a^2$$

or

$$a^2 = 94.77$$

$$a = \sqrt{94.77} = 9.734...$$

Use a calculator to find the square root.
Write down at least four figures.

$$a = 9.73 \text{ cm (to 2 d.p.)}$$

Give the final answer correct to 2 decimal places.

9.73 cm is less than the length of the hypotenuse 14.1 cm and so the answer is sensible.

Example 5

In triangle ABC, angle $A = 90°$, $BC = 17.4$ cm and $AC = 5.8$ cm.
Work out the length of AB.
Give your answer correct to 1 decimal place.

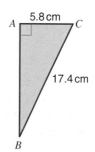

Solution 5

Angle A is the right angle so the hypotenuse is BC.

$$BC^2 = AC^2 + AB^2$$

State Pythagoras' theorem.

$$17.4^2 = 5.8^2 + AB^2$$

Substitute the given lengths.

$$302.76 = 33.64 + AB^2$$

Work out 17.4^2 and 5.8^2.

$$302.76 - 33.64 = AB^2$$

Subtract 33.64 from both sides.

$$269.12 = AB^2$$

$$AB = \sqrt{269.12} = 16.40...$$

Use a calculator to find the square root.
Write down at least four figures.

$$AB = 16.4 \text{ cm (to 1 d.p.)}$$

Give the final answer correct to 1 decimal place.

Exercise 38B

1 Work out the lengths of the sides marked with letters in these triangles.

a 25 cm, a, 24 cm   **b** 12 cm, 37 cm, b **c** 20 cm, 25 cm, c **d** 6.5 cm, d, 2.5 cm

2 Work out the lengths of the sides marked with letters in these triangles.
Give each answer correct to 2 decimal places.

a 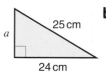 4.8 cm, 10.7 cm, a

b 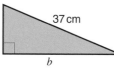 1.8 cm, b, 12.4 cm

c c, 11.3 cm, 8.1 cm

d 8.3 cm, 2.1 cm, d

3 a In triangle ABC, angle $A = 90°$, $AB = 5.9$ cm
and $BC = 16.3$ cm.
Work out the length of AC. Give your answer
correct to 1 decimal place.

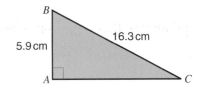

b In triangle DEF, angle $E = 90°$, $DF = 10.1$ cm
and $EF = 7.8$ cm.

    i Draw a sketch of the right-angled triangle DEF and
label sides DF and EF with their lengths.

    ii Work out the length of DE. Give your answer correct
to 2 decimal places.

38.4 Applying Pythagoras' theorem

Pythagoras' theorem can be used to solve problems.

Example 6

A boat travels due North for 5.7 km. The boat then turns and travels due East for 7.2 km.
Work out the distance between the boat's finishing point and its starting point.

Give your answer correct to 2 decimal places.

Solution 6

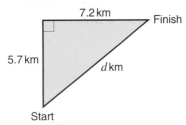

Draw a sketch of the boat's journey.	Remember that the points of the compass are 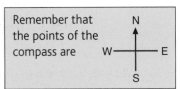

The sketch is of a right-angled triangle so
that Pythagoras' theorem can be used.

$d^2 = 5.7^2 + 7.2^2$

$d^2 = 32.49 + 51.84$

$d^2 = 84.33$

$d = \sqrt{84.33} = 9.183...$

The distance between the starting point and the
finishing point is the length of the hypotenuse of the
triangle. This distance is marked d km in the sketch.

Distance $= 9.18$ km (to 2 decimal places)

Isosceles triangles can be split into two right-angled triangles, in which Pythagoras'
theorem can be used.

Example 7

The diagram shows an isosceles triangle ABC.
The midpoint of BC is the point M.
In the triangle, $AB = AC = 8$ cm and $BC = 6$ cm.

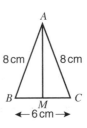

a Work out the height, AM, of the triangle.
Give your answer correct to 2 decimal places.

b Work out the area of triangle ABC. Give your answer correct to 1 decimal place.

Solution 7

Pythagoras' theorem cannot be used in triangle ABC as this triangle is not right-angled.

a

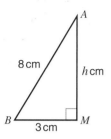

> As M is the midpoint of the base of the isosceles triangle, the line AM is the line of symmetry of triangle ABC. So AM is perpendicular to the base and angle $AMB = 90°$.

> $BM = 3$ cm as M is the midpoint of BC.

> Draw a sketch of triangle ABM.

By Pythagoras

$$AB^2 = AM^2 + BM^2$$
$$8^2 = h^2 + 3^2$$
$$64 = h^2 + 9$$
$$64 - 9 = h^2$$
$$55 = h^2$$
$$h = \sqrt{55} = 7.416\ldots$$
$$h = 7.42$$

> Triangle ABM is right angled with hypotenuse AB. The height, AM, of the triangle is marked h cm on the sketch.

Height of triangle = 7.42 cm (to 2 d.p.)

b

$$\text{area} = \tfrac{1}{2} \times 6 \times 7.416\ldots$$
$$\text{area} = 22.24\ldots$$
$$\text{area} = 22.2 \text{ cm}^2 \text{ (to 1 d.p.)}$$

> area of a triangle $= \tfrac{1}{2} \times$ base $\times$ height

> For triangle ABC base = 6 cm and height = 7.416... cm.

Length of a line joining two points

The diagram shows the points $A(1, 1)$ and $B(9, 5)$. The right-angled triangle ABC has been drawn so that $AC = 8$ and $BC = 4$

Pythagoras' theorem can be used to find the length of AB.

$$AB^2 = 8^2 + 4^2$$
$$AB^2 = 64 + 16 = 80$$
$$AB = \sqrt{80} = 8.94 \text{ (to 2 d.p.)}$$

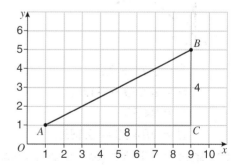

Example 8

Find the length of the line joining $A(3, 2)$ and $B(15, 7)$

Solution 8

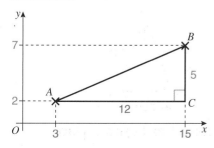

> Draw a sketch showing A and B and complete the right-angled triangle ABC.
> $AC = 15 - 3 = 12$
> $BC = 7 - 2 = 5$

$$AB^2 = 12^2 + 5^2 \quad AB^2 = 144 + 25 = 169$$
$$AB = \sqrt{169} = 13$$

Use Pythagoras' theorem to find the length of AB.

Exercise 38C

1 Find the lengths of the sides marked with letters in each of these triangles. Give each answer correct to 1 decimal place.

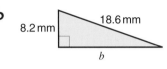

a a, 6.8 cm, 13.4 cm

b 8.2 mm, 18.6 mm, b

c 9.7 cm, c, 6.8 cm

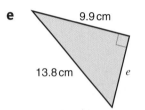

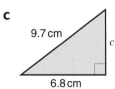

d 11.4 cm, 14.8 cm, d

e 9.9 cm, 13.8 cm, e

f 8.4 cm, 8.4 cm, f

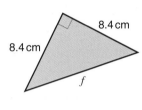

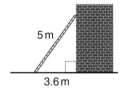

2 The diagram shows a ladder leaning against a vertical wall. The foot of the ladder is on horizontal ground. The length of the ladder is 5 m. The foot of the ladder is 3.6 m from the wall. Work out how far up the wall the ladder reaches. Give your answer correct to 2 decimal places.

5 m, 3.6 m

3 Aiton (A), Beeville (B) and Ceaborough (C) are three towns as shown in this diagram.
Beeville is 10 km due South of Aiton and 21 km due East of Ceaborough. Work out the distance between Aiton and Ceaborough. Give your answer correct to the nearest km.

A, 10 km, C, 21 km, B

4 a Work out the length of the side marked b cm in the triangle. Give your answer correct to 2 decimal places.

b Work out the area of the triangle. Give your answer correct to 2 decimal places.

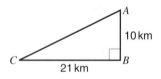

10.6 cm, 14.5 cm, b cm

5 a Work out the length of the side marked a cm in the triangle. Give your answer correct to 2 decimal places.

b Work out the perimeter of the triangle. Give your answer correct to 1 decimal place.

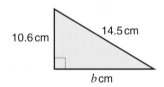

11.7 cm, a cm, 8.3 cm

6

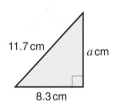

A, 5 m, 2.5 m, P, B, N 2 m C, Q

The diagram represents the end view of a tent, triangle ABC; two guy-ropes, AP and AQ; and a vertical tent pole, AN. The tent is on horizontal ground so that $PBNCQ$ is a straight horizontal line. Triangles ABC and APQ are both isosceles triangles.

$BN = NC = 2$ m, $AN = 2.5$ m and $AP = AQ = 5$ m

a Work out the length of the side AC of the tent. Give your answer correct to 2 decimal places.

b Work out the length of **i** NQ, **ii** CQ.
Give your answers correct to 2 decimal places.

There is a tent peg at P and a tent peg at Q.

c Work out the distance between the two tent pegs at P and Q. Give your answer correct to 2 decimal places.

7 The diagram shows two right-angled triangles.

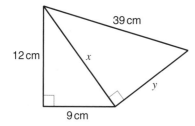

a Work out the length of the side marked x.

b Hence work out the length of the side marked y.

8 Work out the length of the line joining each of these pairs of points.
   a (1, 3) and (5, 6)   **b** (3, 1) and (11, 7)   **c** (2, 1) and (14, 6)

9 Work out the length of the line joining each of these pairs of points. Give your answers correct to 1 decimal place.
   a (3, 5) and (4, 7)   **b** (4, 2) and (7, 5)   **c** (4, 5) and (0, 7)

Chapter summary

You should now know:

★ In a right-angled triangle, the side opposite the right angle is the **hypotenuse**. It is the longest side in the triangle.

You should now be able to:

★ Use **Pythagoras' theorem** in right-angled triangles

$$c^2 = a^2 + b^2$$

- find the length of the hypotenuse when the lengths of the other two sides are known
- find the length of one of the shorter sides of the triangle when the lengths of the other two sides are known

★ Apply Pythagoras' theorem in problems involving right-angled triangles, including the length of a line joining two points whose coordinates are given.

Chapter 38 review questions

1 ABC is a right-angled triangle.
$AB = 4$ cm, $BC = 6$ cm.
Calculate the length of AC.
Give your answer in centimetres,
correct to 2 decimal places.

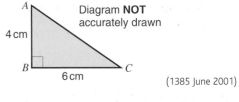

Diagram **NOT**
accurately drawn

(1385 June 2001)

2 ABC is a right-angled triangle.
$AB = 8$ cm, $BC = 11$ cm.
Calculate the length of AC.
Give your answer correct to
1 decimal place.

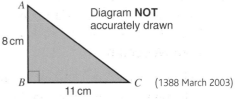

Diagram **NOT**
accurately drawn

(1388 March 2003)

3 ABC is a right-angled triangle.
$AC = 5$ m, $CB = 8.5$ m.

   a Work out the area of the triangle.

   b Work out the length of AB.

Give your answer correct to 2 decimal places.

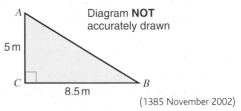

Diagram **NOT**
accurately drawn

(1385 November 2002)

4 The diagram shows triangle ABC
$AC = 16.4$ cm, $BC = 12.6$ cm,
Angle $ABC = 90°$.

Work out the length of AB.

Give your answer correct to 1 decimal place.

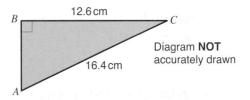

Diagram **NOT**
accurately drawn

5 Calculate the length of AB.
Give your answer correct
to 1 decimal place.

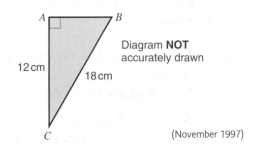

Diagram **NOT**
accurately drawn

(November 1997)

6 $AC = 12.6$ cm,
$BC = 4.7$ cm,
Angle $ABC = 90°$.

Calculate the length of AB.
Give your answer correct to
1 decimal place.

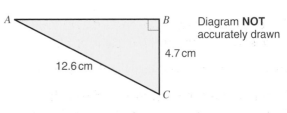

Diagram **NOT**
accurately drawn

(1388 January 2004)

7 Angle $MLN = 90°$,
$LM = 3.7$ m,
$MN = 6.3$ m.

Work out the length of LN.
Give your answer correct
to 2 decimal places.

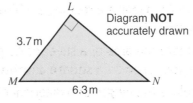

Diagram **NOT**
accurately drawn

(1388 March 2004)

8 Work out the length, in centimetres, of AM.
Give your answer correct to 2 decimal places.

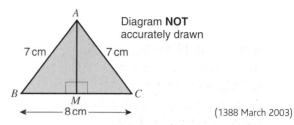

Diagram **NOT** accurately drawn

(1388 March 2003)

9 Ballymena is due West of Larne. Woodburn is 15 km due South of Larne. Ballymena is 32 km from Woodburn.

Calculate the distance of Larne from Ballymena. Give your answer in kilometres, correct to 1 decimal place.

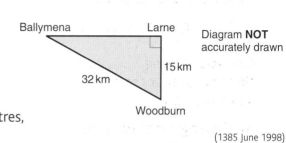

Diagram **NOT** accurately drawn

(1385 June 1998)

10 Sidney places the foot of his ladder on horizontal ground and the top against a vertical wall. The ladder is 16 feet long. The foot of the ladder is 4 feet from the base of the wall.

Work out how high up the wall the ladder reaches. Give your answer correct to 1 decimal place.

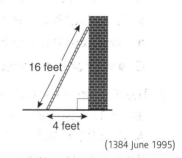

(1384 June 1995)

11 Calculate the length of a diagonal of this rectangle. Give your answer in centimetres correct to 1 decimal place.

12 cm

15 cm

(1384 June 1995)

12 A, B, C and D are four points on the circumference of a circle.
$ABCD$ is a square with sides 20 cm long.

Work out the diameter, BD, of the circle. Give your answer correct to 1 decimal place.

Diagram **NOT** accurately drawn

(1385 November 1998)

13 The diagram shows a rectangle drawn inside a circle. The centre of the circle is at O.

The rectangle is 15 cm long and 9 cm wide.

Calculate the circumference of the circle. Give your answer correct to 1 decimal place.

9 cm

15 cm

Diagram **NOT** accurately drawn

(1385 November 2001)

14 A sheet of A5 paper is a rectangle 210 mm long and 148 mm wide.

  a Calculate the area of a sheet of A5 paper. Give your answer in **square centimetres**.

  b Calculate the length of a diagonal of the rectangle. Give your answer correct to the nearest millimetre.

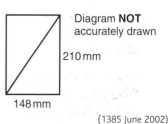

Diagram **NOT** accurately drawn

210 mm

148 mm

(1385 June 2002)

15 ABC is a rectangle.

$AC = 17$ cm. $AD = 10$ cm.

Calculate the length of the side CD.

Give your answer correct
to 1 decimal place.

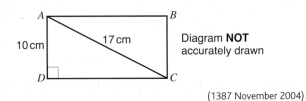

Diagram **NOT**
accurately drawn

(1387 November 2004)

16 The diagram shows triangle ABC and circle, centre O

A, B and C are points on the circumference of the circle.

AB is a diameter of the circle.

$AC = 16$ cm and $BC = 12$ cm and angle $ACB = 90°$.

a Work out the diameter AB of the circle.

b Work out the area of the circle.

Give your answer to the nearest cm^2.

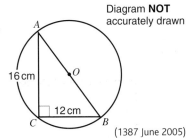

Diagram **NOT**
accurately drawn

(1387 June 2005)

Index

Published by: Edexcel Limited, One90 High Holborn, London WC1V 7BH

Distributed by: Pearson Education Limited, Edinburgh Gate, Harlow, Essex CM20 2JE, England
www.longman.co.uk

© Edexcel Limited 2006

First published 2006
Third impression 2007
ISBN 978-1-903-13398-9

Concept design by Mick Harris. Cover design by Juice Creative Ltd. Index by John Holmes.

Typeset by Tech-Set, Gateshead

Printed in China CTPSC/03

The publisher's policy is to use paper manufactured from sustainable forests.

Live Learning, Live Authoring and Live Player are all trademarks of Live Learning Ltd.

The Publisher wishes to draw attention to the Single-User Licence Agreement below.
Please read this agreement carefully before installing and using the CD-ROM.
We are grateful to the following for permission to reproduce photographs:

Every effort has been made to trace the copyright holders and we apologise in advance for any unintentional omissions. We would be pleased to insert the appropriate acknowledgement in any subsequent edition of this publication.

Alamy Images: pg55 (©PHOTOTAKE Inc.), pg89 (©Aflo Foto Agency), pg131 (©Rodolfo Arpia (Royalty-Free)), pg322 (Dice) (©Leander), (Pool) (©joeysworld.com), (Skyscraper) (©Image State (Royalty-Free)), (Louvre Museum) (©isifa Image Service s.r.o), pg359 (©david sanger photography), pg390 (m) (©cuboImages srl), pg486 (©Hideo Kurihara), pg491 (©Atmosphere Picture Library); **Corbis:** pg46 (©Stephen Hird/Reuters), pg47 (©Stephen Hird/Reuters), pg129 (l) (©Royalty-Free), (m) (©Angelo Hornak), (r) (©Royalty-Free), pg322 (Rubik's Cube) (©Klaus Hackenberg/zefa), pg492 (©Royalty-Free), pg535 (©Royalty-Free); **DK Images:** pg322 (Giant's Causeway) (Photographer:Roger Map, Copyright Holder:Rough Guides); **Pearson:** pg275 (©Pearson Education), pg322 (Toblerone) (©Pearson Education), (Smarties) (©Pearson Education), pg392 (©Pearson Education), pg458 (©Pearson Education); **Punchstock Royalty-Free Images**: pg90 (digitalvision), pg322 (Pyramids) (digitalvision), pg390 (l) (digitalvision)

Picture Research by Karen Jones

advancing learning, changing lives

Series Editors
Trevor Johnson & Tony Clough

Student Book

Edexcel GCSE Mathematics (Modular)

Foundation Tier

Contents